Despite a century of debate and criticism, Marxism as a mass ideological practice has remained an elusive topic. This book examines Marxist socialism as a mode of understanding and self-understanding treasured and transmitted by thousands of anonymous militants. It focuses upon the Parti Ouvrier Français, the 'Guesdists', an archetypical movement of Marxism's 'Golden Age' before the First World War, the period when Marxist socialism evolved from sect to mass movement.

Thousands of French socialists adopted Marxism due to vulgar Guesdist polemic rather than to Marx's profound theoretical works, and entire communities were converted to an austere but messianic socialism which still affects French politics today. This book traces the doctrine's birth through conflict with liberals, proto-fascists, and anarchists; its 'making' of a working class; its attempted seduction of the middle class; its confusion before alternative social visions – issues which today still condition the interpretive triumphs and political tragedies of Marxist ideology.

Frontispiece 'Naufrage de l'ordre bourgeois. Le prolétariat international est en vue du monde nouveau' (From *Le Socialiste*, 23 April 1893)

MARXISM AT WORK

*Ideology, class and French socialism
during the Third Republic*

ROBERT STUART

CAMBRIDGE
UNIVERSITY PRESS

Published by the Press Syndicate of the University of Cambridge
The Pitt Building, Trumpington Street, Cambridge CB2 1RP
40 West 20th Street, New York, NY 10011–4211, USA
10 Stamford Road, Oakleigh, Victoria 3166, Australia

First published 1992

Printed in Great Britain at the University Press, Cambridge

A catalogue record for this book is available from the British Library

Library of Congress cataloguing in publication data

Stuart, Robert S., 1947–
Marxism at work: ideology, class, and French socialism during the
Third Republic/Robert Stuart.
p. cm.
Includes bibliographical references.
ISBN 0 521 41526 8
1. Socialism – France – History – 19th century. 2. Social classes –
France – History – 19th century. 3. France – History – Third Republic.
1870–1940. I. Title.
HX263. s78 1992
335.4′09445 – dc20 91–27093 CIP

ISBN 0 521 41526 8 hardback

HX
263
. S78
1992

For Max and Alice, who taught me that working people could indeed appropriate the best of bourgeois society.

Contents

List of Illustrations   *page* ix
Preface   xi

Part I – In search of French Marxism

1 Ideology, history, and the study of Marxism   3

2 The Parti Ouvrier Français: its history and historiography   20

3 The axioms of class war: class, class consciousness, and class conflict   55

Part II – The making of the French working class

4 The capitalist mode of production and proletarianisation   97

5 Unmaking the working class: lumpenproletarians and labour aristocrats   127

6 A 'class for itself'; trade unions, cooperatives, and the 'labour movement'   180

7 The bourgeois state versus the proletarian party   223

8 Reform and revolution   252

Part III – History and class conflict

9 Vampire-Capital: Marxists indict the bourgeoisie   295

10 Shopkeepers and artisans: the Guesdists and the petite bourgeoisie   350

viii   *Contents*

11 Aristocrats, peasants and labourers: Marxism and rural
   society   388

12 Sales clerks and savants: Marxists encounter the 'new
   middle class'   424

13 The proletarian revolution: from pauperisation to Utopia 459

Conclusion   492

Bibliographical note   503

Index   509

Illustrations

Frontispiece 'Naufrage de l'ordre bourgeois. Le prolétariat international est en vue du monde nouveau' (from *Le Socialiste*, 23 April 1893)

1 'L'évolution du monde capitaliste' (from *Le Socialiste*, 16–23 October 1904)   38

2 'Organisons-nous' (from *Le Socialiste*, 14–21 February 1904)   42

3 'La vertu de Marianne' (from *Le Socialiste*, 30 October – 6 November 1904)   53

4 'À l'Assaut de la Bastille Capitaliste' (from *Le Socialiste*, 28 April 1895)   505

Preface

A preface accords momentary respite from the cool impersonality of the third-person discourse otherwise imposed by stylistic convention, the convention which ensures that facts 'speak for themselves' with decorous academic objectivity. The facts in this study, of course, do not speak for themselves, objectively or otherwise. Instead, they 'speak' through my ventriloquism, through my agency, through the medium of Robert Stuart, '[himself] a fully subjective being, fully historical'.[1] If objectivity, 'that noble dream', is possible, its attainment depends upon confession of bias, upon disclosure of the 'system of reading'[2] which governed research, upon narration of the history of this History.

I embarked upon this enterprise more years ago than I care to remember – a callow student groping anxiously towards a viable PhD topic at the University of Toronto during the early 1970s. But, while indeed callow, I already knew very well (I had recently completed an MA) that post-graduate students rarely survive the agonies of their studies without a masochistic passion for their subject, and I resolved to discover a topic which would retain its allure over years of intensive archival research. I succeeded beyond my wildest dreams: a felicitous choice has sustained my interest for two decades.

Then, as now, three avenues of inquiry tempted me: the baroque intricacies of French history during the decades before the First World War; the austere discipline of social theory, with its endlessly ramifying conceptions of social hierarchy; and, finally, the Promethean promise of Marxist socialism. My devotion to the *Belle Époque* (as passionate today as ever) remains as inexplicable as any

---

[1] R. Barthes, 'Histoire ou Littérature', *Sur Racine* (Paris, 1960), p. 167. Unless otherwise stated, all translations from the French are my own.
[2] *Ibid.*, p. 166.

infatuation, although who would not love the France of those years, once having explored the mysterious convolutions of her body politic? My obsession with social hierarchy, on the other hand, flows from an obvious biographical source. A beneficiary of the economic and educational boom of the 1960s (a *Belle Époque* if ever there was one), I had clawed my way out of the disintegrating post-war working class, determined not to rejoin the printers and cannery workers whose laborious lives retained my sympathies, even my allegiance, but whose labour-constricted horizons never circumscribed my aspirations. 'Upward mobility', however, marks one as indelibly as any other sentence of exile. In my case, the transition from the proletariat to the 'professional managerial class' (the infamous 'PMC' of radical critique) instilled an abiding interest in patterns of social hierarchy, in denunciation and rationalisation of inequality, and in 'second order' analyses of these denunciations and rationalisations. In other words, my social experience had yielded an enduring fascination with ideology, a fascination which has only intensified with time, as capitalism's ideologues have abandoned their obfuscating 'end of ideology' sloganising in favour of the brutal (and no less misleading) edict that 'there is no alternative'. Finally, I had discovered the impassioned science of Marxism, by the early 1970s in triumphant ascendancy among Western intellectuals. Unlike many of my generation, however, I have maintained my loyalty to Marxism's fundamental precepts, confident that Marxist social criticism will endure as long as the capitalism it interrogates.

I determined to write a thesis on how the Marxists of the *Belle Époque* had understood their great mentor's class theory, a topic which promised to sate all three of my intellectual passions. After the usual agonies and ecstasies of post-graduate existence, I successfully defended 400 pages of congealed blood, sweat and tears, convincing an exigent examining panel that the Marxists' Parti Ouvrier had thoroughly misunderstood and misused Marx's insights, that the Guesdists (as posterity has identified the militants of the Party, after their superb polemicist Jules Guesde) fully deserved the contempt heaped upon them since Marx's own exclamation that 'if this is Marxism, then I'm no Marxist!' But, even as I accepted the coveted doctorate, doubts assailed me. Perhaps Marx's legacy was not the coherent, logical measure of militancy portrayed by both his partisans and his detractors? Perhaps the ambiguities, omissions, and contradictions I had discovered in Guesdist discourse (not that I then conceived of the Guesdists' texts as a 'discourse') exemplified the Marxist paradigm (another methodological concept I had yet to discover) rather than betraying it? Perhaps, indeed, the despised 'vulgar Marxism' of the Parti Ouvrier counted for as much in the rise of socialism as the sophisticated products of Marx's scholarly labours? The vulgarities of Guesdism, after all, had animated a socialist party of great contemporaneous force and considerable historical consequence. What had *Theories of Surplus Value* animated, apart from PhD dissertations?

Having stifled these self-destructive qualms as I defended my thesis, I then put them aside altogether as I struggled to establish myself as a teacher, happy enough to escape the succubus which had consumed my energies for so many years. But when I returned to the Parti Ouvrier at the beginning of the 1980s, determined, like thousands of aspiring young academics, to convert my PhD dissertation into a publishable manuscript, I discovered, to my chagrin, that I no longer fully believed my own 'thesis'. Its argument seemed to denigrate the French Marxists' living militancy in favour of an abstract (and largely imaginary) hypostatisation of 'Marxism'; its method to describe the Party's ideological manoeuvres without reference to the social context which defined their purpose and significance; its implicit values to spurn ideological discourse in general as self-contradictory, incomplete, and equivocal.

So, back to the drawing board. Aware of my own paradigm-shift (symptomatically, I now thought in such terms), obedient to the imperatives of the new History of Ideas, I set out to master recent methodological innovations in the study of ideology.[3] Abandoning my naive Marx-centred conception of Marxism, dedicated to a more complex and more tolerant definition of the 'Marxist', I submerged myself in the flood of sophisticated critique which had engulfed study of the doctrine since the 1960s. Repulsed by the passionless intercourse of ideas with ideas, enchanted with the new social history (Perrot, Scott, Lequin, and the brilliant company who have rallied to their cause), I embarked upon an exploration of the social experience which had engendered the Parti Ouvrier and which the Parti Ouvrier in turn had moulded. Above all, I reread the Guesdist texts, astonished and delighted as documents subjected to conceptually renewed exploration yielded fresh insight – an

---

[3] For a brilliant account of this collective project of the 1980s, see Tony Judt's *Marxism and the French Left: Studies in Labour and Politics in France 1830–1981* (Oxford, 1986), p. 14.

utterly convincing practical refutation of simple empiricism. Years passed agreeably as enhanced theoretical sensitivity, accumulated historical instances, and revitalised primary research blended into a thorough reconceptualisation of the social origins, polemical impact, and historical import of Guesdist ideology.

'All good things must end', although dismayed colleagues increasingly doubted the adage as the decade which had begun with the initiation of my project drew to a close without its end in sight. But end it did, in *Marxism at Work*. What have my protracted labours accomplished? Why read their outcome? First, I have attempted to establish the error of distinguishing between 'interpreting the world' and 'changing it'. French Marxists never mounted Parisian barricades, never stormed their Winter Palace, but their decades of dedicated journalism, public meetings, and pamphleteering stirred a powerful current of social critique and socialist (and anti-socialist) militancy which even today flows strongly across the contours of the French polity. I have striven to demonstrate how the Guesdists, in reinterpreting their social world, changed it irrevocably. *Marxism at Work* scrutinises this formative moment and contributes to the general revaluation of discourse presently underway in the human sciences, a revaluation which 'pays as close attention to the cultural conceptions encoded into the social and political order as it does to economic life, or demography, or technological change, or the relative power of different social groups.'[4]

Spurred by these historical and methodological aspirations, I have unravelled (dare I write 'deconstructed'?) the intricate patterns of ambiguity, contradiction, over-emphasis, and omission which characterised both the Guesdists' ideological militancy and the Marxist ideological construct which their movement exemplified. Anti-Marxists should not rejoice, however. Ambiguity and self-contradiction have characterised all ideological discourses, including those of the liberals, conservatives, and non-Marxist radicals who opposed the Parti Ouvrier. Indeed, an entirely self-consistent and unambiguous ideology would have proven impotent and sterile – too simple to engage the complexities of its social order, too simplistic to exploit the opportunities of its polity. I have demolished the Guesdists' ideological edifice to reveal the functionality of its con-

---

4 W. Sewell, 'Property, Labor, and the Emergence of Socialism in France 1789–1848', in J. Merriman (ed.), *Consciousness and Class Experience in Nineteenth-Century Europe* (New York, 1979), p. 60.

ceptual architecture, the coherence of its rhetorical design, the rationality of its polemical foundations: the functionality, coherence and rationality inherent in the movement's most characteristic contradictions and ambiguities.

How does a self-confessed Marxist dissect Marxism, a procedure surely as painful and problematical as a surgeon removing his own appendix? In practice, the incisions must be guided by theoretical awareness and self-awareness, by carefully cultivated mastery of the most sophisticated and most recent criticisms of Marxism, whether composed by anti-Marxists, non-Marxists, or self-critical Marxists. I have not always enjoyed these 'spiritual exercises,' but the precision and depth of my analyses have, I hope, improved with every recondite article absorbed, every gnostic monograph mastered, every intolerant manifesto endured. Unfortunately, this discipline of theoretical rigour evokes historicist suspicion: the fear that imposition of late twentieth-century theory upon late nineteenth-century polemic will result in anachronism, that Guesdist materialism, for instance, will be measured against Althusser rather than against Renouvier. In one sense, I have accepted, even welcomed, this disciplinary dilemma. The 'significance' (the unintended consequences, the implications for posterity) of Guesdist discourse has interested me as much as its 'meaning' (what Guesdists intended, what their immediate audience took them to mean).[5] The triumphs and tragedies of the Parti Ouvrier not only illustrate the adventures and misadventures of Marxism during the *Fin de Siècle*, but also elucidate the grandeur and misery of the doctrine's present.

None the less, like all historians, I have hopelessly hoped to live the lived reality of the past. Daniel Halévy – that acute, if passionately partial, observer – recounts a friend's comment, on beholding banners demanding Justice, Fraternity, Equality, and Liberty preceding a workers' parade, that 'it would be good to know just what those words mean to those men.'[6] I, too, have wished to know the meaning of the Guesdists' words – their meaning to the militants

---

[5] For the distinction, see Quentin Skinner's paradigm-shifting 'Meaning and Understanding in the History of Ideas', *History and Theory*, vol. 8, 1969, pp. 3–53 and the discussion (which does not employ exactly these terms) in J. Pocock, 'Introduction: The State of the Art', in *Essays on Political Thought and History* (Cambridge, 1985), p. 7. For a discerning analysis of the need for both analytical 'present-centred' investigation of past discourses and their illumination by empathic contextualisation, see R. Rorty, J. Schneewind and Q. Skinner, 'Introduction', to R. Rorty et al. (eds.), *Philosophy in History* (Cambridge, 1984), pp. 1–14.

[6] D. Halévy, *Pays Parisiens*, cited in E. Weber, *France: Fin de Siècle* (London, 1986), p. 128.

who wrote or spoke them, their meaning to the workers to whom they were addressed. The endless dialectic between experience and reflection, the most difficult and most fruitful problem in today's social and cultural inquiry, must articulate any study of discourse, including the Guesdists' discourse. Illumination of the Parti Ouvrier's doctrine throws light upon the still obscure world of the movement's militants and audience, while analyses of that world elucidate features of the Parti Ouvrier's doctrine which would otherwise remain inexplicable – a hermeneutic circle which I have traced and retraced.

Unfortunately, the socialist militants who paraded through the streets of late nineteenth-century France and the anonymous workers to whom they spoke, for whom they claimed to speak, have left few personal expressions of their hopes and fears, their loves and hatreds, their ideals and ideas: any community of provincial bourgeois has bequeathed a larger documentary legacy of diaries, letters and memoirs to historians than has the entire French working class of the *Belle Époque*. Deducing the response of French workers to Guesdist polemic, like many other investigations into the reception of discourse, relies primarily upon complex inference rather than upon direct evidence.[7] Happily, *fin-de-siècle* French workers have been studied as have few other classes of few other times and places: the patterns and processes of their militancy and passivity, their working conditions and strikes, even their leisure and family life have been educed from a multitude of historical traces, explicated from a plethora of interpretive angles. Inference founded upon the works of a Joan Scott or a Michelle Perrot is a powerful tool indeed, although I would none the less willingly sacrifice a number of today's histories for a few hours in a Roubaisian *estaminet* during Guesde's bitter reelection campaign of 1898 . . .

Situating Guesdist discourse in its time and place, the search for its 'meaning' in the hermeneutical sense of that sacred word, leads into the clamour and confusion of social and political strife, into the maelstrom of polemics which consumed the Parti Ouvrier's embattled youth and engulfed its bellicose maturity. In an ideal world, I would have studied the polemical legacy of the Guesdists' enemies with the same intensity as that of the POF itself. How else to comprehend the Parti Ouvrier's complex (mis)understanding of

---

[7] Pocock, 'Introduction', p. 18.

'bourgeois democracy' than through intensive study of the French Radicals against whom the POF competed for the allegiance of French workers? I should have read *La Dépêche de Toulouse* with the same attention and exhaustiveness with which I have read and reread *Le Socialiste*, if only to understand *Le Socialiste*'s fanatical detestation of *La Dépêche*. Unfortunately, mastery of the sources for the history of French Marxism has required years of research and reflection; no individual historian could do as much again for all the other ideological movements of the *Fin de Siècle* – for clerical and royalist rightists, Drumont's anti-Semitic militants, proto-fascist Nationalists, Christian Democrats, liberal 'Opportunists', democratic Radicals, an array of non-Marxist socialists, and anarchists. Uneasily, I have relied upon others' research for comprehension of the Guesdists' enemies and competitors. Fortunately, the French political culture of the *Belle Époque* has received extraordinarily detailed investigation from a reassuringly diverse array of historians. I have been well served by my predecessors and colleagues, by modern French political historians and by historians of the politics of modern France, and hope that this study will repay some of my indebtedness to their studies, that my illumination of the ideology of the Parti Ouvrier will by reflection further illuminate the ideologies of the Party's antagonists.

Historians, however, may be alienated by one aspect of this study: its lack of narrative, its decipherment of Guesdist discourse as a unitary phenomenon essentially unchanged between 1882 and 1905. Surely, students of socialist history will argue, the Guesdism of the 1880s differed profoundly from that of the 1890s? How dare I juxtapose material from the two periods to reach conclusions about Guesdist ideology 'in general'? All I can reply is that the rhythms which historians have emphasised in the Party's political behaviour rarely conditioned developments (or lack thereof) in the movement's ideological discourse: the Guesdists' discursive strategy and their everyday practice evolved through radically different periodicities; the unchanging strategic ambiguities of Marxist doctrine authorised far greater tactical mobility than historians of Marxism have conceded. I detected the Parti Ouvrier's apparent doctrinal stasis during my second approach to the movement, and at first could scarcely believe my eyes, so general is the consensus which describes a high-tide of Marxist ideological militancy in the Party's youth, a long reformist ebb during the 1890s as Guesdists revelled thoughtlessly in their political success, and then an abrupt resurgence of revolutionary intransigence at the turn of the century. Could everyone be wrong? Surely not?

I subjected my gathering conviction that the Guesdists had indeed retained an essentially static ideological discourse to two tests – neither conclusive in itself, but convincing in combination. First, I undertook an intensive content analysis of three months of Guesdist publications during November 1896 to January 1897, supposedly the flaccid nadir of the POF, in comparison with its publications between November 1886 and January 1887, during the movement's most sectarian phase – according to the conventional wisdom. In the end, I failed to achieve the precision dear to cliometricians (87 per cent revolutionary and 13 per cent evolutionary political metaphors in 1886–7 as compared to 85 per cent and 15 per cent in 1896–7 . . .), having decided that my evaluation of each instance was too subjective to coalesce into the objectivity of 'hard' statistics. Suffice to say that I discovered no significant mutations in the Party's ideological militancy between the two periods: the movement's fundamental concepts, characteristic lexicon, basic rhetorical tropes, even its favoured exemplars, recurred unchanged across the decade.

Second, I conducted a thematic survey through the entire period of Guesdist militancy. During my rereading of the 1882–1905 run of *L'Égalité* and *Le Socialiste*, the primary sources for any student of Guesdist ideology, I had compiled an index of major articles on a number of themes, including the women's question, peasants, protectionism, anarchism, religion, and nationalism. Determined to confirm or disprove my insight about the *longue durée* of Parti Ouvrier discursive patterns, I reread these sequences, carefully controlling for change between the 1880s and 1890s. Once again, I found few differences between the doctrinal concepts and ideological rhetoric employed during the two periods. Indeed, I discovered (to my surprise and amusement) that the papers' major contributors sometimes recycled decade-old articles – in such cases, a matter not only of little change, but of absolute identity, something I had failed to recognise when reading these weeklies week by week.

Upon reflection, the unchanging nature of Guesdist discourse ceased to surprise me. From the Guesdists' perspective, the French society and polity of 1905 differed not at all from the French political economy of 1882: capitalists still exploited the social order; bourgeois still ruled the state. Nor had the Guesdists' purpose changed: they

still sought to undermine this class society by mobilising its proletariat against capitalist exploitation and bourgeois rule. As Charles
Bonnier, one of Guesde's closest associates, described his Party's
dogged campaign, 'socialist polemic in general takes the form of
repetition, according to the formula: "I always repeat the same
thing because things are always the same".'[8] *Marxism at Work* studies
this pattern of repetition: the Guesdists' constant return to constant
themes.

Historians will also worry about the stark impersonality of my
analysis: no narrative, and no characters. I can still hear the
Chairman of my examining panel informing me that he had been
most impressed by my thesis, but that 'he wondered why it had been
written in the History Department'. Although Guesdist discourse
was itself impersonal (contributions to the Party press often
appeared unsigned; major edicts were written collectively), the Parti
Ouvrier included outstanding individuals, even eccentric individualists, some of whom warrant extended biographies. We still, for
example, lack a serious study of the magnificent Guesde. But I have
focused upon the pattern of discourse which Guesdists shared,
consciously excluding individual eccentricities, except for the
occasional aberrant instance too outré to ignore (and always indicated as such). In practice, I have preferred to cite an archetypical
anonymous comment from a widely diffused pamphlet rather than a
distinctive personal observation from a major theoretical work.
Instead of conducting an exegesis of Paul Lafargue's fascinating and
internationally influential *Les Trusts Américains*, for instance, I have
emphasised the elements of this work which pervaded Lafargue's
occasional journalism, and which recurred frequently in other
Guesdists' analyses of 'monopoly capitalism'. This study employs
texts to explicate a pattern of discourse, not a pattern of discourse to
explicate texts.[9]

I have incurred numerous debts during the past two decades.
Some of these are owed to institutions. Over the years, the kindly
staff at the Internationaal Instituut voor Sociale Geschiedenis in

8 C. Bonnier, 'Leur République', *Le Socialiste*, 27 July – 3 August 1902.
9 For this important methodological distinction, see D. Hollinger, 'Historians and the
   Discourse of Intellectuals', in J. Higham and P. Conkin (eds.), *New Directions in American
   Intellectual History* (Baltimore, 1979), p. 44. There is a useful analysis of the similar
   incompatibility between Lafargue's literary criticism and his socialist polemics in L. Derfler,
   'Paul Lafargue: The First Marxist Literary Critic', *Nineteenth-Century French Studies*, vol. 17,
   1989, p. 377.

Amsterdam and at the Musée Social and the Archives de la Préfecture de Police in Paris have volunteered their informed advice and furnished ideal working conditions. Indeed, individuals on the staff of the Archives Nationales and the Bibliothèque Nationale have left me with warm recollections of support and friendliness. I would like to thank them all, the staff of the former institutions for exemplifying their corporate cultures, the staff of the latter for overcoming theirs. The Canada Council funded my original post-graduate research in Paris, and I owe thanks to the Department of History of the University of Western Australia and to the University itself for funding three extended research visits to my European sources as I laboriously reconceptualised Guesdism. The librarians of my university's Reid Library, above all those in Inter-Library Loan, have met my endless abstruse requests with good-natured competency and true professionalism. Last, but emphatically not least, the secretarial staff of the Department of History at UWA have typed and retyped my chapters more often than they or I care to remember, and I owe them a great deal for their constant good humour and remarkable efficiency.

Other debts are to individuals. First, my thanks to John Cairns, who taught me the rigorous attention to evidence and the obsessive care in its presentation which still defines the historian's craft, despite the theoretical innovations about which he has been so skeptical, and I so credulous. Many hundred students, who have always taken priority over the Guesdists, repeatedly delayed completion of my *magnum opus* – which assumed mythical (in both senses of the word) status with UWA History students, whose avid interest in the intricacies of European ideologies and good-humoured tolerance of my political eccentricities nevertheless did more to sustain my morale than they will ever know. And, preeminently, I would again like to thank the many friends and colleagues who have read, criticised, and occasionally commended the various manuscripts which eventually fused into this book – with particular thanks to Margaret Ashworth, Richard Bosworth, John Hooper, Pat Jalland, Lenore Layman, and Chips Sowerwine, without whose wise advice and moral support in moments of crisis and demoralisation this project would never have been completed. Needless to say, they bear no responsibility for its remaining stylistic infelicities and conceptual awkwardness.

Finally, heartfelt thanks to my family: to Nicole and Suzanne, for their happy disinterest in French Marxism, and to Jan, who struggled valiantly against excessively complex sentences, and who for twenty years has stoically cohabited with the demanding Guesdists.

PART I

In search of French Marxism

CHAPTER I

Ideology, history, and the study of Marxism

Discourses are the complexes of signs and practices which organize social existence and social reproduction. In their structured, material persistence, discourses are what gives differential substance to membership of a social group or class or formation, which mediate an internal sense of belonging, an outward sense of otherness.

R. Terdiman, *Discourse/Counter-Discourse: The Theory and Practice of Symbolic Resistance in Nineteenth-Century France* (Ithaca, 1985), p. 54.

Ideologies will always need to be comprehended through the analysis of their real functions in the world. There are no general laws about this: it will have to be established by historical investigation of specific cases.

I. Schapiro, 'Realism in the History of Ideas', *History of Political Thought*, vol. 3, 1982.

The historical investigation of socialist and labour ideologies – once, with the institutional history of trade unions and parties, the *via regia* of the 'old social history' – suffered an eclipse throughout the 1960s and 1970s as structuralist theory, quantitative methodologies, and populist politics combined to discredit ideology's supposed abstraction from 'real' history. Labour historians' preoccupation with the rediscovered intricacies of the 'labour process' focused scholarly attention upon workers' immediate subjection to capital rather than upon proletarian ideals and aspirations. Cliometricians' disdain for the unquantifiable relegated doctrinal issues to the professional backwaters. And the 'grass roots' enthusiasms of the 'new social historians', practitioners of 'history from below', diverted research from forgotten meeting halls and vanished editorial rooms towards the 'lived experience' of street-life and the intimacies of domesticity. Belatedly, historians cast their handful of graveyard earth into the pit marked 'end of ideology'. The 1980s, however, witnessed

3

ideology's resurrection. Innovations in the sociology of knowledge and the history of science, the advance of semiotics and cultural criticism, the vogue for 'post-structuralist' social and political theory – all revived historians' interest in ideological aspects of the past, a revival prefigured by the most stimulating methodological manifestos of the preceding decades.[1] How might these recent reconceptualisations of ideology aid students of Marxism?

Most significantly, a scholarly consensus has crystallised about the meaning of 'ideology'. This accord must be welcomed after decades of confusion and acrimony, decades during which the concept of ideology inflated to denote culture in general (physics or sculpture as 'ideological practices'), contracted to designate 'transcended' political movements (socialism, for 'end of ideology' liberals; liberalism, for Marxist socialists), or degenerated into a pejorative epithet (I have a world view; you have an ideology).[2] Gross over-expansion of the term proved particularly damaging to historical inquiry: 'ideology' came to mean everything yet nothing.[3] By contrast, current reformulations of the concept of ideology generate formidable heuristic power.

These reformulations define ideologies as the canons governing representation of social and political order (and disorder), as social 'paradigms' which constitute understanding of the 'real', the desir-

---

[1] Seminal theoretical contributions to revival in the study of ideology which have influenced this inquiry included C. Geertz, 'Ideology as a Cultural System', in D. Apter (ed.), *Ideology and Discontent* (London, 1964), pp. 47–76; Q. Skinner, 'Meaning and Understanding in the History of Ideas', *History and Theory*, vol. 8, 1969, pp. 3–53; Q. Skinner, 'Some Problems in the Analysis of Political Thought and Action', *Political Theory*, vol. 2, 1974, pp. 277–303; and, above all, P. Ricoeur, 'Science and Ideology', in *Hermeneutics and the Human Sciences* (Cambridge, 1981), pp. 222–46. The works of William Sewell and Gareth Stedman Jones are exemplary in their assimilation of these insights into historical practice, however controversial their studies have been within the discipline. See the insightful methodological discussions in W. Sewell, 'État, Corps et Ordre: Some Notes on the Social Vocabulary of the French Old Regime', in H.-U. Wehler (ed.), *Sozialgeschichte Heute: Festschrift für Hans Rosenberg zum 70. Geburtstag* (Göttingen, 1974), particularly pp. 50–1 and G. Stedman Jones, 'Rethinking Chartism', in *Languages of Class: Studies in English Working-Class History 1832–1982* (Cambridge, 1983), pp. 90–178. But see the critique of the latter in J. Foster, 'The Declassing of Language', *New Left Review*, no. 150, 1985, pp. 38–41.

[2] Good critiques of these vagaries of usage may be found in G. Lichtheim, 'The Concept of Ideology', *History and Theory*, vol. 4, 1965, pp. 164–95; S. Hall, 'The Hinterland of Science: Ideology and the "Sociology of Knowledge",' in Centre for Contemporary Cultural Studies, *On Ideology* (London, 1978), pp. 9–32; R. Williams, *Marxism and Literature* (Oxford, 1977), pp. 55–71; and J. Larrain, *The Concept of Ideology* (London, 1979), p. 13.

[3] For the need to separate ideology from other cultural regimes, if only to understand how distinct discursive practices interpenetrate, see G. Therborn, *The Power of Ideology and the Ideology of Power* (London, 1980), pp. 2–3 and pp. 70–1.

able, and the possible – paradigms which condition perception of a society, evaluate both the status quo and its alternatives, and assess the possibility of alternative social orders.[4] Ideologies, according to this definition, constitute 'problematics' which edit the infinite number of possible perceptions and statements about a social order into finite (and therefore intelligible) discourses, discourses which necessarily highlight some features of a society while obscuring others.[5] Alternative patterns of emphasis and evaluation define alternative ideologies, embodying 'a process by which different kinds of meaning are produced and reproduced by the establishment of a mental set towards the world in which certain sign systems are privileged as necessary, as natural, ways of recognising a "meaning" in things and others are suppressed, ignored, or hidden in the very process of representing a world to consciousness'.[6] Ideologists, warriors on the battlefields of discourse, struggle against each other for dominance over the grammar and vocabulary of social representation.

This linguistic terminology – description of an ideology as 'the language [individuals] use as an instrument to wrest order from their experience and to present it, in a compelling fashion, to their fellows'[7] – potentially reduces ideological practice to nothing but language, and implies an ontological distinction between 'experience' and its ideological 'signification'. 'Materialists' (by no means all of them Marxists) have exploited this false dichotomy to reduce ideologies to epiphenomenal reflections of social order. Today, the

[4] For application of the Kuhnian concept of 'paradigm' to the study of ideology, see S. Wolin, 'Paradigms and Political Theories', in P. King and B. Parekh (eds.), *Politics and Experience: Essays Presented to Professor Michael Oakeshott on the Occasion of His Retirement* (Cambridge, 1968), pp. 131–52. The concept of 'paradigm' is analysed in relation to the history of ideas by J. Pocock in 'The Reconstruction of Discourse: Towards the Historiography of Political Thought', *Modern Language Notes*, vol. 96, 1981, pp. 964–965 and in 'Languages and their Implications: The Transformation of the Study of Political Thought', in J. Pocock, *Politics, Language, and Time: Essays on Political Thought and History* (London, 1971), p. 18.

[5] The concept of a 'prolematic', by Althusser out of Bachelard, has been widely used in recent 'structuralist' studies of ideology. See, for discussion, J. Rancière, 'On the Theory of Ideology: The Politics of Althusser', *Radical Philosophy*, vol. 7, 1974, pp. 2–14 and P. Hirst, 'Althusser's Theory of Ideology', *Economy and Society*, vol. 5, 1976, pp. 385–412.

[6] H. White, 'The Context in the Text: Method and Ideology in Intellectual History', in H. White, *The Content of the Form: Narrative Discourse and Historical Representation* (Baltimore, 1987), p. 192. For an application of this insight to the study of Marxism, see S. Hall, 'The Problem of Ideology: Marxism Without Guarantees', in B. Matthews (ed.), *Marx: A Hundred Years On* (London, 1983), p. 59.

[7] R. Nichols, 'Rebels, Beginners and Buffoons: Politics as Action', in T. Ball (ed.), *Political Theory and Practice: New Perspectives* (Minneapolis, 1977), pp. 180–1.

more extreme exponents of 'discourse theory' and 'deconstruction', rebelling against discredited reductionisms, proclaim the triumph of text over context, the exorcism of the referent by the signifier, the anarchic reign of intertextuality over the vanquished realm of social causality. Scholars should resist this linguistic extremism, a reductionism quite as tyrannical as the *passé* imagery of 'material bases' and 'cultural superstructures'.[8] Despite its admirable aspirations, the 'linguistic turn' taken by contemporary social thought risks perpetuation of the fruitless conflict between 'idealism' and 'materialism' by merely inverting the epistemological fanaticism of 'vulgar Marxism'.[9] Categorical distinctions between, on the one hand, ideas and language and, on the other, society and experience – whatever their respective priorities, however related to each other – result in historical absurdities, as with the scholar who identifies Christianity as the idea and feudalism as the society of twelfth-century Europe, thereby occluding the institutional ramifications of medieval Christianity and dismissing the ideological discourse of feudalism.[10]

Ideology is indeed language, but not only language. The production, distribution, and consumption of social representation in pamphlets, editorials, and public meetings constitute realms of 'experience' no different in essence from economic practices within factories and bazaars, the deployment of political power within parliaments and party congresses, or reproductive practices pursued within bedchambers and crèches – none reducible to linguistic 'texts'

---

[8] For a particularly extreme manifesto of linguistic imperialism, see R. Robin, 'Langage et Idéologie', in J. Guilhaumou et al., *Langage et Idéologies: Le Discours comme Objet de l'Histoire* (Paris, 1974). A fascinating debate over this issue with particular relevance to labour history has been provoked by Joan Scott's stimulating 'On Language, Gender, and Working-Class History', *International Labor and Working-Class History*, no. 31, 1987, pp. 1–13. See, in particular, the 'Response' by Bryan Palmer, *ibid.*, pp. 14–23 and Professor Scott's 'A Reply to Criticism' in no. 32 of *ILWCH*, pp. 39–45.

[9] See the superb polemic against this tendency in P. Anderson, *In the Tracks of Historical Materialism* (Chicago, 1984), chapter 2. There is discussion of similar critiques of Pocock and Skinner in P. Janssen, 'Political Thought as Traditionary Action: The Critical Response to Skinner and Pocock', *History and Theory*, vol. 24, 1985, pp. 115–46. For a strong argument that Marx himself rejected the base/superstructure metaphor in his actual analyses of history and society, see G. Markus, 'Political-Social Rationality in Marx: A Dialectical Critique', *Dialectical Anthropology*, vol. 4, 1979, p. 256 and J. Larrain, *Marxism and Ideology* (London, 1983), pp. 173–80.

[10] See T. Tholfsen, *Ideology and Revolution in Modern Europe: An Essay on the Role of Ideas in History* (New York, 1984) for a study which repeatedly falls into this confusion – the Christianity-feudalism example occurring on pp. 166–7.

and none explicable by 'intertextuality' alone.[11] A newspaper such as *Le Socialiste* was no more (and no less) 'linguistic' than the steelworks at Le Creusot, although the one produced social rhetoric and the other armour plate. Both socialist journalism and industrial metallurgy in *fin-de-siècle* France deployed complex, distinctive, and indispensable linguistic codes, and both derived from, embodied, and engendered social structures and social experiences irreducible to language. As a consequence, study of Marxist ideology during the *Belle Époque* (not to mention study of Burgundian steelmaking) requires both the 'deconstructionist' sensitivity of contemporary cultural studies and the 'contextualist' insights of social history. Hence the utility of an expansive concept of 'discourse', which explicitly embodies language in experience, systematically synthesises 'ideas' and 'society', self-consciously 'transcend[s] the conceptual prison of "intellectual" versus "social" phenomena'.[12]

The critical procedures which articulate cultural studies, the 'scientific' discipline which disciplines social theory, and the empathic aspirations which animate social history impose reflexivity upon students of ideology: cultural criticism, social science, and historical studies are themselves ideological; scholars study ideology ideologically. Critics, social theorists and historians, however, understandably resist assertions that every system of cultural and social representation, including their own, constitutes an ideological discourse, a systematisation of perspectival partiality and social bias. This instinctive resistance to ideological self-incrimination constitutes the last redoubt of beleaguered positivism, which has traditionally distinguished between ideology, 'partial' and therefore

---

[11] This is one of the most important (and most neglected) points made in Althusser's influential 'Ideology and Ideological State Apparatuses', in *Lenin and Philosophy and Other Essays* (London, 1971), pp. 121–73. Althusser's insight is further developed in Maurice Godelier's impressive 'The Ideal in the Real', in R. Samuels and G. Stedman Jones (eds.), *Culture, Ideology, and Politics* (London, 1982), pp. 12–38. See also, R. Terdiman, *Discourse/Counter-Discourse: The Theory and Practice of Symbolic Resistance in Nineteenth-Century France* (Ithaca, 1985), pp. 28–43.

[12] D. Hollinger, 'Historians and the Discourse of Intellectuals', in J. Higham and P. Conkin (eds.), *New Directions in American Intellectual History* (Baltimore, 1979), p. 58. Similar points are made in P. Ricoeur, 'Science and Ideology', p. 237; J. Pocock, 'Introduction: The State of the Art', in *Essays on Political Thought and History* (Cambridge, 1985), p. 12; C. Taylor, 'Interpretation and the Sciences of Man', *Review of Metaphysics*, vol. 25, 1971, p. 24; R. Williams, *Marxism and Literature*, pp. 20–44 and 61–2; and J. Toews, 'Intellectual History after the Linguistic Turn: The Autonomy of Meaning and the Irreducibility of Experience', *American Historical Review*, vol. 92, 1987, p. 882. For an excellent analysis of 'discourse' as a field of social conflict, see Terdiman, *Discourse/Counter-Discourse*, pp. 25–43.

incapable of 'evaluating information on its own intrinsic merits',[13] and social science (and 'scientific' history), 'objective' and therefore capable of constituting knowledge 'acknowledged as correct even by a Chinese'.[14] Today, few scholars unquestioningly accept this positivist faith; but even fewer abjure the rhetorical constructions 'in fact' and 'in reality'.

Students of ideology should question this attenuated positivism, if only because pretensions to 'scientific objectivity' have underpinned ideological polemics throughout the nineteenth and twentieth centuries, serving liberal political economy, socialist historical materialism, or Nazi racism as the modern equivalent of the religious sanction which legitimised ancient and medieval ideologies. Instead of constructing secure platforms from which to demolish ideological edifices, 'objective' social science erects an 'ideology in the worst sense of the word, that is to say a dogmatic system of eternal and absolute truths'.[15] Social representation, including 'second order' or 'metalinguistic' discourse on discourse such as the History of Ideas, always manifests systematic partiality: partiality in the sense of limitation (historians necessarily represent the past from a temporal and social perspective which accentuates certain 'realities' while diminishing or obscuring others), and partiality in the sense of bias (histories necessarily represent particular interests, if only those of historians).[16] Nor should scholars regret their partiality: only their grounding in time, place, and interest endows their representations with substance and force.[17] Impartiality is not only impossible, but

---

[13] G. Sartori, 'Politics, Ideology, and Belief Systems', *American Political Science Review*, vol. 63, 1969, p. 401.

[14] The quotation is from Max Weber, cited (without exact attribution) in B. Parekh, 'Social and Political Thought and the Problem of Ideology', in R. Benewick et al. (eds.), *Knowledge and Belief in Politics: The Problem of Ideology* (London, 1973), p. 78. For critique of the ideology/social science dichotomy in its positivist form, see A. Schaff, 'La Définition Fonctionelle de l'Idéologie et le Problème de la "Fin du Siècle de l'Idéologie",' *Le Homme et la Société*, vol. 4, 1967, pp. 51–2 and Ricoeur, 'Science and Ideology', pp. 231–9.

[15] A. Gramsci, 'Problems of Marxism', in *Selections from the Prison Notebooks* (London, 1971), pp. 406–7. And see the discussion in Williams, *Marxism and Literature*, pp. 62–4.

[16] J. Hyppolite, 'Le Scientifique et l'Idéologique dans une Perspective Marxiste', in J. Hyppolite, *Figures de la Pensée Philosophique* (Paris, 1971), vol. 1, pp. 360–1 and I. Meszaros, 'Ideology and Social Science', in *Philosophy, Ideology and Social Science: Essays in Negation and Affirmation* (Brighton, 1986), p. 32 and pp. 52–3.

[17] For recognition (from radically contrasting ideological and methodological perspectives) of the fertility of bias, see J. Schumpeter, 'Science and Ideology', *American Economic Review*, vol. 39, 1949, p. 359; L. Althusser, 'Elements of Self-Criticism', in *Essays in Self-Criticism* (London, 1976), p. 121; and Ricoeur, 'Science and Ideology', p. 241.

undesirable – a formula for conceptual impotence and discursive sterility.

Does this conclusion reduce the study of ideology to a game of circus mirrors, to a frustrating or hypocritical exercise whereby the historian's ideological biases reflect, occlude, distort, or exaggerate the ideological biases of the past? Not necessarily. Self-conscious cultural critique, critical social theory, and critically informed historical practice, although fully as ideological as the most unself-critical social polemic, systematically address their own partiality. Theorists, unlike polemicists, search out cases which challenge their own assumptions; criticise their own ambiguities, contradictions, and limitations; and recognise the strengths as well as the weaknesses of rival problematics.[18] Self-criticism, reflection upon the game of mirrors itself, limits and controls the unthinking ideological distortions and occlusions characteristic of polemic. Of themselves, these distinctions need not imply the inherent superiority of theoretical self-awareness over polemical single-mindedness. Self-awareness enhances analytical sophistication, disciplinary openness, and conceptual scope, but precludes polemical efficacy, the efficacy conferred by assertive self-identity and absolute self-certainty. In 'the real world of ideology', defence of social order and advocacy of alternative social orders has required, presently requires, and will always require, polemicists. The necessity or desirability of critical theorists is considerably less obvious.[19]

In principle, however, a self-critical approach to the scholarly study of ideology *is* necessary and desirable, although hardly inevitable in practice. Too many studies of ideology have been thinly-disguised ideological polemics, polemics limited and limiting in their

[18] For the methodological consequences of the recognition that interpretive strategies in the study of ideology are themselves ideological, see White, 'The Context in the Text', p. 191 and p. 194; Ricoeur, 'Science and Ideology', pp. 242–4; and A. Naess, 'Ideology and Rationality', in M. Cranston and P. Mair (eds.), *Ideology and Politics* (Florence, 1980), pp. 137–8. For the application of this insight to Marxist studies of Marxism, see R. Berki, 'The Marxian Concept of Bourgeois Ideology: Some Aspects and Perspectives', in R. Benewick et al. (eds.), *Knowledge and Belief in Politics: The Problem of Ideology* (London, 1973), pp. 88–114.

[19] P. King, 'An Ideological Fallacy', in P. King and B. Parekh (eds.), *Politics and Experience: Essays Presented to Professor Michael Oakeshott on the Occasion of His Retirement* (Cambridge, 1968), pp. 341–94. For the tension between self-critical impotence and polemical efficacy within Marxism, see F. Jameson, 'Science versus Ideology', *Humanities in Society*, vol. 6, 1983, pp. 283–302. And see E. Wright, 'Reflections on *Classes*', in E. Wright et al., *The Debate on Classes* (London, 1989), pp. 69–70, with the critique of his distinction between theory and polemic in M. Burawoy, 'The Limits of Wright's Analytical Marxism and an Alternative', in *ibid.*, pp. 78–99.

naive lack of theoretical self-awareness and self-criticism. By contrast, theoretically informed studies of past ideological polemics offer not only histories 'of change in the employment of paradigms' but self-conscious and explicit 'employment of paradigms for the exploration of paradigms'.[20] If historians of ideology hope to produce such studies, they require 'theories about theories' which will propose 'criteria for assessing the...merits [of ideologies] and situating [them] historically.'[21] By this measure, students of Marxism enjoy a formidable advantage over analysts of other ideological traditions. No social paradigm has undergone such intense scrutiny from theoretically informed antagonists as has Marxism, and the adherents of no other ideology have criticised themselves as ruthlessly as have Marxists: 'second order' languages of critique, theory's primary resource and theory's ultimate product, have assailed Marxist discourse from every side, while proliferating within Marxism itself, at least within the 'Western Marxist' tradition. Marxism, the focus of our epoch's ideological consciousness, has endured a century-long interrogation which has pitilessly exposed its affirmations and lacunae, its coherence and contradictions, its certainties and vacillations. This lavish legacy of criticism and self-criticism furnishes historians of Marxism and Marxist historians with elaborate, sophisticated, and rigorous questions about every conceivable aspect of Marxist ideology.[22]

Criticism empowered by social theory illuminates the internal rationality (and irrationality) of ideological discourses, discourses thereby comprehended as 'texts' with their own inherent logic (and illogic).[23] Yet, just as critics decode literary texts with references to other literary texts, so historians must decipher an ideology by reading it within the matrix of social practices which conditioned and was conditioned by its development. Above all, scholars must locate an ideology in relation to other ideologies, since ideologies exist and evolve primarily through conflict and congress with

---

[20] Pocock, 'Languages and Their Implications', p. 23.

[21] A. Swingewood, *Marx and Modern Social Theory* (London, 1975), pp. 70–1.

[22] For 'second order languages', their utility, and their problems, see Pocock, 'Introduction: The State of the Art', p. 15. There is a superb discussion of the methodological dilemmas faced by a Marxist studying Marxism, of 'second order language' within Marxism, in L. Goldmann, 'Pour une Approche Marxiste des Études sur le Marxisme', in *Marxisme et Sciences Humaines* (Paris, 1967), pp. 220–6.

[23] For the metaphor of the text, see J. Donzelot, 'The Poverty of Political Culture', *Ideology and Consciousness*, no. 5, 1979, p. 74.

alternative ideological discourses. In other words, historians must master not only an ideology's 'problematic', the realm of theory, but its 'conditions of existence', the domain of history.[24] However vital the understanding of an ideology's semantics and syntactics, its distinguishing concepts and their characteristic articulation, historians should also study its pragmatics – its meaning in various historical circumstances, its representative usage.[25] The lapses, vacillations, and ambiguities of an ideological discourse may indicate inherent inadequacies in its fundamental paradigm: lacunae in its social lexicon, contradictions within its order of concepts, discordance between its lexical content and its conceptual form. But the perturbations of ideological practice may also disclose unmastered complexities, even unmasterable contradictions, in the social order addressed by the ideology's 'pragmatics'.[26] Even the most rigorously coherent ideologies engender diverse and contradictory versions of themselves in dissimilar social and historical circumstances. In this sense, ideologies evolve as 'travelling theories', their 'meaning' metamorphosing with their propagation.[27] Once aware of these contingencies, historians must interpret an ideology as an aspect of a particular historical totality, as a part in a particular social whole.[28]

Familiar perils bedevil this 'contextual' method: structuralist determinism and social reductionism have repeatedly ravaged interpretations of past ideological discourses – in some instances, virtually defining ideologies out of existence, and in most cases radically devaluing their social autonomy, internal integrity, and causal

[24] A. Callinicos, *Is There a Future for Marxism?* (London, 1982), p. 189. For a brilliant analysis of the need to comprehend the constitution of an ideological discourse through its contact and conflict with alternative ideologies, see K. Baker, 'On the Problem of the Ideological Origins of the French Revolution', in D. LaCapra (ed.), *Modern European Intellectual History: Reappraisals and New Perspectives* (Ithaca, 1982), pp. 200–3.

[25] J. Dunn, 'The Identity of the History of Ideas', in *Political Obligation in its Historical Context: Essays in Political Theory* (Cambridge, 1980), pp. 13–58.

[26] This study assumes that society as well as thought may be self-contradictory. See the debate over this issue in L. Coletti, 'Marxism and the Dialectic', *New Left Review*, no. 93, 1975, pp. 3–29 and R. Edgley, 'Dialectics: The Contradictions of Coletti', *Critique*, no. 7, 1976–7, pp. 47–52. For exemplary discussion of the relationship between conceptual contradiction and social contradiction, see W. Sewell, *Work and Revolution: The Language of Labor from the Old Regime to 1848* (Cambridge, 1980), pp. 277–84 and W. Reddy, *Money and Liberty in Modern Europe: A Critique of Historical Understanding* (Cambridge, 1987), p. 45.

[27] E. Said, 'Travelling Theory', *Raritan*, vol. 1, 1982, pp. 41–67.

[28] This is the methodology suggested by Lucien Goldmann's *Sciences Humaines et Philosophie: Pour un Structuralisme Génétique* (Paris, 1966). See also J. Merquior, 'The Veil and the Mask: On Ideology, Power and Legitimacy', in *The Veil and the Mask: Essays on Culture and Ideology* (London, 1979), p. 32.

efficacy. No wonder many scholars have renounced the 'scientific' search for structures of determination, venturing forth instead upon the hermeneutic quest for patterns of meaning. Nevertheless, hermeneutics itself, sovereign protection against the iron hand of scientific abstraction, requires exploration of both text *and* context: hermeneutic reconstitution of 'meaning' and revelation of 'intentionality' depend upon interpretation of the reception of discourse, and the study of reception necessarily returns full (hermeneutic) circle to the task of situating an ideology within its textual and social field.[29] Thus, illumination of an ideology's milieu, whether interpreted as deterministic cause or hermeneutic horizon, indicates the only road leading to historical comprehension of ideological discourse. Marxists themselves, the pioneers and most fervent proponents of contextual analysis . . . of others' ideologies, may not exempt Marxism from this discipline.[30]

Contextualisation classically reveals relationships between an ideology and its characteristic bearers, thereby embodying the ideology's texts in its bearers' experience. In pursuing this strategy, historians endeavour to view a society as it once was viewed by an ideology's adherents, to 'think' the social order of the past as it once was thought. Deciphering the past of the past, historians ascertain the historical traditions which moulded ideologists' comprehension of their present and evoked their fears and hopes of the future. And historians, fortunately deaf to post-Althusserian exhortation, delineate both the interests which governed the creation, reception, and comprehension of ideological discourse and the interests engendered by ideological practices. Yet the intricate nexus between an ideology and its advocates and audience will remain problematical: historians should abjure facile answers to questions of contextualisation.

Unfortunately, facile answers abound. Historians have too often assumed that an ideology produced and consumed in a distinctive 'social location' necessarily serves the interests of those located there, that the ideological discourse characteristic of a distinct social category necessarily 'reflects' that category's interests. This *a priori* assumption violates every serious disciplinary protocol in the study

---

[29] Q. Skinner, 'Hermeneutics and the Role of History', *New Literary History*, vol. 7, 1975, pp. 209–32. There is a good critique of the failure of this dialectic in much social history in T. Judt, 'On the Syntax of the History of Socialism', *Historical Journal*, vol. 22, 1979, p. 1025.

[30] See D. LaCapra, 'Marxism and Intellectual History', in *Rethinking Intellectual History: Texts, Contexts, Language* (London, 1983), pp. 325–46.

of the association between social interests and ideological expressions. Restricted social perspective or the iron logic of domination have often (usually?) precluded self-interested representation of society, at least by society's most restricted and dominated subjects.[31] On the other hand, pervasive ideologies do not necessarily serve the interests of society's rulers, as presupposed by disillusioned Marxists, for whom even the most revolutionary ideologies (including their own) inevitably degenerate into the ruling ideas of ruling classes.[32] Despite subjection to 'ideological hegemony', subaltern groups have regularly manipulated dominant political ideas and hegemonic social ideals to their own advantage. The calculus relating historical circumstance, social interest and ideological representation is too complex to allow *a priori* supposition, but not so complex as to preclude its application in scholarly inquiry.[33]

Mention of ideology evokes the imagery of class and class conflict – so completely has assertively Marxist, implicitly Marxisant, or explicitly anti-Marxist scholarship pervaded the study of ideology throughout the twentieth century. Within these limiting parameters, contextualisation of ideological discourse has implied the simple (and sometimes simplistic) reduction of an ideology's social context to class structure, with ideologies equated with varieties of class consciousness. According to this Marxist paradigm, the archetypal 'class for itself' signals its autonomy and manifests its force through the elaboration and deployment of a unique ideology – simultaneously product of its class interest (a class consciousness) and assertion of that interest (an ideological programme).[34] Some of the best recent work on the history of ideologies has invoked the legacy of Antonio Gramsci, the twentieth century's Marxist Machiavelli, subtle theorist of hegemony. The fundamental Gramscian thesis that

[31] I. Balbus, 'The Concept of Interest in Pluralist and Marxian Analysis', *Politics and Society*, vol. 1, 1971, pp. 151–79.

[32] For an excellent elaboration of this association of ideology with the 'ruling ideas of ruling classes', or at least with those of dominant social groups in general, see J. Thompson, *Studies in the Theory of Ideology* (Cambridge, 1984), pp. 73–147. But see the critique of this tradition in N. Abercrombie et al., *The Dominant Ideology Thesis* (London, 1980) and P. Ricoeur, 'Science and Ideology', p. 223.

[33] This vital point is made by J. Elster in 'Belief, Bias and Ideology', in M. Hollis and S. Lukes (eds.), *Rationality and Relativism* (Oxford, 1982), pp. 123–45 and by J. McCarney in *The Real World of Ideology* (Brighton, 1980), pp. 32–3 and chapter 2.

[34] See the useful discussion of this problematic in D. MacRae, 'Class Relationships and Ideology', *The Sociological Review*, vol. 6, 1958, pp. 261–72 and L. Dion, 'An Hypothesis Concerning the Structure and Function of Ideology', in R. Cox (ed.), *Ideology, Politics, and Political Theory* (Belmont, 1969), pp. 319–21.

social order and social protest have always depended to some extent upon the (class) struggle for control of social consciousness, that ideological hegemony and counter-hegemony increasingly articulate class conflict in modern society, has stimulated and validated sophisticated and insightful Marxist studies of culture and class.[35] And, more than two generations after its initial publication, Georg Lukács's *History and Class Consciousness* retains its magnetic influence over Left Hegelians throughout the western world. The Lukácsian assimilation of authentic proletarian class consciousness to revolutionary socialist ideology, by origin an idealist Leninism, has survived slashing Leninist condemnation and the wounding disavowal of its author, living on to inspire the more militant strands of 'Western Marxism'.[36]

But, however fertile these Marxist traditions, historians (including Marxist historians) of socialist ideology, of Marxism, and of working-class cultural expression should resist uncritical conflation of class and consciousness. The Marxist project which historians interrogate has assumed equivalence between class consciousness and social consciousness, between class programme and ideology: Marxist socialism has derived much of its cultural influence and polemical force from the reductionist or relativist implications of these assimilations. Scholars, however, may not perpetrate *a priori* equation of class consciousness and ideological discourse without abandoning an all-important critical perspective. For historians, if not for socialist militants, the relationship between class and ideology must begin (but not necessarily end) as a question, not as an answer.[37]

None the less, social conflict more generally conceived undoubtedly conditions the production, distribution, and consumption of all ideologies.[38] However consensual in their rhetoric, ideologies embody and beget patterns of domination and resistance: they reflect and reflect upon the chronic tensions which pervade social relations and the momentous ruptures which characterise historical mutations. Ideological 'consensus' is as inconceivable as its two

---

[35] For analysis of the Gramscian tradition in the conception of ideology, see S. Hall, B. Lumley, and G. McLennan, 'Politics and Ideology: Gramsci', in Centre for Contemporary Cultural Studies, *On Ideology* (London, 1978), pp. 33–44.

[36] R. McDonough, 'Ideology as False Consciousness: Lukács', in *ibid.*, pp. 33–44.

[37] Ricoeur, 'Science and Ideology', p. 223 and Hall, 'The Problem of Ideology', pp. 77–84.

[38] A point emphasised in Pocock, 'The Reconstruction of Discourse', p. 961, and Skinner, 'Meaning and Understanding in the History of Ideas', pp. 39–48.

preconditions: a society transparent to all its members in all its aspects, and a society free from systemic inequities, iniquities, and dissension. Despite the phantasmagoric imagery of Foucault's discursive fantasies, no historical social order has ever experienced a 'single network of [conceptual] necessities'.[39] Even the social paradigms most all-pervasive in their societies – paradigms as diverse as medieval corporativism, mid-twentieth-century Soviet socialism, or contemporary American liberalism – have displayed extraordinary variations when deployed in different social circumstances and by dissimilar protagonists, and these varied understandings of the 'same' ideologies have fomented 'family feuds' as intense, embittered, and sometimes bloody as the clashes between champions of overtly antagonistic ideological discourses.[40] If historians wish to explain and interpret, as well as describe, they will have to situate an ideology within its characteristic polemical milieu – within the pattern of alternative ideologies against which it struggled, and within the structures of social conflict which these alternatives represented (in both senses of the word).

The location of an ideology within its polemical field of force and in its social environs, its insertion into historical context, inadvertently but inevitably conjures up the spectre of 'false consciousness', that unwelcome revenant from the 'vulgar Marxist' or 'positivist' Dark Ages of the History of Ideas.[41] Hallowed scholarly tradition once ruled that partial representations of society, those conditioned by restricted social perspectives or representative of special interests, must be biased and therefore false, that only objectivity confers 'true consciousness' upon the protagonists of historical dramas. Yet, as we have seen for historians and social theorists themselves, no historical collectivity, no discursive community, has ever enjoyed a vantage unsullied by vulgar interests from which to view society clear and

---

[39] M. Foucault, *The Order of Things* (London, 1974), p. 63. Both the early Foucault of *The Order of Things* and the later Foucault of *Discipline and Punish* often appear to describe structures of representation which dominate their time with totalitarian efficacy.

[40] For the ways in which 'shared meanings' may engender conflict rather than consensus, see Taylor, 'Interpretation and the Sciences of Man', p. 31.

[41] This concept has been particularly important in Marxist theories of ideology, although Marx himself does not seem to have used the term (according to M. Seliger, *The Marxist Conception of Ideology: a Critical Essay* (Cambridge, 1977), p. 30). The question is complicated by the probability that Marx himself advanced several alternative and to some extent contradictory conceptions of ideology and 'false consciousness'. See G. Markus, 'Concepts of Ideology in Marx', *Canadian Journal of Political and Social Theory*, vol. 7, 1983, pp. 84–103.

whole. The Quixotic search for bearers of 'true consciousness' has garnered only frustration and farce: Hegel's universalistic bureaucrats, Lukács's proletarian embodiments of metahistorical reason, Mannheim's socially detached intellectuals – all have bravely come and sadly gone, leaving behind a sour legacy of disillusionment. At the least, recent linguistic theory teaches that social representation as the 'isomorphic recreation'[42] of social order has always resorted, has always had to resort, to the frolic of metaphor, that signifier and signified have never coalesced into transparent equivalence. The mirage of 'true' social consciousness, an evanescent 'noble dream' like historical objectivity itself, has retreated endlessly towards the unapproachable horizon of absolute knowledge and certain self-knowledge.

On the other hand, recognition that all social consciousness (including that of historians) is necessarily partial – both perspectival and interested, and hence ideological in the traditional pejorative sense – potentially domesticates the concept of 'false consciousness', taming its feral menace to empathic scholarship. Too many historians, revolting against the 'enormous condescension of posterity' inherent in attribution of 'false' consciousness, have thrown out the baby with the bathwater – refusing to assess the partiality of past ideologies for fear of claiming a preposterous omniscience, declining to mar the 'lived experience' of the past with anachronistic theoretical insight, repudiating the application of retrospective knowledge to the limitations of past subjectivities. This paralysing methodological reticence violates common sense no less than historiographical prescription. Just as modern epidemiology explains the propagation of the Black Death, so modern social theory and historical insight explain past ideologies, including their 'false consciousness'. In retrospect, historical actors' self-awareness requires explication both by causal contexts of which they were unaware and by outcomes of which they could not have been aware.[43] Absurdly, the more clearly historians of ideas have discerned the relativity, partiality, and bias inherent in their own practice, the less willingly have they attributed these qualities to their subjects.

How might students of ideology amend the 'strategy of suspi-

---

[42] G. Huaco, 'On Ideology', *Acta Sociologica*, vol. 4, 1971, p. 245.
[43] A. MacIntyre, 'The Idea of a Social Science', in *Against the Self-Images of the Age* (London, 1971), pp. 211–29.

cion'[44] which has dominated and increasingly paralysed their craft? Historians might overcome disabling evaluative timidity by manipulating their own disciplinary rhetoric, by substituting the innocuous concept of 'partial consciousness' for the pejorative attribution of 'false consciousness'. A scholar need not consider an ideology 'false' because of its necessarily selective social perspective and its inevitably interested social constitution. Liberalism, for instance, has not 'wrongly' emphasised the formal equality of exchange relations characteristic of capitalist commodity production: this equality has indeed conditioned the distinctive ideals and characteristic contradictions of modern 'Western' social consciousness. Similarly, socialism has not 'wrongly' stressed capitalism's asymmetrical relations of production: this inequality, too, has constituted authentic historical experience. Ideological conflicts, such as the running battle between liberals and socialists, rarely, if ever, evince Manichean rivalries between virtuous truths and vicious falsehoods, but rather the tragic clash of alternative (partial) 'truths'.[45] Liberal and socialist polemicists will never, could never, should never, accept this insight; liberal and socialist historians of ideology, on the other hand, must assent to this methodological precept or accept relegation to the (by no means dishonourable) ranks of the polemicists.

Subjected to these analytical insights, ideologists and their adherents will always appear to be mistaken and ignorant, their preoccupation with particular 'truths' necessarily obscuring others. Just as clearly, the historical fortunes of an ideology will depend upon the outcome of this dialectic between comprehension and incomprehension – upon the scope of the ideology's particular pattern of social revelation and social occlusion, the quality of its maps of social order, the worth of its combat manuals in the war of social ideas and ideals. Nevertheless, no simple correlation prevails between an ideology's 'partial consciousness' and its polemical efficacy. The ideologies which have emerged victorious from the discursive conflicts of the past *may* have been those which best

---

[44] For the need to break the link between the study of ideology and this strategy, see Ricoeur, 'Science and Ideology', p. 223.

[45] This vital point is made in J. Clarke, I. Connell and R. McDonough, 'Misrecognising Ideology: Ideology as Political Power and Social Classes', Centre for Contemporary Cultural Studies, *On Ideology* (London, 1978), pp. 116–18 and in M. Godelier, 'Fétichisme, Religion, et Théorie Générale de l'Idéologie chez Marx', *Annali: Istituto Giangiacomo Feltrinelli* (Milan, 1970), pp. 22–39. Marx's mature views on ideology seem to have evolved towards this conception of conflicting truths. J. Mepham, 'The Theory of Ideology in *Capital*', *Radical Philosophy*, vol. 2, 1972, pp. 12–19.

approximated their social 'reality', as historians usually assume. But not necessarily. In assessing an ideology's social force and its historical fortune, critically informed and historiographically skeptical historians must remember that ideologies prevail not only by 'accurately' mapping society, but by concealing the 'truths' which legitimate alternative ideologies and by camouflaging their own ambiguities, lacunae, and contradictions.[46] Potent fantasies, creative myths, noble lies – these blast open the approaches to the historical treasure-troves indicated on ideological maps. Marxist socialists, no less than positivist liberals, have sincerely believed that 'the truth shall make you free', and that the struggle for freedom opens the way to truth. But 'progressives' may be as socially blinkered as the most purblind reactionaries. As jockeys know, blinkers win races by limiting and directing horses' vision.

In developing this insight, students of ideology should avoid the arrogant empiricist assumption that they know the Truth, the whole Truth, and nothing but the Truth, that they can reveal an ideology's 'distortions' of 'reality' by confronting it with the unimpeachable testimony of 'the' Facts.[47] Instead, historians should compare an ideology with alternative (and equally ideological) representations of its society – both contemporaneous and retrospective, both theoretical and polemical – and interpret the resulting dissonance to reveal the ideology's characteristic contradictions and silences, as well as its distinctive coherence and revelations. In obeying this inquisitorial protocol, the student of ideology follows the procedures of recent method in the history of the physical sciences: 'it is not that we propose a theory and nature shouts NO; rather, we propose a maze of theories, and nature may shout INCONSISTENT'.[48] In any case, historians should respect the ideologies which they study, avoiding the all too common, all too easy, decision to attribute 'patently absurd' social representations to ideologists' lack of social

---

[46] Merquior, 'The Veil and the Mask', pp. 1–38; N. Jennawi-Le Yaouanc, 'Connaissance et Idéologie dans l'Élaboration des Stratégies Socialistes', *Bulletin de la Société d'Études Jaurésiennes*, no. 107, 1987, p. 3; and Ricoeur, 'Science and Ideology', pp. 227–8.

[47] However well taken, E. P. Thompson's criticisms of Althusserian excess, his own defense of empiricist procedure in 'The Poverty of Theory' (in *The Poverty of Theory and Other Essays*, London, 1978) raises many difficulties. See, for example, the important debate provoked in the pages of *History Workshop Journal* by R. Johnson, 'Edward Thompson, Eugene Genovese and Socialist-Humanist History', *History Workshop Journal*, no. 6, 1978, pp. 79–100.

[48] I. Lakatos, 'Falsification and the Methodology of Scientific Research Programmes', in *The Methodology of Scientific Research Programmes* (Cambridge, 1978), pp. 44–5, quoted in A. Callinicos, *Is There a Future for Marxism?*, p. 171.

perspective or to their interested special pleading.[49] Given the nature of social discourse, research will always validate these destructive assessments: all ideologies indeed suffer perspectival limitation and evolve from interests. None the less, theoretical method, as opposed to disguised polemic, requires sympathetic assessment of an ideology's relative truth as well as censorious determination of its 'false' consciousness, empathic illumination of its original rationality as well as critical delineation of its discursive limitations.[50] Empathy, no less than critique, enhances historical understanding.

What protocols, then, should govern the historical study of Marxism as an ideology? Three fundamental requirements emerge from recent theoretical endeavour: first, a clear definition of ideology as representation of social order; second, theoretically informed sensitivity to the internal nuances and intricacies of representation – perception of connotation as well as denotation, of silence as well as emphasis, of contradiction as well as coherence; and, finally, comprehension of ideologies in time and place, their location within the social whole which conditioned their development and was conditioned by that development. These imperatives in themselves, however, remain mere abstractions. For historians of social analysis and for social analysts of history, theoretical introspection and methodological rigour must aid in the authoring of 'close, careful but fully conceptualised concrete studies'.[51] Theory is not an end, but a means – even in the study of theory.

---

[49] Critique of such critiques may be found in A. Naess et al., *Democracy, Ideology and Objectivity: Studies in the Semantics and Cognitive Analysis of Ideological Controversy* (Oxford, 1956), pp. 1–11 and in D. Miller, 'Ideology and the Problem of False Consciousness', *Political Studies*, vol. 20, 1972, p. 433.

[50] Skinner, 'Some Problems in the Analysis of Political Thought and Action', p. 295.

[51] R. Johnson, 'Histories of Culture/Theories of Ideology: Notes on an Impasse', in M. Barrett et al. (eds.), *Ideology and Cultural Production* (New York, 1979), p. 49.

CHAPTER 2

The Parti Ouvrier Français: its history and historiography

Theory . . . becomes a material force as soon as it has gripped the masses.

> Karl Marx, *Contribution to Critique of Hegel's Philosophy of Law. Introduction* (1844).

We have translated the cries [of the suffering proletariat] into words.

> Jules Guesde, untitled, *L'Égalité*, 5 February 1882.

This first encounter between a French [political] culture and Marxism deserves to be recounted: does it not have exemplary value?

> M. Perrot, 'Les Guesdistes: Controverses sur l'Introduction du Marxisme en France', *Annales: Économies, Sociétés, Civilisations*, vol. 22, 1967.

Recent years have witnessed publication of innumerable historical studies of ideology. Unfortunately, most of these works have centred upon individual 'great minds' rather than upon the communities of ideological discourse which such 'minds' exemplified and animated: historians have studied Locke rather than liberalism as a social system of social representation, Burke rather than the generic conservatism which he embodied and engendered, Marx rather than Marxism as a collective enterprise. Yet ideologies advance only as collective enterprises, their force embodied in vulgarisation rather than in the 'received canon of classic texts'[1] worshipped by traditional political theory and adored by the customary history of ideas. Widely-distributed sermons reveal more about the political culture of seventeenth-century England than does the *Two Treatises of Government*, anonymous broadsheets more about the counter-revolution than *Reflections on the Revolution in France*, ephemeral

[1] Q. Skinner, 'Some Problems in the Analysis of Political Thought and Action', *Political Theory*, vol. 2, 1974, p. 280.

pamphlets more about the rise of socialism than *Capital*. As Gramsci insisted, 'for a mass of people to think coherently ... about the real present world, is a "philosophical" event far more important and "original" than the discovery by some "philosophical" genius of a truth which remains the property of small groups of intellectuals'.[2] Historically potent communities of discourse alone beget, empower, and legitimate 'great minds' and 'classic texts'. If historians of ideology accept this insight, they will abandon the ancient questions 'Who really spoke? Is it really he and not someone else? With what authenticity and originality? And what part of his deepest self did he express in his discourse?' Instead, they will ask 'What are the modes of existence of this discourse? Where has it been used, and how can it circulate, and who can appropriate it for himself?'[3] Collective language precedes individual speech, in ideological discourse no less than in everyday usage, yet historians of ideology have repeatedly emphasised ideologies' contingent *parole* rather than their constituting *langue*.[4]

Studies of Marxist socialism have all too frequently exemplified this reduction of doctrine to doctrinaire, focusing obsessively upon the writings of Marx, or even upon some small segment of his textual legacy: entire libraries have been written about the intricacies of Marx's methodological procedures, about the ambiguities of his theory of surplus value, about the ramifications of his concept of class. At their most extreme and absurd, these studies have assumed that 'Marxism was the unique product of the thought of a single individual'.[5] No wonder historians have lavished their energies and intelligence upon textual exegesis! Yet 'the closer we get to what Marx really said, the more difficult it is to assess what he really meant'.[6] Historians of discourse easily resolve this paradox: discovery of 'what Marx really meant' depends upon investigation of

---

[2] Antonio Gramsci, 'The Study of Philosophy', in *Selections from the Prison Notebooks* (London, 1971), p. 325. For good discussion of the collective nature of ideology and the importance of vulgarisation as opposed to high theory, see A. Gouldner, *The Two Marxisms: Contradictions and Anomalies in the Development of Theory* (London, 1980), pp. 275–7.

[3] M. Foucault, 'What is an Author?', in J. Harari (ed.), *Textual Strategies: Perspectives in Post-Structuralist Criticism* (Ithaca, 1979), p. 160.

[4] For the methodological implications of this distinction, see J. Pocock, 'Introduction: The State of the Art', in *Essays on Political Thought and History* (Cambridge, 1985), p. 5.

[5] T. Tholfsen, *Ideology and Revolution in Modern Europe: An Essay on the Role of Ideas in History* (New York, 1984), p. 74.

[6] G. McLennan, 'Philosophy and History: Some Issues in Recent Marxist Theory', in R. Johnson et al. (eds.), *Making Histories: Studies in History-Writing and Politics* (London, 1982), p. 134.

what Marx really meant *to others*, not upon detection of some 'essence' of Marx discerned through ever closer readings of his works. Marxism as a socialist ideology practised by thousands of militants, many of whom had never read Marx, imposes meaning upon Marxist texts; the texts themselves – however widely distributed, however prestigious – are not all-important criteria for evaluating socialism's 'philosophical and methodological divergence from Marx's own ideas'.[7]

Unfortunately, even the best studies of Marxism as a tradition have emphasised the theoretical gymnastics of Marx's ideological progeny rather than the doctrine's constitution as the collective discourse of mass socialist and labour movements: historians of Austro-Marxism, for instance, have focused narrowly upon the theoretical brilliance and high culture of its Viennese intellectuals, while the plodding everyday militancy of thousands of social democrats scattered across the Crown Lands has furnished no more than an untheorised, even unexamined, backdrop to the conceptual exploits of Adler, Bauer, and their dazzling associates.[8] Ironically, Marxist historians have excelled at this 'great man' theorisation of their doctrine's past, whether in party hagiography (Lenin's thought rather than the discourse of Leninism, Luxemburg's legacy rather than the problematic of nascent German communism) or in the more sophisticated endeavours of today's 'Marxism of the Chair' (the Anglo-Marxism of the Communist Historians' Group rather than the world-view of British Bolshevism, the cultural pessimism of the Frankfurt School rather than the death-agonies of the Social Democratic political culture). Historians should reconsider these priorities. After all, Marx himself opted for 'Marxism' while under the influence of the socialist and labour upsurge of the 1840s: his theoretical meditations did not author the social-revolutionary movements of his time, or of any time, however much Marxism has influenced (and been influenced by) the triumphs and tribulations of socialism.[9] Studies of Marxism as an ideology should follow Eric Hobsbawm's suggestion that 'if we want to understand the diffusion

---

[7] D. Morgan, 'The "Orthodox" Marxists: First Generation of a Tradition', in R. Bullen et al. (eds.), *Ideas into Politics: Aspects of European History 1880–1950* (London, 1984), p. 6.

[8] For discussion of the centrality of socialist practice to any Marxist assessment of Marxism, see E. Andrews, 'Marx's Theory of Classes: Science and Ideology', *Canadian Journal of Political Science*, vol. 8, 1975, p. 466.

[9] G. Therborn, 'The Working Class and the Birth of Marxism', *New Left Review*, no. 79, 1973, pp. 3–16.

of Marxism; not just its formal acceptance on the part of organisations but the reality which permeated working class movements, we
must look not only at the works of Marx and of Marxist ideologues
and leaders but also at the concrete reality of the existence and
struggles of the workers and the lessons which they learned from
them'.[10] Understanding of Marxism as a living doctrine, comprehension of its 'diffusion', depends upon this project, given that
'Marxism's contradictions have no pure or simple existence: they
exist only within a *history* of conceptual practice [*une histoire* practico-
théorique]. To grasp [these contradictions] requires a detailed
investigation of that history, which simultaneously involves the
formulation of problems, the usage of concepts, and popular social
practices'.[11]

The requirements of this undertaking are daunting, demanding
theoretical insight into the Marxist paradigm, detailed knowledge of
the movements which have embodied Marxism, and historical
comprehension of their societies. No historian of the doctrine's saga
could possibly accomplish this enterprise alone – although heroic
academic entrepreneurs have attempted the feat. Given historians'
artisanal 'labour processes', comprehensive historical insight into
generic 'Marxism' will have to wait upon illumination of particular
'Marxisms', upon the achievements of individual researchers investigating historically located and socially situated communities of
discourse. This 'case studies' method will serve historical understanding best if concentrated upon times when Marxist socialism
first 'gripped the masses',[12] upon a time such as 'the moment at
which Marxism became the lens through which French socialists saw
and understood their own circumstances and behaviour (a moment
fairly precisely situated between 1881 and 1900)'.[13]

[10] E. Hobsbawm, 'La Diffusione del Marxismo (1890–1905)', *Studi Storici*, a. 15, 1974, p. 269. I
am indebted to Dr Lorenzo Polizzotto for aid in translating this important article.
[11] E. Balibar, 'La Vacillation de l'Idéologie dans le Marxisme', *Raison Présente*, no. 66, 1983, p.
99.
[12] 'Theory ... becomes a material force as soon as it has gripped the masses.' Karl Marx,
'Contribution to Critique of Hegel's Philosophy of Law: Introduction', in Karl Marx and
Frederick Engels, *Collected Works* (London, 1975), vol. 3, p. 182.
[13] T. Judt, *Marxism and the French Left: Studies in Labour and Politics in France 1830–1981* (Oxford,
1986), p. 16. This is not to argue that 'Marxist' socialism only appeared in 1882, as Judt
himself demonstrates (pp. 105–7). See also W. Sewell, *Work and Revolution in France: The
Language of Labour from the Old Regime to 1848* (Cambridge, 1980), pp. 275–6; J.-P.
Courtheoux, 'Naissance d'une Conscience de Classe dans le Prolétariat Textile du Nord
1830–1870', *Revue Économique*, vol. 8, 1957, p. 138; and the very useful discussion in D.
Lovell, 'Early French Socialism and Class Struggle', *History of Political Thought*, vol. 9, 1988,

The Parti Ouvrier Français (the POF or the Parti Ouvrier, the 'Français' being added in the mid-1890s) dominates the intricate story of the birth, apprenticeship, and adventures of Marxist social-ism in France during these years. Its militants, known as 'Guesdists' after their leader Jules Guesde, embodied what they described as 'the only socialism which matters nowadays . . . , the socialism whose basic theses were established by Marx'.[14] The Guesdists' ideological self-image, whether collective or individual, exemplified this em-bodiment: portraits of Marx loomed over Parti Ouvrier meetings; the movement's Thirteenth Congress in 1895 muffled its red banners in black to mark the passing of Engels; and Jean Dormoy, the Guesdist mayor of Montluçon, named his eldest son Marx Dormoy.[15] The Parti Ouvrier, not the better-known Russian or German social democratic movements, pioneered and popularised the symbolism and ceremony of Marxist socialism: the party card (the famous 'carte rouge' which came to symbolise individual socialist commitment), the red flag, the international May Day celebration, and the singing of the *Internationale*.[16] The Guesdists' chief ideologist, Marx's son-in-law Paul Lafargue (with the discreet aid of his self-effacing wife Laura), abridged Engels' *Anti-Dühring* into *Socialism:*

pp. 327–48, particularly pp. 327–30. Indeed, it has been suggested that Marx himself became a 'Marxist' under the influence of the French labour and socialist movement of the 1840s. P. Cousteix, 'L'Introduction du Marxisme en France', *Cahier et Revue de l'Ours*, no. 41, 1973, p. 68 and R. Dangeville, 'Introduction', in R. Dangeville (ed.), *Karl Marx, Friedrich Engels: Le Mouvement Ouvrier Français* (Paris, 1974), vol. 1, pp. 5–36. Nevertheless, it was not until the 1890s that an explicitly Marxist paradigm became dominant among French socialists.

[14] G. Deville, *Principes Socialistes* (Paris, 1896), p. viii. Deville gradually abandoned formal membership in the Parti Ouvrier during the early 1890s, but his work throughout the mid-decade continued to bear the Guesdist stamp and may be adduced in some cases as evidence for Guesdist attitudes. Several of the pieces collected in *Principes Socialistes* had originally appeared in the POF press, and the collection is dedicated to Guesde and Lafargue. For Deville's importance and his relationship to the Guesdist movement, see the excellent study in J. Hall, 'Gabriel Deville and the Development of French Socialism 1871–1905', PhD thesis, Auburn University, 1983.

[15] For the use of Marx's portrait in Guesdist ceremonial symbology, see the description of the opening of the party's fifteenth congress in *La Petite République*, 13 July 1897. For mourning at the Thirteenth Congress, see Anonymous, 'En Mémoire de Frédéric Engels', *Le Socialiste*, 15 September 1895. And on Dormoy, see J. Maitron (ed.), *Dictionnaire Biographique du Mouvement Ouvrier Français 1870–1914* (Paris, 1974), vol. 12, p. 67.

[16] For the origin of the *Internationale* and its association with Guesdism, see G. Delory, *Aperçu Historique sur la Fédération du Nord 1876–1920* (Lille, 1921), p. 77 and the analysis in R. Baker, 'A Regional Study of Working-Class Organisation in France: Socialism in the Nord 1870–1924', PhD thesis, Stanford University, 1967, p. 75. On the origins of May Day within the socialist movement, see M. Dommanget, *Histoire du Premier Mai* (Paris, 1972), pp. 61–4. For the origins of the 'party card', see D. Ligou, *Histoire du Socialisme en France* (Paris, 1962), p. 64.

Utopian and Scientific, the most widely diffused and politically influential Marxist text of the doctrine's 'golden age', while Gabriel Deville's internationally acclaimed abridgement of *Capital* did more to disseminate the arguments of Marx's revered but unread *magnum opus* than did any other publication before or since.[17] The Parti Ouvrier thoroughly deserved its honoured place in the serried ranks of Marxist parties marshalled by the Second International.

Polemicists of genius, Guesdists appropriated notable political events, disruptive strikes, even the everyday chronicle of crime and corruption, processed these raw materials of social perception through their Marxist categories, and retailed the finished product in their newspapers, pamphlets, and incessant public meetings. Decades of this journalistic and oratorical militancy thoroughly justified the Guesdists' self-characterisation as 'soldiers of the Idea',[18] of the 'Idea' of Marxist socialism. The movement's enemies agreed with the Parti Ouvrier's self-estimation: the French political police characterised the POF as 'a party of doctrine [representing] Marxism in France; it is a self-education school where members cooperate in socialist instruction'.[19] The Parti Ouvrier may not have exploded dynamite bombs, erected Parisian barricades, or stormed public buildings, but guardians of order feared the Guesdists' unceasing propaganda and patient organisation of an ever-more militant working class.[20] French Marxists, to their elation, eventually embodied bourgeois visions of the red peril – inheriting the social revolutionary tradition initiated by Babeuf's *Conspiration des Égaux* a century earlier, as feared and hated by the

[17] For the enormous impact of the former, see J. Varlet, 'Préface', in *Paul Lafargue: Théoricien du Marxisme* (Paris, 1933), p. 13, and for that of the latter, J. Hall, 'Gabriel Deville and the Abridgement of *Capital*', *Proceedings of the Western Society for French History*, vol. 10, 1982, pp. 438–48.

[18] 'Le Parti Ouvrier en France – Paris', *Le Socialiste*, 16 June 1895. The 'I' of 'Idée' is capitalised in the original. 'Le Parti Ouvrier en France' – a chronicle of party activities – appeared weekly in the movement's official journal, and provides an invaluable source of information on everyday Guesdist militancy. The POF's intense doctrinal commitment is stressed in C. Willard, 'Contribution au Portrait du Militant Guesdiste dans les Dix Dernières Années du XIXᶜ Siècle', *Mouvement Social*, nos. 33–4, 1960–1, p. 62. Guesdists, however, rarely referred to themselves as 'Marxists', their favourite self-identification being 'collectivist'. For the implications of this terminology, see M. Manale, 'L'Edification d'une Doctrine Marxiste', *Études de Marxologie*, nos. 19–20, 1978, pp. 163–215.

[19] General file on French socialist parties, p. 353, Archives Nationales (henceforth AN) F7 12.855.

[20] See the representative analyses in the reports of 18 May 1885 and 3 November 1890 in the archives of the Paris Préfecture of Police (henceforth APPP), Ba/1135 and file 177300–17 Ba/40.

Republican establishment of the 1890s as the Babouvists had been by the Thermidoreans of the 1790s. Fundamentally transforming France's revered and reviled heritage of popular protest, the POF became the first movement, not only in France but worldwide, to be systematically identified (by its enemies) as Marxist, and the first to welcome the designation.[21]

Assessment by posterity has been less clear-cut. Twentieth-century Marxist militants have cherished the Guesdists' memory (the projected reunification of the Communist and Socialist parties after World War II was to have resulted in a Parti Ouvrier Français, so-called in explicit homage to the first POF, while Leftist municipalities in Greater Paris have named no fewer than thirty-six streets after Guesde). But historians of the movement have gleefully repeated Marx's alleged quip about the Guesdists that 'if this is Marxism, then I'm no Marxist!'[22] At their most critical, some students have ruthlessly denied the POF any part in the introduction of Marxism to France, variously awarding the achievement to Jean Jaurès, Édouard Vaillant, or Georges Sorel.[23] At their most extreme, they

[21] G. Haupt, 'Marx and Marxism', in E. Hobsbawm (ed.), *The History of Marxism: Marxism in Marx's Day* (Brighton, 1982), pp. 269–72 and G. Haupt, 'From Marx to Marxism', in *Aspects of International Socialism 1871–1914* (Cambridge, 1986), p. 5.

[22] Quoted by Engels in a letter to Bernstein, 3 November 1882, cited in *Le Mouvement Socialiste*, 1 November 1900, p. 523, and in virtually every study of French socialism since. In fact, Marx and Engels had a much more positive estimation of the Guesdists than this comment indicates. See the discussion in C. Willard, 'Marx et la Naissance du Parti Ouvrier Français', *Cahiers de l'Institut Maurice Thorez*, no. 10, 1968, pp. 65–9. For the abortive rebirth of the POF after WW II, see J. Duclos, 'L'Héritage de Jules Guesde dans le Mouvement Ouvrier Français: Débat', *Démocratie Nouvelle*, no. 3, 1966, p. 34, and for Parisian street names, C. Willard, 'Paul Lafargue et la Critique de la Société Bourgeoise', in *Histoire du Marxisme Contemporain* (Paris, 1977), vol. 3, p. 199.

[23] For the attribution to Jaurès, see L. Laurat, 'La Pénétration du Marxisme en France', *La Nef*, vol. 7, 1950, pp. 57–59 (there is an excellent study of the ambiguous relationship between Marxism and Jaurès in M. Rebérioux, 'Marxisme et Critique du Marxisme de Jean Jaurès', in *Histoire du Marxisme Contemporain* (Paris, 1977), vol. 3, pp. 205–27); for the attribution to Sorel, see N. McInnes, 'Les Débuts du Marxisme Théorique en France et en Italie (1880–1897)', *Cahiers de l'Institut de Science Économique Appliquée – Série S*, no. 102, 1960, pp. 6–7; and for Vaillant, see J. Howorth's superb *Édouard Vaillant: La Création de l'Unité Socialiste en France/La Politique de l'Action Totale* (Paris, 1982), p. 36 and J. Howorth, 'La Propagande Socialiste d'Édouard Vaillant pendant les Années 1880–1884', *Mouvement Social*, no. 72, 1970, pp. 83–119. The only credible alternative to the Guesdists as propagators of Marxist socialism within the French working class would be Vaillant, simply because of the importance of his 'Blanquist' (a misnomer) movement in the development of French socialism during the period. But Vaillant's Parti Socialiste Révolutionnaire was so closely associated with the Guesdists that contemporaries often saw them as a single movement, as actually became the case after their merger in 1902. A comprehensive study of the 'meaning of Marxism' in France during the period would have to study the PSR as well as the POF, but such a project would be

have ignored the Parti Ouvrier altogether.[24] Even communist scholars, who have contributed most to the study of the POF, have systematically disparaged the Party with invidious comparisons to the Bolsheviks.[25] Why this withering barrage of criticism and denigration? Why have the Guesdists, regarded in their own time as the embodiment of Marxist socialism, lost their credibility among today's students of Marxism and socialist history?

First, historians have charged the Parti Ouvrier with neglecting the study and diffusion of Marx's works, thereby denying the Guesdists any right to Marxist credibility.[26] According to this argument, Guesdist vulgarisation of 'Marxist' first principles rather than learned exegesis of Marx's work reduced the POF's 'Marxism' to 'a series of clichés and stereotyped formulae',[27] a critique variously founded upon the astonishing assumption that Marxist credibility requires 'the reading of Marx's entire oeuvre'[28] or upon the absurd presumption that 'the understanding and characteristic utilisation of Marx and Engels' works allows us to judge the degree

---

unwieldy and would not generate sufficient supplementary insight to warrant the difficulties.

[24] For representative examples of this neglect, see Morgan, 'The "Orthodox" Marxists', and L. Coletti, 'Bernstein and the Marxism of the Second International', in *From Rousseau to Lenin* (London, 1972), pp. 45–108 (which mentions insignificant British Marxists, but virtually ignores Guesdism). Robert Aron's *Le Socialisme Français Face au Marxisme* (Paris, 1971) is a dreadful example of a substantial work (275 pages) which mentions virtually every imaginable socialist from Jesus Christ to Marcuse, but completely ignores the Guesdists. Tony Judt's insightful analysis of French Marxism, however, correctly characterises the POF as 'Jules Guesde's underestimated Parti Ouvrier Français', although Judt fails to remedy this underestimation, his study skipping from Marx's day to the founding of the French Communist Party. T. Judt, *Marxism and the French Left*, pp. 17–18.

[25] Claude Willard's definitive social and institutional history of Guesdism, *Le Mouvement Socialiste en France (1893–1905): Les Guesdistes* (Paris, 1965), is marred by continual critique of the POF for not being the RSDLP (Bolsheviks). See, in particular, pp. 213–15 of this otherwise marvellous study. For similar Leninist indictments, see D. Tartakowski, 'Les Conditions de la Pénétration du Marxisme en France', *Cahiers de l'Institut Maurice Thorez*, no. 28, 1972, pp. 32–43 and L. Figuères, 'Quelques Aspects et Quelques Enseignements de l'Activité de Jules Guesde et du Guesdisme', *Cahiers du Communisme*, vol. 31, 1955, pp. 1,238–62 and pp. 1,392–420.

[26] D. Lindenberg, *Le Marxisme Introuvable* (Paris, 1975), pp. 92–3; M. Perrot, 'Les Socialistes Français et les Problèmes du Pouvoir (1871–1914)', in M. Perrot and A. Kriegel, *Le Socialisme Français et le Pouvoir* (Paris, 1966), pp. 19–20; M. Perrot, 'Les Guesdistes: Controverses sur l'Introduction du Marxisme en France', *Annales: Économies, Sociétés, Civilisations*, vol. 22, 1967, pp. 705–6; and C. Willard, *Les Guesdistes*, pp. 159–60. For a more favourable estimation of the Guesdists' publication record, see J. Kergoat, 'France', in M. van der Linden and J. Rojahn (eds.), *The Formation of Labour Movements 1870–1914: An International Perspective* (Leiden, 1990), vol. 1, p. 170.

[27] M. Dommanget, *L'Introduction du Marxisme en France* (Lausanne, 1969), p. 193.

[28] Cousteix, 'L'Introduction du Marxisme en France', p. 67.

of politicisation and the theoretical and ideological capacity [la capacité théorico-idéologique] of the nascent proletariat'.[29] For socialist scholars and scholarly students of socialism, the Guesdists' cheerful indifference to the enigmatic relationship between Marx and Hegel, their gauche insensitivity to the delicate intricacies of the dialectic, their relaxed unconcern about the unexplored contradictions of advanced value theory, and their other sins against the canons of academic Marxism automatically exclude them from the Marxist Pantheon, a mausoleum reserved for the field marshals of high theory rather than the foot soldiers of low polemic.[30]

These criticisms, although widely accepted, derive from misunderstandings. Marx may exemplify Marxist socialism, but he did not create it; others of his time (and before) independently reached his conclusions about the contradictions of capitalism, the failures of the bourgeoisie, and the liberation of labour: thousands of militants have become 'Marxists' without reading Marx, sometimes without awareness of his existence. Unthinkingly perpetrating reduction of Marxism to Marxology, historians have disdainfully dismissed the 'tranquil assurance with which Guesde claimed to have discovered Marxism at the same time as Marx'.[31] The unfortunate (and grossly unMarxist!) identification of a variety of socialism with a proper name has consistently misled intellectual historians of ideas, too inclined to identify an influential historical movement with the historical influence of a great intellectual. Academic students of Marxism have repeatedly confused the desirable attributes of Marxists with those of Marxologists, failing to recognise that, while the latter indeed require theoretical subtlety and profound knowledge of Marx's texts, the former need only share the fundamental commitments which animated Marx's own socialism. Scholarly 'intellectualism' has defined the prerequisites for Marxist respectability as 'knowledge of political economy, of the dialectic, and of German'![32] 'Marxists' such as Jules Guesde, however, sought the road to

---

[29] T. Paquot, *Les Faiseurs de Nuages: Essai sur la Genèse des Marxismes Français (1880–1914)* (Paris, 1980), p. 31.

[30] M. Kelly, *Modern French Marxism* (Oxford, 1982), chapter 1. The Guesdists receive two short paragraphs in David McLellan's influential *Marxism After Marx* (London, 1979), seemingly on these grounds.

[31] Perrot, 'Les Guesdistes', p. 707.

[32] C. Willard, 'Introduction', in C. Willard (ed.), *La Naissance du Parti Ouvrier Français: Correspondance Inédite de Paul Lafargue, Jules Guesde, José Mesa* (Paris, 1981), p. 21. For the vital distinction between thinking with an ideology and thinking about it, see P. Ricoeur, 'Science and Ideology', in *Hermeneutics and the Human Sciences* (Cambridge, 1981), p. 227.

socialism, not elevation to an Oxford fellowship. Guesdists thought *with* Marxism, not *about* it.

Even communist and socialist scholars, supposedly as sympathetic to popular militancy as opposed to theoretical introversion, have criticised the Parti Ouvrier for vulgarising Marxism, for failing to fight 'on the fundamental front, that of philosophy'.[33] Thus Louis Althusser's lamentations about his youthful ideological education: 'Who were our theoreticians? Guesde? Lafargue?'[34] Virtually caricaturing this genre of critique, Daniel Lindenberg has indicted the Guesdists for failing to contribute to one of the 'few victories' which Marxism won during the *Fin de Siècle*: 'the conquest of a small sector of the intelligentsia during Sorel's Marxist episode'[35] (although Lindenberg concedes that his study ignores the 'relationship ... of French Marxism to ... popular political traditions'![36]) Guesdists themselves applied other criteria of achievement: they welcomed the socialist conversion of the smallest working-class community far more enthusiastically than the ephemeral enthusiasm of Sorel and his circle.

Students of French Marxism have neglected working-class militants 'amongst whom Lafargue could appear as a mandarin' in favour of 'milieux where the exposition of the doctrine could be undertaken in a scientific manner'.[37] Hampered by official harassment, frustrated by workers' disarray, Guesdists would have laughed uproariously if advised that 'police persecution and [lack] of proletarian organisation ... were real difficulties, [but] they were far less heavy with consequences than [the Guesdists'] uncertain mastery of Marxist theory'.[38] These criticisms illuminate the 'theoreticist'

---

[33] Willard, *Les Guesdistes*, p. 168. Willard's enormously important studies of the Guesdists are permeated by this assessment. See *Les Guesdistes*, p. 30, pp. 160–4, and p. 170; C. Willard, 'Paul Lafargue et la Critique de la Société Bourgeoise', p. 187; and Willard, 'Contribution au Portrait', p.62. For similar critiques from sympathetic observers, see S. Bernstein, 'Jules Guesde: Pioneer of Marxism in France', *Science and Society*, vol. 4, 1940, p. 48; G. Delfau, 'Socialisme et Marxisme en France au Tournant du Siècle (1880–1905): Jalons Pour une Problématique Actuelle', *Nouvelle Revue Socialiste*, no. 8, 1975, p. 35; and M. Moissonnier, 'La Longue Marche vers un Parti Ouvrier: Fin du XIXᵉ Siècle', in *La Classe Ouvrière Française et la Politique: Essais d'Analyse Historique et Sociale* (Paris, 1980), p. 50.

[34] L. Althusser, *For Marx* (New York, 1969), p. 23.

[35] Lindenberg, *Le Marxisme Introuvable*, p. 58.

[36] *Ibid.*, p. 10. Lindenberg might well have reached a more serious assessment of the POF if he had actually read some Guesdist material. All his citations are to secondary works and he refers to *Le Socialiste* (the Guesdists' central party publication and the prime source for the movement's ideological development) as *Le Socialisme* (p. 104).

[37] McInnes, 'Les Débuts du Marxisme Théorique', p. 32.

[38] P. and M. Faure, *Les Marxismes après Marx* (Paris, 1970), p. 7.

fixation of today's 'Western Marxists' and the professional biases of academics rather than the daunting dilemmas of socialist militancy during the *Belle Époque*. If able to respond to twentieth-century criticism, Guesdists would have defended their determined 'vulgarity', their dogged determination to arouse the 'vulgar' many rather than enlighten the erudite few.[39]

Ironically, other critics of the POF have indicted the Guesdists for substituting dogmatic doctrinal obsession for considered practical engagement with their own society.[40] The Parti Ouvrier *was* dogmatic at times. Responding to the accusation that his party had failed to elaborate the insights of *Capital*, Charles Bonnier, one of Guesde's closest associates, riposted that 'you might just as easily accuse Christians of not composing a sequel to the Bible'.[41] None the less, unlike their Marxist-Leninist descendants, Guesdists rarely, if ever, fought ideological battles with quotations from their canon of 'sacred' books, if only because neither the Guesdists' friends nor their enemies as yet accorded Marx's works canonical status. French Marxists prided themselves upon their remoteness from doctrinal 'metaphysics' and vaunted their rigorous adherence to 'the experimental method'.[42] The hard 'facts' of social 'reality', not *a priori* dogmas, sanctioned socialism, according to the Parti Ouvrier; Guesdists buttressed their ideological arguments with the mundane

[39] As Madeleine Rebérioux suggests in her 'Le Guesdisme', *Bulletin de la Société d'Études Jaurésiennes*, no. 50, 1973, p. 4. See also J. Raymond, 'Jules Guesde', in J. Maitron (ed.), *Dictionnaire Biographique du Mouvement Ouvrier Français 1870–1914* (Paris, 1974), vol. 12, pp. 350–1; S. Lacore, 'Introduction', in *Jules Guesde* (Paris, 1946), p. 12; and J.-J. Piette, 'L'Héritage de Jules Guesde dans le Mouvement Ouvrier Français: Débat', *Démocratie Nouvelle*, no. 3, 1966, p. 27. The working-class milieu to which the Guesdists appealed demanded 'simplified, even simplistic' versions of ideologies, according to O. Hardy-Hémery, *De la Croissance à la Désindustrialisation: Un Siècle dans le Valenciennois* (Paris, 1984), p. 70. 'If Marxism had been diffused as an analytical programme by the POF, it would have met with a wall of incomprehension [among Roubaisian textile workers]', according to L. Marty, *Chanter pour Survivre: Culture Ouvrière, Travail et Techniques dans le Textile – Rouibaix 1850–1914* (Lille, 1982), p. 206. The ideological needs of working-class communities are beautifully illuminated in this sense by J.-L. Roger in his 'Le Groupe Socialiste de Besançon (1891–1912): L'Évolution Idéologique d'une Section Socialiste au Début du XXᵉ Siècle', *Cahiers d'Histoire de l'Institut Maurice Thorez*, no. 14, 1975, pp. 15–40.

[40] Willard, *Les Guesdistes*, p. 30 and pp. 164–6; G. Lefranc, *Le Mouvement Socialiste sous la Troisième République 1875–1940* (Paris, 1963), p. 51; J. Droz, *Le Socialisme Démocratique* (Paris, 1966), p. 64; and P. and M. Faure, *Les Marxismes après Marx*, p. 17. It has been argued (unconvincingly) that the Guesdists' fundamental ideological legitimacy depended upon their role as the guardians of Marx's theoretical legacy. M. Ymonet, 'Les Héritiers du *Capital*: L'Invention du Marxisme en France au Lendemain de la Commune', *Actes de la Recherche en Sciences Sociales*, no. 55, 1984, pp. 3–14.

[41] C. Bonnier, 'Plus de Catastrophes', *Le Socialiste*, 23–30 March 1902.

[42] J. Guesde, 'Divorse Obligatoire', *Le Cri du Peuple*, 31 December 1883.

force of day-to-day events, not with gnostic evocations of prestigious theoretical arcana. As journalists and public speakers, French Marxists knew very well that vivid anecdotes served their cause far better than did recondite quotations or elaborate speculation: for the Parti Ouvrier, the theory of surplus value led unproblematically towards the evident proletarian misery and bourgeois opulence of Roubaix's textile industry, not into the intricacy of algebraic abstraction. The Guesdists valued Marx because he had been the nineteenth century's finest critic of the bourgeoisie, not because of devout faith in his doctrine; because Marx had been a socialist like themselves, not because they modelled themselves upon the scholarly Marx of the British Museum. As *Le Socialiste* put it, 'socialists are reproached for not having produced a second Marx, as if [his] successor ... was not the socialist movement itself'.[43] Historians of socialism should take this point seriously: individual theoreticians, however epochal, must not obscure the significance of ideological militancy, however 'vulgar'. When 'it becomes necessary ... to ask what exactly Marxism signified in the four decades between the aftermath of the Commune and 1914' the answer is that 'for practical purposes it meant Jules Guesde and his disciples'.[44] Scholars, unfortunately, have neglected those 'practical purposes'.

'Guesdism' first emerged during the later 1870s and the early 1880s as liberal Republicans triumphed over their conservative enemies, a triumph which allowed partisans of the Paris Commune such as Jules Guesde and Paul Lafargue to resume political careers aborted by the catastrophic defeat of 1871 and the subsequent regime of 'Moral Order'. Historical inquiry into the rudimentary French

---

[43] Anonymous, 'La Semaine', *Le Socialiste*, 25 March 1895.

[44] G. Lichtheim, *Marxism in Modern France* (New York, 1966), p. 17 – not a favourable assessment, in Lichtheim's presentation. This was certainly the perspective of historians of French socialism who had lived through the period in question, such as Paul Louis, (*Cent Cinquante Ans de Pensée Socialiste*, Paris, 1939), and Alexandre Zévaès (*De l'Introduction du Marxisme en France*, Paris, 1947). Eminent students of the French working class during the period readily admit the importance of the Parti Ouvrier in the formation of proletarian self-consciousness and awareness of their society. See, for instance, Y. Lequin, 'Classe Ouvrière et Idéologie dans la Région Lyonnaise à la Fin du XIXᵉ Siècle', *Mouvement Social*, no. 69, 1969, p. 3; J. Lhomme, 'Problèmes de la Suprématie d'une Classe', *Revue Économique*, vol. 7, 1956, p. 385; and E. Labrousse, *Le Movement Ouvrier et les Idées Sociales en France de 1815 à la Fin du XIXᵉ Siècle* (Paris, undated), pp. 12–15. Recent overviews of French politics during the period echo these estimations. See J.-M. Mayeur, *La Vie Politique sous la Troisième République 1870–1940* (Paris, 1984), pp. 137–8 and J.-M. Mayeur and M. Rebérioux, *The Third Republic from its Origins to the Great War 1871–1914* (Cambridge, 1984), pp. 137–46.

Marxism of the 1870s has focused narrowly upon the political evolution of Jules Guesde, as if biographical evidence of his gradual abandonment of radicalism and anarchism for socialism suffices to characterise the development of the ideological tendency he eventually personified.[45] When, however, did Marxist socialism first arise as a historical force rather than an individual preference, as a recognisable movement with a significant impact upon the political culture of French workers rather than an isolated coterie of like-minded enthusiasts? When did an independent workers' party dedicated to revolutionary anti-capitalism first assault the bourgeois establishment of the Third Republic? When did the advocates of class warfare first interrupt the embittered dialogue between the heirs of 1789 and their 'reactionary' enemies?

The traditional answer to these questions indicates 1879 as Marxist socialism's birth-year in France, the year when the Congress of Marseilles launched the 'Parti Ouvrier' or 'Party of Labour', the acknowledged progenitor of organised French labour politics.[46] None the less, despite socialist and communist historians' efforts to annex Marseilles to their cause, anti-political anarchists and anti-socialist radicals dominated the infant 'Parti Ouvrier' of 1879, an amorphous movement which included few recognisable Marxists. Nor should this Marxist absence surprise students of the period. Even Paul Lafargue hardly qualified as a 'Marxist' during this early stage in his long political career, and Guesde's newspaper *l'Égalité* remained carefully eclectic throughout the late 1870s, as likely to cite the great utopians as to quote Marx or Engels.[47] The 'Marxist' commitment of Guesde, Lafargue and their comrades evolved slowly and painfully between 1879 and 1882 through rancorous alterca-

---

[45] A prime example of this problem may be found in Samuel Bernstein's otherwise very useful *The Beginnings of Marxian Socialism in France* (New York, 1933), particularly on pp. 187–8. For discussion of this difficult issue in the history of Guesdism, see C. Willard, 'Introduction', to Willard (ed.), *La Naissance du Parti Ouvrier Français*, pp. 9–37.

[46] L. Gaillard, *La Naissance du Parti Socialiste: Marseille Il y a Cent Ans* (Marseille, 1980); R. Joucla, 'Renaissance du Mouvement Français après la Commune: Le Congrès Ouvrier Socialiste de Marseille (Oct. 1879)', *Cahiers Internationaux*, no. 65, 1955, pp. 51–62; and M. Moissonnier, 'Le Congrès de Marseille a Cent Ans', *Cahiers d'Histoire de l'Institut Maurice Thorez*, nos. 32–33, 1979, pp. 198–234.

[47] For Lafargue's politics during the 1870s, see R. Girault, 'Introduction', in R. Girault (ed.), *Paul Lafargue: Textes Choisis* (Paris, 1970), p. 45. Unfortunately, Kolakowski's discussion of Lafargue, unlike most of his illuminating demolition of Marxism, is superficial, and an extreme example of the 'theoreticist' misunderstanding of Guesdism. L. Kolakowski, *Main Currents of Marxism: Its Rise, Growth, and Dissolution* – volume II – *The Golden Age* (Oxford, 1978), chapter 6. The non-Marxist character of the early *L'Égalité* is stressed in M. Manale, 'La Constitution du "Marxisme",' *Études de Marxologie*, no. 18, 1976, pp. 829–31.

tions with former friends and associates – through schism, as first Radicals, then anarchists, and finally anti-Marxist socialists (who first designated the Guesdists as 'Marxists') split away from a 'Guesdist' core loyal to the Party Programme composed by Guesde and Marx and adopted at the Congress of Le Havre in 1880. The distinctively 'Marxist' Parti Ouvrier which contemporaries loved and hated with such passion emerged only in 1882 at the Congress of Roanne – the traumatised offspring of multiple divorces.

Like any ideological movement, the Parti Ouvrier had created itself in struggles against alternative conceptions of social order. No less than French liberals ('les bourgeois libéraux', as the Guesdists characterised the victors of 1789 and their ideological heirs) and conservatives, themselves veterans of a century of mutual mayhem, the Parti Ouvrier had been born in battle, and lived through conflict. As 'soldiers of the Idea', Guesdists fought thousands of 'conférences contradictoires' (the public oratorical contests which informed, excited, and entertained the politically engaged of the *Belle Époque*) – debating ideological gladiators of the clerical and nationalist Right, of the liberal and democratic Republican establishment, and (most frequently) of the non-Marxist movements of the Left. The ephemeral passions of these public encounters persisted in the pages of the Guesdist press, which exhaustively (and tendentiously) reported the debates and recycled the Guesdists' interventions as newspaper articles and pamphlets.[48] Even the Guesdist texts which had not been forged in the oratorical heat of public disputation bore the bloody traces of ideological offensives: French Marxists treasured the metaphors of conflict – the violent language of class *struggle*, the combative discourse of class *war*.

Common sense suggests that the Guesdists' ideological artillery should have lobbed its heaviest projectiles into the encampments of the enemies most hostile to the Parti Ouvrier's 'social democracy' – the warriors of the French Right, with their conservative enthusiasm for social hierarchy. Yet Guesdists tended to disregard, even overtly

[48] For a good discussion of the centrality of debating in French politics, see T. Judt, *Marxism and the French Left*, p. 7. There is a useful analysis of the importance of the 'conférence contradictoire' in creating popular political culture in J. Merriman, *Red City: Limoges and the French Nineteenth Century* (Oxford, 1985), p. 188. For the centrality of these polemics in defining Guesdism, see Willard, *Les Guesdistes*, p. 29 and pp. 136–9 and C. Willard, 'Introduction', in C. Willard (ed.), *Jules Guesde: Textes Choisis* (Paris, 1959), pp. 25–7. The Guesdists themselves recognised the importance of oral propaganda in the triumph of their faith. See, for instance, P. Larlat-Bénaben, 'Que Peut-on Attendre des Réformes?', *Bulletin Mensuel des Élus Socialistes*, deuxième année, no. 23, 1 October 1901, p. 2.

disparage, conservatives, casually dismissing both the threat from the 'Old Right' – clerical, aristocratic, and monarchist – which had menaced the democratic Republic during the 1880s, and the threat from the 'New Right' – nationalist, plebeian, and demagogic – which emerged during the 1890s. Nor did the Parti Ouvrier's artillerymen expend much of their polemical ammunition against the ruling liberals, against Gambetta's 'Opportunist' (later 'Progressist') defenders of bourgeois property and the Republican political order, the 'party' which presided over the French polity throughout the 1880s and 1890s. Why did French Marxists spare their most obvious 'class enemies', concentrating their fire instead upon democratic Radicals, egalitarian anarchists, and fellow socialists?

The POF discounted conservatives and liberals as serious competitors for workers' allegiance: ideologues so patently representative of 'ruling class' interests supposedly posed no threat to the socialist politicisation of the proletariat. Bourgeois would inevitably rally to liberal leadership, bankrupt shopkeepers might enrol in the armies of the nationalist Right, benighted peasants might flock to the standards of clerical reactionaries, but workers would 'naturally' reject these ideologies – ideologies crafted by and for workers' class enemies. Guesdists attacked capitalism with unflagging ardour, but felt little need to discredit its champions. What is more, the POF discerned few advantages in debating agents of the ruling class, who would not, indeed could not, comprehend the logic of their own transcendence. In Charles Bonnier's words, 'there are those with whom one cannot discuss things, simply because there are no common terms of reference'.[49] Neither potential converts nor serious competitors, liberals and conservatives could be safely disregarded.

As a result, Guesdists directed their ideological cannonades against other 'leftists', against the movements which contended with the Parti Ouvrier for the allegiance of French workers, against those who shared the Marxists' commitment to the liberation of labour but rejected the Marxists' conception of the class war. 'Guesdism' hardened its class warriors, blooded its polemical weapons, and perfected its ideological strategy in skirmishes with Radical Republicans such as Georges Clemenceau or Camille Pelletan (who promoted democratic politics and 'mutualist' self-help as remedies for

---

[49] C. Bonnier, 'Incompréhension', *Le Socialiste*, 7–14 June 1903.

the workers' legitimate grievances); in campaigns against anarchists, whether psychopathic terrorists such as Ravachol or pacifist utopians such as Élisée Reclus (who, unlike the Radicals, hated the 'bourgeois' Republic and capitalist property, but also detested the Guesdist programme of political militancy); and in battles with 'Fabian' socialists such as Benoît Malon and Lucien Herr (who, unlike the Guesdists, believed that the established order might evolve gradually and peacefully towards socialism under the influence of enlightened ideals). As potential converts to Marxist socialism and as serious competitors for proletarian endorsement, Radicals, anarchists, and non-Marxist socialists absorbed barrage after barrage of the Guesdists' ideological shellfire.

Guesdists first emerged as distinctive contestants in the French political arena during battles against their erstwhile ally Paul Brousse, whose 'Possibilist' or 'Broussist' supporters wished to discard the 1880 Party Programme which supposedly impeded 'possible' socialist gains and working-class achievements. The Guesdists' *L'Égalité* launched more attacks against the socialist Broussists during the early 1880s than against all the other political movements in France combined – an embittered obsession which foreshadowed the Guesdists' equally intense campaign against the 'Ministerialists', the socialists who supported Alexandre Millerand's participation in the 'bourgeois' Waldeck-Rousseau government at the turn of the century.[50] Radicals, anarchists, and Fabian socialists shared 'common terms of reference' with the French Marxists, questioning the social inequalities praised, excused, or ignored by conservatives and liberals. Hence the virulence of the internecine quarrels between the POF and its fellow movements of the Left – family feuds invariably being the most envenomed and durable of conflicts.

[50] The POF, however, was prepared to cooperate with movements which shared its Marxist commitment, as illustrated by the close relationship between the Guesdists and Vaillant's PSR – apart from the two parties' enduring competition for the allegiance of workers in the Allier, a conflict largely without doctrinal implications. For the friendly personal relationship between Guesde and Vaillant, see J. Howorth, *Édouard Vaillant*, pp. 221–2, although Howorth (over?)emphasises conflict between the POF and PSR as movements. Vaillant was as much a 'Marxist' as Guesde, and it is not surprising that their movements united in 1902, well before the general French socialist unity of 1905. There is a penetrating discussion of Vaillant's impressive Marxism on pp. 98–126 of *Édouard Vaillant*, which is nevertheless grossly unfair to the Guesdists, who are repeatedly set up as strawmen to be knocked down by Vaillant/Howorth. The Guesdists exemplified many of the desirable traits supposedly monopolised by Vaillant, repeatedly advocating non-proletarian recruitment by socialists, for instance (Howorth's presentation of this point seems to be based upon a misunderstanding of Willard's *Les Guesdistes*.)

Despite its passionate polemics, despite its adherents' devotion, the Parti Ouvrier initially amounted to little more than a political sect enrolling fewer than 2,000 members in the mid-1880s, a band of militants incapable of winning more than an infinitesimal proportion of the vote in the national elections of 1885 and 1889.[51] But Guesdists played a more prominent role in the drama of French politics than their meagre numbers and insignificant electoral impact might suggest. Although not yet the household names of the 1890s, Guesde and Lafargue gained the sympathy and admiration of the working-class Left with their imprisonment in 1883 at the hands of authorities outraged by their fiery socialist harangues, a felicitous martyrdom which recalled that of 1878 (when the conservative Republic had imprisoned the two socialists for organising a banned international workers' congress) and foreshadowed that of 1891 (when the liberal Republic would gaol Lafargue for his alleged part in the murderous confrontation between demonstrators and troops at Fourmies).[52] The authorities' hatred of Guesdists unwittingly legitimised Guesdism among those who hated the authorities. Courtroom confrontation between Guesdists and public prosecutors mirrored industrial confrontation between workers and employers: the great strike at Anzin in 1884 and the industrial insurrection at Decazeville in 1886 indelibly imprinted strife between labour and capital, the Guesdists' trademark, onto the political agenda, with considerable assistance from the Parti Ouvrier's assiduous publicists. The French Marxists may have lost election after election during the 1880s, their organisational apparatus may have amounted to little more than Guesde's personal correspondence, but their slogans none the less percolated into the French political consciousness. Faced with crushing electoral humiliation in 1885, Guesde could still cheerfully maintain, with some justice, that 'the basic principle of our politics, that is to say the intervention of society in the economic realm in favour of exploited labour against exploiting capital, is found to a greater or lesser degree in every programme'[53] –

---

[51] The membership estimate is from T. Moodie, 'The Parti Ouvrier Français: The Formation of a Political Sect', PhD thesis, Columbia University, 1966, p. 124.

[52] J. Girault, 'Une Opération de Diversion: L'Instruction du Procès Lafargue-Culine en 1891', *Mouvement Social*, no. 66, 1969, pp. 85–108 is excellent on the importance of these martyrdoms in the spread of Marxist socialism.

[53] J. Guesde, 'Défaite Provisoire', *Le Cri du Peuple*, 11 October 1885. There is a good description of this percolation in L. Portis, *Les Classes Sociales en France: Un Débat Inachevé (1798–1989)* (Paris, 1988), p. 96.

whether as luminous dream to be realised or black nightmare to be exorcised.

Economic circumstance assisted the first tentative flights of the fledgling Parti Ouvrier: the movement launched itself into the turbulence of the acute deflationary crisis of 1882, France's belated exposure to the 'Great Depression' which had spread relentlessly across Europe during the 1870s. Collapsing prices and stagnant markets poisoned the rest of the 1880s, begetting mass unemployment and endemic industrial strife as desperate employers struggled (without great success) to reduce labour costs in proportion to declining prices.[54] The economic conjuncture improved during the 1890s. Aided by the protectionist programme initiated by Jules Méline, prices rallied and production accelerated, an auspicious trend which culminated in a sustained inflationary boom during the decade before the First World War. Unfortunately, the nostalgically remembered prosperity of this *'Belle Époque'* derived in large part from technological innovations which obliterated workers' painfully-acquired skills, from mutations in business organisation which foreshadowed 'monopoly capitalism', and from 'Taylorist' aggressions against workers' traditional practices – innovations, mutations, and aggressions which together inaugurated a 'second industrial revolution' as traumatic for labour as the first. Both cyclical economic fluctuation, the pattern of 'boom and bust', and the secular trend towards increasing labour intensity and accelerating industrial productivity, the 'second industrial revolution', conditioned workers' responses to the Guesdist critique of a triumphant yet troubled industrial capitalism.[55]

---

[54] C. Tilly and E. Shorter, *Strikes in France 1830–1968* (Cambridge, 1974), pp. 74–5.

[55] The thesis that socialist and labour militancy was orientated in new directions by the deflation of the 1880s is argued in M. Lévy-Leboyer, 'L'Héritage de Simiand: Prix, Profit et Termes d'Échange au XIXᵉ Siècle', *Revue Historique*, vol. 243, 1970, pp. 77–8, and in J. Néré, 'Aspects du Déroulement des Grèves en France durant la Période 1883–1889', *Revue d'Histoire Économique et Sociale*, vol. 34, 1956, pp. 286–302. There is a brilliant application of this thesis at the local level in M. Simard, 'Situation Économique de l'Entreprise et Rapports de Production: Le Cas de la Compagnie des Mines d'Anzin (1860–1894)', *Revue du Nord*, vol. 65, 1983, pp. 581–602, and also see M. Pigenet, 'Signification des Votes Ouvrières dans le Département du Cher (1848–1914)', *Revue Française de Science Politique*, vol. 39, 1989, p. 728. For the importance of technological change during the period, see F. Caron and J. Bouvier, 'Les Aspects Contrastés de la Croissance Économique: Les Indices Majeurs', in *Histoire Économique et Sociale de la France:* Tome IV – *L'Ère Industrielle et la Société d'Aujourd'hui (Siècle 1880–1980):* Premier Volume – *Ambiguïtés des Débuts et Croissance Effective (Années 1880–1914)* (Paris, 1979), pp. 117–36, and for its impact upon workers' politics, M. Hanagan, *The Logic of Solidarity: Artisans and Industrial Workers in Three French Towns 1871–1914* (London, 1980), pp. 212–13. Guesdism is described as a response to capitalist triumph in J. Lambert, *Le Patron: De l'Avènement à la Contestation* (Paris, 1969), p. 103.

Dessin de P. Grados.

Le prolétariat. — Dépêchons-nous : il faut que je sois là-bas quand il y arrivera.

Figure 1 'L'Évolution du monde capitaliste' (From *Le Socialiste*, 16–23 October 1904)

Political turmoil compounded economic depression during the late 1880s, as France endured the convulsions of the Boulanger crisis – a catastrophic eruption of virulent chauvinism, radical demands for constitutional revision of the supposedly corrupt and inefficient Republican political order, and plebeian protest against the socio-economic privations of the 'Great Depression'. The regime survived this trial by demagogic fire, but the crisis thoroughly disrupted the long-established Republican and anti-Republican conventions of French politics, unleashing disoriented masses potentially available to the nascent socialist movement. Hundreds of thousands of workers, broken loose from their traditional political identities, bereft of leadership after the demise of the ephemeral Boulangist 'party', suddenly sought alternative political embodiment for their aspirations. Most French socialists, however, had enlisted for or against Boulanger, and the Guesdists' Possibilist and Blanquist competitors (the amorphous 'Blanquist' movement claimed the atheist and insurrectionary heritage of Auguste Blanqui, nineteenth-century France's most celebrated revolutionary) suffered consequent schism and discredit during their moment of greatest opportunity – the Possibilists dividing into a moribund clique of municipal socialists around Brousse and the syndicalist Parti Ouvrier Socialiste Révolutionnaire around Jean Allemane, the Blanquists sundered into a proto-Fascist 'Right' and the impeccably socialist Parti Socialiste Révolutionnaire around Édouard Vaillant.

The Parti Ouvrier, by contrast, had maintained a prickly neutrality throughout the battle between Boulangists and anti-Boulangists (although Lafargue wistfully noted the socialist potential of the Boulangist upsurge, to Engels' dismay[56]), calling down anathemas upon the two 'bourgeois' armies, urging workers to repudiate both contenders for the poisonous prize of Parisian authority ('Ni Rue de Sèze ni Rue Cadet!'), refusing to 'choose between the plague and cholera'.[57] Guesdists denounced Possibilists for succumbing to the hypocritical self-righteousness of corrupt Radical and Opportunist politicians, accusing Brousse and his associates of subordinating the all-important struggle against capital to the incidental struggle against General Boulanger. At the same time, the Parti Ouvrier condemned the Blanquists for surrendering to the demagogic rhetoric of the Boulangist movement, accusing them of having forgotten the anti-bourgeois essence of socialism in their paralysing hatred of a particular bourgeois regime. Manoeuvring brilliantly between the battlelines separating Boulangists and anti-Boulangists, Guesdists survived to scavenge the body-strewn field, gathering up the enduring working-class resentment of a triumphant yet overtly corrupt and selfishly *laissez-faire* 'Opportunist' Republic, but without succumbing to the humiliating Boulangist rout of 1889.[58]

Determinist in their philosophy but activist in their politics, Guesdists laboured mightily to exploit this auspicious conjuncture of

[56] G. Bottigelli, 'Introduction', to E. Bottigelli (ed.), *Friedrich Engels, Paul et Laura Lafargue: Correspondance* (Paris, 1959), p. xxvii. For a defense of Engels' intervention, see L. Figuerès, 'Engels et le Mouvement Ouvrier Français', *Cahiers du Communisme*, vol. 46, 1970, pp. 92–3, and for a more balanced assessment, particularly of Lafargue's refusal to accept Engels' categorical anti-Boulangism, see Girault, 'Introduction', in Girault (ed.), *Paul Lafargue*, pp. 64–8.

[57] Anonymous, 'Un Dernier Mot', *Le Cri du Travailleur*, 14 April 1888, cited in Willard, *Les Guesdistes*, p. 37.

[58] T. Moodie, 'The Reorientation of French Socialism 1888–1890', *International Review of Social History*, vol. 20, 1975, pp. 347–69; Willard, *Les Guesdistes*, p. 59; and P. Hutton, 'The Impact of the Boulangist Crisis upon the Guesdist Party at Bordeaux', *French Historical Studies*, vol. 7, 1971–2, pp. 226–44.

persistent economic depression and endemic institutional crisis. Years of sustained organisational exertion culminated in the Party's Lille Congress of 1890, which established a centralised and rationalised party structure: a still largely notional but none the less impressive pyramid of local sections, departmental federations, and Parisian central apparatus – the first 'modern' party organisation in France, soon to be emulated across the political spectrum. Supplementing the ideological powerhouse of the proletarian party with a corporative 'transmission belt' to the working class, Guesdists animated the first national trade union organisation in France, the Fédération Nationale des Syndicats et Groupes Corporatifs Ouvriers de France, although their dominance of the swelling labour movement eventually collapsed during the mid-1890s under the maximalist assault of 'revolutionary syndicalism'. The Party's municipal programme of 1891, a comprehensive charter for civic social democracy, both reflected and reinforced rapidly expanding Guesdist representation on municipal councils across France – expansion foreshadowed by the Parti Ouvrier's establishment in 1881 of Europe's first Marxist government in the isolated mining town of Commentry. Nor did the Parti Ouvrier confine its militancy to the world of the urban worker: the movement's controversial agrarian programme of 1892 extended the Guesdists' appeal into a rural society profoundly traumatised by the interminable rural depression of the late nineteenth century – an appeal soon answered in socialist villages throughout the traditionally radical Midi. And Guesdists, the 'pionniers du Premier Mai', inaugurated that most potent symbol of working-class solidarity, the May Day demonstration, benefiting mightily as the novel festival of proletarian protest and self-assertion seized the imagination of French workers.[59]

Good fortune, heavily disguised in blood and gunpowder, rewarded the Parti Ouvrier's endeavours during the May Day celebrations of 1891 in the dreary northern textile town of Fourmies, where nervous and poorly officered soldiers fired into a crowd of inoffensive demonstrators, outraging working-class France and con

---

[59] For the importance of the new organisational framework created in 1890, see Moodie, 'The Parti Ouvrier Français', pp. 183–6. There is no history of the FNS, unfortunately. On the popularity of the May First movement in France, see M. Perrot, 'The First of May 1890 in France: The Birth of a Working Class Ritual', in P. Thane et al. (eds.), *The Power of the Past: Essays for Eric Hobsbawm* (Cambridge, 1984), pp. 153–4, and A. Zévaès, *Histoire des Partis Socialistes en France: Les Guesdistes* (Paris, 1911), pp. 59–72.

secrating the Guesdists' ceremony with proletarian blood. A frightened government then compounded its political discredit by indicting Lafargue for inciting the demonstration. In a classic instance of political justice and its consequences, the Guesdist leader was convicted, imprisoned, and then elected to the Chamber of Deputies as a protest candidate in a Lille by-election – inaugurating a national political presence for his Party never to be surrendered, forging a bond between Guesdism and the northern textile proletariat never to be broken.[60] As Lafargue himself interpreted his triumph (in unconsciously Sorelian language): 'students of the origins of religion have a rare opportunity to observe [in these events] the formation of those mythic ideas which mobilise human masses, raise men and women above their milieu and characters, and inspire them to heroic action'.[61] The Guesdists' enemies admitted as much: Paul Leroy-Beaulieu, editor of the authoritative *Économiste Français* and an insightful spokesman for bourgeois interests, fearfully designated Lafargue's election 'the most important event since the Paris Commune', the first fundamental challenge since 1871 to a society and polity founded upon property-ownership.[62]

The Marxist 'mythic ideas' embodied in Lafargue and his Party enjoyed a nation-wide victory during the municipal elections of 1892, when the POF seized control of major industrial cities such as Roubaix and Montluçon and obtained representation in many more, thereby putting down political roots which would nourish the Party throughout its subsequent growth. The newly ensconced Guesdist municipal governments rapidly established minuscule party-states throughout working-class France, sustaining the POF with their patronage while succouring their proletarian supporters with rudimentary welfare state programmes – prefiguration of a social-democratic future. At the same time, the shameful political corruption revealed by the Panama Scandal, which confirmed workers' suspicions about the 'bourgeois Republic', reinforced the Parti Ouvrier's anti-capitalist crusade, as a phalanx of Guesdist deputies invaded the Chamber of Deputies during the decisive legislative elections of 1893. Even when confined to the back rooms

---

[60] The best sources on Foumies are C. Willard, *Le Fusillade de Fourmies* (Paris, 1957) and J. Girault, 'Une Opération de Diversion'.
[61] P. Lafargue, 'Ce Qu'est le ler Mai', *Le Socialiste*, 27 May 1891.
[62] Cited in Varlet, 'Préface', in *Paul Lafargue*, p. 12.

LE CAPITALISTE
et l'ouvrier non-organisé.

L'OUVRIER ORGANISÉ
et le capitaliste.

Figure 2 'Organisons-nous' (From *Le Socialiste*, 14–21 February 1904)

of bistros and to draughty provincial halls, Guesde's powerful speeches had swayed thousands; now he spoke to the nation from the rostrum of the Palais Bourbon as the representative of Roubaix. No longer an isolated sect of soapbox orators and struggling journalists, the triumphant Guesdists would define the political agenda of the mid-1890s.

How did the Parti Ouvrier achieve this electoral breakthrough into political potency? Why the sudden efflorescence of Marxist socialism in France during the early 1890s? Guesdists easily explained their own good fortune: they held that 'communist ideas exist in a latent state in the minds of workers; communist propagandists need only wake them and put them into action'.[63] According to the axioms which governed Guesdist ideology, proletarian 'mentalities', a rich soil deeply ploughed by capitalist exploitation, 'naturally' nourished the seed of Marxist ideology. Although workers' class consciousness lay fallow without ideological insemination, the spontaneous 'common sense' of workers had only to be

---

[63] P. Lafargue, *Le Communisme et l'Évolution Économique* (Lille, 1892), p. 26.

cultivated by Guesdist militants to flower into Marxist socialism.[64] This fundamental assumption explains the generalising tendency of Guesdist propaganda. Unlike the anarchists, who delighted in 'argot', a 'public language' which personified and particularised the general, Guesdists systematically employed formal language to generalise the personal and particular.[65] The Parti Ouvrier may have rhetorically embodied capitalism in the persons of a textile baron such as Eugène Motte of Roubaix or an industrial potentate such as Schneider of Creusot, but only to demonstrate that Motte and Schneider, no less than their employees, danced to the beat of capital, to the compelling music of the utterly impersonal capitalist mode of production. Dedicated to a rigorous conception of 'scientific socialism', French Marxists maintained that workers would triumph only if they subordinated their immediate resentments and hopes – their spontaneous hatred of the Mottes and Schneiders who ruled their impoverished lives, their inchoate aspirations to a future free from capitalist exploitation and bourgeois domination – to a systematic ideology of rational social criticism and revolutionary self-assertion, to the imperatives of Marxist socialism. By the same token, once Marxism permeated its natural proletarian constituency, once the Parti Ouvrier had fulfilled its historical mission of propaganda and organisation, the liberation of labour would follow unproblematically. According to the French Marxists, proletarian mentalities and socialist ideology reinforced each other without discord or contradiction. Guesdists would have been astonished if their appeal had gone unheard by French workers.

Historians should not unquestioningly credit this Marxist orthodoxy: the facile equation of working-class mentalities with Marxist

[64] This thesis was one of the foundations of the Guesdist's social paradigm, and is fundamental to most Marxist political militancy. It will be explored in subsequent chapters of this study. For discussion of the difficult question of the relationship between ideologies and mentalities, and particularly between socialism and working-class mentalities, see M. Vovelle, *Idéologie et Mentalité* (Paris, 1982), pp. 5–17; G. Rudé, *Ideology and Popular Protest* (London, 1980); F. Furet, 'Pour une Définition des Classes Inférieures à l'Époque Moderne', *Annales: Économies, Sociétés, Civilisations*, vol. 18, 1963, pp. 473–4; R. Johnson, 'Three Problematics: Elements of a Theory of Working-Class Culture', in J. Clarke et al. (eds.), *Working Class Culture: Studies in History and Theory* (London, 1979), pp. 230–7; and M. Markovic, 'The Language of Ideology', *Synthèse*, vol. 59, 1984, pp. 86–7. There is a powerful critique of the ideology/mentality dichotomy, described as the rationale for intellectuals' domination of 'ordinary' workers, in A. Gouldner, *The Dialectic of Ideology and Technology: Origins, Grammar, and Future of Ideology* (London, 1976), p. 59.

[65] For the anarchists' linguistic strategies, see R. Sonn, 'Language, Crime, and Class: The Popular Culture of French Anarchism in the 1890s', *Historical Reflections*, vol. 11, 1984, pp. 351–72.

politics appears far less credible from the disillusioning perspective of the neo-liberal 1990s than from the triumphant vantage of the socialist 1890s. None the less, empathic historians should view the Guesdist project from the vantage of Roubaix's working-class tenements, Lyons' industrial suburbs, the mining villages of the Allier and the Gard – from the perspective of the working-class communities which accorded votes, donations, and lives to the Parti Ouvrier; from the viewpoint of the workers whose enthusiasm or indifference determined the force or failure of French Marxism.[66] Why did workers embrace or resist Guesdism? Historians cannot answer this question in terms of *the* proletariat, since French capitalism spawned many working classes: highly-skilled and highly-paid artisans in the luxury trades of Paris and Lyons, with their long tradition of corporative organisation and political militancy; unskilled and poverty-stricken workers in the wool and cotton industries of the Nord and Normandy, disoriented by the harsh world of the nineteenth-century factory; coal miners in the isolated pithead villages of the Pas-de-Calais, their cohesive communities controlling the lifeblood of French industry; isolated and impoverished rural labourers, politically impotent and socially invisible despite their impressive numbers; and many more, their conditions, traditions, and aspirations equally diverse. Were they *all* potential Guesdists, or did French Marxism demonstrate an elective affinity with 'well-defined strata of the working class'?[67]

Social historians once associated the ascendance of working-class socialism with the proliferation of industrialised labourers – accepting the vivid imagery of *The Communist Manifesto* rather than the complex analyses of *Capital*, the Arcadian nostalgia of conservative rhetoric rather than the sober findings of sociological inquiry. The best historians of French labour history have themselves frequently associated the novel Marxist socialism of the Parti Ouvrier with unskilled industrial workers and raw immigrants to industrial conurbations.[68] Recent research, however, has challenged the simple association of tall chimneys with red flags, contending instead

---

[66] There is a definitive description of the geographical implantation of the Parti Ouvrier in Part III of Willard's *Les Guesdistes*. The need to understand French Marxism from the perspective of its local constituencies is convincingly argued in J. Scott, *The Glassworkers of Carmaux: French Craftsmen and Political Action in a Nineteenth-Century City* (Cambridge, Mass., 1974), p. 5.

[67] J. Julliard, 'L'Éternel Guesdisme', *Critique*, no. 234, 1966, p. 950.

[68] M. Perrot, *Les Ouvriers en Grève: France 1871–1890* (Paris, 1974), vol. 2, p. 642.

that skilled tradesmen manned the new socialist movements of the nineteenth century, that workshops rather than factories mustered the proletarian shock troops of the class war, that industrial militancy itself depended upon 'artisans in the factories'.[69] Neither thesis fully illuminates the Parti Ouvrier's constituency, which embraced a startlingly diverse array of supporters and militants, mobilising highly-paid metallurgists from the engineering works of Montluçon and impoverished textile workers from the mills of Roubaix, labourers from large-scale industrial plants and tradesmen from tiny workshops, artisans from the traditional trades in the great commercial cities and raw recruits from the 'green-field' sites of the second industrial revolution, 'white-collar' employees from counting-houses and 'blue-collar' labourers from construction sites. As the Parti Ouvrier, as the 'Party of Labour', the POF defined 'ouvrier' as broadly as possible, opening its ranks to all those who laboured for hire.

At their most ecumenical, Guesdists abandoned the equation between socialist politics and working-class society which they, their supporters, and their enemies otherwise took for granted, instead appealing indiscriminately to everyone victimised by capitalism, to all 'the different categories of the damned in this social hell'.[70] Although undoubtedly a workers' party, the POF did recruit sporadically among land-owning peasants and propertied petits bourgeois, classes with their own heartfelt grievances against the capitalists who presided over the French economy and against the bourgeois who dominated the nation's politics. A peasant could hate the avaricious bourgeois notary who held his mortgage with at least the venom with which an industrial worker detested his exploitative

---

[69] For an interpretation of the POF as the party of the industrial proletariat, see C. Willard, 'Contribution au Portrait', pp. 55–66; P. Sorlin, *La Société Française 1840–1914* (Paris, 1969), pp. 168–74; and C. Posner, 'The Concept of Strategy in the Writings of Marx and Engels and in the French and German Socialist Parties from their Inception to 1905', PhD thesis, University of Essex, 1972, p. 302, although Posner suggests that the POF became limited in this way only after an abortive effort to reconcile artisans and factory proletarians. There is a useful discussion of the political role of the new semi-skilled factory workforce in M. Rebérioux, 'Le Socialisme Français de 1871 à 1914', in J. Droz (ed.), *Histoire Générale du Socialisme:* Volume 2 – *De 1875 à 1918* (Paris, 1974), p. 134. Good statements of the new orthodoxy of the 'protesting artisan' may be found in W. Sewell, 'Social Change and the Rise of Working-Class Politics in Nineteenth-Century Marseille', *Past and Present*, no. 65, 1974, pp. 75–109 and M. Hanagan, *The Logic of Solidarity*, pp. 3–4. This orthodoxy has in turn been challenged. See J. Rancière, 'The Myth of the Artisan: Critical Reflections on a Category of Social History', *International Labor and Working Class History*, no. 24, 1983, pp. 1–16.

[70] J. Guesde, 'Un à Compte', *L'Égalité*, 18 June 1882.

employer; a shopkeeper could fear the all-engulfing capitalist department store with at least the intensity with which a handloom weaver dreaded the industrialist's mechanical loom. Encompassing 'red' landowners from the Var, socialist bistro-owners from working-class *faubourgs*, self-respecting and self-improving tradesmen from the traditional artisanal crafts, brutalised and illiterate women from the notorious slums of Roubaix, the *diversity* of the Guesdists' constituency explains the vagaries of the Parti Ouvrier's ideological militancy – its persistent ambiguities, systematic contradictions, and symptomatic silences. No simple association of Marxist socialism with the factory proletariat or with protesting artisans will suffice.

Several conventional generalisations about the Guesdists' social and political implantation, however, withstand scrutiny. The Parti Ouvrier gained few adherents in Paris, a crippling weakness instanced by historians to illustrate the supposed correlation between non-Marxist socialisms, the 'Proudhonian' or 'Blanquist' traditions which had thrived in the great city since the mid nineteenth century, and the small-scale enterprises and skilled trades characteristic of the capital's industry, a correlation which has further stereotyped Guesdism as the socialism of the industrial proletariat.[71] Yet the POF enjoyed no more support in the raw factory suburbs of Paris such as Saint-Denis or Aubervilliers than in the tradition-bound artisanal central arrondissements: industrial Saint-Denis, no less than the craftsman's Belleville, awarded its allegiance to Possibilists and Blanquists.[72] Guesde himself, although ironically the only major socialist leader of the period to have been born in Paris, complained that 'trying to propagandise Paris was like trying to plough the sea'.[73] Despite Guesde's best efforts, the Parti Ouvrier remained a provincial movement, a geographical limitation with serious political consequences (given the disproportionate weight of Parisian militancy within the labour movement of the *Belle Époque*) but obscure social causes.[74]

---

[71] See, for instance, C. Willard, *Les Guesdistes*, pp. 249–50, although Willard concedes that historical traditions may have played a part along with sociological determinism.

[72] J.-P. Brunet, *Saint-Denis: La Ville Rouge – Socialisme et Communisme en Banlieu Ouvrier 1890–1939* (Paris, 1980), p. 42.

[73] M. Cachin, 'Le Centenaire de Guesde: 11 Novembre 1945', *La Pensée*, vol. 1, 1945, p. 23.

[74] The provincial nature of the party was admitted by Guesdists themselves. See, for instance, 'B' (Bonnier), 'Les Socialistes et le 1er Mai', *Le Socialiste*, 16 April 1893. The police also stressed the contrast between the Guesdists' dominance in the provinces and their virtual absence from Paris. Police Report of 27 September 1898, in file on the POF's 1898 congress,

Second, an unmistakable affinity prevailed between the Parti Ouvrier and workers in the textile industry: Victor Renard's Fédération du Textile was the most substantial and loyal labour organisation associated with the Party, the secure inner bastion of Guesdist syndicalism after every other POF union stronghold had fallen to the insurgent 'revolutionary syndicalists'. Guesdists, their local implantation reflecting the distribution of spinning and weaving mills, constructed a thriving 'counter-society' in the great northern textile conurbation focused upon Lille which equalled, in complexity if not in extent, the powerful Social Democratic political culture of Wilhelmine Germany. Parti Ouvrier union branches, Parti Ouvrier cooperatives, Parti Ouvrier women's groups, Parti Ouvrier brass bands, Parti Ouvrier baptisms combined to mobilise, organise, and inspire the previously apathetic workers in the teeming mill towns of the Flemish plain. The POF garnered no less than a third of its membership from this small, if densely populated, corner of France.[75] Although the Parti Ouvrier never constructed an equivalent alternative society elsewhere, the party successfully infiltrated the smaller textile centres of the eastern Paris Basin and those focused upon Lyons, from Roanne to Grenoble.

The correlation between Guesdist ideology and textile workers' politics may be overstated, however, given that the textile and clothing industries employed between a half and a third of French workers at the end of the nineteenth century.[76] Textile employees would have predominated in *any* working-class political movement of the period, and, indeed, dispatched substantial contingents to various non-Guesdist and anti-Guesdist 'workers' parties – to Christian Democracy in the devout West, to 'National Socialism' in chauvinist Lorraine, to anarchism in insurrectionary Lyons.[77] Nevertheless, the labour processes and industrial relations characteristic of nineteenth-century textile mills profoundly influenced the Parti Ouvrier's perception of industrial France and systematically conditioned the response of industrial France to the Parti Ouvrier.

AN F7 12.886. There is a good discussion of the POF and non-Parisian socialism in P. Brana et al., *Le Mouvement Ouvrier en Gironde (1870–1939)* (Bordeaux, 1971), pp. 15–27.

[75] There is an excellent discussion of this local strength and its importance in R. Baker, *A Regional Study of Working-Class Organisation*, p. vii and p. 75.

[76] In 1901, 43 per cent, according to G. Charle, 'Les Milieux d'Affaires dans la Structure de la Classe Dominante vers 1900', *Actes de la Recherche en Sciences Sociales*, nos. 20–1, 1978, p. 85. For the resulting illusion of textile workers' dominance of labour militancy, see M. Hanagan, *The Logic of Solidarity*, p. 17.

[77] Julliard, 'L'Éternel Guesdisme', p. 955.

Unconsciously relying upon a powerful but deceptive social synec-
doche, upon a 'fallacy of composition', the Guesdists' imagery of
capitalism reduced bourgeois society as a whole to the claustro-
phobic proletarian world of the northern mill towns, a world of
clangorous machines, mass production, and pitiless employer authoritarianism, a world which may have exemplified the capitalist
mode of production at its most oppressive and exploitative, but
which signally failed to encompass the startling variety of social
forms characteristic of capitalist France during the *Fin de Siècle*.[78]
Guesdist rhetoric, not surprisingly, met with eager acceptance in the
grimy streets of Roubaix, where, according to one acute observer,
the 'theoretical impoverishment of the POF fused with the cultural
impoverishment of the Roubaisian working-class community'.[79]
Marxists enjoyed triumphs in most areas of working-class France
during the 1890s (with the glaring exceptions of the anti-Guesdist
capital and ultra-nationalist Lorraine), and even extended their
sway into the traditionally 'Red' but hardly proletarian countryside
of Provence and Lower Languedoc. All the same, Guesdists themselves commented upon the solidity of their bastions in the northern
textile cities, with their 'compact and disciplined movement', in
contrast to the more erratic enthusiasm of the 'ardent Midi'.[80]
Historical memory will always, and rightly, associate the Parti
Ouvrier with Lille and Roubaix, with the Flemish heartland of
Guesdism.

The organisational consolidation and popular success of the Parti
Ouvrier inevitably conditioned the movement's ideological practices: no less than individuals, parties alter (not necessarily for the
better) as they age and prosper. Reinforcing the conventional
equation between maturity and moderation, historians have contended that, as the POF penetrated the Chamber of Deputies and

[78] More than 69 per cent of all textile workers were employed in enterprises of more than 100
employees, and 26 per cent in those of more than 500, according to F.Caron, 'Dynamiques
et Freinages de la Croissance Industrielle', *Histoire Économique et Sociale de la France:* Tome IV
– *L'Ère Industrielle et la Société d'Aujourd'hui (Siècle 1880–1980)*: Premier Volume – *Ambiguïtés
des Débuts et Croissance Effective (Années 1880–1914)* (Paris, 1979), pp. 259–60. The conditions
inflicted upon textile workers are described in D. Vasseur, *Les Débuts du Mouvement Ouvrier
dans la Région de Belfort-Montbéliard 1870–1914* (Paris, 1967), p. 86. Baker (in *A Regional Study
of Working-Class Organisation*, pp. 236–8 and pp. 302–5) suggests that these conditions were
important in conditioning the Guesdists' Marxism.

[79] L. Marty, *Chanter pour Survivre: Culture Ouvrière, Travail et Technique dans le Textile – Roubaix
1850–1914* (Lille, 1982), p. 201. Marty argues the symbiosis of Guesdism and Roubaisian
worker mentalities on pp. 198–206.

[80] P.-M. André, 'La Leçon de Marseille', *Le Socialiste*, 10–17 August 1902.

presided over municipal council chambers, Guesdism – opportunistically eager for useful if compromising political alliances, blindly preoccupied with electoral popularity at the expense of doctrinal principle – ceased to be a 'small messianic sect full of revolutionary intransigence' and degenerated into a 'party integrated into the national life, but losing the revolutionary flame'.[81] The POF undoubtedly demonstrated extraordinary tactical opportunism during its years of prosperity: Guesdists repeatedly struck deals with their 'class enemies', concluding formal electoral pacts with Radicals in the Nord and, in one extreme case, with Monarchists in Bordeaux.[82] None the less, whatever its tactical flexibility, the Parti Ouvrier never discarded its fixed strategy, never abandoned its set principles: the Guesdists' undeviating purpose remained the forging of the proletariat into a self-aware class united against capital; their unalterable goal continued to be the transition to socialism. As the Guesdists themselves expressed their constancy: 'new tactics, same principles'.[83] Throughout the 1890s, Guesde and Lafargue, their journalistic energies flagging with age and responsibility, thriftily recycled articles written during the 1880s: their rhetoric of 1896 differing not at all from that of 1886. In Guesde's own words, 'our language today is the same as yesterday and always'.[84]

Rather than the POF abandoning its Marxist principles, other French socialists, even ultra-moderate former Radicals such as Alexandre Millerand, adopted the Marxists' rhetoric of economic

[81] Willard, 'L'Héritage de Jules Guesde', p. 18. For a sustained argument to this effect, see Willard, *Les Guesdistes*, pp. 139–42 and p. 193 and, for a contemporary view, D. Halévy, *Essais sur le Mouvement Ouvrier en France* (Paris, 1901), p. 223.

[82] For electoral opportunism in the Nord, see Baker, *A Regional Study of Working-Class Organisation*, p. 71, and, for the Gironde, M. McQuillen, 'The Development of Municipal Socialism in France 1880–1914', PhD thesis, University of Virginia, 1973, pp. 109–10. Guesdists had been equally opportunistic during the 1880s, however. The enterprising Girondin Guesdists, for instance, had been as willing to ally with the Boulangists in 1889 as with the Monarchists in the 1890s – as long as the alliances paid off in victories at the expense of the ruling Opportunists.

[83] 'Bernard', 'Nouvelle Tactique, Mêmes Principes', *Le Socialiste*, 28 September 1890.

[84] J. Guesde, 'Ni Contradiction ni Variation', *Le Socialiste*, 4 March 1894. A close analysis and comparison of several months of *Le Socialiste* in 1886–7 and 1896–7 reveals virtually no difference in political rhetoric between the two periods. There is no evidence in this central source to bear out Rebérioux's claim (Rebérioux, 'Le Guesdisme', p. 8) that 'class' gave way to 'the people' as the theme of Parti Ouvrier polemic during the period of 'opportunism' in the 1890s, or Willard's assertion (Willard, *Les Guesdistes*, p. 193) that '*Le Socialiste* from 1894 to 1898 employed the terms "class", "class struggle" and "revolution" with a good deal of discretion'.

contradictions, class conflict, and proletarian politics.[85] As enthused
by the percolation of their ideals and ideas through the ranks of non-
Guesdist radicals as by their own swelling support, Guesdists contended that their Marxist faith had triumphed throughout the Left:

> thanks to twenty years of uninterrupted propaganda, the foundations of
> scientific socialism are absolutely secure. The Parti Ouvrier may be proud
> of its work: it has led the most reluctant to admit that, outside the
> transformation of capitalist property into social property, there can be no
> liberation of labour. At the same time, with rare exceptions, all socialists
> perceive the political action of the organised proletariat ... [as] the
> necessary instrument of that transformation.[86]

Marx's long proxy battle against Proudhon and Bakunin had
apparently drawn to a triumphant close. The century-old predominance of 'populist' rhetoric within the revolutionary Left – the
language of masses rather than classes, of allegiance to the 'People'
rather than the proletariat, of hostility towards elites rather than
exploiters – had succumbed to ascendant Marxism, to the Marxism
of the triumphant Parti Ouvrier Français.

Nor did the Parti Ouvrier's 'bourgeois' adversaries suppose that
the Guesdists' political evolution during the 1890s reduced their
threat to property and social order. Instead, the decade witnessed a
social panic unprecedented since 1871, a frantic anti-socialist scram-
ble to counter the apparently inexorable advance of the Marxist
menace. Desperate to retain labour within the democratic fold, the
'populist' Radicals patented 'Solidarism' as a sovereign remedy
against the socialist contagion. Reconciled by the *Ralliement*
preached by Leo XIII, Catholic conservatives and conservative
Republicans discarded the dispute over clerical authority and
constitutional order which had sundered the French elite since the
eighteenth century, and rallied side by side to the cause of social
defence. Meanwhile, a clamorous array of new political movements
erupted into the French polity, all self-consciously volunteering
their services against Marxist class politics – an array of anti-socialist
'fire-break' parties which included the Christian Democrats
unleashed by Papal reconciliation with the nineteenth century, the

---

[85] L. Derfler, *Alexandre Millerand: The Socialist Years* (The Hague, 1977), p. 104. For Marxism
as the new orthodoxy of French socialism during this period, see Judt, *Marxism and the French
Left*, p. 107.
[86] Circular of the Conseil National (of the POF), 1 July 1898, in the Fonds Guesde of the
Internationaal Instituut voor Sociale Geschiedenis (henceforth IISG), item 287/6.

anti-Semitic movement initiated by Édouard Drumont, and the National Socialist Party launched by Maurice Barrès, the John the Baptist of twentieth-century fascism. Catholics and free-thinkers, authoritarians and liberals, elitists and democrats, monarchists and Republicans leagued to defend property against the ascendant 'collectivism' embodied in the Parti Ouvrier, against the spectre of proletarian revolution conjured by Marxist socialists.[87] From the Guesdist perspective, the ideological coalescence of the working-class Left around Marxist theses and the panic-stricken response of the bourgeoisie, whether of the Right or Left, augured the final apocalyptic confrontation between labour and capital. As the nineteenth century closed, Guesdists confidently anticipated the socialist millennium.

Instead, the Parti Ouvrier suffered a nightmarish crisis which nearly obliterated the movement. The Guesdists' 'time of troubles' began with the Dreyfus Affair, that cataclysm which so disrupted the French polity at the turn of the century without, in the end, greatly altering the fundamental social and institutional foundations of the regime. Guesdists initially ignored the vicious skirmishing between Dreyfusards and anti-Dreyfusards, believing that the Affair amounted to no more than another Boulanger crisis, from which the Parti Ouvrier had abstained to such good effect a decade earlier. Why, Guesdists demanded, should socialists care about injustices inflicted upon a bourgeois officer by his equally bourgeois colleagues, when Dreyfus and his ilk had never protested against the endemic victimisation of working-class conscripts? Why should the working class intervene in a spat between bourgeois factions, now that the proletariat had embarked upon its own socialist venture? But, as the contest between Dreyfusards and anti-Dreyfusards escalated into a choice between democracy and authoritarianism, as the Republic agonised under the assault of anti-Dreyfusard nationalists, socialists (including many prominent Guesdists) abandoned Guesde's abstentionist strategy for enthusiastic engagement in the politics of 'Republican Defence' – the 'old cause' which had enthused French Leftists

---

[87] For the reorganisation of bourgeois politics around anti-socialism, see P. Sorlin, *Waldeck-Rousseau* (Paris, 1966), pp. 359–63; B. Blick, 'What is Socialism? French Liberal Views in the 1890s', in L. Patsouras (ed.), *Crucible of Socialism* (Atlantic Highlands, 1987), p. 386; and H. Lebovics, *The Alliance of Iron and Wheat in the Third French Republic 1860–1914: Origins of the New Conservatism* (Baton Rouge, 1988). There is a brilliant depiction of this reorientation in a working-class constituency in R. Trempé, 'Du Royalisme à la République ou le "Ralliement" du Marquis De Solages', *Annales du Midi*, vol. 29, 1959, pp. 59–70.

since the glorious days of 1793, the democratic militancy which predated socialism as the *Marseillaise* predated the *Internationale*.[88]

Socialist discord exploded into the public arena when Alexandre Millerand, leader with the great tribune Jean Jaurès of the 'Independent Socialists' (who had long tacitly resisted Parti Ouvrier hegemony), joined the historic Government of Republican Defence formed by René Waldeck-Rousseau, a government which extended from Millerand on the Left to the haut-bourgeois 'Progressistes' on the Right, from Millerand to the 'butcher of the Commune' General Galliffet. Overnight, French socialism split into 'Ministerialists', led by Jaurès, who enthusiastically supported Republican Defence and Millerand's reformist programme at the Ministry of Commerce, and 'Anti-Ministerialists', led by the POF, who angrily opposed socialist participation in a 'bourgeois' government. For the Parti Ouvrier, Ministerialism resurrected the moribund reformist illusions once embodied in Brousse's Possibilism, blurred the categorical distinction between revolutionary proletarians and reactionary bourgeois, and paralleled the 'Revisionism' which sapped contemporaneous German socialism – in all these aspects an abomination to Marxist class warriors.[89] Guesdists hated Millerand and the Ministerialists with all-consuming passion.

At first, Millerand's partisans easily defeated the intransigent Parti Ouvrier: many of the Party's most prominent members – from the mayor of Roubaix, that 'Rome of Guesdism', to Alexandre Zévaès, Guesde's youthful *alter ego* – defected to the Ministerialists, demoralising the militants who remained. At the same time, the Guesdists' anti-Ministerialist campaign almost collapsed as workers, stimulated by Jaurès' warming rhetoric, rediscovered their democratic passion, the ardour of 1793 and 1848. As in 1848, workers hoped that the 'bourgeois Republic' would evolve into the 'social Republic', that the retirement benefits, shorter working-hours, and social insurance programmes patronised by Millerand at the Ministry of Commerce promised transition from political democracy to social

[88] There were even disagreements between Guesde and Lafargue. See Lafargue's letter to Guesde of 1 August 1898, Fonds Guesde, IISG, item 288/1. There is an excellent description of the Guesdists' role during the Affair in Willard, *Les Guesdistes*, pp. 422–38.

[89] For the equation of Millerandism and Possibilism, see P.-M. André, '1901–1902', *Le Socialiste*, 6–13 January 1902. These passionate indictments of Ministerialism accord too well with the Guesdists' fundamental rhetorical customs and established doctrinal traditions to justify the claim that POF intransigence depended upon Guesde's jealousy of Jaurès, as claimed in L. Derfler, 'Le "Cas Millerand": Une Nouvelle Interprétation', *Revue d'Histoire Moderne et Contemporaine*, vol. 10, 1963, pp. 100–4.

Dessin de P. Grados.

JEAN PROLO. — Non, mais regardez-moi ça! Et ça voudrait que je protège sa vertu quand les culottes rouges ou les soutanes noires veulent la violer!...

Figure 3 'La vertu de Marianne' (From *Le Socialiste*, 30 October – 6 November 1904)

democracy.[90] Guesdists experienced the opening years of the twentieth century as a nightmare, a nightmare in which rivalry between Catholics and anti-clericals during the 'Separation Crisis' swept class conflict from the centre of the French political consciousness, while a fashionable 'socialism of the intellectuals' flooded the anti-Guesdist cause with professors who professed a better understanding of Marx than the Parti Ouvrier had ever mustered; a nightmare in which the generous eloquence of Jaurès drowned out the astringent oratory of Guesde, while the daily anti-Guesdist diatribes of the Ministerialists' *Petite République* swamped the weekly anti-Ministerialist tirades of the Guesdists' *Socialiste*.

By 1904, however, the Ministerialist tide had ebbed. Disillusioning episodes such as the ruthless repression of working-class unrest in

[90] Disruption of socialist unity and the destruction of Marxist hegemony within the movement was one of Waldeck-Rousseau's purposes in including Millerand in his government, according to Sorlin, *Waldeck-Rousseau*, p. 403 and R. Kaplan, 'France 1893–1898: The Fear of Revolution Among the Bourgeoisie', PhD thesis, Cornell University, 1971, pp. 233–4. There is a graphic description of the damage inflicted upon socialism at the local level by this strategy in J. Sagnes, 'Un Journal Socialiste Héraultais des Années 1900', in *Le Midi Rouge: Mythe et Réalité* (Paris, 1982), pp. 140–1.

Martinique, governmental intervention against the bitter strike at Montceau-les-Mines in 1901, or the shooting of striking workers at Chalon-sur-Saône (a 'second Fourmies', according to the delighted Guesdists), accumulated to discredit the Ministerialists' strategy of 'Republican defence'. As before, the Republic dispatched its police and troops to defend property against labour. The meagre results of the 'social liberalism' practised by Millerand at the Ministry of Commerce, results as disappointing to workers as infuriating to employers, disillusioned the labour movement. As before, political democracy refused to metamorphose into social democracy. And Millerand's evolution towards the Right, the evolution which would eventually lead to his notably reactionary presidency of the Republic, eventually repelled even his partisans. As before, the temptations of power overwhelmed the ideals of the Left. Vindicated by Ministerialist discredit, Guesdists dictated the terms of the long-delayed and long-awaited socialist unification of 1905, while the rhetoric of Marxist socialism regained its hegemony over working-class politics. The class-bound spirit of the Parti Ouvrier, if not its intransigent practice, would preside over the French socialist movement until the late twentieth century.

Thus the story of the POF: a prolonged and agonising birth, an unpromising youth, a prosperous and hopeful maturity followed by apparently terminal crisis and final transfiguration. What goal animated the Parti Ouvrier? What purpose engendered Guesdism? What legacy did the first French Marxists bequeath to their descendants? Guesdists themselves offered a single answer to these questions: 'the separation of the classes upon every terrain and class war aimed at the end of class, [is] the raison d'être of the Parti Ouvrier'.[91] According to the Party's militants, 'the class war ... must ... guide [our] militancy every day, every moment'. Their conception of class conflict constituted 'the only ground upon which we stand, upon which the Parti Ouvrier is organised, upon which we must remain to foresee events and interpret them'.[92] To understand Marxist socialism is to comprehend its apocalyptic vision of the class war – the vision which inspired Guesdists as they put their Marxism to work.

---

[91] G. Deville, 'Aperçu sur le Socialisme Scientifique', introduction to *Le Capital de Karl Marx* (Paris, 1884), p. 23.

[92] J. Guesde, 'Les Deux Méthodes – Conférence de Lille – Discours de Jules Guesde', *La Petite République*, 30 November 1900.

CHAPTER 3

The axioms of class war: class, class consciousness, and class conflict

The history of all hitherto existing society is the history of class struggles.

> K. Marx and F. Engels, *The Communist Manifesto*, in
> *Collected Works* (London, 1976), vol. 6, p. 482.

We must convince the proletariat that every interest *outside* its class is an interest *against* its class.

> E. Fortin, 'La Question Militaire', *Le Socialiste*, 21 January
> 1888.

Students of socialist ideology have agreed that the concepts of 'class', 'class conflict', and 'class consciousness' pervade Marxist doctrine, and historians of the Parti Ouvrier have reinforced this consensus: all the history of French Marxism, at least, seems indeed to have been the history of class struggles. Anti-Marxists, however, have alleged that Marx and his followers rarely, if ever, defined these all-important terms, that Marxists have erected their vast conceptual edifice upon casually unplanned foundations.[1] At first sight, this criticism devastates the Marxist tradition. Generations of social theorists have discovered, to their dismay, that Marx never devised detailed guidelines for the class analysis which articulated his system, and historians may search in vain through decades of Guesdist publications for explicit discussion of the role of class in the Parti Ouvrier's understanding of social order. Until the rise of 'academic' Marxism in the twentieth century, Marxists took 'class' for granted –

---

[1] T. McCarthy, *Marx and the Proletariat: A Study in Social Theory* (Westport, Conn., 1978) is a sustained, though eventually unconvincing, critique along these lines. For good recent statements of the centrality of class to the Marxist paradigm in general, see E. Wright, *Classes* (London, 1985), p. 27, and G. de Ste. Croix, 'Karl Marx and the Interpretation of Ancient and Modern History', in B. Chavance (ed.), *Marx en Perspective* (Paris, 1985), p. 160. On the Guesdists' employment of 'class' as the key term in their socialist discourse, see the perceptive assessment by M. Rebérioux, 'Le Guesdisme', *Bulletin de la Société d'Études Jaurèsiennes*, no. 50, 1973, p. 4.

its salience no more interrogated by socialists than was the primacy of the 'individual' by liberals. Nevertheless, despite neglect of self-critical theoretical reflection, the meaning and significance of Marxism's conception of 'class' – in all its rigour and sophistication, in all its confusion and crudity – emerges from Marxists' *use* of the term. Indeed, exploration of usage opens the only secure avenue to comprehension of an ideology's fundamental ideas: formal definitions – necessarily restrictive, impoverished, and abstract – never disclose ideologies' amplitude, richness, and ambiguity.[2] Scholars must derive an ideology's meaning in its time and its significance in retrospect from inquiry into its deployment in ideological debate.

This inquiry should begin with illumination of the *a priori* assumptions which articulated the Guesdist paradigm of social order, with examinations of the first principles which, for Marxists, identified the inexhaustible day-to-day data of community and conflict as salient or trivial, as meaningful or meaningless, as structured or random. Infinitely various and boundlessly complex, the social world makes sense, becomes visible and comprehensible, only through principles of discrimination and exclusion. Ideologies prevail by imposing their particular principles of partiality upon social perception, always in competition with alternative (and also partial) visions of social order. Excavation of Guesdist 'axiomatics' opens the way towards successful exploration of the labyrinthine complexities of Parti Ouvrier ideology, towards understanding of the intricate elaboration of corollaries which evolved in France from acceptance of Marxist first principles.[3]

This mode of ideological analysis, applied to their doctrine, would have outraged Guesdists, who contended that Marxism had evolved 'not [from] *a priori* concepts, but [from] observation of social

---

2   According to the insightful arguments in H. Draper, *Karl Marx's Theory of Revolution: State and Bureaucracy* (New York, 1977), pp. 505–7, and I. Katznelson, 'Working Class Formation: Constructing Cases and Comparisons', in I. Katznelson and A. Zolberg (eds.), *Working Class Formation: Nineteenth-Century Patterns in Western Europe and the United States* (Princeton, 1986), pp. 13–22.
3   For 'axiomatics' as a tool in the study of ideology, see F. Jameson, 'Science versus Ideology', *Humanities in Society*, vol. 6, 1983, pp. 288–9. There is a similar analysis applicable to the history of ideas in D. Hollinger, 'Historians and the Discourse of Intellectuals', in J. Higham and P. Conkin (eds.), *New Directions in American Intellectual History* (Baltimore, 1979), p. 43, and see the useful discussion of the political implications of social classifications in L. Portis, *Les Classes Sociales en France: Un Débat Inachevé (1789–1989)* (Paris, 1988), pp. 9–10.

phenomena'.[4] According to the Parti Ouvrier, only unregenerate 'idealists' discovered the foundations of social understanding in Pythagorean axiomatics, rather than in 'scientific observation'. Guesdists advanced a thoroughly positivist conception of scientific inquiry; not for them the sophisticated conventionalism of a Poincaré or Mach. Induction, empirical fact, evident 'reality' sanctioned Marxist theory. According to the Parti Ouvrier,

a theory which has no other ambition than to merge as completely as possible with reality, which merges so completely with reality as Marxist theory, incontestably has the right to call itself scientific. That which engenders the force of Marx's scientific doctrine is that . . . it is no less than the correct interpretation of society understood in terms of its material foundations and in all the diversity of its manifestations, without neglecting any.[5]

Guesdists, with occasional spectacular exceptions, prided themselves on their 'materialism'.[6] They systematically reduced 'first principles' and '*a priori* concepts' to epiphenomena of 'material' class interest, to 'idealist' obfuscations of social 'facts'. At their most extreme, Guesdists described themselves as the 'parti du ventre',[7] a self-characterisation seized upon by their enemies, who delighted in portraying the Parti Ouvrier as the 'stomach party'. Guesdist 'materialism', however, usually assumed a more elaborate guise than mere alimentary determinism. The movement, at its most sophisticated, designated ideals such as 'justice' as indispensable concepts inevitably relativised by class interest, rather than indicting them as dispensable metaphysical nonsense. In the words of Charles Bonnier, one of the more subtle Guesdist thinkers,

Tribes, families and fatherlands have all had their own moralities, in the same way that each form taken by society, each form of exploitation, has borne its unique consciousness. The warrior or the nomad . . . had no scruples in seizing the territory of those he defeated. The Roman citizen was

4 A. Zévaès, 'Le Socialisme à l'École de Droit: Réponse à M. P. Beauregard', *Le Socialiste*, 18 February 1894.
5 G. Deville, *Principes Socialistes* (Paris, 1896), pp. xiii–xiv.
6 The most spectacular 'deviation' from Marxist materialism within the Parti Ouvrier was Charles Brunellière, who flirted with spiritualism while leading the POF in Nantes. See C. Willard, 'Introduction', in C. Willard (ed.), *La Correspondance de Charles Brunellière: Socialiste Nantais 1880–1917* (Paris, 1968), p. 11.
7 J. Guesde, 'Candidature Ouvrière et Candidature de Classe', *Le Citoyen de Paris*, c. 1881, in *En Garde!* (Paris, 1911), p. 34, and cited approvingly in various party publications during the intervening thirty years.

persuaded that justice itself had presided at the foundation of his city. The feudal lord had a religion which legitimised serfdom. Finally, the bourgeoisie today sincerely believes that profit excuses any exploitation, however cruel.[8]

If asked if it was sure of the 'truth' of its theses, the Parti Ouvrier, according to Bonnier, would reply 'yes, we have *our* truth'.[9] In any case, whether Guesdists wrote as reductionists or as relativists, they systematically identified ideals and ideas as mere 'symbols behind which hide ... class interests'[10] – an identification which itself served as one of the characteristic first principles governing Guesdist ideology.

Why this dogmatic materialism? The Guesdists' philosophical politics, no less ridiculed by the secular Left than by the theistic Right, did not evolve unproblematically from scientific 'observation of social phenomena', nor arise laboriously from systematic philosophical deliberation. Neither the methodological rigour of the nascent social sciences nor the logical discipline of traditional philosophical reflection attracted Guesdist militants or stirred the Parti Ouvrier's working-class audience. Instead, materialism served polemical purposes: it issued from the clash and clangour of ideas and ideals in conflict. Examination of the context which evoked 'materialist' outbursts from the Parti Ouvrier reveals a consistent pattern: they exploded during ideological battles between the POF and its political competitors, and with good reason – Marxist socialism, to survive and thrive, had to carve out a place in a cultural polity until then monopolised by the secular ethics of French liberalism and the ultramontane moral absolutism of French conservatism. As a newcomer to the philosophical battleground of the French intellect, the Parti Ouvrier struggled to wean socialists and labour militants from a political culture polarised between competing Republican and Catholic moralisms, between the secular idealism represented by Charles Renouvier, philosopher of the liberal Republic and embodiment of the Kantian revival, and the theistic idealism personified by Leo XIII, advocate of the anti-socialist 'Ralliement' and patron of neo-Thomist rationalism. No wonder

---

8 C. Bonnier, 'Morale Collective', *Le Socialiste*, 10 September 1899.
9 C. Bonnier, 'Le Programme d'Erfurt', *Le Socialiste*, 3 November 1901.
10 C. Bonnier, 'Décomposition', *Le Socialiste*, 14 August 1898.

materialism served Guesdist purposes: it discredited the ruling ideas of the ruling class.[11]

This Guesdist struggle for a philosophical identity freed from the previously hegemonic idealisms of Left and Right resolved itself into yet another battle in the class war, into a principled rejection of labour's long quest for 'humane' or 'moral' bourgeois who would address workers' legitimate grievances, whether through Republican enlightenment or through Christian charity. According to Guesdists, the conviction that these abstract ideals might prevail against material interests epitomised naivete and futility, if not bad faith. Ethical socialists such as Benoît Malon or Jean Jaurès, with their idealist and idealistic conviction that rational argument and the bonds of humanity would triumph over bourgeois irrationality and selfishness, deluded themselves and misled others, since 'even if some bourgeois ... have good intentions, they are still ruled by their class and by the economic phenomena which dominate and determine that class'.[12] Ideals, however humane, and ideas, however well-argued, played no part in the Guesdists' conception of social action, where individuals acted as mere 'agents inconscients'[13] of their economic roles. According to the Parti Ouvrier, 'there is not and never can be humane relations between those who produce and those who possess under the present system of production. Sentiments do not guide men; interests do'.[14] The class war precluded ethical community – whether a concord founded upon the Kantian categorical imperative or upon the Christian golden rule.

Penetration of economic rhetoric into the French 'lexique social' reinforced this Guesdist materialism. 'It's study of the economic milieu which must guide us surely and scientifically', French Marxists asserted. 'Such study explains the past, the present, and the future'.[15] Economics, generally accepted in twentieth-century ideo-

---

[11] M. Ymonet, 'Les Héritiers du *Capital*: L'Invention du Marxisme en France du Lendemain de la Commune', *Actes de la Recherche en Sciences Sociales*, no. 55, 1984, p. 4.

[12] Anonymous, 'Bas le Masque', *Le Socialiste*, 18 March 1891. For the strength of moralistic alternatives to Guesdism within French socialism, see Y. Le Bras, 'Jaurès et la Lutte de Classes', *Société des Études Jaurèsiennes: Bulletin*, no. 43, 1971, pp. 40–8, and D. Lindenberg and P.-A. Mayer, *Lucien Herr: Le Socialisme et son Destin* (Paris, 1977).

[13] P. Lafargue, Speech to the Chamber of Deputies, 28 October 1892, *Journal Officiel de la République Française, Chambre des Députés, Débats Parlementaires* (Paris, 1893).

[14] C. Vérecque, 'Les Syndicats Mixtes', *Le Socialiste*, 15 September 1894.

[15] Anonymous, 'Anarchie et Socialisme', *Le Socialiste*, 27 October 1895. For the intrusion of economic rhetoric into French ideological discourse, see J. Dubois, *Le Vocabulaire Politique et Social en France de 1869 à 1872* (Paris, 1969), pp. 50–1.

logical discourse, had only slowly infiltrated the political consciousness of the nineteenth century – as a novelty pioneered by liberal
doctrinaires, a heresy resisted by conservatives and democrats, and
an innovation endorsed by Marxists.[16] Endorsement of 'economic
interest' as the fundamental determinant of social identity, an
endorsement which aligned Guesdists with their liberal enemies such
as Paul Leroy-Beaulieu of *L'Économiste Français* rather than with
revolutionary populists such as Auguste Blanqui, simultaneously
reflected and accelerated trends within the French labour movement, where working-class militants were grudgingly discarding the
'moral economy' of fairness (a fair day's work for a fair day's wage)
in favour of more 'objective' analyses of the social order, while
socialists discarded the 'depreciated currency of supposed eternal
principles' in favour of 'the most vulgar yet most indispensable of
realities, economic reality'.[17] The Marxist materialism of class
interest and class conflict, in effect, endowed French workers with a
'scientific' counter to the liberal materialism of individual interest
and market equilibrium: Christian or Republican moralism might
denounce the iron laws of bourgeois political economy, but Marxism
promised an equally forceful proletarian alternative. Thousands of
labour militants embraced this alternative, convincing themselves,
and persuading others, that socialism represented an economic 'is'
rather than a moral 'ought'. In the words of Paul Lafargue: 'We
[Guesdists] are not prophets, but simply spokesmen translating the
language of economic facts into human language: there, and there
alone, lies the irresistible force of our revolutionary theories'.[18]
French Marxists envisaged themselves as 'mere thermometers indicating the boiling point reached by the masses under the pressure of
the economic phenomena which victimise them'.[19]

---

[16] C. Willard, *Le Mouvement Socialiste en France (1893–1905): Les Guesdistes* (Paris, 1965), pp. 169–80. For a recent, and particularly intemperate, critique of Marxist 'economism', see J. Baudrillard's influential *The Mirror of Production* (St Louis, 1975).

[17] É. Fortin, 'Politique et Économie', *Le Socialiste*, 27 January – 3 February 1901. For the general shift from moralism to economic instrumentalism, see E. Hobsbawm's classic 'Custom, Wages and Work-Load in Nineteenth-Century Industry', in *Labouring Men: Studies in the History of Labour* (London, 1964), pp. 350–1. This tendency is described for France in Y. Lequin, 'Classe Ouvrière et Idéologie dans la Région Lyonnaise à la Fin du XIXᵉ Siècle', *Mouvement Social*, no. 69, 1969, p. 15 and M. Perrot, 'Comment les Ouvriers Parisiens Voyaient la Crise d'après l'Enquête Parlementaire de 1884', in *Conjoncture Économique/Structures Sociales: Hommage à Ernest Labrousse* (Paris, 1974), p. 192.

[18] P. Lafargue, 'La Production Capitaliste: Caractère Fatidique des Misères Prolétariennes Inhérentes à la Forme Capitaliste de la Production Mécanique', *L'Égalité*, 15 October 1882.

[19] J. Guesde, 'Bombe Inutile', *Le Socialiste*, 23 December 1893.

However precocious as socialist champions of political economy, Guesdists enjoyed no monopoly over economic materialism during the *Fin de Siècle*, even among anti-liberals. Maintaining a distinguished tradition, Proudhonian mutualism, the working-class economism of the mid nineteenth century, competed vigorously against the Marxist conception of class interest well into the 1890s, while the proto-fascists of Drumont's anti-Semitic movement discovered the origins of social evil in the occult machinations of high finance. Guesdist Marxism differentiated itself from such competitors by its analytic of labour and property, by its characteristic combination of these fundamental categories into 'modes of production' or, as the Parti Ouvrier preferred, 'systèmes de production'.[20] Against both the precepts of liberal political economists, champions of market exchange, and the gospel of the Proudhonians, enemies of unequal exchange, Guesdists contended that 'the social question . . . is, and always has been, a question of production'.[21] Labour entered Guesdist discourse preeminently as a factor of production, rather than as a tradeable commodity; property, above all else, meant property in the means of production, rather than goods and chattels in general.

The Parti Ouvrier conceded that exchange relations influenced the social order – but conceded the point only rarely, and only when the concession suited Guesdist purposes. The Party sometimes indicted the financial system as a potent instrument of bourgeois domination over small property-owners (when appealing to land-owning peasants and petit-bourgeois shopkeepers) and occasionally denounced merchant capitalism such as the silk manufactory of Lyons (when soliciting support from notionally independent artisans who fearfully anticipated the dismal fate of the Lyonnais canuts). None the less, Guesdists always returned obsessively to 'the relations of production', systematically reducing other social relations to secondary phenomena, when deigning to notice them at all. But why *production*? Why *not* exchange? French Marxists never systematically addressed these questions, their reduction of society's economic foundation to production relations rather than to exchange relations

---

[20] One of the Guesdists' favourite phrases. For explicit defence of its saliency for social understanding, see Anonymous, 'La Marche de la Révolution', *Le Socialiste*, 18 September 1886.

[21] P. Lafargue, 'Le Problème Social', *Le Socialiste*, 2 September 1900. For discussion of contemporaneous critiques of this 'productivism', see C. Prochasson, 'Sur la Réception du Marxisme en France: Le Cas Andler', *Revue de Synthèse*, no. 110, 1989, p. 96.

thereby constituting the preeminent *a priori* assumption of the Guesdists' materialist world-view.

This productivist presumption both reflected and engendered the Guesdists' social location within the French polity: their intimate liaison with the industrial working class. The Marxist accent upon production relations generated powerful criticisms of industrial capitalism and focused the social vision of the French upon the processes of industrial capital accumulation, upon deskilling, mechanisation, authority within the workplace, and the concentration of production – processes obscured by alternative economisms and incomprehensible to traditional moralisms. Textile cities such as Roubaix or Roanne, the seedbeds of the Parti Ouvrier, lent themselves to this productivist paradigm: mill-workers – labouring seventy-two hours a week, fifty-two weeks in a year, throughout a working life begun at the age of twelve – 'naturally' inclined towards the Marxist preoccupation with 'relations of production'. Millions of workers throughout France, bereft of the small-scale productive property which had legitimated Proudhonian 'artisanal socialism', gradually discarded the mutualist detestation of unequal exchange relations in favour of the collectivist critique of exploitative production relations – a transformation of social consciousness which, as a potential, constituted the primary precondition for the implantation of Marxist socialism and, as a realisation, constituted the Marxists' fundamental ideological achievement.[22] Nevertheless, the reductionism implicit in theoretical constructions such as 'social relations of production (i.e. social organisation in its broadest sense)'[23] has always limited Marxists' comprehension or even perception of non-class aspects of their societies – from the microcosm of family life to the macrocosm of international order. The Guesdists' blinkered obsession with production relations effectively restricted their understanding of *fin-de-siècle* French society to class relations and largely confined their constituency to the isolated world of industrial wage-

---

[22] For the evolution of workers' terminology, see M. Perrot, *Les Ouvriers en Grève: France 1871–1890* (Paris, 1975), vol. 2, pp. 618–19, and see J.-P. Courtheoux, 'Naissance d'une Conscience de Classe dans le Prolétariat Textile du Nord 1830–1870', *Revue Économique*, vol. 8, 1957, p. 117 for the preconditions of this 'productivist' mentality. For the dialectic between Marxist socialism and a popular mentality of class conflict, see Portis, *Les Classes Sociales en France*, p. 92.

[23] E. Hobsbawm, 'Introduction', in K. Marx, *Pre-Capitalist Economic Formations* (London, 1964), p. 17.

labour.[24] Like all ideological paradigms, Marxism's most penetrating insights determined its adherents' most characteristic limitations.

Economistic materialism distinguished French Marxism from the traditional moralising philosophies of Left and Right, and the Guesdists' emphasis upon production rather than upon exchange separated them from liberals and socialists who otherwise shared their 'scientific' preoccupation with political economy. Yet other ideologists of the *Fin de Siècle* accepted the coupling of materialism and 'productivism' without adopting their Marxist offspring. The Saint-Simonian tradition, for instance, although self-consciously 'scientific' and 'industrial', categorically refused enlistment in the class war between labour and capital which endowed Marxism with its *raison d'être*. Saint-Simonians such as President Émile Loubet, third generation heir to Saint-Simon's ambiguous legacy, 'perceived, vis-à-vis workers and employers, only one class: the class of labour'.[25] Although consistently respectful of the great utopian's memory, Guesdists angrily denounced contemporaneous Saint-Simonians as treacherous promoters of class collaboration. According to the Parti Ouvrier, the 'class of labour' had long ago fractured into antagonistic camps: separation of labour and property, those fundamental terms in the Marxist conception of social order, had irrevocably sundered 'workers and employers'. This bellicose relationship between labour, the essence of the proletariat, and property, the substance of the bourgeoisie, governed the Parti Ouvrier's perception of nineteenth-century France and its historical conception of all other bourgeois societies. How, then, did the Parti Ouvrier understand 'labour' and 'property' – the contents of its materialist philosophy, the determinants of its conception of social class?

From the Guesdists' Marxist perspective, labour defined humanity, embodied creativity, and generated all wealth: Guesdists unhesitat-

---

[24] For useful critiques of this Marxist essentialism (where every aspect of a society is representative of a dominant factor such as the relations of production), see C. Sabel, *Work and Politics: The Division of Labour in Industry* (Cambridge, 1982), p. 5, and H. Wolpe, 'Introduction', in H. Wolpe (ed.), *The Articulation of Modes of Production* (London, 1980), pp. 1–43.

[25] Speech by President Loubet to a delegation from the class collaborationist 'yellow' unions, 23 December 1901, quoted in Z. Sternhell, *La Droite Révolutionnaire 1885–1914: Les Origines Françaises du Fascisme* (Paris, 1978), p. 248. The Guesdists were infuriated by this speech. See 'P.G.', 'Discours Présidentiel', *Le Socialiste*, 6–13 January 1902.

ingly identified their species as *Homo Laborens*.[26] The Parti Ouvrier, a labour party indeed, perfectly represented the modern western transition from devaluation of labour as a mundane affliction, a punishment for man's sins, to enthronement of labour as a quasi-divine attribute, the essence of Promethean humanity. Why did socialist militants subscribe with such enthusiasm to this near-deification of labour, a rhetorical device traditionally associated with 'bourgeois' denunciations of aristocratic idleness? In effect, Marxism represented a further evolution in the rhetoric of labour, an evolution from its identification with the 'industrious classes' to its arrogation by the 'working class'. Guesdists self-consciously personified 'labour' within the French polity and, less symbolically, represented 'labourers', a constituency highly receptive to the Marxist assertion that workers produced everything of value in society – the practical meaning of the 'labour theory of value'.

For their part, *fin-de-siècle* bourgeois abandoned the equation between labour and value which their ideologists had perfected over the previous 200 years. In its place, neoclassical economists reduced value to price, and derived prices from equilibrium between abstract 'supply' and 'effective demand', seducing and enthusing the propertied and the wealthy, whose extremely 'effective demand' thus became a fountainhead of wealth, rather than its outcome, while labour (read 'workers') became a 'cost of production', rather than the source of value identified by the classical economists from Mandeville to Marx. Labour, or at least the labour movement, required a 'proletarian political economy' to defend itself against this novel 'bourgeois political economy' in which 'it is not labour which produces wealth, but the buying and selling of commodities'[27] – a distortion of 'reality' which was 'tantamount to the claim that it is the rich rather than the workers who are the true producers'.[28] However inadequate they may have been as technical theorists of the economic order, Guesdists served this polemical

---

[26] For rigorous analysis of the link between class and labour in Marxist ideology, see E. Koga, 'Problèmes Théoriques de l'Organisation des Classes et du Travail Productif', *Hitotsubashi Journal of Social Studies*, vol. 4, 1968, pp. 26–43. There is a useful discussion of this issue in the French context in T. Judt, *Marxism and the French Left: Studies in Labour and Politics in France* (Oxford, 1986), pp. 8–10.

[27] C. Vérecque, 'Les Élections Municipales', *Bulletin Mensuel de la Fédération Nationale des Élus du Parti Ouvrier Français*, Première Année, no. 5, 1 April 1900, p. 1. Lafargue gives a fascinating critique of Pareto and Jevons in his 'Plus-Value et Réformisme', *Le Socialiste*, 19–26 March 1905.

[28] Anonymous, 'La Grève des Riches', *Le Socialiste*, 3 July 1886.

purpose with distinction. Their 'scientific' proof that labour alone created value enormously heartened the 'France du travail'[29] – the Parti Ouvrier's self-assigned constituency.

An anomaly arose, however, from within this Guesdist glorification of labour. Paul Lafargue's *Le Droit à la Paresse*, his defence of 'the right to be lazy', endowed the Parti Ouvrier with its only 'best seller', the most widely published and continuously republished of Guesdist pamphlets. Yet the very title of this work violated every tenet of Marxist labourism. How could Lafargue write that 'all social and individual miseries are born of the passion for labour'?[30] By its paradoxical irony, the pamphlet highlighted a momentous ambiguity in Marxist ideology and a crucial ambivalence in working-class mentalities: both Marxists and workers have glorified labour, but both have also dreamed of its abolition. The Marxist utopia, abandoning the work ethic altogether, has promised a world 'where work will be reduced to an absolute minimum', while workers' abstract enthusiasm for labour in general has concealed their embittered antipathy to work in the particular.[31] These discrepancies should not surprise in the context of *fin-de-siècle* France, given the life-long drudgery under appalling working conditions inflicted upon industrialised proletarians. Unlike the songs of traditional artisans, even the music of industrial workers ignored the rhythms and routines of the workplace.[32] Exhausted and sickened by their work, workers understandably translated 'emancipation of

---

[29] *Ibid.* Peter Stearns stresses the importance of pride in labour among late-nineteenth-century workers in his *Lives of Labour: Work in a Maturing Industrial Society* (London, 1975), pp. 234–5, as does Michelle Perrot in 'A Nineteenth-Century Work Experience as Related in a Worker's Autobiography: Norbert Truquin', in S. Kaplan and C. Koepp (eds.), *Work in France: Representation, Meaning, Organisation, and Practice* (London, 1986), pp. 313–14.

[30] P. Lafargue, *Le Droit à la Paresse* (Paris, 1883), p. 11.

[31] P. Lafargue, untitled, *L'Égalité*, 29 January 1882. For this ambiguity in Marxism, see A. Gorz, *Farewell to the Working Class: An Essay on Post-Industrial Socialism* (London, 1982). Tom Bottomore, in his 'Socialism and the Division of Labour', in B. Parekh (ed.), *The Concept of Socialism* (London, 1975), pp. 154–66, suggests that Marx himself believed both in liberation through labour and liberation from labour. For similar ambiguities among French workers, see J. Rancière, 'The Myth of the Artisan: Critical Reflections on a Category of Social History', *International Labor and Working Class History*, no. 24, 1983, pp. 1–16 and the various responses in the subsequent issues of *ILWCH*; M. Perrot, 'La Classe Ouvrière au Temps de Jaurès', in *Jaurès et la Classe Ouvrière* (Paris, 1981), pp. 69–83; and M. Perrot, 'On the Formation of the French Working Class', in I. Katznelson and A. Zolberg (eds.), *Working Class Formation: Nineteenth-Century Patterns in Western Europe and the United States* (Princeton, 1986), pp. 72–4.

[32] L. Marty, *Chanter pour Survivre: Culture Ouvrière, Travail et Technique dans le Textile – Roubaix 1850–1914* (Lille, 1982), p. 22.

labour', the fundamental socialist promise, into 'emancipation from labour', the barely concealed socialist sub-text.

At the same time, Lafargue's pamphlet attacked bourgeois 'labourism', a rhetoric of labour which flatly contradicted the emancipatory (in both senses) promise of its Marxist alternative. Anti-socialist ideologists of the *Belle Époque* perpetuated and embellished the elites' age-old self-interested imagery of the industrious and deferential 'good worker', the 'petit travailleur infatigable' of employers' dreams. Glamorisation of labour in 'bourgeois' discourse legitimised the labour of blacklegs during strikes (*la liberté du travail*, hardly the Marxist conception of labour's liberation), defended the unlimited labour of unrestricted working hours (against the Guesdists' campaign for the eight-hour day), and justified labour sold at the marginal price dictated by an individualised labour market (as opposed to the minimum wage laws and trade agreements advocated by the POF). French Marxists insistently highlighted the profound hypocrisy of this bourgeois 'labourism', a labourism which endorsed the driven lives of French proletarians whose labour subsidised the gilded ease of the bourgeoisie.[33] 'The right to be lazy', as the Parti Ouvrier emphasised, remained a bourgeois monopoly during the *Belle Époque*: workers could only dream of annual leave, 'le weekend anglais', and unhurried evenings. As for the leisured idyll of prewar rentiers, last beneficiaries of the nineteenth-century world of plentiful servants and first beneficiaries of the twentieth-century consumer society – only the most cataclysmic revolution and the most cornucopian utopia might extend their effortless existence to the 'labouring classes': the very revolution and utopia heralded by Guesdist Marxism. When French Marxists such as Lafargue criticised 'labour' and 'labourism', they criticised labour under capitalism, a brutal tyranny which impoverished rather than enriched, or bourgeois labourism, the quintessence of hypocrisy rather than the essence of humanity – not labour in general nor labour as a synonym for the working class.[34]

If idolisation of 'labour' endowed the Parti Ouvrier with its distinctive social orientation, the French Marxists' rigorous and

33 See, for example, P. Lafargue, 'Évolution de la Morale', *Le Socialiste*, 11 December 1886.
34 For Lafargue's polemic in this context, see M. Dommanget, 'Présentation', in *Paul Lafargue: Le Droit à la Paresse* (Paris, 1969), pp. 21–3. The class distribution of leisure is described in E. Weber, *France: Fin de Siècle* (Cambridge, Mass., 1986), pp. 190–1.

sophisticated conception of 'property' supplied them with critical force. The 'property question' has always dominated Marxist social thought, although a century of esoteric debate over the derivation of surplus value has obscured this all-important preoccupation. Social militants by their hundreds of thousands, however, have adhered to the Marxist solution to the property question, not to the algebraic intricacies elaborated in *Capital*. Guesdists, militants rather than theorists, evinced little interest in value theory, not because of sophisticated doubts about its validity (they ferociously defended the concept of surplus value on the few occasions when they discussed the issue), but because of their all-consuming ambition to mobilise the French proletariat against the bourgeoisie. French Marxists flinched from inflicting mathematical abstractions upon semi-literate textile workers. Maldistribution of property and its iniquitous consequences equipped the Parti Ouvrier with a sufficiently potent indictment of the capitalist order and with a more than adequate interpretation of capitalism's traumatic history.[35] The contrast between Eugène Motte's vast textile mills and his employees' impoverishment sufficed to condemn Roubaisian capitalism, without recourse to scholarly meditation upon Motte's manipulation of MCM permutations.

Guesdists had inherited the 'property question' from revolutionary predecessors: it had underpinned successive indictments of bourgeois oppression and exploitation from Babeuf's egalitarian 'agrarian law' to Proudhon's immortal 'property is theft'. The Parti Ouvrier, however, marshalled its entire paradigm, its distinctive social vision, its class conception of society around battle-standards emblazoned with the devices 'le régime de la propriété', 'l'évolution

---

[35] For the centrality of the property question to Marxism, described from radically different theoretical perspectives, see É. Balibar, 'On the Basic Concepts of Historical Materialism', in L. Althusser and É. Balibar, *Reading Capital* (London, 1970), pp. 226–33; A. Hegedus, 'Towards a Sociological Analysis of Property Relations', in T. Bottomore (ed.), *Modern Interpretations of Marx* (Oxford, 1981), pp. 110–24; S. Lash, *The Militant Worker: Class and Radicalism in France and America* (London, 1984), pp. 10–21; and A. Ryan, *Property and Political Theory* (Oxford, 1984), chapters 6–7. In basing their social critique upon property relations rather than upon value relations, Guesdists were 'Roemerites' *avant la lettre*. See J. Roemer, 'Property Relations versus Surplus Value in Marxian Exploitation', *Philosophy and Public Affairs*, vol. 11, 1983, pp. 281–313; J. Roemer, 'Exploitation, Class, and Property Relations', in T. Ball and J. Farr (eds.), *After Marx* (Cambridge, 1984), pp. 198–9; and J. Roemer, 'Should Marxists Be Interested in Exploitation?', *Philosophy and Public Affairs*, vol. 14, 1985, pp. 30–65; as well as the symposium on the Roemer thesis in *Politics and Society*, vol. 11, 1982. This alternative is further developed in T. Carver, 'Marx's Political Theory of Exploitation', in A. Reeves (ed.), *Modern Theories of Exploitation* (London, 1987), pp. 68–79.

de la propriété', or 'la forme de la propriété' – endlessly recurrent images in Guesdist discourse. This emphasis embodied a novel Marxist interpretation of the property system, of property's development, and of property forms – an interpretation which successfully revolutionised the terms of social debate within the French polity, and which threatened to revolutionise the French social order.[36] Guesdists proudly asserted that their interpretation of the property system equipped them with a uniquely potent conceptual framework, that its adoption endowed them with the keys to social revelation and the trigger of social revolution. As Lafargue boasted,

you don't turn to the political reforms or the ethical teaching of bourgeois politicians and moralists if you want to rid society of its evils and man of his vices. Instead, you must overturn the soil which grows such qualities, using the ploughs and mattocks of revolution. And that's why the Parti Ouvrier, the only political party with a philosophical foundation, has the goal of a general recasting of the property system.[37]

Guesdists reiterated this credo in virtually every pamphlet they published, in every issue of *L'Egalité* and *Le Socialiste* they issued, in every *conférence contradictoire* they organised. No wonder. It articulated their promise of 'the transformation of capitalist property into social property'[38] – the heart of the Marxist project.

The Parti Ouvrier's onslaught upon the bourgeois property system provoked the inevitable counter-attack. Exploiting the momentum of the Guesdists' assault, enemies of the POF identified French Marxists as 'partageux', wild-eyed enemies of society who plotted a universal confiscation – the century-old conservative red-herring which now served as well against nineteenth-century socialists as it had once served against eighteenth-century Enragés. After the collectivist revolution, socialist 'partageux' would confiscate and redistribute the modest possessions of provincial petits bourgeois and

---

[36] On the traditional approach to the 'property question' within French radicalism, see A. Cuvillier, 'Les Antagonismes de Classes dans la Littérature Sociale Française de Saint-Simon à 1848', *International Review of Social History*, vol. 1, 1956, pp. 433–63; W. Sewell, 'Property, Labor and the Emergence of Socialism in France 1789–1848', in J. Merriman (ed.), *Consciousness and Class Experience in Nineteenth-Century Europe* (New York, 1979), pp. 45–63; and D. Kelley and B. Smith, 'What is Property? Legal Dimensions of the Social Question in France (1789–1848)', *Proceedings of the American Philosophical Society*, vol. 128, 1984, pp. 200–30. For the novelty of the Marxist reconceptualisation of the issue, see J. Dubois, *Le Vocabulaire Politique et Social*, p. 17.
[37] P. Lafargue, 'Le Parti Ouvrier: La Base Philosophique du Parti', *L'Égalité*, 19 March 1882.
[38] Anonymous, 'Rentrée en Ligne', *Le Socialiste*, 29 November 1896.

the tiny fields of peasant cultivators to the advantage of the shiftless urban poor – according to the apocalyptic visions of anti-Guesdists. Worse yet, anti-socialists charged, the Parti Ouvrier planned the ultimate 'suppression of property'. A socialist future, in this liberal nightmare, would impose an absolute community of goods upon its hapless victims: the clothes they stood in would belong to the collectivity; state-owned barracks would replace private accommodation; women (evidently perceived by bourgeois as property) would undergo a salacious 'nationalisation'. Guesdists angrily rejected these indictments. They mocked the accusation that socialists planned to abolish property, contending, as Guesde hastened to emphasise, that 'what's called property is ... nothing but the relationship between men and things'[39] – a universal relationship which socialists could no more abolish than the laws of nature themselves. Rather than suppressing property, Guesdists intended to *generalise* it by extending ownership of the means of production to the working class, a class 'deprived of [productive] property, that is to say deprived of all liberty and of all well-being'.[40] Like the liberals they so detested, Guesdists identified property-ownership as the only guarantee of independence and the sole assurance of happiness. They aspired to a society 'where all men will be producers, and all men will be propertied'.[41] Despite the hysterical fantasies of anti-socialist propagandists, French Marxists denounced not property-ownership, but exclusion of their proletarian constituents from its manifold advantages.

The Guesdists' conception of property served other socialist purposes. First, its critical force enfeebled 'the natural order created by habit and tradition'[42] – the 'natural order' which had long buttressed social conservation and discredited social revolution, which had legitimated even the most intolerable mechanisms of exploitation and the most oppressive hierarchies of domination, if hallowed by tradition. From the Parti Ouvrier's perspective, a tendentious equation between capital in particular and property in general reinforced the 'natural order' of bourgeois France, whose self-serving advocates proclaimed, to the Guesdists' fury, that

[39] J. Guesde, 'Un Mabouliste', *Le Socialiste*, 27 January 1894.
[40] J. Guesde, 'Bombe Inutile', *Le Socialiste*, 23 December 1893.
[41] C. Vérecque, 'Partage et Salariat', *Le Socialiste*, 27 October – 3 November 1901.
[42] G. Deville, 'Aperçu sur le Socialisme Scientifique', in *Le Capital de Karl Marx* (Paris, undated), pp. 10–11.

'property [and therefore capital] is a social phenomenon immune to the evolutionary law which governs the material and intellectual world'.[43] Liberals and conservatives, however quarrelsome over other issues, heartily agreed that *capital*, the equivalent of property in general, would live on into the distant future as it had lived since time immemorial – inevitable, omnipresent, and eternal. According to Lafargue, however, 'everything continually changes and transforms itself. Property obeys this law; it has changed and, therefore, will change again'.[44] Guesdists employed their concept of property to smash smug assumptions of capitalism's universality, to highlight the historical peculiarity of bourgeois property – 'a very new phenomenon', according to Marxists.[45] Property in general may have characterised human society in general, from Pharaonic Egypt to the industrial present; but capital – bourgeois property, the unique property-form of capitalism – enjoyed no such antique pedigree.

The most common 'history lesson' in Guesdist discourse, an intensely historical genre, contrasted property regimes of the past with those of the present, thereby illustrating the singular properties of capital, and delineating its singularly exploitative attributes. These historical demonstrations sometimes went awry in bestowing unintended praise upon pre-capitalist forms of exploitation. Carried away by the momentum of their assault upon the 'natural order' of bourgeois France, overwhelmed by the potency of their meta-historical thesis, over-enthusiastic Guesdists affirmed that feudal property-owners had foregone the iniquitous absolute right of use and abuse enjoyed by propertied bourgeois, and that slave-owners had self-interestedly cherished the workers they owned, unlike capitalists, who callously mistreated the workers they employed.[46] None the less, these lessons served their purpose – effectively demonstrating that 'capital' had been recently born, and might soon die, although 'property' in the abstract would live forever.

Second, the Guesdist typology of property sharply distinguished capital from other forms of individual property, and thereby erected

[43] P. Lafargue, *Origine et Évolution de la Propriété* (Paris, 1895), pp. 303–4.
[44] P. Lafargue, 'L'Évolution de la Propriété', *Le Socialiste*, 23 November 1890.
[45] C. Vérecque, 'Les Terres Communales', *Bulletin Mensuel de la Fédération Nationale des Élus du Parti Ouvrier Français*, 1 March 1901.
[46] See P. Lafargue, 'La Propriété Bourgeoise', *Le Socialiste*, 29 October 1887 for the superiority of feudal property over bourgeois property, and J. Guesde, 'Liberté et Salariat', *Le Socialiste*, 30 December 1893 for that of slavery over wage labour.

a bulwark against the commonplace accusation that Marxist 'partageux' sought to confiscate the carpenter's saw and the peasant's
plot, that the impending 'collectivisation of the means of production'
menaced the painfully accumulated property of the middle class and
peasantry as ominously as it threatened the ill-gotten gains of the
bourgeoisie, that socialists intended to confiscate the world's wealth
and divide it impartially between the productive and the parasitic,
between the deserving and the undeserving, between the provident
and the shiftless. Proponents of the bourgeois property-system
tendentiously equated the worker's shirt with the capitalist's share
portfolio, seeking thus to recruit propertyless (if beshirted) proletarians into the bodyguard of bourgeois property. Determined to
counter these attacks, Guesdists repeatedly insisted that individu-
ally-worked productive property and individually-owned consumption goods did *not* constitute capital, that the carpenter's saw differed
fundamentally from the capitalist's sawmill, that workers' shirts
differed in kind from bourgeois investment portfolios. Guesdists
advanced a carefully constructed typology of property which clearly
distinguished between saws and saw mills, between shirts and
mining stocks. Their typology differentiated collective property
(ranging from the 'primitive' communal ownership to 'modern'
nationalised enterprise) from individual property, and then disaggregated the latter into property for individual consumption (such
as a shirt), property for individual production (such as a carpenter's
saw), and bourgeois property or 'capital' (such as mining stocks).
According to the Parti Ouvrier, capital was 'worked by employees,
produced commodities, and brought profits to its owners'[47] – it
differed fundamentally from other forms of individual property,
productive or otherwise. If nothing else, possession of capitalist
property implied others' dispossession of the means of production: no
bourgeois mining stocks without proletarian miners. Confronting an
imaginary peasant outraged by the supposedly impending collectivisation of his meagre acres, the hero of one of Adéodat Compère-
Morel's didactic socialist parables argued that

there's property and there's property. Yours, my friend, has the right to
every respect; it's the product of an entire life of labour and privation. But
you don't have much of it. What about his – the property of that fat cat –

47 P. Lafargue, 'L'Évolution de la Propriété', *Le Socialiste*, 23 November 1890.

how did he get it? Five hundred hectares of land, farms, bags of gold – all that, that's the product of *his* labour?[48]

For Guesdists, the legitimacy, freely conceded, of individual property depended upon 'it being *the fruit of the owner's labour* and *exploited by the owner*'.[49] Bourgeois property, by definition, fulfilled neither criterion.

This rigorous typology of property completed the Guesdists' social paradigm: affirmation of economistic materialism lent fashionable 'scientific' certainty to Marxist rhetoric and challenged the traditional liberal and conservative moralisms whose contest had dominated French political culture since the eighteenth century; assertion of labour's social primacy defined the Guesdist's constituency and appealed to workers' pride in their labour; and the Parti Ouvrier's typology of property-forms wrote the protocols for a distinctively Marxist social analytic. When combined with the intersection of socially generative labour and socially distributive property, materialistic economism led with iron logic towards the characteristic Marxist conception of 'class interest' – the fundamental 'material' interest which ruled social order and disorder, conditioned individuals' place in society, and governed the course of history.[50] The concept of class interest elicited empirical insight (and empirical blindness) from Guesdists and imposed normative imperatives upon the Parti Ouvrier, introducing the *dramatis personae* upon the broad stage of French history, and establishing 'what was to be done' by the Marxist players in the drama.[51]

Although the intersection of property ownership and labour power divided individuals into classes, this intersection delineated

---

[48] A. Compère-Morel, 'Paysan et Socialiste', *Le Socialiste*, 10–17 January 1904. For a good description of such a polemical manoeuvre by the Guesdists' enemies, see R. Trempé, *Les Mineurs de Carmaux 1848–1914* (Paris, 1971), vol. 2, pp. 873–4.

[49] A. Compère-Morel, 'Paysan et Socialiste', *Le Socialiste*, 10–17 January 1904 (Compère-Morel's stress).

[50] For the Marxist concept of 'interest', see I. Balbus, 'The Concept of Interest in Pluralist and Marxist Analysis', *Politics and Society*, vol. 1, 1971, pp. 151–79, and G. Wall, 'The Concept of Interest in Politics', *Politics and Society*, vol. 5, 1975, pp. 487–510.

[51] The concept of a 'class interest' which transcends individuals' awareness of their 'immediate interests' has received considerable criticism. See, for example, G. Therborn, *What the Ruling Class Does When It Rules* (London, 1978), p. 146. For critiques of the concept of 'interest' in general, see the thoroughly unconvincing arguments in B. Hindess, 'Power, Interests and the Outcome of Struggles', *Sociology*, vol. 16, 1982, pp. 506–9 and B. Hindess, ' "Interests" in Political Analysis', in J. Law (ed.), *Power, Action and Belief: A New Sociology of Knowledge?* (London, 1986), pp. 112–31.

only a static pattern, with property owners (of various kinds) ranged beside the propertyless. This typology distinguished bourgeois (non-labouring capital owners) from proletarians (propertyless labourers) and both classes from petits bourgeois (labouring owners of individual productive property), but failed to relate these 'classes' to each other, except in abstract definitional terms. If confined to this level of abstraction, Marxist sociology would have degenerated into the gnostic elitism of late antiquity's neo-Platonism or late medieval Scholasticism – reduced to ineffectual spiritual exercise for impotent intellectuals, sterile conceptual masturbation for bloodless savants. Marxist ideology, however – anything but ineffectual or bloodless, sterile or impotent – has always emphasised the clash of interests rather than the conjunction of categories, class conflict rather than class analysis, polemical potency rather than conceptual elegance – at least until its Althusserian metamorphosis. The economistic Marxist conception of 'interest' ensured against introverted abstraction: 'class interests' defined battlegrounds, not categories. As Marx and Engels had written, 'separate individuals form a class only insofar as they have to carry on a common battle against another class; in other respects they are on hostile terms with each other as competitors'.[52] In other words, no class without class conflict.[53]

Unfortunately, this causal relationship between class and class conflict has generated a 'chicken and egg' paradox which has profoundly troubled Marxist theoreticians: no class without the cohesion imposed by class conflict, yet, logically, no class conflict without cohesive classes to conflict.[54] Most Marxists have resolved this apparent paradox by assuming that classes necessarily conflict, that class and class conflict engender each other through the dialectic practised by chickens and eggs. Although never explicitly aware of the original conceptual dilemma, Guesdists implicitly embraced this characteristic Marxist solution to its paradoxical perplexities: they enthusiastically adopted a 'conflict theory' of society in which classes conflicted by definition. Guesdist discourse

[52] K. Marx and F. Engels, *The German Ideology*, in K. Marx and F. Engels, *Collected Works* (London, 1976), vol. 5, p. 77.
[53] For the fundamental importance of the concept of class conflict in Marxist social and political thought, see H. Draper, *State and Bureaucracy*, pp. 162–4, and A. Przeworski, 'Proletariat into Class: The Process of Class Formation from Karl Kautsky's *The Class Struggle* to Recent Controversies', *Politics and Society*, vol. 7, 1977, pp. 343–401.
[54] N. Abercrombie, *Class, Structure, and Knowledge* (Oxford, 1980), pp. 92–113, and B. Hindess, 'The Concept of Class in Marxist Theory and Marxist Politics', in J. Bloomfield (ed.), *Class, Hegemony, and Party* (London, 1977), pp. 95–108.

celebrated clashes and contradictions: military metaphor suffused the Parti Ouvrier's rhetoric; brutal engagements between contradictory class interests animated the movement's conception of historical transformation and its perception of contemporaneous social structure; class collaboration boded stagnation and decadence – in the unlikely event collaboration ever eventuated.

Students of the POF generally agree that, for Guesdists, 'all roads led to the class struggle which assumed such monumental importance as to reduce other issues to virtual insignificance'.[55] Even the most eclectic and undoctrinaire of Guesdist militants, such as Ernest Ferroul, the easy-going Guesdist mayor of Narbonne, identified themselves as 'the men and the party of class conflict'.[56] Like Marx, French Marxists asserted that class struggle alone imposed an 'intérêt commun' upon 'les petites préférences'[57] which otherwise fragmented classes into conflicting individuals and disputatious factions, that the discipline imposed by social conflict and the *esprit de corps* evoked by class war alone prevented the proletariat from disintegrating into a disunited rabble and the bourgeoisie from crumbling into competitive chaos. For Guesdists, the fundamental social relationship of the *Belle Époque* – the escalating antagonism between workers and capitalists, the clash between exploited labour and exploitative capital – generated a dialectical unity-in-conflict: the struggle of the proletariat against the bourgeoisie forced individual bourgeois to forget their 'internecine conflicts',[58] while capitalist exploitation combined individual workers into 'a general force transcending struggles against particular exploiters'[59] – hence the Guesdists' obsessive search for indications of bourgeois coalescence into 'one reactionary mass', indications always interpreted as both cause and consequence of the 'making of the working class'. Noticing

[55] T. Moodie, 'The Parti Ouvrier Français 1879–1893: The Formation of a Political Sect', PhD thesis, Columbia University, 1966, p. 28.

[56] J. Guesde, 'L'Émeute de la Rue Cadet', *Le Socialiste*, 19 December 1891. For Ferroul as a limit case in Marxist commitment within the POF, and his devotion, nevertheless, to the class struggle, see R. Pech, 'Les Thèmes Économiques et Sociaux du Socialisme Férrouliste à Narbonne (1880–1914)', in *Droite et Gauche en Languedoc-Roussillon: Actes du Colloque de Montpellier, 9–10 Juin 1973* (Montpellier, 1975), p. 262.

[57] Manifesto of the Executive Commission of the Guesdist Fédération Nationale des Syndicats, 'Aux Syndicats Ouvriers' (newspaper clipping from *L'Intransigeant* – June 1889), file 177300-9, Ba/39 – Archives de la Préfecture de Police de Paris.

[58] É. Fortin, 'Politique et Économie', *Le Socialiste*, 27 January – 3 February 1901.

[59] P. Grados, 'Syndicats et Groupes', *Le Socialiste*, 25 May – 1 June 1902.

the formation of a nation-wide anti-socialist organisation in 1895, for instance, *Le Socialiste* happily announced that bourgeois, 'once divided by secondary interests', were now 'uniting against their common [proletarian] enemy, giving new and decisive proof of the class war'.[60] For Guesdists, every instance of class solidarity exemplified and amplified class conflict, and every instance of class conflict expressed and enhanced class solidarity – a self-reinforcing chain reaction which, according to the French Marxists, accelerated towards the final Armageddon which would usher in the classless society, the classless society which would inaugurate social peace after millenia of class war.

Unfortunately for Marxist class warriors, the society and polity of *fin-de-siècle* France justified the conclusion that 'the actual form of class politics in much of recent history is not unified struggles between mobilised classes, but fragmented struggles about the process of mobilisation'.[61] Common interests encouraged collaboration between supposedly antagonistic classes, while non-class conflicts fragmented them into antagonistic factions. The 'material interests' of particular firms, of particular trades and industries, or of 'national industry' united employers and employees against other employers and employees, while religious, racial, and gender issues bonded secularist capitalists to anti-clerical workers, anti-Semitic bourgeois to racist proletarians, and male-chauvinist employers to Proudhonian employees. Did the proletariat and the bourgeoisie exist as classes in any meaningful sense when workers and capitalists cooperated, or when they disregarded each other for internecine conflict? Most frequently, Guesdists answered this troubling question by ignoring it: they highlighted instances of class conflict, and disregarded its absence. Marx's celebrated assertion that 'the history of all hitherto existing society is the history of class struggles',[62] in the Guesdists' favourite interpretation of its implications, imposed a brutal reductionism upon the history 'of all hitherto existing society': *all* history exemplified a universal and perennial class war; 'the history of a nation consists *only* of the struggles between the classes

---

[60] J. Sarraute, 'Élimination "En Principe"', *Le Socialiste*, 26 May 1895.
[61] R. Connell, 'The Black Box of Habit on the Wings of History: Critical Reflections on the Theory of Social Reproduction, with Suggestions on How to do it Better', in R. Connell, *Which Way is Up?* (Sydney, 1983), p. 155.
[62] K. Marx and F. Engels, *The Communist Manifesto*, in Marx and Engels, *Collected Works*, vol. 6, p. 482.

which compose it'.[63] On other occasions, however, Guesdists surrendered to a very conditional theoretical pluralism, and grudgingly permitted non-class social identities a degree of autonomy, although an autonomy conditioned by the overriding imperatives of class conflict. Even at its most 'pluralistic', the Parti Ouvrier maintained its rigorous Marxist commitment to the predominance of class struggle within social (dis)order.

Determined to transform France into 'the great battleground of the class war',[64] Guesdists struggled to overcome the theoretical liabilities and empirical improbabilities inherent in their reductionist doctrine of class conflict – and frequently succeeded. Given favourable circumstances and sustained militancy, even the most recalcitrant of the French, even those who benefited most from concealment of the class system, reluctantly enlisted in the class war. Anticipating May Day, that Guesdist-initiated festival of labour, the terrified employers of the northern textile town of Fourmies proclaimed in 1891 that

the undersigned industrialists, abandoning all the political questions or other matters which may divide them during these grave circumstances, swear to defend each other collectively, with solidarity, and materially for the duration of the unjustified and undeserved war which has been declared against them.[65]

Defend each other they did. Nine workers, most of them children or young people, died in the resulting clash between unarmed proletarian demonstrators and the heavily armed regiment deployed to protect the 'undersigned industrialists'. Individual capitalists and workers had coexisted, cooperated, and quarrelled in Fourmies for

---

[63] Anonymous, 'La Lutte des Classes', *Le Socialiste*, 29 August 1885 (stress in original).
[64] 'Socialisme et Patriotisme: Aux Travailleurs de France du Conseil National du POF', 23 January 1893, in Bracke (ed.), *Onze Ans d'Histoire Socialiste* (Paris, 1901), p. 33.
[65] Cited in J. Girault, 'Une Opération de Diversion: l'Instruction de Procès Lafargue-Culine en 1891', *Mouvement Social*, no. 66, 1969, p. 87. *Le Socialiste* cited the same manifesto on 23 April 1891, using it as proof of the overriding nature of the class war. Historians have agreed with this Guesdist assessment of bourgeois cohesion during the 1890s. See, for example, H. Peiter, 'Institutions and Attitudes: The Consolidation of the Business Community in Bourgeois France 1880–1914', *Journal of Social History*, vol. 9, 1976, pp. 512–13; P. Hilden, *Working Women and Socialist Politics in France 1880–1914: A Regional Study* (Oxford, 1986), p. 69 and p. 224; and, above all, H. Lebovics, *The Alliance of Iron and Wheat in the Third French Republic 1860–1914: Origins of the New Conservatism* (Baton Rouge, 1988). For a brilliant theoretical demonstration that 'a classless vision of society is in the class interest of capitalists', see A. Przeworski and J. Sprague, *Paper Stones: A History of Electoral Socialism* (Chicago, 1986), p. 47.

decades before the massacre of 1 May 1891. Afterwards, the town ruptured into antagonistic classes, into a beleaguered bourgeoisie and a militant proletariat – a rupture which testified to the potency of the Guesdists' message, and brought further grist to their ideological mill.

Much against their will, bourgeois Fourmiesiens had learned the meaning of 'class consciousness' – the essence which, for Marxists, pervades social meaning as class conflict pervaded social structure. Yet Marxists have rarely clarified the sense of this all-important concept, although its permutations have ordered their ideological paradigm, itself legitimated as the ultimate distillation of proletarian class consciousness. Did the concept indicate explicit awareness of class?[66] Or did class consciousness indicate consciousness *influenced* by class structure, even if individual or collective subjectivity manifests no overt awareness of class?[67] In other words, did deferential workers who detested socialism reveal a 'consciousness determined by class' similar in essence to Marxist militants' 'consciousness of class' – both categories of proletarians responding in their way to the experience of class domination? Or should theorists limit attribution of 'class consciousness' to the latter case, to self-aware class warriors? Even this second, more restricted, conception of class consciousness has generated puzzling ambiguities in Marxist discourse, notably *vis-à-vis* the genesis of militant class consciousness. Whence arose class warriors? Marx himself evolved three alternative answers to this vexed question, arguing, first, that class consciousness arose spontaneously from social location, that class warriors sprang fully-armed from the fertile soil of class society; second, that class consciousness matured painfully during prolonged experience of class struggle, that class warriors graduated after long suffering in the brutal boot-camps of the class war; and, third, that class consciousness infiltrated its designated class through the agency of autonomous scientific investigation of society, that class warriors mobilised to the drum-beat of theory – three (contradictory?) theses

---

[66] For an acute discussion of this 'Lukacsian' mode of analysis, see H. Lefebvre, *Pour Connaître la Pensée de Marx* (Paris, 1955), pp. 50–1.

[67] There is a brilliant argument for this conception in E. Wood, 'The Politics of Theory and the Concept of Class', *Studies in Political Economy*, vol. 9, 1982, pp. 45–75 and a rigorous statement of its implications in G. de Ste. Croix, 'Karl Marx and the Interpretation of Ancient and Modern History', pp. 166–9.

which have jostled for primacy within the Marxist tradition since its inception.[68]

If their concept of class consciousness inflicted distressing theoretical perplexities upon adherents of the Marxist paradigm, Guesdists encountered equally intractable complexities in applying the concept to their society, particularly in applying it to the complex, ambiguous, and sometimes self-contradictory social mentalities characteristic of the French proletariat during the *Belle Époque*. Did these decades constitute a golden age of proletarian class consciousness, an era when workers attained previously unheard-of and since unmatched separatist self-awareness?[69] Or did these years inaugurate an epoch during which an increasingly hegemonic bourgeoisie increasingly enslaved the minds of French workers – workers newly subjected to compulsory (bourgeois organised) mass education which indoctrinated their children, to an addictive (bourgeois owned) mass media which conditioned their perception of their world, to disruptive (bourgeois imposed) residential patterns which eroded the solidarity of their communities, and to demobilising (bourgeois patronised) leisure activities which undermined their traditional structures of sociability and protest?[70] The complexity and ambiguity of French society during the *Fin de Siècle* has lent credibility to either thesis – confusing contemporaneous militants and perplexing contemporary sociologists. In either case, the working-class consciousness of the *Belle Époque* has proven astonishingly difficult to identify, much less characterise: proletarian 'conscience ouvrière', 'conscience de classe', 'conscience syndicale', and 'conscience politique' overlapped and merged, reinforcing and contradicting each other – to the bemusement of contemporaneous social-

---

[68] According to M. Levin, 'Marx and Working Class Consciousness', *History of Political Thought*, vol. 1, 1980, pp. 499–515. Useful discussion of the importance and the ambiguities of the Marxist concept of class consciousness may be found in I. Meszaros, 'Contingent and Necessary Class Consciousness', in I. Meszaros (ed.), *Aspects of History and Class Consciousness* (London, 1971), pp. 112–17 and H. Wolpe, 'Some Problems Concerning Revolutionary Consciousness', *The Socialist Register*, 1970, pp. 251–80.

[69] Perrot, 'La Classe Ouvrière au Temps de Jaurès', p. 77. Her wonderful *Les Ouvriers en Grève* (Paris, 1974) is permeated by nostalgia for a lost golden age of spontaneous working-class consciousness.

[70] For employer hegemony over working-class consciousness, see R. Martelli, 'Classe, État, Partis: Réflexions sur les Spécificités Françaises des Luttes Politiques', *Cahiers d'Histoire de l'Institut Maurice Thorez*, no. 22, 1977, pp. 158–60 and the telling instance described in M. Pigenet, 'L'Usine et le Village: Rosières 1869–1914', *Mouvement Social*, no. 119, 1982, pp. 33–61. For the decline in working-class identities associated with new residential and community patterns, see M. Hanagan, *The Logic of Solidarity: Artisans and Industrial Workers in Three French Towns 1871–1914* (London, 1980), p. 15.

ists and the bewilderment of contemporary historians.[71] How did Guesdists respond to these unnerving uncertainties in their Marxist ideology and to the even more daunting ambiguities of their complex society?

The facile solution to these conundrums, then as now, equated the consciousness of workers in general with that of the proletarian minority which exemplified the Marxist conception of militant class consciousness, an equation which thereby circumvented the discouraging enigmas of a class interpretation of non-class consciousness and avoided the daunting intricacy of working-class mentalities.[72] Guesdists personified this solution in its most extreme form, even maintaining that workers 'naturally' understood *Capital*, despite its opacity to 'bourgeois intellectuals', since 'each social class always thinks in accordance with its economic situation'[73] – a triumph of wishful thinking over discouraging experience. This reductionist conception of proletarian consciousness absolved the POF from both the demands of social analysis and the discipline of theoretical introspection: simple verities reinforced simplistic concepts. Better yet, this absolutist conception of proletarian consciousness legitimated the absolutes of socialist ideology: 'the proletariat, for a socialist, *is always right*'.[74]

Even when workers spurned socialism? No amount of blind self-confidence could conceal the sad reality that many, even most, French workers rebuffed the blandishments of the Parti Ouvrier, refusing enlistment in the class war for which the Parti Ouvrier recruited. Year after year, decade after decade, Guesdists awaited the 'inevitable' conversion of the French working class to the militant class consciousness exemplified by the POF, and year after year, decade after decade, most workers maintained their supposedly obsolescent faith in Radicalism or reaction, in the ideological visions of the militant enemies of class conflict and class consciousness. Most Guesdists must have endured moments of black despair when, like Étienne Maillard, they cried out 'come on, you workers!

---

[71] G. Haupt, 'La Classe Ouvrière Française au Temps de Jaurès – Annexes', in *Jaurès et la Classe Ouvrière* (Paris, 1981), p. 204.

[72] For the confusions entailed in equating workers conscious of their 'class interest' (as defined by Marxists) with workers in general, see E. Labrousse, 'Observations on a New History of France', *New Left Review*, no. 86, 1974, p. 95.

[73] H. Nivet, *Notions Élémentaires d'Économie Marxiste* (Paris, 1904), p. 5.

[74] P.-M. André, 'Les Grèves', *Le Socialiste*, 16–23 November 1902 (stress in original).

Your lack of consciousness is the root of all our misfortunes. You remain nonentities . . . because of your indifference'.[75] Even at their most demoralised, however, Guesdists never surrendered their conviction that class interest determined social consciousness, retreating instead to the pessimistic but still Marxist conclusion that *bourgeois* class interest might determine *proletarian* consciousness – an admission that capitalists 'control[led] not only the bodies of workers, but their minds as well,'[76] a triumph of discouraging experience over wishful thinking.

Unlike subsequent generations of Marxists, however, this bleak pessimism rarely overwhelmed the Guesdists, who cultivated a determined faith in the inevitability of militant class consciousness – if not a consciousness already inherent in the proletarian mentality, then a consciousness whose birth awaited only the next great strike, the next political scandal, the next May Day demonstration. None the less, even the most optimistic Guesdists – puzzled by the discrepancy between the massive inequities and blatant iniquities of French society, on the one hand, and the enduring passivity and passive endurance of the proletariat, on the other – must sometimes have asked themselves 'why don't the workers revolt?'[77] When French Marxists struggled to answer this troubling question, their responses prefigured the twentieth-century Marxist preoccupation with 'bourgeois hegemony' and occasionally generated sophisticated insights into the complexities of working-class culture and the intricacies of proletarian political consciousness, complexities and intricacies more often ignored by Guesdists in favour of comforting dogma. According to the Guesdists who pursued this demoralising line of inquiry, why *didn't* the workers revolt?

One answer, repeatedly rediscovered as the working class repeatedly ignored Guesdist exhortation, indicted bourgeois brutalisation of working people as the agency of proletarian pacification, as the origin of 'that moral atrophy, that state of resignation, that stupidity which turns a man into a beast and a worker into a beast of burden'.[78] Foreshadowing Marcuse's theory of 'repressive desublimation', the Parti Ouvrier discovered that capitalism could exploit even proletarian exhaustion and 'moral atrophy'. Disgusted by

---

[75] É. Maillard, *Le Prolétariat International et la Journée de Huit Heures* (Bordeaux, 1890), p. 34.
[76] G. Dazet, *Discours de Clôture* (Paris, undated), p. 23.
[77] P. Myrens, 'Les Deux Morales', *Le Socialiste*, 7–14 July 1901.
[78] Maillard, *Le Prolétariat International*, pp. 11–12.

working-class enthusiasm for the 1882 Bastille Day celebrations, for instance, Guesde attributed workers' frenetic participation in that 'bourgeois festival' to 'their need for diversion, their desire to forget themselves in noise and excitement, which is directly proportional to their fatigue, work, and daily toil'.[79] In other words, a debased working-class mentality of escapism, as much the fruit of class society as was socialist militancy itself, might prevail against the assertive realism of class-conscious collectivism: Guesdists unhappily confessed that a proletarian 'class *instinct*' founded upon 'resignation and misery' contradicted the proletarian 'class *consciousness*' founded upon hatred and hope.[80]

Apart from the insidious corruption inherent in 'repressive desublimation', Guesdists discovered more overt bourgeois conspiracies to short-circuit the development of an assertive working-class consciousness. Although the Parti Ouvrier never employed the term in so many words, French Marxists regularly utilised the concept of 'false consciousness' to explain, and to explain away, the discouraging quiescence of the French proletariat. Infuriated by working-class communities which voted for their employers' candidates rather than for those of the POF, angered by proletarians who insisted upon reading *La Libre Parole* rather than *Le Socialiste*, enraged by workers' enthusiasm for Bastille Day military parades rather than May Day marches, French Marxists blamed their Party's lack of immediate success upon an all-pervasive ideological apparatus of priests, teachers and journalists, bourgeois agents who laboured incessantly to 'impose a morality of obedience upon the spirit of the subordinate class, which is thereby constrained to act in the interest of the rich rather than in its own'.[81] Guesde, for instance, having analysed the contents of the primary school civics textbooks imposed upon working-class children in the state educational system, found them permeated with a '*capitalist faith* which is implanted into the budding minds of working-class France ... to secure the greater security and the greater profit of our political and economic exploiters'.[82] Capitalist exploitation of workers accorded capitalists the means to conceal exploitation.

---

[79] J. Guesde, 'Leur Fête!', *L'Égalité*, 16 July 1882.
[80] H. Nivet, 'L'Unité Socialiste', *Le Socialiste*, 6–13 January 1901. For a graphic description of this mentality of resignation, see Marty, *Chanter pour Survivre*, p. 111.
[81] P. Myrens, 'Les Deux Morales', *Le Socialiste*, 7–14 July 1901.
[82] J. Guesde, 'Laïcisation à Faire', *Le Socialiste*, 22 October 1887 (Guesde's stress).

It's terribly easy for bourgeois to mislead workers, to lie to the unfortunate, to credit their theories, to represent us as the enemies of progress and civilisation. Don't they have piles of gold stolen from the serfs of industry, commerce and agriculture to legitimise their crimes? If the working class possessed similar propaganda resources, it's certain that the present social order wouldn't survive for six months.[83]

If the ruling ideas of *fin-de-siècle* France emanated from its ruling class, then socialism and working-class consciousness no longer reinforced each other: workers' minds, no less than their bodies, would obey the bourgeoisie.

The Guesdists' revolutionary optimism, irreplaceable source of the movement's polemical force and ideological stamina, would not have long survived full assimilation of these daunting insights. The Parti Ouvrier's militants, to remain militant, clung desperately to their Marxist materialism, to the 'scientific' certainties which 'guaranteed' that the 'material realities' of class conflict would soon override the degenerate mentalities inculcated by capitalist economic horrors, that class interest would eventually prevail against proletarian escapism and bourgeois brainwashing, that 'material interest' would inevitably disperse the 'false consciousness' imposed by bourgeois cultural hegemony. Indeed, the POF, characteristically overborne by an excess of revolutionary optimism, sometimes affirmed that the working class had *already* escaped its ideological bondage: 'proletarian consciousness is clear to see', proclaimed the assembled Party at its Lyons Congress, triumphantly certain that 'once a class has attained this degree of cohesion and awareness, concrete victory is near'.[84] The *raison d'être* of the Parti Ouvrier resided in this supposed achievement, which, in Guesdist eyes, arose from past socialist militancy and ensured future socialist triumph. 'Our party', boasted Henri Ghesquière, 'can be proud of the class consciousness acquired by workers'[85] – the class consciousness of self-confidence and self-assertion, not the class consciousness of 'moral atrophy, resignation, and stupidity'.

Even in this optimistic mode, however, the Parti Ouvrier confused the causal relationship between the rise of revolutionary class consciousness and the coming of the socialist revolution, a relationship which has posed one of the most vexing issues in Marxist

---

[83] Vandorme, 'Coopération et Socialisme', *Le Socialiste*, 24 September 1899.
[84] 'Le Congrès Socialiste de Lyon', *Le Petit Lyonnais*, 27 November 1891, press clipping in file 1891, Archives Nationales, F7 12.490.
[85] H. Ghesquière, *La Mine et les Mineurs* (Lille, 1901), p. 4.

doctrine. Did consolidation of revolutionary class consciousness constitute a prerequisite for socialist triumph (an implicitly idealist stance in which consciousness not only preceded its 'material' correlate, but caused its occurrence), or did revolutionary class consciousness eventuate from the practice of revolution (an impeccably 'materialist' thesis in which consciousness derived from circumstances)?[86] Characteristically incapable of dialectically reconciling these alternatives, unable to escape the age-old opposition between rationalist idealism and 'vulgar' materialism, Guesdists vacillated helplessly between seemingly antithetical arguments. On most occasions, the Parti Ouvrier contended that the workers' movement 'succeeded only when it has a firm self-consciousness',[87] that the socialist revolution would never eventuate without prior development of revolutionary class consciousness among proletarians – an irrefutable justification of decades of patient Guesdist pedagogy. In so far as French Marxists equated 'the revolution' with ongoing socialist militancy rather than with the final working-class seizure of power, the problem of priorities vanished altogether: revolutionary class consciousness and socialist 'revolution' engendered each other with true dialectical reciprocity.

Unfortunately, Guesdists rarely elaborated this synthesising insight. More often, they swung to the other extreme, arguing that 'intellectual or moral liberation will not precede material liberation. It can only follow the latter'.[88] This reasoning, although it radically diminished the importance of revolutionary pedagogy, comforted Guesdist militants in difficult circumstances. Commenting, for instance, upon a frustrating episode in her campaign to carry the socialist message to female workers, Aline Valette, the Parti Ouvrier's spokesperson on the 'women's question', decided that her repeated fiascoes merely demonstrated 'that the development of consciousness lags behind facts ... [but that] neither [workers'] blindness nor their inertia can stop the march of progress'[89] – a wonderfully comforting conclusion. Polemical considerations reinforced both extremes of the Guesdists' interpretation of the relationship between class consciousness and socialist revolution. Conscious-

---

[86] M. Burawoy, 'Contemporary Currents in Marxist Theory', in S. McNall (ed.), *Theoretical Perspectives in Sociology* (New York, 1979), p. 22, and Levin, 'Marx and Working Class Consciousness', p. 502.

[87] Anonymous, *Socialisme et Sexualisme: Programme du Parti Socialiste Féminin* (Paris, 1893), p. 5.

[88] J. Guesde, *Au Congrès d'Amsterdam* (Paris, 1904), p. 6.

[89] A. Valette, 'À Propos de Syndicat', *Le Socialiste*, 23 June 1895.

ness-raising justified Parti Ouvrier militancy against the 'economist' (in the Leninist sense of the word) tendency within the French labour movement, the tendency which expected workers' self-emancipation to arise spontaneously from the proletariat's immediate economic struggle against capital. At the same time, 'materialist' emphasis upon the origins of a 'mature' class consciousness in revolutionary militancy challenged the 'ethical' socialists who anticipated that workers' liberation would evolve from the progress of moral enlightenment rather than from the clash of material interests. In this respect, the Guesdists' theoretical incoherence served them well, arming them variously against their varied enemies.

'Material interests' articulated by the structural relationship of labour and property ruled the Guesdists' distinctive ideological perception, which viewed the infinite complexity of French society – its wealth and poverty, its hierarchies of power and submission, its communities and conflicts – through the lens of class, through the refractions inherent in that fundamental Marxist concept. Nevertheless, Guesdists, however self-consciously rigorous and aggressively exclusive in their ideological self-discipline, sometimes strayed from the paths of Marxist rectitude into the contaminated slough of eclecticism: the Parti Ouvrier suffered contagion from alternative social paradigms, even while combating them. The political identity of the POF, like that of every other ideological movement, evolved primarily through this dynamic of infection and resistance.[90] What alternatives challenged the Guesdists' imagery of class? To what extent did French Marxists surrender to those alternatives? How did the Parti Ouvrier's long struggle against competing visions of social order influence the development of its Marxism?

The simple contrast of wealth and poverty, as opposed to the intricate dialectic of property and labour, constituted the most potent ideological alternative to class analysis. An 'egalitarian' discourse animated by hatred of ostentatious plutocracy and revulsion against endemic indigence prospered in the late-nineteen-century world of *laissez-faire* individualism and commodification of human relationships, a social milieu which 'naturally' focused

[90] Useful discussions of this interpretive strategy may be found in E. Wright, 'Varieties of Marxist Conceptions of the Class Structure', *Politics and Society*, vol. 9, 1980, pp.324–6, and G. Lichtheim, 'The Concepts of Social Class', in G. Lichtheim, *Collected Essays* (New York, 1973), pp. 247–53.

ideological perception upon individualistic relations of distribution rather than upon class relations of production.[91] Sensitive to 'distributive justice', disciples of the ancient obligations of Christian compassion and devotees of the traditional imperatives of humanitarian philanthropy revolted against the coldly rationalised brutalities of bourgeois political economy, against the iron 'economic laws' which 'proved' that the selfishness of the rich and their trampling of the poor ensured beneficent progress for everyone, against the liberal equation of 'private vices' with 'public virtues'. Empowered both by the passionless predominance of the cash nexus and by the passionate convictions of religious humanists, Dickensian sentimentality competed powerfully against economistic rigour (whether liberal or Marxist) during the *Belle Époque*, an epoch splendid indeed for its rich, but anything but *belle* for its poor. Denunciation of the uncaring affluent and compassion for the uncared-for destitute – the social rhetoric favoured by all non-Marxist socialists, by most democratic Radicals, and by many religious conservatives – superficially resembled the Marxist analytic of property and labour: did not capitalist property generate arrogant plutocratic wealth, and proletarian labour beget demoralising working-class destitution? Outraged by the inequities of bourgeois society and unconcerned with theoretical consistency, socialists utilised Marxist and egalitarian rhetorics interchangeably, or even simultaneously.[92]

All the same, the egalitarian critique of the iniquitous contrast between wealth and impoverishment and the Marxist critique of exploitative class distinctions contradicted each other both in theory and in effect. At the least, the order of classes identified by Marxists clashed with the hierarchy of income delineated by egalitarians, a clash which blurred the outlines of every class and obscured the antagonism between classes. The most highly-paid skilled workers, for instance, earned more in wages than many petty capitalists received in profits, income criteria which thereby obliterated the otherwise clear class distinction between the two categories, smudging the distinction between labour and capital.[93] Worse yet, from a Marxist perspective, vast differentials in wealth and income

[91] C. Bettelheim, 'Idéologie Économique et Réalité Sociale', *Cahiers Internationaux de Sociologie*, vol. 4, 1948, p. 130.
[92] For these distinctions, see J. Dubois, *Le Vocabulaire Politique et Social*, pp. 13–14.
[93] A. Daumard, 'Wealth and Affluence in France Since the Beginning of the Nineteenth Century', in W. Rubinstein (ed.), *Wealth and the Wealthy in the Modern World* (London, 1980), pp. 100–1.

prevailed *within* classes, not least within the proletariat: working-class salaries in the northern industrial centre of Valenciennes, for instance, varied between the 41.50 francs per day received (on extraordinary occasions) by the most highly skilled glass workers and the 1.43 francs per day earned by messenger boys.[94] Egalitarianism encouraged both conflict within classes and class conflict between them, undermining proletarian solidarity between glass workers and messenger boys no less than encouraging their common hostility towards bourgeois opulence. Indeed, egalitarian radicalism favoured intra-class hostilities more than it furthered class war, given that individuals knew their neighbours' incomes far better than they could imagine those of their socially 'distant' class enemies: messenger boys envied the modest prosperity of glass blowers, not the unimaginable affluence of bankers.[95] Marx, with reason, had excluded income from his theory of class structuration: the class system, he contended, did not originate in 'the size of one's purse',[96] although the size of purses undoubtedly originated in the class system. To pursue their distinctive social vision, Marxists had to eschew egalitarianism.[97]

In theory, but not necessarily in practice. More committed to polemical efficacy than to theoretical consistency, many Guesdists lovingly embraced the egalitarian rhetoric which otherwise so distorted their class imagery of society, insistently designating the POF as 'the Party of the Poor'.[98] How could they resist contrasting bourgeois affluence with proletarian poverty – the contrast which symbolised, while not originating, the iniquity of capitalism? The average employer in the footwear industry of Fougères, for instance, enjoyed an income approximately 150 times greater than that of his

---

[94] O. Hardy-Hémery, *De la Croissance à la Désindustrialisation: Un Siècle dans le Valenciennois* (Paris, 1984), p. 46. For further discussion of these differentials, see R. Price, *A Social History of Nineteenth-Century France* (London, 1987), p. 200.

[95] F. Parkin, *Class Inequality and Political Order* (London, 1971), pp. 61–2 and S. Ossowski, *Class Structure in the Social Consciousness* (London, 1963), pp. 30–1 usefully discuss this discouraging aspect of modern social mentalities.

[96] K. Marx, 'Moralizing Criticism and Critical Morality', in Marx and Engels, *Collected Works*, vol. 6, p. 330. See the excellent discussion of this question in A. Wood, 'Marx and Equality', in J. Mepham and D.-H. Ruben (eds.), *Issues in Marxist Philosophy* (Brighton, 1981), vol. 4, pp. 195–214.

[97] This case is well-presented in R. Connell, 'Logic and Politics in Theories of Class', *Australian and New Zealand Journal of Sociology*, vol. 13, 1977, pp. 203–11, and E. Wright and L. Perrone, 'Marxist Class Categories and Income Inequality', *American Sociological Review*, vol. 42, 1977, pp. 32–55.

[98] Vandorme, 'Coopération et Socialisme'.

average employee, an irresistible incitement to (egalitarian) social-ist outrage.[99] Worse yet (or better yet, for the polemicist), the differential between bourgeois and proletarian wealth (property-ownership, as opposed to income) attained nearly astronomical proportions. In Lille, that Guesdist bastion, deceased industrialists left legacies on average 20,000 times greater than those of industrial workers – an outrage by every (egalitarian) socialist criteria.[100] Guesdist journalists tirelessly retailed anecdotal accounts of shame-less bourgeois ostentation, and the spectacular life-style of *fin-de-siècle* plutocrats furnished the Parti Ouvrier with inexhaustible copy.

How, then, did Guesdists differ from Radicals, anarchists, Chris-tian Democrats, and anti-Semites – all of whom enthusiastically adopted similar egalitarian rhetoric? The Parti Ouvrier dis-tinguished itself from its competitors by its integration of the distribution of wealth and poverty into the structure of property and labour, and by its 'materialist' rejection of the essentially moral criticisms deployed by 'genuine' egalitarians. French Marxists held that the maldistribution of income and wealth which disrupted and corrupted French society was overwhelmingly 'determined by the mode of production',[101] thereby explicitly subordinating their movement's periodic outbursts of egalitarian wrath to the 'scientific' rigours of its class theory. Symptomatically, the great egalitarian and redistributionist causes of the *Belle Époque*, most notably the long and acrimonious campaign to reform the iniquitous French taxation system, largely bypassed the Parti Ouvrier – which dismissed such programmes as mistaken or fraudulent, as addressing a superficial symptom, the maldistribution of wealth, rather than the deep-seated disease, the capitalist mode of production.[102] None the less, the Parti Ouvrier sometimes practised egalitarianism with fewer

[99] B. Legendre, 'La Vie d'un Prolétariat: Les Ouvriers de Fougères au Début du XXᵉ Siècle', *Mouvement Social*, no. 98, 1977, p. 21.
[100] F.-P. Codaccioni, *De l'Inégalité Sociale dans une Grande Ville Industrielle: Le Drame de Lille de 1850 à 1914* (Lille, 1976), p. 430. For the vast differentials characteristic of Roubaix, see A. Gronoff, *L'Inégalité Sociale à Roubaix en 1896* (Mémoire de Maîtrise, University of Lille III, 1976), cited in Marty, *Chanter pour Survivre*, p. 68.
[101] A. Zévaès, 'Le Socialisme à l'École de Droit: Réponse à M. P. Beauregard', *Le Socialiste*, 18 February 1894.
[102] One of the few significant discussions of this burning issue during decades of Guesdist journalism occurred with Lafargue's 'L'Impôt Progressif sur l'Héritage' in *Le Socialiste* of 15 December 1894. For a grossly overstated and unsubstantiated characterisation of the POF as egalitarian in its theory and distributionist in its programme, see C. Posner, 'The Concept of Strategy in the Writings of Marx and Engels and in the French and German Socialist Parties from their Inception to 1905', PhD thesis, University of Essex, 1972, p. 275.

Marxist scruples. Discovery of the enormous salary differentials which divided employees of a Parisian department store, for instance, provoked *Le Socialiste* into the outraged comment 'so much for bourgeois equality!'[103] – an outburst ideally calculated to set floor-walkers against sales clerks rather than the store's employees against its proprietors. Most often, however, Guesdists strove to conceal intra-class inequality, carefully limiting their opportunist utilisation of the egalitarian repertoire to illustration and denunciation of the profound inequalities which separated bourgeois from proletarians.

The all-pervasive dichotomy between dominators and the dominated, the age-old distinction between rulers and the ruled, inspired other potent alternatives to the Marxist paradigm of labour and property: the conservative discourse of elitism and the radical discourse of populism. These conceptions of social order and social conflict focused ideological attention upon the relationship between 'elites' and 'masses', upon the clash between 'aristocracies' and 'the people' – relationships highlighted both by conservatives and fascists, on the one (Right) hand, and by anarchists and Radicals, on the other (Left) hand. In theory, Marxists have categorically repudiated this 'Machiavellian' perception of social hierarchy. Their class conception of society has systematically reduced relations of power to relations of production, thereby evoking despair from eclectic Weberians and fury from elitist Paretans. As Marx argued, 'it is always the direct relationship of the owners of the conditions of production to the direct producers ... which reveals the innermost secret, the hidden basis of the entire social structure, and with it the political form of the relation of sovereignty and dependence, in short the corresponding specific form of the state'.[104] Nevertheless, Marx himself, as outraged as Bakunin or Mazzini by aristocratic authoritarianism, frequently employed the populist rhetoric pioneered by his anarchist and democratic antagonists – the rhetoric of the transcended 1848 revolutions rather than the discourse of prospective socialist revolution.[105] What is more, throughout the history of

---

[103] Anonymous, 'À la Belle Jardinière', *Le Socialiste*, 29 October 1887.

[104] K. Marx, *Capital* (Moscow, 1959), vol. 3, p. 791. For critique of this Marxist view of power, and a powerful alternative, see R. Dahrendorf, *Class and Class Conflict in Industrial Society* (Stanford, 1959).

[105] See the instances collected in É. Balibar, 'L'Idée d'une Politique de Classe chez Marx', *Temps Moderne*, vol. 40, 1984, pp. 1357–406.

Marxism, disillusioned adherents of the doctrine have surreptitiously reversed its reductionist principles – reducing class to elite, and exploitation to domination, rather than *vice versa* – thereby lapsing into conservative elitism or anarchist radicalism, depending upon the origin and trajectory of their particular disillusionment.[106]

French Marxists suffered these temptations. Populism, devotion to the virtuous people in their struggle against oppressive elites, pervaded the Left political culture of *fin-de-siècle* France, just as populism had dominated French radicalism since 1789. Most Guesdists had issued from this inchoate populist milieu, struggled valiantly against its ancestral allure, and occasionally reverted to its tutelage. The 'Radical' wing of the Republican movement – where Guesde, Lafargue, and Deville had begun their political lives, and where Deville ended his – represented itself as embodying the 'classe populaire' (a 'classe' which included everyone from paupers to small capitalists) in its age-old struggle against the 'aristocracies' of wealth, power and privilege. This neo-Jacobin social rhetoric, although best exemplified by Radicals such as the early Gambetta or the mature Clemenceau, spilled over into the demagogic Right, the Right of Henri Rochefort's *Intransigeant* and of degenerate Blanquism, and into the socialist movement itself, the socialist movement of Jaurès as the 'people's tribune'.[107] Identification with 'the People' paid handsome political dividends under the democratic Third Republic, where the melodramatic imagery of 'les petits' throwing off the reign of predatory elites played to historical

[106] Robert Michels represents the most theoretically aware instance of the elitist deviation towards Fascism from within the Marxist tradition. For a particularly clear-cut instance of 'Marxist' priority to relations of domination, see the thoughtful arguments in E. Wright, 'Varieties of Marxist Conceptions of Class Structure', pp. 362–5, and the admission and abandonment of this deviation in E. Wright, 'What is Marxist and What is Neo in Neo-Marxist Class Analysis?', in B. Chavance (ed.), *Marx en Perspective* (Paris, 1985), pp. 231–59, and E. Wright, *Classes* (London, 1985), Part I, with the commentary on the resultant controversy in E. Wright, 'A General Framework for the Analysis of Class Structure', in E. Wright et al., *The Debate on Classes* (London, 1989), pp. 3–43. Discussion of this tendency towards 'neo-anarchism' within contemporary Marxism may be found in F. Cardoso, 'Althusserisme ou Marxisme? À Propos du Concept de Classe chez Poulantzas', *L'Homme et la Société*, no. 24–25, 1972, pp. 57–71. Ironically, Frank Parkin's fascinating *Marxism and Class Theory: A Bourgeois Critique* (New York, 1979) is more a defense of the Marxist categories of labour and property against 'neo-Marxist' neo-anarchism than a critique of traditional Marxist class theory.

[107] For the terminology of 'populism' and its diffusion, see Dubois, *Le Vocabulaire Politique et Social*, pp. 16–18 and p. 26, and Portis, *Les Classes Sociales en France*, pp. 102–5. For its utility to both the proto-Fascist and the socialist avatars of the Blanquist tradition, see P. Hutton, *The Cult of the Revolutionary Tradition: The Blanquists in French Politics 1864–1895* (Berkeley, 1981), pp. 3–4 and p. 137.

'memories' of 1789 and to the aspirations of the artisanal working
class, the petite bourgeoisie, and the peasantry – 'classes' thereby
melded into a massive but amorphous 'Peuple'.[108] Even industrial
workers, newly courted by demagogues of every persuasion, often
ignored the property question dear to Marxists in favour of the anti-
authoritarianism favoured by populists, particularly where 'managerial despotism' had supplanted 'bourgeois exploitation' in the
proletariat's litany of grievances.[109]

Studies of the POF have accused the movement of deserting the
hard certainties of the class war for the vacuous phrase-mongering of
Radicalism, of abandoning the austere charms of class analysis for
the baroque temptations of populist demagoguery.[110] This accusation overstates the case: despite their occasional deployment of
populist rhetoric, Guesdists consistently contended that 'the expression "people" is obviously too vague, and no longer has any
correspondence to reality in a society ... based upon class antagonism'.[111] The populist assertion that workers and small capitalists
constituted a single 'class' in conflict with the lords of finance, land,
and religion outraged French Marxists, who relentlessly criticised
the Radical, proto-fascist, and anarchist imageries of an undifferentiated People victimised by aristocratic, Semitic, or power elites.[112]
Guesdists occasionally employed populist rhetoric, but almost
invariably to reinforce their own assault upon class society: for
French Marxists, the proletariat subsumed the People; the People
did not incorporate the proletariat.

A final alternative to the Marxist conception of social order has
evolved from the 'occupational order' and from patterns of community solidarity and inter-communal conflict, patterns which have
fathered 'corporativist' or 'organicist' perceptions of society. Corporativists have advocated occupational solidarity within trades and
organic unity within communities: they have idealised the social

---

[108] M. Perrot, 'Les Classes Populaire Urbaines',in *Histoire Économique et Sociale de la France*,
Tome IV – *L'Ère Industrielle et la Société d'Aujourd'hui (Siècle 1880–1980)*: Premier volume –
Ambiguïtés des Débuts et Croissance Effective (Années 1880–1914) (Paris, 1979), pp. 455–6.

[109] Y. Lequin, *Les Ouvriers de la Région Lyonnaise (1848–1914): Les Intérêts de Classe et la République*
(Lyons, 1977), pp. 154–6.

[110] For the best statement of this common charge, see Réberioux, 'Le Guesdisme', p. 8.

[111] A. Zévaès, 'Révision', *Le Socialiste*, 1 December 1895.

[112] For good instances, see A. Baju, *Principes du Socialisme* (Paris, 1893), pp. 8–17 and G. Deville,
L'Anarchisme (Paris, 1887), pp. 12–25.

harmony which supposedly prevailed between medieval master and man, and have sought to reproduce the sense of mutual obligation which supposedly pervaded the hierarchy of social ranks during the Middle Ages – the social harmony and mutual obligation which contrasted so painfully with the irksome disputes and divisive mentalities of modern 'industrial relations'.[113] Marxists have detested this rhetoric: their dissection of capitalist society has revealed a fundamental rupture between the propertied and the propertyless *within* occupations and communities – thereby elucidating the inevitable antagonism between capital and labour, an antagonism absolutely precluding corporativist harmony and mutuality.[114] Nevertheless, Marxist thought has lent itself to confusion between class and corporation: the concept of 'relations of production', so central to the Marxist paradigm, has indiscriminately fused occupations (social entities founded upon the division of labour) with classes (social entities founded upon property distinctions) – a fusion which has, on occasion, considerably weakened Marxist resistance to contagion by corporativist ideology.[115]

The Guesdists' enemies exploited the anti-Marxist potential of corporativism to the full: both the pseudo-Medieval ideology patronised by Christian Socialists and anti-Semitic Nationalists and the forward-looking 'solidarity' advocated by liberal democrats revived or arose during the *Belle Époque* as explicit alternatives to the class conflict promoted by Marxists. Anti-Marxists, whether of Right or Left, hoped that a rejuvenated guild system tailored to the industrial order and propagation of traditional (or novel) communitarian values would immunise workers against socialism and unite employees with their employers in defence of common interests and common ideals. This class-collaborationist programme tapped a considerable reservoir of proletarian constituents: many (most?) workers primarily identified themselves with their trade (including its employers) rather than with their class, and the heartfelt resonances of 'community' – its sentimental evocation of family ties, hometown memories, provincial traditions, and national fraternity – frequently prevailed over the rationalist interests highlighted by

---

[113] For a rigorous analysis of the development of this tradition, see A. Black, *Guilds and Civil Society in European Political Thought from the Twelfth Century to the Present* (London, 1984), particularly chapter 19.
[114] See, for example, K. Marx, *Capital* (Moscow, 1959), vol. 3, p. 886. The point is elaborated in E. Wright, 'Class and Occupation', *Theory and Society*, vol. 9, 1980, pp. 177–8.
[115] A. Rattansi, *Marx and the Division of Labour* (London, 1982), pp. 14–18 and 53–9.

class theory.[116] The nascent discipline of sociology, struggling to understand and master the social revolution of the nineteenth century, may have discerned the transition from *gemeinschaft* to *gesselschaft*, the replacement of the 'mechanical solidarity' of the village by the 'organic solidarity' of the city, the destruction of status by contract – but the warm intimacy of 'community' relentlessly increased its potency as cultural and political myth, while helplessly surrendering its domain in social and economic practice to the cold anonymity of 'society'.

Guesdists, imperfectly armoured by their doctrine against corporative practices and communitarian myths, occasionally lapsed into opportunist organicist rhetoric, if not into full-fledged corporativist ideology. Charles Bonnier, for instance, usually the most orthodox of Marxists, nevertheless identified the 'nation' as 'a social and economic organism' and advocated 'reforms embracing every organ of the social body'[117] – hardly the language of class analysis. More seriously, Guesdist theory sometimes implicitly accorded the occupational order autonomy from the class system and allowed corporative identities independence from class consciousness, as when Parti Ouvrier labour militants decided to defend the rights of workers 'as much in their corporative forms as in the class war'[118] – a concession which opened a breach in the Marxist paradigm through which corporativists might advance against the primacy of class. None the less, however often Guesdists allowed trades their corporative identity, however frequently Guesdists indulged in organicist metaphor, they consistently abjured corporativism, arguing that corporative identities and corporative organisations, unless clearly subordinated to class identity and class organisation, divided workers from each other while uniting them with their exploiters, to the great advantage of the latter. As for community solidarity, as beloved by social conservatives as by social reformers, as dear to the

[116] For instances of the strength of the corporative and communitarian traditions within the French working class, see R. Gossez, *Les Ouvriers de Paris: L'Organisation* (La Roche-sur-Yon, 1967), p. 253; L. Berlanstein, *The Working People of Paris 1871–1914* (London, 1984), p. 20; W. Reddy, *The Rise of Market Culture: The Textile Trade and French Society 1750–1900* (Cambridge, 1984), chapter 10 and particularly pp. 294–5; N. Papayanis, 'Le Prolétarisation des Cochers de Fiacres à Paris (1878–1889)', *Mouvement Social*, no. 132, 1985, pp. 59–82; M. Perrot, *Les Ouvriers en Grève*, vol. 2, pp. 510–11 and 527–8; and J. Merriman, *The Red City: Limoges and the French Nineteenth Century* (Oxford, 1985), pp. 147–54.

[117] 'B' (Bonnier), 'Nationalisme Politique et Nationalisme Économique', *Le Socialiste*, 11–18 September 1904.

[118] Anonymous, 'Le Socialiste', *Le Socialiste*, 1 January 1887.

Catholic Albert de Mun as to the Radical Léon Bourgeois, as treasured by anti-Semitic nationalists as by Dreyfusard Ministerialists – it evoked Guesdist derision: 'Reciprocity, solidarity, fraternity. Humbug!'[119] In their most optimistic mood, French Marxists confidently declared that Catholic and nationalist prospectives for a class-collaborationist corporative social order, farcical antiquarian fantasies, must come to naught in the competitive maelstrom of capitalism, as must the Radical's programme of social solidarity between employers and employees, a ludicrous figment of the petit-bourgeois imagination. In their less optimistic (or more realistic) moments, however, Guesdists dreaded the corporativist implications even of exclusively working-class trade unions, given the trade unionists' tendency to a narrow professional exclusivity directed as much against other workers as against bourgeois, trade unions' propensity to evolve into 'a sort of closed corporation, as in the Middle Ages'.[120] Social solidarity, whether as carefully cultivated bourgeois myth or spontaneous working-class 'deviation', precluded class consciousness and mortally endangered proletarian pursuit of the class war. No wonder Guesdists fought tooth and nail against the corporativist alternative to class militancy.

Overall, the Marxist axioms of labour and property governed Guesdist discourse with an iron discipline. However tempted by the ideological charms of alien paradigms, Guesdists rarely succumbed: the Parti Ouvrier consistently rejected and reviled non-Marxist and anti-Marxist conceptions of social order. Indeed, the distinctive emphases and silences, the characteristic coherence and contradictions of Guesdist rhetoric evolved from the Parti Ouvrier's long campaign against these alternatives to Marxist socialism, against the social mentalities which fostered intra-class disruption and nurtured class collaboration. Admittedly, French Marxists, against their best intentions, occasionally surrendered to the all-pervasive egalitarian, populist, and corporativist mentalities of their society. Ideological discourses, embodied in erring humanity rather than paradigmatic perfection, inevitably penetrate each other during moments of

---

[119] Anonymous, 'Fouillis Fraternitaire', *Le Socialiste*, 24 July 1886. For a more reasoned critique of the corporatism of Léon Bourgeois's Solidarism, see É. Fortin, 'Solidarité Bourgeoise', *Le Socialiste*, 29 November 1896.

[120] Anonymous, 'Les Instituteurs', *Le Socialiste*, 16 November 1890. For critique of Catholic corporatism, see P. Lafargue, 'La Propriété Féodale', *Le Socialiste*, 22 October 1887, and against the similar ideals of the Nationalists, G. Deville, *Socialisme, Révolution, Internationalisme* (Paris, undated), p. 5.

unguarded laxity or promiscuous opportunism – spawning monstrous hybrids. But Guesdists rarely lapsed from the Marxist rigour of their long-term polemical strategy; upon close examination, even their most egregious lapses reveal short-term tactical manoeuvres designed to harness the popularity of others' rhetoric to the Parti Ouvrier's collectivist juggernaut – tactical manoeuvres which ruthlessly subordinated egalitarianism, populism, and corporativism to the strategy of class war.

What conclusions arise from this overview of the paradigmatic foundations of the Guesdists' conception of social order, from this analysis of the axiomatics of labour and property which engendered the movement's distinctive social rhetoric of class, class conflict, and class consciousness? Above all, 'class' and its corollaries offered the French a coherent and potent alternative to the individualist-egalitarian, elitist-populist, and organicist-corporativist social imageries which had competed for their ideological allegiance throughout the nineteenth century. Despite its formidable force, however, the discourse of class, the rhetoric of labour and property, like all other ideological rhetorics, imposed systematic ambiguities, contradictions, and blind-spots upon its adherents – limitations which, paradoxically, often reinforced the polemical, if not the theoretical, efficacy of the Guesdists' ideological construct.[121] Critical insight into the fundamental conceptual framework which sustained the Parti Ouvrier's intervention in its society – into its strengths and weaknesses, its affinities and inconsistencies, its potential and limitations – illuminates the elaboration of Marxist first principles, thereby elucidating the POF's intricate theses on the making and unmaking of the proletariat, its complex analyses of the propertied classes of capitalist society, and the ambiguities of its ultimate revolutionary project.

---

[121] S. Ossowski, *Class Structure in the Social Consciousness*, p. 87, analyses this seeming paradox in Marxist social thought.

PART II

The making of the French working class

The capitalist mode of production and proletarianisation

The identification of the working class cannot be regarded as an exclusively theoretical exercise. It is a profoundly political question that goes to the very heart of the formation of revolutionary strategy.

A. Hunt, 'Theory and Practice in the Identification of the Working Class,' in A. Hunt (ed.), *Class and Class Structure* (1977).

The concepts of 'class', 'class struggle', and 'class consciousness' have governed the Marxist interpretation of society since Marxism's inception as a doctrine. They have invested Marxist socialism with its impressive polemical force and distinctive theoretical coherence. Axioms in themselves, however, have not answered the two most fundamental strategic questions which have challenged Marxism: who are its potential partisans, and why should these partisans champion the socialist assault upon capitalism? Although socialism might attract anyone as an individual, whatever their class (consider Frederick Engels, wealthy capitalist of Manchester, or Karl Marx, child of the Trier bourgeoisie), Marxists have contended that particular class interests enjoy an elective affinity with socialist politics, and that theoretical misunderstanding of these interests distorts political practice. In the words of the Parti Ouvrier's leader in Nantes, Charles Brunellière, socialists had carefully to

define and delimit the antagonistic classes so that socialism may rapidly encompass new recruits. Without this procedure there's a dual danger: that we'll incorporate the ambitious or ignorant who'll deform the socialist movement ... and that ... we'll exclude workers with a clear class consciousness who might render considerable service to the proletarian cause.[1]

[1] C. Brunellière, 'Bourgeoisie ou Ploutocratie', *Le Socialiste*, 14 May 1899. For an incisive analysis of the linkage between Marxist class analysis and socialist strategy, see N. Poulantzas, 'On Social Classes', *New Left Review*, no. 78, 1973, pp. 33–4, with discussion of

Admittedly, the imperatives of inclusion and exclusion originated in the Marxists' analytic of labour and property: the propertyless, the working class or the proletariat, were by definition potential social-ists; the propertied, the capitalist class or the bourgeoisie, were (again by definition) emphatically anti-socialist. The absolute separation of labour from property, the defining characteristic of the 'capitalist mode of production', automatically and unproblematic-ally furnished socialism with its constituency: capitalism, recruiting its own gravediggers, ensured 'the existence of persons owning their own labour power and nothing else. The proletariat is simply this latter category of persons'.[2]

In practice, however, assertion that 'the proletariat is *simply*' anything has grossly misrepresented the making of the working class. No uniform and united proletariat has ever marshalled its serried ranks against capital. Instead, hierarchies of skill, patterns of authority, and communities of tradition have divided workers against each other, while mobility from class to class and coopera-tion between classes have blurred the sharp dichotomies revealed by the analytic of labour and property. Marxists, both in theory and practice, have had to correlate the elementary absolutes of their first principles with the bewildering intricacies of their societies.[3] Could (or should) socialists appeal to every proletarian or potential prole-tarian – to both the factory-worker and the artisan, the labourer and the skilled worker, the foreman and his charges, the farm-worker and the over-mortgaged peasant, the commercial employee and the near-bankrupt shopkeeper? Why did proletarians so often associate themselves with their putative class enemies, rejecting socialist blandishments in favour of solidarity with their predatory employers? As Marxists, Guesdists inevitably struggled with these quandaries. How did the Parti Ouvrier, in translating its strategic doctrinal presuppositions into tactical polemical practices, under-stand and accomplish the 'making of the French working class'?

Guesdists attributed proletarian class formation to the needs and

this problematic in R. Connell, 'A Critique of the Althusserian Approach to Class', *Theory and Society*, vol. 8, 1979, pp. 303–45 and A. Hunt, 'Introduction', in A. Hunt (ed.), *Class and Class Structure* (London, 1977), pp. 8–9.

[2] G. Deville, *Cours d'Économie Sociale* (Paris, undated), p. 4.

[3] For a useful description of the difficulties which arise in defining class boundaries in particular cases – however absolute they may be in axiomatic terms, see G. Mackenzie, 'Class Boundaries and the Labour Process', in A. Giddens and G. Mackenzie (eds.), *Social Class and the Division of Labour: Essays in Honour of Ilya Neustadt* (Cambridge, 1982), pp. 63–86.

necessities of capital, to 'the law of capitalist production which consumes the manual and intellectual proletariat in the forms which suit [capital]'.[4] According to the Parti Ouvrier, capital had created the working class, workers lived and died to reproduce capital, and proletarians might transcend capital only through capitalism's inherent contradictions: understanding working-class origins, working-class experience, and the working-class destiny meant understanding capitalism; the political economy of capital accumulation governed the history, the sociology and the revolutionary potential of the proletariat. No more than Marx, however, did French Marxists assert that 'capital can actually treat labour-power as a pure and simple commodity that behaves as a passive object completely subjugated to its economic logic.'[5] Guesdists knew perfectly well that workers never responded to capitalist rapacity as 'passive objects' unconditionally subjected to capital's 'economic logic' – after all, propagation and organisation of working-class resistance to capitalist exploitation and bourgeois domination constituted the *raison d'être* of the Parti Ouvrier itself. All the same, for the POF, working-class militancy evolved in dialectical unity with capitalism, shaping that mode of production and shaped by it.

In essence, Guesdists developed an elaborate contrafactual analysis of the capitalist mode of production, an analysis designed to reveal what *might* happen 'if the capitalist regime could work mechanically, without hindrance'.[6] The Parti Ouvrier, pursuing this argument, systematically exaggerated the potency of capital's imperatives, and with good reason. At the least, working-class recognition of worst-case scenarios stimulated the working-class responses which obviated them. But – in theory, if not always in practice – Guesdists analysed the logic of capital as a propensity, as 'a persistent and inevitable tendency',[7] not as an absolute determinant of the proletarian condition. For French Marxists, socialism, as a rational strategy for the 'hindrance' of 'the capitalist regime', depended upon exploration of capital's 'persistent and inevitable tendency'. The Guesdists' 'scientific socialism', 'materialism', and 'economic determinism' resolved themselves into a critique

---

4 J. Guesde, 'La Liberté du Travail', *Le Socialiste*, 31 March 1894.
5 This caricature of Marxist analysis is from C. Mouffe, 'Working Class Hegemony and the Struggle for Socialism', *Studies in Political Economy*, no. 12, 1983, p. 14.
6 C. Bonnier, 'Referendum', *Le Socialiste*, 18 February 1900.
7 Bracke, 'À Travers la Semaine', *Le Socialiste*, 14–21 February 1904.

of capital, the absolute prerequisite of workers' emancipation from capitalist rule. 'What is true for armies is also true for classes', wrote Édouard Fortin. 'The proletariat must govern its organisation, its battle array, its manoeuvres in terms of the development and the power of capital'.[8] 'Know thine enemy' – the cardinal strategic rule of Guesdist ideology.

Guesdism, unfortunately, enrolled no Marxist economists of Hilferding's stature, published no French equivalent of Lenin's masterful *The Development of Capitalism in Russia*, and largely ignored the intricacies of formal value theory – frailties which did not preclude feigned economic precision, as when Guesde wrote of 'the six hours and six minutes out of twelve during which the worker in large scale industry must labour solely for his employer'.[9] But, while French Marxists eschewed econometric intricacy, they focused unerringly upon Marx's fundamental assumption that the capitalist mode of production survived only through the constant and constantly accelerating accumulation of capital.

Accumulate, accumulate! That is Moses and the prophets: accumulation for accumulation's sake; production for production's sake: by this formula classical political economy expressed the historical mission of the bourgeoisie . . . If to classical economy, the proletarian is but a machine for the production of surplus value; on the other hand, the capitalist in its eyes is only a machine for the conversion of this surplus value into additional capital.[10]

Accumulation, for Marx and for his French disciples, ruled the lives of both capitalists and proletarians, the mortal embodiments of abstract capital and abstract labour.

Capitalist accumulation, in the Marxist schema, arose from the exploitative relationship between labour and capital: 'the law of capitalist production', wrote Lafargue, 'is the creation of profit or surplus-value, as Marx calls it. There is only one way of creating surplus value. That is to buy labour power from the worker at the

---

[8] É. Fortin, 'Grosse Artillerie Capitaliste', *Le Socialiste*, 29 September 1895.
[9] J. Guesde, 'Le Collectivisme et la Justice', *L'Égalité*, 8 January 1882. For one of the few explicit discussions in the Guesdist press of the problem of value theory, see A. Delon, 'La Théorie Marxiste de la Valeur', *Le Socialiste*, 24 January 1897. Lafargue's *Fonction Économique de la Bourse* (Paris, 1897), however, constituted an original and significant contribution to Marxist political economy – resolving debate on one aspect of the equalisation of the rate of profit.
[10] K. Marx, *Capital* (Moscow, 1954), vol. 1, p. 558.

cheapest possible price, for the longest possible period'.[11] The accumulation process governed not only the structural relationship between capital and labour, the class identity of the bourgeoisie and the proletariat, but determined their antagonism, the class conflict between bourgeois and proletarians. Capitalists expropriated the economic surplus produced by workers and used it, in part, to expand their exploitative capacity, to expand their capital – an accelerating dynamic which, according to the Parti Ouvrier, governed the history of capitalism, the making of the working class, and the future of socialism. The capitalist mode of production reproduced 'the capital-relation on a progressive scale, more capitalists or larger capitalist at this pole, more wage-workers at that . . . Accumulation of capital is, therefore, increase of the proletariat'.[12] Capitalism and the proletariat grew apace, one the product of the other.[13]

Expanded accumulation, therefore, meant 'proletarianisation' – both the quantitative proletarianisation of society and the qualitative proletarianisation of workers. Capitalists dispossessed small property-owners of their productive assets ('primitive accumulation', in Marx's terminology), thereby proletarianising society as a whole: peasants degenerated into farm labourers, artisans into workers, shopkeepers into employees – all equally subject to capital. This expanding proletariat, the product of capitalist expropriation, in turn suffered intensified proletarianisation as the object of capitalist exploitation. Unchecked, capitalists impoverished their labour force (extracting 'absolute surplus value', once again in Marx's terminology): wages fell below subsistence levels, working conditions deteriorated toward murderous atrocity, working-days expanded to include working-nights – all to capital's benefit. But exponential wage reductions, deterioration in conditions, and lengthening of the working-day inevitably encountered absolute physical limits: priva-

[11] P. Lafargue, 'La Production Capitaliste', *L'Égalité*, 8 October 1882. (Note the confusion of profit with surplus-value.) This summation of Guesdist social thought, published over a number of issues of *l'Égalité* in 1882 and republished several times subsequently, is one of the most useful sources for the Parti Ouvrier's Marxist paradigm.

[12] K. Marx, *Capital* (Moscow, 1954), vol. 1, pp. 613–14.

[13] See, in particular, Gabriel Deville's 'Introduction' to *Le Capital de Karl Marx: Résumé et Accompagné d'un Aperçu sur le Socialisme Scientifique* (Paris, undated) – a powerful and influential summation of the Marxist analysis of the accumulation process. For the impact of Deville's interpretation and abridgement of Marx's great work, see J. Hall, 'Gabriel Deville and the Abridgement of *Capital*', *Proceedings of the Western Society for French History*, vol. 10, 1982, pp. 438–48.

tion and weariness reduced labour productivity and impeded reproduction of the labour force – workers' limits limited capitalists' exactions. Limitation of absolute exploitation impelled capitalists to 'rationalise' the labour process and pursue technological innovation (extracting 'relative surplus value'): expanded accumulation prevailed even against rising real wages, improving conditions, and diminishing working-days – if capital arrogated the lion's share of increasing productivity.[14] Infliction of 'primitive accumulation', exaction of 'absolute surplus value', extortion of 'relative surplus value' – these processes did not necessarily delineate sequential stages in the development of capitalism: primitive accumulation accelerated so long as small property-owners survived for capital to plunder; capitalists pitilessly reduced every defence, whether natural or social, against extraction of absolute surplus value from its proletarian victims; capital continuously transformed the labour process in its ravenous pursuit of relative surplus value. According to Marxists, these mechanisms, the expanded accumulation of capital in its various guises, had revolutionised society for capital; their consequences, the making of the working class, would revolutionise society against capital.[15]

The struggle between workers and employers over the extraction of absolute surplus value had stalemated by the *Fin de Siècle*: real wages had increased even during the depression of the 1880s, while the number of working-hours per day had finally stabilised and begun their slow decline towards the idealised eight-hour norm. Confronted by insurmountable barriers to the expanded extraction of absolute surplus value, French employers insisted that 'the productivity of the human machine be increased'[16] – the search for

[14] For a distinguished study of these processes, rigorous in its use of the Marxist concepts and meticulous in their empirical application, in a context familiar to the Guesdists, see Rolande Trempé, *Les Mineurs de Carmaux 1848–1914* (Paris, 1971), particularly vol. 1, pp. 210–21.

[15] For a discussion and critique of this equation between the progress of capitalism and the advance of socialism, see J. Cohen, *Class and Civil Society: The Limits of Marxian Critical Theory* (Oxford, 1982), chapter 6.

[16] 'Il faut augmenter le rendement de la machine humaine' – the title of a 1905 publication, cited in M. Perrot, 'La Classe Ouvrière au Temps de Jaurès', in *Jaurès et la Classe Ouvrière* (Paris, 1981), p. 70. For the trend of real wages and the decline in working hours during the period, see P. Stearns, *Lives of Labour: Work in a Maturing Industrial Society* (London, 1975), pp. 193–95 and Y. Lequin, *Les Ouvriers de la Région Lyonnaise (1848–1914): Les Intérêts de Classe et la République* (Lyons, 1977), pp. 81–3. None the less, fourteen- and fifteen-hour days were still being imposed upon workers in some industries as late as 1905, according to R. Jonas, 'From the Radical Republic to the Social Republic: On the Origins and Nature of Socialism in Rural France 1871–1914', PhD. thesis, University of California, Berkeley, 1985, p. 163.

relative surplus value superseded extraction of absolute surplus value as the primary locus of capital accumulation. Intensifying the 'industrial revolution' which had both reflected and magnified capitalists' economic hegemony throughout the nineteenth century, French entrepreneurs accentuated the division of labour in their plants, increased managerial authority over the labour process, further accelerated the mechanisation of industry, and generated unprecedented economies of scale by centralising capital and concentrating production. They enjoyed spectacular successes, a multitude of individual entrepreneurial victories subsumed by economic historians in the so-called 'second industrial revolution' – that ultimate 'bourgeois revolution' which triumphantly inaugurated the twentieth-century economic regime of 'big business', mass production, and exponential technological transformation. Advanced firms in the glass industry of the *Belle Époque*, for instance, increased their employees' wages, conceded the eight-hour day, but *tripled* the productivity of each hour worked – a highly profitable conversion of the industry which revolutionised the labour process and obliterated traditional labour practices.[17] Sensitised to transformations of the mode of production by their Marxist convictions, intimately associated with a labour movement traumatised by breakneck technological change, Guesdists fully grasped the scope and importance of these capitalist victories: after all, Lafargue himself had lost a much-needed position with a Parisian insurance company because of a 'rationalisation drive'![18] The Guesdists' critique of capitalism and their consequent depiction of the 'making of the working class' scrutinised, denounced, and exploited every aspect of economic 'rationalisation' (as its bourgeois beneficiaries have designated

[17] J. Scott, *The Glassworkers of Carmaux: French Craftsmen and Political Action in a Nineteenth-Century City* (Cambridge, Mass., 1974), pp. 74–5. For evidence of wide-spread and massive productivity increases throughout industrial France, though not necessarily on the glassworks scale, see P. Sorlin, *La Société Française 1840–1914* (Paris, 1969), p. 118, and A. Cabanis, *Introduction à l'Histoire Économique et Sociale de la France au XIXe et XXe Siècle* (Toulouse, 1977), p. 181.

[18] J. Girault, 'Introduction', in J. Girault (ed.), *Paul Lafargue: Textes Choisis* (Paris, 1970), p. 51. For good instances of the Guesdists' preoccupation with the extraction of 'relative surplus value', see J. Guesde, 'Les Crises', *Le Socialiste*, 20 August 1887 and P. Lafargue, 'La Journée Légale de Travail réduite à Huit Heures', *L'Égalité*, 5 March 1882. Interestingly, both Guesde and Lafargue here argue that it was in the interest of French capitalism to accord shorter working hours to workers, because a reduced extraction of 'absolute surplus value' would result in a 'more modern' pattern of labour exploitation based upon 'relative surplus value'. For an impressive Guesdist survey of various industries which highlighted productivity increases, see Anonymous, 'La Voix des Chiffres', *Le Socialiste*, 19 May 1895.

wresting relative surplus value from labour), the 'rationalisation' inherent in the 'three great facts which have . . . decisively influenced [modern] society: division of labour, mechanisation, and capital concentration'.[19]

No aspect of 'rationalisation' has evoked as much theoretical controversy and social contestation as 'deskilling', the disaggregation of the labour process into its component tasks and the assignment of these simplified jobs to semi-skilled (and cheap) labourers rather than to skilled (and expensive) artisans. Thus rationalised, the omnicompetent artisanal worker, master of his trade, has given way to the specialised general worker, subject of capital. This disintegrative procedure has opened the highroad to productive rationality through successive 'industrial revolutions' – reducing labour costs for innovative entrepreneurs, enhancing their managerial authority over 'their' labour force, and dismantling artisanal barriers to economic 'progress'.[20] Marxists, passionate devotees of economic progress *and* devoted representatives of the working class, have responded ambiguously to capitalist deskilling, simultaneously treasuring the immense increase in productivity associated with the novel labour processes of 'industrial revolution' and denouncing the associated 'dehumanisation' of labour.[21]

To further complicate their response, Marxist socialists, self-proclaimed parasites upon capitalism, fed politically upon the victims of capital's aggression against the artisanate, fattening in proportion to proletarianisation's ever-increasing carnage. Marx himself had described deskilling as essential to the making of a socialist proletariat, contending that destruction of artisanal skills, however cruel in the short term, in the long-term forged proletarian solidarity by eliminating 'trades consciousness'[22] and trades' exclu-

---

[19] A. Valette, 'Une Première Étape', *Le Socialiste*, 26 May 1895.

[20] The classic analysis of deskilling is Harry Braverman's enormously influential *Labor and Monopoly Capitalism: The Degradation of Work in the Twentieth Century* (New York, 1974). For discussion and critique of this aspect of Marxist analysis, see T. Elger, 'Braverman, Capital Accumulation and Deskilling', *Capital and Class*, vol. 7, 1979, pp. 58–99, and D. Lee, 'Skill, Craft and Class: A Theoretical Critique and a Critical Case', *Sociology*, vol. 15, 1981, pp. 56–78.

[21] C. Littler, *The Development of the Labour Process in Capitalist Societies* (London, 1982), pp. 20–5.

[22] K. Marx, *The Poverty of Philosophy*, in K. Marx and F. Engels, *Collected Works* (London, 1976), vol. 6, p. 190. For the unwillingness of labourers to support the militancy of more privileged workers, see M. Perrot, *Les Ouvriers en Grève: France 1871–1890* (Paris, 1974), vol. 2, pp. 507–9.

sivity – the self-defeating hostilities between butchers, bakers, and candlestick-makers – in favour of class consciousness and class solidarity, harbingers of proletarian liberation. And, beyond the horizon of the socialist revolution, capitalist destruction of traditional working-class exclusivities would, by the cunning of historical reason, engender the citizen of the utopian future, 'exercising turn by turn every trade, to the great advantage of his health and intelligence'.[23]

Fully representative of these Marxist ambiguities, Guesdists cheerfully exploited the widespread experience and supposedly universal prospect of deskilling both to indict capitalist mistreatment of skilled workers and to demonstrate the socialist implications of this abuse. Characteristically absolutist in their understanding of the capitalist mode of production, French Marxists contended, against considerable evidence,[24] that all workers – however skilled in their trades, privileged in their enterprises, or protected by labour organisation and industrial regulation – would eventually suffer dequalification; that even the most proficient and honoured workers in *fin-de-siècle* France – typographers, jewellers, even scientists – faced the dolorous fate of eighteenth-century textile tradesmen: deskilling, proletarianisation, and subjugation to triumphant industrial capitalism. 'Soon only one universal skill will remain, that of the mechanic', Lafargue predicted, foreseeing a hive-world of undifferentiated machine-minders in place of the infinitely varied handicrafts which had survived into the *Belle Époque*.[25] With malice aforethought, Lafargue threatened the fundamental values of the French artisanate with his imagery of a hyper-industrial future: the dignity of the trade and pride in mastery of its traditional techniques suffused elite working-class mentalities; socialists recruited easily among artisans terrorised by the prospect, and sometimes the experience, of dequalification.[26]

---

[23] P. Lafargue, 'Le Socialisme et les Intellectuels', *Le Socialiste*, 3 June 1900.
[24] Many workers retained their artisanal privileges even in Roubaix, given the tendency of industrialisation in one sector to increase small-scale enterprise in others. See D. Gordon, 'Liberalism and Socialism in the Nord: Eugène Motte and Republican Politics in Roubaix 1898–1902', *French History*, vol. 3, 1989, pp. 319–20 and L. Marty, *Chanter pour Survivre: Culture Ouvrière, Travail et Techniques dans le Textile – Roubaix 1850–1914* (Lille, 1982), p. 37.
[25] P. Lafargue, 'Le Problème Social', *Le Socialiste*, 2 September 1900.
[26] See the description of the importance of skill in French industry and in workers' mentalities in Y. Lequin, 'Apprenticeship in Nineteenth-Century France: A Continuing Tradition or a Break with the Past?' in S. Kaplan and C. Koepp (eds.), *Work in France: Representation, Meaning, Organisation, and Practice* (London, 1986), pp. 468–71. For the importance of

The Parti Ouvrier, thriftily repackaging this propaganda, addressed its vivid imagery of the proletarianised universal labourer to another, and very different, constituency: semi-skilled workers, especially the textile-industry operatives who populated the northern bastions of the POF, workers whose trades had long-since suffered capitalist rationalisation. From their lowly perspective, the polyvalent mechanic of Lafargue's prediction, if anything, glamorised the 'OS' (*ouvriers spécialisés*, that insulting irony of twentieth-century French industrial terminology) who increasingly staffed French mills and factories.[27] For this audience of the deskilled or the never-skilled, Guesdists discarded nostalgic evocation of artisanal traditions. The novel labour processes of triumphant industrial capitalism, French Marxists promised, laid 'the foundations for the abolition of class and the unification of the human race'[28] – the universal worker of rationalised production embodied both human universality and historical rationality. Just as the Guesdists' delineation of the capitalist dequalification of labour reinforced the paranoia of artisans as yet untouched by deskilling, so the Guesdists' glamorisation of the proletarianised 'proletarian' resonated with the hurts and hopes of labourers devoid of traditional skills. Deskilling, Marxists affirmed, destroyed not only treasured qualifications, but also exclusive trade identities, an assertion with evident force during the *fin-de-siècle* making of the working class, when workers, abandoning indefensible occupational particularism, increasingly conceived themselves as ecumenical 'ouvriers d'usine',[29] as aspirant members of a universal proletariat rather than as privileged incumbents of exclusive professional castes. Dequalification, an unmitigated evil as a tool of capital, promised proletarian solidarity and a utopian future, once transmuted by the alchemy of socialism.

---

workers' resistance to deskilling, see M. Perrot, 'On the Formation of the French Working Class', in I. Katznelson and A. Zolberg (eds.), *Working Class Formation: Nineteenth-Century Patterns in Western Europe and the United States* (Princeton, 1986), pp. 74–83.

[27] The rise of the semi-skilled worker is described in M. Perrot, 'Les Classes Populaires Urbaines', in *Histoire Économique et Sociale de la France*: Tome IV – *L'Ère Industrielle et la Société d'Aujourd'hui (1880–1980)*: Premier Volume – *Ambiguïtés des Débuts et Croissance Effective (Années 1880–1914)* (Paris, 1979), pp. 474–5. For the ambiguities in workers' attitudes towards 'Taylorism', see P. Fridenson, 'Un Tournant Taylorien de la Société Française (1904–1918)', *Annales: Économies, Sociétés, Civilisations*, vol. 42, 1987, pp. 1044–5.

[28] P. Lafargue, 'La Production Capitaliste', *L'Égalité*, 30 July 1882.

[29] Lequin comments on the growing popularity of this rubric (rather than craft identifications) in responses to the census in his *Les Ouvriers de la Région Lyonnaise: Formation de la Classe Ouvrière Régionale* (Lyons, 1977), p. 203.

Disaggregation of the unified skills of artisanal workers into the specialised skills of industrial workers greatly enhanced the role of 'management' – the agency supervising employees who had lost control of the labour process, the nerve centre coordinating the complex organisms of 'industrialised' production, the reason animating 'rationalised' enterprise. 'Employers' in the great industrial enterprises of the *Fin de Siècle* – no longer directly managing the productive process, and often share-owners utterly ignorant of the grimy work which produced their dividends – relied upon an increasingly elaborate apparatus of managing directors, plant managers, and line foremen, themselves salaried employees. The mid-nineteenth-century employer's office, overlooking the shop-floor, gave way to the multi-storey administrative block, often located far from the plants it administered. Marxists have vacillated in their assessment of modern industrial hierarchy and its incumbent managerial authorities, swinging wildly between incompatible theses: at one extreme welcoming the birth of the 'collective worker' – a vast entity amalgamating managerial and supervisory personnel, technical and scientific staff, and manual workers into an awesomely productive 'composite artisan'; at the other extreme, denouncing industrial hierarchy as the essence of bourgeois rule – the intrusion of capitalist domination into the very heart of the labour process.[30] Did the 'emancipation of the workers by the workers themselves' imply workers' emancipation from capital *and* management, or did the slogan imply the emancipation of the collective worker (including managerial staff) from capital alone?

The Marxists' proletarian constituency has shared this morbid fascination with encroaching managerial authority: independent artisans have dreaded their prospective subordination to industrial discipline; skilled workers have resented their loss of control over the labour process (and over their unskilled subordinates); labourers have resisted subordination to supervisors as fiercely as exploitation by bosses, frequently confusing these analytically distinct aspects of capitalist industrialism. Long before the twentieth-century apotheosis of its eponymous theorist, 'Taylorism' terrorised the working class of the second industrial revolution, according to one hypothesis

---

[30] For the former position, see F. Engels, 'On Authority', in Marx and Engels, *Collected Works* (London, 1988), vol. 23, pp. 423–4. For a forceful assertion of the latter position, see S. Marglin, 'What do Bosses Do? The Origins and Function of Hierarchy in Capitalist Production', *Review of Radical Political Economics*, vol. 6, 1974–5, pp. 60–112.

thereby engendering the characteristic defensive militancy of the modern labour movement.[31] France during the *Belle Époque*, homeland of proletarian libertarianism, exemplified this working-class reaction against industrial discipline: French workers – whether as mutualist moderates, revolutionary syndicalists, or Marxist socialists – resented and resisted the despotic practices and authoritarian ambitions of their employers' managerial and supervisory representatives.[32]

Forearmed by their analyses of the capitalist mode of production, Guesdists skillfully exploited working-class anxieties about the evolution of workplace authority. With characteristic polemical overkill, the Parti Ouvrier portrayed virtually all workers as subject to pitiless industrial absolutism, victims of a brutal productive tyranny.[33] The proletariat's allegedly general loss of control over the labour process and the resultant managerial 'despotism' furnished Guesdists with one of their most treasured themes, a theme ideally calculated to mobilise libertarian proletarians against liberal bourgeois. The Party Ouvrier gleefully highlighted the liberals' hypocrisy, contrasting their defence of universal freedom in theory with their safeguarding of work-place tyranny in practice: within the factory, the 'rights of man and the citizen' succumbed to the rights of property. At the least, indictment of managerial autocracy countered the conventional liberal prediction that socialist revolution would inaugurate a nightmarish authoritarianism. Untroubled by the Leninist Taylorism of any 'really existing socialism', Guesdists riposted that the liberals' foreshadowed nightmare already preyed upon factories and workshops across France – at the behest of liberal industrialists.[34] Turning bourgeois myths against the bourgeoisie, the POF heralded the proletarian demolition of the capitalist 'Bastilles' which imprisoned workers under the pitiless supervision of

[31] Z. Bauman, *Memories of Class: The Prehistory and After-Life of Class* (London, 1982), pp. 5–22. For the importance during the *Belle Époque* of worker protest against managerial hierarchy, see B. Palmer, 'Class, Conception and Conflict: The Thrust for Efficiency, Managerial Views of Labor and Working Class Rebellion 1903–1922', *Review of Radical Political Economics*, vol. 7, 1975, pp. 31–49.

[32] For telling instances, see Berlanstein, *The Working People of Paris*, pp. 82–84; P. Hilden, *Working Women and Socialist Politics in France 1880–1914: A Regional Study* (Oxford, 1986), p. 68; and J. Merriman, *Red City: Limoges and the French Nineteenth Century* (Oxford, 1985), p. 221.

[33] Employer authority in the workplace was in many cases very weak. See Berlanstein, *The Working People of Paris*, pp. 79–84.

[34] A. Zévaès, 'Le Socialisme à l'École de Droit: Réponse à M. P. Beauregard', *Le Socialiste*, 18 February 1894.

managerial gaolers: the socialist revolution would extend *liberté, égalité, et fraternité* into the realm of production – the last, and greatest, bastion of exclusive privilege and irresponsible power.

This vista of socialist 'industrial democracy', however, did not open upon unlimited libertarian perspectives. A vague imagery of 'workers' self-management' suffused the Guesdists' rhetorical attacks upon the capitalist present and inspired their fuzzy blueprints of the socialist future, but the Marxist conception of workers' control systematically abjured both Proudhonian nostalgia for individual artisanal independence and anarcho-syndicalist aspirations to industrial 'direct democracy'. Accepting the structural logic of industrialism, assenting to the organisational consequences of the industrial division of labour, French Marxists, at least by implication, concurred with Engels' conviction that 'wanting to abolish authority in large-scale industry is tantamount to wanting to abolish industry itself'.[35] The POF, anti-capitalist but not anti-industrial, intended to abolish *capitalist* authority over workers, but

does it follow that the Parti Ouvrier will profoundly modify the present organisation of production? Obviously not ... The Parti Ouvrier is only committed to freeing this production from the shackles which limit its development.[36]

The socialist revolution would subsume the industrial revolution, replacing capitalist industrial hierarchy with socialist industrial hierarchy. The 'present organisation of production' would prevail even under the future revolutionary property regime: 'management' would manage in the workers' interest, but management would still manage. 'Industrial democracy', for Guesdists, meant exactly that. Just as the Parti Ouvrier's conception of 'industrial *democracy*' served against bourgeois liberals, so its conception of '*industrial* democracy' served against proletarian anarchists. Anarchists, according to the Parti Ouvrier, thoroughly misunderstood the organisational imperatives of modern industrial production: their libertarian aspirations suffered from the same historical illusions and ideological delusions as did the liberals' apologetics.[37]

The Guesdist conception of industrial authority, despite (or

---

[35] Engels, 'On Authority', pp. 423–4.
[36] A. Letailleur, 'Situation du Salarié', *L'Égalité*, 4 June 1882.
[37] This theme underpins Gabriel Deville's incisive *L'Anarchisme* (Paris, 1887).

because of) its ambiguity, tempted French proletarians. Although many workers, increasingly subject to the rigid discipline and close supervision of the panoptic industrial prison, reviled their workplaces as 'petits Mazas',[38] they still dreamed of prison revolts abetted by rebel gaolers: managers, supervisors, and foremen might someday, as the Parti Ouvrier promised, betray their bourgeois masters, thus metamorphosing from servile custodians of capital into benign agents of the 'collective worker'. Nor did all workers resist the Promethean romance of modern industry – the fascination with unlimited mastery of the material world, inhuman scale, and heaven-challenging technique which had transfixed both liberal and socialist ideologues throughout the nineteenth century. After all, a proletarian cog in the vast new 'technico-humain' machines of modern industry, however menial and insignificant, would turn in gear with the most powerful manager – worker and supervisor equally indispensable components of mankind's last and greatest productive apparatus, the cornucopian machinery of unlimited plenty, mechanism of the utopian future.[39] Marxist denunciations of bourgeois authority in the workplace, coupled with enthusiastic acceptance of industrialism purged of capitalist parasites, articulated a potent proletarian mentality of hatred and hope.

The substitution of 'constant capital' for 'variable capital', the replacement of men by machines, has featured in every Marxist analysis of capitalists' extraction of 'relative surplus value' from capitalism's labour force. Indeed, this transformation of the labour process has frequently dominated Marxists' understanding of capital-logic to the near exclusion of other (and equally vital) alterations of the industrial order: the 'second industrial revolution', from this blinkered perspective, collapses into mere technological innovation, into the 'unbound Prometheus' of technocratic enthusiasm.[40]

---

[38] One of the most notorious prisons of Paris. The characterisation and its significance is discussed in M. Perrot, 'Comment les Ouvriers Parisiens Voyaient la Crise d'après l'Enquête Parlementaire de 1884', in *Conjoncture Économique/Structures Sociales: Hommage à Ernest Labrousse* (Paris, 1974), p. 191.

[39] A. Melucci, 'Action Patronale, Pouvoir, Organisation: Règlements d'Usine et Contrôle de la Main-d'Oeuvre au XIXe Siècle', *Mouvement Social*, no. 97, 1976, p. 148.

[40] For arguments stressing the centrality of technology in historical materialism, see W. Shaw, '"The Handmill Gives You the Feudal Lord": Marx's Technological Determinism', *History and Theory*, vol. 18, 1979, pp. 155–76 and J. Sherwood, 'Engels, Marx, Malthus, and the Machine', *American Historical Review*, vol. 90, 1985, pp. 837–65.

Although aspects of Marx's legacy have lent themselves to this conceptual affliction, reduction of historical materialism to technological determinism in theory grossly devalues the labour/property nexus and in practice equates capitalism with industrialism, a profoundly unsatisfactory and un-Marxist equation which distorts the distinctions between capitalism and preceding modes of production and obscures the relationship between capitalism and its prospective socialist alternative.[41] The capitalist mode of production long antedated the industrial revolution, the latter a belated consequence of the former. Whether before industrialism or after, exploitation of labour by private property-owners need not require 'capital goods'. And Marxist theory has postulated, and Marxist practice erected, a mechanised and technological socialism, a socialism founded upon massive 'capital' investment. 'Capital goods', after all, may be collectively owned.

Even if Marx himself had eschewed technological determinism, Guesdists often did not: they repeatedly echoed their master's notorious (and unrepresentative) equation of hand-mills with feudal lords and steam-mills with industrial capitalists.[42] Employing an example more appropriate to the second industrial revolution than to Marx's first, Lafargue, for instance, contended that 'a small machine measuring less than a cubic foot, the turret lathe, has done more to stimulate and disturb humanity materially and intellectually than have all the great thinkers put together, than have all the philosophies and religions piled one atop the other'.[43] Similar instances of technological hyperbole might be multiplied indefinitely: Guesdists, at times, simplistically reduced modern capitalism to 'electricity plus bourgeois power'.

For French Marxists, capitalist technology was not only omnipotent, but omnipresent. With characteristic exaggeration, Guesdists discerned mechanisation everywhere: 'the machine', again according to Lafargue, 'has seized control of all today's industries, from the most primitive and simple to the most artistic'.[44] In a frenzy of technological fervor, the Parti Ouvrier even speculated that a 'calculating machine'[45] might someday supplant the sophisti-

[41] R. Mishra, 'Technology and Social Structure in Marx's Theory: An Exploratory Analysis', *Science and Society*, vol. 43, 1979, pp. 132–57.
[42] Marx, *The Poverty of Philosophy*, p. 166.
[43] P. Lafargue, 'La Production Capitaliste', *L'Égalité*, 15 October 1882.
[44] P. Lafargue. *Le Communisme et l'Évolution Économique* (Lille, 1892), p. 4.
[45] P. Lafargue, 'La Production Capitaliste', *L'Égalité*, 30 July 1882.

cated mathematical skills of astronomers! This speculation, however credible from the perspective of the computer age, grossly exaggerated capital investment in the *fin-de-siècle* French economy, which, if anything, suffered from undercapitalisation. Indeed, the ruthless industrial despotism characteristic of the mill towns of the Nord, the breeding ground of Guesdism, partially resulted from an *absence* of capital intensity: the northern textile proletariat would have benefited if its employers had invested more enthusiastically in technological innovation, rather than relying for their profits upon their workers' long hours and low wages.[46] But Guesdists, unable to imagine that proletarians might ever gain directly from capitalists' transformation of the labour process, doggedly insisted that mechanisation pervaded capitalist France, and everywhere impoverished the proletariat.

On first reading of their rhetoric, Guesdists emulated the most embittered handloom weaver in their hostility towards the machine, characterised by Marxist rhetoricians as the demonic demiurge of capitalist modernity. 'Mechanisation strips the working class of job opportunities and technical skill', *Le Socialiste* angrily charged. 'It engenders unemployment, and reduces the remaining workers to mere labourers'.[47] Capital, the sole beneficiary of ever-accelerating industrialisation, had heedlessly introduced 'industrial applications of engineering and chemistry [which] have transformed the joyous labour of the artisan into a torture [which] exhausts and kills the proletarian'.[48] Worst of all, mechanisation imposed an 'intellectual brutalisation' upon its victims: the worker himself degenerated into 'a machine, or ... the servant of the machine, so that it thinks for him'.[49] Even the few workers who temporarily escaped capital's technological aggression fell victims to its results among their fellows. According to Jean Dormoy, who knew the meaning of unemployment,

every technological innovation, every introduction of a new machine into a factory, inevitably generates unemployed workers who ... are forced to compete with their comrades who have yet to be made redundant by

---

[46] Hilden, *Working Women and Socialist Politics*, pp. 68–69.
[47] Anonymous, 'Faits et Chiffres', *Le Socialiste*, 27 December 1896.
[48] P. Lafargue, *Le Socialisme et les Intellectuels* (Paris, 1900), p. 18.
[49] Lafargue, from a report on the *Conférence Contradictoire* between Lafargue and Edmond Demolins, *Le Socialiste*, 28 May 1892.

machines, by offering themselves at reduced wages. [As a result] disunity and hatred grow between workers.[50]

Guesdists, masters of the telling anecdote, illustrated these themes with innumerable instances of mechanical dequalification of skilled workers, dehumanising mechanised intensification of work, and rampant technological unemployment. 'Under capitalist control', they maintained, 'factories are the proletariat's hell'.[51]

These arguments undoubtedly touched the Guesdists' proletarian constituency. The second industrial revolution terrified many French workers – perhaps most of all those who had yet to experience massive technological change: workshop artisans, thoroughly intimidated by the unpredictable advance of capitalist industrialisation, dreaded the sudden obsolescence of their painfully and pridefully acquired hand-work skills. The miserable tale of the handloom weaver (a tragedy still dragging towards its inevitable denouement in late-nineteenth-century France) haunted the entire artisanal working class as threat, if not yet as reality. But even hereditary factory proletarians, long-wedded to the machine, understandably loathed its clangorous command over their driven lives: thousands of them had died and millions suffered from the brutal working environment associated with *fin-de-siècle* productive technology; ever-accelerating mechanical rhythms deadened and exhausted workers' faculties; sudden unpredictable surges of technologically-driven productivity regularly menaced factory labourers with mass redundancy. When the Guesdist Fédération Nationale des Syndicats questioned its constituent unions on the causes of worsening working conditions, they unanimously identified 'le machinisme' as the primary culprit.[52]

---

[50] J. Dormoy, 'Exploitation des Ouvriers Métallurgistes', *Le Socialiste*, 26 March 1887. On a few exceptional occasions, however, Guesdists argued that mechanisation created as many new jobs as it destroyed. See, for example, 'Dr Z.' (Albert Delon), 'L'Enquête', *Le Socialiste*, 11 March 1891.

[51] P. Lafargue, 'La Production Capitaliste', *L'Égalité*, 13 August 1882.

[52] *Congrès National de Calais, 13–19 octobre 1890. Rapport du Délégué de Nantes*, p. 5, Archives Nationales, F7 12. 491. For the importance of mechanisation in provoking labour unrest, see M. Perrot, 'Grèves, Grévistes et Conjoncture: Vieux Problèmes, Travaux Neufs', *Mouvement Social*, no. 63, 1968, p. 115. Many workers did indeed fear mechanisation as the cause of capitalist authority in the workplace, intensified labour, and increased unemployment. For these fears, see Y. Lequin, *Les Intérêts de Classe et la République*, pp. 39–41 and pp. 88–9; R. Pierre, *Les Origines du Syndicalisme et Socialisme dan la Drôme 1850–1920* (Paris, 1973), p. 62 and pp. 137–8; M. Perrot, 'La Classe Ouvrière au Temps de Jaurès', pp. 72–3; and L. Berlanstein, *The Working People of Paris*, pp. 77–9 and pp. 85–6. For a classic instance of mechanisation destroying artisanal skills and solidarities, see M. Hanagan, *The Logic of*

Nevertheless, Guesdists repudiated Luddism – not for them retreat into an anti-industrial Arcadia where 'working with one's hands rather than with machines'[53] resolved the social question. According to the Parti Ouvrier, the technological transformation of the economy, once begun, inevitably prevailed against the best wishes of bourgeois philanthropists and the most strenuous resistance by proletarian militants. 'Wherever the machine appears', Lafargue contended, 'it makes the rules'.[54] Nor did Guesdist players challenge the rules of the historical game. Like Marx, Guesdists associated industrial revolution with the Promethean bourgeoisie in its ascendancy: 'the capitalist bourgeoisie, the most revolutionary class which has ever oppressed human society, can increase its wealth only by constantly transforming industry with novel applications of mechanical, chemical and physical sciences'.[55] Indeed, for Guesdists, 'so long as the bourgeoisie advanced this [technological transformation], it play[s] a useful [historical] role'.[56] Succumbing to technological determinism in its most extreme form, Guesde, during a speech to the Chamber of Deputies, admitted that

it's the machine which dominates the employer as much as the employee, dominates man and imposes its laws upon him. The discipline which rules the capitalist factory ... will equally prevail in the socialist workshop. [scattered interjections] But it's obvious! Such discipline doesn't have its roots in someone's will or arbitrary edict. It's born of mechanical industry, of the necessity of steam-engines at work.[57]

Like their liberal enemies, Guesdists subscribed to the irreversibility of economic change: workers dissatisfied with capitalist industrialisation would have to advance into the socialist industrialism envisaged

---

Solidarity: Artisans and Industrial Workers in Three French Towns 1871–1914 (London, 1980), pp. 129–37. Even the highly skilled watchmakers of the Jura feared technological progress, a fear fully justified, given the unemployment and degradation associated with the industrialisation of their trade described in J. Charles, *Les Débuts du Mouvement Syndical à Besançon* (Paris, 1962), pp. 56 and 74.

[53] A working-class militant of the period quoted in Y. Lequin, 'À Propos de la Classe Ouvrière du Rhône à la Fin du XIXᵉ Siècle: Conscience de Classe et Conscience Urbaine', in *Colloque Franco-Suisse d'Histoire Économique et Sociale, 1967* (Geneva, 1969), p. 212. For widespread working-class nostalgia for the pre-machine world of manual labour, see M. Perrot, 'Comment les Ouvriers Parisiens Voyaient la Crise', p. 195.

[54] P. Lafargue, 'La Journée Légale de Travail réduite à Huit Heures', *L'Égalité*, 26 February 1882.

[55] P. Lafargue, 'Le Socialisme et les Intellectuels', *Le Socialiste*, 22 April 1900.

[56] 'E.F.' (Fortin), 'La Dernière Marche Funèbre', *Le Socialiste*, 10 April 1886.

[57] *Journal Officiel*, 24 June 1896.

by Marxists, not retreat into the bucolic past imagined by mutualists and anarchists.

Indeed, when attacked by liberal adversaries eager to reduce socialism to an anachronistic fantasy, Guesde responded that 'from every page of our pamphlets emerges the apotheosis of the machine, destined to become the messiah, the redeemer of unfortunate humanity, once it works for everyone as the possession of society as a whole'.[58] In sharp contrast to more backward-looking radicals, Marxists advocated the proletarian seizure of mechanised industry rather than its destruction. The future socialist revolution and the prospective socialist mode of production, far from renouncing the industrial revolution, would arise from its consequences and depend upon its achievements. Returning to the imagery of 1789, the POF proclaimed that

capitalist feudalism has its own Bastilles. In Lille and in Roubaix you may see factories decorated with turrets and battlements, like the old castles. The proletariat must seize them, not to raze them to the ground, but to install itself as their master.[59]

Happily abandoning one aspect of technological determinism, Guesdists ascribed complete social neutrality to technological innovation. Relations of production alone governed whether the forces of production contributed to the betterment or the brutalisation of those who wielded them. Machine-owners, not machines, inflicted technological mayhem upon proletarians: the poisoned paint-worker had no more died of lead than the garroted robbery victim had succumbed to rope – both had been murdered, the latter by a brutal thief, the former by a negligent factory-owner. Machines, instruments of torture in the Guesdists' day, would eventually 'contribute to the happiness of mankind, but only on the day when capitalism has ceased to exist'.[60]

Mechanisation of the labour process, a homeopathic remedy for its own ills, advanced the coming of that happy day. But how could processes which brutalised labour and enhanced capitalist domination of labourers possibly contribute to the socialist revolution? According to the Guesdists, by unifying the proletariat. Machines destroyed craft skills – the elite qualifications which had protected

[58] J. Guesde, 'Hurluberlus', *Le Socialiste*, 4 March 1894.
[59] 'Le Meeting des Élus de L'URS' (Report of speech by Delory), *Le Socialiste*, 8–15 June 1902.
[60] Bracke, 'À Travers la Semaine', *Le Socialiste*, 7–14 June 1903.

labour aristocrats from the depredations of capital and divided privileged artisans from unprotected labourers, thereby fostering artisanal contempt for labourers and stimulating labourers' resentment of artisans. French Marxists anticipated that mechanised industry would so disrupt corporative identities that any worker 'might . . . work outside the trade of his first choice; in his progress through the economy, he would quickly recognise that everywhere he is subject to the same domination; everywhere he is a wage-labourer; everywhere he meets the same forms of exploitation, the same capitalist oppression; he thus acquires the firm idea that he belongs to his class and that the problem to resolve is not particular but general'.[61] Eventually, the uniform triumph of the machine would mould a uniform proletariat, the primary precondition of socialist triumph over the bourgeoisie. And the triumphant proletariat, inheriting the industrial legacy of capitalism, would preside over a realm of plenty until then reserved for the bourgeois beneficiaries of industrialism. In other words, capital-intensive production – even when accompanied by the traumas of deskilling, by brutalisation of the industrial labour force, and by mass unemployment – augured a brilliant future. Under socialism, Guesde predicted, 'the machine, universalised and automated, will no longer manufacture unemployment and servitude; it will confer well-being and leisure, . . . driving from the factory only hours of labour'.[62] The history of Guesdism, undoubtedly an ideology of industrialism, exemplifies the ironic contention that Marxism, if nothing else, has reconciled workers to the machine.[63]

Despite wide-spread working-class anxieties about mechanisation, the Guesdists' favourable assessment of the historical role of the machine encountered a substantial proletarian audience. By the end of the nineteenth century, many, perhaps most, French workers had resigned themselves to the inevitability of technological change.

---

[61] E. Massard, 'L'Électricité et la Concentration Économique', *L'Égalité*, 8 January 1882. There is now a large body of literature attacking the assumption that technology is socially neutral, and that the technologies developed for capitalism may be adopted by socialism. See I. Balbus, *Marxism and Domination: A Neo-Hegelian, Feminist, Psychoanalytic Theory of Sexual, Political and Technological Liberation* (Princeton, 1982); D. MacKenzie, 'Marx and the Machine', *Technology and Culture*, vol. 25, 1984, pp. 498–502; and R. Panzieri, 'The Capitalist Use of Machinery: Marx versus the "Objectivists"', in P. Slater (ed.), *Outlines of a Critique of Technology* (London, 1980), pp. 44–68. For mechanisation as a unifying force within the proletariat, see M. Perrot, *Les Ouvriers en Grève*, vol. 2, p. 511.
[62] J. Guesde, 'Réponse à un Démocrate-Chrétien', *Le Socialiste*, 14 August 1898.
[63] Stearns, *Lives of Labour*, p. 138.

Only the dreamiest utopians dreamed of reversing a century of industrial revolution, and utopians themselves increasingly relied upon electricity and machine tools to construct their promised land: Arcadia surrendered to Metropolis in the proletarian imagery of the future, whether utopian or dystopian. Already servants of the machine or fearful of its intrusion into surviving artisanal handicrafts, workers desperately thirsted for hope that even the lowliest machine-minders might eventually benefit from the mechanised travails of industrial revolution. Whether they tended the machine tools of the second industrial revolution or the mechanical looms of the first, whether employed in the large-scale and high-tech electrometallurgical enterprises of Grenoble or the tiny and antiquated printing shops of old Lyons, thousands of workers enthusiastically embraced the Marxist pledge that capitalism's exploitative technology would eventually transform itself into a cornucopia of socialist plenty.[64]

What is more, some fortunate workers prospered *because* of their epoch's spectacular technological transformation. The capital-intensive industries of the second industrial revolution may have destroyed traditional trades, but they also created novel skills: draymen vanished with their teams of horses, supplanted by lorry drivers; blacksmiths disappeared, to be replaced by auto mechanics; the old-fashioned glass-blower surrendered to the Siemans furnace, but electricians spread along the power grid. Machines occasionally destroyed degrading and dangerous occupations or elevated previously 'unskilled' trades to higher prestige and remuneration: Roubaissian children no longer had to clean wool fibres with their brittle teeth; spinning mills replaced 'unskilled' cottage handworkers with 'skilled' textile operatives.[65] And the Guesdists' imagery of dequalified artisans dragooned into capitalist factories grossly misrepresented the social origins of the 'OS': industrialists recruited semi-skilled machine-minders among unskilled labourers rather than among highly-skilled artisans, thereby initiating a prodigious

---

[64] For the seeming irreversibility of technological change after the collapse of so many handwork industries during the period 1870–1890, see G. Noiriel, *Les Ouvriers dans la Société Française: XIXᵉ–XXᵉ Siècle* (Paris, 1986), pp. 84–5. G. Gras, 'Presse Syndicale et Mentalités: l'Ouvrier Mouleur à Travers le Journal de sa Fédération: *La Fonderie* 1900–1909', *Mouvement Social*, no. 53, 1965, pp. 51–68 describes workers' resignation to this transformation, and M. Perrot, 'Comment les Ouvriers Parisiens Voyaient la Crise', p. 195 and M. Perrot, *Les Ouvriers en Grève*, vol. 2, pp. 578–80 describe their hopes for its outcome.

[65] Marty, *Chanter pour Survivre*, pp. 30–1.

process of social promotion rather than a universal deskilling.[66] Finally, the vast capital costs of the second industrial revolution, so often financed by massive borrowing, guaranteed workers a novel degree of job security and industrial power: employers, quite literally, could not afford to interrupt production. The traditional ironmaster, self-financing and independent, might contemplate extended strikes or 'dead seasons' with equanimity; the corporate colossuses of Lorraine metallurgy, as committed to the continual repayment of debt as to the continuous pour of steel, cringed at the financial implications of industrial disputation.[67]

The electrician, the auto mechanic, the lorry driver, the steel worker, the Breton farm labourer promoted to Saint-Denis engineering employee – all might embrace Marxist critiques of capitalist exploitation or applaud socialist denunciations of bourgeois domination, but none would welcome Luddite attacks upon modern productive technology, their bread and butter, even their *raison d'être*. Working-class mentalities encouraged by industrialised social mobility validated the POF's rehabilitation of the machine, although the Parti Ouvrier systematically ignored the benefits obtained by some workers from capitalist industrialisation – benefits which, if acknowledged, would have blunted the Guesdists' all-out attack upon the relationship between labour and capital. The ambivalent Guesdist conception of the machine, simultaneously instrument of exploitation in the bourgeois present and promise of plenty in the socialist future, reflected these equivocal working-class mentalities while occluding the ambivalent proletarian experience of mechanisation, simultaneously social catastrophe and profitable adventure.

Finally, apart from deskilling, managerial authority, and mechanisation, Marxist analysis of capitalist rationalisation, of capital's relentless quest for 'relative surplus value,' has highlighted the exploitative consequences of the concentration of production and the centralisation of capital-ownership, those supposedly inevitable consequences of economies of scale and the advantages of monopoly. As depicted by Marxist polemicists, these parallel processes deline-

---

[66] Berlanstein, *The Working People of Paris*, pp. 27–9 and pp. 92–5.
[67] For the growing stability of employment in the new capital-intensive sectors, see Y. Lequin, *Les Intérêts de Classe et la République*, pp. 92–93. For the enhancement of labour's industrial potency by mechanisation, see M. Perrot, *Les Ouvriers en Grève*, vol. 1, pp. 54–5.

ated a daunting social vision: the scale of productive units would inflate until gargantuan plants dominated the world economy, while capital would accumulate in fewer and fewer hands until a tiny predatory elite of parasitic plutocrats governed the globe – monopoly and monopolists would reign unbounded and unchecked.[68] Yet Marxists, although hostile to monopolists, have welcomed the historical consequences of monopoly. In their conception of contemporary social transformation, the making of a self-aware working class and the constitution of its socialist project both depended upon the advance of large-scale enterprise: concentration of production concentrated the proletariat, while centralisation of ownership centralised class conflict.

Guesdists exemplified this Marxist fixation upon capital consolidation. Their speeches, their pamphlets, and their journalism obsessively reiterated the causes and consequences of the unchecked economic and political power of the millionaires who exploited the vast mechanised factories of the second industrial revolution, managed entire railroad networks, presided over all-powerful continent-spanning banks, and, incidentally, exploited, managed, and presided over the French state.[69] Plutocratic power – as natural to capitalism as the commodity form, according to French Marxists – followed naturally from the logic of capital accumulation. Capitalist competition ensured that successful enterprises consumed the less successful, a cumulative process driven by ever-increasing capital intensity, ever-expanding economies of scale, and ever-heightening barriers to market entry: bourgeois predators devoured each other until one alone survived; competition negated itself in monopoly.[70] Convinced by the *a priori* logic of their own argument, Guesdists discovered capital concentration everywhere, from railroads to

---

[68] For the important distinction between the pooling of production capacity under capitalist control (concentration) and the tendency towards fewer but richer capitalists (centralisation), see Marx, *Capital*, vol. 1, p. 586. There is a good discussion of the ambiguities of these usages in L. Cahen, 'La Concentration des Établissements en France de 1896 à 1936', *Études et Conjonctures: Série Rouge – Économie Française*, no. 9, 1954, pp. 841–42.

[69] Apart from endless anecdotal accounts, Guesdists usually analysed concentration at the level of the economy as a whole, as with their exploitation of the census of real estate values in 1890, used to demonstrate the decline in the number of factories since the previous census in 1853 and the considerable increase in their value – supposed proof of concentration. P. Lafargue, 'La Propriété Batie de 1853 à 1889', *Le Socialiste*, 3 July 1892. Alternatively, the Guesdists examined specific industries for symptoms of concentration, and always found them. See, for instance, 'Geva', 'La Petite Industrie' (shoe making), *Le Socialiste*, 6 August 1887.

[70] P. Lafargue, 'L'Autonomie', *L'Égalité*, 15 January 1882, is a good example of this argument.

circuses.[71] No field of enterprise – however isolated, specialised, or exotic – might escape eventual imposition of monopoly. Secure in its economic determinism, the Parti Ouvrier mocked the Radicals' advocacy of anti-trust laws, the French democrats' feeble reaction to the predations of France's 'aristocracy of wealth'. According to the Guesdists,

> every metamorphosis of monopoly meets obstacles, and all the great expropriations of the means of production have met legal barriers erected by those who are being victimised. That has not prevented monopoly from establishing itself and eventually prevailing, since it advances with the very evolution of the economy.[72]

Populist assaults upon 'malefactors of great wealth' would no more overpower plutocrats than shopkeepers' protests would deter department stores.

Perhaps. But monopoly during the *Belle Époque* advanced more like a glacier than an avalanche. Despite the Guesdists' imagery of rampant monopolists, all-engulfing factories, and tidal waves of finance capital, monopoly capitalism still lay far in the future as France entered the twentieth century. During the *Fin de Siècle*, millions of the French submerged themselves in a seething cauldron of competitive entrepreneurship: a plethora of small businesses – butchers, bakers, candle-stick makers and all their petit-bourgeois fraternity – proliferated along the main-streets of French towns and the side-streets of French cities; the mercantile exploitation of scattered out-workers, themselves self-employed 'entrepreneurs', thrived alongside factories, themselves usually small-scale and family-owned; peasant farms by their hundreds of thousands spread across the countryside, clawing land away from absentee landlords. Ironically, labour's success in reducing working hours and improving pay and conditions, coupled with factory regulation by the state, precipitated the ruralisation of formally urban industries, coupled with a new lease on life for outworking, thereby reversing the concentration of the means of production foreshadowed by Marxists.[73] In 1906, no less than 29 per cent of the active population

---

[71] 'P.G.' (Grados), 'Barnum', *Le Socialiste*, 8–15 December 1901.

[72] 'Br.', 'A Travers la Semaine', *Le Socialiste*, 10–17 April 1904.

[73] For 'ruralisation', see Jonas, 'From the Radical Republic to the Social Republic', pp. 98 and 127, and, for the proliferation of outwork, see M. Boxer, 'Protective Legislation and Home Industry: The Marginalisation of Women Workers in Late Nineteenth – Early Twentieth-Century France', *Journal of Social History*, vol. 20, 1986, pp. 50–1; Marty, *Chanter pour Survivre*, pp. 57–8; P. Nord, *Paris Shopkeepers and the Politics of Resentment* (Princeton, 1986),

defined themselves as 'patrons', as employers or as self-employed.[74] Despite their *a priori* assumptions, Guesdists occasionally recognised the wide distribution of entrepreneurial property in France, but only when such recognition suited their polemical purposes. The Parti Ouvrier, for instance, furiously denounced the equal representation of employees and employers on the Conseil Supérieur du Travail, which supposedly misrepresented the predominance of workers over capitalists – 'five million workers as against two million employers'.[75] How could the Guesdists sustain their rhetoric of capitalist concentration against these figures? How could the Parti Ouvrier possibly retain its Marxist credibility in this petit-bourgeois world?

French Marxists benefited from a characteristic 'optical illusion' of their period. In the mythology of popular culture, just as in the imagery of Guesdist polemic, the archetypical French capitalist was neither the neighbourhood building contractor nor the local draper, but a captain of industry such as Schneider of Creusot or a plutocratic banker such as Baron Rothschild. The brilliance of a few bourgeois supernovas dimmed millions of faint entrepreneurial stars to invisibility, thereby legitimating the Marxist conception of industrial concentration and financial monopoly. And, in fairness to the Parti Ouvrier, the Guesdists' exploitation of the prominence of great capitalists in the French social mentality emphasised an evident tendency, if not a fully-formed actuality. Schneiders and Rothschilds may have misrepresented the entrepreneurial norm, but they embodied a century-long tendency towards capital concentration, a tendency which would accelerate throughout the twentieth century. This gradual but persistent trend had already overwhelmed the handloom weaver, spawning the northern textile mills of Guesdist notoriety, and concentration would eventually reduce even the proud industrial dynasties of Lille and Roubaix to insignificant pensioners of a few multinational corporations. Paris itself, domain

p. 148; and A. Cottereau, 'The Distinctiveness of Working-Class Culture in France 1848–1870', in I. Katznelson and A. Zolberg (eds), *Working-Class Formation: Nineteenth-Century Patterns in Western Europe and the United States* (Princeton, 1986), pp. 114–23. For the vitality of non-monopolistic enterprise during the *Fin de Siècle*, see the empirical evidence in L. Cahen, 'La Concentration des Établissements', pp. 855–6 and the influential argument in C. Sabel and J. Zeitlin, 'Historical Alternatives to Mass Production: Politics, Markets and Technology in Nineteenth-Century Industrialisation', *Past and Present*, no. 108, 1985, pp. 133–76.

[74] A. Przeworski et al., 'The Evolution of the Class Structure of France 1901–1968', *Economic Development and Cultural Change*, vol. 28, 1980, p. 748.

[75] L. Roland, 'Réforme no. 1', *Le Socialiste*, 11 March 1900.

of the artisanal entrepreneur and the specialist retailer, experienced frightening instances of capital centralisation during the *Belle Époque*, including the proliferation of the Duval restaurants, with their 1,200 staff and 3 million meals a year – a previously inconceivable capitalist assault upon independent restaurateurs.[76] Centralisation of capital and concentration of production advanced indeed, although not yet towards the absolute and universal monopoly of Guesdist myth.

The Parti Ouvrier, however, relied upon theory rather than observation to sustain its absolutist conception of the capitalist mode of production: 'unbiased' observation (that unattainable ideal) would have revealed independent dressmakers in their garrets as well as millionaire mill-owners in their mansions, self-employed masons in villages as well as great construction companies in cities, small-town notaries as well as Parisian merchant bankers. French Marxists, themselves convinced of 'inevitable' monopoly and eager to convince others, clung to their absolutist faith in an absolute conception of capitalist concentration: observation confirmed what Guesdists already knew – that small-scale capital would inevitably surrender to large-scale capital; that production units inevitably inflated exponentially; that monopoly rules OK? These convictions underpinned the Guesdists' all-important theory of proletarianisation, in which 'large scale industry . . . generalise[d] and intensif[ied] the proletarian miseries inherent in the capitalist form of production',[77] thereby generalising and intensifying proletarian anti-capitalism.

According to the Parti Ouvrier, workers' dedication to socialism increased with every increase in the scale of capitalist enterprise: concentration of production intensified the proletariat's exploitation, which in turn augmented proletarians' resistance to their exploiters' exactions. Centralisation of capital envenomed the resulting conflicts, as the paternal relationship between master and man characteristic of small business surrendered to the anonymous authoritarianism characteristic of big business. Finally, not only did capitalist concentration animate and legitimise the workers' struggle for socialism, it ensured their victory. According to the Parti Ouvrier, monopoly capitalism engendered both socialist motives

---

[76] For concentration in the Nord, see Hilden, *Working Women and Socialist Politics*, p. 68. The Duval restaurants are described in Berlanstein, *The Working People of Paris*, pp. 107–8.
[77] P. Lafargue, 'La Production Capitaliste', *L'Égalité*, 6 August 1882.

and socialist means: previously isolated workers, regimented but also mobilised by capital, coalesced into ever larger and ever more homogeneous battalions; previously unenlightened proletarians sensed their class interests, interests once camouflaged by the variety and fragmentation of capitalist enterprise; previously unorganisable employees organised in proportion to the development of capitalist concentration, concentration which heralded a future socialist 'expropriation' facilitated by industry's monopolisation 'by only a few men'.[78] No wonder Guesdists clung to their imagery of all-encompassing industrial plants and all-devouring bourgeois plutocrats. Monopoly capitalism, thus depicted, conjured its own nemesis.

The Parti Ouvrier, however, repudiated reversion to small-scale artisanal production – not for Guesdists the Proudhonian utopia of the patriarchal workshop. Guesdists regularly denounced their ideological competitors – whether anarchists, Radicals, anti-Semites, or Christian Democrats – as pathetic dreamers out of step with the march-past of history, as impotent reactionaries out of sympathy with inevitable 'progress'. Attacking attempts to reverse the concentration of the means of production as 'a crime against humanity', French Marxists asserted that 'one could no more swim against the current of *large-scale commerce* and *large-scale industry* than reverse the tides'.[79] In the Marxist understanding of socialist revolution, 'the proletariat has taken up arms against capitalist concentration, not to destroy the social machine, but simply to give it another leadership'.[80] The impending socialist mode of production would be built upon foundations dug by capitalist monopoly. According to Charles Vérecque,

economic phenomena ... drive towards centralisation and concentration. It would be madness to wish to reverse the process, to turn our backs on progress ... Produced by capitalism, in accord with its facts, but not going beyond them, socialism must base its practice on the forms given to it by capitalist society.[81]

For the Parti Ouvrier, concentration of capital not only mobilised the proletariat against capitalism, but constructed the infrastructure

[78] C. Bonnier, 'La Spéculation', *Le Socialiste*, 14 February 1897.
[79] J. Guesde, 'Socialisez!', *Le Socialiste*, 14 January 1888.
[80] C. Bonnier, 'Art et Socialisme', *Le Socialiste*, 22 April 1900.
[81] C. Vérecque, 'Partage et Salariat', *Le Socialiste*, 27 October – 3 November 1901.

of utopia.[82] Marxists reviled monopoly as proof of capitalist rapacity, and treasured it as foreshadowing the socialist future.

Guesdists expounded a strikingly consistent analysis of the capitalist mode of production, an analysis firmly based upon Marxist political economy. In the Parti Ouvrier's account of its world, capital accumulation, the animating spirit of French society, continually restructured the relationship between labour and capital to capital's advantage: capitalists proletarianised the petite bourgeoisie and peasantry, pauperised already propertyless proletarians, and subjected workers to exploitative 'rationalisation'. Capital's appetites grew as it fed upon its victims – as did capital's ravenous mastery. Already dispossessed of productive property and despoiled of the true value of their labour power, workers increasingly suffered the malignant capitalist processes of deskilling, managerial authoritarianism, mechanisation, and concentration: as their productivity improved, their conditions worsened. Ever-expanding capital accumulation proletarianised society, while further proletarianising proletarians.

And the Guesdists thoroughly approved. However traumatic for its victims, however iniquitous in its immediate effects, capital accumulation generated its own negation, fathered its own nemesis, ensured the expropriation of the expropriators. The Juggernaut advance of capitalist industrialism – with it hideous panoply of deskilling, production authority, mechanisation, and increasing production scale – should not be stopped, indeed *could* not be stopped. Determination to build socialism with the legacies of capitalism sharply distinguished French Marxists from others on the French Left, whether anti-socialist Radicals or anti-industrial socialists. According to the Parti Ouvrier, a proletarianised society free from petit-bourgeois individualism heralded the triumph of collectivism, pauperisation drove capitalism's victims towards socialist revolution, and 'rationalisation' excavated the foundations of utopia. The homogenised labour force of capitalism, a legacy of deskilling, united workers in a common revolutionary cause and

---

[82] There is evidence that large-scale enterprise had the opposite effect – individualising workers rather than combining them into self-conscious masses. See the analysis of the atomisation of the working class by concentration in Y. Lequin, 'Social Structures and Shared Beliefs: Four Worker Communities in the "Second Industrialisation"', *International Labor and Working Class History*, no. 22, 1982, pp. 5–8.

presaged the universalistic social order of the future. And the industrial regime of mature capitalism – highly organised, driven by the technologies of 'industrial revolution', and concentrated into vast enterprises – marshalled workers into a coherent force, incorporated society's productive capacities into the 'collective worker', and promised universal plenty. Capitalism, according to the Marxist interpretation of the accumulation process, produced not only surplus value, but a militant working class and the 'material preconditions' of an alternative mode of production. In effect, socialism arose as an unintended consequence of capitalism.

The Parti Ouvrier's depiction of French society, however exaggerated or distorted, indeed *because* of its exaggerations and distortions, touched the hopes and fears of French workers, and sometimes evoked the generosity and idealism of French bourgeois. Capital accumulation indeed ruled virtually unchecked over a proletarianised society – in Roubaix or Roanne. Some, though not all, workers indeed suffered the processes of 'relative surplus value' extraction: deskilling, rigid industrial discipline, technological revolution of the labour process, and subjection to ever larger units of production.[83] And the 'second industrial revolution' of the *Belle Époque*, by narrowing wage differentials and fostering cooperation between the skilled and unskilled, indeed united previously antagonistic fractions of the working class.[84] Mutation of the mid-nineteenth-century usage 'classes ouvrières' into the late-nineteenth-century 'classe ouvrière', a mutation simultaneously consequence and condition of Guesdist success, reflected a social upheaval, constituted a new ideological order, and, for Marxists, heralded socialist revolution.[85] The Parti Ouvrier convinced itself and persuaded its followers that

---

[83] Good descriptions of proletarianisation which matched the Guesdists' conception may be found in J.-P. Brunet, *Saint-Denis – La Ville Rouge: Socialisme et Communisme en Banlieu Ouvrier 1890–1939* (Paris, 1980), pp. 15–148 and particularly pp. 48–9; P. Barral, *Le Département de l'Isère sous la IIIᵉ République: Histoire Sociale et Politique* (Paris, 1962), p. 209; Scott, *The Glassworkers of Carmaux*, p. 71; and Lequin, *La Formation de la Classe Ouvrière Régionale*, pp. 206–7 and 249–53.

[84] For declining income differentials, see Perrot, 'La Classe Ouvrière au Temps de Jaurès', p. 75; G. Dupeux, *La Société Française 1789–1970* (Paris, 1972), p. 179; and G. Weill, 'Le Rôle des Facteurs Structurels dans l'Évolution des Rémunérations Salariales au XIXᵉ Siècle', *Revue Économique*, vol. 10, 1959, pp. 256–8. For social integration of skilled and unskilled labour through industrial team work, see M. Hanagan, 'Organisation du Travail et Action Revendicative: Verriers et Métallurgistes de Rive-de-Giers à la Fin du XIXᵉ Siècle', *Cahiers d'Histoire*, vol. 26, 1981, pp. 10–11.

[85] J. Dubois, *Le Vocabulaire Politique et Social en France de 1869 à 1872* (Paris, 1969), pp. 19–23.

traversal of capitalism's dark valley, and only that traversal, led to the sunny uplands of socialism.

Guesdist 'industrial socialism' sold as a novelty in the French ideological marketplace. The Saint-Simonian tradition, the 'technocratic' socialism of the École Polytechnique, had praised industrialism, but rejected class conflict. The Babouvist-Blanquist tradition, the Sans-culotte socialism of the Parisian barricades, had advocated class conflict, but resisted industrialism. By combining the anti-bourgeois force of the plebeian revolutionaries with the sociological optimism of the 'bourgeois' Saint-Simonians, by amalgamating vitriolic critique of capitalism's social order with unconditional acceptance of its material triumphs, Marxists promised a positive transcendence of the capitalist mode of production, the appropriation rather than the destruction of bourgeois achievement. Revolutionary workers would inherit a world enriched by capital, but a world freed from capitalist exploitation. No wonder Guesdist ideology 'sold'. The Parti Ouvrier promised the best of both worlds: capitalist productivity combined with socialist solidarity. Socialism, according to the Parti Ouvrier, would arise from 'accumulated capital, the division and the community of labour, mechanisation, all the advances and applications of modern science, and the new men who emerge from this milieu'.[86] 'New men', offspring of modernity, heralds of a transcendent future – the Guesdists' image of the proletariat, and the Guesdists' self-image.

[86] Anonymous, 'Pas de Robinsonnade!', *Le Socialiste*, 12 June 1892.

CHAPTER 5

Unmaking the working class: lumpenproletarians and labour aristocrats

Marx's dissection of the capitalist mode of production bestowed an enormously valuable ideological legacy upon the socialist movement. Revelation of the monstrous anatomy of capitalism, when wielded with force, has repeatedly ruptured the libertarian and egalitarian camouflage which otherwise conceals the system's predatory nature from its proletarian victims. The liberal illusion of equal exchange between the propertied and the propertyless, a bulwark of bourgeois order, has helplessly disintegrated under the assault of Marx's combative concepts. At the same time, the Marxists' critique of capital has revealed how capitalists convert the labour-power they purchase into the proletariat – into a united and self-conscious class, the historical agent destined to expropriate the expropriators. Yet the capitalist mode of production simultaneously 'unmakes' the working class, inflicting an unceasing disaggregation throughout the proletariat from which Marxists have prudishly averted their eyes. Social mobility between classes, internecine conflict between workers, and collaboration between capital and labour have continuously disrupted the working class, just as the accumulation process has continuously consolidated it. How did Guesdists, apostles of proletarianisation, understand 'deproletarianisation'?

At their most dogmatic, French Marxists simply ignored aspects of their society which would otherwise have compelled them to abandon their unilinear theory of proletarianisation. The putting-out system, negation of capital concentration and mechanisation, flourished during the supposedly industrial *Fin de Siècle*. But France's hundreds of thousands of impoverished outworkers might not have existed, for all the attention they received from the POF. Building workers, no less numerous, rarely featured in Guesdist social imagery – although carpenters, masons, and bricklayers had raised the barricades of 1848, fought as Communards, and launched some of

the most aggressive strikes of the *Belle Époque*. Confounding predictions of inexorable deskilling and inevitable industrial hierarchy,
builders have effortlessly preserved their craft traditions and labour
autonomy into the twentieth century – living fossils whose exuberant
vitality apparently refutes the Marxist evolutionary schema.[1] And
the Parti Ouvrier cavalierly disregarded the grievances of those
whom Guesde himself described as that 'special group, which is so
considerable, of restaurant and cafe workers',[2] although 'ouvriers
d'alimentation' sometimes demonstrated extraordinary militancy
during the Guesdists' period.[3] Mechanisation, that Marxist
obsession, played no part in waiting on tables. The individualistic,
even anarchic, experience of exploitation endured by seamstresses,
bricklayers, and waiters, if admitted, would have discredited the
French Marxists' simplistic but powerful imagery of a uniform
capitalist mode of production ceaselessly producing a uniform
proletariat – a proletariat uniformly subjected to deskilling, managerial authority, mechanisation, and concentration.[4] Socialist militants rather than industrial sociologists, Guesdists understandably
preferred polemical efficacy to sociological accuracy. Translating an
exemplary exception into an all-encompassing universal, they subsumed the working-class experience as a whole in the factory
despotism of the northern textile mills.

On other occasions, however, the Parti Ouvrier reluctantly
addressed the diversity of the proletarian experience, and even
confronted 'deproletarianisation'. Ideological enemies menaced the
movement from every side, and without exception mobilised conflict
between workers, cooperation between workers and capitalists, and
social mobility between classes against the Marxist conception of the

---

[1] A. Touraine, *La Conscience Ouvrière* (Paris, 1966), p. 47. Guesdists recognised that building
workers' relative well-being depended upon their insulation from industrialism. See, for
instance, 'Dr Z.', 'L'Enquête', *Le Socialist*, 11 May 1891. The few exceptions to Guesdist
neglect of the construction workers actually demonstrate the Guesdists' priorities by angry
rejection of the exclusive craft traditions of the building trades. See, for instance, H.
Ghesquière, 'À Travers les Métiers: les Ouvriers du Bâtiment', *Le Socialiste*, 15 August 1894.
[2] J. Guesde, 'La Liberté du Travail', *Le Socialiste*, 31 March 1894.
[3] According to L. Moch, 'Urban Structure, Migration, and Worker Militancy: A Comparative Study of French Urbanisation', in M. Hanagan and C. Stephenson (eds.), *Proletarians
and Protest: The Roots of Class Formation in an Industrializing World* (New York, 1986), p. 120
and R. Magraw, 'Socialism, Syndicalism and French Labour before 1914', in D. Geary
(ed.), *Labour and Socialist Movements in Europe* (London, 1989), pp. 91–2.
[4] For a perceptive critique of the persistence of this 'essentialist' understanding of capitalist
society in Marxist ideology, see A. Friedman, *Industry and Labour: Class Struggle at Work and
Monopoly Capitalism* (London, 1977), part 2.

'making of the working class'. The Parti Ouvrier could not resist its enemies, and would never defeat them, without explicit refutation of their visions of deproletarianisation – competitive ideological paradigms inevitably compete. Ever combative, the Guesdists rose to the challenge.

Social mobility, random individual traversals of social order, profoundly perturbed Guesdists – with good reason. The Marxist theory of proletarianisation not only indicated working-class 'places' in society, but implicitly assigned these places to workers who, from birth to death, would experience the social world as proletarians – thereby living the experiential foundation of their class identity. Anti-Marxists, and most Marxists, have assumed that social mobility inhibits class formation, that individual movement across class boundaries, if commonplace, ensures that proletarianisation need not result in a proletarian society, that proletarian 'places' in society might proliferate, but that proletarians might not. Inevitably, individualists and collectivists have disagreed over rates of social mobility, their 'empirical' perceptions of social fluidity or rigidity governed by and governing their ideological presuppositions: liberals have emphasised the prevalence and ease of social mobility in capitalist society; socialists have emphasised its unimportance and improbability.[5] Well aware of the ideological stakes in their contest with Marxist socialism, French liberals and Radicals stressed, indeed grossly exaggerated, the scope for individual advancement inherent in the market economy and democratic polity of the Third Republic: 'careers open to talent' supposedly opened as easily to impecunious textile workers as to ambitious law students.[6]

[5] For the general thesis that persistent and substantial social mobility invalidates Marxist theories of class formation, see R. Dahrendorf, *Class and Class Conflict in Industrial Society* (Stanford, 1959), pp. 57–61; R. Robinson, 'Structural Change and Class Mobility in Capitalist Societies', *Social Forces*, vol. 63, 1984, pp. 51–71; and B. Ollman, 'Towards Class Consciousness Next Time: Marx and the Working Class', *Politics and Society*, vol. 3, 1972, pp. 9–10. For critical discussion of this argument, see J. Kocka, 'The Study of Social Mobility and the Formation of the Working Class in the Nineteenth Century', *Mouvement Social*, no. 111, 1980, pp. 97–117; R. Aberg, 'Social Mobility and Class Structuration', *Acta Sociologica*, vol. 22, 1979, pp. 247–71; and P. Bourdieu, 'Classement, Déclassement, Réclassement', *Actes de la Recherche en Sciences Sociales*, no. 24, 1978, pp. 2–22.

[6] A. Daumard, 'Puissance et Inquiétudes de la Société Bourgeoise', in *Histoire Économique et Sociale de la France*: Tome IV – *L'Ère Industrielle et la Société d'Aujourd'hui (Siècle 1880–1980)*: Premier Volume – *Ambiguïtés des Débuts et Croissance Effective (Années 1880–1914)* (Paris, 1979), p. 411, and P. Sorlin, *Waldeck-Rousseau* (Paris, 1966), p. 375. The Guesdists' vitriolic response to liberal use of social mobility against collectivism may be found, for example, in J. Guesde's representatively titled, 'Imbécile et Malhonnête', *Le Cri du Peuple*, 30 April 1885.

Accepting the conception of individual interest advanced by their liberal enemies, Guesdists agreed that social mobility inhibited working-class solidarity. The comparative ease with which workers had acquired property under the economic *ancien régime* explained, according to French Marxists, why 'the interests of employer and employee [had not been] antagonistic'[7] – every journeyman had aspired to his master's place. Guesde himself, supplementing his Marxism with a Paretan 'circulation of elites', suggested that, even under the ascendant industrial order, 'the capitalist minority can maintain its economic and political dominance only by annexing ... all the most capable elements of the working class. Not to mention that such a haemorrhage drains the proletariat of its best forces and inhibits its revolutionary development'.[8] Although the rapid expansion of proletarian locations in society and the concomitant contraction of bourgeois locations supposedly rendered this strategy of social promotion increasingly illusory, the illusion itself endangered proletarian solidarity. Guesdists feared, correctly, that 'against all reality, the hope of becoming propertied through one's own labour still persists in the dreams of the working class'.[9] So long as bourgeois society offered workers even the dream of escape from the working class into the bourgeoisie, so long would labour solidarity be weakened as enterprising proletarians aspired to the privileges of property-ownership, to individual rather than collective emancipation from the proletarian condition.

How did the French Marxists confront this potentially mortal threat to their theory of proletarianisation? At their most original, Guesdists rejected its fundamental premise, arguing that social mobility *confirmed* the salience of class structure: mobility between classes no more disproved the existence of class inequality than passengers moving between carriages on a train disproved the

[7] L. Greffier, *Petites Conférences Éducatives sur le Socialisme* (Grenoble, 1904), p. 10.

[8] J. Guesde, 'Instruisez', *Le Cri du Peuple*, 9 September 1885. Guesdists recognised that escapees from the proletariat might constitute a particularly anti-socialist category of bourgeois. See, for instance, Anonymous, 'Le Fils de ses Oeuvres', *Le Socialiste*, 5 February 1895.

[9] P. Lafargue, *Les Trusts Américains* (Paris, 1903), pp. 129–30. For the popularity of these 'illusions' among workers during the period, see P. Stearns, *Lives of Labour: Work in a Maturing Industrial Society* (London, 1975), pp. 242–7. Even workers in Guesdist Roubaix worked and hoped for at least their childrens' escape from the proletariat, according to D. Gordon, 'Liberalism and Socialism in the Nord: Eugène Motte and Republican Politics in Roubaix 1898–1912', *French History*, vol. 3, 1989, p. 320.

existence of railway carriages.[10] Proletarian places within the capitalist mode of production, even if filled on a temporary basis, sufficed to damn bourgeois society. But Guesdists rarely advanced this solution to their sociological dilemma. However plausible as egalitarian rhetoric, however unanswerable as social theory, it failed dismally as a theory of class formation: transient proletarians would never evolve a clearly-defined class consciousness or originate sustained class militancy. More often, Guesdists assailed aspirations to social mobility as founded upon pernicious illusion, contending that, apart from self-interested bourgeois fictions, capitalist society confined its passengers to their own (first or second class) railway carriages. Workers, according to the Parti Ouvrier, could not escape from their proletarian condition: the promise of social mobility deceived, apart from the downward social mobility from the petite bourgeoisie to the working class ensured by 'primitive accumulation'. Responding to the liberal boast that 'innumerable people climb and descend the social ladder. Employers return to the proletariat, and workers mount to become employers', Henri Ghesquière retorted that 'innumerable people would like to climb the social ladder, if they weren't continually kicked off by the privileged few on the upper rungs. Employers return to the proletariat, but workers aren't able to mount'.[11] Once workers recognised this 'obvious' truth, surely only a matter of time and socialist enlightenment, liberal illusions would no longer jeopardise working-class solidarity.

The Marxist theory of capitalist concentration armed Guesdists in their struggle against the 'myth' of social mobility. 'Where's the hatter', they asked rhetorically, 'who'd be mad enough to believe in his personal emancipation through possession of the means of production, in the face of immense factories and the millions and millions deployed by capitalist corporations?'[12] Paul Grados, one of the rare Parisian militants of the Parti Ouvrier, imagined a worker told that anyone might aspire to capitalist wealth, if only he exercised prudence and thrift:

The worker listens, stupefied at such audacity. He stares at the pennies in the palm of his hand that are supposed to compensate him for his long daily

[10] Anonymous, 'La Semaine', *Le Socialiste*, 19 August 1900.
[11] H. Ghesquière, 'Société Nouvelle', *Le Socialiste*, 28 July 1894.
[12] Anonymous, 'La Réunion de Saint-Savine: Conférence Contradictoire Charonnat-Pédron', *Le Socialiste*, 27 October 1895.

labours. He thinks of the three or four little stomachs that he needs to fill . . . of small shivering shoulders that must be covered, of the landlord demanding the rent for his slum garret. He thinks of all this, then turns his eyes upon the vast industrial penitentiary which engulfs him every day. He scans the enormous building, its tools and machinery, the warehouses stuffed with raw materials and served by rail, the comfortable offices from which salaries and accounts are paid. He sums it all up, and his arms fall at his sides. They're mocking him, beyond doubt. Even if he didn't have a family, even if there weren't unemployment and illness and accidents to fear, how many working days would it take for him to save the value of these huge workshops and their contents? Several lifetimes wouldn't be enough.[13]

Workers saving their pennies to buy a factory should indeed have despaired: capitalists themselves rarely financed the plant of the second industrial revolution with retained earnings. Yet a few enterprising and lucky workers accumulated spectacular industrial fortunes, thousands more attained the uncomfortable lower rungs of the petite bourgeoisie, and hundreds of thousands crowded eagerly around the base of the social ladder – thereby ensuring that the divisive dream of social ascension through property ownership persisted among workers, perpetuated by tantalising experience.

Although determined to impose their absolutist conception of capitalist society upon working-class political culture, Guesdists could not blindly ignore the popular adulation which surrounded the great self-made men of France, world-renowned figures such as Jean-François Cail, who had begun his career as a mere metal-worker yet died owner of the country's greatest engineering-works. Confronted by Cail and his like, entrepreneurial commanders risen from the proletarian ranks, French Marxists (mixing their metaphors) emphasised that 'the number of those seizing the marshal's baton is so small that people exclaim in astonishment when there's a winner in the great lottery'.[14] Cail's personal triumph, for

[13] P. Grados, 'Moralistes', *Le Socialiste*, 22–9 June 1902.
[14] Anonymous, 'Le Fils de ses Oeuvres', *Le Socialiste*, 5 February 1895. The importance of success stories such as Cail's in the social mentality of the POF's period is stressed in A. Daumard, 'L'Évolution des Structures Sociales en France à l'Époque de l'Industrialisation 1815–1914', *Revue Historique*, vol. 274, 1972, pp. 327–30 and in Y. Lequin, 'Les Villes et l'Industrie: L'Emergence d'une Autre France', in Y. Lequin (ed.), *Histoire des Français XIX—XXe Siècles: La Société* (Paris, 1983), pp. 317–19. Most of our understanding of social mobility in France for the period is impressionistic, since we lack analyses of reconstituted families over generations. See the discussion in M. Perrot, 'Les Classes Populaires Urbaines', in *Histoire Économique et Sociale de la France: tome IV – L'Ère Industrielle et la Société d'Aujourd'hui (Siècle 1880–1980): Premier Volume – Ambiguïtés des Débuts et Croissance Effective (Années 1880–1914)* (Paris, 1979), p. 508 and A. Corbin, 'La Mobilité Sociale en France au

Guesdists, only darkened the already black tragedy of the proletarian condition: for every Cail, a million workers vegetated in impoverished hopelessness. Perhaps. But similar odds have not inhibited working-class enthusiasm for lotteries. Poverty stimulates desperate hopes, even against the odds.[15]

What is more, the Guesdists' systematic equation of social mobility with movement between the industrial proletariat and the capitalist plutocracy was as tendentious as the liberal propaganda which the Parti Ouvrier sought to counter: like the liberals, Marxists obscured the commonplace by highlighting the exceptional. Socially significant mobility in France traversed the indistinct boundary between the upper strata of the proletariat and the lower ranks of the petite bourgeoisie, not the vast gulf separating factory employees from factory owners: enterprising construction workers set up as building contractors; ambitious artisans opened their own workshops; fortunate labourers saved tiny legacies and bought corner-stores.[16] The Parti Ouvrier's denigration of social mobility under capitalism implicitly depended upon the Guesdists' absolutist understanding of 'primitive accumulation' (which supposedly expropriated building contractors, workshop masters, and corner-store owners) and upon their equally absolutist theory of the concentration of production and the centralisation of capital (which supposedly universalised 'the vast industrial penitentiaries' of Grados' discouraging parable). Reduction of individual strategies of social promotion to 'false consciousness' required substitution of an *a priori* theory of capitalist concentration for engagement with France's still largely petit-bourgeois society, thereby reinforcing the

XIXe Siècle', in G. Ritter and R. Vierhaus (eds.), *Aspekte der Historischen Forschung in Frankreich und Deutschland* (Göttingen, 1981), pp. 105–16.

[15] For evidence of blockage, see Corbin, 'La Mobilité Sociale en France au XIXe Siècle', pp. 109–10; Y. Lequin, 'Le Monde des Travailleurs Manuels', in M. Agulhon (ed.), *Histoire de la France Urbaine* (Paris, 1983), vol. 4, p. 517; M. Perrot, 'On the Formation of the French Working Class', in I. Katznelson and A. Zolberg (eds.), *Working-Class Formation: Nineteenth-Century Patterns in Western Europe and the United States* (Princeton, 1986), pp. 104–5; G. Jacquemet, *Belleville au XIXe Siècle: Du Faubourg à la Ville* (Paris, 1984), pp. 324–5; F.-P. Codaccioni, *De l'Inégalité Sociale dans une Grande Ville Industrielle: Le Drame de Lille de 1850 à 1914* (Lille, 1976), pp. 391–2; G. Desert, 'Structures Sociales dans les Villes Bas-Normands au XIXe Siècle', in *Conjoncture Économique/Structures Sociales* (Paris, 1977), pp. 491–513; and, above all, G. Noiriel, *Les Ouvriers dans la Société Française: XIXe–XXe Siècle* (Paris, 1986), pp. 86–8.

[16] G. Dupeux, *La Société Française 1789–1960* (Paris, 1964), p. 161. Codaccioni stresses this 'short-range' mobility, but points out the terrible failure rates for the marginal enterprises accessible to 'upwardly' mobile workers. *De l'Inégalité Sociale*, pp. 190–2.

Guesdists' obsessive reiteration of a simplified, even simplistic, political economy of inevitable and universal monopoly.

If the deproletarianisation inherent in social mobility has posed intractable quandaries for Marxists, structural contradictions within the proletariat and the resulting intra-class conflicts have frustrated them to an even greater extent. Individualist evasion of working-class status, if nothing else, confirmed and highlighted the disparity between proletarian poverty and bourgeois prosperity: no bourgeois has ever struggled to enter the working class. By contrast, systemic conflict between workers systematically undermined the all-important Marxist faith in a unitary proletarian class interest. 'Proletarianisation', the 'making of the working class', the assumption that 'the various interests and conditions of life within the ranks of the proletariat are increasingly equalised [by capital]'[17] – these incantations of the Marxist Cabala have protected Marxists against perception of the disruptive working-class brawls which would otherwise have disrupted their ideological certainties, and (if appropriately intoned) have conjured into existence the class solidarity they supposedly described. Yet even the most blinkered Marxists have occasionally noticed that workers – sometimes more protective of their 'relativities' than opposed to profit, more hostile to foremen than to capitalists, more fond of their masters than of other trades – feud over income differentials, quarrel over authority within the workplace, and ally themselves with their employers against competing workers. Marx himself had concluded that 'the more productive capital grows, the more the division of labour . . . expands. The more the division of labour expands . . . the more competition among the workers expands'.[18] Marx had also predicted that countervailing

17 K. Marx and F. Engels, *The Communist Manifesto*, in K. Marx and F. Engels, *Collected Works* (London, 1976), vol. 6, p. 492.
18 K. Marx, *Wage Labour and Capital*, in K. Marx and F. Engels, *Collected Works* (London, 1977), vol. 9, p. 227. See the useful discussions of Marx's point in R. Mouriaux, 'Livre Premier du *Capital* et Sociologie de la Classe Ouvrière', *La Pensée*, no. 166, 1972, pp. 69–81 and A. Rattansi, *Marx and the Division of Labour* (London, 1982), p. 154. For the critical importance of these doubts about labour solidarity for the Marxist theory of proletarianisation, see F. Parkin, *Marxism and Class Theory: A Bourgeois Critique* (London, 1979), pp. 29–43; A. Giddens, *A Contemporary Critique of Historical Materialism* (London, 1981), pp. 242–3; V. Allen, 'The Differentiation of the Working Class', in A. Hunt (ed.), *Class and Class Structure* (London, 1977), pp. 61–79; H. Wachtel, 'Class Consciousness and Stratification in the Labor Process', in R. Edwards et al. (eds.), *Labor Market Segmentation* (Lexington, 1973), pp. 95–122; and, particularly, W. Roy, 'Class Conflict and Social Change in Historical Perspective', *Annual Review of Sociology*, vol. 10, 1984, pp. 483–506. For arguments (from

tendencies would prevail against disunity, that capital would eventually unite labour against capital, despite the division of labour. But divisions between labourers, the divisive relationships inherent in hierarchies of skill and competition between trades, have continued to haunt Marxist conceptions of the proletariat and enfeeble socialist pursuit of the class war.

Proletarian divisiveness haunted the Guesdists mercilessly. Implicitly, and often explicitly, the Parti Ouvrier's long crusade to unite French workers into a revolutionary proletariat warred against powerful forces of disunity: class disruption defined and delimited the battlefields upon which Marxists campaigned for class solidarity. Indeed, the POF systematically interpreted its own odyssey in these terms. Lafargue, for instance, attributed the schism between Guesdists and Broussists to structural conflicts within the Parisian working class: the Possibilists supposedly representing a backward-looking artisanal elite, with more modern proletarians supporting Guesde's faction – a classic manifestation of the transcended artisans versus ascendant proletariat dialectic repeatedly deployed by Marxists against anti-Marxists within the socialist and labour movement.[19] Guesdists might have preferred to ignore proletarian disunity, but could not. What aspects of the capitalist mode of production in its *fin-de-siècle* French manifestation challenged the POF by turning worker against worker?

Authority within the workplace divided the proletariat of the *Belle Époque*, as it has divided plebeians ever since the appointment of the first overseer at the dawn of history. Workers have always supervised other workers, and workers have always resented and resisted their supervisors: the chain of command from priest-king to worshipping fellaheen, from senatorial aristocrat to latifundial slaves, from Gothic noble to manorial serfs, from merchant prince to handloom weavers has invariably encompassed a complex hierarchy of scribal intermediaries, estate agents, bailiffs, or mercantile factors – themselves often plebeian in origin and status, but usually far more

antithetical perspectives) that Marxism has indeed collapsed because of this flaw in its conceptual foundation, see R. Bendix, 'Inequality and Social Structure: A Comparison of Marx and Weber', *American Sociological Review*, vol. 39, 1974, pp. 152–5 and B. Hindess, 'Classes and Politics in Marxist Theory', in G. Littlejohn et al. (eds.), *Power and the State* (London, 1978), pp. 72–97.

[19] P. Lafargue, letter to F. Engels, 3 November 1882, in *Paul et Laura Lafargue, et Friedrich Engels: Correspondance* (Paris, 1956), vol. 1, p. 92.

bitterly resented by their plebeian charges than were the intermediaries' remote, impregnable, and sometimes revered superiors.
None the less, no previous system of exploitation had relied more
heavily upon supervisory hierarchies than did the nascent monopoly
capitalism of the *Belle Époque,* the capitalism of the 'managerial
revolution'. As the industrial bureaucrat supplemented, and sometimes supplanted, the economic dominion of the entrepreneur,
conflict between workers and 'management' supplemented, and
sometimes supplanted, conflict between workers and employers.
Indeed, shop-floor employees, unconsciously rejuvenating the
antique tradition of 'the good king', frequently appealed to the
undoubted final authority and the (dubious) impartiality of their
employers against the brutalities and exactions of their supervisors.
'If only the king knew . . .'

Under these circumstances, could Marxists view supervisory
employees as 'real' workers? They could indeed. Rigorously applying his concept of the 'collective worker', an entity explicitly
dependent upon 'the labour of coordination', Marx himself had
decided that foremen in industrial enterprises (his period had yet to
experience the more complex industrial supervision of 'monopoly
capitalism') belonged to the working class, although foremen represented not only impersonal coordination of complex labour processes
but capitalist domination of labourers. After all, foremen were
propertyless and themselves subject to capitalist authority. Other
Marxists, however, have contended that 'producers' who exercise
the 'function of capital' became, *ipso facto,* capitalists, even if
unpropertied, thereby inaugurating a debate which has highlighted
both the social ambiguity of supervisory 'workers' and the Marxist
subordination of authority-relations to property-relations (or *vice
versa,* for 'neo-Marxists').[20] How did Guesdists resolve this equivo-
cation in their doctrine and, more importantly, how did they
penetrate this obscurity in their society?

The Guesdist understanding of supervisory workers resembled
Marx's inclusive conception of the proletariat rather than 'neo-
Marxist' exclusivity: the Parti Ouvrier identified foremen as prole-

---

[20] For Marx's position, see *Capital* (Moscow, 1954), vol. 1, pp. 396–400, while the alternative
'neo-Marxist' position is best argued in G. Carchedi, 'On the Economic Identification of
the New Middle Class', *Economy and Society,* vol. 4, 1975, pp. 1–86, an argument discussed
and criticised in T. Johnson, 'What is to be known? The Structural Determination of Social
Class', *Economy and Society,* vol. 6, 1977, pp. 195–233.

tarians simply because 'they too are wage-workers'.[21] In this case, however, imputed class consciousness did not derive unproblematically from evident class condition (unusually for the POF): the Guesdist identification of foremen as 'wage-workers' and therefore as authentic proletarians in no way prejudged the class allegiance of salaried supervisors. Instead, the disjuncture between social status and social role characteristic of foremen demonstrated that 'there are traitors and reactionaries within the working class', although proletarians 'know that their foremen, who are, for the most part, gaolers worse than the boss, are also workers'.[22] Guesdists even noticed the pattern whereby the less control the labour force retained over the labour process, the more capitalists recruited supervisors from the shop-floor, rather than from among their friends and families.[23] Proliferation of working-class supervisory personnel signposted transformation of 'formal' capitalist control over labour into 'real' control, but nonetheless control exercised by proletarians over other proletarians. Foremen, after all, could hardly betray the workers' cause except as workers.

The Guesdists' conception of workplace hierarchy and its place in the class system tapped contradictory working-class mentalities. The expanding authority of foremen and supervisors, viceroys of an increasingly bureaucratic capitalist dominion, evoked intense working-class resentment and hostility.[24] Shopfloor supervisors' petty tyranny, corrupt favouritism or sexual harassment provoked strikes quite as bitter as any directed against employers' exactions. Indeed, *fin-de-siècle* France underwent an acute 'crisis of authority', a French expression of the working-class rebellion against 'Taylorist' managerial innovation which convulsed the industrial world before the First World War.[25] Workers who had only with great difficulty accepted the 'formal' subordination of their labour to the impera-

---

[21] Anonymous, 'À la Belle Jardinière', *Le Socialiste*, 29 October 1887.

[22] Anonymous, 'Candidatures Ouvrières Bonapartistes', *Le Socialiste*, 6 November 1886.

[23] J. Dormoy, 'Exploitation des Ouvriers Métallurgistes', *Le Socialiste*, 26 March 1887.

[24] For description of this mentality, see D. Reid, *The Miners of Decazeville: A Genealogy of Deindustrialisation* (London, 1985), pp. 122–3; L. Berlanstein, *The Working People of Paris 1870–1914* (London, 1984), pp. 103–4; C. Gras, 'Presse Syndicale et Mentalités: L'Ouvrier Mouleur à Travers le Journal de sa Fédération – La Fonderie 1900–1909', *Mouvement Social*, no. 53, 1965, p. 55; J. Merriman, *The Red City: Limoges and the French Nineteenth Century* (Oxford, 1985), pp. 170–1; and R. Trempé, *Les Mineurs de Carmaux 1848–1914* (Paris, 1971), vol. 1, pp. 513–76. The importance of this issue in working-class political culture is discussed in M. Perrot, 'Les Classes Populaires Urbaines', p. 470 and P. Sorlin, *La Société Française 1840–1914* (Paris, 1969), p. 181.

[25] Berlanstein, *The Working People of Paris*, p. 172.

tives of capital accumulation revolted in outrage against its 'real' subordination, against employers' seizure of control over the labour process as well as against capitalist appropriation of labour's product. 'Line management' bore the brunt of this rebellion – its plight symbolised by the fatal defenestration of the eponymous engineer-manager Watrin, hapless victim of the Decazeville miners' outrage against their employers' authoritarian labour-process innovations. For hundreds of thousands of workers, the unfortunate Watrin and the tens of thousands of surviving foremen, supervisors, and managers embodied the iron rule of industrial labour discipline, not the grasping exactions of industrialism's ultimate beneficiaries in the remote, invulnerable, and essentially inconceivable boardrooms of Paris or Lyons.

Why, then, did the Parti Ouvrier refuse to exploit workers' fury? Why the Guesdists' careful incorporation of supervisory staff into the 'collective worker'? First, French Marxists sought to overcome the proletarian mentality which vented its outrage against a Watrin rather than against Watrin's masters. Not for the POF the anarchists' generalised hostility to authority, hostility which explicitly subsumed and implicitly trivialised the Party's campaign against capitalist exploitation. Second, not all workers hated their foremen: many employees respected, even admired, their immediate superiors, although only so long as the supervisory authority of foremen rested upon obvious mastery of the labour process rather than upon mere employer fiat. The highly skilled or highly motivated employees elevated to supervisory roles often retained the esteem and even the loyalty of their former workmates, thereby achieving leadership as well as advancement. Third, promotion from the ranks rarely changed the fundamental social identity of low-ranking supervisory workers, whose remuneration and status closely resembled those of the workers they supervised. Finally, tied by origin, community, and interest to their charges, foremen frequently represented the grievances and aspirations of the shop-floor to senior management, and sometimes sided with the shop-floor in labour disputes.[26] The Parti Ouvrier legitimated its inclusion of super-

---

[26] Respect for skilled foremen is described in R. Trempé, *Les Mineurs de Carmaux*, vol. 1, pp. 200–5. For the social similarities between foremen and other workers, see F.-P. Codaccioni, *De l'Inégalité Sociale*, p. 206 and D. Reid, 'Industrial Paternalism: Discourse and Practice in Nineteenth-Century French Mining and Metallurgy', *Comparative Studies in Society and History*, vol. 27, 1985, p. 593. Foremen defending workers' interests are described in L. Berlanstein, *The Working People of Paris*, p. 81; M. Perrot, 'The Three Ages of Industrial

visory workers within the proletariat by emphasising their lack of property and their productive role, but might also have highlighted their essentially proletarian place within the patterns of class consciousness and class conflict characteristic of French enterprises. Foremen were not invariably 'gaolers worse than the boss'.

In the last analysis, however, the Guesdists' rhetorical incorporation of supervisory personnel into the working class reflected Marxist acceptance of hierarchal production authority, supposedly as necessary for complex labour processes as were conductors for symphony orchestras. According to the POF, the proletariat should defy foremen, supervisors and managers so long as they served capitalists: Guesdists wasted no sympathy upon Watrin, faithful servant of his exploitative employers. But, once the proletariat had overthrown capitalism, supervisory personnel would assume their rightful place among their fellow proletarians as agents of the collectivity rather than lackeys of capital. Guesdists strove mightily to unify the collective worker against capitalist exploitation, not to divide proletarians over 'secondary issues' such as production authority; they worked tirelessly to recruit foremen and supervisors for the socialist cause, not force them further into their employers' embrace.

'Labour aristocrats', in one Marxist tradition, have sapped working-class solidarity far more than have the cancerous ravages of social mobility or fratricidal conflict over workshop authority. A privileged minority's malignant hegemony over proletarian self-consciousness and proletarian self-organisation has supposedly steered the labour movement out of the broad channel of revolutionary class conflict into the stagnant waters of class-collaborationist reformism. In this tradition, while the aristocrats' rare skills and organisational capacity protected them against the worst depredations of capital, they also gained by exploiting the vulnerabilities of less favoured workers. No wonder 'aristocratic' leadership of working-class militancy corrupted proletarian class interest. Labour aristocrats supposedly embodied the most disruptive features of both social mobility and workshop authority: they, more than other workers, dreamed of

Discipline in Nineteenth-Century France', in J. Merriman (ed.), *Consciousness and Class Experience in Nineteenth-Century Europe* (New York, 1979), p. 159; P. Fridenson, 'Un Tournant Taylorien de la Société Française (1904–1918)', *Annales: Économies, Sociétés, Civilisations*, vol. 42, 1987, pp. 1,040–1; and Stearns, *Lives of Labour*, pp. 177–9.

ascension to the bourgeoisie and they, more than other workers, aspired to the foreman's privileges. Marx and Engels themselves had attributed socialist failure in nineteenth-century Britain to the 'lib-lab' political complacency and class-collaborationist social deference of this favoured stratum, which dominated the British labour movement between the mid-century collapse of Chartism and the rise of the 'New Unionism' at the end of the 1880s.[27] Nevertheless, the first generation of Marxists largely ignored this insight, until Leninists rediscovered the labour aristocracy as an explanation of social-democratic 'treason'. Convinced that the capitalist mode of production inexorably homogenised the working class, confident that all workers shared a unitary class interest, the 'Orthodox Marxists' of the Second International failed (refused?) to recognise that workers who sold their labour advantageously often sold out less advantaged workers.[28]

French Marxists infrequently implied that self-satisfied labour aristocrats, disdained by Lafargue as 'half-bourgeois artisans',[29] might disrupt working-class unity. But Guesdists never explicitly elaborated this argument, although it evidently underpinned their pejorative identification of anti-Marxist Possibilists or Ministerialists as political expressions of a reactionary artisanal elite. The French Marxists' only sustained analyses of the 'labour aristocracy' centred upon the United Kingdom, where, like Marx and Engels, they attributed the frustrating political quiescence of the powerful British labour movement to the treason of its aristocrats.[30] Guesdists self-confidently contended that, by contrast, their own 'proletarian elite has already been conquered [for socialism]'.[31] Utterly convinced of the ascendancy of class interest over individual or corporative interests, Guesdists argued that 'the industrial elite does not form an aristocracy, since it cannot liberate itself from capitalist

[27] H. Draper, *Karl Marx's Theory of Revolution: The Politics of Social Class* (New York, 1978), pp. 105–8 describes Marx's views. For critical analysis of the use of this concept in Marxist discourse, see M. Nicolaus, 'The Theory of the Labor Aristocracy', *Monthly Review*, April 1970, pp. 91–101 and H. Moorhouse, 'The Marxist Theory of the Labour Aristocracy', *Social History*, vol. 3, 1978, pp. 61–82.

[28] See the critique of Marxist complacency in A. Friedman, *Industry and Labour*, pp. 53 and 79.

[29] P. Lafargue, untitled article, *L'Égalité*, 1 January 1882.

[30] 'P.L.', 'Les Trades-Unions', *Le Socialiste*, 26 September 1891. The Guesdists never drew Leninist connections between imperialist 'superprofits' and the privileges of the labour aristocracy, being convinced that imperialism 'only benefited the cosmopolitan element of the capitalist class'. Anonymous, 'Au Conseil Municipal – Ivry', *Bulletin Mensuel de la Fédération des Élus du Parti Ouvrier Français*, Première Année, no. 2, 1 January 1900, p. 6.

[31] A. Delon, 'Une Trahison', *Le Socialiste*, 19 January 1896.

oppression without liberating all society with the support of the working-class masses. Indeed, it is from this elite that the natural leaders of the proletarian revolution arise'.[32] The Parti Ouvrier believed in a labour aristocracy, but in a *socialist* labour aristocracy, a 'pure elite of the proletarian class, an elite of intelligence, skill, and spiritual culture, a moral elite, an elite of sobriety and honesty, an elite above all of courage and generosity'.[33] This exalted imagery systematically obscured the top-hatted class-traitors of Victorian trade unionism, undoubtedly intelligent and skilled, usually sober and honest, even cultured and moral, but rarely (by Marxist standards) courageous and generous.

How could Guesdists ignore the divisive role played by privileged workers within proletarian society – a role as evident in the French Republican labour movement as in the British lib-labs, as apparent with Parisian printers as with Birmingham engineers? Easily. The French Marxists' dismissal of the labour aristocracy dilemma arose from their absolutist understanding of the capitalist mode of production. Capitalism supposedly demolished every barrier to extraction of surplus-value, thereby guaranteeing that 'disappearance of some workers' privileged positions will eliminate one of the worst obstacles in our path. From being allies of the bourgeoisie against their fellow workers – from which a relative well-being distinguishes them – these specialised workers ... will take up arms against the common enemy'.[34] In retrospect only a pious hope, this thesis must have enjoyed considerable credibility during the *Fin de Siècle*. 'Elite' workers of various kinds, France's 'labour aristocrats', animated most of the period's labour and socialist militancy: the most highly paid and highly skilled workers in factories initiated the novel industrial unionism which marked the *Belle Époque*, while the workshop artisans who had dominated French labour protest since the eighteenth century sustained the 'socialism of skilled workers' into the twentieth.[35] What is more, once labour aristocrats realised

---

[32] Anonymous, 'Constitution du Prolétariat', *L'Égalité*, 18 March 1880.

[33] A. Delon, 'La Voyoucratie Socialiste-Révolutionnaire', *Le Socialiste*, 6 October 1895.

[34] J. Guesde, 'Quelques Effets de la Loi sur l'Enseignement Primaire Obligatoire', *L'Égalité*, 1 April 1882.

[35] D. Vasseur, *Les Débuts du Mouvement Ouvrier dans la Région Belfort-Montbélliard 1870–1914* (Paris, 1967), p. 50; M. Hanagan, 'Urbanisation, Worker Settlement Patterns, and Social Protest in Nineteenth-Century France', in J. Merriman (ed.), *French Cities in the Nineteenth Century* (London, 1982), pp. 219–20; and R. Aminzade, 'French Strike Development and Class Struggle: The Development of the Strike in Mid-Nineteenth-Century Toulouse', *Social Science History*, vol. 4, 1980, pp. 57–79. This argument is generalised in B. Moss, *The*

the value of working-class solidarity in an age of mass organisation and democratic politics, this minority of the skilled, organised and militant, although traditionally contemptuous of labourers, increasingly sought the support of the unskilled, unorganised, and dependent, thereby legitimating the Guesdists' identification of 'the industrial elite' as 'the natural leaders of the proletarian revolution'.[36] Without the labour aristocracy, the French labour and socialist movements would unquestionably have failed miserably.

Yet the age-old conflict between artisan and labourer persisted: at the extremes, two proletariats coalesced in France during the nineteenth century – one skilled, organised and well-paid; the other unskilled, unorganised, and impoverished.[37] Guesdist discourse implicitly admitted as much in its contrasting theories of proletarian revolution – one of which relied upon the capacities of the working class, repository of all society's creativity; the other reliant upon pauperisation and desperation. But the Parti Ouvrier, against copious evidence, ignored conflicts between the confortable working-class elite and the impoverished proletarian masses, conflicts which none the less permeated working-class society. Many skilled workers of the *Fin de Siècle* (particularly in the building trades) still hired their unskilled helpers, exploiting others' labour even as capitalists exploited theirs – an entrepreneurial framework virtually guaranteed to disrupt class solidarity between, for instance, masons and builders' labourers.[38] No wonder the Parti Ouvrier campaigned relentlessly against this system of 'marchandage', although the Party prudishly veiled the otherwise obvious intra-class conflicts inherent in labour subcontracting. At the same time, despite the levelling effects of the capitalist mode of production, extraordinary

Origins of the French Labor Movement 1830–1914: The Socialism of Skilled Workers (Berkeley, 1976).

[36] This is the basic argument of M. Hanagan, *The Logic of Solidarity: Artisans and Industrial Workers in Three French Towns 1871–1914* (London, 1980), particularly pp. 20–5. See also the fascinating instance illuminated by J.-P. Martin, 'Une Culture Militante à l'Époque du Syndicalisme Révolutionnaire: Les Métallurgistes de l'Ondaine', *Cahiers d'Histoire*, vol. 21, 1982, pp. 316–17.

[37] For the two proletariats, see A. Daumard, 'L'Évolution des Structures Sociales', pp. 330–1 and p. 342. Their disputes are described in P. Stearns, *Lives of Labour*, p. 106; P. Pigenet et al., *Terre des Luttes: Histoire du Mouvement Ouvrier dans le Cher* (Paris, 1977), p. 29; and M. Stein, 'The Meaning of Skill: The Case of the French Engine-Drivers 1837–1917', *Politics and Society*, vol. 8, 1978, p. 409.

[38] M. Hanagan, 'Organisation du Travail et Action Revendicative: Verriers et Métallurgistes de Rive-de-Giers à la Fin du XIXᵉ Siècle', *Cahiers d'Histoire*, vol. 26, 1981, p. 21. For the (disruptive) class implications of this traditional system, see M. Dobb, *Studies in the Development of Capitalism* (New York, 1947), pp. 266–8.

extremes of income and wealth divided proletarian communities. The tiny labour aristocracy of Lille, for instance, owned approximately 75 per cent of the city's working-class wealth – a maldistribution which excavated a gulf between proletarian prosperity and proletarian destitution almost as wide as that between labour aristocrats and bourgeois, and vastly wider than that between labour aristocrats and petits bourgeois.[39] No wonder Guesdists subscribed to the dubious Lassallean 'iron law of wages', the 'law' which supposedly precluded working-class property accumulation. Unskilled workers sometimes even welcomed Taylorisation, the 'rationalisation' of the workplace against which skilled workers struggled so heroically: aspiring labourers understandably viewed destruction of traditional trade practices and simplification of complex labour processes rather more favourably than did privileged artisans.[40] No wonder Guesdists proclaimed the universality of proletarianisation, thereby obscuring the conflict of interest between beneficiaries of the 'primary' and victims of the 'secondary' labour markets. A multitude of privileges and grievances severed the elite of the working class from the bulk of the proletariat – multitudinous reasons for the Parti Ouvrier's systematic shunning of Marx's pessimistic (and perceptive) assessment of the labour aristocracy.

In practice, French Marxists struggled to impose labour solidarity upon a recalcitrant working-class elite, their peremptory theses rhetorically extirpating conflict between proletarian and proletarian by denying its existence, or even its possibility. Paradoxically, the Guesdists' simplistic rhetoric indicated the complexity of the subject they sought to master: labour aristocrats oscillated unpredictably between contradictory patterns of militancy – resisting capital's encroachments as champions of a united working class when economic and political conditions warranted 'inclusionary strategies', exploiting their advantages over other workers by 'exclusionary strategies' when the aspirations of less fortunate proletarians jeopardised 'aristocratic' privileges. Indeed, elite workers have regularly pursued inclusionary and exclusionary strategies simultaneously, although inclusion has understandably predominated

[39] Codaccioni, *De l'Inégalité Sociale*, pp. 204–5.
[40] P. Stearns, *Lives of Labour*, pp. 205–8.

during periods of prosperity and exclusion during depressions.[41]
The Parti Ouvrier, however, never recognised or theorised these
alternatives, although labour aristocrats' inclusionary militancy
legitimated the Guesdist rhetoric of unity while their exclusionary
strategies necessitated it. Solidarity, not sociology, inspired Parti
Ouvrier polemic.

'The industrial reserve army', Marx's classic characterisation of
unemployed workers, has also contributed to the 'unmaking of the
working class' – conflict between the employed and the unemployed
has systematically disrupted proletarian unity throughout the nineteenth and twentieth centuries, thereby posing formidable interpretive quandaries for frustrated Marxists.[42] Strike-breaking by otherwise unemployed blacklegs has discouraged trade unionism; the risk
of dismissal has deterred socialist engagement by vulnerable
employees; while the misery and cost of mass unemployment have
focused social debate upon the imperatives of charity or the evils of
dependency, rather than upon the clash between labour and
property. Conflicts between the defensive employed and the desperate unemployed have generated some of the most envenomed social
conflicts of the past century, above all reinforcing national and racial
hostilities between workers where immigrant labour has swollen the
'industrial reserve army', thus repeatedly discrediting the Marxist
ideal of proletarian solidarity.

Guesdists could not altogether ignore this issue, however much
they may have wished to do so. Although the number of French
unemployed declined considerably after the depression of the 1880s,
most industrial workers expected to suffer unemployment during
their working lives, and the increasing security of the *Belle Époque*

---

[41] For the useful distinction between exclusionary and inclusionary social strategies, see F.
Parkin, 'Strategies of Social Closure', in F. Parkin (ed.), *The Social Analysis of Class Structure
(London, 1974), pp. 24–26. There is discussion of the labour aristocracy in terms of these alternatives in
D. Unger, 'Labor Aristocrats and Class Consciousness', International Labor and Working Class
History*, no. 13, 1978, pp. 26–30 and C. Sabel, *Work and Politics: The Division of Labour in
Industry* (Cambridge, 1983), pp. 167–79. Useful descriptions of this ambiguity among
French labour aristocrats may be found in Vasseur, *Les Débuts du Mouvement Ouvrier dans la
Région Belfort-Montbélliard*, p. 40 and P. Barral, *Le Département de l'Isère sous la III* République:
Histoire Sociale et Politique* (Paris, 1962), pp. 209–10.

[42] K. Marx, *Wage Labour and Capital*, in K. Marx and F. Engels, *Collected Works* (London,
1977), vol, 9, pp. 225–7 and K. Marx, *Capital* (Moscow, 1954), vol. 1, pp. 602–3. See the
useful discussion of Marxist approaches to unemployment in H. Braverman, *Labor and
Monopoly Capital: The Degradation of Work in the Twentieth Century* (New York, 1974), pp.
386–9.

may have rendered this unemployment all the more daunting to proletarians increasingly unaccustomed to its rigours.[43] The permanent pool of unemployed, although contracting at the turn of the century, remained a permanent reservoir of scab labour, thereby sustaining the traditional hatred of 'marginal' (a word with ironic economic connotations) workers among the 'respectable' (and regularly employed) working class. Many enterprises organised themselves around a nucleus of permanently employed skilled workers, precious commodities to be hoarded under all but the worst circumstances, with a penumbra of casual labourers, easily dispensable except during the most sustained booms – thereby establishing a 'dual labour market' which fostered corporative exclusivity among the fortunate 'permanents', passive despair among the 'casuals', and systematic conflict between the two categories.[44] How did Guesdists respond to these structures of labour disunity, to these forces of working-class demobilisation?

They made the best of a bad job, arguing that the systematic generation of unemployment by capitalism raised 'an issue of revolutionary significance',[45] that the mere existence of the 'industrial reserve army' damned capitalism beyond redemption. The atrocious suffering of the unemployed, the endemic insecurity of casual employees, the lurking fear of unemployment among labour aristocrats – all condemned the bourgeois economic regime as inhumane, irrational, and doomed. Few issues of *Le Socialiste* passed without repetition of this passionate indictment. None the less, Guesdists had to concede that unemployment engendered 'hatred

---

[43] M. Perrot, 'La Classe Ouvrière au Temps de Jaurès', in *Jaurès et la Classe Ouvrière* (Paris, 1981), p. 74. Perrot cites estimates of unemployment ranging from 3.4 to 8.5 per cent of the industrial work force for the period in her 'Les Classes Populaires Urbaines', p. 484. Unemployment among industrial workers during the 1880s was even higher, reaching ten per cent, according to G. Noiriel, *Les Ouvriers dans la Société Française*, pp. 88–9. For the unemployed as strikebreakers, even in the most skilled trades, see the striking instance of the Jura watchmakers in J. Charles, *Les Débuts du Mouvement Syndical à Besançon* (Paris, 1962), p. 75.

[44] For this pattern of labour recruitment and its disruptive effects, see the discussion in Stearns, *Lives of Labour*, pp. 91–2 and p. 100; L. Marty, *Chanter pour Survivre: Culture Ouvrière, Travail et Technique dans le Textile à Roubaix (1850–1914)* (Lille, 1982), p. 69; and M. Lévy-Leboyer, 'Innovation and Business Strategies in Nineteenth and Twentieth-Century France', in E. Carter et al. (eds.), *Managerial Hierarchies: Comparative Perspectives on the Rise of the Modern Industrial Enterprise* (London, 1980), pp. 94–5. For the disarray created within the French workers' movement by these labour relations, see Gras, 'Presse Syndicale et Mentalités', pp. 58–9.

[45] P. Lafargue, 'Les Ouvriers Étrangers', *Le Socialiste*, 9 July 1887.

and disunity between workers',[46] that the desperation of unemployed workers bolstered the very capitalist system which had destroyed their livelihood. But, ever optimistic, the Parti Ouvrier anticipated that organisational ties between the unemployed and the employed would eventually counter disunity, that self-interested solidarity would someday prevail against shortsighted selfishness. Led by the POF, the most steadily employed artisans and the most casually employed labourers would enrol together in the socialist campaign against an economic system which begot apprehension and insecurity among the employed and inflicted suffering and demoralisation upon the jobless. 'No workers' organisation', proclaimed the French Marxists, 'may refuse this unity without becoming an accomplice of capitalism'.[47]

Guesdists, however, never analysed the 'objective' interests which sundered the employed from the unemployed. The Parti Ouvrier systematically ignored the high wages and restrictive practices which limited the labour market by confining the wage fund to a privileged circle and by fostering labour-saving innovation. To acknowledge the salience of these labour-market mechanisms, mechanisms so often adduced by 'bourgeois' economists, would, on the one hand, have conceded the existence of a community of interest between capitalist 'rationalisers' and unemployed workers, and on the other, admitted a conflict of interest between the securely employed members of the proletariat and its 'marginal' unfortunates – admissions which would have seriously compromised the Guesdists' Manichean image of French society. Eschewing serious study of the labour-market, French Marxists relied instead upon the anticapitalist community of interest between the employed and the unemployed, the one exploited and the other victimised by capitalism – a rhetorical strategy designed to encourage the harmony which it purportedly described. Yet rhetoric failed. The Parti Ouvrier hardly touched the unemployed, who seldom subscribed to systematic ideologies or participated in sustained militancy. Anarchists, voluntarist and libertarian, captured the sporadic and incoherent protest of jobless workers more often than did socialists, whose intellectual discipline and organisational rigour, however alluring to 'labour

---

[46] J. Dormoy, 'Exploitation des Ouvriers Métallurgistes', *Le Socialiste*, 26 March 1887.
[47] 'Aux Travailleurs de Paris', 1882 handbill in the Fonds Guesde, IISG, no. 551/4.

aristocrats', thoroughly alienated demoralised and desocialised 'marginals'.[48]

The vexed relationship between the employed and the unemployed has repeatedly raised a further issue in Marxist class analysis: the problem of the 'lumpenproletariat', the dependent and 'unemployable' underclass which has characterised capitalism since its inception, the 'dangerous class' of paupers and criminals so often associated with the proletariat in bourgeois polemic. Unfortunately, Marx himself proposed only the most fragmentary and unsatisfactory solutions to the conundrums posed by the lumpenproletariat, and subsequent Marxist social and historical thought has systematically neglected the underclass, relegating it to insignificance as a residual category or ignoring it altogether. Yet the analytic of labour and property which structures the Marxist paradigm has clearly designated 'space' for an underclass of 'unemployed' paupers and criminals, an insalubrious social location inhabited by those who neither laboured (unlike the proletariat and the petite bourgeoisie) nor owned productive property (unlike the bourgeoisie and the petite bourgeoisie). Marxists have failed to explore one of the smaller but more exotic alcoves in their labyrinthine ideological edifice.

Worse yet, on the rare occasions when Marxists have investigated the place of dependency and criminality in the social order, they have rarely exploited the analytical clarity of their own axiomatic, instead conflating marginal elements of the proletariat with the non-working dependent poor and confusing underclass dependency with privileged parasitism. Marx himself often employed the expression 'lumpenproletarian' as an indiscriminate term of abuse, an expletive denoting the servile, predatory, or parasitic social groups he particularly despised – whether deferential servants or bold criminals, the most brutalised elements of the working proletariat or non-working paupers, bourgeois 'adventurers' or plutocratic financiers. Later Marxists have accentuated this unfortunate imprecision, relegating every marginal and 'deviant' denizen of modern society, including economically marginal and socially deviant workers, to the despised

[48] C. Willard, *Le Mouvement Socialiste en France (1893–1905): Les Guesdistes* (Paris, 1965), p. 350. For the anarchism of the unemployed, see Y. Lequin, *Les Ouvriers de la Région Lyonnaise: Les Intérêts de Classe et la République* (Lyons, 1977), p. 283 and J. Kergoat, 'France', in M. van der Linden and J. Rojahn (eds.), *The Formation of Labour Movements 1870–1914: An International Perspective* (Leiden, 1990), vol. 1, p. 189.

lumpenproletariat. Whether Marxists have employed the concept analytically, labelling a distinct non-working and non-property-owning class, or polemically, libelling the marginal and the deviant, they have agreed that the lumpenproletariat possesses no independent historical role equivalent to that of the bourgeoisie or the proletariat. At the most, according to long Marxist tradition, lumpenproletarians would serve those who bribed them most lavishly.[49]

However dependent and parasitic their casting, lumpenproletarians have frequently played walk-on roles in Marxist historical dramaturgy – but only as servile auxiliaries of the wealthy and powerful. Marx's angry and frustrated analyses of mid-nineteenth-century France accorded the lumpenproletariat a significant part in the epic politics of the Second Republic as brutal agents of the bourgeoisie during the reactionary massacres of the June Days and as corrupt militants of Bonapartism during Louis Napoleon's tragi-comic rise to power, an interpretation of underclass politics which foreshadowed similar analyses of Blackshirts and Stormtroopers by equally angry and frustrated Comintern theorists. Guesdists, by contrast, awarded lumpenproletarians far less prominence in their portrayals of *fin-de-siècle* politics. Why this hiatus? The Parti Ouvrier's relative indifference to the lumpenproletariat undoubtedly reflected changes in the French social structure since Marx's mid-century: the 'dangerous class' of paupers and criminals which had so frightened and disgusted *bien pensant* bourgeois and moralistic socialists during the 1840s and 1850s had dwindled in numbers and influence by the *Fin de Siècle*.[50] Lumpenproletarians mattered less to Guesdists than they had to Marx because lumpenproletarians mattered less to turn-of-the-century French society.

All the same, beggars, criminals, and paupers had hardly vanished from France's church steps, prisons and slums: at least 100,000 *clochards* (bums) survived on the streets of Paris at the

[49] H. Draper, 'The Concept of the "Lumpenproletariat" in Marx and Engels', *Économies et Sociétés: Cahiers de l'ISEA – Série S*, no. 15, 1972, pp. 2285–302; F. Bovenkerk, 'The Rehabilitation of the Rabble: How and Why Marx and Engels Wrongly Depicted the Lumpenproletariat as a Reactionary Force', *Netherlands Journal of Sociology*, vol. 20, 1984, pp. 13–41; and D. Hodges, 'Class Analysis and its Presuppositions', *American Journal of Economics and Sociology*, vol. 20, 1960, pp. 23–8.

[50] P. Sorlin, *La Société Française 1840–1914*, pp. 121–2 and M. Perrot, 'Les Classes Populaires Urbaines', in *Histoire Économique et Sociale de la France: Tome IV – L'Ère Industrielle et la Société d'Aujourd'hui (Siècle 1880–1980): Premier Volume – Ambiguïtés des Débuts et Croissance Effective (Années 1880–1914)* (Paris, 1979), pp. 462–4.

dawning of the twentieth-century, importuning the prosperous and sleeping rough; wild bands of 'apaches' descended from the noisome heights of Belleville to terrorise the capital (or so feared readers of the popular press); the indigent proliferated during the 1880s and 1890s even in the Guesdist stronghold of Lille, that archetypical industrial metropolis; and the nascent welfare state engendered the 'welfare class' which would eventually feature so prominently in the class-consciousness of 'post-industrial' society.[51] Fixated upon the working class rather than the underclass, Guesdists systematically neglected the latter. But French Marxists realised that the lumpen-proletariat existed, and on occasion recognised its numerical weight: scrutinising official statistics, the Parti Ouvrier calculated that 6 per cent of the French population vegetated as 'indigents, mendiants et vagabonds'.[52] How did Guesdists portray this considerable 'class' on the rare occasions when they conceded its significance?

First, they rarely defined the group with any precision: as in Marx's more intemperate outbursts, 'lumpenproletariat' served French Marxists as a catch-all term of abuse. The 'parasitic fleas' which sucked the blood of the 'bourgeois fleas' which preyed upon the proletariat included, according to Lafargue, 'statesmen, soldiers, magistrates, lackeys, and prostitutes',[53] a hate-list fully as haphazard and untheorised as any formulated by his father-in-law. Once embarked upon this course, Guesdists dumped virtually everyone they despised (apart from industrialists) into the lumpen-proletarian dust-bin, a strategy which indiscriminately jumbled ragged beggars with sleek establishment politicians, jewel thieves with the criminal police who pursued them, lawyers with the prostitutes they patronised and prosecuted – associations developed to the great advantage of Guesdist polemic but to the considerable detriment of Guesdist theory. By any serious theoretical criterion, the penumbra of privileged retainers which radiated from the bourgeois monolith differed enormously from the detritus of indigent underlings at its feet.

---

[51] For the bums of Paris, see Perrot, 'Les Classes Populaires Urbaines', p. 463; on the 'apaches', G. Jacquemet, 'Belleville Ouvrier à la Belle Époque', *Mouvement Social*, no. 118, 1982, pp. 61–77; and for Lille, F.-P. Codaccioni, *De l'Inégalité Sociale*, pp. 206–27 and pp. 392–4.

[52] 'La Semaine', *Le Socialiste*, 2 April 1899.

[53] P. Lafargue, 'La Production Capitaliste', *L'Égalité*, 24 September 1882. (Reprinted word for word as 'Caractère Fatidique des Misères Prolétariennes', *Le Socialiste*, 18–25 September 1898).

Lafargue's identification of 'lackeys' as lumpenproletarians illustrated a further ambiguity of Guesdist usage (as the rarity of the
reference highlighted the systematic Guesdist neglect of servants).
On the face of it, domestic employees laboured as archetypical
proletarians – working long hours under their employers' supervision, selling their labour for miserable salaries, bereft of productive
property. By the criteria which the Parti Ouvrier applied, how did a
housemaid employed by a Roubaix textile baron differ from a
worker in his mill? The analytic of labour and property apparently
assigned both maidservant and textile worker to the proletariat.
Indeed, domestic servants constituted one of the largest categories of
employees in *fin-de-siècle* France, and one of the worst-paid and
worst-treated.[54] Why, then, did the Parti Ouvrier relegate them to
the despised lumpenproletariat? Unlike some twentieth-century
Marxists, Guesdists never contended that servants' wages derived
from bourgeois 'revenue' (the personal income of individuals) rather
than from 'variable capital' (the wage-bill of enterprises), and that
'lackeys' thereby fell into a different class from 'real' workers.[55]
Guesdists evinced little interest in the value theory which had
fascinated Marx, and demonstrated still less skill in its manipulation
– not for Guesdists the subtle distinctions between 'productive' and
'unproductive' labour characteristic of *Theories of Surplus Value* or
twentieth-century 'neo-Marxism'.

Instead, the Parti Ouvrier, for once a faithful reflection of its
constituency's mentality, excluded servants from the working class
because Guesdists shared the widespread popular contempt for
domestics, long despised by artisans and even labourers for their
dependency and servility. The most impoverished textile worker
considered herself superior to the most superior upper servant:
however poor, however insecure, she lived independently; no
employer supervised her private life. What is more, Guesdists had no
hope of mobilising 'lackeys' into the labour movement, even if the
Parti Ouvrier had cared to attempt this unlikely feat. Despite their
impressive numbers, servants demonstrated no organisational potential or awareness of collective interest, and for good reason: domestic

---

54 For the importance of servants during the period, see T. Zeldin, *France 1848–1945: Ambition
   and Love* (Oxford, 1973), p. 14. Their working and living conditions are described in Perrot,
   'Les Classes Populaires Urbaines', pp. 460–461 and Codaccioni, *De L'Inégalité Sociale*, pp.
   205–6.
55 This distinction receives a useful discussion and critique in J. O'Connor, 'Productive and
   Unproductive Labor', *Politics and Society*, vol. 5, 1975, pp. 297–336.

employees, working individually or in groups of two or three, enjoyed little contact with other servants; many had migrated from the provinces to metropolitan stations, and enjoyed none of the community solidarities which empowered the labour militancy of more rooted employees; most were girls or women, many of whom envisaged their time in service as a transient opportunity to accumulate savings before returning to their villages and marriage; and all suffered the stifling tyranny of incessant close supervision by their employers.[56] The French Marxists' relegation of servants to the despised lumpenproletariat indicated the centrality of independent organisation and self-assertive militancy in the Guesdist conception of the proletariat, as well as the limits of that conception.

Indeed, according to the Parti Ouvrier, lumpenproletarians in general lacked organisational potential and collective identity.[57] French Marxists saw no opportunity to recruit among the destitute, the dependent, and the criminal. The mere existence of paupers and prostitutes indicted bourgeois society, but beggars and whores supposedly lacked both the inclination and the capacity to challenge the social order which impoverished and brutalised them. Not that the Parti Ouvrier would have welcomed lumpenproletarians to its ranks; Guesdists cordially detested those who resorted to crime or charity to sustain themselves. Confronted by pauperism, dependency, and social 'deviance', the Parti Ouvrier fastidiously turned away. Charles Bonnier spoke for his comrades when he wrote peremptorily that 'we will have nothing to do with such types'.[58] Why this categorical Guesdist disparagement of the underclass? How did the Parti Ouvrier justify its calculated indifference towards the most degraded victims of capitalism?

In theory, lumpenproletarians, who neither owned property nor worked, might have aligned themselves with either propertyless

---

[56] For Guesdists' attitudes, see, for instance, P. Lafargue, 'M. Herbert Spencer et le Socialisme', *L'Ère Nouvelle*, no. 5, 1894, pp. 45–6. The impossibility of organising domestic servants is stressed in Sorlin, *La Société Française*, p. 155 and in Perrot, 'Les Classes Populaires Urbaines', pp. 460–1. But see the challenge to this orthodoxy in J. McMillan, *Housewife or Harlot: The Place of Women in French Society 1870–1940* (New York, 1981), p. 73. For working-class hostility towards domestic servants, see M. Perrot, 'On the Formation of the French Working Class', pp. 98–9.

[57] The one exception to this general indictment occured in an investigation by 'J.P.' (Phalippou) into the extent of destitution and dependency among the non-working poor of Paris. The researcher concluded that 'if this army of charity cases joined with the wage workers' then capitalist society could easily be overthrown. 'J.P.', 'La Misère à Paris', *Le Socialiste*, 15 January 1899.

[58] 'B' (Bonnier), 'Les Vêpres d'Aigues-Mortes', *Le Socialiste*, 6 January 1894.

workers or with non-working bourgeois. But, in practice, Guesdists assumed that the dependent underclass survived as 'parasites on the parasites',[59] that parasitic lumpenproletarians inevitably gravitated towards the parasitic bourgeoisie: prostitutes 'naturally' sought wealthy clients, thieves rich victims, beggars affluent benefactors – lumpenproletarian survival depended upon bourgeois affluence. At its most conspiratorial and paranoid, the Parti Ouvrier even alleged that capitalists intentionally nurtured the lumpenproletariat 'in order to fulfil [the bourgeoisie's] double function as non-producer and over-consumer'.[60] Bourgeois vice and bourgeois largess supported the 'undeserving' poor, and they in turn supported the bourgeoisie. Under these circumstances, the ruling class always 'found [lumpenproletarians] ready to hand when they need a riot to frighten the shopkeepers, or when they need an *agent-provocateur*'.[61] Maurice Barrès's account of the rough vitality and picaresque imagination of the Parisian underworld evoked the acerbic Guesdist retort that such empathy with lumpenproletarians might be expected from a licensed mouthpiece of the bourgeoisie, but that, for socialists,

these milieux . . . offer us little of interest. We consider them to be the direct product of capitalism, and the beings who compose them provide nothing useful for us. If [Barrès] had studied some socialist literature . . . he would have realised that there is a term for such types . . . used by Marx: the 'lumpenproletariat'. This might be poorly translated as 'canaille', the sweepings of pimps, journalists, prostitutes, lackeys, and psychological writers, in brief, all the gang who support the bourgeoisie because they are supported by it.[62]

Guesdists frequently reiterated this theme of symbiosis between under-class and ruling class, a theme which blackened the bourgeoisie by inverting the century-old conservative fusion of working class with 'dangerous class'.

Forceful Guesdist polemic, like Marx's similar usage, often violated the fundamental categories of Marxist theory, as with the peculiar list of lumpenproletarians in *Le Socialiste*'s intemperate critique of Barrès. Professional prostitutes, for instance, (at least those exploited by brothel-owners) lived archetypal, if not exemplary, proletarian lives as employees of a classically commodified

59 J. Guesde, *Le Problème et la Solution* (Paris, 1895), p. 14.
60 P. Lafargue, *Le Droit à la Paresse* (Paris, 1883), p. 31.
61 'Bernard', 'Le Cinquième État', *Le Socialiste*, 20 March 1892.
62 'B.', 'Noël Anarchiste', *Le Socialiste*, 30 December 1893.

service industry: they owned no productive property apart from their labour-power; they laboured to produce a commodity owned by their employers; and capital exploited them to produce surplus value. Thus understood, the *maisons surveillées* of Paris, in (Marxist) essence, differed not at all from the textile mills of Roubaix. In theory, Parti Ouvrier militants should have recruited along the Rue Saint-Denis, and Guesdist trade unionists should have encouraged *Syndicats des Prostituées*. In practice, however, French Marxists relegated 'working girls' to the despised lumpenproletariat, to the twilight world of poverty and criminality. Why?

Puritanical hostility towards the unrespectable working class, the undiscriminating Guesdist slogan 'le parasitisme, voilà l'ennemi!',[63] excluded professional prostitutes from the proletariat, just as 'respectable' proletarians excluded them from their communities. Working people had despised and feared the sordid milieu inhabited by prostitutes, criminals, and paupers for centuries, and with good reason. The working class abominated mendicancy, prostitution, and criminality because the three great underworld 'occupations' constituted integral and bitterly resented aspects of the everyday proletarian condition: workers' indigence and dependency awaited only ill-fortune, old-age, or illness; thousands of impoverished working women resorted to casual prostitution during social or personal crises; the endemic alcoholism of the proletarian male eventuated in endemic (bourgeois defined) criminality; and the most brutalised and impoverished workers (male and female) subscribed to the 'irresponsible' mores and hardened conduct of the non-working underclass.[64] Workers' tenuous sense of self-worth depended upon the cultural barriers they raised between themselves and lumpenproletarians, barriers high in proportion to the intimate interpenetration of the two classes. Barrès might well romanticise the Parisian *canaille* – unlike Parisian workers, he did not risk its realities. In the Guesdist approach to the lumpenproletariat, the prejudices, fears, and aspirations of the respectable working class, the seed-bed of socialism, overwhelmed the theoretical imperatives of the Marxist

---

[63] 'Appel aux Travailleurs de France, du Conseil National, le 13 mars 1892', in G. Bracke (ed.), *Onze Ans d'Histoire Socialiste: Aux Travailleurs de France* (Paris, 1901), pp. 19–20. For this mentality among the constituents of the POF, see M. Perrot, *Les Ouvriers en Grève: France 1871–1890* (Paris, 1974), vol. 2, p. 546.

[64] For the impossibility of separating less fortunate workers from the underclass, see Jacquemet, *Belleville au XIX' Siècle*, p. 336.

analytic. The designation lumpenproletarian served as an emblem of cultural exclusion rather than a mark of social understanding.

Finally, the challenge to Marxist class analysis and class politics posed by a nascent 'welfare class' assumes considerable importance in retrospect, although at the time constituting only a minor theme in the Guesdist analysis of dependency. The twentieth-century welfare state has fundamentally reoriented social consciousness since the Guesdists' era: centring political polemic upon the suffering of the dependent 'poor' (or upon their cost to society) rather than the grievances (or iniquities) of the working class, organising social debate around the allocation of welfare entitlements rather than the conflict between labour and capital, focusing proletarian hatred of parasitism upon dependent 'welfare cases' rather than exploitative bourgeois. Foreshadowing the dilemmas of their social democratic descendants, Guesdist militants who worked in their Party's municipal welfare programmes developed a prescient awareness of how 'bourgeois society ... by leaving to charity and public assistance all the victims it has created, destroys [working-class] morale and makes the formation of social solidarity increasingly difficult'.[65] Bureaucratic surveillance and social services may have tamed the 'classe dangereuse' which had so disturbed Marx and so dismayed his generation's bourgeois social observers, but the poverty and dependency of the unemployed and the unemployable, more than ever, continued to 'give a false direction to the ... interests of the subordinate class'.[66] The insufferable sufferings of the nonworking poor challenged not only Marxist theory, but socialist practice – a challenge which would mount throughout the twentieth century.

The universal commodity market which has increasingly articulated the capitalist mode of production has also increasingly divided the working class, at its most extreme fragmenting an individual worker into self-antagonistic producer and consumer, roles embodying apparently conflicting interests. At the least, higher wages for some workers have implied higher prices for others, if employers could pass on their costs to the market. By other criteria, lower wages for some workers have meant cheaper goods for others, if compe-

---

[65] H. Ghesquière, 'L'Assistance Sociale à Lille', *Bulletin Mensuel de la Fédération Nationale des Élus du Parti Ouvrier Français*, no. 5, 1 April 1900, p. 3.
[66] P. Myrens, 'Les Deux Morales', *Le Socialiste*, 7–14 July 1891.

tition ruled price-fixing.[67] Butchers' well-being imposed expensive meat upon bakers, while bakers' impoverishment bestowed cheap bread upon butchers – no recipe for labour solidarity in the food industry. Conflict between workers as consumers and workers as producers has repeatedly disrupted the labour movement, for all Marx's lifelong conviction that production, not consumption, governed the proletarian condition. Despite the best efforts of socialists, an individualist 'consumer mentality' has too often prevailed against collectivist producer solidarity, thereby fundamentally challenging the Marxist conception of the 'making of the working class'.[68]

France did not escape this logic of disintegration, although the labour movement between the mid-nineteenth-century eclipse of traditional popular protest and the twentieth-century rise of 'consumerism' apparently embodied (male) workers preeminently as producers, to the virtual exclusion of their role as consumers. But, behind the organisational facade of trade unions and beneath the ideological rhetoric of socialist parties, tensions evoked by 'the cost of living' permeated the everyday life of working-class *faubourgs*, and prices obsessed the proletarian women who fought so heroically in the front line of their class's daily battle to make ends meet – tensions and obsessions which culminated in the great revolt of 1911–1912 against 'la vie chère'. Well aware of their employees' desperate preoccupation with the tragic mismatch between low wages and high prices, militant employers diverted proletarians from trade union demands and socialist propaganda by indicting the workers' movement as selfish in the short term and short-sighted in the long term, its transient victories more likely to victimise proletarian consumers than harm capitalist 'exploiters' – an indictment which struck home among the hundreds of thousands of working-class families which teetered insecurely on the border between subsistence and destitution.[69] How did the Parti Ouvrier, productivist to its ideological core, master these dispiriting circumstances?

On rare occasions, Guesdists recognised the 'antagonism between seller and buyer'[70] which sundered various categories of workers. This antagonism justified the Parti Ouvrier's determined opposition

---

[67] For an elaboration of this contradiction, see A. Gorz, 'Work and Consumption', in P. Anderson and R. Blackburn (eds.), *Towards Socialism* (Ithaca, 1966), pp. 317–53.

[68] For this Marxist assumption in Marx's case, see K. Marx, *A Contribution to the Critique of Political Economy* (Moscow, 1970), p. 200.

[69] Perrot, 'La Classe Ouvrière au Temps de Jaurès', pp. 74–5.

[70] J. Guesde, *Double Réponse à MM. de Mun et Paul Deschanel* (Paris, 1900), p. 13.

to the 'premature' establishment of publicly-owned enterprises. Guesdists, for instance, violently attacked the creation of municipally-owned bakeries in Paris, a favourite scheme of their 'Possibilist' enemies, those archetypical 'gas and water socialists'. The Parti Ouvrier maintained that this proposal, if implemented, would direct the animus of a hungry Parisian working class against communally employed bakery workers, who would 'naturally' exact the highest possible price for their labour and its product, thereby forcing socialists into a Hobson's choice between two proletarian constituencies, one composed of producers and the other of consumers.[71] The corrosive secretions of the cash nexus would dissolve the proletariat, if workers bought from workers.

Guesdists, however, denied that friction between workers as consumers and workers as producers jeopardised proletarian solidarity so long as the means of production remained in private hands. Competition between capitalists supposedly ensured that wage increases for some workers would not result in higher prices for others: bakery workers might triumph over their (private) employers without the slightest harm to the poorest proletarian shopper. Hence, according to *Le Socialiste*, 'workers shouldn't worry about increasing the price of goods by increasing their own pay. It's only the employers' profits which will suffer from an increase in salaries, and that should be the least of workers' concerns'.[72] This argument may have heartened striking bakers and reassured impoverished buyers of *baguettes*, but it blithely violated the Guesdists' conviction that the capitalist mode of production tended inexorably towards monopoly, that capitalists increasingly set prices in spite of rather than because of competition, and that trade unionists laboured futilely, like Sisyphus, to shove wages up an inflationary hill. As so often in Guesdist discourse, the urgent imperative of polemical efficacy prevailed over the abstract necessity of theoretical consistency.

French Marxists, fortunately, never faced the agonising choices imposed by war, invasion, and occupation, the fate of their predecessors in the First International and their successors in the SFIO

---

[71] J. Guesde, 'Un Dernier Mot', *Le Cri du Peuple*, 10 October 1884 and J. Guesde, 'Pour la Taxation', *Le Socialiste*, 25 June 1887.
[72] Anonymous, 'Les Salaires et le Prix des Marchandises', *Le Socialiste*, 27 February 1886.

and the Comintern. Better yet, Guesdists, unlike the Russian or Austrian Marxists, escaped the immense theoretical and practical difficulties of erecting a socialist edifice upon multinational foundations. But the 'national question' none the less forced itself upon the French Marxists. The problem of immigrant labour, in particular, undermined proletarian solidarity, as hundreds of thousands of foreign workers 'invaded' France during the *Belle Époque*. This invasion lacked the grandeur of Sedan or the Marne, but none the less evoked its own outpouring of chauvinist hysteria, provoked its own resistance movement, and wrote its own casualty lists of dead and wounded. By the 1880s, in the depths of depression, foreign labour already furnished 7 or 8 per cent of France's industrial workforce.[73] And, as the economic boom of the 1890s coincided with the consequences of France's relative demographic stagnation, the figure rapidly increased to 10 per cent, the highest level in Europe.[74] By the early twentieth century an invasion force of 1,150,000 foreign workers had penetrated France – Spaniards and Italians bivouacking in the vineyards of Languedoc and Provence, Belgians consolidating their entrenchments in the northern textile industry, Poles infiltrating the mines and steelworks of Lorraine.[75]

This wave of immigrant labour inundated the industrial citadels of Guesdism, sometimes with catastrophic consequences. The availability of virtually unlimited Belgian labour in Roubaix, for instance, created a cut-throat local labour market 'as close as anyone could come to an ideal Marxist scheme of capitalist exploitation'.[76] The 'reserve army' of labour mobilised by capital in the Nord consisted largely of mercenaries, not conscripts. Under these circumstances, foreign workers weakened trade unionism (their transience, vulnerable legal status, and linguistic disabilities discouraged organisation) and broke strikes (they were frequently recruited as strike-breakers) – characteristics which earned them an unenviable sobriquet as the

---

[73] Perrot, 'Les Classes Populaires Urbaines', p. 459.
[74] Perrot, 'La Classe Ouvrière au Temps de Jaurès', p. 69.
[75] Sorlin, *La Société Française 1840–1914*, p. 167.
[76] D. Landes, 'Religion and Enterprise: The Case of the French Textile Industry', in E. Carter et al. (eds.), *Enterprise and Entrepreneurs in Nineteenth and Twentieth-Century France* (London, 1976), p. 48. For the overall problem of immigrant labour in Roubaix, see J. Reardon, 'Belgian and French Workers in Nineteenth-Century Roubaix', in L. and C. Tilly (eds.), *Class Conflict and Collective Action* (London, 1981), pp. 167–83 and Marty, *Chanter pour Survivre*, pp. 75–80.

'providence of strike-bound factories'.[77] Xenophobic invective suffused workers' discourse at the turn of the century: even thoroughly French strike-breakers were vilified as 'Italians'.[78] Understandably embittered by their increasing subjection to an international labour market, French workers ferociously resisted the alien threat to their precarious well-being, concentrating their fear and fury upon vulnerable foreign labourers rather than the well-protected capitalists who imported them. Inter-communal conflict between French and alien proletarians escalated in proportion to the swelling influx of foreigners, an escalation which sometimes ended in murderous violence.[79] Guesdists would have preferred to ignore these distressing fracas, but could not. Working-class communities which mobilised against foreigners resisted socialist mobilisation: xenophobia and anti-socialism fed upon each other.[80]

For all their internationalism, Guesdists very occasionally succumbed to xenophobia themselves, describing alien workers, in one shameful instance, as 'a jealous and hostile mob which ... having lived off us and spied upon us, will return arms in hand'.[81] This paranoid tirade was an aberration, however. Guesdists usually sym-

---

[77] Contemporary saying cited in Y. Lequin, *Les Ouvriers de la Région Lyonnaise: La Formation de la Classe Ouvrière Régionale* (Lyons, 1977), p. 153. See the discussions of this problem in M. Perrot, 'Les Rapports entre Ouvriers Français et Ouvriers Étrangers (1871–1893)', *Bulletin de la Société d'Histoire Moderne*, vol. 58, 1960, pp. 5–9; R. Trempé, *Les Mineurs de Carmaux 1848–1914*, vol. 1, pp. 159–60; and Perrot, *Les Ouvriers en Grève*, vol. 1, pp. 170–1.

[78] Perrot, *Les Ouvriers en Grève*, vol. 2, p. 519.

[79] There is evidence (Lequin, *Les Intérêts de Classe et la République*, pp. 90–1 and Kergoat, 'France', p. 170) that such conflict increased during the founding years of the POF. And violence against foreign workers was concentrated in areas of Guesdist strength, particularly in the Nord and Pas-de-Calais (Gordon, 'Liberalism and Socialism in the Nord', p. 319 and J.-P. Courtheoux, 'Naissance d'une Conscience de Classe dans le Prolétariat Textile du Nord', *Revue Économique*, vol. 8, 1957, pp. 130–1); Nantes (Y. Guin, *Le Mouvement Ouvrier Nantais*, Paris, 1976, p. 252); and the South-East (Y. Lequin, *Les Intérêts de Classe et la République*, p. 91 and P. Barral, *Le Département de l'Isère sous la IIIe République*, pp. 211–12).

[80] See the discussion of this congruence in C. Collot, 'Le Socialisme en Meuse avant 1914', *Bulletin des Sociétés d'Histoire et d'Archéologie de la Meuse*, no. 5, 1968, pp. 104–5. For useful theoretical analyses of Marxism's engagement with the 'national question', see H. Davis, *Nationalism and Socialism: Marxist and Labor Theories of Nationalism to 1917* (New York, 1967); H. Lefebvre, 'Classe et Nation depuis le *Manifeste* (1848)', *Cahiers Internationaux de Sociologie*, vol. 38, 1965, pp. 31–48; M. Lowy, 'Marxism and the National Question', in R. Blackburn (ed.), *Revolution and Class Struggle: A Reader in Marxist Politics* (London, 1978), pp. 136–60; E. Hobsbawm, 'What is the Worker's Country?', in E. Hobsbawm, *Worlds of Labour: Further Studies in the History of Labour* (London, 1984), pp. 49–65; E. Hobsbawm, 'Some Reflections on Nationalism', in T. Nossiter et al. (eds.), *Imagination and Precision in the Social Sciences: Essays in Memory of Peter Nettl* (Atlantic Heights, N.J., 1972), pp. 49–65; and S. Bloom, *The World of Nations: A Study of the National Implications in the Work of Karl Marx* (New York, 1941) – still one of the best studies of the subject.

[81] A. Delon, *La Revue Philosophique et le Socialisme Intégral* (Paris, undated), p. 729.

pathised with the immigrant worker, described as having been forced into 'the most repugnant and dangerous jobs',[82] character-ised as 'isolated, most often without his family, ignorant of even the language and customs of the country to which he is brought, and thus unable to defend himself. This factory-fodder from Belgium, Italy, Germany, Switzerland – and they haven't given up dreams of China – is perfect for French employers, who can exploit it at will without fearing resistance'.[83] For their part, Guesdists strove to encourage the resistance of this 'factory-fodder', not least by welcoming non-French recruits into the POF. Self-consciously opposing working-class xenophobia, the Parti Ouvrier justifiably prided itself on its foreign membership. Italians and Belgians, responding to their welcome, significantly reinforced the Party in the South-East and the North, reinforcement which supposedly proved that 'for socialism and the Parti Ouvrier Français, there are no frontiers'.[84] Apart from its often remarked filiation with the German Social Democrats, the Parti Ouvrier also assiduously cultivated its Italian connection. Guesde himself had spent part of his Communard exile in Italy, and the POF rejoiced in the continuing interpenetration of the French and Italian socialist move-ments. *Le Socialiste* included occasional Italian-language articles, proudly highlighting the number of Italian Guesdists in POF strongholds such as Grenoble at a time when French workers would

[82] P. Lafargue, 'Les Ouvriers Étrangers', *Le Socialiste*, 9 July 1887.

[83] J. Guesde, 'Misérables et Imbéciles', *Le Cri du Peuple*, 21 February 1885.

[84] 'Le Parti Ouvrier en France – Savoie', *Le Socialiste*, 29 July 1900. For the importance of Belgians in the POF, see C. Strikwerda, 'Regionalism and Internationalism: The Working-Class Movement in the Nord and the Belgian Connection 1871–1914', *Proceedings of the Western Society for French History*, vol. 12, 1984, pp. 221–30. The Parti Ouvrier paid a high political price for its internationalism, its enemies systematically identifying its socialism as 'foreign', and particularly as German in inspiration if not in allegiance. See B. Blick, 'What is Socialism? French Liberal Views in the 1890s', in L. Patsouras (ed.), *Crucible of Socialism* (Atlantic Highlands, 1987), pp. 388 and 392. Even otherwise sensible historians continue to argue that the POF was a sickly German graft upon the spreading tree of French socialism – its 'new imported Marxism' (R. Magraw, 'Socialism, Syndicalism and French Labour before 1914', p. 71) having to be learnt like a foreign language (M. Perrot, 'Controverses sur l'Introduction du Marxisme en France', *Annales: Économies, Sociétés, Civilisations*, vol. 22, 1967, p. 707). See the discussion of this problem in M. Rebérioux, 'Le Socialisme Français de 1871 à 1914', in J. Droz (ed.), *Histoire Générale du Socialisme: Volume II – De 1875 à 1918* (Paris, 1974), p. 148 and the striking instances of its perversion of historical understanding in L. Laurat, 'La Pénétration du Marxism en France', *La Nef*, vol. 7, 1950, pp. 55–63 and D. Lindenberg, 'Marx et les "Mystères de Paris"', in B. Chavance (ed.), *Marx en Perspective* (Paris, 1985), pp. 571–83. Tony Judt is surely correct in arguing that Marxism is no less French than any other general system of thought. T. Judt, *Marxism and the French Left: Studies in Labour and Politics in France 1830–1981* (Oxford, 1986), pp. 17–18.

much rather have driven their Italian 'comrades' back over the Alps than embrace them.[85] Commenting upon the visit to France of a former Italian Guesdist, now a socialist deputy in Rome (Rinaldo Rigola), *Le Socialiste* rhapsodied that '[whether] Parti Socialiste Italien or Parti Ouvrier Français, we are all members of the same nation, the nation of labour'.[86] 'No socialist worker, no trade unionist', the French Marxists optimistically asserted, 'will perceive an Italian [worker] as an enemy, but rather as a brother in suffering'.[87] Always ready to ascribe the characteristics of its militant elite to the working class as a whole, Guesdists attributed their own studied internationalism to French workers in general, who supposedly had 'always disdained the barbarous prejudices of race and nationality',[88] who had 'never asked for the passport of any worker before opening their ranks to him and making room for him at their side'.[89]

None the less, some French workers, for all their supposed internationalism, *did* murder their foreign 'comrades', and some immigrant labourers, ignoring the bonds of proletarian solidarity, *did* break strikes. How did Guesdists cope with these awkward incidents? How did they incorporate the endemic conflict and the occasional violence which sundered French from immigrant workers into their Marxist conception of the working class? Their favourite strategy, apart from assuming a blissful ignorance, devalued these unfortunate phenomena, reducing brawls between French and foreign workers to trivial local exceptions which proved the all-important internationalist rule. After all, Guesdists assured their readers, 'the foreigners who drive down wages are a tiny minority. And if the foreign colony provides its quota of traitors ready to submit to the capitalists, then there are ... French who do the same'.[90] But French Marxists could not easily denigrate tragic affrays such as the Aigues-Mortes massacre of Italian immigrant labourers in 1893 as merely 'regrettable conflicts which hardly have

---

[85] See, for an instance which defends this internationalist practice, 'Operai Italiani', *Le Socialiste*, 17 July 1886.

[86] Anonymous, 'Vive l'Internationale!', *Le Socialiste*, 17 June 1900.

[87] Anonymous, 'L'Assassinat Politique', *Le Socialiste*, 30 June 1894. A comment on Caserio's assassination of President Loubet.

[88] Anonymous, 'Organisation Corporative ou de Métiers', *L'Égalité*, 21 May 1882.

[89] J. Guesde, 'Patriotisme Patronal', *Le Cri du Peuple*, 21 February 1884.

[90] Geva, 'Les Ouvriers Étrangers', *Le Socialiste*, 20 November 1886.

the importance attributed to them',[91] although the Parti Ouvrier strove to diminish even this calamity. When unable to dismiss or devalue such vicious atrocities, Guesdists denied that workers committed them. According to the Parti Ouvrier, vagrant 'lumpen-proletarians'[92] had murdered the Italians at Aigues-Mortes, not 'real' workers – a further instance of the Marxist tradition of hiding awkward or embarrassing aspects of the proletarian condition behind the vague silhouette of the polymorphic lumpenproletariat.

Indeed, at their most extreme, French Marxists systematically rejected *any* geographical identity for workers, including regional identities within the French working class itself, although hundreds of thousands of workers conceived of themselves as Bretons or Parisians first and workers only second, if at all.[93] Workers' diatribes against 'foreign' labour sometimes actually referred to 'immigrants' from other parts of France: urban craftsmen hardly distinguished Italian building workers from Breton labourers.[94] In Parti Ouvrier parlance, however, *ouvrier* always prevailed over *français* or *Breton*. Workers partook of class identity, but never of identities compounded of 'blood and soil' – not for Guesdists the Barrèsian mystique of 'la terre et les morts'. Acutely aware of the slightest threat to proletarian unity, French Marxists fiercely criticised a socialist such as Paul Brousse who exploited his local identity against 'outsiders': a socialist militant, by (Marxist) definition, represented the universal proletariat, not a Parisian arrondissement.[95] The usual Parti Ouvrier response to working-class nationalism generalised this cosmopolitan absolutism. According to Guesde,

[91] *Ibid.*, for an earlier killing. The Aigues-Mortes atrocity is described in P. Milza, 'Le Racisme Anti-Italien en France: La "Tuerie d'Aigues-Mortes" (1893)', *Histoire*, no. 10, 1979, pp. 23–31. For the POF's embarrassed analysis of the incident, see Anonymous, 'Rivalités Internationales', *Le Socialiste*, 2 September 1893.

[92] 'B,' 'Les Vêpres d'Aigues-Mortes', *Le Socialiste*, 6 January 1894.

[93] The localism of the French working class is stressed in Moss, *The Origins of the French Labor Movement*, p. 20 and Perrot, *Les Ouvriers en Grève*, vol. 2, pp. 512–13. For the roots of proletarian regionalism in the very capitalist political economy understood by the Guesdists as a homogenising force, see the excellent study in W. Brustein, 'A Regional Mode-of-Production Analysis of Political Behaviour: The Cases of Western and Mediterranean France', *Politics and Society*, vol. 10, 1981, pp. 355–98.

[94] P. Hutton, 'The Impact of the Boulangist Crisis upon the Guesdist Party in Bordeaux', *French Historical Studies*, vol. 7, 1971, p. 237.

[95] Anonymous, 'Le Droit du Logement', *Le Socialiste*, 26 December 1885 for an attack on Brousse, and H. Ghesquière, 'Unité et Fédéralisme', *Le Socialiste*, 30 March-6 April 1902 for a powerful critique of localism in general .

there are no longer nations, above all today, nineteen years after the creation of the great Working Men's International. [Guesde, of course, ignored the collapse of the First International in the 1870s.] There are only classes, corresponding to the growing conflict of interest upon which society is based. There are capitalists – possessors who, by their postal conventions and telegraphic agreements, by their trade treaties, and so on, inter-nationalise their exploitation to a greater and greater extent. And there are proletarians – non-possessors suffering from the same evils, subjected to the same yoke, victims of the same robbery, obliterating frontiers in the community of their solidarity.[96]

According to the Guesdists, nationalism, in a world dominated by capitalism, had become as obsolete as tribalism: it survived only as anachronism and mystification – not for Guesdists that 'absurd slogan "Wright [sic] or wrong, my country!" '[97]

On occasion, however, Guesdists had to retreat from doctrinaire intransigence, thereby conceding the unpleasant prevalence of work-ing-class xenophobia. In so far as 'genuine' workers perpetrated nationalist violence against foreigners, the Parti Ouvrier pleaded with them to come to their senses, to realise that they acted 'against their own class to the great profit of the bosses'.[98] Workers injured themselves when they injured immigrants: only the bosses benefited, adding a welcome division of the working class to the profits extorted from foreign labour. Lapsing into their paranoid mode, Guesdists ascribed working-class xenophobia to a cunning bourgeois plot: 'employers encourage the divisions and hatreds which ... arise between workers of different nationality', contended the Party's *Programme*, 'since these conflicts prevent any combination for the defence of the workers' labour power'.[99] If the bourgeoisie bene-fited, then bourgeois must be responsible – the recurrent logic behind the Guesdists' conspiracy theory of capitalist society.

The Parti Ouvrier, however, occasionally recognised 'objective' causes for inter-communal conflict, thereby admitting that prole-tarian nationalism transcended any mere 'false consciousness' incul-cated by bourgeois propagandists. Competition between workers in the labour market, Guesdists recognised, 'naturally' ignited

[96] J. Guesde, 'Nations et Classes', *Le Citoyen*, 3 April 1882.

[97] 'B.' (Bonnier), 'Nationalisme Politique et Nationalisme Économique', *Le Socialiste*, 11 September 1904. Charles Bonnier enjoyed showing off his English, occasionally with unanticipated results.

[98] Anonymous, 'Rivalités Internationales', *Le Socialiste*, 2 September 1893.

[99] J. Guesde and P. Lafargue, *Programme du Parti Ouvrier: Son Histoire, Ses Considérants, Ses Articles* (Paris, undated), pp. 90–1.

fratricidal conflicts between low-wage immigrants and the French workers they displaced. Characteristically shifting gears from revolutionary exhortation to reformist pragmatism, the Parti Ouvrier proposed a minimum wage which would 'put an end to the [ethnic] conflict which so often bloodies our construction sites. Peace will thus be restored within the great family of workers'.[100] Contractors would no longer have an incentive to hire cheap Italians, no longer cheap. The POF likewise urged the extension of employer liability to foreign victims of industrial accidents, coverage which would have eliminated one of the major labour-market 'advantages' of immigrant workers, largely unprotected by France's rudimentary labour laws.[101] Once foreigners entered the French labour market on equal terms with French workers, conflict between immigrants and natives would cease, to the great advantage of the labour movement and socialist militancy.

These proposals, coming from the Parti Ouvrier, possessed little credibility, and deserved less. Whether Guesdists hoped that such reforms would inhibit the hiring of foreign labour is unclear; French Marxists, at least in public, never admitted that the protection of labour resulted in labour protectionism, an argument reserved for proponents of 'national economics' and their laissez-faire opponents. In any case, Guesdists, profoundly skeptical of reformism in general, quite obviously believed that the bourgeois Third Republic, with its callous record of indifference or hostility toward social amelioration, would never implement measures to defend foreign workers from the rapacity of French employers or protect French labour from the cutthroat competition of cut-price foreign workers. Proposals of labour market regulation, in the hands of the Parti Ouvrier, served by their rejection, and were so intended to serve; their utterly predictable unacceptability illustrated cold-blooded Republican complicity in the brutal exploitation of both French and foreign workers. Faced with 'bloody conflict on French construction sites', French Marxists, apart from half-hearted reformist manoeuvres, retreated to the pious hope that 'foreigners working in France will link themselves with the [socialist organisation and militancy of the] French, which will eliminate the old hatreds'.[102]

[100] 'La Semaine', *Le Socialiste*, 20 May 1893.
[101] Anonymous, 'Les Ouvriers Étrangers', *Bulletin Mensuel des Élus Socialistes*, no. 23, 1 October 1901, p. 6.
[102] Geva, 'L'Internationalisme', *Le Socialiste*, 19 February 1887.

Workers, of course, in their most fundamental identity are biological organisms, organisms destined to be born, mature, reproduce, and die. Biology was indeed destiny during the *Belle Époque*: reproduction, in the seductive guise of sex roles or as the pitiless march of the generations over their aging predecessors, determined workers' lives with at least the tyrannical rigour of the capitalist mode of production. French proletarians – whether as dependent children, as mothers and fathers, or as the incapacitated aged – depended upon fragile strategies of family survival whose internal contradictions and vulnerability to the capitalist labour market generated constant friction between children and their parents, between wives and husbands, between the aged and their offspring – friction which wore away the proletarian solidarity necessary for socialist victory in the class war. Marxists, strategists in that war, necessarily detested this 'permanent strife within the working-class family'.[103] How did Guesdists comprehend this 'permanent strife'? How did they hope to overcome the tensions between impatient youth and repressive age, between dominant males and subordinate women – the tensions which divided worker from worker and occasionally united workers with bourgeois?

The age-old antagonism between youth and age disturbed the Parti Ouvrier least: Marxists, from Marx until at least 1968, have traditionally disregarded generational stratification and generational conflict, the pattern of communal hierarchy and field of social struggle delimited by aging and inheritance.[104] The Parti Ouvrier, however, neglected generational interests to an unusual extent, even for Marxist socialists, never encouraging or even trusting its own ephemeral youth movement – and this during a period which experienced the birth of youth organisations across the continent, from the *wandervogal* to the boy scouts.[105] Guesdists, however, did highlight the pernicious effects of the class system upon the young, and with good reason. The French of the *Belle Époque* – their families adapting with difficulty to a new world of universal primary education, stringent child labour laws, and increasingly anonymous

[103] P. Lafargue, 'Les Révolutionnaires', *Le Socialiste*, 20 May 1891. For the conflicts which engendered this concern, see L. Tilly, 'Structure de l'Emploi, Travail des Femmes et Changement Démographique dans Deux Villes Industrielles: Anzin et Roubaix 1872–1906', *Mouvement Social*, no. 105, 1978, pp. 33–58.
[104] For a useful exception, see J. Reynolds, 'Youth as a Class', *International Socialist Journal*, February 1968, pp. 47–80.
[105] Willard, *Les Guesdistes*, pp. 103–4 and Kergoat, 'France', p. 178.

patterns of labour recruitment and labour discipline – incessantly debated the meaning of childhood and the place of children in their parents' world. The plight of working-class children particularly perturbed the *fin-de-siècle* conscience. No wonder. Not only did Lille and Roubaix have the highest infant mortality rates in France, but this dreadful index of deprivation and suffering actually worsened during the 1890s.[106] Ever eager to intervene in the issues of the day, the Parti Ouvrier imposed its own socialist preoccupations upon this debate: revelations that near-infants laboured under appalling conditions for uncaring capitalists furnished French Marxists with heaven-sent polemical opportunities.[107] Guesdists exploited these opportunities to the full, emphasising the capitalist preference for just such cheap and vulnerable (because young) workers, indicting the entire 'capitalist mode of production' for their dreadful plight, promising to rescue 'working-class youth from the capitalist ogre'.[108] Images of undernourished and sickly proletarian children recurred throughout the Guesdist corpus – children doomed, at worst, to an early death from tuberculosis and industrial accidents or, at best, to premature ageing from brutalising working-conditions and endless working-days. The gaunt and tormented visage of the child-worker stared out of innumerable Marxist indictments of capitalist exploitation.

Determined to abolish the bourgeoisie by universalising its privileges, the Parti Ouvrier sought to extend the novel bourgeois ideal of a carefree childhood from its privileged beneficiaries to the children of the proletariat. The Guesdists' campaign, however, may have swayed conscience-stricken bourgeois rather more than child-rearing workers: hardly a year passed during the *Belle Époque* without parliamentary debate over child-protection laws, press campaigns against child labour, and dismayed public discussion of 'degenerating' proletarian families – accumulated (bourgeois) public discourse which, unusually for the Third Republic, actually resulted in genuine social improvement. Not that reform satisfied the Guesdists,

---

[106] For the saliency of child labour in the conscience of the period, see E. Accampo, *Industrialization, Family Life, and Class Relations: Saint Chamond 1815–1914* (Berkeley, 1989), pp. 141–2. The mortality rates are from C. Willard, *Les Guesdistes*, p. 230.

[107] See the horrifying material in J.-P. Brunet, *Saint-Denis: La Ville Rouge 1890–1939 – Socialisme et Communisme en Banlieu Ouvrier 1890–1939* (Paris, 1980), pp. 102–4 and Jacquemet, *Belleville au XIXᵉ Siècle*, p. 335. The ease with which the labour laws governing child labour could be evaded is illustrated in R. Cazals, *Avec les Ouvriers de Mazamet* (Paris, 1978), p. 23.

[108] Anonymous, 'Action Socialiste dans les Corps Élus', *Bulletin Mensuel de la Fédération Nationale des Élus du Parti Ouvrier Français*, Première Année, no. 2, 1 January 1900, p. 6.

always fearing the worst from 'bourgeois politics', always convinced that any law passed under bourgeois auspices would benefit only the bourgeoisie. 'Thus,' Lafargue contended, 'the law on child labour which seems to be designed to aid workers, has been supported and praised by Dollfus and the other great manufacturers only because it will guarantee them future generations of ... slaves'.[109] Guesdist rhetoric met a more ambiguous response from workers. Many favoured the expulsion of child labour from the labour market, yet most, at some stage in their lives, also depended upon supplementary income from their children, so often an indispensable resource for hard-pressed working-class families.[110] Confronted by proletarian resistance to age limitations on employment, the Parti Ouvrier exploded in paternalist outrage. 'The socialist party has to ignore workers' weaknesses', argued Bonnier. 'There has not been a single public health measure or social reform which hasn't evoked the hostility of workers, blinded by momentary advantages, sacrificing their class [interest] to their [immediate] interest'.[111] Not for the first nor last time, the Guesdists' visionary project exceeded the limited aspirations of the Guesdists' class-bound constituency.

Apart from their indictments of child labour, French Marxists ignored generational dynamics within the labour market, dynamics which systematically disrupted working-class unity during the later nineteenth century. The conflicts between youth and maturity once associated with family hiring patterns and (literally) paternal labour discipline had declined by the *Fin de Siècle*: outside the construction trades, fathers rarely hired their sons and supervised their work as labour subcontractors for their own employers, thereby eliminating one institution of paternal power and patronage which had long galled working-class youth. But the deskilling of 'artisans in the factory' and the associated 'crisis of apprenticeship' triggered new clashes between younger employees and their elders, struggles now unmediated by family solidarity: youthful (and therefore cheap) workers willingly cooperated with employers to dismantle traditional seniority systems, while 'labour aristocrats', determined to protect their trade monopolies, fiercely opposed 'excessive

[109] Report of a speech by Lafargue, 'Mouvement Social – France: Paris', *Le Socialiste*, 27 November 1886.
[110] For the ambiguity of working-class attitudes towards child labour, see Marty, *Chanter pour Survivre*, p. 71.
[111] C. Bonnier, 'Referendum', *Le Socialiste*, 18 February 1900.

apprenticeships'.[112] The POF prudishly averted its eyes from these intra-class disputes, never once exploring the ramifications of inter-generational working-class antagonisms, and with good reason: these disputes and their associated tension would have tarnished the Guesdists' bright image of 'bourgeois society collapsing before the combined efforts of bold youths and aware adults'.[113] French Marxists never conceded that working-class 'bold youths' might challenge their fathers and mothers, that proletarian 'aware adults' might dread youthful competition.

The 'war between the sexes' further complicated the Guesdists' pursuit of the class war. Female employment posed particularly intractable problems for the Parti Ouvrier during the *Belle Époque*, as women increased from 30 per cent of the waged labour force in 1866 to 38 per cent in 1911,[114] an increase characteristically exaggerated in Guesdist polemic, which sometimes alleged that 'women had virtually replaced men in industrial work'.[115] How could the POF

---

[112] Peter Stearns's *Lives of Labour*, pp. 62–3 and 257–63 is excellent for the general problem of generational conflict within the working class. The decline of traditional forms of intergenerational labour recruitment is described in M. Perrot, 'The Three Ages of Industrial Discipline in Nineteenth-Century France', in J. Merriman (ed.), *Consciousness and Class Experience in Nineteenth-Century Europe* (New York, 1979), pp. 153–5. For intergenerational conflict created by deskilling and the decline of the apprenticeship system, see Y. Lequin, *Les Intérêts de Classe et la République*, p. 89; J. Scott, *The Glassworkers of Carmaux: French Craftsmen and Political Action in a Nineteenth-Century City* (Cambridge, Mass., 1974), pp. 79–80 and p. 101; Perrot, *Les Ouvriers en Grève*, vol. 2, p. 463; and Merriman, *Red City*, pp. 218–19. Lequin has recently questioned the existence of a 'crisis of apprenticeship'. Y. Lequin, 'Apprenticeship in Nineteenth-Century France: A Continuing Tradition or a Break with the Past?', in S. Kaplan and C. Koepp (eds.), *Work In France: Representation, Meaning, Organisation, and Practice* (London, 1986), pp. 457–74.

[113] H. Bès, 'Le Parti Ouvrier en France – Castres', *Le Socialiste*, 26 February 1899. There is some evidence that the union of ardent youth and wise age had some reality in the northern textile industry, where there were relatively few occupational barriers between youthful and mature workers. Perrot, *Les Ouvriers en Grève*, vol. 2, p. 462.

[114] M. Guilbert, *Les Femmes et l'Organisation Syndicale* (Paris, 1966), p. 14. For the centrality of the issue of female workers in the labour movement of the *Belle Époque*, see M. Perrot, 'La Classe Ouvrière au Temps de Jaurès', p. 69.

[115] A. Valette, 'Force Ignorée', *Le Socialiste*, 8 September 1895. She supports her point with columns of detailed statistics from across France, all of them drawn from the food and clothing/textile industries! On the other hand, Guesdists largely ignored home workers, whose numbers and femininity would have strengthened this case. For the particular problems of this category which was so neglected by the POF, see M. Boxer, 'Protective Legislation and Home Industry: The Marginalization of Women Workers in Late Nineteenth-Century France', *Journal of Social History*, vol. 20, 1986, pp. 45–65. The best overall critiques of the Guesdists' reaction to the 'women's question' are P. Hilden, 'Rewriting the History of Socialism: Working Women and the Parti Ouvrier Français', *European History Quarterly*, vol. 17, 1987, pp. 285–306 and, above all, C. Sowerwine, *Sisters or Citizens? Women and Socialism in France Since 1876* (Cambridge, 1982), pp. 54–66. See also M. Boxer, 'Socialism Faces Feminism: The Failure of Synthesis in France 1879–1914', in M. Boxer

interpret, evaluate, even exploit this gendered transformation of the proletariat? Should socialists welcome this 'industrialisation of women'? Would the frequently fraught relationship between male and female employees evolve to favour proletarian class unity? Did working women possess distinct interests which justified their distinct organisation? Bewildered by the ambiguities of their society and confused by the implications of their ideology, Guesdists vacillated between, on the one hand, glamorisation of working women as agents of both proletarian revolution and women's liberation and, on the other hand, the most 'traditional' portrayals of 'true women' as homemakers rather than 'real' workers. The POF's bewilderment and confusion seriously impeded its development: the Party's periodic feminism alienated chauvinist labour militants, while its occasional paternalism demobilised potentially militant women. This demobilisation hurt the Guesdists most in their heartland, the textile cities of the Flemish plain, where women furnished a disproportionate share of the labour force but, after an auspicious beginning, never played an equal role in the region's socialist militancy.[116]

Nevertheless, French Marxists, unlike most of their contemporaries, generally welcomed the 'industrialisation' of women, at least in theory; the Parti Ouvrier rejected exclusion of women from the industrial labour force, in sharp contrast to both 'bourgeois' reformers, frightened by the social and demographic consequences of female factory employment, and non-Marxist labour militants, terrified by the influx of cheap and docile female factory-fodder. Better yet, the Guesdists vigorously defended women's right to jobs, not least because 'wherever female labour has been tried, it has been at least as proficient as male labour, and almost always [women]

---

and J. Quataert (eds.), *Socialist Women: European Socialist Feminism in the Nineteenth and Early Twentieth Centuries* (New York, 1978), p. 80. There are illuminating discussions of Marxism's engagement with gender in H. Hartmann, 'The Unhappy Marriage of Marxism and Feminism', in L. Sargent (ed.), *Women and Revolution: A Discussion of the Unhappy Marriage of Marxism and Feminism* (Boston, 1981), pp. 1–41 (see also the other contributions to this collection) and A. Kuhn and A. Wolpe, 'Feminism and Materialism', in A. Kuhn and A. Wolpe (ed.), *Feminism and Materialism: Women and Modes of Production* (London, 1978), pp. 1–10.

[116] For the predominance of female employment in these areas, see M. Perrot, 'De la Nourrice à l'Employée: Travaux de Femmes dans la France du XIXe Siècle', *Mouvement Social*, no. 105, 1978, pp. 3–10 and M. Guilbert, 'La Présence des Femmes dans les Professions et ses Incidences sur l'Action Syndicale avant 1914', *Mouvement Social*, no. 63, 1968, pp. 127–8. Patricia Hilden, in her fine studies of the area, *Working Women and Socialist Politics in France 1880–1914: A Regional Study* (Oxford, 1986), has convincingly described lost Guesdist opportunities in the class war convulsing the Nord.

have been more adroit',[117] a comment carefully calculated to enrage exclusionary male trade unionists. The slogan 'Women – out of the factory!' was, according to the Guesdists, both 'brutal and stupid'.[118] More importantly (from a Marxist perspective), the Parti Ouvrier argued that women, when restricted as housewives, inevitably feared strikes and demonstrations as mortal threats to the security and well-being of their households: timid 'homemakers' would not only resist trade union and socialist blandishments, but would demobilise their more committed menfolk. By contrast, women, once fully integrated into wage labour, would understand the imperatives of union organisation and socialist militancy, their households' only sure defences against capitalist aggression: *ouvrières*, like *ouvriers*, would willingly sacrifice their restricted leisure and their meagre resources to their now-evident class interest. Capital redoubled the strength of its working-class enemy by 'industrialising' women, thereby freeing them from the constraints of domesticity so that they, in turn, could free the proletariat from the constraints of capital. The Parti Ouvrier practiced what it preached: one of the most bitter conflicts between the early Guesdists and the Possibilists turned upon the POF's decision to have its newspaper printed by a firm employing female typographers, typography having degenerated into a particularly bloody battleground in the sex war. Confronted by Possibilist criticism of this supposed betrayal of the labour movement, the French Marxists acerbically responded that 'just because typographers behaved stupidly, there is no reason for socialists to follow suit'.[119] At its most stringent, *Le Socialiste* even compared the relationship between men and women to that between capitalists and proletarians: 'just as capitalists have made concessions to labour only when constrained by circumstances, so men will never surrender their privileges of their own free will, but will be forced to do so by the [coming] economic independence of women'.[120] Guesdists, no doubt, evolved this *ouvriériste* feminism to some extent because of the peculiarities of their ideology's social implantation. Conditions

---

[117] Anonymous, 'La Question de la Femme', *Le Socialiste*, 30 October 1886.

[118] A. Zévaès, 'Une Élucubration d'Yves Guyot', *Le Socialiste*, 7 April 1894.

[119] Anonymous, 'Une Explication', *Le Socialiste*, 3 October 1885. There is some evidence that female industrial employment did, in fact, encourage labour militancy, if only because the resultant augmented financial resources of working-class families allowed individual workers (male or female) greater freedom to participate in strikes. Moch, 'Urban Structures, Migration, and Worker Militancy', p. 116.

[120] 'La Semaine', *Le Socialiste*, 7 April 1894.

in the northern textile industry, with relatively restricted sex-segregation in the workplace and comparatively little patriarchy within the working-class community, legitimated sexual egalitarianism: the rigid separation between female domestic labour and male paid employment exemplified by mining villages and the highly-paid artisanal trades of Paris, milieus resistant to Marxism, never typified Lille or Roubaix.[121]

All the same, working-class men in the Nord, whose wives and daughters laboured alongside them in the textile mills and whose *compagnes* joined them in the local estaminet after work, still subscribed, however abstractly, to age-old stereotypes. Labour militants, those of the Guesdist Fédération Nationale du Textile no less than elitist Lyonnaise printers or brawny miners, sometimes accused female workers of impoverishing the working class by flooding the labour market, and denounced the 'innate' female passivity and timidity which effectively precluded not only women's mobilisation but that of their menfolk. Social conditions legitimated this working-class misogyny, as they legitimated egalitarianism in other circumstances: the 'feminisation' of a trade invariably indicated deskilling and lower wages. However unjustified their prejudiced interpretation of the phenomenon, male workers rightly feared women workers as unwitting agents of capital's assault upon labour's last bastions of autonomy and relative privilege.[122] Worst of all, women workers, like the unfortunate foreign labourers they so resembled in cost and malleability, sometimes served employers as strike-breakers: working women, far from consolidating labour's unity, frequently disrupted the fragile solidarity upon which the nascent trade union movement depended.[123] These distressing circumstances, however

---

[121] See W. Reddy, 'Family and Factory: French Linen Weavers in the *Belle Époque*', *Journal of Social History*, vol. 8, 1975, pp. 102–12; P. Hilden, 'Class and Gender: Conflicting Components of Women's Behaviour in the Textile Mills of Lille, Roubaix and Tourcoing 1880–1914', *Historical Journal*, vol. 27, 1984, pp. 379–81; and Hilden, *Working Women*, pp. 90–1.

[122] For the profound ambiguity of workers' attitudes, see Marty, *Chanter pour Survivre*, pp. 86–7. For the association between deskilling, low wages and female labour, see Merriman, *Red City*, p. 168 and Guilbert, *Les Femmes et l'Organisation Syndicale*, pp. 228–36. The new department stores hired women quite explicitly for their docility, according to T. McBride, 'A Woman's World: Department Stores and the Evolution of Women's Employment 1870–1920', *French Historical Studies*, vol. 10, 1978, p. 668.

[123] Guilbert, *Les Femmes et l'Organisation Syndicale*, pp. 228–230; Marty, *Chanter pour Survivre*, p. 82; and M.-H. Zylberberg-Hocquard, *Féminisme et Syndicalisme en France* (Paris, 1978), pp. 256–9.

attenuated in the Guesdists' heartland, inculcated deep-seated anti-*ouvrière* prejudices.

At the same time, many working women distrusted class warriors, seeking instead more pacific representatives. Such representation lay ready to hand. Socialist militants resentfully pointed out that the class-collaborationist Catholic trade unions recruited largely among female employees, a correlation which reinforced the Left's traditional association of femininity with religious irrationality.[124] Why this correlation? Why the apparent alienation of so many *ouvrières* from socialism and labour militancy? First, proletarian women, victims of the epidemic alcoholism of the male workforce, inevitably associated militancy with bistros: party-meetings in convivial backrooms resulted in immediate individual drunkenness as well as eventual collective organisation. And working-class wives and mothers, almost exclusively responsible for their families' provisioning, inevitably associated strikes with privation: work-stoppages, however justified, resulted in hungry children as well as proletarian self-assertion.[125] Guesdists were well aware of these problems, worrying that 'women are the enemies of disturbance and distrust the consequences of social conflict ... They view social battles involving their loved ones with maternal horror, and that horror explains why they so frequently oppose the social task that workers, impelled by their class instinct, have set themselves.'[126] Women's marginality in the labour force and their domestic responsibilities all too often precluded sustained militancy. The clerical austerity and unaggressive ideology of Social Catholicism promised women exemption from the lusty recklessness of (male) labour insurgency – no wonder the Christian trade union movement recruited so successfully among *ouvrières*.

Finally, women employees, subject to the most degrading and least remunerative working conditions in the French economy, understandably sought to escape the proletarian condition altogether. Paid employment, undertaken in youth as an ongoing dowry

---

[124] M. Weitz, 'Varieties of Class-Collaborationist Ideology in the French Labor Movement Before World War I', PhD thesis, City University of New York, 1977, pp. 409–15. The labour movement's equation of religion and women is described in M. Perrot, 'L'Éloge de Ménagère dans le Discours des Ouvriers Français au XIXᵉ Siècle', *Romantisme*, nos. 13–14, 1976, pp. 113–14.

[125] Perrot, *Les Ouvriers en Grève*, vol. 2, p. 507 and, for a striking example, J. Quellien, 'Un Milieu Ouvrier Réformiste: Syndicalisme et Réformisme à Cherbourg à la Belle Époque', *Mouvement Social*, no. 127, 1984, p. 82.

[126] P.-M. André, 'Le Vote des Femmes', *Le Socialiste*, 14–21 July 1901.

and resorted to after marriage as an unwelcome expedient, served women of the working class as an inevitable and burdensome supplement to their reproductive roles as wives and mothers, not as a personality-affirming career. *Ouvrières* doubted whether industrial labour liberated anyone, male or female: at the least, tedious work under constant supervision in clangorous textile mills offered 'liberation' in a most unattractive guise. Under these circumstances, the ideal of 'la femme au foyer' inevitably seduced both working women, who dreamed of individual liberation from (wage) labour through a good marriage, and male labour militants, who dreamed of matrimonial bliss and constricted labour markets. Equally alienated by the workplace, proletarian men and women shared an inequitable fantasy of domestic escapism.[127] Labouring women, more than any other workers, exemplified the proletariat's profound ambivalence towards labour.

Guesdists faithfully mirrored these fears and fantasies, but as ideologists rather than as escapists: theorising their own surrender to the domestic ideal, they discovered a fundamental 'economic antagonism' between male and female workers which 'expand[ed] and intensif[ied] in proportion to the development of capitalism',[128] a thesis which completely contradicted the Guesdists' alternative assumption that capital, an irresistible homogenising agent, inevitably united working men with working women, dissolving their differences with the gender-blind solvent of the labour market. As always when called upon to explain discord within the proletariat, Guesdists blamed the bourgeoisie: conflicts founded upon gender identities, no less than those derived from nationality, allegedly served the very capitalism which supposedly erased sexual and national commonalities. Following the logic of this argument, the Parti Ouvrier happily blamed their class enemies for the 'industrialisation of women', for the invasion of the family by industrial capitalism so dreaded both by male workers, terrified of low-wage competition and the erosion of traditional family strategies, and by *bien pensant* 'public opinion', traumatised by horrid visions of 'racial degeneration' and 'social anarchy'. Once embarked upon this polemical manoeuvre, Guesdists unthinkingly adopted the paternalist rhetoric otherwise more characteristic of their Proudhonian

---

[127] C. Sowerwine, 'Workers and Women in France before 1914: The Debate over the Couriau Affair', *Journal of Modern History*, vol. 55, 1983, p. 413.
[128] P. Lafargue, *La Question de la Femme* (Paris, 1904), p. 5.

enemies, condemning capitalism for 'the unfortunate way in which women are replacing men in so many areas of human endeavour'.[129] Not surprisingly, this rhetoric led towards the ultimate male-chauvinist nightmare in which 'men are driven from the workshop, so that to survive they have to depend upon the salaries of women and children'[130] – towards a world turned upside down, not a world redeemed. Torn between women's liberation by labour and women's liberation from labour, the Parti Ouvrier collapsed into incoherence, an incoherence which disclosed both the ambiguities of proletarian family-life and the contradictions of the Guesdists' polemical strategy.[131]

To compound Marxist confusion, capitalism has not only pitted worker against worker, but united workers and capitalists around common economic interests. 'Class collaboration' arises as naturally from the capitalist mode of production as does class conflict, however intense the Marxist conviction that the weight of the accumulation process relentlessly shifts the equilibrium between the two relationships towards conflict. Marx, who devoted a lifetime to the struggle against class collaboration, optimistically identified cooperation between exploited workers and their capitalist exploiters as proof of proletarian 'immaturity', a necessarily transient failure of class consciousness.[132] Unfortunately for his successors, class collaboration has persisted, despite the rosy hopes of class theory and the best efforts of socialist practice, its persistence legitimating generations of anti-Marxist critique and anti-socialist militancy.[133] Class conflict or class collaboration? – the alternatives which sum up the fundamental question dividing Marxist socialists from their many enemies.

These enemies have battened upon the collective identities which transcend the divisive relationship between wages and profits:

---

[129] H. Ghesquière, *La Femme et le Socialisme* (Lille, 1893), p. 7. We have an excellent study of this aspect of Guesdist polemic in L. Grani, 'Jules Guesde, Paul Lafargue et les Problèmes de Population', *Population*, vol. 34, 1979, pp. 1024–44.

[130] P. Lafargue, 'La Journée Légale de Travail réduite à Huit Heures', *L'Égalité*, 26 February 1882.

[131] For Guesdist confusion, see Hilden, 'Rewriting the History of Socialism', p. 286. Parti Ouvrier ambivalence paralleled the confusion within the French working class itself described by Guilbert in 'La Présence des Femmes', p. 130.

[132] See, for instance, Marx, *The Communist Manifesto*, p. 492.

[133] For a classic, and influential, development of this argument, see T. Marshall, 'The Nature of Class Conflict', in T. Marshall, *Class Conflict and Social Stratification* (London, 1938), pp. 97–112.

collective mentalities such as those, for instance, founded upon nationality or gender. Worse still, from a Marxist perspective, profit-takers and wage-earners – French *bourgeoises* and French *ouvrières*, for instance – have shared common 'economic' interests, apart from their common communal identities as French nationals and a common gender identity as women. Bourgeois and proletarians have both relied for their livelihoods upon the success of particular capitalist enterprises, and upon the success of capitalist enterprise in general. Secure employment and decent wages, most workers' first priorities, have depended upon their employers' profitability and upon an adequate rate of profit throughout the economy, although profit has functioned as a necessary rather than a sufficient condition of proletarian welfare – workers' relative share of their firms' net product and of society's wealth being determined by the outcome of class struggle.[134] In other words, workers might starve while capitalists prospered, but workers necessarily starved when capitalists failed. The capitalist mode of production evokes both class collaboration and class conflict, however obsessively Marxists have obscured the former by emphasising the latter.

The practices of French capitalists, no less than those of French workers, reflected this dialectic between conflict and cooperation. Although Guesdists portrayed the bourgeoisie as utterly indifferent to workers' welfare, the French *patronat* in practice utterly failed to evolve a consistent strategy of labour relations. At one extreme, employers treated workers as mere units of labour-power, as ciphers to be purchased on an impersonal market, used and abused at will, and discarded without compunction – an approach to labour relations which effectively reinforced the Guesdist indictment of capitalism. But, at the other extreme, employers (sometimes the same employers in different circumstances) practised an industrial 'paternalism' designed to reinforce the bonds of community and augment the interests which married labour to capital, associated employees with employers, and bound the proletariat to the bourgeoisie. These managerial alternatives, *laissez-faire* ruthlessness or the

[134] This point has been cogently argued in the recent work of Adam Przeworski. See, in particular, his 'Material Interest, Class Compromise, and the Transition to Socialism', *Politics and Society*, vol. 10, 1980, pp. 133–7 and A. Przeworski and E. Wallerstein, 'The Structure of Class Conflict in Democratic Capitalist Societies', *American Political Science Review*, vol. 76, 1982, pp. 215–38. For the prevalence of 'industrial patriotism' in workers' attitudes towards their firms and industries, see M. Perrot, *Les Ouvriers en Grève*, vol. 2, p. 443.

conciliatory search for community, reflected the same contradiction in the capitalist mode of production which evoked a French labour movement torn between class conflict and class collaboration: as workers oscillated between self-interested identification with the success of 'their' firms and equally self-interested determination to assert their rights against their employers, so capitalists vacillated between self-interested loyalty to the employees upon whom their profits depended and equally self-interested reduction of workers to interchangeable factors of production.[135] In any case, paternalist enterprise – protecting its employees against the vicissitudes of the labour market, educating and housing their families, and guaranteeing their welfare against the ravages of disease, accident and old age – undermined fundamental Guesdist assumptions about the impersonal rapacity of capitalism. At the same time, the enthusiastic welcome extended by many workers to bourgeois proposals of 'social partnership' blurred the Marxists' stark image of the 'making of the working class', an image of irreconcilable estrangement between capital and labour, not of their connubial felicity.[136] How, then, did the Parti Ouvrier decipher the mysterious political economy of class collaboration?

Understandably, Guesdists detested capitalist advocacy of 'social solidarity', which they denounced as the 'attempted embourgeoisement of the working class'.[137] Hundreds of articles in *Le Socialiste* over the years denounced or (more frequently) mocked employers' attempts to seduce the employees they exploited. Significantly, however, the Parti Ouvrier reserved its most concentrated vitriol for workers who succumbed to bourgeois seduction. Perennially frustrated in their millenarian expectations of imminent socialist revolution, Guesdists decided that capitalist society survived its otherwise fatal contradictions only because workers periodically abandoned the class war for illusory peace settlements with the bourgeoisie: capitalism, Guesde bitterly concluded, 'lives, and can only live,

---

[135] A. Melucci, 'Action Patronale, Pouvoir, Organisation: Règlements d'Usine et Contrôle de la Main-d'Oeuvre au XXᵉ Siècle', *Mouvement Social*, no. 97, 1976, pp. 140–1.

[136] For a powerful description of authoritarian paternalism in action, see L. Berlanstein, 'The Formation of a Factory Labor Force: Rubber and Cable Workers in Bezons, France (1866–1914)', *Journal of Social History*, vol. 15, 1981, pp. 163–86. The extent of class-collaborationist sentiment in the labour movement is described in M. Weitz, 'Varieties of Class-Collaborationist Ideology'.

[137] *Rapport au XIXᵉ Congrès National, Fédération du Nord* [of the POF], p. 6 (in AN F7 12.522, file on Congress of Roubaix, 1901).

through conscious or unconscious treason ... among workers'.[138] By
Marxist criteria, bourgeois 'naturally' sought to delude their proletarian prey: 'class collaboration', however fraudulent, reflected
capitalists' vested interest in the perpetuation of the class system over
which they presided; workers, by contrast, betrayed their interests
every time they abandoned the class war and accepted their
subordinate place in bourgeois society, whatever the terms of their
armistice with the class enemy. Given these uncompromising precepts, Guesdists resolutely deployed their polemical artillery against
the turncoats within the workers' movement who 'wished to substitute "class cooperation" for class conflict'.[139] In the class war, as in
any war, combatants have hated traitors far more intensely than
they have hated the enemy.

If nothing else, these betrayals of class interest undermined the
deterministic foundations of the Guesdists' doctrine: in theory, and
by definition, class interest prevailed over all other considerations –
all history was the history of class struggle. Why then did workers
double-cross each other? Why did recent French history encompass
so much class collaboration? French Marxists frequently 'solved' this
conundrum by denying its existence. In their most simplistic model of
social order, capitalist exploitation of workers absolutely precluded
collaboration between bourgeois and proletarians – an astonishing
triumph of theory over experience. According to *Le Socialiste*, 'all
efforts at bourgeois reconciliation with the proletariat will inevitably
leave the workers completely cold: first because such attempts can
only be traps, and ... second, because ... the bourgeoisie must
follow the dictates of its own class interest.'[140] Unfortunately for the
Guesdists' peace of mind, experience repeatedly discredited this
comforting conviction: despite the incantatory force of 'inevitably',
workers regularly warmed to reconciliation with the bourgeoisie.
Guesdists needed to explain, not ignore, incidents such as the
alliance of bakers and their employees against the price controls
imposed by the Flaissières administration in Marseilles, a municipal
government enthusiastically supported by the POF.[141]

The charms of class collaboration occasionally seduced even

[138] J. Guesde, 'Un Candidate Ouvrier', *Le Cri du Peuple*, 29 August 1885.
[139] L. Greffier, *Petites Conférences Éducatives sur le Socialisme*, p. 16.
[140] Anonymous, 'Bas le Masque', *Le Socialiste*, 18 March 1891.
[141] See the bitter commentary on this incident in Anonymous, 'La Défaite des Affameurs', *Le Socialiste*, 5 February 1893.

Guesdist class warriors. Addressing employers in the printing trade, for instance, the Toulousain Guesdist Lucien Dejean urged: 'Come on, bosses! Wake up and turn your subordinates into associates. The workers are as interested as you are in the development and growth of the firm, since they can expect better conditions from it. And, if the firm fails, they'll have to look elsewhere for work, hardly an attractive prospect'.[142] Not the language of social revolution! Even Guesde, the class war embodied, succumbed to the temptations of class collaboration, suggesting on one astonishing occasion that workers and employers of the northern textile enterprises collaborate to impose a nation-wide salary scale upon their industry, thereby eliminating low-wage competition from elsewhere in France – an implicit admission that the capitalist mode of production induced solidarity between employers and employees (not to mention competition between low-wage and high-wage workers) as well as class conflict between labour and capital.[143]

But these exceptions proved the rule: Guesdists hated class collaboration. They furiously denounced every institution which associated labour with capital – profit sharing within individual firms, 'mixed unions' of employers and employees, the corporative organisation of a trade – as 'instruments of servitude, of starvation, and of death'.[144] Yet denunciation rarely, if ever, resulted in explanation. Guesdists (apart from startlingly aberrant cases like Dejean) systematically ignored the common interests which tied employees to employers: according to the Parti Ouvrier, workers did *not* share an interest with their boss in 'the development and growth of the firm', nor did workers and employers in the same industry share an interest in aggressive price-fixing. Confronted with unpalatable evidence to the contrary, Guesdists habitually retreated into the dogmatic conviction that class conflict, the fundamental reality of the capitalist mode of production, would inevitably prevail over class collaboration, a mere epiphenomenon of false consciousness. In the dismissive words of Alexandre Zévaès: 'To substitute a harmony of interests for the class war, for the economic conflicts which neces-

---

[142] L. Dejean, *Étude et Exposé des Conditions de Travail dans l'Industrie du Livre* (Toulouse, 1899), p. 65.
[143] J. Guesde, 'Aux Serfs de l'Industrie Textile', *Le Socialiste*, 17 October 1891.
[144] J. Guesde, 'Les Bons Apôtres', *Le Cri du Peuple*, 17 September 1884. For the development and influence of these class-collaborationist schemes in France during the period, see the biting account in S. Elwitt, *The Third Republic Defended: Bourgeois Reform in France 1880–1914* (London, 1986), pp. 85–113.

sarily result from the division of contemporary society into classes . . . What a dream!'[145] For Guesdists, a 'harmony of interests' required the establishment of socialism, and socialism would arise only through class conflict.[146] Mesmerised by their revolutionary aspirations to social transcendence, governed by the polemical imperatives of class war, distrusting social explanation as political justification, the French Marxists signally failed to evolve a coherent theory of class collaboration.

Controversies over the constitution and decomposition of the working class – over its construction and destruction, its cohesion and disintegration, its historical potential or lack thereof – have governed the long debate between socialists and anti-socialists, not least during the *Belle Époque*. Confident in the verities of their Marxist political economy, Guesdists contended that the working class inflated to virtually all-inclusive proportions, that the capitalist mode of production united the proletariat while decisively sundering capital and labour, and that capitalism self-destructively forced workers to challenge its exploitation of their labour power. In reply, enemies of the Parti Ouvrier asserted that the French working class constituted a small and declining fraction of the population, that workers shared at least as many interests with their employers as they shared with each other, and that proletarians, no less than bourgeois, prospered under the beneficent rule of capital.[147] By the 1890s, the French political culture turned around these issues – a triumph of Guesdist polemic, but no assurance of Guesdist triumph.

As usual in ideological controversies, the 'facts' validated both Marxist and anti-Marxist contentions. *Industrial* workers, narrowly defined, increased in number from 3,032,000 in 1881 to only 3,143,000 in 1901, so that their proportional share in the economically active population declined – grist to the anti-Marxist mill.[148] During the same period, however, the number of wage and salary earners – the *salariat*, as the Guesdists called them – grew from 9,131,000 to 12,092,000, while their share of the economically active population, by one calculation, increased from 56.7 per cent to 63.3

[145] A. Zévaès, 'Blague Bourgeoise', *Le Socialiste*, 1 September 1895.
[146] J. Guesde, 'La Participation aux Bénéfices', *La Revue Socialiste*, 20 February 1880, p. 8.
[147] For an explicit Guesdist description of this polemical terrain, see J. Guesde, 'Les Deux Armées', *Le Socialiste*, 29 July 1891.
[148] Retrospectively confirmed by J.-C. Toutain, 'La Population de la France de 1700 à 1959', in J. Marczewski (ed.), *Histoire Quantitative de l'Économie Française* (Paris, 1963), table 77.

per cent – 'proof' of the Guesdists' contentions.[149] In other words, clerical workers, waiters, and shop assistants proliferated, while the number of 'archetypical' industrial proletarians stagnated as their vast increases in per capita productivity encountered the constricted markets of the *Fin de Siècle*. Guesdists, however, assumed that all workers (defined as those who sold their labour) suffered, or would soon suffer, from all the relations of production characteristic of 'mature' industrial capitalism, from deskilling, managerial authority, mechanisation, and the centralisation and concentration of capital and production – although most wage and salary earners evaded at least one of these aspects of capital accumulation, and some escaped them all.

Why this Guesdist assumption? Quite simply, a proletariat rent by conflicts between the skilled and the unskilled, artisans and industrial workers, supervisors and the supervised, the employed and the unemployed, French and foreigners, men and women, a proletariat as tempted by individual social mobility or class collaboration as spurred by class conflict – this proletariat would never, could never, attain the historical destiny assigned to the working class by Marxism. Guesdists, during moments of discouraged lucidity, occasionally conceded that the capitalist mode of production disaggregated the proletariat as well as 'making the working class', demoralised proletarians as well as mobilising workers against capital, co-opted employees as well as alienating them from the bourgeois order. But the Parti Ouvrier flinched from theorising the working-class 'betrayals' which confounded the movement's sanguine convictions. In the last analysis, both the polemical force and the theoretical fragility of French Marxism derived from the Guesdists' tacit assimilation of a fragmented and conflict-ridden *salariat*, explicitly encompassing all those who worked for wages, to a united and homogeneous proletariat, implicitly identical to the industrial working class.

---

[149] J. Maréchal and J. Lecaillon, *La Répartition du Revenue National: Les Salariés* (Paris 1958), p. 81. The decline of property-owners and the proportional increase in wage and salary earners, however, has been paralleled by a large increase in the economically 'inactive' population (dependent adults, students, and the retired), so that the proportion of the proletariat within the population as a whole has remained relatively static over the past century. See the analysis of this little-recognised pattern in A. Przeworski et al., 'The Evolution of the Class Structure of France 1901–1968', *Economic Development and Cultural Change*, vol. 28, 1980, p. 750.

CHAPTER 6

A 'class for itself': trade unions, cooperatives and the 'labour movement'

> Economic conditions had first transformed the mass of the people of the country into workers. The domination of capital has created for this mass a common situation, common interests. This mass is thus already a class as against capital, but not yet for itself. In the struggle ... this mass becomes united, and constitutes itself as a class for itself. The interests it defends become class interests. But the struggle of class against class is a political struggle.
>
> Karl Marx, *The Poverty of Philosophy* (1847).

Analysis of the capitalist mode of production illuminates the making of workers, but not the making of the working class. By Marxist criteria, individual proletarians, however numerous, do not constitute a full-fledged class while still unorganised and unaware of their potential force. The proletariat only emerges as 'a class for itself' (an organised unity conscious of its own class interest), rather than vegetating as 'a class in itself' (a collection of individuals with a potential but unrealised common identity), through the aggregation of particular workers and particular labour disputes into a united front of workers in general against capital in general.[1] This all-important process of class formation begins, according to Marx (who nevertheless wrote surprisingly little on the rise of the trade unions), with the 'strikes, combinations and other forms in which the proletarians carry out before our eyes their organisation as a class.'[2]

---

[1] Marx never employed the phrase 'class in itself' in contradistinction to his 'class for itself' ('This mass [of workers] is thus already a class as against capital, but not yet for itself', K. Marx, *The Poverty of Philosophy*, in K. Marx and F. Engels, *Collected Works* (London, 1976), vol. 6, p. 211) although the former term has been used in this way by generations of Marxists. For rigorous discussion of this distinction, see E. Wood, 'The Politics of Theory and the Concept of Class', *Studies in Political Economy*, vol. 9, 1982, p. 61 and E. Wright, 'Class and Occupation', *Theory and Society*, vol. 9, 1980, pp. 189–90.

[2] Marx, *The Poverty of Philosophy*, p. 211. The relative neglect of trade unionism in Marx's work is pointed out in J. Banks, *Marxist Sociology in Action: A Sociological Critique of the Marxist*

Born simultaneously with the union movement during the second half of the nineteenth century, Marxist socialism has presupposed generalisation of industrial militancy as a precondition for its programme of class war: the expropriators could not be expropriated, or even challenged, until capitalism's victims organised against capital's exactions.

Should workers organise, and, if so, why? Liberals, at their most dogmatic, have denied the necessity or desirability of trade unions: the free labour market, the invisible hand of supply and demand, ensures that the labourer is worthy of his hire – and *vice versa*. Marxists, by contrast, have asserted that the fundamental asymmetry in the relationship between employers and employees constrains workers to organise themselves collectively against the exploitative consequences of individual dependency: a 'free' labour market where isolated workers compete against each other for employment and preferment would reduce all workers to impoverishment and insecurity. Without labour organisation, the 'laws of capital' would rule proletarians without mercy and without appeal: deskilling, managerial authoritarianism, and mechanisation would accelerate exponentially, while the resulting cornucopia would empty exclusively into the greedy maw of the bourgeoisie. Only proletarian solidarity and workers' organisation could obstruct 'the incessant encroachments of capital'[3] upon labour's prerogatives and labourers' livelihoods.

Marxists have consistently advocated labour organisation – in this defensive role. But they have also repeatedly criticised labour solidarity as an end in itself, as a substitute for socialist revolution, a substitute whereby unionised workers acquiesce in their own exploitation, once they have obtained a marginal degree of control over the capitalist mode of production. Indeed, Marxists have feared that the more securely the working class fortifies itself within the trench system of trade unionism, the less aggressively the proletariat will assail its class enemy: by Marxist criteria, the union movement, defensive by definition, has single-mindedly constructed a social

---

Approach to Industrial Relations (London, 1970), p. 47. The best guide to Marx's scattered writings on this subject is H. Draper, *Karl Marx's Theory of Revolution: The Politics of Social Class* (New York, 1978), pp. 81–146.

3   K. Marx, *Instructions for the Delegates of the Provisional General Council: The Different Questions*, in K. Marx and F. Engels, *Collected Works* (London, 1985), vol. 20, p. 191. For discussion of this fundamental Marxist thesis, see D. Booth, 'Collective Action, Marx's Class Theory and the Union Movement', *Journal of Economic Issues*, vol. 12, 1978, pp. 163–85.

Maginot Line – massively impressive, technically flawless, and perfectly calculated to lose the class war. Marxist analysts of the capitalist mode of production and the bourgeois polity have consistently advocated priority investment by the working class in the mobile strike force of the socialist party, rather than in the static defence system of the trade unions. This ambiguous, if not contradictory, combination of hostility towards the trade union movement as an agent of working-class (negative) integration into bourgeois society *and* enthusiasm for unions as instruments of working-class defence and proletarian class formation has sounded a discordant leitmotiv throughout the history of Marxist socialism, repeatedly disturbing the harmony between socialism and unionism advocated by Marx.[4] How did the Guesdists, representatives of Marxism in the homeland of Proudhonian 'mutualism' and 'revolutionary syndicalism', manipulate the all-important dialectic between labour organisation and class formation, with its promise of a proletarian 'class for itself' and its potential for class collaboration?

If nothing else, the Parti Ouvrier, itself born from the labour congress of Marseilles in 1879, exemplified the fragile Marxist symbiosis between industrial organisation and class politics.[5] French Marxism and French trade unionism intertwined throughout the *Belle Époque:* no labour disturbance erupted without the rapid arrival of Guesdists determined to guide the floodtide of working-class anger into socialist channels; *L'Égalité* and *Le Socialiste* supported virtually every significant strike which broke out during the *Fin de Siècle*, publicised and encouraged newly-founded unions, and reported the innumerable labour congresses of the *Belle Époque*; while the first nation-wide French trade union organisation, the Fédération Nationale des Syndicats et Groupes Corporatifs Ouvriers de France, worked closely with the Guesdists between its foundation

---

4 This ambiguity is discussed in R. Hyman, *Marxism and the Sociology of Trade Unionism* (London, 1971), p. 34, and M. Mann, *Consciousness and Action Among the Western Working Class* (London, 1973), pp. 19–23.
5 The intimate connection between the rise of socialism and the development of trade unions is a commonplace in the social history of the *Belle Époque*. For particularly telling examples relevant to Guesdism, see Y. Lequin, *Les Ouvriers de la Région Lyonnaise (1848–1914): Les Intérêts de Classe et la République* (Lyons, 1977), pp. 286–287; J.-M. Gaillard, 'La Pénétration du Socialisme dans le Bassin Houiller du Gard', in *Droite et Gauche en Languedoc-Roussillon: Actes du Colloque de Montpellier 9–10 Juin 1973* (Montpellier, 1975), pp. 277–9; and S. Derruau-Boniol, 'Le Socialisme dans l'Allier de 1848 à 1914', *Cahiers d'Histoire*, vol. 2, 1957, pp. 146–7.

in 1886 and its dissolution in 1894–95.[6] Symptomatically, however, French Marxists altogether ignored informal working-class resistance to capital. The systematic indiscipline, covert sabotage, frequent job-hopping, and endemic absenteeism with which workers indicated their resentments and coerced their employers never interested the POF, although these patterns of individual protest far exceeded unionism and strikes in their extent and in their effect upon labour relations before the First World War.[7] On the other hand, Guesdists devoted inordinate attention to abortive or moribund labour organisations, such as the ineffectual 'Secrétariats du Travail' or the archaic 'campagnonnages', institutions of little contemporaneous significance.[8] True to their teleology of class formation, Guesdists focused upon labour organisation in particular, however ephemeral and fruitless, rather than upon labour protest in general, however widespread and vigorous. By Marxist criteria, workers who joined a union, or even a compagnonnage, reinforced their class; workers who stayed in bed on Mondays or left a spanner in the works merely inconvenienced their bosses – organisation heralded labour's liberation; insubordination simply highlighted workers' subservience.

The Parti Ouvrier, confident in its determinist analysis of bourgeois society, fondly imagined that the capitalist mode of production produced organised labour as surely as it produced commodities: workers 'naturally' progressed from the futility of individual protest against employers to the potency of collective self-defense against

[6] The FNS has been almost totally forgotten. Georges Lefranc, the doyen of French labour historians, for instance, failed to mention its inglorious history in his 'Marxisme et Syndicalisme', *La Nef*, vol. 7, 1950, pp. 64–78 (although the organisation's failure would have greatly reinforced his thesis in this interesting study), and even more recent and far more substantial works mention the Federation only in passing.

[7] A. Cottereau, 'The Distinctiveness of Working-Class Culture in France 1848–1900', in I. Katznelson and A. Zolberg (eds.), *Working-Class Formation: Nineteenth-Century Patterns in Western Europe and the United States* (Princeton, 1986), pp. 123–42 for a general discussion, and O. Hardy-Hémery, *De la Croissance à la Désindustrialisation: Un Siècle dans le Valenciennois* (Paris, 1984), pp. 55–8 for a useful instance.

[8] *Le Socialiste*, between 1890 and 1895, devoted inordinate space to the Secretariats, which were supposed to collect labour statistics for the trade union movement, but which never became a serious reality. The Guesdist response to the compagnonnages, secret societies of journeymen artisans dating to the *ancien régime*, is particularly interesting, since the POF completely failed to develop a coherent approach to these living fossils. They were sometimes denounced for their hierarchy and mysticism, and at other times praised as ancestors of modern trade unionism. See, for the former approach, Anonymous, 'Organisation Corporative ou de Métiers', *L'Égalité*, 21 May 1882 and, for the latter, H. Ghesquière, 'Corporations et Syndicats 1776–1791–1884', *Le Socialiste*, 13 October 1894.

capitalism. 'Countering the rigours of the economic regime', proclaimed *Le Socialiste*, 'stands the resistance of the human herd which
will no longer tolerate its own decimation, which everywhere
opposes the free play of economic forces . . . with the solidarity of the
exploited.'[9] Reinforcing this unintended consequence of capitalist
exploitation, socialists had to foster working-class solidarity. According to the Guesdists' Congress of Roanne:

Considering that the organisation of workers by trade is a necessary and
natural consequence of capitalist production;

Considering that those organisations will be a powerful ally in the economic
and political battles which are inevitable. . .

The Congress declares that the Parti Ouvrier must encourage the trade
unions by every means in its power in all their activities: congresses, strikes,
etc.[10]

This imperative, established during the founding Congress of the
Guesdist movement, supposedly ruled the POF throughout its
tumultuous history. The Party unconditionally seconded its ally in
the Fédération Nationale des Syndicats when that organisation
declared that

the fate of the working class is in its own hands. . . Given its number and its
power, the world will belong to it if it so wishes, but without the unity and
solidarity of all its elements, it will never be able to raise itself above the
condition of inferiority and increasing misery inflicted upon it by the salary
system. Let each of us fulfil our primary class obligation by joining the
union of our trade. Let each union join with the others of its locality to form
a local federation. Finally, let every union in the nation unite in a powerful
national federation. These are the tasks to which workers conscious of their
true interests and of their rights and duties must devote their activity,
devotion, and sacrifices. Long live the liberation of the workers by the
workers themselves![11]

Trade unions reinforced socialism, while socialists reinforced trade
unionism. Or did they?

In practice, the Parti Ouvrier and the nascent trade union
movement quarrelled incessantly from the battles between Guesdists
and liberal 'Barberetists' during the early 1880s to the struggle

[9] Anonymous, 'Le Minimum de Salaire', *Le Socialiste*, 28 July 1894.
[10] Excerpts from the proceedings of the Roanne Congress of 1882 in File 177300–6–2, Ba/39 of
    the Archives de la Préfecture de Police de Paris.
[11] Le Conseil National (of the FNS), 'Appel aux Travailleurs de France', *Bulletin Mensuel de la
    Fédération Nationale des Syndicats et Groupes Corporatifs Ouvriers de France*, no. 3, 25 July 1890.

between Marxists and revolutionary 'anarchosyndicalists' at the beginning of the twentieth century. Contemporaneous observers portrayed the Guesdists as systematically hostile to unionism, an assessment since seconded by labour historians.[12] Critics have charged the French Marxists with autocratically reducing the union movement to a mere auxiliary of their Party, indicting them for ruthlessly sacrificing the needs of industrial militancy to the imperatives of socialist politics.[13] Secure in their mechanistic understanding of the 'making of the working class', Guesdists angrily rejected such charges: socialist politics, according to the French Marxists, flowed 'naturally' from the deep reservoir of labour militancy without need of socialist pump-priming. Indeed, the Parti Ouvrier self-confidently advocated a clear separation between trade unions, 'the community of suffering', and the socialist movement, 'the community of aspirations'.[14] Despite its name, the Parti Ouvrier was not a 'labour party' representing trade union affiliates on the twentieth-century British model. Guesdists even asserted that 'such a union of the occupational and political organisations of the proletariat ... would destroy both'.[15]

Why this apparent commitment to trade union autonomy? Why did the Parti Ouvrier ostensibly repudiate organic unity between the industrial and political militancy of the working class? As usual, French Marxists reacted to polemical imperatives and opportunities: their enemies' indictment, the charge that Guesdists sought to subordinate the unions to their Party, evoked an exaggerated

---

[12] For the contemporaneous view from very different perspectives, see L. de Seilhac, *Les Congrès Ouvriers en France de 1876 à 1897* (Paris, 1899), p. vii and E. Berth, *Les Nouveaux Aspects du Socialisme* (Paris, 1908), pp. 14–15. Examples of labour history on the same theme are G. Lefranc, *Le Mouvement Syndical sous la Troisième République* (Paris, 1967), p. 34; J. Bruhat and M. Piolet, *Esquisse d'une Histoire de la CGT* (Paris, 1967), p. 42; A. Dubief, *Le Syndicalisme Révolutionnaire* (Paris, 1969), p. 18; and M. Branciard, *Syndicats et Partis: Autonomie ou Dépendance* – Tome I – *1879–1947* (Paris, 1982), chapter 1.

[13] L. Rioux, *Notions d'Histoire du Mouvement Ouvrier Français: Les Cahiers du Centre d'Études Socialistes* (Paris, 1962), p. 9; C. Willard, *Le Mouvement Socialiste en France (1893–1905): Les Guesdistes* (Paris, 1965), p. 355; P. Stearns, *Revolutionary Syndicalism and French Labor* (New Brunswick, 1971), p. 15; and M. Moissonnier, 'La Longue Marche vers un Parti Ouvrier: Fin du XIXᵉ Siècle', in *La Classe Ouvrière Française et la Politique: Essais d'Analyse Historique et Sociale* (Paris, 1980), p. 69.

[14] G. Deville, 'L'Organisation Corporative', *Le Socialiste*, 27 August 1887. For a historical perspective on this question, see G. Haupt, 'Socialisme et Syndicalisme: Les Rapports entre Partis et Syndicats au Plan International – Une Mutation', in *Jaurès et la Classe Ouvrière* (Paris, 1981), pp. 29–67, and P. Schöttler, 'Politique Sociale ou Lutte des Classes: Notes sur le Syndicalisme "Apolitique" des Bourses du Travail', *Mouvement Social*, no. 116, 1981, pp. 16–17.

[15] J. Guesde, 'L'Autre Côté de la Question', *Le Petit Sou*, 27 December 1900.

response – advocacy of total separation between trade unionism and socialism. But Guesdists genuinely recoiled in horror from proposals to submerge their 'disciplined and organised forces' in the ideologically heterodox and organisationally incoherent union movement.[16] Only a fraction of the French working class belonged to trade unions during the *Belle Époque*, but the unions' membership dwarfed that of the POF, so that unionists would have overwhelmed socialists in any fusion of the industrial and political movements. An all-inclusive French 'Labour Party' would have drowned the French Marxists in a sea of working-class Radicals and anarchists as the followers of Émile Basly and Émile Pouget overwhelmed those of Guesde and Lafargue.

What is more, Guesdists argued that organised labour's adoption of a political programme, even a socialist programme, would greatly retard the ongoing organisation of labour. Abandoning its unproblematic linkage between labour militancy and socialism, the Parti Ouvrier admitted that 'when a trade union is endowed with a political credo, it divides the workers rather than uniting them'.[17] Convinced that class coalescence preceded class politics, but that the latter followed inevitably from the former, Guesdists did not fear that the political neutrality of organised labour would preclude the eventual socialist mobilisation of the working class. In the words of Charles Bonnier:

a trade union must be representative, which is to say that it must welcome every opinion. How could you mobilise an entire trade if it's fragmented into reds and yellows, into Catholics and free thinkers? This [argument] appears to go against our [Marxist] interests ... but, once united in the same cause, the proletariat will never again be separated – Catholic and conservative workers [will be] united with their class brethren.[18]

Once united, workers would necessarily rebel against their capitalist tormentors, and their unity would ensure their victory. Thus, under Guesdist guidance, the Fédération National des Syndicats ruled that 'unions which are already formed or those in the process of formation must not associate with any political party whatsoever'.[19]

[16] Compère-Morel, 'À Quelques Camarades de la Campagne', *Le Socialiste*, 10–17 February 1901.
[17] J. Guesde, *Questions d'Hier et d'Aujourd'hui* (Paris, 1911), pp. 13–14.
[18] C. Bonnier, 'Propos d'Organisation', *Le Socialiste*, 23–30 April 1905.
[19] *Fédération Nationale des Syndicats et Groupes Corporatifs Ouvriers de France: Troisième Congrès National – Bordeaux Octobre 1888* (Bordeaux, 1888), p. 3.

So much for theory. In practice, Marxist militants systematically politicised the unions within which they enjoyed influence, so that the Fédération du Textile, in particular, eventually functioned as a potent ally of the Parti Ouvrier: Victor Renard, leader of the textile workers, represented the POF no less than his powerful union. Trade unions, despite the Marxists' repudiation of an organic tie between industrial and political organisations, sent delegates to all POF gatherings, controlling more than half the mandates at the Party's 1892 Congress.[20] The POF rejected union affiliation in general, but eagerly incorporated *Guesdist* unions. The Parti Ouvrier press, ignoring its own endorsement of trade union political neutrality, enthusiastically pressed socialist politics upon the labour movement, advocating 'politics, still more politics, always and everywhere politics, but class politics alone'.[21] And the FNS itself, although advocating neutrality in principle, supported Parti Ouvrier electoral campaigns in practice, backing Guesdist politics even while locked in life-and-death struggle with the anti-political anarchosyndicalists.[22] How did Guesdists reconcile these partisan practices with the preconditions of labour solidarity?

The two strategies, neutrality and partisanship, usually coexisted in happy contradiction: Guesdists, given the opportunity, zealously proselytised among unionists, and, when challenged, affirmed their undying commitment to labour solidarity through political absten-tion. Cornered, or troubled by their own ideological dissonance, French Marxists resolved the contradiction by redefining 'politics': they distinguished between the factional conflicts characteristic of the bourgeois Republic, politics which workers should firmly abjure, and socialism, not politics in the pejorative sense understood by union militants.[23] According to Guesde and his comrades, only

---

[20] Willard, *Les Guesdistes*, p. 115.

[21] 'J. G.', 'De La Politique!', *Le Socialiste*, 21 November 1892.

[22] The *Bulletin Mensuel* of the FNS was dominated by an article on 'Les Élections Municipales et les Syndicats' in its April 1896 issue – at the very moment when the organisation struggled for its life against the anti-political unionism of the CGT. See also the lengthy panegyric to 'Le Parti Ouvrier à la Chambre' in the *Bulletin Mensuel* of July 1894, immediately before the crucial labour congress of Nantes which destroyed Guesdist hegemony over the national labour movement.

[23] For the assumption that 'socialism' excluded 'politics', see J. Dubois, *Le Vocabulaire Politique et Social en France de 1869 à 1872* (Paris, 1969), p. 58; P. Schöttler, *Naissance des Bourses du Travail: Un Appareil Idéologique d'État à la Fin du XIXᵉ Siècle* (Paris, 1985), pp. 169–177; M. Rebérioux, 'Le Socialisme Français de 1871 à 1914', in J. Droz (ed.), *Histoire Générale du Socialisme – De 1875 à 1918* (Paris, 1974), p. 148; and M. Perrot, *Les Ouvriers en Grève: France 1870–1890* (Paris, 1974), vol. 2, p. 607 and pp. 334–5.

socialist 'anti-politics' would allow labour to escape from the sterile 'politics' which divided unionists into Royalists and Republicans, Boulangists and anti-Boulangists, Dreyfusards and anti-Dreyfusards; unions could only function as the 'real educators and defenders of the working class within capitalism' once they realised the 'role they will play in transcending that society'[24] – unionist anti-politics presupposed socialist anti-capitalism. Understandably, non-socialist labour militants, and even many non-Guesdist socialists, rebuffed this jesuitical distinction between bourgeois politics and non-political (because non-bourgeois) socialism. By the mid-1890s, workers' hostility towards Guesdist politics had wrecked the FNS and instituted the transient but spectacular reign of the anarchosyndicalists.

Nevertheless, Parti Ouvrier ambiguities had not impeded the symbiosis of unionism and Marxism during the preceding decade, when Guesdists had not only dominated the FNS but presided over the establishment of the first national trades federations and even founded Bourses du Travail, subsequent bastions of anarchosyndicalism.[25] Why, then, did the contradiction between labour solidarity and socialist militancy prove so disruptive of Marxist unionism during the 1890s? Perhaps Guesdist 'politics' changed between the two periods. Historians have suggested that the 'bureaucratic practices' of the Parti Ouvrier – its aspirations to centralisation, discipline, and uniformity – thoroughly alienated a labour movement devoted to autonomy, spontaneity, and diversity.[26] The Party's bureaucracy, however, would have alienated no one during the 1880s, when it largely consisted of Guesde's personal correspondence. But the POF's increasing organisational solidity of the 1890s – its Parisian national council (complete with permanent secretariat), its regularly convened annual conferences, its novel departmental federations – undoubtedly antagonised unionists, who profoundly distrusted the potential authoritarianism of socialist leaders seconded by a nascent 'party-state.' And the Guesdist electoral successes of the early 1890s, the establishment of Parti Ouvrier municipal governments and ascension of prominent POF personalities to the Chamber of Deputies, reinforced this distrust. Unionists

[24] Manifesto of the National Council of the Party, June 1, 1897 in the Fonds Guesde of the Internationaal Instituut voor Sociale Geschiedenis, item no. 275/10.

[25] The Guesdists' enthusiasm for the Bourses evolved towards indifference or even hostility as the Parti Ouvrier increasingly viewed them as too heterogeneous to suit the POF's political model. Schöttler, *Naissance des Bourses du Travail*, pp. 101–2.

[26] Bruhat and Piolet, *Esquisse d'une Histoire de la CGT*, p. 39.

dreaded their reduction to mere election fodder, and with good reason: Guesdists openly downgraded unions to training formations, contending that 'a trade union is to a socialist group what a rifle club ... is to an infantry regiment'.[27] Ironically, the more successfully the Parti Ouvrier regimented working-class voters, the more completely it alienated trade unionists.

The Guesdist argument that socialist commitment precluded 'politics' also carried more conviction during the 1880s than during the 1890s. The fledgling unions of the early Third Republic rightly feared manipulation by the ruling Opportunists or the Opportunists' clerical and authoritarian enemies, so that socialism, a novel intrusion into the political culture of the period, offered workers escape from the oppressive patronage of the newly dominant liberals or the recently dominant conservatives.[28] Guesdist 'anti-politics' allowed workers to bypass 'bourgeois' brawls such as the Boulanger Affair. During the 1890s, however, as Guesdists, Allemanists, Blanquists, and Independent Socialists jostled each other in their pursuit of trade union endorsement, political factionalism within the working class increasingly arose from competition between socialist sects rather than from bourgeois party-politics. In 1882, workers had followed Guesde to avoid the Hobson's choice between Gambetta's disciples and Chambord's partisans; in 1889, workers followed Guesde to escape the competition between Ferry and Boulanger; but, in 1902, workers faced the choice between Guesde and Jaurès, whereupon many labour militants, disgusted by socialist divisiveness, opted for anarchosyndicalist autonomy. Well aware of the growing competition from Independents and Allemanists which challenged the transient Marxist hegemony over the labour Left, Guesdists blamed the destruction of the FNS in 1894–95 on their ascendant socialist competitors, competitors supposedly envious of the alliance between the Federation and the POF.[29] Labour militants, understandably, shied from such self-interested competition for their allegiance.

[27] P. Grados, 'Syndicats et Groupes', *Le Socialiste*, 25 May – 1 June 1902.
[28] Perrot, *Les Ouvriers en Grève*, vol. 2, p. 436.
[29] R. Lavigne, 'Le Congrès Corporatif de Nantes', *Le Socialiste*, 13 October 1894. For the importance of this issue, see B. Moss, *The Origins of the French Labor Movement 1830–1914: The Socialism of Skilled Workers* (Berkeley, 1976), pp. 138–44; C. Geslin, 'Les Syndicats Nantais et le Congrès Corporatif de Nantes 1894', *Cahiers d'Histoire*, vol. 22, 1977, pp. 260–7; J. Howorth, 'Édouard Vaillant: le Socialisme et le Mouvement Syndical *c.* 1888–1907', *Nouvelle Revue Socialiste*, nos. 12–13, 1975, p. 97; and J. Howorth, *Édouard Vaillant: La Création de l'Unité Socialiste en France/La Politique de l'Action Totale* (Paris, 1982), p. 200.

The Guesdist response to unionists' alienation from socialist politics proved ineffectual, even counter-productive. The POF advocated single-party socialism as the panacea for labour's ills: once French workers unanimously embraced Marxism, labour unity would follow automatically, a thesis which incidently contradicted the Guesdists' assumption that proletarian political unity followed upon industrial solidarity, the former a consequence of the latter. Henri Carrette, the Guesdist leader in Roubaix, seriously suggested that traditional centres of labour militancy (and of labour politics) such as Lyons and Paris, with their energetic unionism and crippling political factionalism, should copy the example of the Nord, with its single socialist party: all would be well once the POF's dominance in Roubaix prevailed throughout proletarian France.[30] Inevitably, this advice further alienated non-Guesdist trade union militants, already profoundly perturbed by the hegemonic aspirations of French Marxism. Events confirmed their worst fears: the Guesdists' willingness to split the labour movement rather than compromise with their enemies during the 1894 Congress of Nantes which destroyed the FNS apparently confirmed the incompatibility between politics, even socialist politics, and unionism, even revolutionary unionism. United by their common hostility to socialist politicisation of trade unions, 'anarchosyndicalists' who rejected revolutionary *politics* and Republican moderates who rejected *revolutionary* politics excluded Marxists from the leadership of French labour for a generation. Fernand Pelloutier, anarchist theorist of revolutionary syndicalism, and Auguste Keufer, liberal leader of the class-collaborationist Printers' Union, successfully leagued their otherwise antagonistic forces against Jules Guesde and his Marxist project.

The failure of the Guesdists' trade union strategy illuminated a fundamental contradiction in the Guesdist linkage between working-class industrial organisation and proletarian class formation, and highlighted a serious flaw in the Marxist conception of the 'making of the working class'. The Parti Ouvrier, following Marx, enthusiastically advocated trade union solidarity: unionism represented workers' only defence against the daily exactions of capital,

---

[30] *Ve Congrès National des Syndicats et Groupes Corporatifs Ouvriers de France tenu à Marseille du 19 à 22 Octobre 1892. Compte Rendu Recueilli dans les Archives de la Bourse du Travail de Marseille* (Paris, 1909), pp. 59–60. The title of this report is in error, the Congress having taken place in September 1892.

and constituted the prime prerequisite for the proletariat's embarkation upon its ultimate historical mission – the supersession of capitalism. But the POF, again following Marx, simultaneously pressed political militancy upon the labour movement. Trade unions, despite anarchosyndicalist counsels, could not avoid politics, if for no other reason than the all-important role of the state in defining the institutional parameters of industrial militancy: apolitical or anti-political unionism, as Guesdists occasionally realised, constituted a contradiction in terms.[31] But politics divided workers and thereby undermined the solidarity which alone sustained trade unionism. Neither Marxist theory nor Guesdist practice resolved this contradiction between working-class industrial solidarity and proletarian political mobilisation – a contradiction which dissipated Marxist hegemony over the unions during the 1890s.

Compounding their difficulties, Guesdists forfeited trade unionists' allegiance by adopting a distinctly ambivalent approach toward strikes, toward the industrial militancy which had assumed such unprecedented saliency in the working-class political culture of the *Fin de Siècle*. During these early years of the trade union movement, work stoppages were far more than negotiating ploys in banal disputes over wages and conditions: strikes served as a major mode, perhaps as *the* major mode, of workers' self-assertion against a social order dominated by their employers. Despite the suffering and privation which industrial militancy inflicted upon employees (as yet unprotected by strike-funds or personal financial reserves), strikes exploded as spontaneous festivals of liberation, festivals which convincingly asserted proletarian autonomy and self-reliance.[32] The great strikes of the *Belle Époque* announced the arrival of a new and forceful contender for power: they represented the decisive disassociation of the 'social question' from the pathos of the 'dangerous class' – from poverty, deviance, and charity – and its inextricable association with workers' rights, with the assertive claims of a labour *movement*. Industrial conflict repeatedly marked

---

[31] The close linkage between the changing political context and patterns of labour militancy is cogently argued in C. Tilly and E. Shorter, 'Les Vagues de Grèves en France 1890–1968', *Annales: Économies, Sociétés, Civilisations*, vol. 28, 1973, pp. 857–87 and in P. Stearns, 'Against the Strike Threat', *Journal of Modern History*, vol. 40, 1968, p. 476.

[32] This is the underlying theme of Michelle Perrot's *Les Ouvriers en Grève*. But see L. Marty, *Chanter pour Survivre: Culture Ouvrière, Travail et Techniques dans le Textile – Roubaix 1850–1914* (Lille, 1982), pp. 109–10 for a challenge to this interpretation.

decisive moments in the socio-political transformation of *fin-de-siècle* France: the murderous violence of the Decazeville strike of 1886 shattered the illusion that Republican institutions guaranteed class harmony, thereby legitimising the Marxist conception of class war; the patient perseverance of the Carmaux strikers in 1892 inaugurated a sustained working-class assault upon the 'bourgeois Republic', thereby validating the Marxist conception of the 'making of the working class'; and the bitter strike at Montceau in 1901 discredited the class-collaborationist 'social liberalism' of the Waldeck-Rousseau ministry, thereby rescuing French Marxism from the 'Ministerialists'. How did the Parti Ouvrier evaluate the place of strikes in a capitalist polity and how did the Party assess their role in the transition to socialism?

Superficially, the POF maintained a uniform and consistent approach to strikes: it unconditionally supported them. The strike, according to the Parti Ouvrier, armed workers with their 'only weapon of protection'[33] against employers' rapacity. Deprived of the power and privilege accorded by property-ownership, proletarians could coerce the property-owners upon whom they depended for employment only by collectively reappropriating workers' sole asset – their labour power. Better yet, from a Marxist perspective, strikes disrupted the officially sanctioned 'myth of civil and political harmony'[34] between labour and capital. Every strike, however insignificant in itself, illustrated the inherent conflict between wage-rates and the rate of profit and thereby illuminated the contradictory class interests which sundered workers from capitalists. Lightning bolts bursting from the dark sky of capitalist society, strikes periodically revealed the impassable chasm separating the proletariat from the bourgeoisie. Finally, strikes forced workers to organise and discipline themselves, serving as a 'veritable military school' which drilled proletarians in 'organisation and solidarity'.[35] Once enrolled in the harsh academy of industrial militancy, workers would quickly master the strategy of the class war

---

[33] 'J. G.' (Guesde), untitled, *L'Égalité*, 18 December 1881.
[34] J. Guesde, 'Le Résultat', *Le Cri du Peuple*, 18 April 1884. Strikes were indeed instrumental in destroying the association between workers and the Radical Party – that great obstacle to socialist politics in France. See, for instance, the graphic description of one such disassociation in G. Dupeux, *Aspects de l'Histoire Sociale et Politique du Loir-et-Cher 1848–1914* (Paris, 1962), pp. 521–2.
[35] J. Guesde, *Services Publics et Socialisme* (Paris, 1884), p. 28.

and the tactics of class conflict. Guesdists, officer-instructors as well as recruiting sergeants for the proletarian army, summed up their teleology of working-class mobilisation as 'strikes today, electoral conflict tomorrow, armed struggle eventually, but discipline, organisation and concentration always'.[36] Industrial disputation supplied Guesdist polemicists with their bread-and-butter theme and Guesdist theorists with their most convincing argument: with considerable justification, French Marxists assumed that strikes blasted open the road along which workers would march towards socialism.[37]

Nevertheless, Guesdists, even at their most enthusiastic, consistently described work stoppages as *defensive*, as reactions to an endless litany of 'workers unjustly fired and reductions in wages'.[38] Strikes, it seemed, schooled proletarian class warriors in fortification technique, not invasion strategy. Professionally pessimistic about the workers' lot under capitalism, French Marxists rarely admitted that strikes occasionally increased workers' salaries or enhanced their working conditions. Industrial militancy, according to the Parti Ouvrier, might prevent employers from reducing their employees to absolute dependency and impoverishment, but could not gain workers an increased share or, by definition, a *fair* share of their product: the exploitative relationship between labour and capital would survive the most successful strike. Uneasily contemplating the industrial unrest of the *Belle Époque*, French Marxists concluded that

[36] J. Guesde, 'Le Salut', *L'Égalité*, 8 January 1882. There is evidence that many workers shared the Guesdists' conviction that strikes foreshadowed the revolution. Perrot, *Les Ouvriers en Grève*, vol. 2, pp. 630–3.

[37] For arguments stressing the strong connection between strikes and the implantation of socialism in regions relevant to Guesdism, see R. Jonas, 'From the Radical Republic to the Social Republic: On the Origins and Nature of Socialism in Rural France 1871–1914', PhD thesis, University of California, Berkeley, 1985, p. 385; T. Judt, 'The Development of Socialism in France: The Example of the Var', *Historical Journal*, vol. 18, 1975, pp. 74–5; L. Loubère, 'Coal Miners, Strikes and Politics in Lower Languedoc 1880–1914', *Journal of Social History*, vol. 2, 1968–69, p. 50; J.-M. Gaillard, 'La Pénétration du Socialisme dans le Bassin Houiller du Gard', pp. 271–87; and R. Pierre, 'Aux Origines du Mouvement Ouvrier dans la Drôme: Les Ouvriers Chapeliers du Bourg-de-Péage et de Romans (1850–1890)', *Cahiers d'Histoire*, vol. 17, 1972, pp. 357–60. The simple connection between strikes and socialist organisation is challenged in D. Vasseur, *Les Débuts du Mouvement Ouvrier dans la Région de Belfort-Montbéliard 1870–1914* (Paris, 1967), pp. 25 and 75; Perrot, *Les Ouvriers en Grève*, vol. 2, pp. 643–644; and in P. Ponsot, 'Organisation et Action dans le Mouvement Ouvrier: Réflexion sur le Cas de Monceau-les-Mines au Tournant du XIXᵉ et du XXᵉ Siècles', *Mouvement Social*, no. 99, 1977, pp. 11–16, with discussion of Ponsot's point in *ibid.*, pp. 16–22.

[38] Anonymous, 'Grèves', *Bulletin Mensuel de la Fédération Nationale des Syndicats et Groupes Corporatifs Ouvriers de France*, no. 3, 25 July 1890.

workers risked confusion between defensive tactics and offensive strategy, that the vogue for strikes might jeopardise the socialist mobilisation of the proletariat.

In the POF's most schematic analyses of the making of the working class, the Party predicted that 'the further we advance towards political organisation, the more workers discard the strike'[39] – industrial and political militancy were mutually exclusive, the former a transcended evolutionary stage towards the latter. At their most negative, Guesdists completely reversed their otherwise favourable assessment of strikes as an important, if secondary, front in the class war. Charles Bonnier, for instance, wrote that Parti Ouvrier involvement in industrial disputes would trap Guesdists in a labour of Sisyphus, that 'a strike may be general, local, governmental, capitalist, or syndical; it can never be socialist. A class party, organised and conscious, will never expend its time and money on this unknown and shifting terrain'.[40] French Marxists, in this critical mode, questioned the utility of the strike even as a defensive weapon. According to the Parti Ouvrier, employers – scheming to diminish burdensome inventories, cut labour costs, and dismantle nascent trade unions – intentionally provoked many (if not most) labour stoppages: strikes exhausted trade union resources and destroyed labour morale; workers should abjure them in favour of more 'profitable' militancy. These doubts and apprehensions featured in most labour and socialist thought of the *Fin de Siècle:* theorists and militants, if not their followers, dreaded a tactic which required enormous sacrifices at great risk for minimal returns.[41] But the Guesdists' qualms also revealed profound hostility to the unplanned spontaneity and unregenerate localism of most turn-of-the-century labour unrest, which rarely manifested 'discipline, organisation, and concentration'. French Marxists dreamed of carefully planned strikes targeted against entire industries and sustained by nation-wide solidarity, and criticised industrial action which failed to match this ideal. Given the embryonic character of French trade

---

[39] Copie du Rapport de Delory au Congrès Fédéral de Denain, 28 August 1898 (AD du Nord, M 154/82, pièce 3) cited in Willard, *Les Guesdistes*, p. 351.

[40] C. Bonnier, 'La Grève Patronale', *Le Socialiste*, 12–19 May 1901.

[41] Examples of employers provoking strikes may be found in M. Hanagan, *The Logic of Solidarity: Artisans and Industrial Workers in Three French Towns 1871–1914* (London, 1980), pp. 153 and 170 and in Perrot, *Les Ouvriers en Grève*, vol. 2, p. 681. The general disjuncture between leadership qualms about strikes and the enthusiasm of local militants for this mode of action is discussed in Perrot, *Les Ouvriers en Grève*, vol. 1, p. 64. Guesdist doubts about the strike weapon are discussed and criticised in Branciard, *Syndicats et Partis*, pp. 26–7.

unionism, these criteria effectively condemned most strikes as irrational in conception and counterproductive in effect.

The ambiguities characteristic of the Parti Ouvrier's approach to industrial militancy manifested themselves most catastrophically in the barely concealed Guesdist glee occasioned by failed strikes. How could socialists dedicated to working-class militancy rejoice in working-class defeats? Why this astonishing lack of sensitivity, which undoubtedly cost the POF dearly in unionist sympathy? Essentially uninterested in everyday industrial relations, French Marxists expected defeat in strikes to force workers out of corporative defence at the point of production into political offensives against bourgeois society as a whole: disillusioned trade unionists would supposedly emerge from defeats as militant socialists. 'Agreed that strikes harm workers', admitted *Le Socialiste*, 'but from this evil we derive an advantage – workers realise that they cannot expect anything from their employers until they seize power. It's what we call in today's pedagogy: "an object lesson".'[42] Hence, for instance, the Parti Ouvrier's pleasure at the disastrous coal miners' strike of November 1893, which virtually demolished the northern miners' union (a bastion of anti-Guesdism), but supposedly ensured that 'trade unionists have become socialists ... not a negligible result for our party'.[43] This approach, wherever and whenever applied, proved to be tactless, counter-productive, and, usually, incorrect: the failure of industrial militancy disorganised and demoralised local socialist movements as well as disorienting and disrupting the reformist or anti-political trade unions against which socialists competed.[44] Guesdists' enthusiasm for failed strikes – their slogan 'End of the Strike, Beginning of the Revolution!'[45] – demonstrated both polemical insensitivity and theoretical incomprehension.

Overall, Guesdists fundamentally misunderstood the place of

[42] 'B.', 'Contradictions Capitalistes', *Le Socialiste*, 13 January 1895.
[43] 'A. Z.' (Zévaès), 'Résultat', *Le Socialiste*, 11 November 1893.
[44] There are numerous instances of this conjunction of the defeat of labour militancy and the decline of socialist politics during the *Belle Époque*. See, for example, R. Pierre, *Les Origines du Syndicalisme et Socialisme dans la Drôme 1850–1920* (Paris, 1973), p. 90; R. Parize, 'La Stratégie Patronale au Creusot pendant les Grèves de 1899–1900', *Cahiers d'Histoire de l'Institut Maurice Thorez*, no. 24, 1978, pp. 13–46; Derruau-Boniol, 'Le Socialisme dans l'Allier de 1848 à 1914', p. 151; J. Sagnes, 'Le Syndicalisme Ouvrier dans le Bassin Minier de Graissessac des Années 1890 à la Première Guerre Mondiale', in *Le Midi Rouge: Mythe et Réalité* (Paris, 1982), pp. 185–213; and J. Merriman, *Red City: Limoges and the French Nineteenth Century* (Oxford, 1985), chapter 8.
[45] Anonymous, 'Fin de Grève', *Le Socialiste*, 15 May 1886.

strikes in the mentality of the French proletariat. The Parti Ouvrier's ambiguous combination of enthusiastic support for striking workers in particular cases coupled with denigration of the long-term efficacy of industrial militancy in general confused and alienated labour militants. Paul André undoubtedly antagonised many of his fellow railway workers (never an enthusiastic audience for Guesdism) when he patronisingly wrote that

it's always worthwhile for the proletariat to mobilise against employers' exploitation: first, because that's the way to impose a limit on exploitation; second, because the strike, an elementary but very clear form of the class war, gives workers their first understanding of social conflict; and, finally, because the inadequacy of that double-edged weapon is obvious from experience, which convinces the working class of the necessity of other means of action.[46]

'Economistically' reducing strikes to (fruitless) exercises in wage bargaining, the Parti Ouvrier underestimated the role of industrial militancy as an affirmation of working-class autonomy and failed (or refused) to recognise that workers often struck to influence 'public opinion' and summon state intervention, that proletarians compelled public recognition of their needs and enhanced political awareness of their grievances through symbolic industrial insurrection.[47] In turn, few labour militants ever understood the complex rationale which simultaneously justified enthusiastic and unconditional Guesdist support for particular strikes *and* Guesdist attacks upon the rationality and efficacy of industrial militancy in general. This mutual incomprehension precipitated the collapse of Marxist trade unionism during the 1890s, simultaneously destroying Guesdist credibility and the Fédération National des Syndicats.[48] Why did the Parti Ouvrier so clumsily alienate the labour movement, a movement so central to its project of constructing a self-assertive proletariat?

---

[46] P.-M. André, 'Les Grèves', *Le Socialiste*, 14–21 December 1902.
[47] For a superb discussion of this failure of Guesdist understanding, see W. Reddy, *The Rise of Market Culture: The Textile Trade and French Society 1750–1900* (Cambridge, 1984), pp. 296–7, 309, and 324. For evidence that state intervention in strikes tended to advantage workers, see G. Friedman, 'The State and the Making of the Working Class: France and the United States 1880–1914', *Theory and Society*, vol. 17, 1988, p. 411, and G. Friedman, 'Strike Success and Union Ideology: The United States and France 1880–1914', *Journal of Economic History*, vol. 48, 1988, pp. 7–8.
[48] J. Bron, *Histoire du Mouvement Ouvrier Français* (Paris, 1970), vol. 1, p. 63 and Anonymous, 'Introduction', in *Jules Guesde et les Grèves* (Paris, 1949), p. 7.

The Parti Ouvrier's denigration of the strike as an adequate response to exploitation possessed considerable force – at particular times and in particular places. The depressed economic circumstances of the 1880s apparently justified the Guesdist critique of industrial militancy: strikes during the 'Great Depression' usually reacted against employers' desperate efforts to reduce wages in parallel with price deflation (thereby reinforcing the Marxist identification of strikes as essentially a defensive weapon), and usually failed (thereby reinforcing the Marxist devaluation of industrial militancy).[49] But the Parti Ouvrier did not revise its negative assessment of strikes during the economic boom which began in the 1890s, years when successful offensive strikes proliferated throughout the French economy.[50] Appropriate circumstances sometimes validated the Party's critique of strikes, but evidently did not engender that critique.

A discouraging industrial relations environment in the Parti Ouvrier's northern bastions, which prevailed throughout the *Belle Époque* in sharp contrast to circumstances elsewhere, further deepened Guesdist pessimism.[51] Employers in the Nord successfully frustrated the development of textile unionism in major centres such as Tourcoing; strikes by textile workers consistently failed as their industry entered its slow twentieth-century decline; and the state repressed textile workers' militancy with a brutality Paris rarely dared to impose upon more powerful working-class communities. Voting for Guesdists was the only form of protest readily available to workers suffering these employment conditions – little wonder that the Fédération du Textile, alone in the labour movement, refused to

---

[49] For labour conditions in the 1880s, see J. Néré, 'Aspects du Déroulement des Grèves en France durant la Période 1883–1889', *Revue d'Histoire Économique et Sociale*, vol. 34, 1956, p. 290, and Perrot, *Les Ouvriers en Grève*, vol. 1, p. 67, pp. 92–4, and 158–9. Graphic regional examples of the difficulties encountered by labour militancy during the 1880s may be found in C. Geslin, 'Provocations Patronales et Violences Ouvrières: Fougères (1887–1907)', *Mouvement Social*, no. 82, 1973, pp. 17–83 and J. Charles, 'Les Débuts de l'Organisation Ouvrière à Besançon 1874–1904', *Mouvement Social*, no. 40, 1962, p. 21.

[50] See the statistical tables in Perrot, *Les Ouvriers en Grève*, vol. 1, p. 66.

[51] See the case for such an explanation of responses to various labour strategies in J. Julliard, 'Théorie Syndicaliste Révolutionnaire et Pratique Gréviste', *Mouvement Social*, no. 65, 1968, p. 65, and G. Weill, 'Le Rôle des Facteurs Structurels dans l'Évolution des Rémunerations Salariales au XIXe Siècle', *Revue Économique*, vol. 10, 1959, pp. 558–9. The unskilled and semi-skilled workers who predominated in the northern bastions of the POF had a particularly poor success rate in their strikes, according to Perrot, *Les Ouvriers en Grève*, vol. 2, p. 647.

abandon the POF during the 1890s.[52] All the same, Guesdists ignored victorious strikes elsewhere in France, never analysed the peculiarities of industrial relations in the stagnant textile industry, and never contrasted labour markets characterised by trade union successes with those typified by setbacks. The Parti Ouvrier's only systematic analysis of the relative success rate of various industrial strategies under varying economic circumstances appeared in an isolated examination of the *American* labour movement. Elsewhere, anecdote reigned unchecked.[53] Once again, appropriate circumstances validated the Guesdists' pessimistic assessment of strikes, but patently did not originate that assessment.

In practice, the Guesdist denigration of industrial militancy rested upon two alternative but equally *a priori* interpretations of the capitalist labour market, not upon empirical examination of conjuncture and milieu. In the more simplistic interpretation, which unrealistically presupposed monopolistic price-fixing throughout the French economy, workers could not improve their circumstances through collective bargaining because higher wages and better working conditions immediately inflated prices, with no net gain to workers – a thesis as favoured by employers as by Marxists. Untrained and uninterested in labour economics, Guesdists never admitted that this argument, although possibly defensible in the aggregate (although only by abstracting the rate of profit and ignoring changes in productivity), did not apply to any particular group of workers: even if overall real wages remained unchanged, real wage increases for metal workers might incur equally real wage reductions for textile employees. As usual, French Marxists fastidiously evaded economic logic which disclosed potential conflict between workers.

The more sophisticated thesis employed by Guesdists in their analyses of the (il)logic of industrial militancy conceded that wage increases need not yield higher prices, given unrelenting competition between employers (an implicit admission that France had not yet attained 'monopoly capitalism'). French Marxists even developed

[52] Reddy, *The Rise of Market Culture*, pp. 309, 322, and 329. For graphic descriptions of the discouraging industrial environment in the northern textile industry, see P. Hilden, *Working Women and Socialist Politics in France 1880–1914: A Regional Study* (Oxford, 1986), p. 91, and R. Pierreuse, 'La Situation Économique et Sociale à Roubaix et Tourcoing à la Belle Époque', *Revue du Nord*, vol. 55, 1973, p. 424.

[53] Anonymous, 'Les Grèves aux États-Unis', *Bulletin Mensuel de la Fédération Nationale des Syndicats et Groupes Corporatifs Ouvriers de France*, no. 3, 15 July 1890.

the surprisingly modern contention that higher wages forced capitalists into productivity-enhancing (and labour-saving) investments, so that salary increases *cheapened* commodities over the long term.[54] In this 'market-forces' scenario, wage increases reduced profits rather than inflating prices.[55] Guesdists, again as usual, eagerly seized upon economic logic which disclosed potential class conflict between capitalists and workers. But even this dynamic, in the Guesdist analysis of capitalist political economy, would fail to improve labour conditions in the long term. The conjunction of higher wages, lower profits, and labour-substituting investment necessarily (according to the POF) generated accumulation crisis and depression, economic phenomena which victimised the very workers who had shortsightedly sought advantages *within* the capitalist economic order.[56]

In any case, Guesdists contended, although strikes might have succeeded in the past, when 'small-scale industry led to the proliferation of employers', they necessarily failed in a present dominated by 'large-scale mechanical industry concentrated in a few hands'.[57] Workers' solidarity had prevailed against isolated and disunited workshop masters: striking workers had easily obtained alternative employment, while strike-bound employers had faced ruin at the hands of unaffected competitors. But these conditions belonged to the archaic past. In the brave new world of concentrated and centralised capital, militant trade unionists and strikers quixotically challenged the vast resources of monopolists: striking workers succumbed to blacklegs, blacklists, and starvation, while embattled employers retreated into the invulnerability of their vast financial reserves and rigorously managed markets. Worse still, monopoly

---

[54] P. Lafargue, 'Le Taux des Salaires et le Prix des Marchandises', *L'Égalité*, 28 May 1882 and J. Guesde, 'Les Crises', *Le Socialiste*, 20 August 1887. The French Marxists enjoyed pointing out how 'bourgeois' economists retreated from their obsession with prices determined by supply and demand in favour of price determination by cost – when it was a question of wages. See, for example, Anonymous, 'Les Salaires et le Prix des Marchandises', *Le Socialiste*, 27 February 1886.

[55] *Ibid.*

[56] 'B'. (C. Bonnier), 'Les Grèves en Angleterre en 1890', *Le Socialiste*, 14 February 1892. Guesdist analyses coincided with real patterns within the French labour market of the time, according to J. Lambert, *Le Patron: De l'Avènement à la Contestation* (Paris, 1969), pp. 43 and 91–3.

[57] J. Guesde, 'Une Nouvelle Loi Chapelier', *Le Cri du Peuple*, 26 February 1884. The tyrannical labour relations characteristic of great plants such as that at Le Creusot confirmed this pessimistic diagnosis. See, for example, J. Dereymez, 'Les Syndicats Ouvriers de Saône-et-Loire 1899–1914', *Cahiers d'Histoire de l'Institut de Recherches Marxistes*, no. 16, 1984, p. 43.

capitalists replied to strikes by radically transforming workplaces vulnerable to industrial disruption – enforcing novel managerial hierarchies, deskilling strategic trades, and replacing intransigent workers with docile equipment. Profoundly pessimistic at the best of times about the workers' lot under capitalism, Guesdists concluded that 'strikes are virtually impossible nowadays, given that science so easily replaces men by machines.'[58]

This thesis, although well-tailored to suit the technological anxiety of skilled workers, profoundly misread the nascent industrial relations of twentieth-century monopoly capitalism. Apart from the Guesdists' gross overestimation of mechanisation in their nation's industry, they systematically ignored the ways in which the vast capital investment and oppressive debt burden associated with the second industrial revolution conferred unprecedented industrial power upon its employees. Ironically, 'monopoly capitalism' awarded 'monopoly' power to small groups of strategically situated workers, whose strikes could both disrupt production on a national scale and interrupt the flow of investment income which sustained the new order's fragile symbiosis between industry and finance. Far from dooming unions, 'Fordism' (as capital-intensive mass production has come to be known) inaugurated the golden age of industrial unionism, a radiant dawn mistaken by Guesdists for the blackest night.

The role of the 'bourgeois state' in industrial relations clinched the Guesdist argument against strikes. As subscribers to a thoroughly reductionist political theory, Guesdists assumed that French public authority necessarily represented the capitalist 'ruling class', that capitalists, by definition, enjoyed governmental support during labour conflicts. Misinterpreting the motivation behind many strikes, Guesdists could not conceive that workers might appeal to public authority against their otherwise invincible employers, that industrial action often constituted an implicit (and sometimes explicit) appeal for state intervention against intransigent bosses. In the Marxists' demonology, the state, a fiend only one rank below the satanic bourgeoisie itself, 'provoke[d] strikes, starve[d] workers, and oppress[ed] them politically'[59] – no less than intransigent

---

[58] Comment by Roussel, *IIe Congrès National des Syndicats Ouvriers de France, tenu à Montluçon en Octobre 1887. Compte Rendu Officiel* (Montluçon, 1888), p. 39.
[59] P. Dramas, 'La Grève de Carmaux', *Le Socialiste*, 18 August 1895.

employers, prefects and police chiefs bedevilled industrial militancy. How did Guesdists sustain this polemical reduction of the Ministry of the Interior to the Ministry of Strikebreaking?

Their thesis, however untenable in general, undoubtedly reinforced resentments evoked by workers' experience, and in turn was reinforced by these resentments: the state may have favoured conciliation in many conflicts, but every significant strike during the *Belle Époque* mobilised police and troops to defend employers' property against occupation and protect strike-breakers against irate strikers. Entire army corps, detached from their supposed task of national defence, deployed against insurgent French workers, occupying mining villages, mill towns and industrial faubourgs as if encamped in enemy territory. The resultant skirmishes between strikers and the 'forces of order', skirmishes marked by substantial and exclusively proletarian casualty lists, apparently confirmed the Guesdist assertion that French capitalists sheltered behind an impenetrable rampart of 'soldiers, gendarmes, police, and judges'.[60] According to the Parti Ouvrier, employers 'can withstand any strike with the backing of the government, the army, and the police'.[61] Delighted by further 'object lessons' in the futility of strikes, Guesdists actually cheered when police blocked 'the unionist dead-end into which too many workers threaten to rush'.[62] Industrial militancy, however massive and however sustained, would never overcome the coercive powers of the ruling class: only socialist revolution could challenge the 'bourgeois state'. 'Defeated in a strike, that unequal conflict', Guesdists argued reassuringly,

---

[60] Rapport du citoyen Mazelier, *IIe Congrès National des Syndicats*, p. 60. Significantly, the state's repression of labour militancy was most consistently applied in the textile industry, that bastion of Guesdism, while conciliation was often attempted in more strategic areas of the economy – coal miners enjoyed both more industrial and more political muscle than textile workers. See E. Shorter and C. Tilly, 'Le Déclin de la Grève Violente en France de 1890 à 1935', *Mouvement Social*, no. 76, 1971, pp. 109–11.

[61] C. Bonnier, 'La Grève de Crimmitschau', *Le Socialiste*, 21–28 February 1904. In fact, there were many cases in which workers sought government intervention and arbitration against their employers – the relationship between state power and industrial relations was by no means as unilateral as Guesdists assumed. For illuminating examples of embattled workers pressing for government intervention in labour disputes, see E. Shorter and C. Tilly, *Strikes in France* (London, 1974), pp. 29–33; R. Trempé, 'Le Réformisme des Mineurs Français à la Fin du XIXᵉ Siècle', *Mouvement Social*, no. 65, 1968, p. 99 and p. 104; and F. Caron, 'Essai d'Analyse Historique d'une Psychologie du Travail', *Mouvement Social*, no. 50, 1965, pp. 3–40.

[62] Guesde, interviewed in *Le Matin*, cited in G. Lefranc, *Le Mouvement Socialiste sous la IIIᵉ République 1875–1940* (Paris, 1963), p. 57.

'workers will be victorious some day upon another terrain',[63] the political terrain controlled by Marxist generals.

At their most extreme, Guesdists proclaimed that trade unions and strikes 'harmed workers not only when [they] fail, but when [they] succeed'.[64] Once diverted into the dead-end of trade unionism, the workers' movement would drag to a halt, its impasse indicated as much by the fury as by the futility of its periodic industrial insurrections. In one astonishing instance of this argument, the Parti Ouvrier, adducing the harrowing evidence of British poverty revealed by Booth and Rowntree, alleged that this proletarian distress derived, not from inadequate industrial organisation, but from the great *strength* of the British trade unions. The British workingman's investment in work-place militancy had supposedly impoverished him. According to *Le Socialiste:* 'this [misery] proves that the more the proletariat perfects its union and cooperative organisation, the more unhappy it is'.[65] But, however effectively this thesis served against anti-revolutionary French craftsmen who dreamed of emulating their British peers, it simultaneously alienated labour militants in general, the vital constituency of the Marxist project, and contradicted the fundamental Guesdist commitment to industrial organisation and labour militancy, the mould of class formation and weapon of class defence. Why this self-destructive polemical extremism? Why this systematic pattern of self-contradiction?

Changing French circumstances and unchanging socialist principles undoubtedly conditioned both the Parti Ouvrier's most fervent denunciations of unions and its most unconditional endorsements of unionism: the contingencies of the economic environment and the ambiguities of Marxist doctrine engendered systematic Guesdist ambivalence towards industrial militancy and industrial organisation. At the same time, however, the POF's vacillations arose from the polemical imperatives which governed the development of French Marxism. Parti Ouvrier labour militancy – the attempted synthesis of unionism and socialism, of labour solidarity and revolutionary militancy – contended fiercely against vigorous alternative strategies for labour: against deferential workers and

---

[63] P.-M. André, 'Impuissance Gouvernementale', *Le Socialiste*, 10–17 February 1901.
[64] C. Carlier, *Contre la Grève Générale* (Lille, 1901), p. 21.
[65] L. Deslinières, 'Où Mène le Capitalisme', *Le Socialiste*, 29 December 1901 – 6 January 1902.

authoritarian capitalists who combined within the traditional framework of employer paternalism; against Social Catholics, 'national socialists,' and Republican 'Solidarists' who patronised competing models of corporatist or class-collaborationist trade unionism; and against 'mutualists' and 'revolutionary syndicalists' who repudiated socialist politics in favour of workers' self-emancipation through labour organisation alone. The Parti Ouvrier's assaults upon these anti-Marxist labour strategies generated the peculiar combination of dogmatic rigidity and programmatic incoherence which consistently undermined and eventually destroyed the Guesdists' influence within the French trade union movement.

Paternalism had reigned, at least as rhetoric, over labour relations since the earliest separation of capital and labour. Hierarchical conceptions of mutual dependency and mutual obligation inherited from feudal ideology, if not from feudal practice, had long structured the dialogue between the lords of capital and 'their' workers, serving the former as a stratagem of overt domination of labour and the latter as tactics of covert manipulation of employers.[66] Large French enterprises, particularly in mining and metallurgy, had traditionally dominated their employees by combining punitive surveillance – designed to exclude 'trouble makers', preclude unionisation, and repress labour unrest – with company housing, company insurance against sickness, accident and old age, and company-sponsored religious education – all calculated to reward loyalty, inculcate deference, and retain the allegiance of valued workers.[67] Although the constraints of competition and the *laissez-faire* principles of nineteenth-century entrepreneurs repeatedly jeopardised this strategy, paternalistic labour regimes survived into the *Belle Époque*, reinforced by both the self-interest and the religious convictions of French industrialists.

---

[66] L. Bergeron, *Les Capitalistes en France 1780–1914* (Paris, 1978), pp. 149–152, and Lambert, *Le Patron*, pp. 95–7.

[67] For the nineteenth-century background to employers' efforts to dominate working-class communities through 'paternalistic' labour strategies, see E. Accampo, *Industrialization, Family Life, and Class Relations: Saint Chamond 1815–1914* (Berkeley, 1989), p. 213; L. Murard and P. Zylberman, *Le Petit Travailleur Infatigable ou le Prolétaire Régénéré: Villes, Usines, Habitat, et Intimités au XIXᵉ Siècle* (Fontenay-sous-Bois, 1976), and, for instances from the Guesdists' period, see 'Transformations Industrielles et Sociales à Saint-Étienne à la Fin du XIXᵉ Siècle', in P. Héritier et al., *150 Ans de Luttes Ouvrières dans le Bassin Stéphanois* (Saint-Étienne, 1979), p. 117; D. Reid, 'Industrial Paternalism: Discourse and Practice in Nineteenth-Century French Mining and Metallurgy', *Comparative Studies in Society and History*, vol. 27, 1985, pp. 597–607; and P. Stearns, *Lives of Labour: Work in a Maturing Industrial Society* (London, 1975), pp. 173–7.

Paternalism encountered a favourable, even enthusiastic, reception from many workers, who trustingly confided their welfare to the patronage of powerful employers rather than to the uncertainties of independent labour organisation. Despite the revolutionary heritage of French proletarians, despite memories of the Lyonnais Canuts and the Parisian Communards, deference endured and often prevailed in working-class mentalities and in the labour-relations of *fin-de-siècle* France. Even the most revolutionary workers, although hostile to the 'patronat' in general, sometimes esteemed their 'patrons', a word which retained its favourable connotations even within militant labour discourse.[68] The symbiotic relationship between paternalist employers and deferential proletarians challenged the Guesdists' interpretation of the making of the working class: at the least, paternalistic labour practices violated the Marxist assumption that capital treated labour solely as a commodity; at the most, they devalued the emancipatory imperative which governed the Marxist project. More outraged by working-class deference than by employer authoritarianism, more troubled by the paternalism which defied their Marxist paradigm than by the exploitation which confirmed it, Guesdists violently attacked both the workers who accepted employers' patronage and the employers who offered it, with their most savage assaults reserved for the former. This ongoing Marxist struggle against the symbiosis between deferential workers and paternalistic employers accounts for the most vehement Guesdist arguments in favour of unionism, for the POF's periodic adherence to the virtues of trade unions and industrial militancy, however non-socialist or even anti-socialist.

Paternal discipline, however, declined in importance and prevalence throughout the French industrial economy during the later nineteenth century, thereby diminishing its salience in Guesdist discourse. Employers, even in redoubts of neo-feudal practice such as Decazeville or Le Creusot, decided that dominance over workers' lives beyond the factory gate, the *sine qua non* of efficacious paternalism, cost more in capital and political credit than it returned in employee deference and loyalty. At the same time, paternalism, traditionally favoured by capitalists with Bonapartist or Royalist sympathies, incurred the hostility of the triumphant Republicans, of liberals and democrats ideologically allergic to overt hierarchy and

---

[68] M. Perrot, 'Le Regard de l'Autre: Les Patrons Français vus par les Ouvriers (1880–1914)', in *Le Patronat de la Seconde Industrialisation* (Paris, 1979), pp. 294–5.

pragmatically unwilling to surrender the working class to the tutelage of wealthy enemies. Finally, paternalist practices, however well-intentioned, increasingly evoked violent protest or passive resistance from workers who had absorbed the Republican principles of civic equality and consequently resented their reduction to *de facto* minors.[69] Collective working-class self-assertion empowered by Republican institutions and inspired by Republican ideals dissolved the individual bond between 'master and man' which had sustained French paternalism.

The capitalists of the *Belle Époque*, of course, continued to resist labour militancy, which, at the least, jeopardised their profits and, at the most, menaced the survival of their class. But their resistance increasingly depended upon 'co-partnership' schemes rather than pseudo-feudal authoritarianism: Catholic employers abandoned the age-old nostrums of charity and obedience in favour of Christian-Social 'mixed unions,' which would supposedly associate capital with labour in Christian brotherhood; Catholics and Nationalists revived (or invented) the 'corporatist' traditions of the *ancien régime*, which would supposedly articulate the common interest of workers and capitalists in the welfare of their firms, their trades, and their nation; while the ruling liberals patronised 'business unionism', which would supposedly couple pragmatic labour leaders to conciliatory businesspeople as separate but equal partners, partners equally dedicated to the prosperity of the capitalist economy and the sanctity of Republican institutions. Abandoning their aspirations to extra-mural domination, capitalists of every religious and political persuasion hoped that newly-organised labour would cooperate with newly-threatened capital, once employees and employers associated freely as (Christian or Nationalist or Republican) equals.[70] The

---

[69] A useful discussion of these changes in employer strategy may be found in D. Reid, 'Decazeville: Company Town and Working Class Community 1826–1914', in J. Merriman (ed.), *French Cities in the Nineteenth Century* (London, 1982), pp. 193–207. On the overall collapse of employers' paternalist 'Le Playan' programmes during the 1890s, see L. Portis, *Les Classes Sociales en France: Un Débat Inachevé (1789–1989)* (Paris, 1988), pp. 80–1. For overt treatment of workers as minors by paternalistic capital, and workers' consequent resentment, see J. Dereymez, 'Les Syndicats Ouvriers de Saône-et-Loire', p. 32.

[70] J. Quellien, 'Contribution à l'Histoire du Mouvement Ouvrier en Basse-Normandie: La Naissance du Mouvement Ouvrier Bas-Normand à la Fin du XIXᵉ Siècle', *Annales du Normandie*, vol. 23, 1983, pp. 22 and 44–7. Class collaborationist unionism was usually only tried once repression had failed, however – according to Vasseur, *Les Débuts du Mouvement Ouvrier*, p. 104 and R. Trempé, *Les Mineurs de Carmaux 1848–1914* (Paris, 1971), vol. 2, p. 752.

Parti Ouvrier, as hostile to class collaboration as to working-class deference, ferociously attacked every project associating capitalists with organised labour, even on 'equal' terms, projects which the French Marxists denounced as mere 'camouflage' for exploitation.[71] Many of the Guesdists' most exaggerated critiques of trade union malignancy derived from their campaigns against unionism's class-collaborationist implications.

The POF expended little polemical ammunition against the labour movements associated with the embryonic Social Catholics and nascent 'national socialists', although 'Christian Socialists' and proto-fascists constructed formidable industrial organisations in the Guesdists' domains, particularly in the Nord, where both movements had evolved in symbiotic response to Marxist vitality. The Parti Ouvrier, self-confidently dismissive of 'antiquated' religion, dismissed Catholic 'mixed unions' of employers and employees as historically doomed, as unworthy duelling partners for Marxist class warriors. According to the POF, these corporative organisations clearly contradicted the laws of the capitalist economy which they surreptitiously defended, and would not survive this crippling contradiction: the heartless calculations of capitalist rationality precluded the sentimental attachments of Christian brotherhood.

The 'yellow unions' patronised by the ascendant proto-fascist nationalists frightened Guesdists more than did the supposedly foredoomed Christian Social movement. But the Parti Ouvrier relegated even the national-socialist labour movement to the dustbin of history, despite its spectacular growth during a period which witnessed the precipitous decline of socialist unionism. According to the French Marxists, the 'yellow unions' – corporatist, anti-semitic, nationalist, and profoundly anti-socialist – depended upon company corruption and police provocation. Class conflict between nationalist employers and nationalist workers supposedly doomed this corporatist confidence trick as surely as the class war damned the Christian Socialists' analogous subterfuge. In the event, circumstances justified Guesdist contempt: employers repudiated the concessions to their employees which would have legitimised nationalist class collaboration; the yellow unions collapsed in a spasm of internal discord; and 'yellow' and 'red' workers blended into an

[71] J. Sarraute, 'Élimination "En Principe",' *Le Socialiste*, 26 May 1895.

aggressive 'green unionism' during industrial conflicts.[72] Anti-Republican corporatism enjoyed no sustained popularity among French workers, whether under the patronage of the Catholic's Notre-Dame de l'Usine or the protection of the Nationalists' Jeanne d'Arc.

The class collaboration championed by Republican 'business unionists' imperilled Marxist unionism far more than did the transient corporatist successes of the Catholic and nationalist Right. Determined to include the burgeoning labour movement in the Republican consensus, forsaking repression for propitiation, far-sighted French liberals discarded their traditional laissez-faire dogmatism in favour of a novel pluralism which encouraged collective organisation, even the collective organisation of workers: Republican harmony would, in the future, rest upon the formalised association of cooperative interest groups rather than upon the informal intersection of competitive individual interests; the visible hand of arbitration and conciliation would replace the invisible hand of the free market. Initiated by Opportunists unsettled by the revival of industrial radicalism after 1879, this strategy occasioned the so-called Waldeck-Rousseau law of 1884 which removed the restrictions which had crippled labour organisation since the draconian Le Chapelier law of 1791.[73] Similar calculations inspired the 'Solidarist' programme popularised by Léon Bourgeois and his associates during the 1890s (a programme since described as the 'official ideology of the Third Republic') and justified the policy of social conciliation pursued during Millerand's tenure as Minister of Commerce. The Radicals of the Republican Left, the prime patrons of Republican trade unionism from the Opportunists' betrayal of the Belleville Programme until Clemenceau's disillusioning career as the 'strike-breaker', explicitly hoped for an 'American' solution to the social question, a solution in which free trade unions would buttress

---

[72] L. de Seilhac, *La Grève du Tissage de Lille* (Paris, 1910), pp. 43–4, cited in Hilden, *Working Women and Socialist Politics*, p. 117. For the Nationalist challenge to Marxism within the labour movement, see Z. Sternhell, *La Droite Révolutionnaire (1885–1914): Les Origines Françaises du Fascisme* (Paris, 1976), pp. 245–318 and G. Mosse, 'The French Right and the Working Classes: *Les Jaunes*', *Journal of Contemporary History*, vol. 7, 1972, pp. 185–208.

[73] P. Sorlin, *Waldeck-Rousseau* (Paris, 1966), pp. 264–6 and 473–4. The Guesdists understood the class-collaborationist purpose behind the reform of industrial relations during the 1880s, and ferociously opposed the law. See J. Guesde, 'Une Nouvelle Loi Chapelier', *Le Cri du Peuple*, 16 February 1884.

the liberal-democratic (and capitalist) order rather than second its socialist enemies.[74]

This project met with widespread acceptance, even widespread enthusiasm, from the French working class, a class long schooled in Republican ardour by repressive Monarchist and Bonapartist masters. Liberal and Radical trade unionists assumed that labour, the spearhead of nineteenth-century Republicanism, would gain a respectable and profitable place within the Republican political system and the capitalist economic order, that a secure Republic would ensure working-class security. At the same time, they 'sold' their conciliatory programme to employers by promising that 'unionisation equals an end to strikes',[75] that both proletarians and capitalists would benefit from the harmony of Republican class collaboration. The Union des Chambres Syndicales Ouvrières de France, established with government backing in 1880 to reverse the socialist turn taken by organised labour at the Marseilles Congress of 1879, embodied this Republican unionism during the infancy of the POF.[76] But, even after the demise of the UCSOF, destroyed by its overly close association with the unpopular Opportunists, powerful forces within organised labour continued to defend the anti-socialist Republican cause.[77] Revolutionary unionism, whether socialist or anarchist, confronted its most formidable working-class obstacle in proletarian endorsement of a social order in which 'labour negotiates with capital, as equal to equal, for the prosperity of the country and the grandeur of the Republic'[78] – a social order where organised labour, accepted by capitalists and bourgeois Republicans, in turn accepted capitalism and the bourgeois Republic.

Founded upon categorical rejection of the 'bourgeois Republic',

---

[74] For 'Solidarism', see J. Hayward, 'The Official Social Ideology of the French Third Republic', *International Review of Social History*, vol. 6, 1961, pp. 19–48. On the Radicals' social ideal, see L. Loubère, 'The French Left-Wing Radicals: Their Views on Trade Unionism 1870–1898', *International Review of Social History*, vol. 7, 1962, pp. 203–30.

[75] According to the Republican journalist Joseph Barberet, who enjoyed a long career as a labour publicist in the Opportunists' service, quoted in Lefranc, *Le Mouvement Syndical*, p. 23.

[76] The UCSOF lacks a historian. The best accounts are in *Les Associations Professionelles Ouvrières* (Paris, 1899–1904), vol. 1, pp. 248–50, and M. Weitz, 'Varieties of Class-Collaborationist Ideology in the French Labor Movement before World War I', PhD thesis, City University of New York, 1977, pp. 72–114. For the Guesdists' bitter hostility to the organisation, see J. Guesde, 'Eux Aussi!', *Le Cri du Peuple*, 7 December 1884.

[77] Trempé, 'Le Réformisme des Mineurs Français', p. 93.

[78] Speech by the northern miners' leader Émile Basly in 1891, cited in J. Michel, 'Syndicalisme Minier et Politique dans le Nord-Pas-de-Calais: Le Cas Basly (1880–1914)', *Mouvement Social*, no. 87, 1974, p. 14.

the Parti Ouvrier denounced this working-class ideal as 'treason and delusion'.[79] For Guesdists, the Republican labour movement, deprived of socialist weaponry and confined to defence of immediate industrial interests, resembled a 'soldier sent into battle with no other arm than a shield'[80] – labour leaders who advocated this suicidal programme consciously or unconsciously served the class enemy. Even if Republican 'business unions' could successfully defend the proletariat's short-term corporative interests, workers would 'remain enclosed within the narrow limits of their partial and particular requirements ... [which] completely hide the grandiose future'[81] – arbitration and conciliation forfeited revolution and socialism, an outrageously inequitable exchange. Infuriated by the 'treasons' committed and the 'delusions' fostered by Republican unionists, Guesdists repeatedly exploded in wrath against the French 'lib-labs', and sometimes, at their most intemperate, denounced trade unions in general.

Yet most Guesdist attacks upon the labour movement criticised strategies which upheld 'the emancipation of the workers by the workers themselves', strategies which explicitly accepted the inevitability of conflict between the bourgeoisie and the proletariat. In its infancy, the Parti Ouvrier's 'collectivism' had defended itself and defined itself against 'mutualism', the 'associationist' ideology which had pervaded the independent French labour movement for most of the nineteenth century. Mutualists renounced bourgeois competition in favour of a cooperative political economy founded upon voluntary association in producer cooperatives, credit unions, and consumer co-ops, institutions which would replace the ruthless and inequitable regime of liberal economic individualism with a harmonious cooperative commonwealth of solidarity and mutual aid. Convinced that cooperation would eventually prevail over competition, mutualists anticipated gradual rather than revolutionary replacement of capitalist exploitation by cooperative mutuality: their new social order would ripen within the dissolving body of the old. Mutualism, however, although overwhelmingly dominant in the labour movement of mid-nineteenth-century France, had sadly withered by the *Fin de Siècle*, abandoned by most of its adherents after a century of capitalist industrialisation and two generations of

[79] J. Guesde, 'Efforts Perdus', *Le Cri du Peuple*, 14 January 1884.
[80] P. Grados, 'Syndicats et Groupes', *Le Socialiste*, 25 May – 1 June 1902.
[81] P. Larlat, 'Les Travailleurs du Livre', *Le Socialiste*, 18–25 August 1901.

cooperative failure. But mutualist ideals had appeared thoroughly realistic to hundreds of thousands of workers and socialists during the mutualists' mid-century ascendancy, when most trades required little fixed capital and skilled workers managed the labour process, and chastened mutualists survived into the twentieth century in artisanal backwaters and within the flourishing consumer cooperative movement.[82]

Why this Guesdist hatred of the mutualists, antagonists who shared the POF's intense dislike of capital and who aspired to the Party's official goal of working-class self-emancipation? After all, Marx himself had sympathised with the cooperative movement, and his few vague descriptions of the future socialist mode of production delineated an essentially associationist society.[83] The Parti Ouvrier itself had evolved out of a predominantly mutualist labour movement, and, during the 1880s, French labour militants, including many Guesdists, consistently confused the traditional mutualist ideal of producer cooperation with the novel Marxist 'nationalisation of the means of production'. Even the youthful Lafargue had once advocated credit unions as the road to working-class liberation, a road paved with 'free credit' in fine Proudhonian style.[84] Yet French Marxists, disavowing their origins, commonly disowned the mutualist tradition. Emergent Guesdism campaigned as fervently against its mutualist forebears as against its Possibilist competitors.[85]

Bonapartist and liberal patronage of mutualism had tarnished cooperation in the eyes of many socialists. 'Bourgeois reformers' had long solved (in prospect) the 'social question' with workers' thrift and the pooling of individual proletarian savings to found cooperative enterprises – every worker an entrepreneur, Samuel Smiles as

---

[82] For a brilliant analysis of the origins of the mutualist ideal, see W. Sewell, *Work and Revolution in France: The Language of Labour from the Old Regime to 1848* (Cambridge, 1980). Its subsequent development through the period of the POF is carefully analysed in Moss, *The Origins of the French Labor Movement*.

[83] Marx, *Instructions for the Delegates of the Provisional General Council*, p. 190. Marx's relationship to the associationists is discussed in T. Lowitt, 'Marx et le Mouvement Coopératif', *Cahiers de l'Institut de Science Économique Appliquée – Série S (6)*, no. 129, 1962, pp. 79–104.

[84] P. Lafargue, 'Un Moyen de Groupement', *L'Égalité*, 12 March 1882. The general confusion between producers' cooperatives and 'collectivist' nationalisation of the means of production played a large role in the socialist victory over labour moderates at the Lyons Congress of 1886 which established the FNS. See the police report to the Ministry of the Interior of November 20, 1886. AN F7 12.491.

[85] There is a superb description of the conflict between 'collectivism' and an increasingly conservative mutualism in Moss, *The Origins of the French Labor Movement*, chapter 3.

cooperator.[86] Nevertheless, most Guesdist critiques of the mutualist project relied upon Marxist political economy rather than guilt by association. Cooperation, according to the POF, could never compete successfully against capitalist enterprise: employers, the favoured beneficiaries of capitalist finance, tapped vast reservoirs of credit unavailable to workers' co-ops; and capitalists, untrammelled by mutualist scruples, exploited their labourers far more ruthlessly than genuinely cooperative enterprises ever could. Under these circumstances, workers' aspirations to become 'their own capitalists' constituted 'a mystification, one of our century's greatest'.[87] The Parti Ouvrier contended that the relentless advance of the capitalist mode of production had reduced mutualism to no more than a nostalgic dream, an escapist fantasy which diverted workers from more realistic (Marxist) remedies for their social agony.

This denigration of the cooperative movement, like many Guesdist polemics, rested upon problematical empirical foundations. Despite the triumphs of capitalism, three hundred and thirty-eight production cooperatives with approximately 20,000 members survived (and sometimes thrived) in France as late as 1906 – no validation of the mutualists' programme, but also no proof of the Guesdists' critique.[88] The mutualist ideal, and to some extent mutualist practice, retained a mid-nineteenth-century vigour in the skilled trades of industries such as construction and printing, industries where an irreducibly artisanal labour process or sustained working-class resistance had precluded capitalist deskilling of the labour force and thwarted the concentration of the means of production. Symptomatically, these 'mutualist' milieus resisted both capitalist concentration *and* Guesdist collectivism: Proudhon prevailed against Marx in thousands of workshops, even as France entered the collectivist twentieth century. Indeed, as the working-class 'aristocracy' and the petite bourgeoisie began to accumulate personal savings, credit unions themselves, the ultimate expression of the Proudhonian ideal, proliferated in centres such as Lyons and

---

[86] Weitz, *Varieties of Class Collaborationist Ideology*, pp. 35–6; Lequin, *Les Intérêts de Classe et la République*, p. 190; and J. Stone, *The Search for Social Peace: Reform Legislation in France 1890–1914* (Albany, 1989), pp. 64–5.

[87] J. Guesde, 'La Coopération', *Le Cri du Peuple*, 9 September 1886. The best expression of this Guesdist critique of production cooperation may be found in G. Deville, 'Un Atelier Collectif', *L'Égalité*, 1 January 1882.

[88] M. Perrot, 'Les Classes Populaires Urbaines', in *Histoire Économique et Sociale de la France: Tome IV – L'Ère Industrielle et la Société d'Aujourd'hui (Siècle 1880–1980): Premier Volume – Ambiguïtés des Débuts et Croissance Effective (Années 1880–1914)* (Paris, 1980), p. 523.

Paris, reinforcing the mutualist infrastructure of those traditionally anti-collectivist redoubts. Finally, the *Belle Époque* witnessed a spectacular expansion of the consumer cooperative movement, not least spectacularly in the Guesdists' northern strongholds, where co-ops such as 'La Paix' of Roubaix buttressed the proletarian countersociety otherwise articulated by the trade unions and the Parti Ouvrier itself. Workers by their thousands, including thousands of Guesdists, joined co-ops even as the POF preached the impossibility of cooperation to an increasingly persuaded audience. Paradoxically, mutualism declined precipitously as labour ideology while expanding rapidly as working-class experience.[89]

In its less dogmatic moments, the Parti Ouvrier grudgingly conceded that cooperatives might survive and even prosper within the capitalist mode of production, that mutualism might supplement (if not supplant) capitalism. But recognition of the cooperative movement as a commonplace proletarian practice never implied approbation of mutualism as an alternative proletarian ideology. Jealous for their collectivism, Guesdists regularly denounced the social and political implications of even successful cooperation, reserving their most concentrated venom for the ideological penumbra which surrounded producer co-ops. According to Édouard Fortin,

in such associations, workers abandon their radical location in society, along with the enormous power embodied in the universal nature of their class, to defect to the class enemy. They faithlessly seek to solve egotistically the problem which must be resolved collectively, and thereby become in their turn enemies of the proletariat.[90]

In other words, production cooperatives parodied capitalist corporations. Guesdists – citing the Parisian cooperative of spectacle-makers, owned by 60 'cooperators' but employing 1,400 workers – demonstrated that production co-ops inevitably evolved into bourgeois companies: in any successful mutualist enterprise, cooperators began by hiring auxiliary labour, then withdrew from the immediate labour process in favour of management and profit-taking, and finally degenerated into completely parasitic capitalists indis-

---

[89] G. Jacquemet, *Belleville au XIXᵉ Siècle: Du Faubourg à la Ville* (Paris, 1984), p. 363 highlights the paradox. For the continuing popularity, however, of mutualism among artisanal 'labour aristocrats', see J. Charles, *Les Débuts du Mouvement Syndical à Besançon* (Paris, 1962), p. 120.

[90] 'E. F.' (Fortin), 'L'Avenir des Prévoyants', *Le Socialiste*, 26 February 1887.

tinguishable from shareholding bourgeois.[91] In one of their more dubious displays of Marxist political economy, Guesdists even contended that producer co-ops exploited their workers more intensively than did even the ultra-capitalist railway companies, given that the co-ops employed (on average) two employees for every cooperator, while railway shareowners considerably outnumbered railway workers![92]

What is more, even if every French worker someday enjoyed cooperator status, the resulting cooperative utopia of associated producers would still violate collectivist principles: a mutualist triumph would only ensure that 'the faults of individual property would reappear', wrote Gabriel Deville, 'notably because of the unequal distribution resulting from the differential productivity of the various means of production'.[93] Coal miners, exploiting their 'natural' monopoly, would exploit steel workers; rural cooperatives, secure in their ownership of the fields, would starve their urban counterparts into submission; and transport workers, masters of society's infrastructure, would pillage society as a whole – a dog-eat-dog world of mutualists would replace the dog-eat-dog world of capitalists. Sworn enemies of exploitation, Guesdists repudiated any society which allowed the 'exploitation of certain categories of workers', even at the hands of more strategically situated proletarians.[94] In sum, the Parti Ouvrier cordially detested the mutualists' alternative political economy, envisaged as a 'milieu both bourgeois and anarchist'.[95]

Guesdists focused their hostility towards mutualism upon producers' cooperatives, the vital heart of the mutualist project but only a peripheral part of the *fin-de-siècle* cooperative movement. On the

[91] J. Phalippou, 'Banqueroute Coopérative', *Le Socialiste*, 27 November 1898.

[92] 'P.L.', 'Tous Propriétaires! Plus de Classes!', *Le Socialiste*, 11 February 1900. For evidence supporting the Guesdist indictment, see Jacquemet, *Belleville au XIXe Siècle*, p. 372, and the instances of the 'Mine aux Mineurs' of Rive-de-Giers between 1886 and 1898 (Lequin, *Les Intérêts de Classe et la République*, pp. 277–8), the 'Verrerie Ouvrière' of Albi between 1896 and 1914 (J. Scott, *The Glassworkers of Carmaux: French Craftsmen and Political Action in a Nineteenth-Century City* (Cambridge, Mass., 1974), pp. 181–7), and the bakers' and masons' cooperatives of the Cher (C. Pennetier, *Le Socialisme dans le Cher 1851–1921* (Paris, 1982), p. 97).

[93] G. Deville, preface to *Le Capital de Karl Marx* (Paris, 1883), p. 21.

[94] P. Lafargue, 'Le Communisme et les Services Publics', *L'Égalité*, 2 July 1882.

[95] J. Martin, 'Les Deux Coopérations', *Le Socialiste*, 13–20 October 1901. On rare occasions Guesdists adopted a less jaundiced view of production coops, admitting that Marxists had not 'insisted sufficiently on the distinction between cooperation and the usage that bourgeois politicians wished to make of it'. P. Lafargue, 'La Coopération', *Le Socialiste*, 9 September 1900.

whole, the Parti Ouvrier tolerated the rapidly expanding consumer co-ops, although with uneasy reservations about their liability to mutualist exploitation. The Parti Ouvrier certainly savaged cooperators who advanced consumer organisation as the solution to the 'social question'. Cooperation might supplement socialism, but never supplant it: for Marxists, the 'relations of distribution' mastered by consumer cooperation hardly mattered compared to the relations of production which engendered capitalist exploitation and bourgeois domination.[96] Consumers' associations, however widespread and however successful, would never overcome these fundamental evils: at the best, cheaper bread and annual dividends might attenuate workers' torments within the capitalist purgatory. According to the Parti Ouvrier, proletarians who abandoned socialisation of the means of production for collectivisation of the means of consumption deserted the class war, thereby forfeiting their sole hope of salvation.

In practice, while the socialist party threatened the bourgeoisie, undermining the hegemony of industrialists and bankers, the consumer cooperative movement challenged the petite bourgeoisie, sapping the livelihood of butchers and bakers. The POF, far less hostile towards petits bourgeois than towards bourgeois, agonised about the threat to small business from consumer cooperatives – a disquiet, needless to say, shared by butchers and bakers. If nothing else, consumer co-ops, by ruining small retailers and forcing them into the 'reserve army of labour', supposedly allowed employers to reduce wages at least in proportion to the reduction in prices achieved by cooperation. Thus, Guesde asserted, 'what working class cooperators "gain" as consumer, they lose (and more) as producers'.[97] Only bourgeois, masters of the mode of production, would gain from consumer association, as the price of labour's subsistence and the price of labour depreciated together.

Sound political reasons further accentuated Guesdist distrust of consumers' cooperation: the Parti Ouvrier had gained its ascendancy over the rapidly expanding consumer cooperative movement of the Northern textile cities just as the Party's newly elected municipal

---

[96] See the debate between Guesde and the cooperative leader Fongerousse at Roubaix in 1891, as reported in Anonymous, 'La Fête de La Paix', *Le Socialiste*, 20 May 1891. For consumer cooperation as an anti-socialist alternative, see Pierre, *Les Origines du Syndicalisme et Socialisme dans la Drôme*, pp. 61–2 and C. Prochasson, 'Sur la Réception du Marxisme en France: Le Cas Andler', *Revue de Synthèse*, no. 110, 1989, p. 96.

[97] J. Guesde, 'La Coopération', *Le Cri du Peuple*, 9 September 1886.

governments discovered a shopkeeper constituency – key to electoral success in marginal constituencies, prerequisite of popular solidarity against capital in even the most working-class faubourg. Unfortunately, once the hypothetical Marxist 'socialisation of the means of production' fused with the all-too-real cooperative 'collectivisation of the means of distribution', butchers and bakers, although hostile to bourgeois 'monopolists' since at least the eighteenth century, discovered an anti-collectivist class interest which bound them to industrialists and bankers. French Marxists, unwilling to surrender the petite bourgeoisie to capitalism, reacted nervously to this petit-bourgeois allergy to cooperation: the Guesdist-controlled cooperative La Paix, for instance, withdrew from the grocery trade because of the political mobilisation of Roubaissian *détaillants* against cooperative competition.[98] What gained workers, the Parti Ouvrier asked, if they obtained cheap bread and lost bakers' support against capital?

Nevertheless, consumer cooperatives constituted an integral part of the 'counter-society' constructed by workers in the northern textile towns; Guesdists, political representatives of this alternative social order, could hardly disavow the cooperative movement unconditionally. Indeed, the Parti Ouvrier, characteristically inconsistent, evinced periodic outbursts of enthusiasm for cooperation, recurrent moments of Marxist mutualism. According to Lafargue's authoritative dictum, cooperatives manifested 'the superiority of socialist solidarity over individual autonomy'[99] – they inculcated collectivist values in the face of bourgeois hegemony and founded collectivist institutions in the heart of bourgeois society. Better yet, consumer co-ops erected arenas of class conflict, arenas where bourgeois selfishness duelled against 'socialist solidarity' in every annual general meeting. Working-class cooperators, to Guesdist delight, repeatedly employed profits collectively rather than distributing them as dividends.[100] Best of all, consumer cooperatives warred against employers' 'economats', the class war evident in the

---

[98] R. Baker, 'A Regional Study of Working Class Organization in France: Socialism in the Nord 1870–1924', PhD thesis, Stanford University, 1967, p. 158. Guesdists, however, vehemently denied that they inhibited the cooperative movement in order to pacify the petite bourgeoisie. J. Phalippou, 'Petit Commerce, Coopératives et Socialisme', *Le Socialiste*, 12 March 1899.

[99] P. Lafargue, 'Un Moyen de Groupement', *L'Égalité*, 12 March 1882.

[100] Vandorme, 'Coopération et Socialisme', *Le Socialiste*, 24 September 1899.

purchase of every baguette.[101] At their most self-confident, Guesdists strove to annex the mutualist project rather than demolish it.

The Parti Ouvrier, moreover, possessed a substantial vested interest in consumer cooperation, an interest frequently revealed with brutal candour. Just as bourgeois politicians battened upon the surplus value extracted from the proletariat by their capitalist patrons, so the POF depended upon the profits of socialist cooperative enterprise: Guesdist printing works, Guesdist publications, Guesdist organisers, Guesdist congresses, Guesdist committees – all subsisted upon cooperative largess. In Compère-Morel's forthright words,

consumer cooperation possesses utility ... only when it brings something concrete to the Party. If it doesn't give a venue to workers interested in discussing their class interests; if it doesn't furnish subsidies ... to the workers' industrial and political organisations; if it doesn't contribute, materially and morally, to the diffusion of socialist ideas; if it's not a weapon in socialist hands to be used against the bourgeoisie, then it's not worth the trouble.[102]

As thorough-going theoretical materialists, the Guesdists thoroughly understood the material requirements of practical militancy – and esteemed their paymasters accordingly.

Even at their most 'mutualist', however, the Parti Ouvrier limited cooperatives to the same subsidiary role awarded to trade unions: coops served as instruments of class formation and supports for socialist politics, but never as ends in themselves. As a palliative, as a remedy for proletarian misery, cooperatives would either disappoint, or, succeeding, prolong the capitalist disease which they supposedly cured. And the Marxist assumptions which governed Guesdist collectivism damned the mutualists' aspiration to working-class self-emancipation through peaceful association: anti-capitalist cooperation would either fail or, in succeeding, itself become capitalist. For Guesdists, cooperatives posed the same danger as trade unions: both co-ops and unions potentially integrating workers into the bourgeois order, a potential confirmed by Radical ideologues'

[101] For the 'class war' which developed between workers' cooperatives and employers' economats, see Hardy-Hémery, *De la Croissance à la Désindustrialisation*, p. 41.

[102] Compère-Morel, 'La Coopération dans les Milieux Agricoles', *Le Socialiste*, 4–11 January 1903. For the importance of the northern consumer coops in the funding of the Guesdist apparatus, see Baker, 'A Regional Study of Working Class Organization,' p. 158, and Willard, *Les Guesdistes*, p. 490.

insatiable appetite for mutualist and unionist nostrums. The Guesdists' sustained campaign against cooperation as an alternative to socialist revolution accounts for some of their otherwise puzzling hostility towards working-class corporative organisation.

Mutualism, an increasingly conservative ideology, had virtually vanished from the working-class Left by the 1890s, its place usurped by 'revolutionary syndicalism', a novel movement dedicated to the general strike as the ultimate weapon of the class war and aspiring to a social order founded upon trade-union democracy. As with earlier conflict between mutualists and the Parti Ouvrier, the hostility between revolutionary syndicalists and Guesdists which dominated labour politics throughout the 1890s appears, at first sight, inexplicable. The two movements shared a common working-class constituency, a common understanding of class and class conflict, and a common hostility towards the bourgeoisie and the 'bourgeois state' – commonalities which might have wedded revolutionary syndicalists and revolutionary socialists in a common anti-capitalist cause. Fernand Pelloutier himself, the embodiment of anarchosyndicalist ideals and revolutionary syndicalist militancy, had served his ideological apprenticeship in the POF, as had other notable syndicalist ideologists such as Aristide Briand.[103] Why did Pelloutier end his brief life as bitter an enemy of the Parti Ouvrier as of capitalism? Why did the POF attack revolutionary syndicalists, themselves fanatical enemies of 'bourgeois reformism', with all the hatred the Party usually reserved for class-collaborationist traitors?

One necessary and sufficient *casus belli* suggests itself: the role of politics in the 'making of the working class'. As Marxists, Guesdists incarnated a single and all-important political imperative: the mobilisation of the proletariat into a socialist political party, into a 'Parti Ouvrier'. Revolutionary syndicalists, by contrast, denounced socialist politics as, at best, a diversion from the true path of proletarian emancipation and, at worst, a trick whereby workers legitimised their own subordination to the bourgeois state and its capitalist masters. For anti-Guesdist ideologues such as Pelloutier, only trade unions, through their direct democracy, distilled the true essence of proletarian class interest – not the socialist party; only trade unions, through their strikes, challenged the routine hegemony

---

[103] F. Ridley, 'Syndicalism, Strikes and Revolutionary Action in France', in W. Mommsen and G. Hirschfeld (eds.), *Social Protest, Violence and Terror in Nineteenth and Twentieth-Century Europe* (London, 1982), p. 233.

of capitalist property relations – not socialist militancy; only trade unions, through the general strike, would rupture the bulwarks constructed around capital by the bourgeois state – not the socialist revolution; and only trade unions, through workers' control, would articulate the post-capitalist society of self-governing producers – not the socialisation of the means of production.[104] Flaunting this 'anarchosyndicalist' credo, revolutionary syndicalists hijacked the Fédération National des Syndicats at the Congress of Nantes in 1894, successfully usurping the transitory Guesdist command over the national labour movement established during the 1880s.[105] The Confédération Générale du Travail, born from this Parti Ouvrier defeat and nurtured by revolutionary syndicalists, was to resist Marxist blandishments for a generation – excluding socialists from the most conspicuous positions of labour leadership, denying collectivism its self-proclaimed birthright as the ideology of organised labour. How did the anarchosyndicalists prevail? Why the Guesdist debacle?

Revolutionary syndicalists skillfully manipulated their protean strategy: in anarchosyndicalist hands, the 'general strike' easily and instantly metamorphosed from 'le grand soir', the apocalyptic revolutionary moment of the anarchist tradition, into a mundane sectorial strike for corporative goals, 1891's 'Grève Générale des Omnibus', for instance.[106] Like Marxists, revolutionary syndicalists combined messianic dreams with hard-headed pragmatism – not least in the Bourses du Travail, institutions founded and funded by reformist municipal councils, for all the Bourses' ultra-revolutionary rhetoric.[107] Given this felicitous ambiguity, the general strike appealed across the entire spectrum of the labour Left, winning praise from both eclectic reformists such as Jean Jaurès and rigorous revolutionaries such as Jean Allemane. Its charms seduced even

---

[104] J. Julliard, *Fernand Pelloutier et les Origines du Syndicalisme d'Action Directe* (Paris, 1971), chapter 5.

[105] *Compte Rendu des Travaux du Congrès tenu à Nantes du 17 au 22 Septembre 1894* (Nantes, 1894) and various press reports on the Congress in the dossier of the Musée Social. For the destruction of the FNS and its vanquishers' social and political context in the Loire-Inférieure, see Y. Guin, *Le Mouvement Ouvrier Nantais* (Paris, 1976), pp. 279–88 and 306–17.

[106] For a good discussion of the amazing fluidity of the concept of the general strike, see the argument developed in B. Mitchell, *The Practical Revolutionaries: A New Interpretation of the French Anarchosyndicalists* (New York, 1987); J. Maitron, 'Introduction', in R. Brécy, *La Grève Générale en France* (Paris, 1969), p. vii; and Perrot, *Les Ouvriers en Grève*, vol. 2, pp. 489–498.

[107] N. Papayanis, *Alphonse Merrheim: The Emergence of Reformism in Revolutionary Syndicalism 1871–1925* (Dordrecht, 1985), chapter 1.

Guesdists, particularly during the early 1890s, despite the overt conflict between Marxist socialism and revolutionary syndicalism. After all, the seeds of the 1890s enthusiasm for the general strike had been implanted via Marxist carriers during the Montluçon labour congress of 1887, an initially unproblematic planting, as the new strategy for labour germinated not only within the FNS but within the POF itself.[108] The Parti Ouvrier commenced its doomed campaign against the general strike only in 1890, and the Guesdists' proud advocacy of a general work stoppage on 1 May, their vocal enthusiasm for the great suffrage strikes in Belgium, and their unconditional support for a 'general strike' of coal miners as a revolutionary tactic all confused the issue at the peak of the Marxists' conflict with revolutionary syndicalism.[109] Revolutionary syndicalists even infiltrated a fifth column into the POF itself: dedicated Guesdists – Farjat of Lyons, Treich of Limoges – succumbed to the insurrectionary aura of the general strike, not least because of the tactical void in their own movement's revolutionary strategy.[110] Aware of the momentum behind revolutionary syndicalism, Jean Jaurès, while still closely associated with the POF, advised the Party to coopt the popular new programme, rather than pay the price of obstructionist negativism.[111] Why did the French Marxists reject his wise advice, at terrible cost to socialist unionism?

First, Guesdists belittled the general strike as a redundant irrelevancy. As Léon Greffier, POF leader in the Isère, wrote at the peak of revolutionary syndicalism's popularity: 'if some central committee or other has so much popular influence that it can obtain such an

---

[108] *IIe Congrès National des Syndicats*, p. 12. Alexandre Zévaès, who should have known better, claimed that the POF opposed the general strike from the beginning. A. Zévaès, *Histoire des Partis Socialistes en France: Les Guesdistes* (Paris, 1911), p. 97.

[109] For linkages between the general strike and the May First demonstration, see R. Brécy, *La Grève Générale en France*, pp. 23–4; G. Lefranc, *Grèves d'Hier et d'Aujourd'hui*, pp. 47–8; and Perrot, *Les Ouvriers en Grève*, vol. 1, pp. 11 and 97–100. The Marxists realised that the equation was being used against them, and bitterly protested at such sleight of hand. See the intervention by Lavigne in *Compte Rendu des Travaux du Congrès tenu à Nantes*, p. 39. For the Guesdist position on the Belgian strikes, see J. Guesde, 'Suffrage Universel ou Grève Générale', *Le Socialiste*, 14 January 1891. For the miners' strike and revolution, see *Huitième Congrès National du Parti Ouvrier tenu à Lille le Samedi 11 et Dimanche 12 Octobre 1890* (Lille, 1890), p. 33.

[110] See the police report on the 1892 FNS Congress, which predicted an eventual split between the Party and its trade union base over the issue. Report of 25 September 1892, File 1892, AN F7 12.490. For the popularity of the general strike among Guesdist militants, see Lequin, *Intérêts de Classe et la République*, pp. 298–9.

[111] Police report on the debates at the POF's Nantes Congress. 17 September 1894, file on Nantes Congress, AN F7 12.490.

effort [the general strike] at a given moment, then we are dealing with a highly class-conscious proletariat totally dominated by its class interest'.[112] By Marxist calculations, socialist revolution would eventuate long before this ideal state of class solidarity (a rare Guesdist admission of the actual 'immaturity' of the French working class, all too often characterised as already 'totally dominated by its class interest').[113] Second, organisation for the remote possibility of a general strike or, worse yet, abortive attempts to realise its revolutionary promise would inflict grievous harm upon the working-class movement: the mirage of the general strike would entice workers away from the fertile promise of socialist militancy into the sterile cul-de-sac of anarchosyndicalism; a failed general strike would obliterate both trade unionism and independent working-class politics. Finally, revolutionary syndicalism, according to the POF, undermined the day-to-day activities of trade unions, diverting workers from the immediate interests of the workshop towards the chimerical fantasies of the wineshop – although this critique lacked credibility, emanating from a party which ruthlessly subordinated the mundane requirements of industrial organisation to the glittering promises of socialist politics.[114]

On balance, the revolutionary syndicalists' antithesis between industrial militancy and political 'corruption' alienated the Guesdists most categorically. Assimilating advocacy of the general strike to advocacy of anarchosyndicalism, French Marxists rejected synthesis between revolutionary syndicalism and revolutionary socialism: Guesde's repudiation of the general strike mirrored Pelloutier's renunciation of socialist politics, a self-destructive pattern of reciprocal anathema not uncommon in the development of Parti Ouvrier ideology. For Guesdists, the general strike had degenerated into another anarchist absurdity, 'economic abstention' seconding 'political abstention', both irrationalities perfectly calculated to emasculate the working-class movement.[115] Guesdists even feared that the vogue for the general strike, like anarchism itself, represented a carefully calculated police provocation, that ostensibly anti-bourgeois revolutionary syndicalists covertly served anti-revo-

---

[112] L. Greffier, *Petites Conférences Éducatives sur le Socialisme* (Grenoble, 1904), pp. 33–4.
[113] J. Guesde, 'Réponse Ouverte', *Le Socialiste*, 16 October 1892.
[114] Carlier, *Contre la Grève Générale*, p. 16.
[115] Anonymous, 'À l'Assaut du Sénat', *Le Socialiste*, 3 January 1897.

lutionary bourgeois.[116] But, whether as absurdity or as provocation, anarchosyndicalism, both cause and consequence of workers' inability to progress from industrial militancy to political self-assertion, signalled proletarian immaturity – according to the Parti Ouvrier.

Demoralised by unfavourable circumstances and discredited by their own contradictions, the revolutionary syndicalists eventually lost control of French labour – their leaders and ideologists deserting anarchosyndicalist principles for bourgeois opportunism (Briand), tepid reformism (Merrheim), or Bolshevik rigour (Lagardelle); their sporadic industrial insurgencies humiliatingly defeated by the 'bourgeois state'; their constituency among militant skilled workers eroded by triumphant 'Taylorism'.[117] But, however warranted in retrospect, the Guesdist crusade against this 'new anarchist campaign in the guise of the general strike'[118] failed catastrophically at the time. The Parti Ouvrier's self-defeating denigrations of working-class industrial organisation derived from rhetorical overkill: the Guesdists' brutal denunciations of the anarchists' revolutionary syndicalism, like their vociferous campaign against the Radicals' 'business unionism', frequently escalated into abuse of trade unionism in general, an escalation which alienated thousands of labour militants, disrupted the POF's theoretical synthesis of unionism with socialism, and discredited the Guesdists' practical combination of working-class industrial organisation with proletarian politics.

Guesdists advanced a superficially coherent theory of working-class industrial organisation and labour militancy: trade unions and cooperatives defended proletarians against capitalist aggression and, in the process, forged the working class into an organised and self-conscious entity, although unionists, however revolutionary, and mutualists, however proletarian, would never, could never, liberate labour from capitalist exploitation, an emancipatory mission reserved for socialist revolutionaries. Guesdists, however, signally

---

[116] In fact, the police did advise that 'the government should struggle against the socialists on their own ground, in propagating the idea of the general strike, a chimerical idea, impossible according to the socialists themselves'. Police report of 20 September 1894, AN F7 12.490.

[117] Y. Lequin, 'À Propos de la Classe Ouvrière du Rhône à la Fin du XIXᵉ Siècle: Conscience de Classe et Conscience Urbaine', in *Colloque Franco-Suisse d'Histoire Économique et Sociale – Genève 5–6 Mai 1967* (Geneva, 1969), p. 218, and J.-P. Martin, 'Une Culture Militant à l'Époque du Syndicalisme Révolutionnaire: Les Métallurgistes de l'Ondaine', *Cahiers d'Histoire*, vol. 21, 1982, p. 317.

[118] Anonymous, untitled, p. 1 of *Le Socialiste*, 13 October 1894.

failed to synthesise corporative solidarity and Marxist class politics. Instead, the Parti Ouvrier oscillated wildly between vehement unionist exhortations and equally vehement denunciations of the futility of trade union organisation and cooperative association. These socialist contradictions empowered anti-socialist labour strategies: 'business unionism' promised workers contentment within capitalist society, while anarchosyndicalism promised them liberation without socialist politics. Ferocious Guesdist onslaughts upon these anti-socialist strategies further disorganised the fragile Guesdist association between political militancy and corporative solidarity, creating a vicious circle of polemical excess and theoretical distortion, a vicious circle both cause and consequence of French unionism's alienation from socialism.

CHAPTER 7

The bourgeois state versus the proletarian party

In searching for the sources of social domination in the ostensibly egalitarian polities constructed by nineteenth and twentieth-century liberals and democrats, Marxists have discovered the secret of modern oppression in Marx's observation that 'the economical subjection of the man of labour to the monopoliser of the means of labour ... lies at the bottom of servitude in all its forms'. They have concluded, with Marx, that 'the economical emancipation of the working classes is ... the great end to which every political movement ought to be subordinated'.[1] But how to achieve this end? Unquestioningly associating class emancipation with a 'political movement', Marxist socialists have advanced a single answer to this question:

in its struggle against the collective power of the propertied classes, the working class cannot act as a class except by constituting itself into a political party, distinct from, and opposed to, all old parties formed by the propertied classes. This constitution of the working class into a political party is indispensable in order to ensure the triumph of the social revolution, and of its ultimate end, the abolition of classes.[2]

Ever since the First International proclaimed this principle, Marxists have postulated that class interest in general, whether bourgeois or proletarian, lies dormant unless embodied in political militancy, and that proletarian class interest in particular withers without

---

[1] K. Marx, *General Rules and Administrative Regulations of the International Working Men's Association*, in K. Marx and F. Engels, *Collected Works* (London, 1988), vol. 23, p. 3.
[2] K. Marx and F. Engels, *Resolutions of the General Congress Held at the Hague*, in K. Marx and F. Engels, *Collected Works* (London, 1988), vol. 23, p. 243. Indeed, since only the working class has an interest in organising politics around class issues, class will not appear in political discourse without the presence of a proletarian party. See J. Przeworski and J. Sprague, *Paper Stones: A History of Electoral Socialism* (Chicago, 1986), p. 11 for this argument.

mediation by a proletarian political party.[3] According to this dictum, capitalists prey at will upon politically unorganised workers, hampered only by the negative force of proletarian industrial militancy. By contrast, workers organised into a class party might not only challenge the predatory rule of capital, but eventually realise the 'abolition of classes', the ultimate socialist aspiration.

Dying without having written his promised *Politics*, Marx never systematically addressed the most troubling issues raised by his conception of class domination, issues which have preoccupied the subsequent generations of Marxists who have struggled so valiantly to constitute 'the working class into a political party' under conditions radically different from those posited by the founders of their ideology.[4] How should socialists conceive the state, the supposed quintessence of class power, after the establishment of the democratic franchise? As the 'managing committee of the bourgeoisie', the directorate of a hidden class dictatorship? Or as the trophy in the contest between bourgeois and proletarian political parties, the victor's prize in the class war? Should the 'distinct political party' of the proletariat cautiously limit its membership to workers? Or should 'proletarian parties', advancing bravely into the unknown terrain opened up by universal suffrage, enrol everyone with a grievance against capital, whether petit bourgeois, peasant, or even bourgeois? Finally, once constituted 'into a political party', how should the proletariat 'act as a class' within a parliamentary democracy: through campaigns for social reforms 'within the system', or through revolution against it? As the first major Marxist movement to emerge within a liberal democratic polity, the Parti Ouvrier confronted these enigmas with only rudimentary guidance from Marx, who had deployed his political thought in battles against the exclusive property franchise or outright authoritarianism, against

3 This equation has recently become intensely controversial – evoking a debate which has brilliantly illuminated the problems in the Marxist conjuncture between class and politics. See, for exemplary instances, A. Cutler et al., *Marx's Capital and Capitalism Today* (London, 1977), vol. 1, p. 237; B. Hindess, 'Classes and Politics in Marxist Theory', in J. Littlejohn et al. (eds.), *Power and the State* (London, 1977), pp. 72–97; P. Hirst, 'Economic Classes and Politics', in A. Hunt (ed.), *Class and Class Structure* (London, 1977), pp. 125–54; and S. Hall, 'The "Political" and the "Economic" in Marx's Theory of Classes', in A. Hunt (ed.), *Class and Class Structure* (London, 1977), pp. 15–46.
4 The best presentation of Marx's relevant work may be found in H. Draper, *Karl Marx's Theory of Revolution: Volume I – State and Bureaucracy* (New York, 1977), and *Karl Marx's Theory of Revolution: Volume II – The Politics of Social Classes* (New York, 1978), which place Marx's political thought firmly in its historical context.

the Whiggish liberalism of a Guizot or the despotic caesarism of a Louis Napoleon.

'The proletariat can act as a class only by constituting itself as a distinct political party ...' The Parti Ouvrier self-consciously embodied this imperative, its very name affirming class politics. Apostles of Marx's revelation, Guesdists 'read' the most abstract ideals as disguised class interest: to the Parti Ouvrier, the liberals' sacrosanct 'freedom' meant freedom to exploit; the Radicals' all-encompassing 'democracy' reflected petit-bourgeois hatred of both bourgeois oligarchy and proletarian collectivism; while the conservatives' deified 'authority' concealed the rule of property. Convinced that political order was social order made manifest, French Marxists reduced the Republican and anti-Republican factions whose disputes periodically convulsed the Third Republic to mere epiphenomena of the capitalist mode of production: royalists and Republicans, Boulangists and anti-Boulangists, Dreyfusards and anti-Dreyfusards – all represented fractions of the bourgeoisie, all embodied interests alien to the proletariat. Substituting social determinism for individual will, Guesdists deprived even the most eccentric or powerful politicians of their distinctiveness: the anti-Semitic popularity of Édouard Drumont represented the death-cry of the petite bourgeoisie, not the success of a clever demagogue; the aloof authoritarianism of President Jean-Paul-Pierre Casimir-Perier flaunted the arrogance of the haute bourgeoisie, not the aristocratic personality of a political dynast; and the Machiavellian manoeuvres of Prime Minister René Waldeck-Rousseau reflected the hegemony of capital over French society, not the skill of France's premier parliamentarian. The Parti Ouvrier strove unremittingly, and with success, to convert potential class identity into actual class politics – finding a society whose political culture turned upon the traditional opposition between elites and 'the masses', leaving a nation preoccupied by the politics of class struggle.[5] How did Guesdists accomplish this purpose? What ideological legerdemain converted France's rulers from 'notables' to 'bourgeois' and its ruled from the 'people' to 'proletarians'?

First, Guesdists denied priority or even autonomy to the political

---

[5] For the relative intensity of class politics in France, see D. Gallie, *Social Inequality and Class Radicalism in France and Britain* (Cambridge, 1983), pp. 5–8 (although Gallie, pp. 185–7, attributes this peculiarity to the militancy of 1918–20 rather than to the Guesdists) and S. Lash, *The Militant Worker: Class and Radicalism in France and America* (London, 1984).

realm, affirming instead that 'the political order is only the reflection, the moon, of the economic order'.[6] Challenging the assumptions which had governed French popular radicalism from eighteenth-century protests against 'famine plots' to the nineteenth-century enthusiasm for the 'Social Republic', the Parti Ouvrier disputed the presumption that social inequality and economic injustice derived from political domination. Instead, political domination, according to French Marxists, emanated from exploitative relations of production: protest movements in pre-revolutionary France had mistaken feudalism for monarchical despotism, while post-revolutionary radicals had mistaken capitalism for electoral privilege. Marx had pioneered his reduction of authority to exploitation while Europe's exclusive or authoritarian politics had apparently legitimated this equation, just as the property franchise or monarchical tyranny had seemingly legitimated the Republicans' reduction of exploitation to political authority (causality may run either way in the dialectic of polity and economy). Marx and his radical enemies had agreed that authority and exploitation mirrored each other, but disputed which was image and which reality.

Guesdists, however, confronted a very different milieu from the world of Guizot and Louis Napoleon which had informed Marx's thought: a 'bourgeois democracy' founded upon universal manhood suffrage, simultaneously the optimal opportunity for labour's liberation *and* the most formidable embodiment of capitalist rule, in the paradoxical Leninist formulation.[7] Workers' enfranchisement, on the one hand, enormously enhanced proletarian political potency. But liberal democracy, on the other hand, imposed an all-important dilemma on Marxist political strategists: how could an egalitarian political order 'reflect' capitalist exploitation and oppression? Might the conjunction of democratic politics and capitalist economics validate the liberals' presumption that freedom depended upon 'free enterprise', their anti-Marxist version of economic determinism? How did the Parti Ouvrier resolve this conundrum?

The Party's simplest solution denied the reality of political

---

[6] J. Guesde, 'Lettre de Bordeaux', *Le Socialiste*, 31 December 1887.
[7] For the inadequacy of Marxist thought on liberal democratic politics, see A. Hunt, 'Marx – The Missing Dimension: The Rise of Representative Democracy', in B. Matthews (ed.), *Marx: A Hundred Years On* (London, 1983), pp. 87–110; A. Hunt, 'Taking Democracy Seriously', in A. Hunt (ed.), *Marxism and Democracy* (London, 1980), pp. 7–9; and G. Therborn, 'The Rule of Capital and the Rise of Democracy', *New Left Review*, no. 103, 1977, pp. 3–41.

democracy in capitalist society, thereby resolving the puzzle of 'bourgeois democracy' by its rhetorical abolition. Enthusiastically pursuing this strategy, Guesdists categorically rejected the democratic pretensions of the Third Republic, denouncing its liberal forms as camouflage for the reality of social despotism, indicting its leaders as puppets who danced on strings manipulated by capitalist tyrants. French Marxists caustically criticised the deeply rooted Republican ideals (the French political culture equated democracy and the Republic) of the French Left, arguing that social democracy would only prevail once the democratic Republic had been discredited as *the* balm for working-class agonies. Unhappy experience justified this diagnosis: socialism, with its critique of capitalist exploitation, superseded democratic Republicanism, with its critique of privileged authority, only where and when the defence of 'Republican liberties' ceased to govern popular politics, a condition which rarely obtained during the *Belle Époque*.[8] Working-class Republicanism, a potent legacy from the sans-culottes and the '48ers to the plebeian French, repeatedly frustrated Marxist socialists: workers rallied to the Republic against the resurgent Monarchists in 1885, reducing the POF to insignificance in the movements's first major electoral test; alternative visions of the Republic mesmerised proletarian opinion during the Boulanger Affair, forcing the Parti Ouvrier onto the sidelines during the most intense economic and social crisis of the *Fin de Siècle*; and the defence of the democratic Republic against nationalist and clerical reactionaries virtually destroyed the painfully constructed Guesdist political apparatus at the turn of the century, awarding proletarian political leadership to Jaurès rather than Guesde. Tormented by antagonists sustained by a century of accumulated Republican memories, French Marxists desperately sought to discredit 'bourgeois democracy', the heavily fortified political outworks which protected the 'reality' of social autocracy.

Fully aware of the infelicitous conjuncture between liberal demo-

---

[8] Y. Lequin, 'Classe Ouvrière et Idéologie dans la Région Lyonnaise à la Fin du XIXᵉ Siècle', *Mouvement Social*, no. 69, 1969, p. 17; M. Rebérioux, 'Le Socialisme Français de 1871 à 1914', in J. Droz (ed.), *Histoire Générale du Socialisme: Tome II – De 1875 à 1918* (Paris, 1974), pp. 134–136; J. Howorth, 'Socialists and the Republic in the Twentieth Century: Instrument of Integration, Agent of Alienation, or Road to Revolution?', *Proceedings of the Eighth Annual Conference of the Western Society for French History*, vol. 8, 1980, pp. 452–63; and J. Howorth, 'From the Bourgeois Republic to the Social Republic', in S. Williams (ed.), *Socialism in France from Jaurès to Mitterrand* (London, 1983), pp. 1–14.

cratic traditions and Republican anti-socialism which sustained Marxism's Opportunist and Radical enemies, Guesdists aimed their ideological heavy artillery against the memories bequeathed by the revolutions of 1793, 1848 and 1870. For French Marxists, the First Republic, despite the Jacobins' egalitarian rhetoric, had embodied the bourgeois revolution, its anti-proletarian essence summed up in the infamous Le Chapelier Law; the Second Republic, despite Louis Blanc's blandishments, had revealed its true nature in the working-class dead of the June Days; and the Third Republic, repudiating transformation of the social order from its inception, had baptised itself with the blood of 25,000 murdered Communards.[9] Guesdists ostentatiously boycotted July Fourteenth celebrations, individual party-members being expelled for participating in this 'bourgeois festival' and POF municipalities closing their town halls for the day. For workers, *Le Socialiste* claimed, 'the Fourteenth of July ... will always be *the celebration of others*'.[10] Consciously constructing an alternative to the Republican myth which had enthralled the French Left since the eighteenth century, the Parti Ouvrier founded its own historical mythology upon a chronicle of bourgeois repression which unrolled its bloody scroll from the Champ de Mars massacre of 1791 to the killings at Fourmies in 1891, a century-long working-class martyrdom which consecrated the socialist indictment of the Republican regime.[11] For Guesdists, murder and myth sustained the 'bourgeois Republic', not liberty and equality.

Turning from cruel memories to the harsh present, French Marxists illustrated their theoretical criticisms of liberal democracy with contemporaneous Republican practices, practices by no means always liberal or democratic. In Deville's embittered words, written during the nadir of his Party's political fortunes:

---

[9] For a self-consciously historiographical example of anti-Republican rhetoric, see Anonymous, 'M. Aulard et la Révolution Sociale', *Le Socialiste*, 30 April 1893. For discussion of this anti-Republican stringency, see J.-M. Mayeur, *La Vie Politique sous la Troisième République 1870–1940* (Paris, 1984), pp. 142–3.

[10] Anonymous, 'Leur Fête', *Le Socialiste*, 15 July 1891. For expulsion from the Party for 'complicity' in 14 July celebrations, see the account in 'Le Parti Ouvrier en France: XVIIIᵉ Arrondissement', *Le Socialiste*, 14–21 September 1902, and for municipal hostility, see the recollections of Mireille Osmin in 'L'Héritage de Jules Guesde dans le Mouvement Ouvrier Français: Débat', *Démocratie Nouvelle*, no. 3, 1966, p. 35.

[11] For the potency of this martyrology in working-class political culture, see Y. Lequin, *Les Ouvriers de la Région Lyonnaise (1848–1914): Les Intérêts de Classe et la République* (Lyons, 1977), p. 284 and J. Stone, 'Political Culture in the Third Republic: The Case of Camille Pelletan', *Proceedings of the Western Society for French History*, vol. 13, 1985, p. 219.

all this democracy is a mystification. Democratic forms are an optical illusion which projects an image of universal equality, while the reality is that two classes embody, under conditions of profound inequality, the two factors of the mode of production: capital and labour. Disguising class with democratic rhetoric is duping the masses with false appearances – hiding from one class that it is being sacrificed to another, thereby protecting the latter from the continuous rebellion which would be inevitable if the truth were not hidden from the eyes of the victims.[12]

Republican democracy, in other words, equalled bourgeois hegemony. Above all, the patent prejudice of the judicial system, an integral component of the bourgeois order in the Guesdists' schema, regularly confirmed the Parti Ouvrier's equation of polity and economy: workers indicted for transgressions against property and socialists accused of infringements of 'social order' could expect little mercy from examining magistrates and the courts, but the law rarely charged and less often convicted bourgeois who violated France's rudimentary labour laws.[13] The French state after 1879, although firmly controlled by the liberals and democrats whose forebears had once filled Bonapartist and Monarchist gaols, retained the repressive apparatus developed by the preceding authoritarian regimes, and deployed it ruthlessly against the nascent socialist movement: by the 1890s most Guesdist leaders had served an apprenticeship in the Sainte-Pélagie prison, repository of the Republic's political enemies. Welcoming this repression in an overt *politique du pire*, Guesdists never forgot and never forgave these violations of the Republic's self-proclaimed libertarian norms, violations which proved, according to the POF, that 'indirect bourgeois rule in the form of a monarchy or empire differs not at all from direct bourgeois rule under a republic'.[14] For *Le Socialiste*,

there's nothing to choose between the monarchists of the rue Transnonain, the Bonapartists of La Ricamarie and D'Aubin and the Republicans of Fourmies and Paris [this editorial was written on the occasion of the violent closure of the Paris Bourse du Travail by the Dupuy government]. It's impossible to see any difference between them any longer. They're sealing their shameful union with your blood and upon the ruins of your trade unions.[15]

---

[12] G. Deville, 'La Loi Militaire', *Le Socialiste*, 18 June 1887.
[13] J.-P. Machelon, *La République contre les Libertés? (1879–1914)* (Paris, 1976) and M. Perrot, *Les Ouvriers en Grève: France 1871–1890* (Paris, 1974), pp. 453–4.
[14] J. Guesde, 'Lettre de Bordeaux', *Le Socialiste*, 31 December 1887.
[15] J. Guesde and P. Lafargue, 'Pour Nos Élections', *Le Socialiste*, 15 July 1893.

Workers' blood, whether shed by monarchist sabres or Republican bullets, ran just as red.

Animated by their hatred of the hypocritical 'bourgeois Republic', Guesdists decided that liberal democracy secured capitalist tyranny far more reliably than had authoritarian reaction: Republicans, wolves in sheep's clothing, camouflaged the mechanisms of exploitation behind false promises of universal freedom and equality; reactionaries, wolves in wolves' clothing, revealed the true nature of an exploitative and oppressive society. The former were the workers' 'most jesuitical and dangerous of enemies'.[16] Tracing the logic of this insight to its ultimate conclusion, French Marxists lapsed into full-blown catastrophism: at their most extreme, they expressly hoped for the victory of the Republic's Monarchist, Boulangist, or nationalist enemies, a victory which would establish an obvious congruence between the political and social orders, with an authoritarian polity corresponding to a despotic economy. Foreshadowing the lethal errors of the Parti Ouvrier's Communist descendants during the Comintern's 'Third Period', Guesdists hoped that 'the triumph of reaction from on high might precipitate the triumph of revolution from below'[17] – a *politique du pire* with a vengeance.

This extremism recurred in Guesdist rhetoric, most frequently during the great crises of 'Republican defence' which periodically convulsed French politics. But the dream of a providential 'reaction from on high' rarely predominated in Parti Ouvrier visions of revolution: its terrible logic antagonised potential supporters; its bloodcurdling implications frightened the most sanguine of Guesdists; while the POF itself had been born of French Radicalism, and never altogether abandoned its birthright to the language of liberty. In any case, the protean Marxist theory of proletarian politics contained an alternative or complement to the Guesdists' indictment of liberal democracy as a malignant fraud: the thesis that 'bourgeois democracy' alone supplied 'the necessary political form of the proletariat's liberation'.[18] How did the French Marxists justify this conclusion, which seemingly contradicted their more fevered criticisms of the 'bourgeois Republic'?

First, in this democratic rationale for revolution, authoritarian regimes, far from enhancing the prospects of autonomous working-

[16] P. Lafargue, 'Exploitation Politique de la Classe Ouvrière', *Le Socialiste*, 18 February 1900.
[17] Anonymous, 'Vive la Sociale!', *Le Socialiste*, 30 June 1894.
[18] Bracke, *Onze Ans d'Histoire Socialiste: Aux Travailleurs de France* (Paris, 1901), p. 4.

class politics, compelled workers to exhaust themselves in struggles for civic and political liberty, struggles inevitably fought in alliance with bourgeois liberals and petit-bourgeois democrats. In other words, reactionary regimes recruited for liberal democracy, not for socialism. Social democracy, the ideology of anti-capitalism, would move onto the historical agenda when proletarians realised that political democracy, the ideology of anti-despotism, could not supply workers with a panacea for the malady of exploitation, a realisation which required sustained prior exposure to the inadequacies of 'bourgeois democracy'.[19] Second, liberal democracy, despite its hypocrisy, furnished unprecedented opportunities for working-class mobilisation against capital: the Republic, despite the bloodshed at Fourmies and the restrictions of the Waldeck-Rousseau Law, allowed far greater latitude to socialist militancy and labour organisation than had any preceding regime. Not unappreciative of these advantages, the POF 'defended liberties not for themselves, but for their revolutionary utility'.[20] Thus, once superficial disputes over the polity had dissipated, the proletariat could and would finally embark upon its ultimate revolutionary mission, turning bourgeois political forms against bourgeois society. When 'political conflict is over', presaged the Parti Ouvrier, 'economic conflict begins: employees against employers, exploited workers against exploiting parasites, class against class, Revolution against the Republic'.[21] From this perspective, a victorious Republic doomed Republicanism.

Unfortunately for the French Marxists, the Third Republic, menaced by resurgent Monarchists and the demagogic Boulangists during the 1880s and savaged by proto-fascist nationalists during the Dreyfus Affair, rarely appeared unconditionally victorious during the *Belle Époque*. Faced by the apparent reality of 'reaction from on high', Guesdists sullenly defended a regime they hated, yet which they found 'preferable to an Orleanist monarchy'.[22] Tolerance of reactionaries, a consistent *politique du pire*, would have discredited the

---

[19] For evidence of this phenomenon, see R. Jonas, 'From the Radical Republic to the Social Republic: On the Origins and Nature of Socialism in Rural France 1871–1914', PhD thesis, University of California, Berkeley, 1985, p. 93.

[20] P.-M. André, 'Ni Lutaud, Ni Régis', *Le Socialiste*, 2–9 June 1901.

[21] J. Guesde, 'Le Résultat', *Le Cri du Peuple*, 27 January 1885. For an excellent description of exactly this transition from conflict about the political regime to conflict about the social order, see P. Hutton, 'Popular Boulangism and the Advent of Mass Politics in France', *Journal of Contemporary History*, vol. 11, 1976, pp. 98–101.

[22] P. Lafargue, 'Les Endormeurs Possibilistes', *Le Socialiste*, 10 December 1887.

POF, already suspect in liberal and Radical circles as an unwitting agent of the anti-Republican Right. And a principled policy of abstention, the programme attempted during the Boulanger Affair with the slogan 'Ni Rue Cadet, Ni Rue de Sèze!', usually proved impossible in practice, however desirable in theory: particularly during the Dreyfus Affair, the Party fragmented as groups and militants opted for one side or the other, while workers who misunderstood the POF's withdrawal from the fray abandoned the aloof Guesdists for more activist factions. Cowed by these daunting circumstances, the Parti Ouvrier periodically reversed itself, on the occasion of the October 1898 crisis even assuming the lead in organising working-class resistance to the anti-Dreyfusard mob.[23] Once having abandoned systematic anti-Republicanism, Guesdists sought to annex the democratic tradition to their novel socialist ideology, arguing that the Parti Ouvrier alone embodied the 'Social Republic', the last and highest manifestation of the democratic ideal. Indeed, according to the POF, *only* the socialist working class under Guesdist leadership could or would defend the Republican political order, since bourgeois, aware themselves of the socialist consequences of democracy, had retreated into authoritarian reaction. Once challenged by Marxist socialists, 'bourgeois democracy' supposedly degenerated into a contradiction in terms; the political bankruptcy of the bourgeoisie converting French politics 'into a steeple chase between military dictatorship and revolutionary dictatorship'.[24] Guesdists, tracing the consequences of this thesis, predicted that 'the Republic will become the [socialist] Revolution, or it will cease to be'.[25]

Overall, French Marxists were in two minds about liberal democracy: they treasured its opportunities for socialist mobilisation, but damned its masking of bourgeois domination – an ideological schizophrenia the symptoms of which recurred with every political crisis between 1882 and 1905. In retrospect, historians have denounced these Guesdist inconsistencies: communists condemning the POF's periodic submission to the Republican political consensus, liberal democrats reviling the Party's stubborn adherence to 'outmoded' revolutionary intransigence. Yet the Parti Ouvrier's contradictions, however dubious theoretically, enhanced the movement's

---

[23] A. Noland, *The Founding of the French Socialist Party* (Cambridge, 1956), pp. 76–7.
[24] 'C.', 'Dictature', *Le Socialiste*, 5 March 1899.
[25] Anonymous, 'Révolution ou Monarchie', *Le Socialiste*, 10 October 1885.

appeal to the French proletariat, whose own disposition towards the Republic vacillated between uncritical enthusiasm and disenchanted hostility. Workers valued the Republic's combination of liberal civil rights and democratic political equality, the liberal democratic combination which allowed relatively unrestricted assertion of proletarian interests after a century of repression: if nothing else, interested workers could now freely read *Le Socialiste*. Yet workers' 'betters' enjoyed political advantages to which proletarians could never aspire, advantages which generated resentment and hostility as workers took their first stumbling steps into a political realm still governed by wealth, education, and 'connections'. Given this ambiguous working-class political culture, absolute Parti Ouvrier commitment to the Republic would have disarmed Marxists before anti-political revolutionary syndicalists and anti-democratic Nationalists, while absolute Guesdist anti-Republicanism would have awarded much of the working class to Radicals or Independent Socialists. The Parti Ouvrier, both reflecting and enhancing its constituency's self-contradictory political mentality, argued, as Guesde put it in his famous debate with Jaurès, that,

following Marx, the Republic is *the ideal terrain* for our revolution, because it brings the classes face to face in their direct and collective antagonism, without their inevitable conflict being distorted by dynastic calculations and manoeuvres. But ... if ... the proletariat abandons its own struggles, renounces its efforts to create its own Republic, in order to tie itself down in the defence of its masters' regime, *the Republic, thus understood and practised, would become the worst of governments.*[26]

Or, as Lafargue wrote, in his suitably paradoxical style: 'the bourgeois republican order is the most corrupt and dishonest regime which could possibly exist, and the Parti Ouvrier will support it in preference to all others, until the day when we will be strong

---

[26] J. Guesde, 'Rectification', *Le Socialiste*, 4–11 September 1904 (Guesde's stress). For workers' ambiguous reaction to their Republican rights, see J. Julliard, 'Les Ouvriers dans la Société Française: Intégration et Autonomie', in *Histoire Sociale, Sensibilités Collectives et Mentalités: Mélanges Robert Mandrou* (Paris, 1985), pp. 423–30; Jonas, 'From the Radical Republic to the Social Republic', p. 423; W. Reddy, *The Rise of Market Culture: The Textile Trade and French Society 1750–1900* (Cambridge, 1984), p. 296; M. Pigenet, 'Signification des Votes Ouvriers dans le Département du Cher (1848–1914)', *Revue Française de Science Politique*, vol. 39, 1989, pp. 730–1; and D. Tartakowski, 'Le Mouvement Ouvrier Français et l'État de la Commune à la Première Guerre Mondiale', *Cahiers d'Histoire de l'Institut des Recherches Marxistes*, no. 11, 1972, p. 18.

enough ... to overthrow it and establish the dictatorship of the proletariat'.[27]

The Guesdist obsession with the Republican form of government, whether interpreted as a bulwark of bourgeois rule or as the seedbed of socialist revolution, exemplified the perennial Marxist preoccupation with the state, a preoccupation which has systematically precluded a broader socialist understanding of politics as collective decision-making.[28] This reduction of politics to the struggle for control of public authority undoubtedly reflected widespread working-class convictions, and mirrored the vastly expanded competency of public authority during the *Fin de Siècle*. The Third Republic's state, that precocious offspring of the modern leviathan, inexorably penetrated every aspect of French 'civil society', not excepting the internal regulation of the workplace, once laissez-faire's most secure refuge.[29] Nevertheless, although in keeping with the times, the restriction of Guesdist political thought to analyses of the relationship between state and society dulled the French Marxists' sensitivity to the 'politics of everyday life' – to the patters of domination and submission, authority and resistance, consensus and conflict characteristic of families, informal sociability, and voluntary organisations. This refusal or inability to discern how 'politics' suffused civil society foreshadowed the tragic 'statism' of successful twentieth-century Marxist revolutionaries, who have proven signally unwilling or unable to articulate autonomous social politics with the authority of the revolutionary state. Nor did the Guesdists' acuity of focus compensate for narrowness of vision: their conception of public authority, although central to their political perceptions, remained blurred and distorted.[30] The state embodied 'the public coercive power created by class division'[31] – so much was clear, at least to

[27] P. Lafargue, 'La Politique de la Bourgeoisie', *L'Égalité*, 18 December 1881.

[28] For a strict critique of this blinkered approach, see R. Gunn, 'Marxism and the Ideas of Power and Participation', in J. Bloomfield (ed.), *Class, Hegemony and Party* (London, 1977), p. 21.

[29] D. Tartakowski, 'Le Mouvement Ouvrier Français et l'État', p. 15 describes the impact of this process upon the workers' movement. For the substitution of public law for private regulation within capitalist enterprise, see J. Lambert, *Le Patron: De l'Avènement à la Contestation* (Paris, 1969), p. 115.

[30] For the general difficulties in conceptualising the state experienced by French Marxists, see T. Judt, *Marxism and the French Left: Studies in Labour and Politics in France 1830–1981* (Oxford, 1986), p. 47. The Guesdists' particular difficulties are discussed in M. Moissonnier, '1898–1905: Tours et Détours de l'Unité Socialiste en France', *Cahiers d'Histoire de l'Institut des Recherches Marxistes*, no. 20, 1985, pp. 53–80.

[31] G. Deville, 'L'État et le Socialisme', *Le Socialiste*, 26 May 1895.

Marxists. But what structures, which processes, linked state power to class rule? Here clarity succumbed to ambiguity, confusion, and contradiction, those attendant demons or guardian angels of ideological discourse.

The favoured Guesdist presentation of the relationship between public authority and class structure identified the state as 'the expression of a dominant class, [which] exists only to maintain [that class's] domination by force'.[32] But why this strict reduction of public authority to class domination? As so often happened in Parti Ouvrier discourse, theory bowed to polemic: the thesis strengthened the Guesdists against their competitors for the allegiance of French workers. Radicals and reformist socialists, who affirmed their faith in the democratic Republic and opposed the Parti Ouvrier's programme of social revolution, wilted before the icy logic of the Guesdists' political theory, while the powerful anti-political current in the French labour movement, which invested its hopes in the abstentionist construction of an alternative society and opposed the Parti Ouvrier's campaign for proletarian political mobilisation, stood condemned as naive at best and complicit at worst in its negative approach to the 'bourgeois state'. How did the Parti Ouvrier manipulate its class-reductionist theory of public authority against these antagonists?

In campaigning against their Republican enemies of the working-class 'Right', Guesdists maintained that French governments, although thoroughly democratic in their rhetoric, would 'never act against the capitalist lords of whom they [were] ... agents'.[33] Proletarians supposedly deluded themselves if they anticipated alleviation of their lot by a regime subordinated to capital: they might as well expect liberation by their employers as by their employers' political proxies. At the same time, campaigning against their anti-political working-class enemies, Guesdists contended that the proletariat could liberate itself only through seizure of the 'bourgeois state', given that 'political power [was] indispensable for the transformation of society'.[34] Anti-political revolutionary syndicalists and Proudhonian mutualists who relied upon trade unions and cooperatives to construct an alternative society apart from or

[32] Anonymous, 'La Semaine', *Le Socialiste*, 3 June 1900.
[33] Anonymous, 'Lendemain d'Arbitrage', *Le Socialiste*, 5–12 November 1899.
[34] Manifesto of the Parti Ouvrier – Fédération Socialiste Révolutionnaire du Nord, 5 February 1884, in file 177300–7–1 Ba/39 Archives de la Préfecture de Police de Paris.

against political authority supposedly misled themselves and deluded others: the bastions of bourgeois social power would never fall without a preparatory assault upon the citadel of bourgeois political sovereignty. Finally, Guesdists promised that, 'on the day when [the workers] seize power, they will be able to utilise it for the realisation of their own class interest'.[35] Workers who naively indicted power itself as the origin of social evil, the anarchist heresy, supposedly precluded labour's liberation: they connived at their own subordination to capital. For the Guesdists,

the state, garrisoned by the capitalist class, can best be compared to those fortresses which loomed over Medieval cities. If you occupied the town, but failed to take the fortress at the same time, you had nothing. On the other hand, if you had the fortress, you had the city without having to seize it.[36]

Skirmishes for footholds within bourgeois society mattered not at all unless they contributed to the siege of the state: reformists and anarchists, although dissimilar in their motives, embodied a common strategic error in their opposition to the proletarian seizure of public authority.

Guesdists, however, failed to explain systematically and explicitly *why* the state served as an instrument of bourgeois class rule, a lapse which indicated their failure to grapple with one of the most difficult and controversial issues in Marxist thought. Implicit assumptions abounded, however. Parti Ouvrier rhetoric, rarely theoretically rigorous, frequently implied a simple equivalence between the political elite and the capitalist class: for Guesdists, the French polity and French society both obeyed a homogeneous 'classe capitaliste et gouvernementale' or 'bourgeoisie patronale et gouvernementale'. This rhetoric misled. Several of the Guesdists' most prominent entrepreneurial enemies – including Eugène Motte, deputy for Roubaix, vanquisher of Guesde – indeed sat in the Chamber of Deputies, and the symbiosis of state and capital found a classic instance in Maurice Rouvier, simultaneously finance minister and president of the Banque Française pour le Commerce et l'Industrie. But late nineteenth-century France experienced an overall withdrawal of capitalists from political office, a tendency towards managerial specialisation or rentier irresponsibility accompanied by a consequent 'professionalisation' of politics: the palmy days of the

---

[35] Anonymous, 'La Semaine', *Le Socialiste*, 3 June 1900.
[36] J. Guesde, 'Révolution et Maraude', *Le Cri du Peuple*, 26 November 1884.

July Monarchy when bourgeois notables had run the state as a side-line to their business interests had long passed. Gambetta, Clemenceau, Waldeck-Rousseau, men who had spent their lives manipulating political power, exemplified the political leadership of the Third Republic. While dedicated to the defence of private property and the free market, they themselves were not and never had been capitalists.[37]

French Marxists, however, developed a more sophisticated answer to the troubling question of the relationship between the bourgeoisie and the 'bourgeois state'. Reverting to their habitual economic determinism, the Guesdists frequently contended that the primacy of the mode of production compelled a political order superimposed upon a capitalist economy to function in the interest of capital, no matter whence the polity recruited its governing elite. Whether aristocrats or petits bourgeois, whether professionals or even workers, political leaders necessarily served capital so long as the economy served capitalists. In the aptly entitled article 'République et Propriété', *Le Socialiste*, embroidering a *leitmotif* repeated in hundreds of other polemics, concluded that 'so long as the bourgeoisie exists, that is to say so long as property retains its individual character, the bourgeoisie will be the ruling class. The government, whether a monarchy, an empire, or a republic, will serve the capitalists and oppress the workers'.[38] Determined to construct an autonomous working-class politics, Guesdists systematically exploited this thesis to divorce workers from their traditional allegiances. According to the Parti Ouvrier, so long as capital ruled the economy, so long as capitalists exploited workers, it mattered not a jot whether rural clerical or urban secular politicians filled the Chamber of Deputies, whether aristocratic monarchist or capitalist Republican bureaucrats staffed the ministries, whether bourgeois moderate or petit-bourgeois Radical statesmen presided over the state – all represented capitalism.

These equations of class power and political domination, whether through homology between class and elite or through reduction of polity to economy, have suffered biting criticisms, both during the Guesdists' period and since. According to the indictments of

---

[37] The withdrawal of capitalists from overt involvement in politics is described in J. Lambert, *Le Patron*, pp. 113–14. For discussion of this contentious issue in Marxist theory, see R. Miliband, *Marxism and Politics* (Oxford, 1977), pp. 68–74.
[38] Anonymous, 'République et Propriété', *Le Socialiste*, 19 June 1886.

Marxism's critics and the confessions of self-critical Marxists, subordination of politics to the mode of production has rendered 'the relative autonomy of the state' virtually inconceivable: the independent interests of political actors have disappeared from view, thereby impoverishing Marxist analyses of social order and disorder and hindering Marxist comprehension of historical change and continuity. At the same time, economic reductionism has preempted discussion of the internal logic of alternative political orders: Marxists have never devoted the intensive research, intellectual rigour and creative insight characteristic of their investigations of modes of production to the study of 'modes of rule'.[39] Empirical discordance paralleled theoretical inadequacy: the Parti Ouvrier's assimilation of the regime to the ruling class ignored the frequently fraught relationship between the Third Republic and the French bourgeoisie, a bourgeoisie by no means fully reconciled to the swelling domain of political democracy. If the state necessarily served capital, as the Parti Ouvrier contended, then capitalists should logically have welcomed the expansion of public authority, supposed guarantor of their interests. Instead, French employers, terrified that political democracy would award proletarians mastery over the propertied, fearing that bureaucracies responsive to the masses would supersede free markets responsive to economic power, fiercely resisted the expanding authority of the state.[40] The Parti Ouvrier, while usually ignoring this evidence against their fundamental political theory, occasionally admitted that 'the anarchy of bourgeois society'[41] generated contradictions between capital and the state, an institution intrinsically hostile to 'anarchy'. But these unusual intuitions, insightful exceptions which proved the blinkered rule, rarely modified the French Marxists' equation of state and capital. Frightened liberals who denounced the 'creeping socialism' inherent in democratic politics understood the logic of their times

---

[39] For representative critiques of this Marxist inadequacy, see R. Miliband, 'State Power and Class Interests', in R. Miliband, *Class Power and State Power*, pp. 63–78; G. Therborn, 'What does the Ruling Class do when it Rules? Some Reflections on Different Approaches to the Study of Power in Society', *Insurgent Sociologist*, vol. 6, 1976, pp. 3–16; and N. Poulantzas, 'The Problem of the Capitalist State', in R. Blackburn (ed.), *Ideology in Social Science* (Bungay, 1972), p. 246. There is an excellent defence of an essentially 'Guesdist' conception of the 'ruling class' in J. Hoffman, 'The Problem of the Ruling Class in Classical Marxist Theory: Some Conceptual Preliminaries', *Science and Society*, vol. 50, 1986, pp. 342–63.

[40] P. Sorlin, *Waldeck-Rousseau* (Paris, 1966), p. 376.

[41] P. Lafargue, 'Une Enquête sur Fourmies', *Le Socialiste*, 17 June 1891.

better than did Guesdists, convinced as the Marxists were that the state's defence of order necessarily meant defence of bourgeois order.[42] Why did the POF favour a political theory which virtually precluded political theorising?

Above all, the Guesdist equation of political elite and economic class reinforced common working-class suppositions which greatly facilitated socialist militancy. Workers, however ambitious, however optimistic, no more aspired to prefectural or ministerial posts than to the millions of a Rothschild: they knew that, whoever staffed the 'ruling class', proletarians need not apply. Illogically yet understandably, workers deduced that a political and administrative elite as closed to the working class as the plutocracy itself must constitute part of the 'bourgeoisie patronale et gouvernementale', that portmanteau Guesdist characterisation of the ruling class. At the same time, French business increasingly recruited its management cadres from the ranks of the senior civil service, thereby further reinforcing the proletarian equation of state and business.[43] Finally, the close working association between private property and 'law and order' during the *Fin de Siècle* validated the Guesdist merger of these two 'establishment' evils. A striking Roubaisian textile worker, defeated by an intransigent employer supported by the Republican police and the national army, easily bracketed exploitative capital with despotic state. Overall, the Guesdist postulate that bureaucrats and bosses constituted a single 'ruling class' yielded forceful and credible Marxist polemic, if dubious political sociology. Rigid subordination of the state, a dependent variable, to capital, the ultimate demiurge of society, rendered routine politics, the politics of 'Possibilism', irrelevant or noxious: socialist revolution alone would arm workers against that ferocious ideological hybrid – the 'bourgeois state'.

All the same, Guesdists, implicitly accepting an 'underdetermined' relationship between polity and bourgeois society which contradicted this revolutionary purism, sometimes portrayed public authority as a 'gauge' by which 'the power . . . of a class is measured

[42] For the general problem created by these bourgeois attitudes for Marxism's theory of the 'capitalist state', see C. Crouch, 'The State, Capital, and Liberal Democracy', in C. Crouch (ed.), *State and Economy in Contemporary Capitalism* (New York, 1979), pp. 25–8 and A. Przeworski and I. Wallerstein, 'The Structure of Class Conflict in Democratic Capitalist Societies', *American Political Science Review*, vol. 76, 1982, pp. 235–6.

[43] C. Charle, 'Les Milieux d'Affaires dans la Structure de la Classe Dominante vers 1900', *Actes de la Recherche en Sciences Sociales*, nos. 20–1, 1978, pp. 83–96.

by what it can demand [of the state]'.[44] The social orientation of the
state, in this contingent conception of power, indicated the relative
weight of the working class and of the bourgeoisie in the balance of
sociopolitical might. Capitalist economic power conferred a natural
advantage upon the bourgeoisie, but a sufficiently well-organised,
self-conscious, and militant proletariat might eventually bend public
authority to its will – a powerful argument for the class politics
advocated by the Parti Ouvrier, and one regularly deployed against
anarchists and revolutionary syndicalists. Experience reinforced
polemical logic: French Marxists occasionally noticed labour disputes in which the state intervened against employers in favour of
protesting workers. Commenting, for instance, upon a labour dispute during which employers had been singularly unreasonable and
workers admirably conciliatory (according to the FNS), Guesdist
unionists conceded that 'the Prefect has done everything in his
power to encourage conciliation and to force the bosses to realise
that it's odious and unjust to refuse collective bargaining'.[45] The
May Day demonstrations pioneered by the POF, with their ostentatious working-class delegations to the public authorities in favour of
the eight-hour day, reinforced this strategy of protest and influence,
a strategy which clearly sapped the rigid premises underlying the
rhetoric of the 'bourgeois state'.

French Marxists noticed the consequences, although they failed to
analyse the causes, of the state's responsiveness to labour protest
during a period when aggrieved workers, despite the exhortations of
revolutionary syndicalists, desired, expected, and sometimes
obtained public arbitration of labour disputes, arbitration in which
workers' political weight compensated for their employers' industrial
muscle. Unfortunately, the Parti Ouvrier never synthesised these
instances into the systematic articulation of class conflict and politics
which might have supplemented or replaced its reductionist equation of class and polity. Instead, returning to their close correlation
of political power and capitalist rule, French Marxists usually

[44] J. Guesde, 'L'État Providence', *Le Cri du Peuple*, 26 January 1884. See the discussion of this
alternative view of the state in N. Yennawi-le Yaouang, 'Les Divergences sur la Nature de
Classe de l'État dans le Polémique entre Jaurès et les Guesdistes', *Bulletin de la Société d'Études
Jauréssiennes*, no. 95, 1964, pp. 3–10. For analysis of this approach to the state within the
Marxist tradition, see S. Clarke, 'State, Class Struggle, and the Reproduction of Capital',
Kapitalistate, nos. 10/11, 1983, pp. 113–30.
[45] 'Les Ouvriers Verriers de Bordeaux et des Landes', *Bulletin Mensuel de la Fédération Nationale
des Syndicats et Groupes Corporatifs Ouvriers de France*, no. 3, 25 July 1890.

argued that the state *had* to intervene against irrationally brutal employers to secure the conditions for more 'normal' exploitation: prefects and ministers supposedly disciplined particular bourgeois to protect the bourgeoisie as a whole against the consequences of individual irresponsibility. In the words of the Guesdist railroad worker and publicist Paul André, 'bourgeois order demands condemnation of [such irresponsible] bosses'. But, he continued, this condemnation in no way refuted the Guesdists' class diagnosis of the ills associated with the 'bourgeois state': 'a few bosses have been condemned: fine, but it's not enough! It's the bosses in general who are at fault'.[46]

Governed by their polemical purpose, Guesdists necessarily rejected the 'gauge' model of the state when criticising 'reformists', however well the model served them in their struggle against anarchists: non-Marxist socialists such as Brousse and Millerand repeatedly and successfully employed the idea of a neutral government, measure of relative class power, against Marxist advocates of a duel to the death between the proletariat and the 'bourgeois state'. Just as the Parti Ouvrier discovered an audience for its intransigence among workers habituated to governmental indifference or repression, so Possibilists and the Independents gained a following among more fortunate proletarians: the Parti Ouvrier rarely overcame the Republican convictions of workers, such as the northern coal miners, whose numbers, organisation, or strategic location in the economy ensured state protection against politically reactionary or industrially despotic employers.[47] In practice, Marxist advocacy of revolutionary socialism required acceptance of an 'instrumentalist' interpretation of political power, an interpretation in which public authority existed to defend exploitation, but never to defend workers. Obeying this imperative, the Parti Ouvrier rarely conceded that democratically elected governments might occasionally favour the interests of labour over those of capital.

Marx himself, passionately devoted to his conception of the organisational prerequisites for both labour reformism and socialist revolution, had designated proletarian political mobilisation as the only sure antidote to the poisons of bourgeois hegemony ('the

[46] P.-M. André, 'Patrons Condamnés', *Le Socialiste*, 27 November–4 December 1904.
[47] M. Simard, 'Situation Économique de l'Entreprise et Rapports de Production: Le Cas de la Compagnie des Mines d'Anzin (1860–1894)', *Revue du Nord*, vol. 65, 1983, p. 597.

proletariat can act as a class only by constituting itself as a distinct political party'). Despite the ambiguities and lacunae in Marx's conception of the proletarian party, both Marxism's enemies and its adherents have associated the ideology with party-building, with the intricate dialectic between labour movement and socialist party.[48] This Marxist preoccupation with proletarian political organisation has evoked vexing questions. Did workers spontaneously organise their own political party, given the imperatives imposed upon them by a bourgeois polity which otherwise consigned the unorganised poor to political irrelevancy? Or did overt proletarian class consciousness and class organisation, latent at best without political manifestation, depend upon prior 'agitation and propaganda' by socialist parties? The overwhelming salience of these questions has evoked debates between 'Leninists' and anti-Leninists, between champions of communist discipline and of 'Luxemburgist' spontaneity, between proponents of 'Stalinist' bureaucratic centralism and of 'Trotskyist' proletarian democracy.[49] But Guesdists wondered 'what was to be done' about the proletarian party while Lenin, still Vladimir Ulyanov, was writing essays for his Samara school teachers rather than political manifestos for the Russian Social Democratic Labour Party. The organisational dilemmas which have plagued twentieth-century socialist revolutionaries have derived from the founding Marxist political project, not from some Russian distortion of its original meaning.

As authentic embodiments of the Marxist political tradition, Guesdists devoted themselves with zeal to constructing a solidly organised, tightly disciplined, and ideologically coherent socialist party: Guesde never spoke publicly without recruiting for the POF; *Le Socialiste* rarely appeared without accounts of membership drives, organisational meetings, and recent enlistments in the Marxist army; and the centralised party structure evolved in embryo during the early 1890s, with its armature of departmental federations supervised by a national council, evoked the pride and joy of Guesdist militants, fully aware of the novelty and import of their

---

[48] For discussion of this Marxist preoccupation, see M. Johnstone, 'Marx and Engels and the Concept of the Party', *Socialist Register*, 1967, p. 121 and K. von Beyme, 'Karl Marx and Party Theory', *Government and Opposition*, vol. 20, 1985, pp. 70–87.

[49] These alternatives are discussed in W. Grytting, 'Midwives, Vanguards, and Class Consciousness', in N. Fischer et al. (eds.), *Continuity and Change in Marxism* (Brighton, 1982), pp. 97–111; C. Harman, 'Party and Class', in T. Cliff et al., *Party and Class* (London, 1971), pp. 47–66; and R. Miliband, *Marxism and Politics*, chapter 5.

innovative political technology, a technology soon to be adopted across the political spectrum. By the mid-1890s, the POF – national in scope, uniform in structure, obeying common principles and a single leadership – not only dominated the amorphous French socialist movement, but constituted the 'first modern political party' in French experience. Yet, despite the practical achievements of Guesdist party-building, the Parti Ouvrier never fully solved the ideological conundrums posed by equating a political movement with a social class, the equation rendered explicit by the very term 'proletarian party'.

How, for instance, did French Marxists respond to the awkward question of the origin of class-conscious working-class political organisation? Was the 'party of labour' the spontaneous by-product of the proletarian condition, or was it the contingent outcome of socialist agitation and propaganda? Guesdists, reiterating Marx's predominant view, sometimes contended that socialist militancy emerged unprompted from the everyday lives of workers, that independent proletarian politics arose spontaneously from the routine working-class experience of capitalist authoritarianism and exploitation and from the everyday exclusions and repressions of the bourgeois state. In this conception of politics, the bourgeoisie itself recruited for the socialist party – an ironic formulation most frequently deployed against *bien-pensant* accusations that Guesdists, as 'outside agitators', had corrupted otherwise docile working-class communities. 'Don't blame us! Blame yourselves!' sums up the Parti Ouvrier's response to the bourgeois terror and outrage occasioned by the development of anti-capitalist proletarian politics.

Guesdist political discourse, however, rarely addressed bourgeois interlocutors: the Parti Ouvrier's discursive protocols discouraged dialogue with the class enemy and its political agents. But Guesdists, forever fearful of competitors for the proletariat's political allegiance, frequently argued with and against antagonists on the Left who challenged the Guesdist merger of proletarian class interest with socialism, antagonists who thereby questioned the *raison d'être* of the Parti Ouvrier. While debating these fraternal enemies – while contending against anti-political anarchists and against populist Radicals – French Marxists, characteristically indulging in polemical overkill, sometimes depicted a working class incapable of defying or even discerning capitalist exploitation without 'outside agitation' by socialists. In this proto-Leninist formulation, the 'education of the masses' depended upon the prior existence of 'a party whose scientific theory furnishes a reasoned strategy'.[50] An untutored working class – ignorant of the wider society which determined its lot, subordinate to the 'ruling ideas' of the ruling class, dominated by the 'bourgeois state' – would inevitably vegetate as an amorphous and helpless aggregate of competing individuals and contending factions, mere prey for the depredations of capital. From this perspective, Guesdists argued fiercely that 'the socialist party must educate the proletariat, not the opposite'.[51] Workers informed by socialist party-education could guard themselves against their adversaries in the malignant capitalist present, and, in the not-too-distant future, would erect a radiant post-capitalist society; by contrast, uninstructed workers would oscillate hopelessly between passive acquiescence to bourgeois hegemony and futile anarchistic revolts against superficial symptoms of capitalist exploitation. Without the disciplined and rational militancy of socialist organisation, without the 'Parti Ouvrier, that is to say the proletariat having achieved self-consciousness',[52] the working class hardly existed in its own right, and would never act as a potent historical subject, as the transcendent embodiment of a 'future which sings'.

These theses consummated the Guesdists' near deification of political organisation: the Parti Ouvrier, the hypostatised embodiment of workers' class interest, blazed forth as the proletariat's sole hope of salvation, as the firm promise of a transfigured future. Working-class militants, apostles of the socialist creed, owed their faith and allegiance to

the Parti Ouvrier, always more powerful and numerous, admirably organised and equipped for both education and struggle, unceasingly elaborating its doctrine and its programme . . . If a socialist representative does his duty, if he faithfully executes the party programme, he cannot go wrong, for he would be going wrong along with all his party.[53]

---

[50] *Septième Congrès National du Parti Ouvrier tenu à Roubaix du Samedi, 29 Mars, au Lundi, 7 avril 1884* (Paris, undated), pp. 16–17. For an unconvincing critique of the allegedly circular argument whereby the party constitutes the class by giving it self-expression, while the class constitutes the party by giving it its *raison d'être*, see M. Ymonet, 'Les Héritiers du *Capital: L'Invention du Marxisme en France au Lendemain de la Commune*', *Actes de la Recherche en Sciences Sociales*, no. 55, 1984, p. 14.

[51] C. Bonnier, 'Antagonismes', *Le Socialiste*, 21 October 1900.

[52] J. Guesde, 'Dîme et Corvée Capitalistes', *L'Égalité*, 18 December 1881. We have a superb description of the POF's party-building activities in C. Willard, *Le Mouvement Socialiste en France: Les Guesdistes* (Paris, 1965), pp. 219–342.

[53] Anonymous, 'Les Élus Socialistes', *Bulletin Mensuel de la Fédération Nationale des Élus du POF*, no. 16, 1 March 1901, p. 4.

'The party is always right'. French Marxists, professing the Word of proletarian class interest and affirming the POF as its messenger, invented 'party line' politics *avant la lettre*.

Guesdists, however, encountered a potentially devastating heresy during their transubstantiation of proletariat into party: the heresy of 'ouvriérisme' – an extreme class reductionism which posited that only the proletarian saved could enter into the 'proletarian party', that non-workers would contaminate the purity of the working-class movement. A Parti 'Ouvrier', many proletarians reasoned, should be confined to 'ouvriers'. How else could workers ensure that 'their' party genuinely represented their interests? Marx himself – no proletarian by birth, 'life-style', or labour – had suffered 'workerist' denunciations: how, his enemies had demanded, could the son of a prosperous Jewish lawyer, the soft-handed scholar of the British Museum, instruct 'real' workers about their class interests? Anti-Guesdists, a generation later, repeatedly deployed the heavy artillery of *ouvriériste* rhetoric against the notably non-proletarian leadership of the POF: how, they asked, could Guesde, journalist son of a schoolmaster, and Lafargue, the 'millionaire of Draveil', presume to lead the French working class?[54] Paradoxically, class-collaborationist Republican labour leaders particularly favoured this exclusionary class extremism, which served them well as a defence against Parti Ouvrier attacks upon their alliance with 'bourgeois' liberals.[55] Émile Basly, miners' leader and sponsor of working-class Republicanism, may have consorted with the rich and the powerful. But unlike his bitter enemy Guesde, Basly had been born into the working class, been raised as a worker, and still bore the callouses of manual labour. According to Basly and his ilk, workers should ignore the proletarian rhetoric of 'bourgeois' socialists such as Guesde and Lafargue in favour of leadership by their

[54] For Marx's response to *ouvriériste* attacks, see Draper, *The Politics of Social Classes*, pp. 545–50. For the largely non-proletarian social origins of the POF's leading cadres, see Willard, *Les Guesdistes*, pp. 344–5, and for the characterisation of Lafargue, p. 133. There is a vitriolic response to a characterisation of Guesde as a 'bourgeois de Paris' in *Le Socialiste* of 9 September 1893. The strength of *ouvriériste* sentiments in French working-class political mentalities is stressed in M. Offerlé, 'Illégitimité et Légitimation du Personnel Politique Ouvrier en France avant 1914', *Annales: Économies, Sociétés, Civilisations*, vol. 39, 1984, pp. 692–4, and there is an interesting instance described in M. Pigenet, 'Signification des Votes Ouvriers', pp. 730–1.

[55] For the association of *ouvriérisme* with the 'Right' of the workers' movement, see M. Weitz, 'Varieties of Class-Collaborationist Ideology in the French Labor Movement Before World War I', PhD thesis, City University of New York, 1977, p. 102.

own, such as Basly – even if Basly's leadership led them into the arms of the bourgeoisie.

Wounded to the quick by challenges to their proletarian credentials, Guesdists riposted by emphasising that 'even if the workers exclude potential traitors originating in the bourgeoisie, they'll still leave the door wide open for working-class traitors [a reference to class-collaborationist unionists]'.[56] Unlike *ouvriéristes*, Guesdists judged recruits by their political destination, not by their social origin: the POF welcomed 'all men of good will, even if born capitalists'.[57] French Marxists repeatedly emphasised that many of the proletariat's greatest champions – including Frederick Engels, bourgeois of Barmen, manufacturer of Manchester – had defected from capital, and sadly reminded the proletariat that some of the working class's worst enemies – including France's own Senator Tolain, bronze engraver, ally of the butcher Thiers – had originated in the working class.[58] Nevertheless, Marxist class warfare unintentionally legitimated *ouvriériste* introversion: the Parti Ouvrier's class theory of political representation, its faith that the socialist party directly embodied workers' class interest, necessarily exposed French socialism to the exclusionary logic of 'workerism'.

The French political culture, with its diffuse party system, posed further dilemmas for the Parti Ouvrier's theory of politics. The Guesdists' equation of class and party, coupled with their reduction of class conflict to the war between capital and labour, implied a two-party system: a capitalist party versus a labour party. Given one class interest per class, one party should have represented each. Yet this polarisation never characterised the Third Republic, in which parties, factions and coteries proliferated indiscriminately – emerging, disintegrating, dividing, and reuniting without obvious class logic.

---

[56] J. Guesde, *En Garde! Contre les Contrafaçons, les Mirages et la Fausse Monnaie des Réformes Bourgeoises* (Paris, 1911), p. 33. It is obviously not the case, as is argued by Annie Kriegel, that the Marxist critique of *ouvriérisme* dates from Lenin. A. Kriegel, 'Fonction Révolutionnaire de la Classe Ouvrière et Ouvriérisme', in *Conjoncture Économique/Structures Sociales: Hommages à Ernest Labrousse* (Paris, 1974), p. 515. Nor is it true that the Guesdists were themselves 'ouvriériste', as alleged in L. Kolakowski, *Main Currents of Marxism: Its Rise, Growth and Dissolution* – volume 2 – *The Golden Age* (Oxford, 1978), pp. 22–3.

[57] J. Guesde, 'Pas d'Erreur!', *Le Cri du Peuple*, 4 May 1884. The POF literally welcomed capitalists into its ranks, as with Charles Brunellière, shipowner of Nantes – see the discussion of his business career in C. Willard, 'Introduction', to C. Willard (ed.), *La Correspondance de Charles Brunellière* (Paris, 1968), pp. 8–9, and Y. Guin, *Le Mouvement Ouvrier Nantais* (Paris, 1976), pp. 255–6.

[58] For the Guesdists' hatred of Tolain, 'la trahison faite sénateur', see Anonymous, 'Les Violents', *Le Socialiste*, 4 December 1886.

In particular, 'bourgeois class interest', according to the Guesdists' own unsolicited testimony, disseminated itself across a plethora of political movements, movements ranging from the declining Bonapartists to the ascendant Independent Socialists. The 'Opportunist/ Progressiste' current of French liberalism, the 'party' of Gambetta and Waldeck-Rousseau which governed France throughout the 1880s and 1890s, undoubtedly best exemplified bourgeois class interest, but the Opportunists never represented the entire capitalist class, which continuously shed influential bourgeois to both the anti-Republican Right and the Radical Left. No more united by the ideological marketplace than by the commodity market, capitalists distributed their allegiance across virtually the entire political spectrum of the *Belle Époque* – from the Royalism favoured by conservative merchant bankers nostalgic for Louis Philippe to the 'Millerandism' advocated by 'enlightened' industrialists in search of class-collaborationist partners. How did Guesdists, newest players in the intricate French party game, reconcile a multitude of 'bourgeois' parties with their Manichean political paradigm?

More interested in the imperatives of socialist propaganda than in the exigencies of political science, French Marxists frequently 'solved' this riddle by ignoring its existence. The Parti Ouvrier devoted little attention to the intricacies of bourgeois politics: for all the mention they received in *Le Socialiste*, conflicts between Republicans and Orleanists, Opportunists and Gambetta's enemies, or Radicals and Progressistes might never have electrified the French hustings and divided the Chamber of Deputies. Guesdist rhetoric regularly lumped every non-socialist political movement, from the democratic Radicals to the most conservative monarchists, into a single 'reactionary mass',[59] into a fictitiously unified 'party of capital'. Even on the rare occasions when the Parti Ouvrier reluctantly conceded that bourgeois *did* divide their political allegiance between, at least, anti-Republican conservatives and Republican liberals, Guesdists belittled the gravity of friction between 'Monarchists and Republicans, those two wings of the same bird of prey, capital'.[60] Bourgeois politicians and bourgeois factions might com-

[59] For an explicit attribution of the phrase to Lassalle, see Anonymous, 'La Masse Réactionnaire', *Le Socialiste*, 7 July 1894. The image was not without its cogency: ideologues of the French bourgeoisie indeed formed a relatively cohesive group when confronted by militant labour. See the discussion of this unity in J. Stone, *The Search for Social Peace: Reform Legislation in France 1890–1914* (Albany, 1988), pp. 52–4.

[60] P. Lafargue, 'Les Étapes de l'Internationale', *Le Socialiste*, 25 September–2 October 1904.

pete against each other for influence over the state, but, like the bourgeois state itself, they represented a unitary class interest.

All the same, Guesdists sporadically recognised that class interest, however fundamental to social order, rarely exhausted the grounds of political representation, that 'although capitalists have general interests in common, which weld them into a hostile class vis-à-vis the proletariat, they are divided by particular interests which fragment them into sub-classes, whose economic antagonisms are translated into parties and political conflicts'.[61] In this conception of party politics, economic determinism assured a plurality of bourgeois parties rather than a monolithic capitalist party opposed to a unified labour party. This pluralism, once recognised and accepted as the reality of French politics, profoundly troubled the Guesdists, who unhappily concluded that bourgeois factionalism facilitated capitalist domination: 'classes which have obtained power', the Parti Ouvrier decided, 'augment their defensive force by dividing politically'.[62] But why? Should not Guesdists have rejoiced at their enemies' divisions?

According to the Parti Ouvrier, the 'defensive force' inherent in bourgeois political pluralism derived from occlusion of class conflict by lesser issues, from reduction of politics to superficial quarrels between factions of the ruling class, rather than to fundamental conflict between rulers and ruled. The brawl over industrial and agricultural protection during the 1890s, for instance, which divided Lyonnais bourgeois from those in Lille, which set urban Radicals against rural agrarians, and which provoked a confused melee of self-interested trade associations, also diverted proletarians from the class war. Workers in free-trading Lyons united with their employers against protectionist Lillois workers and employers, cotton textile workers supporting protectionist capitalists against free-trading silk-workers and silk-merchants; Parisian artisans backed anti-protectionist wholesalers against Méline's agrarians, who in turn recruited among farm labourers. This superficial decomposition of the bourgeois polity disaggregated the working class, but reinforced bourgeois social hegemony: bourgeois, not workers, led the innumerable interest groups which proliferated upon the interface between economy and polity during the *Fin de Siècle*. At their most conspiratorial,

---

[61] POF Resolution at the General Socialist Congress of 1899, in *Le Socialiste*, 24–31 December 1899.

[62] Anonymous, 'La Liste', *Le Socialiste*, 12 September 1885.

Guesdists portrayed 'secondary' disputes such as the 1890s' debate over protection as capitalist intrigues calculated to prevent the development of independent working-class politics, following a logic whereby, if bourgeois rule benefited from a debate, then bourgeois must have contrived the debate to that end. According to this thesis, capitalists invested wisely by distributing their political favours widely; 'the capitalist class rule[d] by dividing itself'.[63]

If the Parti Ouvrier's theory of bourgeois party politics vacillated erratically between 'one reactionary mass' illusions and conspiracy-theory paranoia, its understanding of the intricacies of proletarian political diversity failed completely. Mesmerised by its compelling conception of unitary class interests reflected in unified political movements, Guesdists developed no equivalent for working-class politics of their rudimentary theory of the bourgeois party system: they never seriously suggested links between the four or five socialist parties in France – the Guesdists, Possibilists, Allemanists, Blanquists, and Independents – and economically determined 'sub-classes' of the proletariat. On rare occasions, Guesdists speculated that reformists' anti-Marxism reflected the 'immaturity' of some segments of the French working class, that Brousse or Millerand represented the still quasi-artisanal Parisian labour aristocracy, unaware of its dismal historical prospects and thus willing to compromise with its exploiters. But the Parti Ouvrier, dedicated to class mobilisation rather than to political sociology, usually refused to recognise social distinctions within the proletariat, much less accept socially justified working-class political pluralism.

Given the imperatives of the Marxist theory of the 'making of the working class', Guesdists could not conceive that political pluralism might strengthen the workers' cause as it supposedly strengthened the class enemy's. The proletariat, according to the Parti Ouvrier, would never prevail against the formidable alliance between capital and the state until workers united behind a single political programme: in Guesde's words, 'a class programme, by definition unique, is indispensable to the class war in which we are engaged'.[64] French Marxists angrily disavowed the idea that alternative inter-

---

[63] P.-M. André, 'La Dernière de Waldeck', *Le Socialiste*, 27 January–3 February 1901. Lafargue attributed the weakness of Marxist socialism in Paris to workers' involvement in the bourgeois politics which preoccupied the capital. P. Lafargue in *Die Neue Zeit*, vol. 2, no. 36, as cited in C. Willard, *Les Guesdistes*, p. 251.

[64] 'J.G.' (Guesde), 'Le Congrès de Reims', *L'Égalité*, 11 December 1881.

pretations of proletarian class interest legitimised multiple labour and socialist movements: a class programme, by definition, *had* to be 'unique'. The tedious tale of the Guesdists' sectarianism – their Party's emergence after multiple splits with Radicals, mutualists, anarchists, and Possibilists between 1879 and 1882, its long campaign to impose its class programme upon recalcitrant socialists and labour militants during the 1880s and 1890s, its intemperate rejection of Jaurès's eclectic vision of socialist unity during the 'Millerand Affair', its final imposition of its Marxist programme upon the SFIO in 1905 – testifies to this categorical rejection of socialist pluralism. Like their Communist heirs at the Congress of Tours, Guesdists rejected unity with those who rejected their conception of revolutionary Marxism.[65] Ironically, Guesdist single-mindedness alienated socialists who refused the POF 'party line', thereby fomenting the very factionalism which supposedly precluded forceful proletarian politics. Trapped between their passionate desire for working-class political unity and their equally passionate commitment to an exclusive 'programme unique', Guesdists exemplified the perennial contradiction between Marxist political theory, which has exalted solidarity above all other virtues, and Marxist political rhetoric, which has unremittingly assailed every non-Marxist version of socialism.

How, then, did Guesdists explain the French phenomenon of a supposedly unitary proletarian class interest coexistent with undeniably multiple proletarian parties? The Parti Ouvrier usually resolved the conundrum with obfuscation: a historian reliant upon scattered issues of *Le Socialiste* might conclude that the French socialist movement equalled the POF. At their most tolerant, French Marxists imagined a nebulous 'Parti Socialiste' which incorporated the Parti Ouvrier as one element, albeit the decisive element. Guesdists, writing *ex cathedra* on faith and doctrine, then symbolically 'excommunicated' socialists who opposed the Marxist interpretation of class politics from this fictitious socialist 'broad church': Possibilists or Ministerialists, heretics at best and infidels at worst, did not represent alternative socialisms; they were not socialists at all. By a

[65] For a (favourable) equation of Guesdist intransigence with Bolshevik rigour, see Rappaport in the *Revue Communiste* of 1921, as cited in T. Paquot, *Les Faiseurs de Nuages: Essai sur la Genèse des Marxismes Français (1880–1914)* (Paris, 1980), p. 153. Noland stresses the Guesdists' repeated withdrawal from any grouping which they could not control. Noland, *The Founding of the French Socialist Party*, p. 132.

similar sleight of hand, French Marxists figuratively annexed non-Guesdist socialists who endorsed the POF's Marxism, such as Édouard Vaillant and his comrades of the Parti Socialiste Révolutionnaire, to an imperially expanded Parti Ouvrier – clever polemic, if unconvincing political theory.[66] Guesdist rhetoric, reliant upon journalism rather than bayonets, none the less foreshadowed the late and unlamented 'Socialist Unity' parties of 'actually existing socialism'.

Overall, the Guesdists devised a powerful, if schematic, political model: a stark opposition between the 'bourgeois state', guardian of economic exploitation, and the proletarian party, guarantor of social liberation. The Manichean simplicity of this dichotomy undoubtedly abetted the Parti Ouvrier in its mission to wean French workers from their long infatuation with the 'bourgeois Republic'. But unequivocal equation of bourgeois class interest with the state and categorical identification of proletarian class interest with the POF generated unresolvable dilemmas for Guesdist ideologists, who never successfully jettisoned their own Republican and democratic legacies, never fully deciphered the ambiguous relationship between bourgeois polity and capitalist society, and never satisfactorily explained why proletarian politics should be restricted to the Parti Ouvrier when the Parti Ouvrier refused to restrict itself to the proletariat – dilemmas as attributable to the strengths of the Marxist political paradigm as to the frailties of Guesdist political practice.

---

[66] Vaillant frequently contributed to the Guesdist press. See, for instance, his 'Tzarisme et Républicanisme', *Le Socialiste*, 23 September 1893, where he is virtually identified as a member of the POF. This rhetorical approach to socialist unity is analysed in R. Huard, 'La Genèse des Partis Politiques Démocratiques Modernes en France: Y a-t-il une Specificité Populaire?', in *La Classe Ouvrière Française et la Politique: Essais d'Analyse Historique et Sociale* (Paris, 1980), p. 12. Guesde is reported to have covertly planned the annexation of the other socialist parties. Informer's report of 12 July in the file on the Guesdists' 1897 Congress. AN F7 12.886.

CHAPTER 8

Reform and revolution

[We are] neither bomb-throwing anarchists who substitute the
violence which kills individuals for the revolution which kills
classes, nor shortsighted reformists seeking to obtain from the
capitalist state what it is [un]able to give. [Instead] we are
revolutionaries in the exact sense of the word, class revolutionaries. For this reason, and despite the red herrings of
anarchists and Radicals, the Parti Ouvrier Français has fused
the two formulae which indicate its goal: *the transformation of
capitalist property into social property* combined with *the organisation
of the proletariat into a class party for the conquest of political power.*
Joseph Sarraute, 'Révolutionnaires', *Le Socialiste*, 13
December 1896.

Many of the conundrums posed by the Guesdist doctrines of the
bourgeois state and the proletarian party arose from peculiarities in
the French political culture – a culture characterised by indelible
memories of the liberal revolution of 1789 and the democratic
revolution of 1793, an astonishingly fluid and amorphous political
'establishment', and an exceptionally creative yet irredeemably
fragmented labour and socialist movement. In essence, however, the
vacillations and contradictions of Guesdist political thought exemplified the uncertain entry of Marxism, born during the politically
exclusive or authoritarian nineteenth century, into the democratic
twentieth. As property-franchise liberals mutated into liberal
democrats, as aristocratic conservatives developed into demagogic
fascists, so sectarian socialists evolved into 'social democrats', an
evolution marked by agonising extinctions and traumatic transformations. Torn between inherited revulsion against the 'bourgeois
state' and tempting integration into the democratic Republic,
Guesdists manifested every variation of this Marxist evolutionary
adventure, variations ranging from ultra-revolutionary intransigence befitting Lenin or Rosa Luxemburg to the reformist moder-

ation proper to Léon Blum or Friedrich Ebert, thereby foreshadowing the protean political future of Marxist social democracy.

The Guesdist political paradigm rested upon an apparently simple relationship between the leviathan state, embodiment of bourgeois class interest, and the socialist party, representative of the proletarian alternative – a relationship simple in theory but enormously complex in practice. How did the 'bourgeois state' and 'proletarian party' relate to each other? Was their relationship one of unmitigated hostility: socialist revolutionaries confronting capitalist counter-revolutionaries? Or might the proletarian party work constructively for socialist ends within the bourgeois state, thereby deferring or even obviating the revolutionary apocalypse? Did revolutionary militancy evoke bourgeois intransigence and thereby impede reform, or did the threat of revolution stimulate capitalist concessions? Did reform strengthen bourgeois hegemony and demobilise the proletariat, or did reformist gradualism undermine the capitalist mode of production and enhance the revolutionary potential of the working class? These portentous questions have ensured that the dichotomy between reform and revolution has consistently structured Marxist political debate, debate which has unfailingly generated more factional dissonance than dialectical synthesis.[1]

The Parti Ouvrier's detractors, then and now, have criticised the movement for oscillating between sterile revolutionary sectarianism and flaccid opportunism. Professionally dedicated to chronology as causality, historians have attributed this oscillation to changing circumstances: the Guesdists' revolutionary intransigence supposedly arose from the impossibility of any credible reformist political strategy during the electorally frustrating 1880s, while their parliamentary opportunism resulted from socialist electoral successes during the early 1890s.[2] This plausible and generally accepted thesis, possibly valid when applied to Parti Ouvrier political manoeuvre, seriously misrepresents Guesdist political rhetoric. Careful comparison between Parti Ouvrier discourse of the mid-1880s and that of the mid-1890s reveals few differences: oscillation between

---

[1] See the useful critique of the dichotomy in C. Mercer, 'Revolutions, Reforms or Reformulations? Marxist Discourse on Democracy', in A. Hunt (ed.), *Marxism and Democracy* (London, 1980), pp. 101–37.

[2] C. Willard, *Le Mouvement Socialiste en France (1893–1905): Les Guesdistes* (Paris, 1965), chapter 11; L. Derfler, 'Reformism and Jules Guesde 1891–1904', *International Review of Social History*, vol. 12, 1967, pp. 66–80; and A. Noland, *The Founding of the French Socialist Party* (Cambridge, 1956), pp. 56–7.

reformist moderation and revolutionary intractability characterised *both* periods. The instability of Guesdist political language derived as much from the dialectical (or contradictory) logic of Marxist ideology as from varying Guesdist political fortunes.

This Marxist logic has, in theory, consistently denied any systematic contradiction between social reform and socialist revolution, instead promoting their harmonious integration. Marx himself despised purist abstention from reformist agitation as much as he detested timid rejection of revolutionary activism – an attitude exemplified by his enthusiasm for legislative limitation of the working day[3] or, indeed, by his composition of the POF's founding charter, with its classic combination of reformist minimum and revolutionary maximum programmes. Guesdists, heirs to this programmatic synthesis, strove mightily to fuse the short-term tactics of their 'minimum programme' with a maximalist long-term strategy of socialist revolution. As they proclaimed in 1903, during the climactic battle between Marxist socialists and the reformist 'Ministerialists',

it's not a matter, as some pretend who wish to spread confusion, of opposing revolution to reforms, the one excluding the other. Reform and revolution, far from being mutually exclusive, complement and complete each other. Forced from the class enemy, even limited reforms increase the liberty of action, courage and ardour of the struggling proletariat. Refused, reforms, in establishing the impotence or bad faith of the ruling bourgeoisie, encourage militancy among the workers, motivated to liberate themselves in full battle.[4]

Foreshadowing the more sophisticated reformist Marxism of twentieth-century 'Left Social Democrats', the Parti Ouvrier argued that workers challenged capital because of their strength, as well as because of their exploitation, and that the achievement of reforms augmented their challenging potency. According to Guesde, 'reductions in workers' subjugation within the factory, the physical and mental development of the proletariat, more leisure, all of this can and must aid and hasten the development of the proletariat as a

---

3   K. Marx, *Capital* (New York, International Publishers, 1967), vol. 1, chapter 10. See the discussions of the reformist Marx in R. Miliband, *Marxism and Politics* (Oxford, 1977), p. 160 and G. Therborn, 'Why Some Classes are More Successful than Others', *New Left Review*, no. 138, 1983, pp. 37–9.
4   'Aux Travailleurs Socialistes: Déclaration du Conseil Central [of the POF]', *Le Socialiste*, 26 April – 3 May 1903.

force, as a revolutionary army.'[5] Workers' struggle for social reform disciplined and unified the proletariat, the concession of reforms limited the social sovereignty of capital and thereby weakened the bourgeoisie, and the results of reforms enhanced proletarian organisational and ideological capacity. Just as victorious battles prefigured triumph in war, so reformist triumphs foreshadowed victory in revolution, initiating 'a triumphal march to the conquest of the state, to the dictatorship of the proletariat'.[6] 'We are reformist', Guesdists confidently declared, 'because we are revolutionary'.[7]

In pursuing this synthesising strategy, Guesdists contended that, just as the possibility of revolution increased with every successful social reform, so successful reforms depended upon the increasing menace of revolution: in Guesde's words, 'the firmer one's support for the Republic, the fewer [reforms] the Republic undertakes'.[8] French Marxists, hard-headed materialists all, loathed naive Reformists who anticipated that bourgeois would address the 'social question' out of the goodness of their black capitalist hearts. According to the Parti Ouvrier, ethical socialists who coerced the ruling class with moral exhortations rather than with revolutionary barricades misunderstood the lesson of history: only looming insurrection, not the Kantian categorical imperative, might force a ruling class to disgorge some of its wealth and power so as to preserve the rest, would compel the bourgeois order 'to change so that things will remain the same'. In Charles Bonnier's colourful metaphor, 'the Parti Ouvrier has to put workers' desire for reform to the throat of every government and demand: your money or your life! And, at the first sign of resistance, carry out the threat'.[9] Deprived of its revolutionary weapon, the workers' movement – disarmed,

---

5   J. Guesde, untitled, *L'Égalité*, 5 February 1882. For elaboration of this conception by one of its best contemporary exponents, see C. Offe, 'Theses on the Theory of the State', *New German Critique*, vol. 6, 1975, pp. 137–47.
6   J. Sarraute, 'Réformes!', *Le Socialiste*, 29 November 1896.
7   Sarraute, 'Réformes!'. Howorth's attribution of a categorical *politique du pire* to the Guesdists, in which they welcomed immiseration as the key to socialist advance, is unfair, their uneasy synthesis of meliorative reform and revolutionary activism being very similar to Vaillant's 'action totale'. J. Howorth, *Édouard Vaillant: La Création de l'Unité Socialiste en France/La Politique de l'Action Totale* (Paris, 1982), pp. 159–60.
8   J. Guesde, 'Le Parti Ouvrier en France', *Le Socialiste*, 6 October 1894.
9   C. Bonnier, 'Parlementarisme et Socialisme', *Le Socialiste*, 25 January – 1 February 1903. The other 'bourgeois' response to socialist revolutionaries is, of course, repression. Marxists, including the Guesdists, have never successfully theorised the variables which might result in reformist or repressive responses to revolutionary 'threats'. See the analysis of this failure in C. Mainfroy, 'Sur le Phénomène Radical: L'Approche de Marx et Engels dans les Années 1871–1895', *Cahiers d'Histoire de l'Institut des Recherches Marxistes*, no. 1, 1980, p. 38.

powerless, and vulnerable – would resemble a cutthroat without his dagger.

In summation, Guesdists categorically supported workers' struggles for social reform, but unconditionally hated 'Reform*ism*' as an alternative to socialism. French Marxists thoroughly detested those within the French Left who intended to humanise, civilise and reform the bourgeois order, those such as the Radicals who advocated 'capitalism with a human face'. According to the Parti Ouvrier, 'reforms sought for themselves, whether improvements in wages or even limitations of the working day, are necessarily sterile if they are not part of a socialist programme; if they are not means but ends'.[10] Guesdists subscribed to a simple and coherent programmatic formula: reforms yes, Reformism never.

However elegant in theory, formulae must be applied in practice, and French Marxists rarely practised what they preached: Guesdist polemics against Reformism frequently, indeed usually, degenerated into attacks upon reforms. At their most extreme, French Marxists, in agreement with liberal doctrinaires, contended that the logic of capital, the unbending laws which governed the modern world, absolutely precluded social reform: capital exerted 'a mysterious force which laughs at all legislative measures seeking to limit its power'.[11] 'Everything which the law might accomplish with a "good legislature", industrial evolution – which has no heart – will defeat'.[12] Even social reform in the long-term interest of capital itself would inevitably be frustrated by the 'bestial egotism of the bosses'.[13] Mocking the Belleville Programme during the 1880s, deriding the 'social liberalism' of Léon Bourgeois during his brief ministry of 1895, ridiculing Ministerialist expectations of Millerand, Guesdists contended that reformist parliamentarians, modern King Canutes, could no more alleviate the proletariat's lot than they could master the tides. Only revolutionary violence, the 'forceps de

---

[10] 'B.' (Bonnier), 'L'Idée et la Réforme', *Le Socialiste*, 23 April 1892. For the distinction between reforms and Reformism, see Willard, *Les Guesdistes*, p. 57. The strength of Reformism in the French labour and socialist movements is stressed in J. Stone, *The Search for Social Peace: Reform Legislation in France 1890–1914* (Albany, 1985), p. 156.

[11] H. Pécry, 'À Propos d'Usuriers', *Le Socialiste*, 5 February 1895. For a particularly clear elaboration of this extreme position, see P. Larlat-Bénaben, 'Que Peut-on Attendre des Réformes?', *Bulletin Mensuel de la Fédération Nationale des Élus du POF*, no. 22, 1 September 1901, p. 1.

[12] J. Sarraute, 'Réformes!', *Le Socialiste*, 29 November 1896.

[13] P. Lafargue, 'La Journée Légale de Travail Réduite à Huit Heures', *L'Égalité*, 12 March 1882.

la rue',[14] would extract the working class from the cramped womb of bourgeois oppression and capitalist exploitation.

This denial of the existence or even possibility of reformist meliorism, however passionately argued, wavered in the face of popular social reforms such as provision of free medical assistance for pregnant women, limitations on child labour, establishment of employer liability for industrial accidents, and Millerand's ten-hour day law – reforms which proved the possibility of practical Reformism. Retreating to a more empirically defensible position, the Parti Ouvrier denounced such reforms as too little and too late, as meaningless palliatives which left exploitation untouched, pathetic irrelevancies in a society dominated by a capitalist despotism which no reform would ever seriously mitigate. 'Everything undertaken by the bourgeoisie, above all in humanitarian guise', French Marxists warned, 'is shifty and suspect by definition'.[15] According to Guesdists, pregnant proletarian women needed liberation from capital rather than a few transient months of medical care before returning to the uncaring workplace; working-class children required a non-capitalist future rather than a few short years of freedom from the factory's tyranny; injured employees needed socialist security rather than a few francs compensation for their sacrifices to the capitalist Moloch; and ten hours a day working for capital were ten hours a day too many. No reform of the proletarian condition compensated for the condition of being proletarian.

Counterattacking ferociously against its reformist enemies, the Parti Ouvrier asserted that social reforms were *worse* than useless, that they actually precluded working-class liberation. How could Guesdists justify this assertion? How could they promulgate a doctrine which so completely disrupted their attempted synthesis of reform and revolution, a synthesis predicated upon the explicit assumption that social reform both attenuated capitalists' social domination and enhanced proletarians' revolutionary potential? Untroubled by self-contradiction, the POF contended that workers' expectation of a soon-to-be civilised capitalism inhibited their adherence to revolutionary socialism (an understanding shared by intelligent liberals such as René Waldeck-Rousseau and by Fabian

---

[14] J. Guesde, 'Parlementarisme et Révolution', *Le Socialiste*, 10 November 1894. Guesde knew Marx's famous assertion that force had always been the midwife of history. J. Guesde, 'Les Exigences du Maroquin', *Le Cri du Peuple*, 23 July 1885.

[15] C. Bonnier, 'Pas de Collaboration', *Le Socialiste*, 2–9 August 1903.

socialists[16] such as Millerand). What profited the proletariat, Marxists asked, to gain a reduced working day and forfeit the socialist future? In this stringent critique of meliorism, reforms, far from undermining bourgeois hegemony, raised 'the last rampart of the bourgeois class'.[17] Carried to this extreme, the Guesdists' struggle against Reformism compelled the Parti Ouvrier to adopt the rhetoric of its anarchist enemies. The elegant simplicity of 'reforms yes, Reformism never' disintegrated into strident and incoherent negativism.[18]

Once in this intransigent posture, Guesdists refused to distinguish between 'bourgeois' reformers such as Léon Bourgeois, who wished to perfect and defend the capitalist regime by correcting its more self-destructive and unpopular side-effects, and reformist socialists such as Paul Brousse, who advocated gradual change within the existing order as the best or only way to found a post-capitalist society. In all justice, the Parti Ouvrier should have distinguished between social liberals and gradualist socialists: the French Marxists' conflict with the former concerned ends; their quarrel with the latter concerned means. But Guesdists, convinced that all was fair in love and (ideological) war, systematically equated anti-socialist Solidarists with 'Fabian' socialists, thereby exploiting working-class disillusionment with the Radicals to discredit anti-Marxist Possibilists and Independent Socialists. Unfortunately, these tactics of 'guilt by association', however fruitful as polemic, precluded reasoned comprehension of the strengths and weaknesses of anti-capitalist gradualism, otherwise a logical extrapolation of the Guesdists' own synthesis of reform and revolution.

In their more cautious moments, however, French Marxists recognised that reforms which evoked enthusiastic working-class approval could not be opposed or even criticised without cost: pregnant working-class women may have preferred a socialist utopia to prenatal care, but the latter was immediately available and the former only a distant promise. Systematic Guesdist negativism

---

[16] The Guesdists themselves drew the analogy between French reformist socialists and the British Fabians. See P. Lafargue, *Le Socialisme et la Conquête des Pouvoirs Publics* (Lille, 1899), p. 10.

[17] Anonymous, 'Sur Toute la Ligne', *Le Socialiste*, 5 February 1895.

[18] Such confusion and dismay have been the repeated Marxist response to reformist success. See the analysis of this syndrome in C. Crouch, 'The State, Capital, and Liberal Democracy', in C. Crouch (ed.), *State and Economy in Contemporary Capitalism* (New York, 1979), pp. 31–6.

would have alienated proletarians unable or unwilling to tolerate an unyielding policy of 'all or nothing'. And, just as the Parti Ouvrier struggled against Fabian socialists who emphatically repudiated revolution, even socialist revolution, so they opposed ultra-revolutionary anarchists who categorically rejected political engagement with the bourgeois polity, even for socialist ends. When attacking anarchists, Guesdists resembled the most gentle of socialist gradualists: the often-remarked moderation of the Parti Ouvrier during the early 1890s derived as much from Marxist campaigns against sporadic anarchist terrorism and nascent anarchosyndicalism as from electoral and parliamentary opportunism. In this emollient mode, Guesde himself wrote that, if socialism 'flowed freely, like a broad river with gentle currents', France might 'reach the new society without violence'.[19] But Guesdists, even at their most gradualist, never displayed the categorical rejection of revolution characteristic of their 'Fabian' enemies. Loyal to its vision of the class war, the Parti Ouvrier refused to limit its demands to 'those reforms acceptable to the wealthy classes'[20] – the only reforms tolerable within a bourgeois polity, according to the determinist tenets of French Marxism. Unaccepted reforms promoted social revolution by their very unacceptability. Reversing this social causality, Guesdists contended that even the most acceptable reforms ultimately depended for their realisation upon the menace of revolution. 'It is not through collaboration with the capitalist class', argued the Guesdist *Normalien* Alexandre-Marie Desrousseaux, that workers would improve their lot, but 'through threats'.[21] In the hands of the Parti Ouvrier, gradualism itself turned revolutionary.

But what did Guesdists mean by 'revolution', the most potent yet most ambiguous term in their ideological lexicon? Like most modern ideologues and theorists, they employed the expression in alternative and possibly contradictory ways to denote either a violent political change (the French Revolution, for instance) or a fundamental

---

[19] J. Guesde, *Le Collectivisme au Palais-Bourbon* (Paris, undated), p. 22. See the insightful discussion of these Marxist ambiguities in J. Howorth, 'From the Bourgeois Republic to the Social Republic', in S. Williams (ed.), *Socialism in France from Jaurès to Mitterrand* (London, 1983), p. 3 and note 6.

[20] P. Lafargue, 'La Journée Légale de Travail réduite à Huit Heures', *L'Égalité*, 5 March 1882. For analysis of this characteristic Marxist distinction between reforms possible or even desirable within capitalism and those which are destructive of the system, see G. Esping-Anderson et al., 'Modes of Class Struggle and the Capitalist State', *Kapitalistate*, nos. 4/5, 1976, pp. 198–207.

[21] Bracke (A.-M. Desrousseaux), 'L'Étape', *Le Socialiste*, 21–28 June 1903.

social transformation (the Industrial Revolution, for example). Anti-Marxists – playing upon this ambiguity, equating 'revolution' with insurrection as exemplified by the storming of the Bastille or the seizure of the Winter Palace – have mocked the absence of Marxism's 'inevitable' proletarian revolution. Marx himself suffered this mockery, and its polemical potency has increased with every passing year, at least in the stable heartlands of world capitalism. Marxists, however, while sometimes playing into their critics' hands by themselves implicitly equating revolution with insurrection, have explicitly understood 'revolution' to be 'any transition from one mode of production to another . . . however long it takes'.[22] Political insurrections might contribute to revolutionary social transitions, but, in principle, insurrection and revolution have played fundamentally unequal roles in Marxist thought – the former as mere froth upon the surface of history's flow, the latter as the very substance of 'world-historical' change.

Obedient to this subordination of political epiphenomena to socioeconomic structural transformation, Guesdists explicitly repudiated the insurrectionary conception of revolution, asserting that 'workers organised into the class party know perfectly well that the collectivist society will not be built all at once in a single act upon the ruins of the old capitalist society. They realise that the new society takes form, develops, matures within the very breast of the old'.[23] In the Parti Ouvrier's political paradigm, this development and maturation, in themselves, constituted revolutionary social transformation: the socialist revolution meant 'the incessant and tireless organisation of the proletariat into the class party throughout society'.[24] Historians who reiterate contemporaneous disdain for a 'revolu-

---

[22] J. Stevens, *The Transition from Capitalism to Socialism* (London, 1980), p. 6. For the ambiguities of Marx's own usage, see E. Hobsbawm, 'Revolution in the Theory of Karl Marx', in B. Chavance (ed.), *Marx en Perspective* (Paris, 1985), p. 558 and R. Dangeville, 'Introduction', in R. Dangeville (ed.), *Karl Marx, Friedrich Engels: Le Mouvement Ouvrier Français* (Paris, 1974), vol. 1, pp. 5–36. Willard denounces the incoherence of the Guesdists' own conception of revolution in C. Willard, 'Engels et le Mouvement Socialiste en France (1891–1895), à travers la Correspondance Engels-Lafargue (Tome III)', *Annali: Istituto Giangiacomo Feltrinelli*, 1960, pp. 761–3.

[23] A. Compère-Morel, 'Candidatures de Classe', *Le Socialiste*, 9–16 March 1902. For a particularly careful development of the thesis that the socialist revolution did not necessarily involve insurrection, but that it was a long drawn-out process of class conflict and socialist construction, see G. Crépin, 'Stratégie Contre-Révolutionnaire', *Le Socialiste*, 4 September 1886. This point was made as often during the Guesdists' allegedly ultra-revolutionary phase during the 1880s as during their supposedly gradualist 1890s.

[24] J. Sarraute, 'Révolutionnaires', *Le Socialiste*, 13 December 1896.

tionary' Party which built no barricades, stormed no Bastilles, and never invaded the Chamber of Deputies as sans-culottes had once invaded the National Convention should seriously consider the Guesdists' self-understanding: when asked by mocking enemies when their 'final' revolution would finally arrive, Guesdists replied that it had already begun, that the glacial advance of working-class self-organisation would carry all before it, in sharp contrast to the ephemeral fireworks of revolutionary *journées*.[25]

In theory, this 'revolution' of patient organisation, ideological education, and everyday militancy might last for centuries – a virtually imperceptible accretion of institutional and ideological changes which would eventually, by the dialectical transformation of quantity into quality, 'revolutionise' society. In practice, however, time-frames on this vast macro-historical scale demoralised the thousands of anonymous working-class militants who sacrificed their precious leisure, their meagre incomes, and occasionally their liveli-hoods or even their lives to the socialist cause. The most heroic party-workers hesitated at the daunting prospect that their sacrifices would bear fruit only in the distant future, that even their children and their children's children would never enter the socialist king-dom. Instead, the millenarianism of the 'grand soir', that dream of sudden and imminent revolutionary transcendence, justified and validated their years of suffering, frustration, and abnegation far better than did the stoic perspective of social transformation over near-geological time-spans.[26] A century of Parisian insurrections greatly enhanced this revolutionary messianism: four successful 'revolutions' in less than a century augured well for the insurrec-tionary aspirations of late nineteenth-century French social radi-cals.[27] In retrospect, the property-based social order and liberal political establishment of the early Third Republic foreshadowed twentieth-century norms; at the time, however, the Republic

---

[25] 'Bernard', 'La Révolution Commencée', *Le Socialiste*, 22 April 1891.

[26] For a fascinating discussion of the influence of various individual, social and institutional time-frames upon ideological development, see A. Gouldner, *The Dialectic of Ideology and Technology: The Origins, Grammar, and Future of Ideology* (London, 1976), pp. 78–9. The need among French labour militants for hope in imminent revolution is discussed in J. Maitron, 'La Personnalité du Militant Ouvrier Français dans la Seconde Moitié du XIXᵉ Siècle', *Révolution Prolétarienne*, no. 147, 1960, pp. 17–21 and no. 148, 1960, pp. 17–23, and, for the terrible pressures upon working-class militants, see M. Perrot, *Les Ouvriers en Grève: France 1871–1890* (Paris, 1974), vol. 2, pp. 477–8.

[27] Dangeville, 'Introduction', pp. 16–20.

enjoyed no more historical solidity than the other transient regimes which had come and gone during the previous century.

Mesmerised by memories of barricades, entranced by the mystique of 1793, 1830, 1848 and 1870, Guesdists sometimes depicted the advent of socialism as if workers would merely be taking their predestined turn on a clockwork revolutionary device. As *Le Socialiste* anticipated, sixteen years after the Republican victory of 1870, 'we overthrow a government every eighteen years in France. The eighteen years of the bourgeois Republic are ending. We'll profit from the occasion to establish the workers' Republic'.[28] Paul Lafargue, perhaps because of his dilettantish historical interests, suffered with particular intensity from the delusion that French revolutions ensued with 'the regularity of celestial motion'.[29] But most Guesdists, historians *manqué* or not, periodically equated social-ist revolution with political insurrection, and eagerly anticipated the imminent arrival of the great day of class judgment. At the very inception of their movement, French Marxists confidently presumed that 'one can already count on one's fingers the number of months which separate us from the definitive triumph of the social revol-ution'.[30] Undaunted by the passage of the decades, they continued counting as their Party entered the twentieth century. Guesdists characteristically never reconciled their sober long-term conception of revolution with their millenarian short-term expectation of its advent. The two metahistorical visions, however contradictory in theory, both reinforced revolutionary *esprit de corps* in practice: 'momentary' defeats lost their sting, once integrated into the per-spective of a centuries-long transition to the socialist mode of production, while tactical victories bolstered militants' hopes that those now living might enter the socialist promised land.

Inheriting Marx's lacunae and foreshadowing twentieth-century Marxist travails, the Parti Ouvrier largely failed to devise a compre-hensive and coherent political rhetoric: Guesdist attempts to walk the unstable tightrope between reform and revolution wavered

---

[28] Anonymous, 'À Limoges', *Le Socialiste*, 9 October 1886. Guesde himself fell prey to this periodic illusion. See J. Guesde, 'Lettre de Bordeaux', *Le Socialiste*, 31 December 1887.

[29] P. Lafargue, 'Le Lendemain de la Révolution', *Le Socialiste*, 19 September 1892. See the commentary on this aspect of Lafargue's political thought in R. Girault, 'Introduction', *Paul Lafargue: Textes Choisis* (Paris, 1970), p. 64 and M. Perrot, 'L'Introduction du Marxisme en France et les Débuts du Parti Ouvrier Français (1882–1889), à travers la Correspondance Engels-Lafargue (Tomes I et II)', *Annali: Istituto Giangiacomo Feltrinelli*, 1960, p. 742.

[30] E. Massard, 'Projets', *L'Égalité*, 11 December 1881.

erratically between reformist opportunism and revolutionary sectarianism, depending upon whether the Party engaged anti-socialist Reformists or anti-reformist anarchists. Throughout the development of the POF, its conception of socialist revolution mutated continuously – at one moment breathing insurrectionary fire, at the next secreting icy analyses of long-term structural transformation. At their other political extreme, French Marxists vacillated uncertainly between intemperate hostility towards Reformists and uncritical enthusiasm for social reforms, sometimes within the compass of a single pamphlet. None the less, however reformist their rhetoric, French Marxists never subscribed to Reformism: both reform, when advocated, and revolution, however conceptualised, derived legitimacy from their contributions to the transition from the capitalist to the socialist mode of production. Even provision of free school meals for working-class children, its practitioners swore (with good reason), constituted 'creeping socialism' – today *potages des légumes*, tomorrow the revolution![31] Guesdist militants pledged 'to go on until the end. So long as a single vestige of the exploitation of man by man remains, so long as hands and minds create wealth and well-being for privileged parasites, our work will not be done. Socialist militants will only lay down their arms with the final abolition of class'.[32] Whether gradualist and reformist or inflammatory and insurrectionary, Guesdists strove for the transition to socialism.

Unfortunately for French Marxists, no opportunities for socialist revolution and few for social reform transpired during the *Belle Époque*. Guesdist militants exhausted themselves in organisation seemingly without outcome and propaganda seemingly without issue: attainment of the new socialist world appeared as distant in 1905 as it had in 1882. Admittedly, workers marshalled themselves in increasing numbers behind Guesdist standard-bearers. But their disciplined phalanxes stormed none of the bourgeois bastions protecting the capitalist mode of production and conquered none of the institutional outworks defending the bourgeois polity, instead advancing noisily from one electoral skirmish to another, accumulating votes as battle trophies. Unintentionally parodying their own revolutionary pretensions, Guesdists urged 'Aux urnes, citoyens,

---

[31] This is not to denigrate the provision of school lunches, 732,104 of which were served in Roubaix in 1900, according to Willard, *Les Guesdistes*, p. 349.
[32] J. Sarraute, 'Nos Réformes!', *Le Socialiste*, 4 August 1895.

formez vos bataillons!'[33] Circumstances dictated this 'electoralist' strategy in the Guesdists' war of attrition against the 'bourgeois state'. French workers, despite their new socialist organisations and novel socialist ideology, deployed few arms apart from their vote. Ignoring this constraint, anarchists, flourishing their dramatic dynamite bombs, and revolutionary syndicalists, promising an all-conquering general strike, categorically condemned Guesdist 'electoralism'. According to the anti-political Left, self-interested socialist politicians such as Guesde and Lafargue reduced the working class to mere election fodder: their preoccupation with winning elections precluded genuine revolutionary militancy.[34] How did Guesdists defend their suspect practices from these corrosive criticisms?

Staunchly contesting the anarchists' advocacy of electoral abstention, the Parti Ouvrier flatly denied that its electoral commitments violated revolutionary principles. Elections, according to the POF, allowed socialist candidates to flaunt the red banner of revolution; electoral campaigns mobilised workers against their bourgeois masters and solidified working-class organisation and proletarian self-consciousness; while electoral outcomes measured the relative strength of the contending class armies. Every electoral skirmish between representatives of the bourgeoisie and the working class, for the POF, prefigured the final revolutionary battle: Guesdists, as they frequently pointed out, supported 'electoral action precisely because we are revolutionaries'.[35] No less than strikes, elections were clashes in the social war, clashes to be fought 'with the weapons of the class candidature and the class programme'.[36] A Guesdist candidate, explicitly representing working-class interests (the 'class candida-

---

[33] Maussa, 'Sur un Adjectif', *Le Socialiste*, 2 June 1895, substituting 'urnes' – ballot boxes – for the 'armes' of *La Marseillaise*. The Guesdists never systematically rejected the socialist utility of universal suffrage, as claimed in N. Birnbaum, 'Universal Suffrage, the Vanguard Party and Mobilisation in Marxism', *Government and Opposition*, vol. 20, 1985, p. 60. For the uncertainties of Marxists during this early stage of democratic electoral politics, see A. Przeworski and J. Sprague, *Paper Stones: A History of Electoral Socialism* (Chicago, 1986), p.15.

[34] For description of the by no means revolutionary Guesdist election campaigns, see C. Willard, *Les Guesdistes*, pp. 379–80.

[35] 'Mouvement Social – France', *L'Égalité*, 11 December 1881. For an excellent analysis of how elections not only allowed the Guesdists to measure their strength, but also constituted the 'entity' of a socialist electorate which in turn served as the *raison d'être* of the POF which had brought it into existence, see M. Offerlé, 'Le Nombre de Voix: Électeurs, Partis and Électorat Socialiste à la Fin du XIXᵉ Siècle en France', *Actes de la Recherche en Sciences Sociales*, nos. 71–2, 1988, pp. 5–21.

[36] *Septième Congrès National du Parti Ouvrier tenu à Roubaix du Samedi 29 Mars au Lundi 7 Avril 1884* (Paris, undated), p. 17.

ture'), would sharply distinguish himself from the various 'bourgeois' who solicited the proletarian vote, thereby forcing them to reveal the class biases concealed behind their obfuscating political rhetoric. The Parti Ouvrier's socialist call-to-arms (the 'class programme') heralded 'the class war among workers ignorant of its principles'[37] – universal suffrage apparently universalised revolutionary socialism. Socialist electoral victories spurred hardened class warriors to further triumphs, while mobilising the previously apathetic or demoralised into the advancing Guesdist legions. Even socialist electoral defeats, however unwelcome, revolutionised the terms of political debate, as 'fear of their electors forces a few socialist ideas into the heads of some . . . legislators and . . . will compel them to accomplish those social reforms possible within capitalism'.[38] Elections, whether won or lost, wedded revolutionary consciousness-raising to reformist influence over the Republic – a distinctively Guesdist marriage of convenience.

All the same, 'bourgeois' candidates repeatedly humiliated Guesdist electoral warriors, even in solidly proletarian constituencies: over the decades, millions of workers spurned both the 'class candidature' and the 'class programme'. The Guesdists' stoic conviction that the process of electoral struggle justified itself in the long term, whatever its short-term outcome, faltered under the impact of these demoralising defeats. Embittered by rejection, Parti Ouvrier militants sometimes blamed their frustrations upon a 'peuple imbécile' who richly deserved their inevitable pillaging by the bourgeois representatives they foolishly elected.[39] Despairing of both revolutionary consciousness-raising and reformist influence, Guesdists sadly asked themselves 'why this living corpse [the proletariat], from which the capitalist vampire has sucked most of the blood, persists in dragging itself to the ballot box in order to cast a vote for its torturers? When will the eternally humbled speak as master?'[40] What answers did disappointed Guesdists propose to this dispiriting question?

The Parti Ouvrier, probing the undemocratic essence of 'democratic' politics, suggested an embryonic theory of 'bourgeois hege-

---

[37] Report of a conference by Chauvin and Zévaès at Le Mans, 'Le Parti Ouvrier en France – Le Mans', *Le Socialiste*, 8 December 1895.

[38] P. Lafargue, 'L'Action Parlementaire du Parti Socialiste', *Le Socialiste*, 10 September 1899.

[39] Anonymous, untitled, *Le Socialiste*, 5 December 1885, reflecting upon the Socialists' crushing defeat in the 1885 legislative elections.

[40] P. Myrens, 'Capital et Pouvoir', *Le Socialiste*, 15–22 December 1901.

mony', thereby foreshadowing one of the most fruitful themes in twentieth-century Marxist political thought. Guesdists argued that,

> so long as the nation is divided into two classes, one of them monopolising society's wealth and the resulting electoral advantages, and the other doomed to salaried labour, and thus unable to devote itself to politics or exercise its vote in freedom, then universal suffrage will be a limited suffrage ... The possessing class, a tiny minority, will control in its interest the votes of the immense majority of the nation.[41]

The Parti Ouvrier tirelessly denounced the electoral advantages enjoyed by the bourgeoisie: capitalism's intellectuals controlled the rapidly expanding state school system, where the 'civic education' curriculum indoctrinated future voters with capitalist values; capitalism's editors managed the great daily newspapers which increasingly dominated public perception of the political world, management as productive of electoral influence as of profit; capitalism's agents manipulated the electoral process itself (France had yet to institutionalise the secret ballot), marshalling capitalists' employees in the struggle for power and place as noblemen had once mustered their retainers in battles for land and lordship.[42] According to the POF, the formal democracy of the ballot-box concealed the *de facto* autocracy of capital: despite appearances, democratic polity indeed reflected despotic economy.

At their most disillusioned, Guesdists portrayed elections as part of the problem of bourgeois domination, rather than as part of its solution. Like many later Marxists since the consolidation of 'bourgeois democracy', Guesdists feared that the political effervescence of election-time masked or even reinforced the structural solidity of the capitalist mode of production.[43] Electoral fever, in this argument, demobilised potentially revolutionary workers, pacified by the illusion of political equality and incapable of articulating their 'non-

---

[41] Anonymous, 'Le Suffrage Universel', *Le Socialiste*, 17 October 1885.

[42] Agricultural workers, in particular, came to be known as 'electoral slaves', according to J. Smith, 'Work Routine and Social Structure in a French Village: Cruzy in the Nineteenth Century', *Journal of Interdisciplinary History*, vol. 5, 1975, p. 376. For industrialists' manipulation of their employees' votes, see Perrot, *Les Ouvriers en Grève*, vol. 2, p. 662 and the vivid instance described in M. Pigenet, 'Signification des Votes Ouvriers dans le Département du Cher (1848–1914)', *Revue Française de Science Politique*, vol. 39, 1989, p. 729.

[43] For discussion of this theme in Marxist thought, see B. Jessop, 'Capitalism and Democracy: The Best Possible Shell?', in G. Littlejohn et al. (eds.), *Power and the State* (London, 1978), p. 21; A. Przeworski, 'Social Democracy as a Historical Problem', *New Left Review*, no. 122, 1980, pp. 27–58; and Birnbaum, 'Universal Suffrage, the Vanguard Party, and Mobilisation in Marxism', pp. 53–69.

political' resentment of economic domination and social hierarchy. By the same token, the goal of electoral victory compelled ambitious socialists to dilute their anti-capitalist message. How else could they seduce the broadest possible constituency and pander to a 'public opinion' controlled by their enemies, seduction and pandering which fixed socialist attention upon an amorphous fantasy of 'the people' rather than upon the rigorous reality of the proletariat? Worse yet, elections precluded working-class militancy unsanctioned by electoral legitimacy: politics, even class politics, shrivelled into a stilted melodrama staged every four years by bourgeois impresarios.

Dismayed by these predicaments, Guesdists bemoaned 'the all too complete conversion of France to parliamentarianism. This conversion has changed an essentially revolutionary people into one which is susceptible only to electoral fever. Manipulated by the nominal sovereignty and the nominal equality consecrated by universal suffrage, workers can think of nothing but their vote'.[44] French Marxists may have supported 'electoral action precisely because [they were] revolutionaries', but the majority of the French people participated in elections precisely because they were *not* revolutionary. Discarding its attempted synthesis of electoral militancy and revolutionary aspirations, the Parti Ouvrier abandoned itself to unrestrained attacks upon pernicious electoral illusions. These onslaughts upon the electoral carapace of 'bourgeois democracy' undoubtedly wounded the Guesdists' Republican enemies, enemies who denied the very existence of class domination once all Frenchmen had attained formal equality before the (electoral) law. Unfortunately, Marxist assaults upon 'electoralism' all too closely resembled those of the anarchists, whose opposition to electoral participation Marxists otherwise vehemently criticised.

This confused oscillation between electoralism and anti-electoralism bore some relation to the success or failure of Parti Ouvrier candidates: the Guesde of 1893, newly elected from Roubaix, more easily equated revolutionary militancy with electioneering than did the Guesde of 1898, evicted from the Chamber of Deputies by the hated Eugène Motte. But Guesdists, dismissing fleeting political contingencies in favour of the structural imperatives revealed by their ideological vision, defended electoral participation even after defeats, even defeats as demoralising as the decade-long frustration

44 G. Deville, 'À Qui la Faute', *Le Socialiste*, 3 December 1887.

of the 1880s or the terrible reversals of the Millerand years. And French Marxists denounced the exclusively electoral politics defended by their reformist enemies even after Guesdist triumphs, even triumphs as intoxicating as the great socialist breakthroughs of the 1892 municipal and 1893 legislative elections. Vacillation between unreasoning hostility towards 'electoralism' and uncritical enthusiasm for electoral politics arose from the practice of class war within a 'bourgeois democracy', as the Parti Ouvrier campaigned against both timid limitation of proletarian militancy to the ballot box and purist opposition to working-class electoral participation – a two-front war the complex strategy and demanding tactics of which regularly overwhelmed the Guesdist officer corps.

Guesdists, despite their qualms and despite 'bourgeois hegemony', did, on occasion, win elections. By the mid-1890s a socialist invasion force had blasted its way into the Palais-Bourbon. But successful 'class candidatures' posed a new dilemma for Guesdists: how could socialists advance their cause once they had penetrated the last redoubt of the 'bourgeois Republic' – the Chamber of Deputies? Could a socialist deputy represent his constituency in the prosaic routines of the hemicycle, while still embodying the embattled proletariat? Marxists have never satisfactorily answered these questions: they have been criticised, and have criticised themselves, both for placing too much faith in the efficacy of parliamentary representation and for denigrating its democratic legitimacy.[45] Guesdists, the first Marxists to penetrate a democratically-elected national legislature, already suffered these criticisms to the full: anarchists attacked them as parliamentary place-seekers, as opportunists seduced by the deputy's privileges and mystique; while 'moderate' socialists denounced them as a barbarous survival in the brave new world of parliamentary democracy, as a deluded sect clinging desperately to the violent political rhetoric of a vanished era. How did French Marxists defend themselves against this withering crossfire?

Wounded by anarchist denunciations of their parliamentary participation, Guesdists vehemently denied that involvement in the highest institution of the 'bourgeois' Republic tarnished socialists' revolutionary integrity: 'any means are revolutionary', Guesde

---

[45] See B. Hindess, 'Marxism and Parliamentary Democracy', in A. Hunt (ed.), *Marxism and Democracy* (London, 1980), pp. 21–54.

maintained in his aptly entitled 'Parlementarisme et Révolution', 'when they are directed towards the revolution'.[46] As the French Marxists regularly pointed out in one of their favourite slogans: 'The POF [would] use any means to establish socialism – even Parliament'. According to the Guesdists, 'there [were] two parliaments in parliament, just as there [were] two nations in the nation'[47] – socialist deputies constituted an 'anti-parliament', an alien intrusion into the Republican order destined first to disrupt and then to destroy bourgeois political hegemony. Conflict between an insurrectionary working-class parliament, the advance guard of the proletarian party, and a reactionary capitalist parliament, the general staff of the bourgeois state, ensured that 'the class war, otherwise scattered from one end of the country to the other and submerged in thousands of local and transient issues, assumes manifest form'.[48] In this conception of parliamentary politics, a Guesdist deputy did not represent a particular locality, and emphatically did *not* speak on behalf of a unitary 'national interest', the grandiose myth which sustained 'bourgeois' parliamentarians. Instead, he represented 'all workers, all the exploited, all the dispossessed'.[49] Class warriors rather than corrupt place-seekers, stalwart proletarian militants rather than self-seeking electoral entrepreneurs, socialist parliamentarians served as the 'pathfinders of a proletariat fighting for the conquest of political power'.[50]

What weapons did these courageous scouts deploy as they infiltrated capitalism's parliamentary citadel? They captured their most explosive munitions from the enemy: deputies' institutional privileges and political prominence enormously amplified Guesdist propaganda, a priceless advantage for ideologists who regarded themselves as evangelists of the socialist gospel, as 'workers for the working class'.[51] The free rail passes enjoyed by deputies, for instance, transformed POF parliamentarians into 'the travelling salesmen of socialism',[52] a privilege exploited to the maximum (and

[46] J. Guesde, 'Parlementarisme et Révolution', *Le Socialiste*, 10 November 1894.
[47] J. Guesde, 'Le 11 Février 1886', *Le Cri du Peuple*, 11 February 1886. Guesdists sometimes claimed that socialists were not really part of parliament at all, but 'come only as observers'. Anonymous, 'Échec Colossal', *Le Socialiste*, 9 January 1893.
[48] J. Sarraute, 'Un Mot de Tactique', *Le Socialiste*, 21 February 1897.
[49] P. Grados, 'Eux et Nous', *Le Socialiste*, 15–22 June 1902.
[50] *Onzième Congrès National du Parti Ouvrier tenu à Paris du 7 au 9 Octobre 1893* (Lille, 1893), pp. 17–18.
[51] 'Jules Guesde devant ses Électeurs – Discours de Guesde', *Le Socialiste*, 1 September 1894.
[52] C. Vérecque, 'Action Parlementaire', *Le Socialiste*, 10–17 January 1904.

often to the detriment of constituency business) as proselytising Guesdist deputies descended onto station platforms in virtually every French town and city. Defending his record (unsuccessfully) before his Roubaissian electors in 1898, Guesde vividly recounted how a socialist deputy such as himself 'spread the socialist idea across the entire nation... He goes from department to department, from commune to commune, preaching the new gospel, teaching the lowly, the suffering, and the exploited about the possibility and the necessity of a new society based upon the well-being and liberty of all'.[53] During the *Fin de Siècle*, when popular political culture turned around parliamentary debate as never before (or since), a vocal role in the Chamber of Deputies conferred genuine national prominence. Jules Guesde, as obscure editor of *Le Socialiste*, preached only to the converted, an audience of thousands; Jules Guesde, as spellbinding parliamentary orator, addressed the French people as a whole, an audience of millions. According to the Parti Ouvrier, seats won in parliament

constitute as many tributes from which our ideas of liberation are easily proclaimed. They are recruiting stations for the doctrines of our party. From the heights of the official rostrum – however modest the orator – the socialist message is always heard and likely to gain adherents, to recruit fighters for our banner. Thanks to the *Journal Officiel* and to the press of every persuasion which is compelled to notice us, our speeches carry into the smallest hamlets and make known our militants and the end they fight for.[54]

Angrily rebuking anarchist advocacy of political abstention, French Marxists refused to evacuate the strategic salient occupied by their parliamentary representatives.

Thus deployed against the anti-political proletarian Left, Guesdists remained vulnerable to the reformist working-class Right, which contended that workers' representation in parliament signposted the best or the only road to social felicity. Campaigning against the 'Radical-Socialists' and Independent Socialists who reduced proletarian politics to parliamentary manoeuvre, Guesdists invented the sin of 'parliamentarianism'. At the best, Guesdists suggested, this blinkering strategy devalued the extra-parliamentary

53 *Travailleurs de Roubaix et de Wattrelos 1898.* (Election poster for Guesde's 1898 re-election campaign, in the Fonds Guesde of the IISG, item no. 63813).
54 C. Vérecque, 'Action Parlementaire', *Le Socialiste*, 10–17 January 1904.

organisation and propaganda which alone empowered socialist deputies. At the worst, 'parliamentarianism' would altogether preclude socialist militancy, reducing the 'proletarian party' to little more than one of the ephemeral electoral clubs which supported bourgeois notables. In essence, Guesdists decided, 'parliamentarianism is the specific governmental form of the bourgeois class'[55] – no socialist should succumb to its blandishments. Instead, in the words of Charles Bonnier, militant socialists should 'destroy the bourgeois state by using the parliamentarianism which until now has protected it', rather than rely upon 'the meliorative value of parliamentarianism, a worm-eaten and decrepit rampart fit only to be overturned upon those it protects'.[56] Having demonstrated how socialists could exploit 'parliamentarianism' in the class war, socialists would soon reveal, Bonnier predicted in a retrospectively sinister formulation, 'how it could be destroyed, once it no longer proves useful [to socialists] as a weapon'.[57] For Marxists, real power resided in the streets and barracks, in factories and counting houses, not in councils filled with impotent yet self-important parliamentarians: socialists who anticipated a new society founded upon votes in the Chamber of Deputies evoked 'Marx's quip about "parliamentary cretinism"'.[58]

Yet Guesdists, despite their Marxist convictions, sometimes behaved as 'cretinously' as their most anti-revolutionary parliamentary antagonists. In practice, Parti Ouvrier deputies devoted their time and energy to the parochial concerns of their constituents: the secret delights of the pork-barrel often prevailed over the public interests of the proletariat. Guesdist parliamentarians, when not evangelising for socialism, proposed prosaic amendments to obscure bills, conscientiously fulfilling their legislative role within the 'bourgeois state'. And Guesdist deputies, despite their self-proclaimed indifference to the factional coloration of capitalist rule, surreptitiously participated in the intricate French game of governmental musical-chairs – contributing to the fall of Jules Ferry, patently preferring the sympathetic Léon Bourgeois to the hated Charles Dupuy, and voting for the detested Waldeck-Rousseau ministry when the alternative meant voting with the right.[59] Why did POF

---

[55] P. Lafargue, 'L'Action Parlementaire du Parti Socialiste', *Le Socialiste*, 10 September 1899.
[56] C. Bonnier, 'La Conquête des Pouvoirs Publics', *Le Socialiste*, 17 January 1897.
[57] *Ibid.*
[58] Anonymous, 'Les Réformes,' *Le Socialiste*, 8–15 December 1901.
[59] See, for examples, J. Guesde, *Quatre Ans de Lutte de Classe à la Chambre 1893–1898* (Paris, 1901) – a collection of Guesde's parliamentary speeches which often belies its title.

parliamentarians so regularly desert their Party's ostensible politics of 'class against class'?

They had little alternative. Determined to conserve their revolutionary 'tribunes', Guesdist parliamentarians needed to satisfy the everyday concerns of their electors: impoverished proletarians craved sustenance from the state's nourishing pork-barrel no less (and perhaps far more) than did affluent bourgeois. Parliamentarians among other parliamentarians, socialist deputies unconsciously adapted to the norms of the established political culture, norms instanced by the astonishment and outrage provoked when the Guesdists' Christophe Thivrier, the 'deputé en blouse', wore his worker's tunic into the Chamber. And a few Guesdist deputies succumbed to the illicit temptations placed in the way of successful Third Republic politicians, while every POF parliamentarian knew full well that his constituents would never understand, approve, or forgive 'irresponsible' votes against reforming Republican ministries.[60] In extreme cases, these pressures and temptations forced or seduced Guesdist deputies into abandoning not only revolutionary socialism, but socialism itself: Gabriel Deville, with Guesde equal founder of the Parti Ouvrier, ended his political career as the anti-Guesdist member for Paris's fourth arrondissement. In despair over the deviations and defections of socialist parliamentarians, the Parti Ouvrier angrily denounced the 'dire spirit of personal vanity and the hunger for advantages'[61] which polluted the Chamber of Deputies.

The Party's despair climaxed during the Millerand Affair, which witnessed a massive conversion of Guesdist parliamentarians to 'Ministerialism', that archetypical expression of socialist 'parliamentarianism', if not of 'parliamentary cretinism'. But Guesdists denounced parliamentary politics even at the peak of their electoral success in the early 1890s, just as they displayed episodic enthusiasm

[60] For the integration of working-class interests into the Republican political system via a supposedly revolutionary socialism (negative integration, as the concept has been developed vis-à-vis the SPD), see R. Rémond, 'La Société d'avant 1914', in Centenaire de la Troisième République: Actes du Colloque de Rennes, 15–17 Mai 1975 (Paris, 1975), p. 204. 'Pork barrel politics' are related to Guesdist representatives in R. Jonas, 'From the Radical Republic to the Social Republic: On the Origins and Nature of Socialism in Rural France', PhD thesis, University of California, Berkeley, 1985, p. 407 and pp. 421–2. The conformist pressures which weighed upon socialist deputies are described in M. Offerlé, 'Illégitimaté and Légitimation du Personnel Politique Ouvrier en France avant 1914', Annales: Économies, Sociétés, Civilisations, vol. 39, 1984, pp. 681–713. For the manipulation of socialists' parliamentary ambitions by the liberal political elite, see P. Sorlin, Waldeck-Rousseau (Paris, 1966), pp. 379–80 and pp. 473–4.

[61] 'Rapport Ghesquière', Le Socialiste, 20–27 August 1899.

for parliamentary militancy even during the electorally sterile 1880s and during the Millerand Affair itself.[62] Vacillation between altern- ative rhetorical strategies derived in large part from constants in the Guesdists' milieu and ideology, not necessarily from conjunc- tural factors. In its milieu, the Parti Ouvrier's ambivalence reflected (and reinforced) a deeply-seated but incoherent working-class pol- itical mentality: workers rejoiced when their representatives forced their way into the highest council in the land, incursions which apparently promised that the (Social?) Republic might finally address itself to the social question; but the working class also shared the cynical popular assumption that parliamentarians represented their own selfish ambitions rather than their constituents' needs, that socialist deputies might come to have more in common with bourgeois deputies than with socialist workers.[63] This uneasy com- bination of proletarian hope and proletarian cynicism, a confused mentality embodied in the fragile politics of working-class communi- ties and embedded in the contradictory consciousness of individual workers, energised the self-destructive rivalry between parliamen- tary socialism and revolutionary syndicalism in the decades before World War I, but also legitimised the Parti Ouvrier's profoundly ambivalent political rhetoric: workers' hopes justified Guesdist parliamentarianism; their cynicism sanctioned Guesdist anti- parliamentarianism.

At the same time, the conflicting polemical strategies imposed by the Parti Ouvrier's two-front war against both exclusively parlia- mentary Reformism and anti-political anarchism twisted Guesdist political practice, reinforcing the ambivalence inherited from the POF's social milieu: the Marxist discourse appropriate for denuncia- tion of Ravachol's indiscriminate terrorist atrocities conflicted with the discourse appropriate for diatribes against Millerand's oppor- tunist rejection of revolutionary socialism. Guesdists defended par- liament against Ravachol's dynamite, yet lobbed rhetorical bombs towards Millerand's prideful place in the Chamber of Deputies. More fundamentally, Guesdist ambivalence towards parliamentary practices reflected an impasse inherent in the combination of

---

[62] See the discussion of this point in M. Perrot, 'Les Socialistes Français et les Problèmes de Pouvoir (1871–1914)', in M. Perrot and A. Kriegel, *Le Socialisme Français et le Pouvoir* (Paris, 1966), p. 55.

[63] C. Landauer, 'The Origin of Socialist Reformism in France', *International Review of Social History*, vol. 7, 1962, p. 88.

Marxist class politics with the institutions of liberal democracy: the novel political order embodied in the Third Republic elevated socialist leaders to national prominence, but, as the Parti Ouvrier ruefully recognised, simultaneously discredited their struggle for a proletarian 'dictature de classe'.[64] The Parti Ouvrier's slogan of 'struggling against parliamentarianism by parliamentarianism itself'[65] proved as profoundly problematical as superficially para-doxical, however well-crafted it may have been to resonate with workers' uncertain appreciation of 'bourgeois democracy'.

Despite the Guesdists' firm conviction that national politics mapped the best (or only) terrain suitable for socialist offensives in the class war, Marxists won their most substantial and most lasting victories within the constricting confines of France's municipalities: Guesdists inaugurated the world's first Marxist government in the remote mining town of Commentry in 1881, and, while Marxist parliamen-tarians never constituted more than an isolated party of skirmishers in the Chamber of Deputies, Marxist municipal councilors swept the battlefields of Roubaix or Montluçon, establishing socialist bastions which would retain their solidity for generations. Nevertheless, the Parti Ouvrier retained a residual hostility towards 'municipal social-ism', a hostility which dated from the early fratricide between Guesdists and Possibilists, the latter firmly based in the Paris Municipal Council, where Possibilism exemplified the 'gas and water socialism' pioneered during the 1880s. By the early 1890s, however, the capture of town halls in working-class communes enthused Guesdists as it had once bewitched Brousse and his Parisian supporters – an enthusiasm embodied in the POF's 1891 Municipal Programme, the first formulated by any Marxist party,[66] and

[64] Anonymous, 'La Dictature du Prolétariat', *Le Socialiste*, 14 May 1899. Interestingly, the article dates the 'parliamentary degeneration' of socialism to Engels' famous 1895 'Preface' to Marx's *La Lutte des Classes en France*. See the discussion of the dilemmas posed by the combination of parliamentarianism and socialist militancy in D. Tartakowski, 'Le Mouve-ment Ouvrier Français et l'État de la Commune à la Première Guerre Mondiale', *Cahiers d'Histoire de l'Institut des Recherches Marxistes*, no. 11, 1982, p. 16.

[65] 'B.' (Bonnier), 'Parlementarisme', *Le Socialiste*, 31 March 1894.

[66] According to M. McQuillen, 'The Development of Municipal Socialism in France 1880–1914', PhD thesis, University of Virginia, 1973, p. 74. There are useful discussions of Guesdist municipalism in M. Moissonnier, 'Les Guesdistes et la Bataille Municipale (1891–1900): Réflexions sur les Fluctuations d'une Doctrine', *Cahiers d'Histoire de l'Institut Maurice Thorez*, no. 19, 1976, pp. 25–60; J. Scott, 'Social History and the History of Socialism: French Socialist Municipalities in the 1890s', *Mouvement Social*, no. 111, 1980, pp. 145–53; and J.-Y. Nevers, 'Notes sur la Démocratie Locale, l'Hégémonie Bourgeoisie et les Luttes de

rewarded by triumphs in great provincial cities such as Lille or Marseilles and representation in isolated links in the future Paris 'Red Belt' such as Ivry or Courbevoie (although the Paris Municipal Council itself remained inviolate, the preserve of Possibilists and Blanquists). How did these victories influence Parti Ouvrier political discourse?

Anticipating that a socialist municipality in Lille foreshadowed a socialist government in Paris, Guesdists welcomed these victories enthusiastically, although with puzzlement and some dismay at the disproportion between their local popularity and their national impact: workers, hedging their bets, often voted for the POF locally and for 'bourgeois' candidates nationally.[67] 'We now have in this fragment of government granted by universal suffrage', Guesde none the less rejoiced, 'the lever with which we can raise the entire world of labour'.[68] Carried away by his Party's electoral triumph in Lille, Charles Bonnier even identified the city's newly-elected Guesdist municipal government as 'the dictatorship of the proletariat', fitting heir to the Paris Commune itself.[69] In practice, however, the vicissitudes of Guesdist local politics posed grave ideological dilemmas for French Marxists, dilemmas considerably more serious than those posed by the central state, since the Parti Ouvrier assumed responsibility in dozens of local governments, but never in the national administration. Municipal rule confronted Guesdists with that ultimate Marxist political predicament: governmental responsibility without revolutionary authority. How did French Marxists resolve this dilemma? How did they bind the politics of the parish pump to the politics of the class war?

Municipal Guesdism hardly differed from the Possibilist gradualism and localism so often denounced by the Parti Ouvrier during the 1880s: the *Bulletin Mensuel de la Fédération Nationale des Élus du Parti Ouvrier Français* usually read as a compendium of mundane social welfare reforms, rarely as an incitement to socialist revolution. Establishment of public kitchens, student loan schemes, marriage advice bureaux, public libraries – these prosaic concerns, not the

---

Classe sous la Troisième République', *Annales Publiées par l'Université de Toulouse-Le Mirail*, vol. 14, 1978, pp. 59–77.

[67] R. Baker, 'A Regional Study of Working Class Organization in France: Socialism in the Nord 1870–1924', PhD thesis, Stanford University, 1967, pp. 47–8.

[68] J. Guesde, 'À l'Oeuvre', *La Question Sociale*, 5 June 1892, cited in M. Perrot, 'Les Socialistes Français et les Problèmes de Pouvoir', p. 50.

[69] 'B.', 'La Dictature du Prolétariat', *Le Socialiste*, 3 January 1896.

strategy of socialist revolution or the prospects of a post-capitalist order, preoccupied the contributors to the *Bulletin*.[70] Deferring the transition to the socialist mode of production, Guesdist municipalities strove mightily to enhance the everyday living conditions of

workers in general, but in particular, children, the aged and invalids. School lunches for workers' children; shoes and clothes for poverty-stricken youth; seaside recuperation for sickly children; aid for working-class mothers and families in the form of nursery schools and day-care centres; free public baths; pensions for aged and indigent workers of both sexes; improvements in the condition of aged-homes; improved working regulations for municipal employees; subsidies for unions; legal aid; public kitchens distributing cheap and healthy meals in working-class quarters; refuges for the homeless; slum improvement; support for the families of active-duty reservists; elimination or reduction of consumption taxes; etc., etc. – such are the fruit of socialist entry into municipal government.[71]

Foreshadowing the historical mission of European social democracy, Guesdists pioneered the twentieth-century welfare-state in their newly conquered urban domains, replacing failing traditions of community solidarity and inadequate institutions of individual self-help with the benevolent, if bureaucratic, care of the state.

Municipal political responsibility evoked the Parti Ouvrier's most reformist persona, thereby further foreshadowing the evolution of twentieth-century social democracy.[72] At their most conciliatory and pacific, Guesdist municipal leaders abandoned the rhetoric of class conflict altogether, a betrayal of Marxist principles rarely if ever committed by national instances of their Party. Even the Guesdist local authorities of Roubaix, that 'Rome of French Marxism', depicted their town as 'never having been so calm as since the socialists came to power. The most intransigent bourgeois have got along perfectly well with the workers' administration'.[73] Co-

---

[70] A single issue (no. 2) of the *Bulletin* contained projects for public kitchens, student loans, marriage advice bureaux, and lending libraries. The fifth series of *Le Socialiste* included a 'Bulletin Municipal' which publicised such innovations. And see the special double issue of *Le Socialiste* (29 April and 6 May 1900) devoted to the welfare achievements of the Guesdist municipalities.

[71] C. Vérecque, 'Le Pouvoir Communal', *Le Socialiste*, 21–28 February 1904.

[72] The reformist tendencies supposedly characteristic of the POF during the mid-1890s have been attributed to the influx of local-authority staff into the Party during this period. See M. Perrot, 'Les Socialistes Français et le Problème de Pouvoir', pp. 57–8 and R. Pech, 'Les Thèmes Économiques et Sociaux du Socialisme Férrouliste à Narbonne (1880–1914)', in *Droite et Gauche en Languedoc-Roussillon: Actes du Colloque de Montpellier 9–10 Juin 1973* (Montpellier, 1975), pp. 256–61.

[73] G. Siauve, *Roubaix Socialiste* (Lille, 1896), pp. 62–3.

operation from local entrepreneurs (usually more eagerly sought than given) proved to be invaluable as Guesdists 'calmly' constructed their mini-welfare states in Roubaix, Lille, or Narbonne. And no wonder. Ernest Ferroul, socialist crusader against a conservative municipal government, represented the proletariat struggling against class oppression; but Ernest Ferroul, mayor of Narbonne, represented his community, including both its workers and (perhaps particularly) its entrepreneurs: class collaboration followed unavoidably from the socialist assumption of governmental responsibility without social revolution.[74] The Parti Ouvrier, true to its Marxist convictions, systematically rejected class-collaborationist welfare-state Reformism in national politics, if only because this programme never seemed a realistic prospect in *fin-de-siècle* France, except at the behest of dedicated anti-Marxists such as Léon Bourgeois or Alexandre Millerand, whose projects themselves failed miserably once confronted by the adamantine self-interest of the French bourgeoisie. But the Guesdists' cogent critiques of Bourgeois' 'Solidarism' and Millerand's 'Ministerialism' might just as well have been directed against the 'municipalism' of Guesdist local governments, which patently shared the reformist goals and gradualist practices of the 'Radical-Socialists' and Independent Socialists. Guesdist local politics, the unstable foundation of the Parti Ouvrier's nascent political culture, prefigured the achievements, frustrations, temptations, and betrayals inherent in the exercise of socialist political power within the capitalist mode of production.

Despite (or because of) the overt class-collaborationist Reformism of Guesdist local councillors, the Parti Ouvrier desperately sought to integrate the theory and practice of municipal socialism into its overall revolutionary project. According to Guesdist doctrine, socialist municipalities, for all their admirable aspirations, could never themselves prevail against the bourgeois class interest embodied in the national government – a doctrine firmly founded upon prolonged and bitter experience. Just as workers' desperate need for social security reinforced workers' reformist expectation of local government largess, so prefectural rejection of socialist local government initiatives reinforced the Marxists' pessimistic assessment of municipal socialism's potential. The national government, through

---

[74] For Ferroul, see P. Guidoni, *La Cité Rouge: Le Socialisme à Narbonne 1871–1921* (Toulouse, 1979), pp. 105–10.

its omnipresent and nearly omnipotent Prefects, regularly intervened to abort municipal aid for striking workers, veto redistributive fiscal measures by local governments, and, indeed, frustrate virtually any municipal project designed to redress the imbalance of social power between capital and labour. Implacable Ministry of the Interior versus reforming socialist council – this recurrent one-sided contest validated recurrent Marxist admonitions on the priority to be accorded to struggle against the 'bourgeois state'. According to the POF, the socialist seizure of Paris alone would empower socialism in Lille or Montluçon. From this systemic perspective, municipal socialism seemed as much a palliative, even a dead-end, as trade unions or cooperatives, those other favoured instruments of 'Possibilism'. Municipal politics, Guesdists decided, were 'at the best, worth no more than strikes as a training ground for our soldiers'[75] – hardly high praise, coming from the Parti Ouvrier.

Guesdists, as 'economistic' as ever, reinforced this dismissive argument with their rigid version of Marxist political economy, which conclusively demonstrated that the mechanisms of capital accumulation transcended the greatest city, that the ultimate engagements in the class war would have to be fought on national and international battlefields.[76] Reliance upon local politics as the womb of social revolution, the 'federalist' ideal of Bakunin and the (failed) legacy of the Commune, had, by the *Fin de Siècle*, supposedly become as obsolescent as reliance upon local fairs to distribute commodities. At the most, the Parti Ouvrier decided, socialist municipalities might reinforce the proletarian army during the final battle: 'our victory will be easier', Charles Vérecque concluded, 'if, in place of a single commune like Paris in 1871, thousands of others rise at our call'.[77]

Guesdist ambivalence towards municipal socialism illustrated in microcosm the ambiguity of class politics in a 'bourgeois democracy'. The Parti Ouvrier could not ignore local politics and municipal reform: indifference to workers' communal traditions and local interests led towards political oblivion, while school lunch programmes filled ballot boxes with POF votes as well as filling

[75] J. Guesde, 'La Fin d'une Erreur', *L'Égalité*, 7 May 1882.
[76] C. Vérecque, 'Le Pouvoir Communal', *Bulletin Mensuel de la Fédération Nationale des Élus du Parti Ouvrier Français*, no. 3, 1 February 1900, pp. 1–2. Prefectural control of Guesdist municipalities is described in Willard, *Les Guesdistes*, p. 186.
[77] C. Vérecque, 'Le Pouvoir Communal', *Le Socialiste*, 13–20 March 1904.

proletarian children with vegetable soup.[78] Nor did the POF wish to adopt the anarchists' hostility towards political participation, local or otherwise: conflict between municipal socialists and their resident bourgeoisies graphically illustrated the class war and mobilised the working class against both easily-personified local capitalists and prefectural representatives of the 'bourgeois state'.[79] Nevertheless, the political, financial and administrative imperatives imposed by local responsibilities dragged Guesdist councils into a morass of 'opportunism', corruption and overt class collaboration: the discreet temptations of the municipal council chamber, no less than the grandiose enticements of the Chamber of Deputies, seduced class warriors from their stern obligations.[80] Dismayed by these dilemmas, Guesdists desperately sought to subordinate local politics to their overall strategy of 'class against class', and occasionally retreated into the categorical hostility towards municipal socialism which had characterised the nascent POF.

Changing circumstances undoubtedly conditioned the evolution of Marxist political rhetoric during the *Belle Époque*, but far less than historians have assumed. The vacillations characteristic of Guesdist discourse – vacillations from vitriolic anti-republicanism to republican dedication, and back; from sectarian revolutionary intransigence to bland reformist moderation, and back; from anti-electoral cynicism to idealistic electoralism, and back; from anti-parliamentary extremism to parliamentary pragmatism, and back – followed logically from constants in the history of the POF, constants as characteristic of 1882 as of 1905. Guesdists vacillated because of the ambiguities inherent in fighting the class war within a liberal democratic polity, because of the profoundly ambivalent political mentalities of the French working class, and because of the

---

[78] For the desperate need for municipal services among urban workers, and the popularity of their introduction, see L. Berlanstein, *The Working People of Paris 1871–1914* (London, 1984), p. 48.

[79] See the discussion in Y. Lequin, 'Les Villes et l'Industrie: L'Émergence d'une Autre France', in Y. Lequin (ed.), *Histoire des Français XIX-XXᵉ Siècles: La Société* (Paris, 1983), p. 422.

[80] Baker, *A Regional Study of Working Class Organization in France*, pp. 79–82; M. Moissonnier, 'La Longue Marche vers un Parti Ouvrier: Fin du XIXᵉ Siècle', in *La Classe Ouvrière Française et la Politique: Essais d'Analyse Historique et Sociale* (Paris, 1980), pp. 70–1 (for the POF's difficulties in coping with its sudden municipal success); and (for a description of the mercurial nature of Guesdist municipalism) Guidoni, *La Cité Rouge* – which brilliantly depicts the 'class-collaborationist' degeneration of Ferroul's municipality.

contradictory strategic imperatives imposed upon the Parti Ouvrier by its polemical milieu, strategic imperatives inherent in the Guesdists' long campaign against the Radicals and anarchists who continually and successfully contested the POF's exclusive right to its proletarian constituency. The Marxists' corrosive hatred of the anarchist aversion to class *politics* and their intense dislike of Radical antipathy to *class* politics inspired the Guesdists' unvarying rhetorical variations.[81]

By the end of the nineteenth century, anarchism, empowered by endemic popular hostility towards France's unusually centralised political structure and the nation's immemorial tradition of bureaucratic rule,[82] had emerged as a formidable contestant in the nation's political culture. A galaxy of brilliant anarchist thinkers entranced educated opinion with their destructive critiques of authority, relaying a recurrent intellectual fashion which would eventually extend from the eighteenth-century scandal over the mysterious Meslier to today's vogue for the sibylline Foucault; 'anarchosyndicalists' attained their transient dominance of the organised labour movement, supplanting the Guesdists' unlucky Fédération Nationale des Syndicats in the process; and half-mad 'propagandists of the deed' bloodily obliterated personifications of bourgeois power and wealth, including a president of France and randomly selected patrons of expensive cafés.[83] Why did the Parti Ouvrier oppose anarchism, a movement which patently shared the Guesdists' hatred of capitalism and detestation of the 'bourgeois state', a movement with impressive revolutionary credentials thoroughly authenticated by the Sainte-Pélagie prison and the guillotine itself?

Anarchists, class warriors in dispersed order, may have fought the *Fin de Siècle*'s social war with a vigour at least equal to that of Guesdism's own regimented combatants, but anarchists and Marxists did not fight as allies. Guesdists, true to their reductionist 'vulgar Marxist' convictions, discovered the ultimate source of social

---

[81] A close textual analysis of the third series of *L'Égalité* in 1881–1882 reveals a few polemics against the liberal Opportunists, many against 'Radical' critics of the governmental Republicans, and virtually no mention of the still potent Right. A decade later, a similar analysis of *Le Socialiste* demonstrates that it targeted Radicals and anarchists, and largely ignored the centre and right of French politics.

[82] P. Birnbaum, 'States, Ideologies and Collective Action in Western Europe', *International Social Science Journal*, vol. 32, 1980, p. 677 and Tartakowski, 'Le Mouvement Ouvrier Français et l'État', p. 15.

[83] For a superb discussion of the importance of anarchism during the *Belle Époque*, see J. Maitron, *Histoire du Mouvement Anarchiste en France* (Paris, 1975), vol. 1, parts II and III.

suffering and political oppression in the capitalist mode of production, with the state merely an epiphenomenon of the ultimate evil – exploitation. Once conquered by the POF, the state itself would metamorphose into 'the instrument of [the proletariats'] redemption'.[84] By contrast, anarchists identified bourgeois economics as merely a subset of the overlapping categories of hierarchy and domination, with capitalist exploitation itself merely an epiphenomenon of the ultimate evil – authority. Anarchists, logically enough by these premises, categorically repudiated adoption of authoritarian means in the proletariat's struggle against exploitation: for libertarians, the Marxists' construction of a centralised and disciplined working-class party and the impending socialist seizure of the state would merely replace one tyranny by another. Marxists, for their part, derided the anarchist rejection of disciplined organisation as at best naive and at worst suicidal, given the awesome power of bourgeois economics and political institutions.[85] Marxists and anarchists may have shared common goals, but their means to these ends differed so completely that mortal conflict between the two movements proved inescapable.

How did the Parti Ouvrier conduct its long campaign against the anarchists? What arguments justified its fratricidal onslaught upon working-class libertarianism? Anarchism, the Parti Ouvrier contended, was purely gestural: its terrorists left the bourgeois state untouched, or even reinforced its repressive power, while less violent 'propaganda of the deed' was merely pathetic. As Deville wrote, in his characteristically mordant style,

anarchism salivates tremendously. Aside from their tongues being the only things of theirs which really work, and work overtime, Anarchists use spit on the rare occasions when they venture beyond demagoguery. Their most serious attack upon the government occurred at the Salle Chaynes, where they took turns spitting on a poster advertising the names of the ministry. Their efforts weren't rewarded. The ministry hasn't bogged down, and not a single capitalist has had to put up his umbrella.[86]

[84] J. Guesde, 'Réponse Ouverte', *Le Socialiste*, 16 October 1892.
[85] See the excellent discussion of this century-old debate in E. Hobsbawm, 'Should Poor People Organise?', in *Worlds of Labour: Further Studies in the History of Labour* (London, 1984), pp. 282–96. For all the discordance between anarchism and socialism, most bourgeois of the time could not readily distinguish anarchists from socialists, or at least refused to make the distinction. B. Blick, 'What is Socialism? French Liberal Views of the 1890s', in L. Patsouras (ed.), *Crucible of Socialism* (Atlantic Highlands, 1987), pp. 395–6.
[86] G. Deville, *L'Anarchisme* (Paris, 1887), pp. 6–7.

Neither anarchist dynamite nor libertarian spit, according to the Parti Ouvrier, armed workers against their class enemies. Only a proletarian counter-power, laboriously constructed through patient party-organisation and incessant socialist propaganda, could challenge bourgeois rule over French society: rationally calculated political militancy, not gestural anti-politics, alone opened a road to the post-capitalist future.

Anarchist opposition to organisation and discipline, according to the Parti Ouvrier, demoralised socialist assault troops while leaving bourgeois fortifications unscathed. Worse yet, capitalists founded their ideological hegemony over French society upon the libertarian illusions of *laissez-faire* economics and individual 'freedom' – illusions reinforced by the anarchists' libertarianism, by their 'hatred of all social solidarity, by [their] horror of anything smacking of socialism and organisation',[87] the hatred and horror which revealed the 'elective affinit[ies]' which drew bourgeois and anarchists together.[88] Guesdists repeatedly riposted against the damaging bourgeois equation of anarchism and socialism by counter-charging that capitalism's 'unrestrained individualism, its "each for himself and all against all"', secreted anarchism as naturally as the 'Ganges delta produced cholera'.[89] For Marxists, 'anarchism, no less than alcoholism, was the morbid product of an abnormal society'[90] – repressing anarchists would no more suppress anarchism than quarantining alcoholics would eliminate alcoholism. Society could detoxify itself of anarchism only through socialist revolution: 'the bourgeoisie is disorder', Guesdists trumpeted, 'socialism order'.[91] Workers who, misled by anarchist rhetoric, translated their hatred of the bourgeois organisation and discipline lurking behind liberal illusions into a generalised hatred of all organisation and discipline would prove incapable of the self-organisation and self-discipline necessary for any proletarian assault upon capital and the state. By (Marxist) definition, an anarchist proletariat – inchoate and unruly, fit neither for social revolution nor for socialist construction – never would, never could, become a 'class for itself'. Whatever anarchists' theories may have claimed, anarchist disorder challenged bourgeois

[87] Anonymous, 'Le Véritable Attentat', *Le Socialiste*, 16 December 1893.
[88] 'B.', 'Le Lien Moral', *Le Socialiste*, 25 November 1893.
[89] J. Guesde, 'Entre Anarchistes', *Le Socialiste*, 25 August 1894.
[90] 'G. D.', 'Bêtise de Classe', *Le Socialiste*, 23 December 1893.
[91] P. Dramas, 'Le Socialisme c'est l'Ordre', *Le Socialiste*, 16 December 1893.

order neither in principle nor in practice. In effect, and perhaps in intent, anarchism even served as yet another agency of bourgeois hegemony and domination: anarchists and policemen, overt enemies, complemented each other as covert allies against social-ism.[92] Fashionable bourgeois enthusiasm for anarchist philoso-phers, according to Guesdist analysis, proved the point, demonstrat-ing 'the sympathy which the bourgeoisie always manifests towards the misdirected efforts of the working class'.[93] Anarchists, Guesdists concluded in their more unrestrained polemics, jeop-ardised the progress of socialism far more seriously than did counter-revolutionaries: the latter might temporarily block the advance of the workers' army; the former forestalled its mobilisation.[94]

If anarchists betrayed the proletariat's class interest, why did so many workers subscribe to anarchism? Why the subterranean popularity of Ravachol's insane bombing campaign against the Parisian bourgeoisie? Why the easy anarchosyndicalist triumph over the Guesdists' unfortunate Fédération Nationale des Syndicats? Mesmerised by their unproblematical equation of working-class society with socialist politics, Guesdists rarely addressed, or even perceived, this embarrassing puzzle. When they did concede the reality and potency of French libertarianism, however, French Marxists advanced a series of alternative and contradictory explana-tions for the enigma posed by the proliferation of proletarian anarchists. First, the Parti Ouvrier, thriftily consolidating its critiques of the libertarians to its Left and the Reformists to its Right, blamed anarchist popularity upon the influence of the Marxists' moderate enemies within the socialist movement: the Parisian cult of Ravachol supposedly responded to the squalid treason of Brousse's municipal councillors, while Pelloutier's anarchosyndicalism evolved from the sordid compromises of Jaurès's parliamentary socialism. 'The abortion of reformist hopes recruits for anarchism', alleged the Guesdists, and 'the recantations of socialist politicians [allow] libertarians to tar the futile politics of class collaboration and class politics with the same brush'.[95]

---

[92] National Council of the POF, 'Aux Travailleurs de France', in Bracke (ed.), *Onze Ans d'Histoire Socialiste: Aux Travailleurs de France* (Paris, 1901), p. 28.
[93] 'B.', 'Contradictions Capitalistes', *Le Socialiste*, 13 January 1895.
[94] R. Chauvin, *Sans Patrie* (Lille, 1894), p. 11.
[95] P.-M. André, 'Le Congrès de Bourges', *Le Socialiste*, 18–25 September 1904.

Second, French Marxists, searching for the etiology of anarchism within plebeian society itself, construed working-class libertarianism as an affliction both caused by and causing proletarian backwardness, a malignancy indicating workers' social immaturity or political corruption. Reacting to bourgeois denunciations of the 'troublemaking bad workers' supposedly responsible for the spread of socialism, *Le Socialiste* riposted that

the bad worker, the 'sublime', has never been much more than the invention of overheated journalism. If there have been a few such workers about, they're found among the Anarchists, who have, for many reasons, an elective affinity with what Marx called ... the 'lumpenproletariat' ... But this lot are never attacked in the bourgeois press, since they form the muddy moat around the capitalist fortress.[96]

Certain aspects of *fin-de-siècle* society did indeed associate anarchists and 'lumpenproletarians', particularly during the sinister conjunction of common criminals, police informers, and anarchist terrorists of the early 1890s. But the Guesdist equation between criminals and anarchists amounted to little more than name-calling: most proletarian anarchists, whether stalwarts of the informal study groups and *ad hoc* action committees which articulated the anarchist political culture or anarchosyndicalist trade union militants, emerged from the same milieu of self-educating skilled workers which supplied the socialist movement with its own cadres.[97]

Finally, abandoning this convenient but implausible equation of anarchist anti-politics with working-class degeneracy (an equation uncomfortably similar to that favoured by the 'bourgeois' press), Guesdists more charitably attributed proletarian anarchism to the last desperate hopes of artisanal workers clinging to the ideals and practices of petty commodity production, to 'economic conditions which have had their day'.[98] Anarchosyndicalists and anarchist adepts such as Kropotkin, Élisée Reclus, or Jean Grave, for all their

---

[96] 'B.', 'Les Mauvais Ouvriers', *Le Socialiste*, 25 December 1892.

[97] For links between the 'lumpenproletariat' and anarchism, see R. Pierre, *Les Origines du Syndicalisme et Socialisme dans la Drôme 1850–1920* (Paris, 1973), p. 70; Maitron, *Histoire du Mouvement Anarchiste en France*, pp. 473–76; and R. Sonn, 'Language, Crime, and Class: The Popular Culture of French Anarchism in the 1890s', *Historical Reflections*, vol. 11, 1984, pp. 351–72. The social similarity of anarchist and socialist cadres is, however, convincingly argued in Y. Lequin, *Les Ouvriers de la Région Lyonnaise (1848–1914): Les Intérêts de Classe et la République* (Lyons, 1977), p. 281 and pp. 285–6.

[98] Deville, *L'Anarchisme*, p. 6.

self-assertive modernity, supposedly represented the dying gasp of a moribund Proudhonism. According to the French Marxists, socialist discipline and organisation alone, not anarchist spontaneity and libertarianism, could survive in the new world of capitalist industrialisation and bureaucratic authority; only Marxism, not anarchism, corresponded to the flight of history away from 'the private domain which once encompassed everything' but which had been 'reduced century by century, absorbed bit by bit, function by function, into the public domain'. This flight, Guesdists asserted, traced 'the evolutionary law of our species'.[99] A generation after the fragmentation of the First International, Marx's faction was historically destined finally to prevail against Bakunin's, despite the apparent anarchist vitality of the *Fin de Siècle*. Entranced by the congruence between their disciplined Marxist convictions and the centralising forces of their age, Guesdist ideologues never once imagined that libertarian sentiments might intensify in proportion to the progress of bureaucratic industrialism.

This decades-long Guesdist campaign against the anarchists animated the Parti Ouvrier's enthusiastic advocacy of electoral participation, parliamentary activism, and reformist gradualism, advocacy which otherwise contrasted so strangely with the French Marxists' caustic criticism of 'bourgeois' institutions. In practice, the Guesdists' critique of the libertarian sectarians to their Left, when moderately formulated, moderated the Parti Ouvrier's own tendency to sectarian rigidity. But, forced to extremes, this critique forced the POF into accord with the Reformism the Party otherwise detested. More seriously, the Marxists' intemperate critique of anarchism legitimated the restrictive Guesdist reduction of politics to the fraught relationship between bourgeois state and proletarian party, a reduction which diverted Guesdists from more subtle libertarian analyses of the 'politics of everyday life'. The Marxist thesis that workers had to organise politically in a world where the state dominated society while capital dominated the state was incontrovertible: abstention from politics, however much it might gladden proletarian purists, would result in workers' de facto submission to bourgeois governance and consequent capitulation to the capitalist masters of the 'bourgeois

[99] Anonymous, 'Anarchie et Socialisme', *Le Socialiste*, 27 February 1886.

state'.[100] Unfortunately, the very strength of this thesis inclined Guesdists to neglect 'non-political' forms of protest and to equate proletarian class interest with the POF party-line. The Marxist self-righteousness engendered by anarchist 'absurdities' blinded the Parti Ouvrier to its own political limitations.

The 'populist' programme advanced by French Radicals challenged Guesdist class politics even more fundamentally than did anarchist libertarianism: Ravachol's bombs may have outraged the Marxists' rationalist understanding of militancy, but Clemenceau's democratic alternative to socialism threatened the POF's very survival as an ideological force. Radicalism's populist conception of social order negated Marxism's stern dichotomy between proletariat and bourgeoisie, systematically amalgamating workers, peasants, and small businessmen into 'The People' – a vast, amorphous and virtuous entity menaced by malignant clerical, aristocratic, bureaucratic, and monopolistic elites. Following the political logic inherent in this social vision, Radicals claimed to represent the 'classe populaire' against the elites, rather than the proletariat against the bourgeoisie: they advocated democracy against privilege rather than socialism against capitalism.[101] France's democratic populists traced their ideological ancestry to the Jacobins of 1793 and the Republicans of 1848, not to the militants of the First International or the Communards of 1871: they flew the Tricolore, not the Red Flag. Radicals, the legitimate heirs of Saint-Just and Raspail, were indeed politically 'radical', but not socially revolutionary, a socio-political orientation ideally calculated to confuse and seduce the Guesdists' working-class constituency, itself deeply imbued with Republican traditions and long-accustomed to the neo-Jacobin's populist categories of social analysis. Newcomers to a political culture over-

---

[100] For the success of these arguments in reducing the appeal of libertarian protest in favour of socialist practice, see R. Huard, 'La Genèse des Partis Politiques Démocratiques Modernes en France: Y a-t-il une Specificité Populaire?', in *La Classe Ouvrière Française et la Politique: Essais d'Analyse Historique et Sociale* (Paris, 1980), p. 37.

[101] For the ubiquity of populist rhetoric in France, see J. Dubois, *Le Vocabulaire Politique et Social en France de 1869 à 1872* (Paris, 1969), pp. 16–18, and P. Hutton, *The Cult of the Revolutionary Tradition: The Blanquists in French Politics 1864–1893* (Berkeley, 1981), pp. 3–4 and p. 137. The theoretical disjuncture between Marxism and populism is described in E. Laclau, 'Towards a Theory of Populism', in *Politics and Ideology in Marxist Theory* (London, 1977), pp. 143–98, and B. Jessop, 'The Political Indeterminacy of Democracy', in A. Hunt (ed.), *Marxism and Democracy* (London, 1980), pp. 55–80.

whelmingly dominated by a century-long struggle between democracy and authority, French Marxists had to dispel the Radicals' hegemony over the French Left before they themselves could emerge as a significant ideological force.

Like the Guesdists' dispute with the anarchists, the Parti Ouvrier's campaign against the Radicals assumed the unforgiving attributes of a family feud: Marxist socialists and Radical 'neo-Jacobins' not only competed for the same working-class constituency, but shamefacedly shared a common parentage in the undifferentiated political promiscuity of the mid-nineteenth-century French Left,[102] while family associations and personal loyalties at the local level continued to marry socialist militants to their Radical counterparts long after the two movements had separated in national politics.[103] Even in national politics, however, many Radicals continued to share the socialists' hostility towards powerful capitalists, although 'real' Radical-Socialists such as Camille Pelletan justified their sporadic attacks upon the ruling 'two hundred families' by the clerical and anti-Republican politics of the haute bourgeoisie rather than by any serious concept of exploitation.[104] For their part, most Guesdists – including Guesde, Lafargue, and Deville – had begun their political careers as Radicals, and some, like Deville, ended by returning to the fold. Misled by these continuities and connections, Marx and Engels themselves had hoped that Georges Clemenceau, the epitome of French Radicalism, might some day lead the nascent socialist movement – a hope rendered unreasonable only by anachronistic familiarity with the aged 'Clemenceau brisseur des

---

[102] For examinations of the relationship between Radicalism and working-class politics, see R. Sandstrom, 'Radicalism and Socialism in the Var 1871–1914', *First Annual Meeting of the Western Society for French History*, 1974, pp. 338–45 and T. Judt, *Marxism and the French Left: Studies in Labour and Politics in France 1830–1981* (Oxford, 1986), chapter 1. A series of articles in issue 35 (1980) of the *Cahiers d'Histoire de l'Institut des Recherches Marxistes* is particularly useful in this regard. See, in particular, Rebérioux, 'Sur le Radicalisme', pp. 117–19 and Sagnes, 'Aspects du Radicalisme Héraultais sous la IIIᵉ République', pp. 65–84.

[103] For examples, see P. Bernard, 'Les Élections de 1881–1882: Du Radicalisme au Socialisme', *Mémoires de la Société Académique du Nivernais*, vol. 63, 1981, pp. 73–85 and L. Comby, 'Les Socialistes-Révolutionnaires d'Alfortville, à l'Aube du XXᵉ Siècle', *Études de la Région Parisienne*, vol. 44, 1970, pp. 10–17.

[104] As described in L. Loubère, 'Left-Wing Radicals, Strikes, and the Military 1880–1907', *French Historical Studies*, vol. 3, 1963–64, pp. 93–105. For Pelletan, see J. Stone, 'Political Culture in the Third Republic: The Case of Camille Pelletan', *Proceedings of the Western Society for French History*, vol. 13, 1985, pp. 217–27.

grèves', Clemenceau the strike-breaker.[105] Finally, electoral competition between Radicals and socialists divided the Left to the
advantage of their common conservative enemies, a political disaster
for both movements. As a result, self-righteous 'Republican defence'
or embarrassed opportunism sanctioned 'Republican [electoral]
unity' between liberal-democratic populists and Marxist class
warriors, antagonists who none the less regularly suspended their
ideological hostility for the duration of the second-round balloting
which determined their parliamentary representation.[106] The
neologism 'Radical-Socialist' indicated both doctrinal similarities
and practical imperatives in *fin-de-siècle* France, despite the ideological differences and political conflicts which otherwise divided
Radicals from socialists.

All the same, Guesdist polemic remained unrelentingly hostile to
Radicalism, described in one memorable polemic as 'that succubus
of socialism'.[107] According to the Marxists, Radicals compromised
the integrity of socialism *because* of their links with the workers'
movement: the aristocratic conservatism of René de la Tour du Pin
or the bourgeois liberalism of René Waldeck-Rousseau could never
seduce proletarian militants from their socialist obligations as easily
as would the populist Radicalism of Georges Clemenceau. In
Charles Bonnier's rueful words, 'all of us ... have the blood ... of
bourgeois radicals in our veins; we have been raised under their
influence and must continually struggle not to succumb once
again'.[108] But why struggle? Why not succumb to the populist
charms of the Radical succubus? Repeatedly challenged by precocious advocates of a *fin-de-siècle* 'Popular Front', the Parti Ouvrier
justified its unabated hatred of the French 'Extreme-Gauche'
(Guesdist use of this anachronistic term indicated the extent to
which they excluded themselves from the conventionally accepted
spectrum of French parties) by stressing the class-collaborationist

---

[105] Engels to Bernstein, 22 September 1882 and Marx to Engels, 20 September 1882, in *Marx/Engels et la Troisième République* (Paris, 1983), pp. 123–5. For discussion of this hope, see Mainfroy, 'Sur le Phénomène Radical', pp. 8–51.

[106] For a superb analysis of this rationale in operation in the very heartland of Guesdism, see R. Vandenbussche, 'Une Élection de Combat dans le Nord: 27 avril et 11 mai 1902', *Revue du Nord*, vol. 56, 1974, pp. 131–40.

[107] C. Bonnier, 'Fausse Manoeuvre', *Le Socialiste*, 28 July – 4 August 1901.

[108] 'B.' (Bonnier), 'Erreurs Radicales', *Le Socialiste*, 7 July 1895.

implications of populist politics.[109] As French Marxists never tired
of emphasising, Radicals unreservedly welcomed capitalists into
their ranks, along with anyone else apart from priests and the exiled
royal families, so long as recruits honestly subscribed to the anti-
clerical and democratic precepts of French neo-Jacobinism. Democratic populists would welcome the most unregenerately exploitative
industrialist into their American-style utopia, if only he abandoned
the anti-democratic politics once hereditary to his class. Radicals
would have cheerfully confessed to this indictment: their doctrine of
'Solidarisme' constituted the *Belle Époque*'s most sophisticated programme of class collaboration, a programme explicitly designed to
unite labour and capital in a common defence of the democratic
(and capitalist) Republic against assaults by both elitist reactionaries from the extreme Right and revolutionary socialists from the
(new) extreme Left.[110] Guesdists realised full well that 'the class
war . . . is the *raison d'être* of the Parti Ouvrier; without it, [the Party]
would become no more than a fraction [of Radicalism]'.[111]

Circumstances abetted the Guesdists' onslaught against the populist biases of the French Left. Paradoxically, the Radicals' passionate
advocacy of 'social solidarity' as an ideal indicated a dramatic
decline in social cohesion as a practice: Radical ideology, for once
confirming Marx's classic metaphor, inverted 'reality' as through a
camera obscura. *Fin-de-siècle* labour militancy, anathema to small
businessmen as well as to great capitalists, alienated Radicals from
their traditional working-class associates: the mass strikes which
punctuated these years forced populists to choose between capital
and labour, and most Radicals unhesitatingly chose capital.[112] And
the contemporaneous upsurge of Marxist socialism, itself both cause
and consequence of the populists' turn to the Right, fostered hitherto
unthinkable alliances between Radicals and 'bourgeois' moderates,

[109] For the antithesis between the Radicals' populism and the Marxists' class paradigm, see J. Stone, *The Search for Social Peace: Reform Legislation in France 1890–1914* (Albany, 1984), pp. 56–7.
[110] For the Guesdists' hatred of this programme, see Éd. Fortin, 'Solidarité Bourgeoise', *Le Socialiste*, 29 November 1896. On Solidarism, see J. Hayward, 'Solidarity: The Social History of an Idea in Nineteenth-Century France', *International Review of Social History*, vol. 4, 1959, pp. 261–84; J. Hayward, 'The Official Social Philosophy of the French Third Republic: Léon Bourgeois and Solidarism', *International Review of Social History*, vol. 6, 1961, pp. 19–48; Stone, *The Search for Social Peace*, chapter 2; L. Portis, *Les Classes Sociales en France: Un Débat Inachevé (1789–1989)* (Paris, 1988), pp. 61–5; and S. Elwitt, *The Third Republic Defended: Bourgeois Reform in France 1880–1914* (London, 1986), pp. 170–216.
[111] Anonymous, 'Catastrophe', *Le Socialiste*, 21 May 1899.
[112] M. Rebérioux, *La République Radicale? 1898–1914* (Paris, 1975), pp. 111–15.

alliances forged from their shared hatred of 'collectivism'. As Radicals quarrelled over whether to cooperate with the new 'extreme Left' against the increasingly conservative Republican 'centre' or ally themselves with their former Opportunist enemies against the 'Reds', socialists (and many non-socialists) decided that the imposing Radical monolith would soon fragment and erode away, crushed between the irresistible force of the advancing socialist proletariat and the immovable object of the anti-labour bourgeoisie.[113] Radicals denied the inevitability of their own supersession, but every Radical, whether opting for the Left or the Right, categorically rejected the Guesdists' Manichean programme of class against class. Given the Radicals' refusal to enlist in the class war, Guesdists relentlessly advocated 'that hatred of Radicalism which is the beginning of wisdom for the French proletariat'.[114]

How did the Parti Ouvrier account for the Radicals' potency within the French political culture? According to the Guesdists, Radical 'radicalism' represented petit-bourgeois protest against modernity rather than proletarian aspiration to a better future. The prevalence of Radical rhetoric within the French political culture supposedly responded to the contemporaneous destruction of artisanal enterprise by industrial capital, the decline of shopkeeping before the department store, the suffocation of the small-holding peasantry by capitalist agriculture, and the expropriation of traditional rentiers by financial speculators. These centralising tendencies in the capitalist mode of production, according to Guesdist analyses, provoked the populists' peculiar combination of hostility towards monopoly-power with enthusiasm for property-ownership, the unstable ideological configuration characteristic of petit-bourgeois politics.[115] Unable to adjust to its hyper-capitalist milieu, unwilling to accept the socialist alternative to capitalism, Radicalism repre-

---

[113] For the Radicals' reaction against militant labour, see L. Loubère, 'Les Radicaux d'Extrême-Gauche en France et les Rapports entre Patrons et Ouvriers 1871–1900', *Revue d'Histoire Économique et Sociale*, vol. 42, 1984, pp. 102–3. For a very premature Guesdist obituary for Radicalism, see Anonymous, 'La Mort du Radicalisme', *Le Socialiste*, 9 September 1893. Liberal agreement with the Guesdists' prognosis for Radical longevity is described in Sorlin, *Waldeck-Rousseau*, p. 381.

[114] C. Bonnier, 'Fausse Manoeuvre', *Le Socialiste*, 28 July – 4 August 1901.

[115] *Almanach du Parti Ouvrier pour 1894* (Lille, undated), pp. 29–30. For analysis of the Marxist logic which governed this argument, see W. Schonfeld, 'The Classical Marxist Conception of Liberal Democracy', *Review of Politics*, vol. 33, 1971, pp. 364–75 and S. Berstein and A. Prost, 'Radicalisme et Couches Moyennes', *Cahiers d'Histoire de l'Institut de Recherches Marxistes*, no. 35, 1980, pp. 85–115.

sented a historical impasse. Secure in their alliance with History, Guesdists derided 'this strange party, crushed between the past and the future, wishing neither the one nor the other, contradicting the course of capitalist development ... Arising from determinant economic circumstances, the Radical party must disappear at the same time as the material conditions from which it draws its life and its necessity'.[116] The sooner workers abandoned their long infatuation with the ageing neo-Jacobin succubus, Guesdists argued, the better for labour and socialism. In Bonnier's gruesome metaphor, it was 'not healthy for a young and vigorous entity like the POF to have too much contact with these revenants from times past. The Radical corpse is beginning to stink'.[117]

Authentic spokesmen for the French petite bourgeoisie indeed, Radicals dreamed of a world made safe for the shopkeeper: not for them the industrial socialism of the POF, a socialism at least as inimical to small-scale enterprise as was monopoly capitalism itself. But, even assuming the practicality of the Radicals' utopia of petty property, a practicality rarely conceded by the Parti Ouvrier, the populist ideal of a 'République à l'Américaine'[118] outraged and frightened Guesdists. Its most 'radical' variant, that of the 'Radicaux-Socialistes', still negated 'real socialism', that of the Parti Ouvrier.[119] For Guesdists,

the social revolution will be an immediate possibility only if the workers remain true to themselves; class against class, proletariat against the bourgeoisie, battling our enemies on the Left as well as our enemies on the Right. We have always been a class party devoted to the hastening of the final liberation, rather than its retardation by criminal and dangerous compromises [with Radicals].[120]

The siren song of Republican democracy which had enchanted the French Left since 1793, the neo-Jacobin populism which had incited Parisian insurrections throughout the nineteenth century, the Radical mystique which would confine the proletariat to the political

[116] J. Sarraute, 'Le Parti Radical', *Le Socialiste*, 7 July 1895.

[117] 'C.B.' (Bonnier), 'Le Bilan Radical', *Le Socialiste*, 25 August – 1 September 1901.

[118] J. Guesde, 'L'Automaniaquisme', *L'Égalité*, 28 May 1882.

[119] An explicit confrontation between democracy and class socialism may be found in the fascinating debate between Tony Révillon and Guesde in 'Radicalisme et Socialisme (Conférence Contradictoire)', *L'Égalité*, 25 December 1881. For a Guesdist critique of the brief Bourgeois government, see A. Zévaès, 'Radicalisme et Socialisme', *Le Socialiste*, 10 November 1895.

[120] C. Vérecque, *Trois Années de Participation Socialiste à un Gouvernement Bourgeois* (Paris, 1904), p. 38.

bounds of the 'bourgeois Republic' – all compromised class politics; all precluded socialist revolution.

Just as disputes with anarchists impelled the Parti Ouvrier to adopt a moderate rhetoric resembling that of French Reformism at its most class-collaborationist, so disputes with Radicals inspired Guesdists to rhetorical excess more characteristic of anarchism than of Marxist socialism. Determined avoidance of 'criminal and dangerous compromises' with the French Radicals engendered the Marxists' visceral anti-electoralism and anti-parliamentarianism, their uncompromising hostility to the 'bourgeois' Republic, and their simplistic confusion between advocacy of social reform and adherence to 'Reformism' – sectarian 'deviations' which repeatedly disoriented the POF's Marxist strategy of turning 'bourgeois' political forms against the bourgeoisie, but which also precluded the Guesdists' assimilation into the amorphous banality of neo-Jacobin 'populism', the fate of most protest movements on the French Left during the nineteenth century. None the less, Guesdism, while undoubtedly devoted to its novel politics of 'class against class', had matured within a liberal-democratic political order which rewarded the use of populist rhetoric, a political order which forced ideologues to define their constituency as broadly as possible. Falling prey to their origins within the neo-Jacobin Left and to the predominant political culture of French democracy, Guesdists occasionally succumbed to the implicit equation of 'the people, that is to say, the proletariat',[121] thereby returning to the populist womb from which they had been born. Radical petits bourgeois and socialist workers, the Parti Radical et Radical-Socialiste and the Parti Ouvrier, shared too many common interests and opposed too many common enemies for the firm dichotomies of class theory to triumph unconditionally over the fluid compromises of populist practice.

Polemical imperatives explain the inconsistent extremes of Parti Ouvrier political rhetoric. The Guesdists' Marxist understanding of the working class – the primary victim of bourgeois rule and capitalist economics, while unorganised, but mankind's ultimate saviour from domination and exploitation, once mobilised – required construction of a disciplined working-class party and capture of the 'bourgeois state', an intensely political programme which outraged the anti-political anarchists. Clashes between

---

[121] 'Le Parti Ouvrier en France – Montluçon', *Le Socialiste*, 10 October 1891.

Marxists and anarchists, clashes fought throughout the life-span of the POF from Guesde's youthful separation from the Jura Federation in the 1870s to his Party's final campaign against the anarchosyndicalist CGT at the beginning of the twentieth century, drove the Parti Ouvrier towards democratic Reformism. At the same time, the Guesdists' tenacious pursuit of the war between capital and labour, the *raison d'être* of French Marxism, divided the populists' sacrosanct 'People' into antagonistic classes, while disrupting the alliance between bourgeois employers and proletarian employees against 'aristocratic and clerical' authoritarians which had sustained French democracy since the days of the sans-culottes, a divisive class programme which outraged the populist Radicals. The battles between Radicals and Marxists which resulted, battles which punctuated the development of the POF from the Marseilles Congress of 1879 to the Party's insurgency against the Combes Ministry, impelled the Parti Ouvrier towards sectarian repudiation of liberal-democratic ideals and institutions. Torn between powerful competitors, caught in the cross-fire of a two-front war, French Marxists struggled heroically (if inconsistently) against both anti-political anarchists and class-collaborationist populists, but never vanquished them, nor altogether purged anarchist and populist rhetoric from the Parti Ouvrier's own political discourse.

In the words of one of the best historians of nineteenth-century French labour militancy, 'socialist political practice [during the Guesdists' period] ... reveals not the limits of socialist imagination but the power of French capitalism and the state'.[122] The history of the Parti Ouvrier indeed illustrates the dilemmas of a revolutionary party in a non-revolutionary society – a party too weak to accomplish the socialist transformation its theory called for, yet incapable of obtaining the reforms for which its constituents ached. The equivocations and contradictions characteristic of Guesdist political rhetoric also stemmed, however, from dilemmas inherent in the Marxist project of practising working-class politics within a liberal democratic polity.[123] How did the capitalist mode of pro-

---

[122] J. Scott, 'Mayors versus Police Chiefs: Socialist Municipalities Confront the French State', in J. Merriman (ed.), *French Cities in the Nineteenth Century* (London, 1982), p. 245.
[123] This point is made very effectively in T. Judt, *Marxism and the French Left*, pp. 111–12. Unfortunately, Judt (p. 112) links this point to the absurdly reductionist proposition that 'the consciousness of the French working class emerged out of encounters with the political superstructure, with the economic infrastructure quite absent from the equation'.

duction condition the 'bourgeois' state? What linked the proletariat with 'its' party? What strategy of reform and (or?) revolution best satisfied the political requirements of a socialist party enmeshed in the institutions of a capitalist yet democratic regime? Clear and consistent answers to these questions never emerged from the Parti Ouvrier's rhetoric, as much because of the inherent lacunae and ambiguities of the Guesdists' Marxist doctrine as despite its evident force and rationality.

PART III

History and class conflict

Vampire-Capital: Marxists indict the bourgeoisie

> The specific economic form, in which unpaid surplus-labour is pumped out of direct producers, determines the relationship of rulers and ruled, as it grows directly out of production itself and, in turn, reacts upon it as a determining element. Upon this, however, is founded the entire formation of the economic community which grows up out of the production relations themselves, thereby its specific political form. It is always the direct relationship of the owners of the conditions of production to the direct producers ... which reveals the innermost secret, the hidden basis of the entire social structure ...
>
> Karl Marx, *Capital* (Moscow, 1959), vol. 3, p. 791.

Ideologists have always employed metahistorical weaponry – weaponry which has included the cyclical 'eternal return' wielded by traditional conservatives against optimistic radicals, the linear progress of the 'Whig interpretation of history' deployed to such effects by liberals and socialists against guardians of the *status quo*, and the catastrophism launched by millenarians and anarchists against corrupt, intolerable but apparently all-powerful elites. Established and aspirant social orders, whether hierarchical, individualist, or collectivist, have always required both *arche* and *telos*, both a usable past and an anticipated future, while the ideologues who have served order or revolt, from Plato to Popper, have always relied upon visions of history, extrapolations of the trajectory from past to future, to comprehend, evaluate, and transform their societies. A study of ideology may begin with elucidation of first principles and continue through analyses of conceptions of social structure, but must end with exploration of metahistories.

From Marx to Marcuse, Marxists have exemplified the symbiosis of ideology and historical vision: their dialectic of property and labour, the foundation of Marxist social thought, has underscored both the mutability of social order and the common lineage of societies in production, exploitation, and domination; their concept of 'modes of production', the crux of the Marxists' social analytic, has delineated both the harsh contours of the exploitative past and the Elysian Fields of a post-revolutionary future; and their dynamic of class conflict, the outcome of exploitative modes of production, has supposedly driven humankind from the limbo of 'primitive communism', through the purgatorial realms of slavery, feudalism, and capitalism, to the golden gates of the socialist paradise.[1] Classes have embodied this metahistorical myth, not the epochal *Weltanschauungen* of idealist conservatives or the 'great men' of empirical liberals, albeit Marxists have on occasion lapsed into *Geistesgeschichte* or hero worship. In this Marxist historical drama-turgy, classes have assumed a life of their own: they have literally made history. Ruling classes, once having played their role in the succession of modes of production, have aged and died; revolution-ary classes, vigorous newcomers upon the stage of history, have seized power from their senile predecessors; while 'non-historic' classes, without capacity for either rule or revolution, have played their supporting parts in the ongoing drama of the class war.

The Parti Ouvrier certainly exemplified ideological history-mindedness, both in the movement's rhetoric and in its conceptual repertoire. Anachronistic historical imagery permeated Guesdist polemic: capital reduced workers to 'slaves' or 'serfs'; bourgeois paraded in the togas of senatorial slave-owners or the robes of *ancien régime* aristocrats; and factories, lurid backdrop to the drama, bore the crenellations of medieval fortresses.[2] History, not surprisingly, always spoke in the Guesdists' favour. In one astonishing example, Lafargue, determined to discredit Paul Brousse's 'municipal social-ism', wrote an extended description of the disastrous urban insur-

---

[1] For an insightful analysis of the historical philosophy implicit in the Marxist project, see W. Shaw, *Marx's Theory of History* (London, 1978).

[2] See, for a striking example, J. Guesde, untitled, *L'Égalité*, 13 August 1882. For an interesting discussion of the 'uses of history' in the development of French socialism, see R. Kaes, 'Mémoire Historique et Usage de l'Histoire chez les Ouvriers Français', *Mouvement Social*, no. 61, 1967, pp. 12–32. Workers often used the same anachronistic identification of capitalists as feudal lords, according to M. Perrot, *Les Ouvriers en Grève: France 1871–1890* (Paris, 1974), vol. 2, p. 581. Capitalists unintentionally encouraged the analogy by embellishing their factories with crenellations and towers. See the photograph of Eugène Motte's enterprise in L. Marty, *Chanter pour Survivre: Culture Ouvrière, Travail et Techniques dans le Textile – Roubaix 1850–1914* (Lille, 1982), p. 25.

rections of Medieval Flanders, thereby supposedly demonstrating the impotence of local politics![3] What conception of history underlay this picturesque rhetoric? What patterns did the Parti Ouvrier discern in the past?

First, Guesdist historical thought, as materialistic and 'scientific' as every other element in the Parti Ouvrier's ideology, advanced a strikingly determinist interpretation of historical process and metahistorical progress: societies, like the Newtonian natural world, supposedly obeyed laws which admitted no exceptions, which allowed no latitude for random accident. Unswayed by 'bourgeois' notions of free-will, French Marxists discovered an 'absolute determinism in the social order'.[4] As always, metahistorical vision discerned or (better yet) created a 'usable past', a past which predicted, even constituted, a desired future. For Guesdists, the social revolution of which they dreamed could be predicted with the certainty of an eclipse, and could no more be prevented: revolution was as fixed in the inevitable future as 1789 was fixed in the unchangeable past. Inexorable historical 'laws' had ruled over the birth of *fin-de-siècle* France, and the same laws would govern its future, laws which guaranteed the 'revolutionary situation which must develop' as 'the inevitable result of the upheavals convulsing contemporary society'.[5]

'Inevitable'? 'Historical inevitability', long one of the most criticised aspects of 'orthodox Marxism', if it determined nothing else, certainly determined the Guesdist vision of past, present and future. This Second International faith in History, a Marxist version of divine providence, supposedly fostered a debilitating historical *attentisme*, a self-confident passivity which precluded both reformist tinkering with the capitalist present and revolutionary activism directed towards the socialist future. According to their many critics, the Marxists of the Menshevik faction of the RSDLP, Bebel's SPD, the Social Democratic Federation, and, not least, the POF itself awaited a *deus ex historia* who would accomplish the tasks which, in reality, depended upon their own will and initiative.[6] Although

3 P. Lafargue, 'Les Luttes de Classes en Flandre', *L'Égalité*, 22 January and 29 January 1882.
4 'B' (Bonnier), 'Les Lendemains de la Révolution', *Le Socialiste*, 10 July 1892.
5 *Septième Congrès National du Parti Ouvrier tenu à Roubaix du Samedi 29 Mars au Lundi 7 Avril 1884* (Paris, undated), pp. 16–17.
6 For this critique applied to the Guesdists, see D. Lindenberg, *Le Marxisme Introuvable* (Paris, 1975), p. 66 and P. Cousteix, 'L'Introduction du Marxisme en France', *Ours*, no. 41, 1973, p. 69.

popular with Leninists and historians of socialism, this indictment
lacks credibility. 'Determinist' faiths have animated every successful
ideology: devout belief in providence, fate, or progress has always
inspired religious, political and social activists.[7] *'Deus Le Veult!'*
resounded across Palestinian battlefields, not through the scriptoria
of medieval schoolmen; the subtlety of 'Western Marxism', not the
certainty of Second International orthodoxy, has reflected and
reinforced ideological passivity among socialists. French Marxists of
the *Belle Époque*, crusaders of the class war, persevered in the face of
recurring defeat *because* their historical vision had revealed a secular
providence which guaranteed their eventual victory.[8]

Guesdists fought on in the conviction that 'those of us who have
been taught by history how classes are born, develop, and die feel no
uneasiness about the final outcome'.[9] This teleology structured the
Parti Ouvrier's determinist metahistory, its all-encompassing overview of past and future in which 'progressive' modes of production
sired revolutionary classes which, upon seizing power, presided over
their society as ruling classes until destroyed, in turn, by further
progress and new revolutionary classes. Priest-kings, slave-owners,
feudal lords, and capitalists had succeeded each other upon the
bloody stage, precursors of the final act in which the proletariat
would bring down the curtain upon the age-old play of exploitation
and domination. Class war, embodied in both the conflict between
ascending and transcended ruling classes and the struggle of the
exploited against their exploiters, supplied the 'condition of historical movement'[10] in the same way that biological competition drove
the evolutionary process, a Darwinian analogy frequently repeated
in Guesdist discourse. 'Historical development has been solely the

---

[7] A. Gouldner, *The Two Marxisms: Contradictions and Anomalies in the Development of Theory*
(London, 1980), pp. 108–50 and R. Jacoby, 'The Politics of Crisis Theory', *Telos*, no. 23,
1975, p. 4 and p. 29. The ideology of the POF effectively refutes Coser's identification of
'determinist' Marxists with reformism and 'volunteerist' Marxists with revolution, as well
as his identification of determinist reformists with Western Europe and revolutionary
volunteerists with the East. L. Coser, 'Marxist Thought in the First Quarter of the
Twentieth Century', *American Journal of Sociology*, vol. 78, 1972, pp. 172–201.

[8] For the importance of faith in the future to Guesdist militants, see C. Willard, *Le Mouvement
Socialiste en France (1893–1903): Les Guesdistes* (Paris, 1965), p. 382 and P. Hutton, 'The
Impact of the Boulangist Crisis upon the Guesdist Party in Bordeaux', *French Historical
Studies*, vol. 7, 1971, p. 231.

[9] Anonymous, 'L'Expérience Radicale', *Le Socialiste*, 24 October 1885 – the Guesdists'
response to their crushing defeat in the 1885 legislative elections.

[10] P. Lafargue, *La Lutte Sociale* (Paris, undated), pp. 4–5.

result of social conflicts inherent in successive modes of production', Guesdists asserted. 'Prevention of the class war which embodies these conflicts would freeze history.'[11]

Like Darwinian evolution, the class war ensured the survival of the fittest: class conflict was inherently progressive. Just as the best-adapted organisms prevailed in the dog-eat-dog natural world, so classes representative of the most productive modes of production triumphed in the strife-ridden social world. Progress (and French Marxists of the *Fin de Siècle* believed in progress as devoutly as did most Victorians) depended upon the dethroning of senile ruling classes, embodiments of antiquated relations of production, and the enthronement of vigorous and creative revolutionary classes, pregnant with the future. But, unlike evolution, historical progress moved towards a goal and an ending. Guesdists, like Marx himself, believed that they lived the last days, that capitalism, the culmination of the dialectic between progress and exploitation, heralded the end of history as class war. The metahistorical drama, in the last hours of its three-thousand year run, would culminate in 'the battle between the two enemy camps which have little by little come to include all society: the capitalist bourgeoisie and the proletariat'.[12]

But what about the rest of the cast?[13] Proletarians, after all, constituted only a substantial minority of the French population, and bourgeois only a tiny minority. For their part, the 'middle and intermediate strata' which 'obliterate lines of demarcation everywhere',[14] repeatedly stumbled onto the stage, disrupting the classic simplicity of the Marxist denouement with low comedy. Petits bourgeois and peasants, not to mention lumpenproletarians and white-collar employees – 'non-historic classes' because they neither commanded the present, the role of the bourgeoisie, nor represented the future, the role of the proletariat – were mere bit-players, but bit-players who often stole the show by sheer weight of numbers.

[11] G. Deville, *Philosophie du Socialisme* (Paris, 1886), p. 25. Despite a common allegation, the Guesdists were not infected with Social Darwinism. See their angry refutation of this creed in Anonymous, 'Edward Aveling', *Le Socialiste*, 20 February 1886.

[12] G. Deville, *Aperçu sur le Socialisme Scientifique*, in G. Deville, *La Capital de Karl Marx* (Paris, undated), p. 12.

[13] For acute discussions of the problems posed to Marxist historical understanding by dichotomous class analysis, see A. Giddens, *Capitalism and Modern Social Theory: An Analysis of the Writings of Marx, Durkheim and Max Weber* (Cambridge, 1975), pp. 38–9; R. Dahrendorf, *Conflict After Class* (London, 1967), p. 5; and W. Wesolowski, *Classes, Strata and Power* (London, 1979), pp. 14–16.

[14] K. Marx, *Capital* (Moscow, 1959), vol. 3, p. 885.

None the less, Guesdists, as devoted adherents of a historical star-system, focused their attention upon villain and hero, upon the bourgeoisie and the proletariat.

More specifically, the Marxist interpretation of modern history has focused upon a theory of the bourgeoisie: Marxists may have identified with the proletariat, but the origins, mechanisms, and fate of capital have dominated their conception of social transformation. Marx himself, determined to discover the source of exploitation and domination in nineteenth-century Europe, devoted his life to investigating the bourgeoisie and the logic of its society; he consistently construed the proletariat as a derivative of the bourgeois past and the capitalist present, whatever its promise of a post-capitalist future.[15] Building upon this legacy, the first generation of Marxists likewise devoted themselves to the critique of the bourgeoisie, neglecting the history and sociology of the working class, and virtually ignoring the 'non-historic' classes. No wonder. Marx's studies of the capitalist ruling class had bequeathed unresolved questions rather than definitive answers. Were the terms 'capitalist class' and 'bourgeoisie' identical, mere synonyms for the modern ruling class? Or was the latter term more inclusive, encompassing the auxiliaries of capital: bureaucrats, lawyers, army officers, and other non-propertied 'bourgeois'?[16] How united was the bourgeoisie, however it was conceptualised? Marxists, unsure of the answer to this question, have long debated the relationships between industrial, commercial, and financial capital, those *frères ennemies*.[17] And why was the bourgeoisie doomed to defeat in its class war against the proletariat? What contradictions in the capitalist mode of production foreshadowed its transcendence?

Guesdists exemplified Marxist preoccupation with these unresolved questions. They lived, by their own estimation, in the last

[15] R. Duhac, 'Bourgeoisie et Prolétariat à Travers l'Oeuvre de Karl Marx', *Cahiers Internationaux de Sociologie*, vol. 30, 1961, pp. 147–66.

[16] G. Cole, *Studies in Class Structure* (London, 1955), pp. 90–2 provides a good analysis of this ambiguity. The best exegesis of Marx's use of the terms 'bourgeoisie' or 'capitalist class' is in H. Draper, *Karl Marx's Theory of Revolution: The Politics of Social Classes* (New York, 1978), pp. 169–287.

[17] S. Ossowski, *Class Structure in the Social Consciousness* (London, 1963), p. 81. For a good analysis of this difficulty in the Marxist problematic, see R. Crompton and J. Gubay, *Economy and Class Structure* (London, 1977), pp. 64–98.

years of 'the bourgeois century',[18] a century which had experienced the apogee of capitalist power and the beginning of its end. Offspring of their epoque, French Marxists inevitably viewed their society through spectacles crafted by bourgeois opticians: Guesde himself maintained a decades-long running commentary on the eminently bourgeois *Économiste Français*, just as Marx had perused the London *Economist* throughout his long British exile; and the Parti Ouvrier relied upon statistics provided by the 'bourgeois state' in elaborating its depiction of the French political economy, just as Marx had depended upon parliamentary enquiries for the evidence which sustained his magisterial portrayal of capitalism. How, in their turn, did the Guesdists conceptualise the French ruling class? First, French Marxists rarely identified and delineated their enemy with clarity. Reacting daily to the practice of polemic rather than the discipline of theory, the Parti Ouvrier sank into a bottomless terminological morass. *Le Socialiste*, on occasion, explicitly dismissed lexical rigour: 'proprietors and non-proprietors, capitalists and the salaried, bourgeois and proletarians, it doesn't matter much which terms are used to identify the antagonists'.[19] 'Proprietors', 'capitalists', and 'bourgeois' – these categories certainly overlapped, but they did not necessarily coincide: petits bourgeois were proprietors, but not capitalists; lawyers were bourgeois, but not proprietors. Guesdists, on other occasions, recognised that terms did 'matter', that 'bourgeois' and 'capitalist' might, indeed, designate different strata in society, and that the distinction could be of capital importance. How else could French Marxists have depicted, or even perceived, 'the rapid replacement of the bourgeois regime by capitalist rule'[20] – the destruction of the Third Republic's 'property-owning democracy' by capitalist plutocracy? Moving from one terminological extreme to the other, the Parti Ouvrier even denounced the very word 'bourgeoisie' (otherwise one of their favourite usages) as a

---

[18] P. Lafargue, 'Le Matérialisme de Marx et l'Idéalisme de Kant', *Le Socialiste*, 25 February 1900. A. Daumard discusses this widely accepted understanding of the French nineteenth century in 'Les Structures Bourgeoises en France à l'Époque Contemporaine: Évolution ou Permanence?', in *Conjoncture Économique/Structures Sociales: Hommage à Ernest Labrousse* (Paris, 1974), p. 449.

[19] Anonymous, 'La Lutte des Classes', *Le Socialiste*, 29 August 1885. The French working class tended to use the terms 'bourgeois' and 'capitalist' interchangeably, according to Perrot, *Les Ouvriers en Grève*, vol. 2, p. 623.

[20] C. Brunellière, 'La Question Agraire', *Le Socialiste*, 13 October 1895.

mystification invented to disguise the distinction between capitalist predators and their petit-bourgeois victims.[21]

How, then, did French Marxists portray their class enemy, however it was designated? What content filled the empty terms? Guesdists, in practice, employed two radically opposed rhetorical modes when they depicted the 'bourgeoisie' or the 'capitalist class'. On the one hand, they personalised the class, embodying its exploitative whole in its most spectacular representatives. On the other hand, the Parti Ouvrier more often than not stripped the ruling class of any specific referents: bourgeois, personifications of capital rather than personalities, represented only 'the economic interests of their class'.[22] Why this abstraction, which sometimes afflicted the Parti Ouvrier's journalism with a peculiar lifelessness? Why did Guesdists, dedicated to vulgarising their doctrine, adopt the deadly sterility of the 'ism' rather than the lively vitality of the example?

Despite its rhetorical weakness, abstraction served the Guesdists well in their long campaign against class-collaboration and its ideologues. From 'National Socialists' on the extreme Right to 'Ministerialist' socialists on the moderate Left, class collaborationists agreed that the proletariat and the bourgeoisie shared common interests, in both the workplace and the broader society. Enemies of the class war attributed the inequities and iniquities which marred capitalist society to the irresponsibility of unrepresentative capitalists: indictments of bad bourgeois supplanted indictment of a bad system; moralising replaced the critique of political economy. Class warriors first and always, Guesdists detested this thesis, and abominated its corollary that socialists might work with 'progressive bourgeois' to prevent 'abuses' of the system – the fundamental premise underlying the hated 'reformism' of the anti-Marxist Left. For French Marxists, capitalists in general bore responsibility for all the sins of capitalism; 'no particular employer', Lafargue asserted, 'can be blamed for this state of affairs'.[23] By the same rationale, no individual capitalist, however kindly, or faction of the bourgeoisie, however enlightened, could mitigate capitalism's systemic evils. Before or after Christmas, Scrooge remained the enemy.

The alternative rhetorical mode favoured by Guesdists personal-

[21] C. Brunellière, 'Bourgeoisie ou Ploutocratie', *Le Socialiste*, 14 May 1899.
[22] P. Lafargue, speech to the Chamber of Deputies, *Journal Officiel*, 28 October 1892.
[23] P. Lafargue, 'Le Programme Municipal', *Le Socialiste*, 9 April 1892.

ised the entire capitalist class. French Marxists, for instance, described their archenemy Eugène Motte as 'the embodied patronat'.[24] True to its origins in the provincial industrial cities of France, the Parti Ouvrier usually identified great industrialists as its exemplary bourgeois, Schneider of Creusot most often sharing the 'honour' with Motte of Roubaix. These alternative rhetorical modes, abstraction and personification, did not contradict each other, but the latter implied that less powerful bourgeois than Motte or Schneider might escape Marxist strictures, an implication which served the POF admirably when the Party sought to turn petits bourgeois, potential allies of the revolutionary proletariat, against haut-bourgeois plutocrats. On the other hand, personification allowed a rhetorical sleight-of-hand which indicted *every* employer, however benevolent, with the class despotism characteristic of Roubaisian textile manufacture or Le Creusot's metallurgy – a usage reinforcing rather than contradicting the rhetoric of abstraction. Parti Ouvrier propagandists, no more troubled by rhetorical inconsistency than by theoretical contradiction, relentlessly rang the changes on this ideological carillon.

These rhetorical ambiguities pale to insignificance before glaring Guesdist indecision over the composition and cohesion of the bourgeoisie. Was it a homogeneous mass of parasitic property-owners, fused into absolute solidity by common interests, common attitudes, and common institutions? Or was it a loose alliance of quarrelling factions, riven by internal discord? Guesdists never decided this question, despite their conviction that the socialist campaign against the capitalist mode of production depended upon clear analysis of the 'economic structure of our bourgeoisie'.[25] They most often described the bourgeois ruling class as 'a single reactionary mass' (French Marxists adored the Lassallean phrase), a mass mobilised, organised, and disciplined by its interest in the private ownership of the means of production and the on-going exploitation of wage-

---

[24] P. Lafargue, 'L'Affaire Dreyfus: Le Nouveau Spectre Rouge', *Le Socialiste*, 3 June 1900. Eugène Motte, leader of the Roubaix employers in their campaign against socialism, was indeed the virtual embodiment of textile manufacturing – that archetypical industry of the capitalist industrial revolution. For the ways in which Motte typified a certain kind of patronat, see R. Priouret, *Origines du Patronat Français* (Paris, 1963), p. 212.

[25] P. Dramas, 'L'Action Sénatoriale', *Le Socialiste*, 13 December 1896. There is an excellent discussion of Marxism's analyses of divisions within classes in S. Resnick and R. Wolff, *Knowledge and Class: A Marxian Critique of Political Economy* (Chicago, 1987), pp. 117–32.

labour. The Parti Ouvrier, when pressed, conceded the novelty of this capitalist unity. Once upon a time, bourgeois had indeed preyed upon bourgeois, capitalists had indeed pillaged other capitalists: bankers had looted industrialists' treasuries, merchants had mobilised against finance, and industrialists had denounced parasitic mercantile middlemen. But class conflict, a life and death matter, had finally prevailed (according to Marxists) over intra-class disputes, superficial and transient by comparison. Thus, Guesde asserted, 'the more the [proletariat] is "deindividualised", the more the exploiters will forget their divisions ... and think only of what unites them, that is the defence of their profits against the workers who are determined to reduce them to a minimum before abolishing them altogether'.[26] The POF itself thus claimed credit for bourgeois concord: 'wherever the Parti Ouvrier Français has penetrated, there the unity of the capitalist class has been consolidated'.[27] Challenged by the advancing red flags of socialism, bourgeois had abandoned the fratricidal disputes of their hegemonic period for the unity demanded by class war, thereby coalescing into 'one reactionary mass'.

This conviction, embedded in the *a prioris* of Marxist class theory, lacked empirical force. Apart from exceptional moments such as the May Day of Fourmies, French bourgeois quarrelled as ferociously over market-shares, access to political power, and alternative visions of the Good Society during the *Belle Époque* as at any time during the preceding century. Fiercely individualistic, French capitalists even remained without institutional representation until 1898, when a National Association of Chambers of Commerce finally embodied the French 'business community'.[28] This ineffective organisation, however, more often served as a forum for inconclusive debate than a weapon in the class war. The French bourgeoisie, despite the best efforts of its more far-sighted or more frightened leaders, entered the

[26] J. Guesde, 'Classe contre Classe', *Le Socialiste*, 24 June 1891. For discussion of this dialectic of class formation during the *Fin de Siècle*, see H. Peiter, 'Institutions and Attitudes: The Consolidation of the Business Community in Bourgeois France 1880–1914', *Journal of Social History*, vol. 9, 1976, pp. 512–13; J. Lambert, *Le Patron: De l'Avènement à la Contestation* (Paris, 1969), p. 121; and M. Gillet, 'L'Affrontement des Syndicalismes Ouvriers et Patronales dans le Bassin Houiller du Nord et du Pas-de-Calais de 1884 à 1891', *Bulletin de la Société d'Histoire Moderne*, vol. 56, 1957, p. 8. There was an almost complete lack of employer solidarity before the 1890s, according to Perrot, *Les Ouvriers en Grève*, vol. 2, pp. 678–9.
[27] J. Martin, 'L'Unité Capitaliste', *Le Socialiste*, 1–8 December 1891.
[28] R. Magraw, *France 1815–1914: The Bourgeois Century* (London, 1983), p. 230.

twentieth century thoroughly divided.[29] Guesdists, however, largely ignored this divisiveness, or even denied its reality. Why? How could the Parti Ouvrier cling so devotedly to its imagery of 'one reactionary mass' in the face of daily bourgeois altercations with bourgeois?

The Guesdists' unwavering political vision depended upon social myopia. French Marxists practised an integral class politics, the politics of class against class, of capitalists versus anti-capitalists, 'without wishing to recognise', Paul André unwittingly confessed, 'the divisions within capitalism'.[30] After all, these divisions fragmented the working class as well as the bourgeoisie: workers in export industries allied themselves to their free-trading employers against protectionist proletarians and Méliniste capitalists; Nationalist employees and chauvinist bourgeois united against 'Ministerialist' workers and Dreyfusard employers. The class war, according to Guesdists, could only be fought to a conclusion once these debilitating side-issues had been forgotten. Rejoicing (prematurely) in the disappearance of disruptive secondary disputes from the bourgeois political culture, *Le Socialiste* maintained that 'revolutionary socialists now have the considerable advantage of no longer confronting a divided enemy, which can give them only facile and transient victories. Instead, they face, in Lassalle's words, a single reactionary mass ... The battle is joined on a single front, and every blow will count'.[31] Once workers and bourgeois forgot other issues, unconditional class war would break out and the proletariat would prevail.

Even during the mid-1890s, when Guesdists assumed most confidently that class blocs had hardened into crystalline rigidity, conflicts of interest, tradition, and expectations still fractured the French bourgeoisie.[32] Should France establish protection for 'national enterprise', or should she cling to free trade? Should Republicans welcome the Catholic Church into the national community, or should they adhere to their traditional Voltairian anti-clericalism?

---

[29] G. Lefranc, *Les Organisations Patronales en France: Du Passé au Présent* (Paris, 1976), p. 21 and pp. 45–7.

[30] P. André, 'Le Rôle des Élus', *Bulletin Mensuel des Élus Socialistes*, deuxième année, no. 24, 1 November 1901, p. 1.

[31] Anonymous, 'La Nouvelle Convention', *Le Socialiste*, 9 September 1893.

[32] Eugène Motte himself had considerable difficulty in uniting the Roubaisian bourgeoisie against Guesde. See D. Gordon, 'Liberalism and Socialism in the Nord: Eugène Motte and Republican Politics in Roubaix 1898–1912', *French History*, vol. 3, 1989, p. 314.

Should capitalists embrace social reform as the alternative to social revolution, or should they avoid it as the antechamber of insurrection? These issues fragmented the ruling class and engendered long-lasting antagonism between Mélinistes and free traders, Ralliés and reactionaries, Radicals and Progressistes – the inexplicably divided representatives of a supposedly unified bourgeoisie. However self-deluding, however socially myopic, socialists could not completely ignore the clashes between bourgeois which periodically convulsed the French polity. Discovering virtue in necessity, Marxists wondered whether the internecine quarrels of their enemies might be turned to socialist advantage.

In pursuing this logic, the Parti Ouvrier evolved a rhetorical strategy which flatly contradicted its imagery of a 'single reactionary mass'. Rather than emphasising the unity of the bourgeoisie as the correlative of proletarian solidarity, Guesdists cheered bourgeois factionalism as the precondition of socialist revolution. French Marxists hoped that intra-bourgeois brawls would facilitate the demolition of bourgeois rule, just as quarrels between Church, monarchy, and aristocracy had enabled the bourgeoisie to overthrow the *ancien régime*. Carried away by this happy speculation, Guesde himself, otherwise a fervent champion of 'one reactionary mass' imagery, decided that internal divisions within the bourgeoisie had 'virtually paralyse[d] the class as a whole'.[33] Lafargue, for his part, held that revolutionary socialists should welcome ruling class dissension. 'The Parti Ouvrier has an interest in aggravating the conflicts which tear apart the bourgeoisie', he commented, since 'these antagonisms disorganise the ruling class'.[34] A divided enemy was a weakened enemy.

The furious debate between free-traders and protectionists which convulsed entrepreneurial France during the 1890s exemplified the Guesdists' quandary over whether to base their revolutionary strategy upon bourgeois unity or bourgeois dissention. Foreign competition preoccupied the business community in the Guesdist bastion of the Nord, where the all-important textile industry competed directly against the previously hegemonic British and aggressive cheap-labour newcomers such as Russian Poland. The industrialists of Lille, Roubaix, and Tourcoing struggled at least as violently against the free-trading merchants of Lyons and Bordeaux as they fought against

33 J. Guesde, 'L'Explication', *Le Cri du Peuple*, 1 March 1886.
34 P. Lafargue, 'Le Communisme et les Services Publics', *L'Égalité*, 25 June 1882.

local socialists: the latter may have threatened textile magnates with eventual expropriation, but the former threatened them with imminent bankruptcy.[35] Yet Guesdists, at least in their national press, dismissed the 1890s' noisy argument over protection as sound and fury signifying nothing. They asserted that 'socialists have no business being protectionists or free-traders, since these varied relationships between the owners – or robbers – of industry and commerce don't affect – don't modify in the slightest – the relationship of robber and robbed which prevails between capitalists and proletarians'.[36] For the POF, discord over free trade and protection served only to divert workers from their revolutionary vocation.[37]

The Parti Ouvrier, however, itself fell prey to this diversion. Guesdists in the Nord, for instance, joined in the region's apprehensive hostility towards foreigners' 'unfair' trading practices, practices which jeopardised the livelihood of Roubaisian workers as much as (indeed, far more than) they threatened the profits of Eugène Motte (who owned factories in Lodz). Guesdists in other cities, where proletarians worked in export industries and suffered from the high food prices associated with the Méline tariffs, denounced protection as a cynical ploy by the new barons of agrarian capital, as the cruel instrument of a rural bourgeoisie determined to victimise already impoverished urban workers. The Guesdists' enemies gleefully highlighted the POF's inconsistencies, and met with only the most feeble and embarrassed of responses.[38] The clashing business interests of free-traders and protectionists indeed disrupted the workers' movement, including the Parti Ouvrier itself.[39]

Logically, the 'one reactionary mass' image of the bourgeoisie should have predominated during the Guesdists' supposedly 'sectarian' period during the 1880s, while emphasis upon ruling class fragmentation should have coincided with their alleged 'opportunist'

---

[35] Lefranc, *Les Organisations Patronales en France*, pp. 34–5, and M. Smith, 'La Haute Bourgeoisie Capitaliste in the Late Nineteenth Century: A Prosopographic Inquiry', *Proceedings of the Third Annual Meeting of the Western Society for French History*, vol. 3, 1975, pp. 354–5.

[36] J. Guesde, 'L'Échéance de 1892', *Le Socialiste*, 4 March 1891.

[37] There is a good description of the manipulation of protectionism against socialism in H. Lebovics, *The Alliance of Iron and Wheat in the Third French Republic 1860–1914: Origins of the New Conservatism* (Baton Rouge, 1988), pp. 46–7.

[38] For Lafargue's discomfiture, see the debate on Lafargue's motion to abolish agricultural protection in the *Journal Officiel*, 16 February 1892.

[39] For the impact of the debate over protection upon Guesdist support, see A. Baker, 'Organize for Revolution: The Threat of Syndicalism before the *Belle Époque*', *Proceedings of the Third Annual Meeting of the Western Society for French History*, vol. 3, 1975, pp. 453–4.

deviations during the 1890s. A strategy founded upon exploitation of intra-bourgeois divisions allowed or even required political 'flexibility', as socialists manipulated capitalists' internecine quarrels, while the imagery of 'one reactionary mass' implied a *pur et dur* 'class against class' revolutionary intransigence. Yet both strategies, both that based upon ruling class cohesion *and* that based upon the debilitating dissension of a fragmented bourgeoisie, characterised Parti Ouvrier polemic from 1882 to 1905, with very little variation in their relative emphasis. Torn between contradictory rhetorics, Guesdists retained only the certainty that 'there is a single ground upon which the bourgeoisie forms a homogeneous class: that it is obliged to maintain the existence of a class without the means of production, the proletariat'.[40]

Guesdist perplexities were compounded by the intricate inter-relationships between the 'functional' fractions of capital which Marx had delineated: industry, commerce, finance, and (possibly) land-ownership. How did the very different historical roles of these 'fractions' condition the Parti Ouvrier's portrayal of the French ruling class? How did the Parti Ouvrier describe, understand, and exploit the always complex and often conflict-ridden nexus between industrialists, merchants, bankers, and landowners?[41] Here the Parti Ouvrier fell victim to an *a priori* assumption derived from its Marxist political economy. Marx's classic dictum that 'it is always the direct relationship of the owners of the conditions of production to the direct producers ... which reveals the innermost secret, the hidden basis of the entire social structure' necessarily focused Marxists' attention upon industrialists – the direct exploiters of the proletariat. Factory and workshop proprietors appropriated the surplus value of labour upon which non-industrial bourgeois supposedly depended for their sustenance; industrialists divided their ill-gotten gains with land-owners (through rent), financiers (through interest payments), and merchants (through wholesale and retail

[40] É. Fortin, 'Politique et Économie', *Le Socialiste*, 27 January – 3 February 1901.
[41] The Guesdists also occasionally discovered a conflict between 'productive' capitalists and parasitic 'rentier' capitalists, although this dichotomy contradicted their portrayal of capitalists as parasitic by definition – a rare deviation which resulted on one occasion in the POF associating 'les commerçants et les industriels', as productive capitalists, with equally productive workers in a vast alliance of 'all those who work and produce' directed against parasitic rentiers. Anonymous, 'L'Impôt sur les Rentiers', *Le Socialiste*, 5 September 1885.

profits).[42] By (Marxist) definition, industrialists were the primary stratum of the bourgeoisie; other strata were secondary.

Unquestioningly obedient to this highly questionable postulate, Guesdists predicated their analysis of the bourgeoisie upon the presumption that, although 'the industrial capitalist is the appropriator of surplus value' he could not 'pocket it in its entirety'.[43] According to Gabriel Deville's authoritative exegesis of *Capital,* 'all the various elements of the bourgeois class . . . are connected to the exploitation of wage labour, since they more or less evenly divide the product of the industrialist's robbery of his workers'.[44] This connection potentially united 'the industrial and agrarian bourgeoisie, the commercial and shopkeeping bourgeoisie, and the financiers – all of whom subsist upon the labour of industrial and rural labourers'.[45] But, concurrently, the connection forced bourgeois into 'irresolvable conflicts between the masters of production and the masters of exchange, between factory owners and merchants'.[46] Industrialists begrudged every interest payment to bankers, every centime of rent to landlords, every markup imposed by distributors; financiers sought absolute hegemony over the entire circuit of capital; wholesale merchants strove to dominate their suppliers as they dominated their customers; and landowners' exploitation of the absolute scarcity of their asset disadvantaged other property-owners far more than it disadvantaged the propertyless (hence periodic bourgeois enthusiasm for public landownership). Like bandits, bourgeois fought over the division of the spoils, spoils plundered from the workers by capitalist industry.

French industrialists, however wealthy and powerful from the perspective of the proletariat, would have sadly disavowed the Marxist presumption that they dominated the bourgeois polity of the *Belle Époque,* although they would have ruefully agreed that their profits underpinned its prosperity. From their perspective, a potent mercantile interest had consistently prevailed over French industry throughout the nineteenth century: the industrial dynasties of

[42] Resnick and Wolff, *Knowledge and Class,* pp. 124–7 and their elaboration of the argument in S. Resnick and R. Wolff, 'Classes in Marxian Theory', *Review of Radical Political Economics,* vol. 13, 1982, pp. 1–18.

[43] Deville, 'Aperçu sur le Socialisme Scientifique', p. 96.

[44] *Ibid.*

[45] P. Lafargue, 'La Politique de la Bourgeoisie', *L'Égalité,* 18 December 1881.

[46] 'E. F.' (Fortin), 'La Dernière Marche Funèbre', *Le Socialiste,* 10 April 1886.

Saint-Étienne or Roubaix carried little weight in Paris by comparison with the great trading houses of Marseilles, Bordeaux, or Lyons.
Industry, industrialists would have contended, had regularly suffered from the allocation of credit by French banks, which had
always preferred the fabulous profits of Russian or Egyptian state
finance to the pedestrian business of industrial credit. And landowners, buttressed by the electoral weight of the French peasantry,
had triumphed during the prolonged nineteenth-century debates
over agricultural protection, thereby substantially increasing the
price of labour for industrialists.[47] Deaf to the grievances of their
class enemies, Guesdists systematically ignored the wrongs suffered
by French industrialists at the hands of their fellow bourgeois. The
Parti Ouvrier's political economy, focused almost exclusively upon
the nexus between wage-labour and private property in the means of
production, grossly underestimated the exploitative power of commerce, finance, and landownership (including their capacity to
exploit industrialists), and substantially overestimated industry's
potency within the capitalist class as a whole.[48]

Why these misjudgements? How could Guesdists so misunder-
stand the bourgeois balance of power? Apart from its Marxist first
principles, the Parti Ouvrier's misconception derived from its role as
a Parti *Ouvrier*, from its solid implantation within the industrial
working class and its consequent alienation from peasants and petits
bourgeois, who might otherwise have enlightened Marxist ideologues about the diversity and complexity of exploitation. The
POF's depiction of industrial capital's omnipotence coincided with
the mentality of the French proletariat, and in turn reinforced
proletarians' daily experience. Workers, at the end of the nineteenth
century, never entered banks and rarely owned real estate, while
their everyday contact with 'commerce' was confined to local shops.
By contrast, industrialists dominated proletarians' workplaces and
often sought to dominate their home-lives, their religious convictions, and their meagre entertainments. Seen from the Paris

---

[47] R. Priouret, *Origines du Patronat Français*, pp. 180–90 and M. Lévy-Leboyer, 'Innovation
and Business Strategies in Nineteenth and Twentieth-Century France', in E. Carter et al.
(eds.), *Enterprise and Entrepreneurs in Nineteenth and Twentieth-Century France* (London, 1976), p.
102.

[48] J. Roemer, 'Exploitation, Class, and Property Relations', in T. Ball and J. Farr (eds.), *After
Marx* (Cambridge, 1984), pp. 184–211 criticises these *a priori* assumptions, so common in
Marxist political economy over the past century.

Bourse, Eugène Motte appeared as merely another provincial businessman; seen from a Roubaisian *estaminet*, he was lord of creation.[49]

Preoccupied by industrial capital, Guesdists neglected commercial enterprise: merchants, however wealthy and influential, rarely featured in the Marxists' demonology. Admittedly, the Parti Ouvrier recognised that mercantile capital had dispossessed the peasants and artisans whose 'free labour' (free from property) had constituted the labour force of nascent eighteenth and early nineteenth-century industry – the 'primitive accumulation' depicted so brilliantly in the historical chapters of *Capital*. Commercial capitalism, in this 'neo-Smithian' version of the Marxist creation myth, fathered industrial capitalism.[50] Guesdists even acknowledged that 'primitive accumulation' continued as long as small property-owners survived. But Guesdists rarely elaborated this thesis, apart from anecdotal accounts of shopkeepers withering in the shade cast by the vast new Parisian department stores. Essentially uninterested in the commercial circuit of capital, Guesdists ignored the powerful wholesalers who dominated French foreign trade, French internal markets, and French chambers of commerce.[51] The Parti Ouvrier never feared that commercial hypertrophy might extinguish the life-force of French industry, that the commerce which had fathered industrialism might eventually devour its offspring – the supposed fate of sixteenth-century Venice, eighteenth-century Holland, and twentieth-century Britain, according to one influential Marxist interpretation of the life-cycle of capitalist social formations.[52]

Why did the Parti Ouvrier neglect commerce, except as a superannuated relic of the proto-capitalist past or a peripheral

---

[49] Lambert, *Le Patron*, pp. 92–3.

[50] See, for instance, the discussion of this process in P. Lafargue, *Origine et Évolution de la Propriété* (Paris, 1895), pp. 485–98.

[51] Lefranc, *Les Organisations Patronales*, p. 31.

[52] Marxists, in general, have neglected evidence that commercial and financial capital has sometimes dominated industrial capital or even precluded its development. See the discussion of this incomprehension and its costs in G. Ingham, 'Divisions within the Dominant Class and British "Exceptionalism"', in A. Giddens and G. MacKenzie (eds.), *Social Class and the Division of Labour: Essays in Honour of Ilya Neustadt* (Cambridge, 1982), pp. 209–27. There is a useful discussion of the permutations of relationships between industrial and commercial capital in C. Colliot-Thélène, 'Contribution à une Analyse des Classes Sociales', *Critique de l'Économie Politique*, no. 21, 1975, pp. 96–7.

aspect of the industrial present? First, merchants enjoyed less social visibility than did industrialists, though not necessarily less social importance. Apart from the owners of Parisian department stores, most merchant capitalists, however wealthy and powerful, concealed themselves too well within the hidden machinery of the French economy to attract the attention of Guesdist ideologists, mesmerised by the lurid glare cast by the blast furnaces of Le Creusot. A genuine *société anonyme*, wholesale merchants, whose buying and selling rarely impinged upon the consciousness of French industrial workers, presented few targets for Marxist invective. Eugène Motte, that exemplary capitalist, dominated Roubaix from his impressive town house; the wool traders who dominated Eugène Motte rarely visited the town.

Office workers in the counting-houses of Le Havre or Marseilles, producers of surplus labour if not of surplus capital, might well have taught the Guesdists something of the contemporaneous power of merchant capital, if the Parti Ouvrier had ever asked their opinion. But the POF made few converts among white-collar employees – a deficiency both cause and consequence of the Party's indifference towards commercial capital. Marxist *a prioris* exaggerated the social myopia peculiar to movements based upon industrial workers: the presumption that commerce depended upon industry, that merchants were parasitic upon industrialists, diverted the Parti Ouvrier from white-collar employees, themselves defined as marginal by their place in the commercial circuit of capital. Circumstance and theory reinforced each other, blinding Guesdists to the might of commercial capital and the plight of its proletariat.

Despite this self-inflicted blindness, Guesdists occasionally admitted that commerce appropriated surplus value in its own right, thereby emancipating itself from capitalist industry and (potentially) acquiring a more central place in the Parti Ouvrier's political economy and social rhetoric. Paul Lafargue, for instance, described how wealthy merchants exploited the small entrepreneurs of the Lyonnais silk industry, the *canuts* of nineteenth-century revolutionary fame. Control of the *fabrique's* world-wide market by dynasties of silk traders had reduced ostensibly independent silk-manufacturers to a total dependency resembling that of true proletarians: Lyonnais artisans wove their wonderful fabrics on their own looms with their own labour and that of a few employees, but the profits accrued to commercial capitalists, mere intermediaries who none the less completely controlled the industry.[53] The relationship between self-employed small-scale entrepreneurs and merchant-capitalists, by these criteria, resembled the exploitative mutual dependency which tied wage-labourers to industrialists: exploitation proceeded apace, even without capitalist expropriation of the 'direct producers'.

Nor did the Parti Ouvrier totally ignore the exploitative relationship between commercial capitalists and their employees. Sales clerks, like mill hands, worked long hours for low wages under often dreadful conditions to enrich property-owners. But only exceptional circumstances diverted the Parti Ouvrier's attention from the factory floor to the sales counter. On one such occasion, Guesdists, outraged by the flood of public acclaim which accompanied the donation of the vast Boucicaut legacy, derived from the profits of the Bon Marché department store, to the employees of that enormous enterprise, inquired acidly how Madame Boucicaut had obtained her millions in the first place. Answering their own questions, they attributed her wealth to the exploitation of thousands of foot-sore sales-clerks, a few of whom would now receive back a tiny portion of their own product.[54] In other words, French Marxists, goaded by spectacular episodes such as the Boucicaut legacy, recognised that commercial employees, like industrial workers, contributed to the accumulation of capital.

The Parti Ouvrier, however, never elaborated or theorised these scattered insights. When they deigned to notice capitalist commerce, Guesdists stressed its expropriation of petit-bourgeois shopkeepers, not merchant capitalism's exploitation of independent producers and commercial employees. This one-eyed rhetorical focus explains the Guesdists' otherwise inexplicable complacency about the predations of merchant capital. Forgetting the dreary world of the shop assistant and the desperate plight of small producers caught in the webs of all-powerful wholesalers, Guesdists rejoiced at commerce's proletarianisation of the petite bourgeoisie, a guarantee of an ever-increasing working class, and welcomed the world of readily available cheap commodities promised by mass retailing. This latter response paralleled the unobtrusive birth of a novel proletarian mentality, a 'consumer mentality' which no longer associated capitalist commerce with grain speculation but with the glittering

[53] See, for instance, P. Lafargue, 'Notes Économiques', *L'Égalité*, 19 February 1882.
[54] J. Guesde, 'Les Libéralités Boucicaut', *Le Socialiste*, 17 December 1887.

emporia on the boulevards of every French city, glamorous worlds of discount prices and infinitely varied self-indulgence. The upper ranks of the working-class, following the petits bourgeois, already shopped in down-market versions of the Bon Marché, and dreamed of the riches available through mail-order catalogues. 'Commercial concentration, even in its present capitalist form', Guesdists admitted, 'has advantages for every consumer'.[55] Perhaps Printemps of Paris knew what it was doing when the great department store advertised in *Le Socialiste* . . .[56]

Only finance challenged the importance of industry in the Guesdist morphology of capital, although French Marxists most often relegated financiers to the same secondary and essentially parasitic place assigned to merchants: 'finance is not . . . a cause, but an effect', Guesdists usually concluded. 'Financial centralisation derives from industrial centralisation'.[57] By these protocols, finance was not only temporally secondary, but structurally derivative: 'the *haute-banque* exists only by stealing from the robbers of the working class'.[58] On occasion, however, the Parti Ouvrier elevated finance, in Guesde's words, to the ranks of 'master of the capitalist world'.[59] High finance, in this deviant interpretation, 'dominates production and exchange by draining capital from the small entrepreneur; agglomerates capitals and imperiously manipulates them; and presides over internal and external policy'.[60] 'Credit', according to *Le Socialiste*, was 'the living spirit of the social body'. It

attracted and centralised . . . all the nation's liquid capital; then distributes it throughout the realm wherever it's needed. The class which controls credit is the sovereign master of the country's property: no commercial, industrial or agricultural enterprise could live nowadays without credit. The credit system established and perfected by the bourgeoisie is the most powerful instrument ever invented for dominating the globe.[61]

[55] Anonymous, 'Les Grands Magasins', *Le Socialiste*, 4 February 1888.
[56] *Le Socialiste*, 28 May 1892 (almost certainly a quickly corrected error by the intensely conservative management of the enterprise).
[57] Report of a speech by Guesde, in Anonymous, 'Antisémites et Socialistes', *Le Socialiste*, 17 July 1892.
[58] A. Zévaès (quoting Guesde), 'M. Drumont et le Socialisme', *Le Socialiste*, 11 October 1893.
[59] J. Guesde, 'Pro Domo Sua', *Le Citoyen*, 9 April 1882.
[60] Deville, 'Aperçu sur le Socialisme Scientifique', pp. 15–16.
[61] Anonymous, 'Expropriation Économique de la Bourgeoisie', *Le Socialiste*, 12 September 1885.

Why did Guesdists occasionally abandon their fixation on factories for the ancient critique of usury, when they almost completely ignored merchant capital, like finance supposedly derivative from industry? Not because the POF enrolled more bank clerks than shop assistants: the black-coated proletariat of the financial districts, desperate for respectability and promotion, rejected socialist blandishments with horror. Nor did the Guesdists' discovery of 'interest slavery' represent a Parti Ouvrier perception of transition from 'industrial capitalism' to 'finance capitalism', that 'final stage' of the capitalist mode of production discerned by Marxists elsewhere in Europe.[62] Not for the Guesdists Hilferding's careful analyses of the banks' dominance over industry through interlocking director-ates, perhaps because the symbiosis of high finance and capital-intensive industry already characteristic of Imperial Germany at the turn of the century had as yet only begun to unfold in France.

Instead, the Guesdists' preoccupation with banking reflected their immediate political concerns. First, they stressed the depredations of finance not because of its role in the terminal stages of 'late' capitalism, but because of its contribution to 'primitive accumu-lation', because of its part in the destruction of the petite bourgeoisie, that formidable fortification against proletarian revolution. Finance, from this perspective, acted as

the revolutionary agent *par excellence*. It is [finance] which, by emptying the mattresses of the peasantry and rifling petit-bourgeois savings, alone can remove the barrier to communist progress constituted by the middle class which forms a shock-absorber between the proletariat and capital and thereby retards the liberating concussion. It is [finance] which, in incorpor-ating industrial property, reveals the uselessness of its owners, tied to production only by their dividend coupons ... It is [finance] which, by accumulating, by centralising ... the nation's wealth in fewer and fewer hands, will allow the easy 'nationalisation' of that wealth.[63]

Finance capital, tricked by the cunning of historical reason, under-mined the fortifications which defended its plutocratic commanders:

---

[62] A. Granou, *La Bourgeoisie Financière au Pouvoir et les Luttes de Classe en France* (Paris, 1977), pp. 13–22. For the rapid development of financial concentration during the period and its implications for the nation's class structure, see P. Sorlin, *La Société Française 1840–1914* (Paris, 1969), p. 143. The POF, despite its critique of finance, has been criticised for its failure to develop a more sophisticated understanding of the role of banking in French capitalism. Willard, *Les Guesdistes*, pp. 175–6.

[63] Anonymous, 'La Question Juive', *Le Socialiste*, 26 June 1892 – culled from Anonymous, 'Vive la Finance!', *Le Socialiste*, 26 June 1886.

bankers devoured petits bourgeois by the thousands, reducing
society to the stark opposition between parasitic beneficiaries of
bursting trust funds and destitute victims of an endless series of
Panama scandals. No wonder Guesdists, as interested in proletarianisation as in the proletariat, turned fascinated eyes from
industrialists' despotism to financiers' machinations.

Second, the broader French political culture, profoundly hostile
to 'usury' in general and large-scale capitalist banking in particular,
stimulated and reinforced the Guesdist assault upon finance.[64]
Increasingly dependent upon investment loans rather than retained
earnings for their expansion, industrialists detested their resultant
vulnerability to the Paris money market. Anxious to compete in
rapidly expanding commodity markets, merchants sank deeper and
deeper into a morass of commercial credit. Struggling to survive the
falling prices of the agricultural depression, landowners over-
borrowed to expand their overproduction. And, endlessly short of
liquidity, petits bourgeois endlessly dreaded bankruptcy at the
hands of their bankers. Even industrial workers, although insulated
by poverty from the credit system, succumbed to this wide-spread
hatred of bankers. An entrenched proletarian 'monetarist' mentality
explained unemployment, wage-reductions, and economic crises by
restriction of the money supply at the hands of all-powerful financiers, who thereby enhanced their own profits and power.[65] Everyone, from hard-pressed industrialists to penurious millhands, hated
bankers, those bloated descendants of the medieval usurer.

Guesdist exploitation of this hatred sometimes occasioned diatribes indistinguishable from those of 'National Socialists' such as
Maurice Barrès and Édouard Drumont, ideologues who fought to
unite France's affluent industrialists, aristocratic landowners, back-
woods peasants, petits bourgeois, and poverty-stricken workers
against their supposed common enemy: the cosmopolitan lords of
finance. Unwittingly providing grist for the national-socialist mill,

---

[64] For hostility towards finance during the *Belle Époque*, see G. Palmade, *Capitalisme et
Capitalistes Français au XIXe Siècle* (Paris, 1961), pp. 205–23; J. Bouvier, 'L'Extension des
Réseaux de Circulation de la Monnaie et de l'Épargne: Système Bancaire et Marchés
d'Argent', in *Histoire Économique et Sociale de la France: Tome IV – L'Ère Industrielle et la Société
d'Aujourd'hui (Siècle 1880–1980): Premier Volume – Ambiguïtés des Débuts et Croissance Effective
(Années 1880–1914)* (Paris, 1979), p. 162; and J. Bouvier, *Un Siècle de Banque Française* (Paris,
1973), pp. 14–21.

[65] M. Perrot, 'Comment les Ouvriers Parisiens Voyaient la Crise d'Après l'Enquête Parlementaire de 1884', in *Conjoncture Économique/Structures Sociales: Hommage à Ernest Labrousse* (Paris,
1974), p. 196.

Guesdists demonstrated that the prosperity of the financial oligarchy varied inversely with the health of the French economy, that the prosperity of bankers resulted from the penury of the French in general and the impoverishment of French industry in particular – a conclusion reached by comparing statistical series on bankruptcies, the discount rate, and dividend payments by the Bank of France.[66] Guesdists, entrapped by the cross-class logic of this argument, momentarily abandoned their advocacy of proletarian revolution to call for revolt against 'the lords of finance who treacherously conceal themselves within the Bank of France to pillage the nation and rob merchants and industrialists'.[67] This programme suggested a populist alternative to working-class socialism: the mobilisation of virtually everyone, from the poorest proletarian to the richest industrialist, against financiers, whom Lafargue denounced as 'despots dominating the law and robbing without pause or mercy all those with property'.[68] Guesdist adoption of this ancient rhetoric may have implied a more sophisticated theory of exploitation than did the more common Parti Ouvrier reduction of capitalism to industrialism. But these polemics also endorsed a class alliance between workers and 'healthy' (national?) industrialists, the people's friends, against 'parasitic' (Jewish?) finance, everyone's enemy. Barrès and Drumont would have enthusiastically approved; Marx and Engels would not have.

Finally, Guesdists might have conceived of rent and real estate as one buttress, and not the least, of France's formidable capitalist edifice. Urban land-speculation had enriched bourgeois for centuries, and real estate continued to prove a highly profitable investment during the *Belle Époque's* sustained campaign of 'urban improvement', particularly in Paris, with its new Métro and vast suburban expansion. The same speculative opportunities arose, however, upon the Guesdists' home ground: Roubaix's doubling of population during its boom years undoubtedly reflected and depended upon the prosperity of the textile industry, but this spectacular urban growth also greatly enriched bourgeois wealthy enough and sufficiently well-connected to exploit the accompanying

---

[66] Anonymous, 'Les Profits de la Banque', *Le Socialiste*, 12 September 1885.
[67] P. Lafargue, 'La Banque de France', *Le Socialiste*, 18 February 1891.
[68] P. Lafargue, 'Les Financiers', *Le Socialiste*, 31 October 1891.

astronomical escalation in the value of development land. At the same time, rent from the agglomerations of dismal working-class housing which sprang up in industrial faubourgs generated cash flows which sometimes eclipsed the profits of the associated factories. How did the Guesdists, determined to challenge all exploitation, depict the role of land speculators, developers, and landlords in the constitution of the French bourgeoisie?

In practice, the Parti Ouvrier virtually ignored 'real estate' and its beneficiaries. In an implicit rank order headed by industry and followed by finance and commerce, real estate trailed a distant fourth. Land speculation did receive sporadic attention from the Guesdists, albeit only *vis-à-vis* the periodic scandals surrounding Parisian 'development' (scandals which, to Marxist delight, sometimes implicated Possibilist municipal councillors). Diverted from their all-consuming campaign against capitalist industry by the irresistible temptation of corrupt 'reformists', Guesdists condemned developers' huge profits as the fruit of publicly-funded municipal growth and illicit political deals, not of productive enterprise.[69] Despite the connotations of this rhetoric, Guesdists explicitly repudiated 'Henry Georgeism': they never aspired to cure the ills of the bourgeois property system by amputating its diseased speculative member. Socialist revolutionaries, not petit-bourgeois advocates of 'single tax' panaceas, would soon sweep away land speculators, along with the corrupt municipal governments upon which they battened.[70] For Guesdists, land-ownership possessed none of the privileges conferred by land's absolute scarcity: real estate and its profiteers were a minor aspect of the bourgeois property system – hardly worth mentioning in their own right.

Repudiation of the classic distinction between property which resulted from enterprise and property (such as land) which gained its value from natural scarcity clearly depended upon the Parti Ouvrier's class bias: the distinction mattered most to property-owners, but hardly at all to propertyless proletarians. But why did Guesdists neglect rental income, the long-term payoff which justified

[69] For instance, P. Lafargue, 'La Dette Publique de Paris', *Le Socialiste*, 25 June 1887. There is a useful theoretical analysis of the Marxist engagement with landownership in Resnick and Wolff, *Knowledge and Class*, pp. 127–8.

[70] J. Guesde, 'Un à Compte', *L'Égalité*, 18 June 1882. The POF explicitly criticised George and his analyses. Anonymous, 'La Candidature de Henry George', *Le Socialiste*, 2 October 1886.

short-term speculation?[71] After all, payment of rent embittered the lives of virtually every French worker during the *Belle Époque*, and expensive yet grossly inadequate housing remained the bane of working-class existence and the surest sign of proletarian impoverishment long into the twentieth century, when nourishment and clothing no longer separated working-class poverty from petit-bourgeois comfort. Rent subordinated workers to capital accumulation as surely as did the wage-system, as Guesde himself had once recognised: 'by deploying the means of habitation which they monopolise to exploit their tenants ... landlords ... behave no differently from the industrialists and merchants who use and abuse the means of production and means of consumption which they monopolise to exploit workers and consumers'[72] – an invaluable insight, but an insight soon forgotten. Did Guesdists ignore Monsieur Vautour (the popular name for the landlord) the better to indict the boss? Did they obscure the conflict between landlords and tenants because they wished to highlight the clash between employers and employees, the 'real' locus of exploitation and class domination in the Parti Ouvrier's overly-simple conception of the bourgeois order? Or did the Parti Ouvrier's Marxist political economy so dominate its perception of society that the Party simply failed to notice the daily struggle between rent-collectors and proletarian families, a struggle which the least literate and least politically conscious worker perceived with cruel clarity? No other explanations account for this astonishing void in the Guesdist analysis of the bourgeoisie.

Marxists have not confined themselves to rhetorical exemplification of the capitalist ruling class or dissection of the bourgeoisie into its component fractions. They have indicted bourgeois domination of society for its exploitative crimes and predicted capitalism's inevitable transcendence: the question 'what is?' has always evoked

---

[71] Lafargue had a brief and not-to-be repeated enthusiasm for rent as an issue for socialist militancy in 1882. See, for instance, P. Lafargue, 'La Question des Loyers', *Le Citoyen*, 12 June 1882. There is a good discussion of this episode in W. Cohn, 'Paul Lafargue: Marxist Disciple and French Revolutionary Socialist', PhD thesis, University of Wisconsin, 1972, pp. 192–7. Apart from this instance, anarchists rather than socialists tended to preempt anti-landlord agitation. J. Kergoat, 'France', in M. van der Linden and J. Rojahn (eds.), *The Formation of Labour Movements 1870–1914: An International Perspective* (Leiden, 1990), vol. 1, p. 189.

[72] J. Guesde, 'Un à Compte', *L'Égalité*, 18 June 1882.

the question 'what is to be done?'[73] But why an indictment? Why transcendence? What aspects of the bourgeois order rendered capitalism intolerable? What contradictions within the capitalist mode of production doomed the bourgeoisie?

Marxists have proffered three alternative, although complementary, answers to these all-important questions. First, they have alleged that the bourgeoisie long ago forfeited the universality whereby

it fraternises and merges with society in general, becomes confused with it and is perceived and acknowledged as its *general representative* [Marx's stress]; a moment in which its demands and rights are truly the rights and demands of society itself; a moment in which it is truly the social head and the social heart. Only in the name of the general rights of society can a particular class lay claim to general domination.[74]

But bourgeois class interest and the general interest of society, which had corresponded during the struggle against the *ancien régime*, no longer coincided by Marx's day. Dominion by a 'non-universalistic' class such as the mid-nineteenth-century bourgeoisie engendered social irrationalities which both justified and facilitated revolution against its rule.[75] More concretely, the capitalist mode of production itself contained internal contradictions which condemned bourgeois society to eventual destruction. Underconsumption, the inevitable result of capital accumulation at one pole of society and the accumulation of misery at the other, climaxed in overproduction, crises and unnecessary suffering – the preconditions of revolution. And the bourgeois property regime, founded upon individual ownership of the means of production, clashed with the increasingly 'socialised' forces of production – the preconditions of a new social order. These contradictions condemned capitalists as socially malignant, economically parasitic, and historically doomed. According to Marx, bourgeois would inevitably follow aristocrats into the dustbin of history.

Guesdists, carried away by their passionate hatred of the French

---

73 For argument that this theme constitutes the heart of any Marxist understanding of society, see B. Harris, 'Alienation of the Capitalist Class: Towards a More Careful Reading of Marx', *Social Praxis*, vol. 7, 1980, pp. 77–90.

74 K. Marx, 'A Critique of Hegel's Philosophy of Law: Introduction', in K. Marx and F. Engels, *Collected Works* (London, 1975), vol. 3, p. 184.

75 This attack on capitalist irrationality is discussed and its limitations exposed in A. Gouldner, *The Dialectic of Ideology and Technology: Origin, Grammar, and Future of Ideology* (London, 1976), p. 51.

ruling class, occasionally denounced the bourgeoisie in ways which would have perturbed Marx himself. Marx, at least, had portrayed capitalists as historically progressive during their ascendancy, lauding youthful capitalism to the skies in famous passages in the *Communist Manifesto*. Guesdists, by contrast, sometimes argued that capitalism suffered by comparison with preceding modes of production, that the bourgeoisie was 'the most egotistical and limited class which has ever ruled France'.[76] Most often, however, Guesdists conceded, with Marx, that the bourgeoisie had once exemplified progress, albeit only during the feudal past and during the heroic age of bourgeois creativity. But this bourgeois golden age, according to French Marxists, no longer existed except as myth. The modern bourgeoisie ruled only by corruption, oppression and historical inertia. Like 'vampires'[77] ruling over terrorised villages from mouldering castles, bourgeois sustained their overlong reign by draining the vigour of the still vital proletariat. The Parti Ouvrier envisaged a future free from superannuated bourgeois parasites, contending that 'the present ... relationship between man and ... property [has] had [its] day and demand[s] renovation. Every institution which survives beyond its initially necessary role as an element of order becomes an element of disorder on the eve of its disappearance'.[78] A senile ruling class, an obvious 'element of disorder', poisoned the society over which it ruled: France suffered from 'the crimes of the bourgeoisie, which are all its acts, without exception';[79] 'capitalist property' was 'the sole cause of suffering and of all the material and moral disorders plaguing our species';[80] and, in the end, 'once [the bourgeoisie's] useful role has been completed, [and it] becomes oppressive and malignant, it must go'.[81]

Guesdists, like Marx himself, adduced an impressive ensemble of reasons why the bourgeoisie's 'useful role' had, by the late nineteenth century, exhausted itself. First, they denounced bourgeois for having subordinated 'general emancipation [to their] own

---

[76] P. Lafargue, 'La Journée Légale de Travail réduite à Huit Heures', *L'Égalité*, 12 March 1882.
[77] Geva, 'Échos de l'Atelier: Le Patron', *Le Socialiste*, 5 November 1887.
[78] J. Guesde, 'Formes Vieillies', *Le Cri du Peuple*, 18 November 1886.
[79] J. Guesde, 'La Liberté du Travail', *Le Socialiste*, 5 October 1890.
[80] J. Guesde, 'L'Expropriation Révolutionnaire à l'Hôtel de Ville', *Le Cri du Peuple*, 22 June 1884.
[81] J. Sarraute, 'Le Droit Historique', *Le Socialiste*, 9 June 1895.

emancipation',[82] as Guesde and Lafargue wrote with specific reference to 1789, thereby initiating a critique of the bourgeoisie's
historical role which unconsciously echoed that of the 'young Marx'.
The French bourgeoisie, according to the Parti Ouvrier, had signally
failed as a 'universal class'. Whatever its hegemonic pretensions, the
bourgeoisie no longer represented historical rationality and social
progress, as it had done during its long campaign against feudalism.
Instead, bourgeois – as they resisted the advance of labour, harbinger
of the future – embodied the same social irrationality and historical
reaction as had their erstwhile aristocratic enemies. French Marxists,
in elaborating this teleological theme, touched upon the 'ethical' and
'philosophical' critiques of bourgeois society which would eventually
beguile twentieth-century 'Western Marxists', although Guesdists,
unlike later 'humanist socialists', rarely abandoned 'economism' for
the empyrean realm of the human essence.

First, the Parti Ouvrier attacked the commodification of society,
denouncing capitalism's tendency to degrade every human activity,
from sexuality to artistic creativity, into a sordid cash transaction.
Carried away by polemical enthusiasm, Guesdists grossly exaggerated the extent to which 'everything is merchandise, everything
can be bought and sold: ideas as well as manual labour, love as well
as domestic service'.[83] They ignored the sectors of social activity
upon which the market had as yet to gain purchase, and remained
oblivious to the uncommodified domestic domain, that supposed
'haven in a heartless world'. French Marxists, despite (or because of)
their exaggerations, elaborated a potent critique of society's perversion by commodity exchange. At their most sophisticated, they even
rediscovered 'commodity fetishism', the fascinating, if mystifying,
theme of Part I of *Capital* which would later inform the development
of Marxist philosophy during the 1940s and 1950s. Guesdists,
without abandoning their critique of exploitation, described producers as having been 'enslaved by their own products',[84] products
which had seized phantom sovereignty over the (false) consciousness
of deluded workers and self-deluding bourgeois.

[82] P. Lafargue and J. Guesde, 'Essai Critique sur la Révolution Française du XVIIIᵉ Siècle',
Études Socialistes, March–April 1903, p. 68.
[83] P. Grados, 'Plaies Sociales', *Le Socialiste*, 20–7 November 1904. For a good critique of
Guesdist exaggeration of the commodification of French society, see W. Reddy, *The Rise of
Market Culture: The Textile Trade and French Society 1750–1900* (Cambridge, 1984), pp. 296–7
and pp. 323–5.
[84] G. Deville, *Principes Socialistes* (Paris, 1896), p. 28.

This capitalist commodification of the world, according to the POF, soiled every aspect of society: human relations, mediated by the market, became purely instrumental and impersonal; love itself walked the streets, debased to a mere monetary transaction; while the cash nexus, that poisonous solvent, dispersed communities and dissolved solidarities upon which men and women had depended for their emotional security and material sustenance since time immemorial.[85] Guesdists contended that love, friendship and mutual aid had evaporated under the baleful glare of commercial calculation and greed, while the profit motive, sole guide to production under capitalism, had corrupted every product, destroying craftsmanship along with craftsmen. The quality of life had fled, replaced by quantity, that bourgeois fetish. This theme, more in keeping with the conservative glamorisation of traditional *gemeinschaft* than with the Marxist dialectic of labour and property, harmonised badly with the Guesdists' *leitmotiv* of production and exploitation, but resonated so well with *fin-de-siècle* anxieties that the Parti Ouvrier regularly employed it in denouncing the capitalist present and predicting the socialist future. Capitalist decadence supposedly foreshadowed capitalism's demise: 'bourgeois dilettantes claim that [this decadence] is *fin-de-siècle:* for [Guesdists], however, it's the *fin de régime*'.[86]

According to the Parti Ouvrier, the bourgeois reduction of social relations to market relations, the essence of capitalist 'rationality', spawned social irrationality on a historically unprecedented scale. Capitalists and their proletarian dupes – 'individuals' constituted as isolated human commodities, functioning as mere units of 'human capital' – forgot the social bonds which defined their humanity and enabled them to pursue a humane existence. Lafargue, horrified by the inhuman logic of bourgeois society, bemoaned the way in which 'individuals consider themselves autonomous in capitalist society. They recognise only one law: that of their immediate personal interests; and, in order to satisfy those immediate personal interests, they enthusiastically sacrifice not only the general interest but even

---

[85] For an excellent example of the 'cash nexus' argument (although the term itself is not used), see the report of a speech by Guesde in 'Mouvement Social', *L'Égalité*, 9 July 1882.

[86] 'Dr Z', 'L'Enquête', *Le Socialiste*, 11 May 1891. The decline in product quality associated with capitalist commodity production is powerfully argued in P. Lafargue, 'La Production Capitaliste', *L'Égalité*, 5 November 1882. This critique must have had considerable appeal to the artisanal elements of the French working class, which detested the shoddiness of large-scale capitalist production. See L. Weissbach, 'Artisanal Responses to Artistic Decline: The Cabinetmakers of Paris in the Era of Industrialization', *Journal of Social History*, vol. 16, 1982, pp. 67–81.

their own long-term personal interests'.[87] For Guesdists, the 'contradiction between the public interest and private interest' inherent in capitalism 'suffice[d] in itself to condemn individual property in the means of production'.[88] Guesdists failed to recognise that their deployment of 'general interests, the higher and lasting interests of the national community and humanity'[89] against the class interest of the bourgeoisie violated the spirit, if not the letter, of their Marxist materialism.

The POF illustrated this argument with a horrifying array of contemporaneous social irrationalities, irrationalities which exemplified the malignant dominion of a decaying bourgeoisie while fortuitously subverting its rule. Guesdists, ever optimistic, held that 'a class loses its intelligence when it is declining. Its vices, mistakes and crimes then all help to precipitate its fall'.[90] Paradoxically, French Marxists contended that 'it's better for humanity that capitalists are burdened with moral and intellectual vices than it would be if they were graced with every virtue'.[91] Guesdists never seriously considered the terrifying possibility that the degenerate vices to which the bourgeoisie had become addicted might seduce others, that decadent bourgeois might consort with decadent proletarians, thereby banishing all hope of social redemption. Dismissing the imagery of universal corruption, the Parti Ouvrier attributed every social ill afflicting France to bourgeois degeneration alone. Guesdists even blamed actual medical 'ills' upon capitalist contagion: Paul Lafargue, doctor of medicine, pointed out that 'the appearance of syphilis in Europe coincided with the birth of the capitalist bourgeoisie, and since then the number and extent of man's illnesses has continued to increase'.[92] The Parti Ouvrier in particular blamed tuberculosis, that proletarian pestilence of the nineteenth century, upon capitalism – not without some justification, given the abominable sanitation, nutrition, and housing characteristic of France's working-class *faubourgs*. Guesdists painted a picture in which not only plague, famine and war, but death itself rode through the proletarian world as capital's avatar.

[87] P. Lafargue, 'La Journée Légale de Travail Réduite à Huit Heures', *L'Égalité*, 12 March 1882.
[88] J. Guesde, 'La Bourgeoisie et ses Avocats en Province', *L'Égalité*, 6 August 1882.
[89] Zévaès, interpellation of 1 December 1898, *Journal Officiel 1898*.
[90] *L'Almanach du Parti Ouvrier pour 1894* (Lille, undated), p. 45.
[91] P. Lafargue, 'Évolution de la Morale', *Le Socialiste*, 11 December 1886.
[92] P. Lafargue, 'Le Programme Municipal', *Le Socialiste*, 9 April 1892.

More seriously, Guesdists attributed 'all the afflictions' of the *Belle Époque* to 'the contradiction between the form of labour and the form of property'.[93] According to the Parti Ouvrier, prostitution, a large and successful industry during the *Fin de Siècle*, augmented its sordid dominion through bourgeois corruption of impoverished proletarian women; alcoholism, epidemic among workers by the end of the nineteenth century, stemmed from the miseries attendant upon proletarianisation (as well as from the unhealthy liquors peddled by bourgeois profiteers);[94] and crime, that dread obsession (and thrill) of bourgeois still terrorised (and fascinated) by *la classe dangereuse*, represented the final desperate expedient of capital's most brutalised victims. Summing up, *Le Socialiste* charged that 'capitalists produce, among other nice things, the prostitute, the alcoholic, and the street-child'.[95] This indictment, replicated in hundreds of articles based upon the same *faits divers* which titillated readers of the 'capitalist' press, reversed common bourgeois (and peasant and petit-bourgeois) prejudices about the working class: prostitution, drink, and crime arose from capitalist degeneracy, not from working-class irresponsibility. Immorality, alcoholism, and violence 'were not inherent in the working class, but in the capitalist form of production; they will not disappear until the capitalist form of production has been shattered'.[96] This reversal undoubtedly salved workers' injured pride and soothed their status anxieties, while simultaneously advancing a powerful case against the capitalist enemy, now culprit rather than prosecutor. Guesdists, sensing the needs of their audience, wrote many of their most potent and appealing, if least intellectually rigorous, polemics on this theme of proletarian innocence and bourgeois depravity.

Capitalist 'irrationality', according to the Parti Ouvrier, permeated the heights of French cultural and intellectual achievement

---

[93] J. Guesde, 'Réponse à un Démocrate-Chrétien', *Le Socialiste*, 14 August 1898.

[94] For alcoholism as a working-class issue, see B. Mitchell, *The Practical Revolutionaries: A New Interpretation of the French Anarchosyndicalists* (New York, 1987), pp. 81–5 and Kergoat, 'France', p. 165.

[95] Maussa, 'Réflexions', *Le Socialiste*, 11 August 1895.

[96] P. Lafargue, 'La Production Capitaliste', *L'Égalité*, 8 October 1882. Guesdists repeatedly attributed alcoholism, another proletarian plague like tuberculosis, to the miseries of capitalist exploitation. Guesdists remained hostile to the temperance movement, however, arguing that only the end of capitalism would solve the problem of alcohol abuse. Their hostility undoubtedly reflected the importance of *cabaretiers* among the POF's cadres, as well as general working-class attitudes. P. Prestwich, 'French Workers and the Temperance Movement', *International Review of Social History*, vol. 25, 1980, pp. 35–52.

as well as the sordid depths of the daily *faits divers*. Guesdists, themselves fanatical rationalists, detailed how the degenerate bourgeoisie, abandoning all pretence of rationality, patronised the revival of religious enthusiasm, the vogue for spiritualism and the occult, and the philosophical abandonment of scientific method which characterised the *Fin de Siècle*. This spiritual malaise, like epidemic social deviance, indicated bourgeois senescence: high-society decadence, embodied in the fashion for masses and black masses, constituted a bourgeois confession of historical incompetence, *prima facie* proof that sane Frenchmen and Frenchwomen would have to dethrone France's ruling class if they hoped to escape its irrational fancies. In the vivid, not to say fevered, words of an anonymous contributor to *Le Socialiste:* 'fetid miasmas hover over putrid cess-pits. In the same way, ideas and ethics derived from mental degeneration and moral rot appear in societies which are disaggregating and decomposing'.[97] The putrefying bourgeoisie would poison everyone unless buried in the graveyard of history by proletarian undertakers.

Two minor themes in this attack upon bourgeois irrationality sound surprisingly familiar to late twentieth-century ears. The Parti Ouvrier foreshadowed the modern consumer movement, denouncing dangerous goods, poor quality products, and planned obsolescence: 'commodity production, with its competition among retailers', Bracke asserted, 'leads inevitably to falsification'.[98] False labelling, false measures, and false promises pervaded the capitalist market, from Parisian department stores to village shops: 'commerce', according to Lafargue, could 'live only through lies. It lies when it buys, and lies when it sells; it always lies'.[99] Bad meat, contaminated canned goods, poisonous drink flooded from capitalist abattoirs, canneries, and distilleries: capitalism threatened to 'poison the entire species'.[100] As capitalism 'perfected its technology', it 'falsified and degraded its product'.[101] Socialism alone could restore integrity to production and distribution. What is more, a rudimentary 'Green Guesdism', once again foreshadowing the radicalism of the late twentieth century, contended that the bourgeoisie, driven by

[97] Anonymous, 'Signes de Gâtisme-Social', *Le Socialiste*, 21 November 1885. This particular article focused upon the popularity of spiritualism.
[98] Bracke, 'À Travers la Semaine', *Le Socialiste*, 12–19 April 1903.
[99] P. Lafargue, 'Propos Socialistes', *Le Socialiste*, 4 March 1891.
[100] 'B.', 'Rivalités Internationales', *Le Socialiste*, 2 September 1893.
[101] Anonymous, 'Le Congrès Catholique de Liège', *Le Socialiste*, 9 October 1886.

its insatiable desire for wealth, brutally ravished nature herself, an even more helpless victim than the working class. *Le Socialiste* reported that the number of bird species in Manchester had declined from 71 to 6 between 1850 and 1882, commenting that 'capitalism seems to have the mission not only of deforming man, but nature herself'.[102] As precocious eco-Marxists, Guesdists charged that 'capitalist civilisation corrupts and pollutes everything, air and water, no less than love'.[103] The socialist revolution alone would terminate capitalists' unthinking exploitation of nature, as well as ending their carefully considered exploitation of mankind. Alcoholism, criminality, prostitution, cultural and intellectual insanity, corruption of the human and the natural worlds – Guesdists, outraged by a decadent bourgeois society, predicted 'the end of a class in this infected swamp'.[104]

Despite the unquestionable potency of the Parti Ouvrier's denunciation of the social corruption and cultural degeneracy of capitalist rule, economic analysis furnished the Guesdists with their favourite ideological weaponry. Bourgeois depravity made good journalistic copy, but suggested no mechanism which necessarily propelled history from capitalism, however decadent, towards socialism, however virtuous: procurers, universally despised by self-respecting workers, provided Guesdist journalists with wonderful villains, but prostitutes, also thoroughly disdained by the 'respectable working class', could hardly be marshalled as revolutionary heroines. 'Working girls of the world, unite!' – a slogan which would have to await late twentieth-century Hamburg. Guesdists themselves scathingly criticised anti-Marxists who based their hostility towards bourgeois society upon ethical and philosophical foundations: impersonal economic processes, not personal failings, doomed the bourgeoisie to decline and dispossession; socialists would prevail, not because of their virtues, but because they represented the inevitable advent of a

---

[102] Anonymous, 'Le Capitalisme et les Oiseaux', *Le Socialiste*, 31 July 1886.
[103] P. Lafargue, 'Le Programme Municipal', *Le Socialiste*, 9 April 1892. In their anti-Malthusian mode, however, Guesdists were anything but 'green', suggesting that population could never outstrip resources because 'the production of meat and vegetables is that much more abundant the more industrialised the district; the waste products of the primary materials become fertiliser for the earth and nutrients for the animals'. P. Lafargue, 'La Production Capitaliste', *Le Socialiste*, 24 September 1882.
[104] 'H. G.', 'La Peur dans les Petites Chambres', *Le Socialiste*, 13 January 1895.

mode of production already inherent in both the triumphs and the catastrophes of capitalism.

The great strength of the Marxist comprehension of capitalism has stemmed not so much from its demonstration of the unprecedented social malignancy of the bourgeoisie, but from revelation of the economic contradictions which undermined bourgeois rule and prediction of the 'inevitable' crises which would facilitate proletarian revolution.[105] As Lafargue articulated this thesis,

economic phenomena [are]the terrible revolutionaries which undermine every . . . routine and all the secular foundations of society. We communists of the school of Marx and Engels, we are only the spokesmen of these economic phenomena. If, like seabirds predicting a storm, we announce the tempest which will obliterate ruling class privileges, it is not we who have raised it.[106]

This economic meteorology in place of social moralising sharply distinguished Guesdists from their competitors within the French political culture. Denunciations of the inhuman cash nexus and its iniquitous consequences characterised virtually every critic of French society, from the most reactionary Legitimist to the most revolutionary anarchist. French Marxists, however, not content with moral outrage, distinguished themselves from their radical and conservative enemies by the conviction that internal economic contradictions sapped the strength of the capitalist mode of production, economic contradictions which would inevitably find their resolution in socialist revolution.

The Parti Ouvrier derived an 'underconsumptionist' creed from its Marxist 'crisis theory', to the virtual exclusion of Marx's more sophisticated (and less accessible) theses on the 'falling rate of profit' – further proof of the Guesdists' blank indifference to value theory. Guesdists contended that the capitalist mode of production doomed itself because capitalists, however humane and benevolent as individuals, could not raise the incomes of the producers who laboured for them in proportion to increases in production, despite (or because

---

[105] For the importance of crisis theory in the Marxist critique of the bourgeoisie, see E. Wright, 'Historical Transformations of Capitalist Crisis Tendencies', in E. Wright, *Class, Crisis and the State* (London, 1978), pp. 111–80; D. Yaffe, 'The Marxian Theory of Crisis, Capital and the State', *Economy and Society*, vol. 2, 1973, pp. 186–232; R. Jacoby, 'The Politics of Crisis Theory', *Telos*, no. 23, 1975, pp. 3–52; and P. Bell, 'Marxist Theory, Class Struggle and the Crisis of Capitalism', in J. Schwartz (ed.), *The Subtle Anatomy of Capitalism* (Santa Monica, 1977), pp. 170–94.
[106] P. Lafargue, *Le Communisme et l'Évolution Économique* (Lille, 1892), p. 25.

of) the vast increase in labour productivity achieved by capitalism's ever-accelerating transformation of the forces of production. Production of goods expanded exponentially, while their consumption expanded not at all, or even contracted as capitalists pursued the extraction of absolute surplus value, thereby reducing workers to unprecedented poverty. Even the most sophisticated forms of capitalist exploitation, those based upon the extraction of relative surplus value, presupposed a more rapid growth in productivity than in workers' remuneration. By its very success as a mode of exploitation, capitalism condemned its workers to impoverishment and itself to ever-deepening crises of overproduction.

This underconsumptionist political economy, ironically, armed the Parti Ouvrier with yet another moral critique of bourgeois rule. Glaring contrasts between the rapidly accumulating wealth of the *fin-de-siècle* bourgeoisie and the immemorial poverty of its proletarian victims illustrated hundreds of Guesdist pamphlets and articles, sometimes literally in mordant cartoons. Aware that individual tragedies struck home with more force than abstract collective suffering, Parti Ouvrier journalists specialised in anecdotal accounts of proletarian misery juxtaposed with bourgeois affluence: they contrasted starving vagrants with pet dogs fattened upon gourmet food, denounced incidents in which unemployed workers assaulted police to gain the food and shelter of gaol, and bemoaned the fate of girls forced into prostitution by destitution and the wiles of enterprising procurers – a never-ending litany of unnecessary proletarian poverty amid unlimited bourgeois plenty.[107] French Marxists, however, transcended this time-honoured but essentially banal rhetoric of injustice, which had hardly altered since Old Testament jeremiads. 'Scientific' as well as righteous, Guesdists detailed the mechanisms of 'overproduction' and 'underconsumption' inherent in the capitalist economy and delineated the cyclical crises and ever-deepening depressions characteristic of the bourgeois era – collective expression of millions of individual working-class tragedies; faults which not only damned capitalism as inhuman and inhumane, but as inefficient and self-destructive; failings which augured capitalism's inevitable transcendence. Economic crises, Guesdists knew,

---

[107] Anonymous, 'Chiens Chics', *Le Socialiste*, 31 July 1886 for bourgeois dogs; Anonymous, 'Les Beautés de la Civilisation Capitaliste', *Le Socialiste*, 3 June 1891 for gaol as refuge from poverty; and Anonymous, 'Récompense', *Le Socialiste*, 19 February 1887, among many others, for prostitution.

'furnish[ed] communists with their supreme argument against capitalist society, an argument without a reply, an argument against which the bourgeoisie can do no more than file silently towards the common grave where transcended classes lie buried'.[108] The capitalist mode of production would give way to socialism not because of its injustice, but because of its self-destructive internal logic.

Guesdists maintained that 'underconsumption', which derived from the inadequacy of 'the working masses' consumption power',[109] had characterised the bourgeois order from its inception. In this respect, capitalism, according to French Marxists, suffered by comparison with preceding modes of production; 'feudalism', Lafargue noted, 'had maintained an interest in the well-being of its serfs, [while] the bourgeoisie, by contrast, has an interest in increasing the workers' misery to obtain cheaper labour'.[110] Subject to unrelenting competitive pressure from other capitalists, every individual capitalist strove to reduce his wage bill to the absolute minimum, with the unintended but inevitable consequences of general underconsumption, recurrent crisis, and endemic misery: the individual strategies pursued by bourgeois ensured the collective bankruptcy of the bourgeoisie. For Guesdists, this contradiction, a self-destructive dialectic inherent in the capitalist mode of production, confirmed

our conclusions about the impossibility of capitalism containing its developing industrial forces, and about the inevitability of an approaching rupture of the system. It foreshadows the end of a world which has only been able to create extreme misery among the producers with its superabundance of production, a world the order of which is now and will increasingly be . . . permanent disorder.[111]

An anarchy of unbridled competition, vast expansion of the forces of production, general impoverishment of workers – no wonder capitalism lurched from crisis to crisis, condemned as 'a social order so absurd that it can't utilise all its producers or consume all its products'.[112]

Guesdists never supported this thesis with rigorous economic analysis: they lacked both the necessary skills and the inclination to

[108] 'E. F.' (Fortin), 'La Dernière Marche Funèbre', *Le Socialiste*, 10 April 1886.
[109] J. Guesde, 'Qu'ils Rient', *Le Cri du Peuple*, 1 February 1885.
[110] P. Lafargue, 'La Propriété Bourgeoise', *Le Socialiste*, 29 October 1887.
[111] J. Guesde, 'Fin du Monde', *Le Cri du Peuple*, 3 April 1886.
[112] J. Guesde, 'Faites vos Malles!', *Le Socialiste*, 3 September 1887.

undertake such an enterprise. But their underconsumptionist political economy sometimes evolved the rudiments of a Guesdist 'Keynesianism', an interpretation of economic crises founded upon indictment of 'insufficient demand' and implying reformist strategies of 'demand management'. In the hands of the Parti Ouvrier, however, even 'Keynesianism' served revolutionary purposes. When 'bourgeois' reformers advocated working-class savings programmes (the credit unions, pension funds, and illness and unemployment insurance schemes dear to 'mutualists') as sovereign remedies for proletarian poverty, the POF responded that, if workers saved at the expense of consumption, their circumstances would worsen, in both the short and long terms. In the short term, the financial bourgeoisie would ruthlessly appropriate proletarian savings (given the nature of the credit system), thereby immediately deepening the relative, if not absolute, poverty of the working class. In the longer term, working-class thrift would accentuate the characteristic capitalist disproportion between production and consumption, a disproportion which would soon disrupt production, eventually sink the economy into ever deepening depressions, and throughout intensify working-class misery.[113] Worse yet, proletarian savings, invested by financiers, would end as new capital equipment 'introduced into factories to the detriment of the workers, who will be forced out'.[114] Proletarian 'accumulation', according to these arguments, could not salve the wounds inflicted upon workers by capitalist accumulation. Instead, working-class thrift could only intensify the crises and misery inherent in bourgeois economics.

Guesdists deployed the same quasi-Keynesian 'underconsumptionist' schema against employers' perennial plea for 'wage restraint'. According to the French Marxists, higher incomes for workers, far from darkening the business climate, would ensure abundance for all. If unrestrained by avaricious employers, workers' demand might come to match workers' production – a recipe for general prosperity. 'Wage restraint', by contrast, spelled general depression. Potentially, the POF had discovered the political economy of twentieth-century social democracy, with its commitment to working-class prosperity *within* capitalism: underconsumptionist

[113] J. Guesde, 'La Bourgeoisie et ses Avocats en Province', *L'Égalité*, 6 August 1882.
[114] J. Guesde, 'Encore l'Épargne', *Le Salariat*, 24 November 1889, cited in Y. Marec, 'Le Socialisme et l'Épargne: Réactions de Jules Guesde', *Revue d'Économie Sociale*, no. 5, 1985, p. 47.

economics led away from socialist revolution towards the welfare
state, redistributive taxation, and 'business' unionism – all supposed
guarantees of both working-class well-being and capitalist wealth.
Guesdists, however, rarely abandoned revolutionary socialism for
reformist social democracy. French Marxists assumed that capitalists
would not, indeed could not, redistribute wealth to their workers,
even to save themselves from economic bankruptcy, social crisis, and
socialist revolution. The competitive nature of capitalism, the 'anarchic state of modern production',[115] forestalled bourgeois from
attaining any long-term view of their own ultimate interests. A few
farsighted capitalists might discern their dilemma, but the individualist pattern of accumulation which ruled their mode of production
forced even the most prescient capitalist into business practices
which impoverished his workers and which, when generalised
throughout the economy, detonated ever more explosive underconsumptionist crises, thereby ensuring the eventual self-destruction of
capitalism.

Nor, according to Guesdists, would international trade or imperial expansion save the bourgeoisie from this underconsumptionist
logic: foreign markets could not compensate for the structural
inadequacy of domestic demand. The Parti Ouvrier buttressed its
faith in underconsumption crises with a rudimentary 'Leninist'
interpretation of the world market. As every capitalist economy
sought to resolve its internal contradictions by exporting excess
production, the international market became as competitive as the
domestic, forcing capitalist states to resolve this expanded pattern of
contradiction with the protectionist policies of the late nineteenth
century – the economic logic behind the self-destructive trade wars
and escalating international tensions of the *Fin de Siècle*.[116] The
capitalist imperative to compete for every market, whether domestic
or global, guaranteed ever more intense crises, both global and
domestic.

According to the Guesdists' economics, no solution short of
socialism would resolve the contradictions of capitalism. Overproduction and underconsumption arose inevitably from the relationship between capitalists and workers, the relationship
between capitalists, and the relationship between capitalist economies. Crises flared at every level of the capitalist mode of production,

[115] J. Guesde, 'Qu'ils Rient', *Le Cri du Peuple*, 1 February 1885.
[116] See, for example, C. Bonnier, 'Catastrophe', *Le Socialiste*, 17 June 1900.

precipitating increasingly calamitous bankruptcies, depressions, and trade wars. According to *Le Socialiste*,

the bourgeoisie is condemned, by the logic of its own development, to augment industrial power and to increase productive potential to its highest level of development. Production today is beyond control and without limit. But the absorptive power of the market cannot correspond to this production without bounds or reason. This creates the economic crises which have occurred repeatedly since the beginning of the century, and which today have a tendency to become permanent.[117]

Capitalist exploitation, according to the Parti Ouvrier, elicited its own retribution.

In retrospect, Guesdist crisis theory appears thoroughly wrong-headed. Economically untrained and overly influenced by ideological *partis pris*, the French Marxists never fully recognised that entrepreneurial profits, although undoubtedly dependent upon limitation of proletarian consumption, not only sustained bourgeois gluttony, but underwrote investment – a self-inflicted blindness with two major consequences for the Guesdists' (mis)understanding of capitalist economics. First, the Parti Ouvrier, clinging to its conviction that bourgeois rapacity necessarily issued in stagnation and crisis, refused to admit that the chain of successful exploitation, higher profits, and expanded investment underwrote economic growth, the Guesdists' own primary measure of historical 'progress'. How could French Marxists concede that capitalist accumulation, under favourable circumstances, not only enriched bourgeois, but created the possibility (which, admittedly, eventuated only through class conflict) of higher wages and better conditions for the workers whom capitalists exploited? How could Guesdists admit that, in this limited sense, capitalists' interests and the general interest indeed coincided?[118] The Parti Ouvrier's astonishing neglect of investment, its *a priori* assimilation of profits to bourgeois consumption, arose from self-interested ideological limitations as well as from untutored economic obtuseness.

Second, Guesdists failed to recognise that capitalists' profits, once

[117] Anonymous, untitled, *Le Socialiste*, 6 February 1886.

[118] A. Przeworski, 'Material Bases of Consent', in A. Przeworski, *Capitalism and Social Democracy* (Cambridge, 1985), p. 139. Eugène Motte, during his campaign against Guesde, argued that industrialists would not invest in a socialist Roubaix, a powerful argument. D. Gordon, 'Liberalism and Socialism in the Nord: Eugène Motte and Republican Politics in Roubaix 1898–1912', *French History*, vol. 3, 1989, p. 328.

invested, generated their own pattern of demand. French Marxists assumed that working-class consumption provided the (inadequate) outlet for working-class production, apart from the luxury market servicing bourgeois, humanly incapable of consuming the surplus (the difference between working-class production and consumption) extorted by capitalist exploitation. Guesdists conveniently forgot that the surplus could be invested as well as consumed. The market for investment goods, in the 'real world' of imperfect entrepreneurial knowledge, may not have necessarily compensated for shortfalls in the market for consumption goods, but neither did the two markets together inevitably fall short of production. Far from lapsing into endemic recession, the French economy actually 'overheated' during the first decade of the twentieth century, years when booming investment and strong consumer demand exceeded supply, producing shortages and inflation rather than overproduction and depression. Say's Law, that Panglossian denial of contradiction and crisis, did not rule the economy of the *Belle Époque*: given levels of production did not inevitably create perfectly equivalent markets; the bourgeois utopia of economic harmonies remained just that – a utopia. But neither did the simplistic underconsumptionist logic of Guesdist political economy prevail within a crisis-wracked capitalist France: no mechanism ensured that production automatically exceeded demand; economics refused to play its role as *deus ex machina* in the Marxist revolutionary drama.

Apart from its theoretical inadequacy, the thesis that French capitalism had exhausted its potential and sunk into permanent crisis, the explicit conclusion of the Guesdists' *a priori* economics, lacked empirical credibility after the recession of the 1880s.[119] The 'Great Depression' which had so traumatised Europe after 1873 and France after 1882, far from marking the exhaustion of the capitalist mode of production (as Guesdists fondly imagined), unleashed the wave of technological and organisational innovation, economic growth, and unprecedented profits which made the *Belle Époque* so *belle* – for the bourgeoisie. Demolishing stereotypes about her 'economic retardation', France emerged as one of the most economically dynamic capitalist economies of the period: only her demographic

---

[119] J. Bouvier, 'Les Crises Économiques: Problématiques des Crises Économiques au XIXe Siècle et Analyses Historiques – Le Cas de France', in J. Le Goff and P. Nora (eds.), *Faire de l'Histoire* (Paris, 1974), vol. 2, p. 47.

stagnation supported the illusion that she lagged behind her continental rivals.[120] French capitalism emergèd from the stagnant markets and deflation of the 1880s immeasurably strengthened, and the French enjoyed sustained commercial expansion throughout the 1890s and into the twentieth century, decades of prosperity which rendered the Parti Ouvrier's crisis theory increasingly unsustainable. Rapid industrial growth, astonishing technological innovation in the vital new industries of the second industrial revolution, minimal industrial unemployment, booming profits, rapidly expanding domestic markets and burgeoning foreign trade – French society may have suffered crises, but it was not a society in crisis.[121]

Why, then, did Guesdists cling to their theoretically inadequate and empirically untenable conception of capitalist crisis? Quite simply, its polemical potency compensated for its deficiencies as economics and its shortcomings as a model of the French economy. Uninterested in academic economics and econometric 'realities', Guesdists discovered a rationale for revolution in the contradictory dynamic of capital accumulation. Ignoring all evidence to the contrary, Marxists confidently affirmed that 'each industrial crisis poses the following challenge: the bourgeoisie, master of all society's wealth, is incapable of administering it – it must be expropriated, and it will be'.[122] Evidence could always be unearthed to validate this burning conviction: superficial fluctuations of the Paris Bourse, defaults by distant Latin American states, or the bankruptcies of prominent financiers all foreshadowed 'the final crisis of capitalism' – in the Guesdist imagination. Commenting, for instance, on the stock market speculation associated with the Panama Canal company, *Le Socialiste* concluded that

it recalls the gigantic debacle of Law and his system, which contributed more than a little to the revolution of 89–93. Every end of a regime is marked by and precipitated by crashes of that nature and of that proportion. The Panama Company . . . will be our Mississippi Bank. It will

---

[120] M. Lévy-Leboyer, 'Le Processus d'Industrialisation: Le Cas d'Angleterre et de la France', *Revue Historique*, vol. 239, 1968, pp. 281–98. The buoyancy of the rate of profit was a particularly telling indication of the capitalist prosperity characteristic of the *Belle Époque*. See J. Bouvier et al., *Le Mouvement du Profit en France au XIXe Siècle: Matériaux* (Paris, 1965), pp. 273–4.

[121] A. Daumard, 'L'Évolution des Structures Sociales en France à l'Époque de l'Industrialisation 1815–1914', *Revue Historique*, vol. 274, 1972, p. 346.

[122] Anonymous, 'Expropriation Économique de la Bourgeoisie', *Le Socialiste*, 12 September 1885.

mortally wound the capitalist order and open, through its ruins, the road to the workers' revolution.[123]

The crash, when it came, certainly facilitated the Guesdist election victories of 1893, but it no more mortally wounded French capitalism than had any of the preceding panics.

French Marxists, perhaps unconsciously aware of their own vulnerability, reacted with fury to socialist 'revisionists' (they employed the term with explicit reference to Bernstein and his French apologists) who believed that capitalist economies might evolve indefinitely without catastrophic crises, a belief which, for the Parti Ouvrier, suggested 'that socialism was losing its purpose in the face of growing prosperity'.[124] Apparently convinced that bourgeois prosperity precluded the transition to socialism, Guesdists flatly refused to imagine the possibility, much less accept the reality, of an economically stable and permanently dynamic capitalist order. In clinging to their underconsumptionist economics, Guesdists equated capitalism with crisis, and crisis with socialist revolution. Marc Delcluze, Parti Ouvrier leader in Calais, summed up his movement's convictions in one lapidary formula: 'crises come, and with them and by them comes socialism'.[125]

Yet Guesdist crisis theory suffered from two major liabilities, even as political rhetoric, liabilities which undoubtedly inclined the Parti Ouvrier to seek alternative theories of capitalist transcendence. First, the Marxist appetite for capitalist crises ('socialism was losing its purpose in the face of growing prosperity') clearly implied a lack of confidence in working-class militancy. Guesdists, after all, might have (indeed, often had) decided that the capitalist mode of production, whether crisis-ridden and impoverished or stable and prosperous, necessarily evoked a socialist response from its workers. In this alternative conception of the relationship between capitalists and their employees, the proletariat needed no extra stimulus from cyclical unemployment and periodic suffering to challenge the

---

[123] Anonymous, 'Ça Mord', *Le Socialiste*, 31 July 1886. Willard comments on this feature of Guesdist discourse (*Les Guesdistes*, p. 30), but contrasts it with the 'real' Marxism of Marx and Engels, who nevertheless were as much given to allowing their hopes to dominate their reason as were the Guesdists.

[124] C. Bonnier, 'Crise et Chômage', *Le Socialiste*, 16–23 February 1902.

[125] M. Delcluze, 'Le Parti Ouvrier en France: Calais', *Le Socialiste*, 21 September 1890. Indeed, Guesdists, applying economic determinism to their own history, attributed the birth of the POF to workers' responses to the acute economic crisis of 1882. Deville, 'Aperçu sur le Socialisme Scientifique', p. 15.

exploitation inherent in bourgeois economics: capitalism, however buoyant, however stable, inevitably alienated its working-class victims. Implicitly far more pessimistic, crisis theory challenged this inevitability: its first principle postulated that routine, and particularly routine growth, however exploitative, however repressive, reinforced the capitalist mode of production; that crises, stagnation, and economic decline alone disrupted bourgeois hegemony over the working class.[126] French Marxists, if confronted by this implication made explicit, would have rejected it out of hand. At the most fundamental level of the Guesdist creed, crisis theory was both unnecessary and disturbing.

Second, crisis theory disregarded the ways in which the depressions which have repeatedly discredited capitalism have simultaneously 'depressed' labour militancy: during economic crises, workers compete with each other for scarce work, employers thankfully lay off 'trouble makers', and day-to-day survival assumes precedence over aspirations to a better world. The revolutionary potential of the working class has weakened during the cyclical depressions which have discredited bourgeois management of the economy, while labour's industrial organisation and political power have climaxed during the booms which have legitimised and consolidated capitalism: the trade cycle and the political cycle, capitalist crisis and labour militancy, have seldom coincided to socialist advantage; unemployment, insecurity, and misery have occasionally given workers compelling motives for revolution, but rarely the opportunity.[127] Quite apart from its theoretical flaws and empirical inadequacy, the Guesdists' crisis theory suffered from crippling political defects.

No doubt reflecting (and reinforcing) the anxieties of workers traumatised by memories of past depression or terrified of crashes to come, Guesdists refused to abandon their crisis theory, despite its

---

[126] B. Moore, *Injustice: The Social Basis of Obedience and Revolt* (New York, 1978), p. 365. For a rigorous argument that workers have no interest in attacking capitalism while it still has potential for development, see A. Przeworski, 'Material Interest, Class Compromise, and the Transition to Socialism', *Politics and Society*, vol. 10, 1980, pp. 125–53.

[127] P. Stearns, *Lives of Labor: Work in a Maturing Industrial Society* (London, 1975), pp. 104–105. There are good descriptions of how the economic cycle fuelled workers' grievances just when they could not express them safely in M. Hanagan, *The Logic of Solidarity: Artisans and Industrial Workers in Three French Towns* (London, 1980), pp. 152–3 and E. Accampo, *Industrialization, Family Life, and Class Relations: Saint Chamond 1815–1914* (Berkeley, 1989), p. 199.

theoretical contradictions, empirical inadequacy, and political ambiguities. Nevertheless, the Parti Ouvrier formulated an alternative and considerably more plausible delineation of the bourgeoisie's transient place in modern society, a prediction founded upon a rudimentary analysis of 'monopoly capitalism'. This analysis, although never elaborated with the sophistication and rigour of its more famous Central European exponents, none the less brilliantly highlighted the role of corporations, trusts, and monopolies in the transition from nineteenth-century entrepreneurial to twentieth-century managerial capitalism, a radically new version of the capitalist mode of production with all-important, if as yet ambiguous, social and political consequences.

These observations, in themselves, were banal. Virtually everyone who examined the French polity and economy at the turn of the century agreed that free-enterprise individualism belonged to the past, that the twentieth century would be characterised by corporate economics, although observers disagreed over the import of the novel forms of capital which had developed during the 'second industrial revolution': conservatives, reinvigorated by the decline of *laissez-faire* liberalism, denounced the corrupting hegemony of (semitic) finance capitalism, or welcomed the felicitous coincidence of corporations and corporatism; liberals, uneasily awaiting the end of 'the bourgeois century', bemoaned the decline in economic individualism, or praised the diffusion of property inherent in the limited liability company; while radicals, determined to seize the twentieth century for democracy, raged against the new robber barons, or cheered the replacement of parasitic property ownership by meritocratic 'management'. Why did Guesdists, in the midst of this cacophony, conclude that the new economic order foretold capitalism's 'catastrophic end'?[128]

French Marxists elaborated two theses which connected the novel developments in property-ownership with the 'inevitable' transition to a socialist mode of production. First, Guesdists, developing a theme already implicit in their general conception of class conflict, asserted that 'organised capitalism' (as Hilferding would name the new economic order) generalised and intensified the class war: workers who struck against their local employer often laboured under the illusion that their grievances arose from individual

---

[128] P. Lafargue, 'Trust et Socialisme', *Le Socialiste*, 6–13 December 1903.

iniquity, rather than from the logic of capital; workers who rebelled against the nation-wide or world-wide tyranny of a great monopoly would suffer no such delusion – for them, capitalists in the particular would equal capital in general. 'While rival enterprises give rise to partial labour conflicts localised in this or that region', discovered a delighted Paul Grados, 'trusts . . . generate conflicts of interest on an incomparably greater scale.'[129] The accelerating organisation of capital accelerated the organisation of labour against capital.

Second, the new capitalism, paradoxically, functioned without 'capitalists'. Early industrial capitalism, the system dissected by Marx, had combined capital accumulation with direction of production: factory owners had also worked as factory managers, and, as such, had presided over the all-important revolution in the forces of production so treasured by Marxists. But 'organised capitalism', monopolistic rather than individualistic, stripped bourgeois of their entrepreneurial role by separating the ownership of capital from the management of production. Once profit-taking had freed itself from profit-making, bourgeois property-owners degenerated into dependent parasites, functionless in their own mode of production (Guesdists never discovered the 'investment function', once again confusing capitalist profits with bourgeois consumption). According to Lafargue,

the stock owner doesn't have the slightest contact with production. He can completely ignore where it takes place, and even its nature . . . The joint-stock limited liability company severs the last connections between proprietor and property, and depersonalises the latter . . . [These companies] demonstrate . . . the complete uselessness of the capitalist proprietor and illuminate the parasitic character of the capitalist class. It's no longer the owners but the non-owners who are useful in capitalist production. Social revolution will relieve production of these parasites.[130]

Lafargue reiterated this thesis in *Le Socialiste*, in pamphlets, and in his major economic works (*La Fonction Économique de la Bourse* and *Les Trusts Americains*), and other Guesdists echoed his conclusions: this 'redundancy theory' of the bourgeoisie permeated Parti Ouvrier discourse.

The Party assumed, in its authoritative *Programme*, that 'the individual form of property' which had engendered capitalism 'was being eliminated by [the] industrial progress' in turn engendered by

---

[129] 'P. G.' (Paul Grados), 'La Semaine', *Le Socialiste*, 21–8 July 1901.
[130] P. Lafargue, 'La Propriété Capitaliste', *Le Socialiste*, 7–14 June 1903.

that capitalism.[131] The bourgeoisie, a parasitic residue, decayed into the corruption once characteristic of 'the Romans of the imperial decadence',[132] and, like the useless but pampered senatorial aristo-crats of the later Empire, their decay poisoned their society. 'The capitalist class has become superfluous', asserted Guesde, 'and, as a consequence, it [has become] noxious'.[133] Reaching back into France's socialist past, Guesdists enthusiastically recycled Saint-Simon's famous parable of the uselessness of 'les oisifs' by comparison with the indispensability of the 'classe productive': if France awoke one morning to discover the bourgeoisie gone, France would be the healthier for the discovery; by contrast, the disappearance of the proletariat would precipitate immediate social catastrophe.[134] As homely parable or as sophisticated theory, this thesis depended upon three assumptions: that capitalists no longer served a useful function in the capitalist mode of production; that bourgeois, as a conse-quence, burdened rather than enriched society; and that progress would sweep the bourgeoisie into the dustbin of history, as preceding parasitic classes had been dispossessed and discarded. These assump-tions suffered from theoretical and empirical inadequacies, but their combination undoubtedly appealed to the French working class, elements of which had long reviled the bourgeoisie as 'vampire-capital'[135] bleeding workers of their product. Sensitive to the ideo-logical sensitivities of their constituency, eager to support the antipathies of their supporters, Guesdists denounced capitalist vampirism in their every depiction of the French economy and polity.

Yet problems plagued this 'redundancy theory' of the bourgeoisie. First, it implied that employers who managed their own enterprises (as most did at the turn of the century, despite Guesdist rhetoric) functioned as productive workers in their managerial role, as well as preying upon (other!) workers as exploitative property-owners.[136]

---

[131] Guesde and Lafargue, *Le Programme du Parti Ouvrier*, pp. 31–32.
[132] J. Guesde, 'La Bourgeoisie Désarmée', *Le Cri du Peuple*, 20 March 1884.
[133] J. Guesde, *Le Collectivisme* (Lille, 1891), p. 12.
[134] See, for example, Anonymous, 'La Grève des Riches', *Le Socialiste*, 3 July 1886.
[135] J. Guesde, 'Un Mabouliste', *Le Socialiste*, 27 January 1894. For workers' use of this image, see M. Perrot, 'Le Regard de l'Autre: Les Patrons Français vus par les Ouvriers (1880–1914)', in *Le Patronat de la Seconde Industrialisation* (Paris, 1979), pp. 298–9 and M. Perrot, 'On the Formation of the French Working Class', in I. Katznelson and A. Zolberg (eds.), *Working Class Formation: Nineteenth-Century Patterns in Western Europe and the United States* (Princeton, 1986), p. 100.
[136] For class-collaborationist use of the equation of capitalist 'workers' with workers in general, see Lebovicz, *The Alliance of Iron and Wheat*, p. 66. See the interesting theoretical analysis of this issue in B. Hindess and P. Hirst, *Modes of Production and Social Formation: An Auto-Critique of Pre-Capitalist Modes of Production* (London, 1977), pp. 67–72.

Unwilling to concede the slightest positive attribute to the hated bourgeoisie, the Parti Ouvrier refused to draw this conclusion. At the most, Guesdists, searching for the sources of proletarian 'false consciousness', admitted that 'a fair number of workers still believe in the utility [of employers]'.[137] This belief, which so convincingly legitimised the bourgeois economic order, undoubtedly explains Guesdist exaggeration of the 'managerial revolution' in French enterprise: French Marxists expected that working-class respect for employers would evaporate once workers realised that capitalists had lost their 'managerial and administrative qualities', qualities which they had delegated to 'directors, managers, and foremen'.[138] Proletarians, victims of painstakingly inculcated 'false consciousness', had been misled by a tendentious amalgamation of petits bourgeois, who by definition melded labour and property-ownership, with parasitic bourgeois, alien to both manual and managerial labour (although Guesdists, no friends of the petite bourgeoisie, maintained that even the artisanal employer 'hardly supervises his workshop any longer'[139]). Bourgeois propagandists cynically presented capitalists as 'travailleurs spéciales' contributing indispensable organisational skills to the productive process, when bourgeois property owners no longer functioned 'even as producers of guano – since the invention of artificial fertilizers'.[140]

This imagery required considerable creative imagination on the part of its intended recipients, who had to picture capitalists as the animated money-bags of Guesdist cartoons, rather than as the hardworking, if hard-driving, employers who managed the scattered workshops and small factories which employed the vast majority of French proletarians. Yet this dissociation between ideological imagery and everyday experience succeeded – where Guesdism succeeded. Many workers, even while respecting their own 'patron', came to detest the noxious class to which he belonged: a signal victory for Marxist ideology over bourgeois hegemony. The Guesdist indictment of the bourgeoisie as parasitic rather than productive triumphed where proletarians equated capitalists with the despised habitués of Parisian café society; it failed dismally where workers

---

[137] Geva, 'Échos de l'Atelier: Le Patron', *Le Socialiste*, 5 November 1887.

[138] P. Lafargue, 'La Propriété Capitaliste', *Le Socialiste*, 7–14 June 1903.

[139] Geva, 'Échos de l'Atelier: Le Patron', *Le Socialiste*, 5 November 1887.

[140] J. Guesde, 'L'Exécution de Waldeck', *Le Cri du Peuple*, 22 January 1885. The Guesdists enjoyed this image of the capitalist as good only for what Lafargue called 'intestinal labour'. P. Lafargue, 'Justice et Injustice de l'Échange Capitaliste', *L'Égalité*, 9 April 1882.

viewed capitalists as hard-working wealth creators. No wonder Guesdist cartoonists so often dressed their bourgeois money-bags in formal evening clothes, the accoutrements of decadent parasitic luxury.

The new structures of enterprise erected yet another obstacle to the Marxist assault upon the bourgeoisie: the supposed 'democratisation' of capital through extension of share-ownership to modest citizens who, previously, would never have dreamed of participating in capitalist entrepreneurship.[141] Responding to the Marxist analysis of 'monopoly capitalism', anti-socialists contended that the new economics, far from concentrating property in fewer and fewer hands, actually generalised ownership of the means of production: France, under the beneficent economic regime of the limited-liability company, was evolving into a 'stock-owning democracy' – every Frenchman, potentially, could purchase his share in corporate capitalism.[142] Share-ownership indeed expanded during the *Belle Époque*, the number of shareowners growing from 700,000 in 1870 to more than two million in 1913.[143] Extrapolating this curve, the day would come when everyone owned a personal portfolio – no more workers and capitalists, but a universal property-owning middle class.

Undaunted by this bourgeois fantasy, the Parti Ouvrier confidently refuted predictions of a 'people's capitalism'. Small investors in joint-stock companies, Guesdists argued, far from participating in capitalist accumulation, fell victim to a ruthless confidence-trick perpetrated by monopoly capitalists: the plutocrats who owned controlling interests in corporations and trusts mobilised, managed, and eventually appropriated the painfully acquired patrimonies of the petite bourgeoisie. 'Whether the bourgeoisie owns the totality or only a part of the shares of industrial and commercial enterprises', Guesdists asserted, 'they alone direct and administer them'.[144] 'The diffusion of stock', according to Lafargue, '[was] the most powerful instrument imaginable for concentrating capital in fewer and fewer

---

[141] The importance of this issue to Marxists is emphasised and analysed in M. De Vroey, 'The Separation of Ownership and Control in Large Corporations', *Review of Radical Political Economics*, vol. 7, 1975, pp. 1–10. The legal minimum for share prices in France was reduced from 500 francs to 100 for large companies and from 100 to 25 for small in 1893, expressly to encourage share-ownership.

[142] This propaganda is described in P. Sorlin, *Waldeck-Rousseau* (Paris, 1966), p. 375.

[143] Sorlin, *La Société Française*, p. 145.

[144] Anonymous, 'Expropriation Économique de la Bourgeoisie', *Le Socialiste*, 12 September 1885.

hands'.[145] Plutocracy rather than democracy would characterise twentieth-century capitalism. This debate between socialists and anti-socialists dragged on without resolution, an outcome to be expected, given the ambiguities associated with the new patterns of capital ownership. On the one hand, 'monopoly capitalism' undoubtedly did allow hundreds of thousands of *rentiers* to share in the profits generated by novel entrepreneurial forms – a phenomenon which indeed considerably extended the privileges of bourgeois property ownership. But, on the other hand, corporate capitalism undoubtedly did concentrate control of this wealth in the hands of a tiny plutocratic elite of French 'robber barons', and small investors' savings indeed fattened the bank accounts of bourgeois speculators during the Third Republic's innumerable financial scandals.[146] The transformation of French capitalism's organisational forms, a vastly complicated process, supplied ammunition for both socialists determined to discover creeping economic oligarchy and anti-socialists resolved to reconcile democracy with bourgeois property-ownership.

The transformation of the French bourgeoisie, its transition from the individualism of its early entrepreneurial phase to the managerialism of 'organised capitalism', was virtually complete by the early twentieth century – according to the Guesdists. In one of the Parti Ouvrier's most characteristic interpretations of the *fin-de-siècle* economy, monopoly had already superseded the market, managers had already replaced entrepreneurs, and corporations had already supplanted family firms. Yet the vast majority of French businesses at the turn of the century were still owner-operated and subject to intensely competitive markets. Far from declining, entrepreneurship, the organic connection between profit-making and profit-taking, arguably increased its role in the French economy during the *Belle Époque*, as economic boom and the proliferation of 'sunrise' industries opened unprecedented opportunities for businesspeople.[147] Guesdists, however, ignored the buoyant entrepreneurship of their times, entrepreneurship as characteristic of Grenoble's

---

[145] P. Lafargue, 'Trust et Socialisme', *Le Socialiste*, 6–13 December 1903.

[146] R. Pernoud, *Histoire de la Bourgeoisie en France: Les Temps Modernes* (Paris, 1962), vol. 2, pp. 575–9 and Bouvier, 'L'Extension des Réseaux de Circulation de la Monnaie et de l'Épargne', pp. 196–7.

[147] According to L. Cahen, 'La Concentration des Établissements en France de 1896 à 1936', *Études et Conjonctures: Série Rouge – Économie Française*, no. 9, 1954, pp. 846–7. But see the evidence to the contrary in J. Bouvier et al., *Le Mouvement du Profit*, pp. 271–2. For the weakness of 'big business' in France during the *Belle Époque*, see M. Lévy-Leboyer, 'The Large Corporation in Modern France', in A. Chandler and H. Daems (eds.), *Managerial*

'high-tech' electro-technical industries as of Roubaix's 'old-fashioned' textile mills. Enchanted with bourgeois redundancy as the key to socialist revolution, entranced by the assumption that 'socialised' production led inexorably towards socialised property, French Marxists proclaimed the final victory of monopoly over the market as early as 1883 – at least half a century before the tentative inauguration of a fully-fledged 'organised capitalism' in France.[148]

Guesdists, characteristically, undertook few explorations of monopoly power in particular industries, and presented no instances of managerial control over particular corporations, although developments in some sectors of the French economy, such as the steel industry, would have validated their depiction of the concentration and centralisation of capital.[149] The Guesdist imagery of capitalism continued to draw upon the grim factories of the northern textile industry – still family-owned, still entrepreneurial, and still market-oriented, exemplary legacies of the first industrial revolution – rather than the titanic blast furnaces erected in Lorraine by the organisationally innovative steel industry – an industry which indeed depended upon corporate forms to raise its colossal capital requirements, hired France's first great manager-industrialists, and relied upon national or even international cartelisation to protect its mammoth investments from the insecurities of 'unbridled competition'.[150] The Guesdists' inappropriate imagery may have reflected the POF's weak representation among the workers of the second industrialisation: the Parti Ouvrier recruited few of Lorraine's steel workers. Guesdists, however, ignored the peculiarities of steel-making Longwy or high-tech Grenoble not so much because few Guesdists worked in those cities' novel industries (the POF dominated Grenoblois socialism), but because French Marxists assumed that no peculiarities existed. Governed by their treasured economic 'science' and encouraged by their political presuppositions, Guesdists sincerely believed that monopoly capitalism ruled Roubaix as well as Longwy, a belief which underpinned the

Hierarchies: Comparative Perspectives on the Rise of the Modern Industrial Enterprise (London, 1980), pp. 117–60.

[148] G. Deville, 'Aperçu sur le Socialisme Scientifique', p. 15.

[149] H. Morsel, 'Le Patronat Alpin Français et la Seconde Révolution Industrielle 1869–1939', in M. Lévy-Leboyer (ed.), *Le Patronat de la Seconde Industrialisation* (Paris, 1979), pp. 201–8 and H. Morsel, 'Contribution à l'Histoire des Ententes Industrielles', *Revue d'Histoire Économique et Sociale*, vol. 54, 1976, pp. 118–20.

[150] For the continuing entrepreneurial dominance of *fin-de-siècle* Roubaix, see Marty, *Chanter pour Survivre*, p. 252.

conviction, fundamental to Guesdist socialism, that Roubaisian workers could soon, would soon, dispense forever with Eugène Motte and his ilk.

Close reading of the Guesdists' portrayal of 'monopoly capitalism' reveals its dependence upon *a priori* theory and prejudged polemical strategies. According to Marxist political economy, the capitalist mode of production naturally concentrated and depersonalised capital: 'free' competition inevitably ended in monopoly, as successful capitalists devoured their less successful competitors, the scale of production inevitably escalated in proportion to this concentration of capital, and large-scale production inevitably divorced capital-ownership from management. Capitalist success reduced the need for successful capitalists. Polemical imperatives reinforced these *a priori* theoretical presuppositions. As recruiting sergeants for the class war, Guesdists *wanted* to reach these conclusions, *needed* to believe that capitalists no longer played any productive role within capitalism. A perception that capitalists functioned as both exploitative capital-accumulators and productive managerial workers (a perception inherent in Marx's own discussion of the capitalist's role) would have fatally confused the POF's class warriors. It could not be accepted: 'capitalist', in the Guesdist lexicon, remained synonymous with 'parasite', never with 'entrepreneur', and emphatically not with 'managerial worker'.

Quite apart from the empirical and theoretical flaws in their portrayal of monopoly capitalism, Guesdists misconstrued the political implications of the nascent twentieth-century productive order. The Parti Ouvrier, ever optimistic, had predicted that fat, parasitic, coupon-clipping bourgeois would prove easy prey for socialists, that the managerial revolution augured the socialist revolution, and that corporations, cartels, and monopolies foreshadowed a post-capitalist mode of production. Developments have frustrated these great expectations: 'monopoly capitalists' have proven to be far more formidable foes of socialism than the nineteenth-century competitive variety analysed by Marx. Why? How did 'organised capitalism' presage a new lease on life for the bourgeoisie, rather than its demise? What had the Guesdists overlooked? First, the separation of management and ownership – the separation which, for Guesdists, destined bourgeois for redundancy and dispossession – instead insulated capital from its enemies by focusing proletarian hostilities upon managerial and bureaucratic authority, evident daily on the factory floor and in working-class communities, rather than upon bourgeois exploitation and ostentation, increasingly divorced from the sites of production and remote from the everyday life of the proletariat.[151] Eugène Motte, embodied symbol of bourgeois hegemony, had ruled his workers directly; by contrast, his corporate descendants preside over the pathetic remnants of the Roubaisian textile industry from anonymous Parisian or international head-quarters – symbols of nothing, apart from the abstract omnipotence of late twentieth-century capital.

Second, Guesdists themselves recognised that monopoly capital-ism reduced, if it did not altogether eliminate, the 'anarchy of production' upon which Marxists had counted for revolutionary crises: the vast new corporations planned production in ways unimaginable for traditional family firms, cartels and trusts organ-ised markets to ensure economic stability and corporate profita-bility, while 'monopoly capitalism' aspired to direct entire econo-mies and societies. The all-powerful 'visible hand' of the technocratic manager replaced the failing 'invisible hand' of the competitive market. These novel forms of capital, Guesdists admitted, endowed bourgeois society with an indispensable 'element of order' because of their capacity to 'dominate the market, fix prices, allocate orders, limit and organise production'.[152] At their most apprehensive, French Marxists suffered nightmares in which capitalists, by organ-ising society as they had once organised individual factories, escaped altogether from the 'anarchy of production', from economic crises, and (eventually) from any conceivable challenge to their rule. Guesdists, however, stifled their apprehensions and clung to their determinist faith that the socialised productive organisation of advanced capitalism guaranteed transition to socialised property relations.

Despite its failings, the Guesdist critique of the bourgeois ruling class served French socialists well: it indicted capitalism for every ill or crime afflicting French society, demonstrated that bourgeois rule produced self-destructive economic crises as surely as capitalism produced commodities, and proved that the internal logic of capital

---

[151] See the interesting discussions of this disjuncture in R. Aminzade, *Class, Politics and Early Industrial Capitalism: A Study of Mid-Nineteenth Century Toulouse, France* (Albany, 1981), pp. 271–2 and Perrot, *Les Ouvriers en Grève*, vol. 2, pp. 673–4.

[152] A point made in the 'Resolution on the Role of Trade Unions' during the *Quinzième Congrès National du Parti Ouvrier Français tenu à Paris du 10 au 13 Juillet 1897* (Lille, 1897).

rendered the bourgeoisie economically redundant, socially noxious, and politically vulnerable. Conceptual ambiguities and contradictions riddled this indictment, and its empirical credibility was highly questionable. All the same, Guesdists, in exploiting its many-sided potential, spoke to the anxieties and hostilities of French workers, who welcomed a bourgeois scapegoat for their afflictions, dreaded the onset of economic crises and dreamed of a socialist solution to their recurrence, while fearing the depredations of an all-powerful but parasitic 'vampire-capital'. Under these circumstances, the sociological inadequacy of the Guesdist denunciation of the bourgeoisie actually enhanced its potency as revolutionary ideology.

CHAPTER 10

Shopkeepers and artisans: the Guesdists and the petite bourgeoisie

> Each time that scientific socialists encounter shopkeepers and
> small industrialists, each time that they can demonstrate to
> them, as they know all too well, that they are being obliterated
> by large-scale commerce and industry, these bourgeois come to
> understand that the socialists are the only people defending
> their interests, even when they demand the expropriation of
> capitalists and the socialisation of the means of production.
>
> J. Guesde, 'Fureur Impuissante', *Le Socialiste*, 2 October 1886.

The bourgeoisie may have reigned over the Third Republic, but
bourgeois hardly predominated in French society, where they
constituted, by any definition, only a tiny minority of the population. Nor did the working class incorporate the majority of Frenchmen and Frenchwomen, despite the Parti Ouvrier's assiduously
fostered illusion of universal proletarianisation. Most of the *fin-de-
siècle* French retained an affiliation, however tenuous, with independent enterprise and small-scale property-ownership: a massive petite
bourgeoisie of shopkeepers and self-employed artisans in the towns
and a yet more massive small-holding peasantry in the countryside
dominated France, in number, if not in economic power. At their
most schematic and dogmatic, French Marxists sometimes ignored
these petits bourgeois and peasants altogether, a feat of perceptual
legerdemain accomplished only by withdrawal from the social
reality accepted by most of the Guesdists' contemporaries. More
often, however, the Parti Ouvrier wrestled resolutely with the
dilemma posed for socialists by small property-ownership, a dilemma whose solution was crucial to the successful deployment of
Guesdist polemic.

Analysis of Guesdist perception of non-proletarians must discrimi-
nate between the issues raised, respectively, by petits bourgeois,
peasants, and white-collar employees. The petite bourgeoisie – an

'intermediate class sharing the proletariat's labour and the capitalist's property',[1] as the Guesdists conceived it – constituted a distinctive, although hardly uniform, class in its own right. The great variety of shopkeepers and independent artisans in France, however much they differed in their particular enterprises, shared a common economic identity, common values, and, increasingly, common politics. Grocers who prepared their own foodstuffs (the rule during the nineteenth century) resembled artisans, and cobblers who sold shoes (as many self-employed artisans sold their products directly to the market) resembled shopkeepers: grocers and cobblers both participated in small-scale commodity production and exchange, both worked to fructify their own small property, both shared a common fear of 'proletarianisation', and both, during the *Fin de Siècle*, were tempted by the paranoid politics of middle-class defence.

Landowning peasants, on the other hand, who resembled shopkeepers and artisans by combining property with labour in their own distinctive 'mode of production', may not be equated with the petite bourgeoisie of the towns. The rural and urban societies of France, despite their intricate interconnection, not only retained their separate identities throughout the *Belle Époque*, but engaged in a long-drawn-out and pitiless contest over the distribution of wealth and power between city and countryside. In the light of this systemic conflict, peasants, by definition and by self-perception, were not *bourge*ois of any kind, petit or otherwise. They, and other country people, require their own analysis. For similar reasons, amalgamation of independent property-owners and salaried 'white-collar' employees into a vast and amorphous 'middle class', a conceptual strategy as common in twentieth-century sociology as in Third Republic polemic, obscures crucial social relations in *fin-de-siècle* France and implies problematical political conclusions.[2] The 'new middle class' ('new working class'?) of white-collar workers, a complex historical subject in its own right, demands separate consideration.

The Parti Ouvrier, when the movement escaped from its fantasies of general proletarianisation, devoted considerable attention to the

[1] Anonymous, 'La Petite Bourgeoisie', *Le Socialiste*, 9 October 1886.
[2] For a critique of this amalgamation, see F. Bechhofer and B. Elliott, 'Petty Property: The Survival of the Moral Economy', in F. Bechhofer and B. Elliott (eds.), *The Petite Bourgeoisie: Comparative Studies of the Uneasy Stratum* (New York, 1981), pp. 182–200.

petite bourgeoisie. After all, that class held a central place in the logic of property and labour which structured the Guesdist world-view: between a propertied non-labouring class (the bourgeoisie) and a propertyless labouring class (the proletariat), the Marxist paradigm of social hierarchy allowed, even demanded, a propertied labouring class (the petite bourgeoisie). Experience reinforced theory: family ties and neighbourhood solidarity bonded propertied petits bourgeois to propertyless proletarians, despite the evident conflicts of interest which opposed workers to small businesspeople. Working-class aspirations reinforced these bonds: skilled workers dreamed of owning their own workshops, while millions of proletarians aspired to the independence, however precarious, conferred by the proprietorship of a corner grocery store or bistro, those traditional sanctuaries against the insecurity and dependency of wage-labour. Both Marxist theory and working-class mentalities mandated Guesdist preoccupation with the petite bourgeoisie, however much the Parti Ouvrier would have preferred to conceive of France as divided exclusively into capitalists and proletarians.

Petits bourgeois, whose shops and workshops lined the streets of every French town and city, far outnumbered the bourgeoisie and eclipsed the working class itself in all except the most industrialised urban centres. Their consequent political weight ensured them a pivotal place in Guesdist ideology: Marxist militants could not ignore their petit-bourgeois neighbours, whose votes swung elections and whose weight, some day, might prove decisive in the ultimate confrontation between labour and capital. Whether as obstacle to be overcome or as ally to be courted, the petite bourgeoisie, in its millions, stood astride the road to the socialist transformation of society. How did the Guesdists address this 'middle class' of small businesspeople, a class characterised by its combination of labour and property, the labour and property whose *separation* otherwise governed the Marxists' analytic of bourgeois society?

First, the predominant social mentalities of the late nineteenth century, still permeated by a 'gradational' perception of class, posed a formidable barrier to the infiltration of Marxist ideology. At one extreme, this schema united petit *bourgeois* and bourgeois, 'the thin and the fat of the same possessing class',[3] in one immense entre-preneurial mass, an extreme reduction occasionally reached by

---

[3] Anonymous, 'La Petite Bourgeoisie', *Le Socialiste*, 9 October 1886, although this reference stressed their impending divorce.

Guesdists themselves, but usually rejected as 'a confusion which must be dispelled'.[4] Less radically, gradational protocols assigned most capitalists to the *petite* bourgeoisie because, compared to 'real' capitalists, they owned little capital and employed few workers. At the other social extreme, the 'respectable' working class, although it owned no capital and employed no one, acceded to the petite bourgeoisie by virtue of its 'life-style'.[5] These notions of the petite bourgeoisie expanded its scope to include virtually everyone except the dependent poor and ultra-capitalist plutocrats, a conception of the French social order which ensured that both the working class and the haute bourgeoisie lost the prominence and historical destiny accorded them by Marxist ideologues.

This gradational delineation of the petite bourgeoisie, so widely accepted within the French political culture, threatened to marginalise or obliterate the Parti Ouvrier itself. Campaigning against the socialist threat, Radicals challenged the priority awarded to the working class by Marxist ideology, and maintained that 'we are all middle-class now', that small employers, peasants, shop-keepers, artisans, and most workers constituted a single vast 'class' united by common cultural values, common political interests, and a common standard of living remote from both plutocracy's corruption and poverty's degradation.[6] Only thus could the neo-Jacobins mobilise the broad 'middle-class' coalition which underpinned their campaigns against both the ruling oligarchy and the nascent labour movement. Only thus could Radicals fabricate the democratic politics which they now wielded as effectively against bourgeois liberals and proletarian socialists as against their traditional reactionary foes.

Guesdists detested this conception of a virtually all-inclusive middle class: they insisted upon separate identities for the diverse social categories – small employers, petits bourgeois, and workers – which had been amalgamated by anti-socialist populists into the 'couches moyennes' who, although meek enough in the oligarchic

[4] C. Brunellière, 'Bourgeoisie ou Ploutocratie', *Le Socialiste*, 14 May 1899.

[5] These conceptual problems are theorised in W. Wesolowski, *Classes, Strata and Power* (London, 1979), p. 14 and S. Ossowski, *Class Structure in the Social Consciousness* (London, 1963), p. 76. The ambiguities of the term 'petite bourgeoisie' in the French context are discussed in J. Dubois, *Le Vocabulaire Politique et Social en France de 1869 à 1872* (Paris, 1969), pp. 14–15.

[6] For discussion of this ideological tactic, see S. Berstein and A. Prost, 'Radicalisme et Couches Moyennes', *Cahiers d'Histoire de l'Institut de Recherches Marxistes*, no. 35, 1980, pp. 85–6.

present, were to inherit the earth. By Marxist criteria, the proletariat, not the middle class, swallowed up society, and the working
class, not the petite bourgeoisie, would rule the future. Édouard
Fortin, translator of Marx and one of Guesde's most faithful
lieutenants, argued that 'even if the petit-bourgeois ideal ... could
be realised ... and all wage-earners were to become thoroughly
middle-class, this would still imply a superior class. Thus the social
question arising from the existence of classes, one exploiting the
other, would continue to exist unchanged ...'[7] These rhetorical
games conducted during the *Belle Époque* on petit-bourgeois playing-
fields involved high stakes: the ultimate victory of 'bourgeois democracy' or proletarian socialism.

Other aspects of the petite bourgeoisie challenged Guesdist perceptions of the capitalist present and socialist future, even without
the anti-socialist amalgamation of petits bourgeois and skilled
workers into an all-inclusive 'middle class'. First, petits bourgeois not
only resisted recruitment by socialists, but reacted angrily to the
Guesdist campaign against the property system, thereby furnishing
the bourgeoisie with a mass base for its anti-socialist politics.
Shopkeepers and master artisans, not bankers and industrialists,
sustained the anti-collectivist counter-offensive launched during the
1890s. Second, petits bourgeois' ambiguous status as both property-
owners and workers blurred popular perception of the antagonism
between capital and labour, thereby muting the class conflict which,
for Guesdists, ensured the socialist revolution. French Marxists
regularly described the petite bourgeoisie as a shock absorber
intruded between capital and labour. Finally, small businesspeople,
by escaping the supposedly inexorable laws of capital concentration,
baffled the Marxist social analytic which otherwise so brilliantly
illuminated the vexed relationship between capitalist property and
wage labour, thereby refuting (for anti-socialists) Marxism's pretensions to constitute a general science of society.[8] The political
economy of bakeries repelled the theoretical and polemical arma-
ments forged for assaults against factories.

Just as the petite bourgeoisie's place in society challenged Marxist
assumptions, so its historical significance placed the class at the
centre of the Guesdists' theoretical preoccupations: its evolution

[7] É. Fortin, 'La Grande Industrie', *Le Devenir Social*, 1896, pp. 704–5.
[8] This issue is stressed in A. Przeworski et al., 'The Evolution of the Class Structure of France 1901–1968', *Economic Development and Cultural Change*, vol. 28, 1980, pp. 725–52.

from the undifferentiated urban 'people' of pre-capitalist society had coincided, as a correlative, with the emergence of the modern working class.[9] Where would its evolution take the petite bourgeoisie? Did it face extinction as the last remnant of a pre-capitalist mode of production, its myriad shopkeepers and artisans scurrying helplessly before the leviathan predators of capitalism? Did petits bourgeois constitute an integral and permanent aspect of capitalism, with small businesses proliferating under the aegis of big business? Or did the self-employed entrepreneur prefigure a post-capitalist society of universal independence, competition, and individualism, with the enterprise and agility of the petite bourgeoisie prevailing triumphantly against big business' inherent dis-economies of scale and wage labour's inherent dependency and sloth?[10]

No Marxist has ever defended this final projection of the middle-class historical trajectory, a fantasy of free-enterprise utopians. But Marxist ideologists have subscribed, sometimes simultaneously, to both alternative theses, although the Guesdists themselves neglected Marx's insight that the advance of capitalism's big battalions presupposed the support of petit-bourgeois skirmishers.[11] Guesdists favoured the alternative thesis in which the petite bourgeoisie, a remnant of pre-capitalist petty commodity production, would vanish from society, ground out of existence beneath the tread of capital. French Marxists confidently relied upon 'the axiom in which the transformation and disappearance of small property [under capitalism] is inevitable'.[12]

Yet the petite bourgeoisie refused its role as an endangered species: petits bourgeois, in their millions, continued to dominate most towns, apart from unrepresentative hyper-industrial centres such as Roubaix, and, in France as a whole, continued to eclipse the

---

[9] M. Rebérioux, 'Les Socialistes Français et le Petit Commerce au Tournant du Siècle', *Mouvement Social*, no. 114, 1981, p. 58.

[10] F. Bechhofer and B. Elliott, 'Persistence and Change: The Petite Bourgeoisie in Industrial Society', *European Journal of Sociology*, vol. 17, 1976, p. 77. For these ambiguities in a French context, see L. Portis, *Les Classes Sociales en France: Un Débat Inachevé (1789–1989)* (Paris, 1988), pp. 105–8.

[11] For Marxism's overall approach, see R. Scase, 'The Petty Bourgeoisie and Modern Capitalism', in A. Giddens and G. MacKenzie (eds.), *Social Class and the Division of Labour: Essays in Honour of Ilya Neustadt* (Cambridge, 1982), pp. 148–61. Marx's argument that the petite bourgeoisie remained integral to even advanced capitalism may be found in *Capital* (Moscow, 1954), vol. 1, p. 586, and see the discussion in J. Tomlinson, 'Socialist Politics and "Small Business"', *Politics and Power* (Henley, 1980), pp. 165–9.

[12] C. Bonnier, 'La Question Agricole', *Le Socialiste*, 29 January 1899.

industrial working class.[13] Worse yet, from a Marxist perspective, the absolute size of the petite bourgeoisie and (by some estimates) its relative share of the population actually increased during the *Belle Époque:* the number of small businesses, a primary measure of the vitality of the propertied middle class, grew at roughly twice the rate of population growth between 1881 and 1910.[14] These enterprises increased from 1,750,000 in 1866–69 to 2,138,000 in 1900, while 'patrons' (admittedly defined far too broadly by the census authorities) expanded their share of the economically active population from 40·5 per cent in 1876 to 42·2 per cent in 1911.[15] The nineteenth century has been characterised as the 'golden age of the shopkeeper', a period during which France experienced a six-fold increase in the number of café-owners, a four-fold increase in grocers, a three-fold increase of butchers, and a doubling of the number of bakers and innkeepers – hardly evidence for the death of the petite bourgeoisie.[16] Charles Gide, one of the period's most eminent economists, calculated only half facetiously that, if late nineteeth-century trends continued for 200 years, every Frenchman and Frenchwoman would keep shop by the end of the twenty-first century![17]

Apart from their number, the grievances and aspirations of small property-owners heavily influenced French politics during the pre-war Third Republic, as they had done since the revolutionary exploits of the sans-culottes, or perhaps since the seizure of Paris by the sixteenth-century Catholic League. Every 'bourgeois' political party in France, from the extreme nationalist Right to the democratic Radicals, claimed to represent the virtuous small businessperson. In consequence, the petite bourgeoisie, by the turn of the century, enjoyed unprecedented influence in the councils of the

[13] A. Daumard, 'L'Évolution des Structures Sociales en France à l'Époque de l'Industrialisation (1815–1914)', *Revue Historique*, vol. 247, 1972, p. 344.

[14] A. Daumard, 'Puissance et Inquiétudes de la Société Bourgeoise', in *Histoire Économique et Sociale de la France: Tome IV – L'Ère Industrielle et la Société d'Aujourd'hui (Siècle 1880–1980): Premier Volume – Ambiguïtés des Débuts et Croissance Effective (Années 1880–1914)* (Paris, 1979), p. 403.

[15] The absolute number of businesses is from the *Annuaire Statistique de la France: Resumé Retrospectif* (Paris, 1951), p. 468, cited in L. Cahen, 'La Concentration des Établissements en France de 1896 à 1936', *Études et Conjonctures: Série Rouge – Économie Française*, no. 9, 1954, pp. 846–7. For the proportion of patrons, see G. Dupeux, *La Société Française 1789–1970* (Paris, 1972), p. 155.

[16] H.-G. Haupt, 'The Petite Bourgeoisie in France 1850–1914: In Search of the *Juste Milieu?*', in G. Crossick and H.-G. Haupt (eds.), *Shopkeepers and Master Artisans in Nineteenth-Century Europe* (London, 1984), p. 98.

[17] Cited without exact attribution in R. Pernoud, *Histoire de la Bourgeoisie en France: Les Temps Modernes* (Paris, 1962), p. 584.

nation: France, not Britain, had become the archetypical 'nation of shopkeepers'. The Guesdists' conviction that the petite bourgeoisie had been reduced to a 'non-historical' class, impotent in the present and doomed in the future, seemed absurd or at least grossly overstated to virtually everyone but POF ideologues and the more hysterical or manipulative representatives of middle-class interest-groups. Why did the Parti Ouvrier subscribe to this apparently untenable thesis? How could Guesdists possibly believe in the imminent demise of that boisterous and healthy class, the petite bourgeoisie of the *Belle Époque*?

The French Marxists' deterministic political economy misled them. It taught *a priori* that 'competition leads directly to monopoly',[18] that a small business, if competitive, evolved into a big business or, if not, disappeared into the bankruptcy court. In a capitalist world structured by this law of self-destructive competition, small-scale enterprise, by definition, faced the most dismal prospects: 'the progress of large-scale industry', predicted *Le Socialiste*, 'will leave none but a tiny number of parasites beyond its high and sombre walls'.[19] Cobblers, unable to compete with industrial shoe-making, would soon be engulfed by huge leather-goods works; watch-makers in the Jura, tied to an antiquated handicraft, would soon succumb to capitalist horology; and the cabinet-makers of the Faubourg Saint-Antoine, burdened by their proud tradition of individual craftsmanship, would soon disappear into the maw of Parisian furniture factories. As for shopkeepers, department stores doomed them as textile mills had once doomed the handloom weavers – a prospect actually welcomed by Guesdists, since it promised the removal of 'useless and costly intermediaries, [thereby] reducing the general cost of distribution'.[20] The neighbourhood draper would never compete successfully against the glamour, variety, and discounted prices available in the vast halls of Printemps or the Galeries Lafayette.

If capitalist industry and commerce failed to exterminate the petite bourgeoisie, capitalist finance would administer the *coup de grâce* by expropriating middle-class savings and appropriating the commercial liquidity of small businesses. Financiers and speculators, according to the Parti Ouvrier, preyed upon petit-bourgeois

---

[18] 'E. M.', untitled, *L'Égalité*, 19 March 1882.
[19] Anonymous, 'Leur Fête', *Le Socialiste*, 15 July 1891.
[20] J. Guesde, 'Socialisez!', *Le Socialiste*, 14 January 1888.

frugality as malignant parasites, and eventually consumed their unwilling hosts. Guesdists dismissed any possibility of petit-bourgeois self-defence against these all-consuming monsters: small business-people, dispersed over hundreds of thousands of scattered enterprises and divided by intense competition, could never unite to protect their fragmented and amorphous interests; small-business organis-ations and commercial cooperatives, if they could be formed, would inevitably bow in submission before the might and majesty of capitalist monopoly.[21] Guesdists, characteristically, opposed the very idea of halting this onward march of capital concentration, ridiculing petit-bourgeois dreams of taxing large-scale competitors out of existence, since 'artificially reconstituting antiquated shopkeeping would be as silly as restoring the stage coach, the spinning wheel, and the flail of times past upon the ruins of the railways, textile mills, and steam-powered threshing machines of today'.[22] The petite bourgeoisie had no future, and not much of a present.

This proposition possessed a superficial plausibility in *fin-de-siècle* France: some artisanal trades did indeed disappear, obliterated by novel capitalist technologies and organisation; shopkeepers them-selves panicked before the spectacular advance of large-scale retail-ing symbolised by Parisian department stores; and speculative bubbles such as the Panama Affair, which engulfed petit-bourgeois fortunes by the thousands, appeared to confirm the Guesdist diag-nosis of terminal capital concentration.[23] Nevertheless, the Marxist doom cast upon the middle class ignored three aspects of the French political economy which ensured the long-term vitality of small-scale industry and commerce. First, industrialism, the combination of increasing capital intensity and large-scale organisation which Marxists foresaw as the universal destiny of every productive endeavour, could not be sensibly applied in many, even most, enterprises, including those in vital sectors of the economy such as

---

[21] For a good instance of this argument, see A. Compère-Morel, *Du Socialisme* (Breteuil, 1894), pp. 12–17.

[22] J. Guesde, 'Socialisez!', *Le Socialiste*, 14 January 1888.

[23] J. Guesde, 'La Tire-Lire Cassée', *Le Socialiste*, 16 November 1890. Guesde demonstrated an acute understanding of how knowledge of the market and advantages in liquidity allowed speculators to prey upon small business. See J. Guesde, 'Le Vol Aux Métaux', *Le Socialiste*, 7 January 1888. For the crisis of artisanal industry, see G. Noiriel, *Les Ouvriers dans la Société Française* (Paris, 1986), p. 86, and for shopkeeper panic, P. Nord, 'Le Mouvement des Petits Commerçants et la Politique en France de 1888 à 1914', *Mouvement Social*, no. 114, 1981, pp. 35–55, and P. Nord, *Paris Shopkeepers and the Politics of Resentment* (Princeton, 1986), pp. 81–2 and p. 268.

construction, with its tens of thousands of small businesses. Indeed, the rapid expansion of capitalist industry evoked an even more rapid multiplication of building contractors, as mechanical spinning had once evoked the explosive propagation of hand-loom weaving. Second, the most concentrated and monopolistic industries, including exemplary manifestations of the 'second industrial revolution' such as steel or electrochemistry, spawned hosts of sub-contractors, thereby creating entirely new opportunities for petit-bourgeois entrepreneurship. The vast new steelworks of Lorraine arose within a penumbra of associated small businesses. Finally, the rapidly accelerating commodification of everyday life, a genuinely inexorable and universal attribute of capitalism, opened up a plethora of tempting opportunities for specialised small-scale retailing and services. For every Printemps or Bon Marché, a thousand boutiques opened their doors.[24] Mesmerised by their myth of universal capitalist aggression and general capital concentration, Guesdists remained blissfully unaware of these processes, which ensured the survival and, indeed, the proliferation of petits bourgeois.

The Parti Ouvrier did observe other tendencies which assured the survival of small business within the rapidly changing economy and society of the French 'second industrial revolution', including the labour regime specific to small-scale independent businesses and the impact of technological change upon petit-bourgeois enterprise. But Guesdists perversely mistook guarantees of small-business vitality for symptoms of petit-bourgeois morbidity. According to French Marxists, the appalling conditions endured by many petits bourgeois, such as the sixteen-hour working days inflicted by bakers upon themselves and their families, demonstrated the terminal agony of the middle class. These afflictions, however, actually insulated the self-employed against competition from large-scale commerce and in-

---

[24] For the survival of small enterprise in areas resistant to industrialisation, see R. Scase and R. Goffee, *The Entrepreneurial Middle Class* (London, 1982), pp. 32–69. On the ways in which capitalist industry creates opportunities for small business, see A. Friedman, *Industry and Labour: Class Struggle at Work and Monopoly Capitalism* (London, 1977), p. 24. The French artisanal petite bourgeoisie seems to have benefited considerably from the subcontracting associated with the large new enterprises of the 'second industrial revolution'. See, for instance, 'Transformations Industrielles et Sociales à St-Étienne à la Fin du XIXᵉ Siècle', in P. Heritier et al., *150 Ans de Luttes Ouvrières dans le Bassin Stéphanois* (Saint-Étienne, 1979), p. 114, and R. Priouret, *Origines du Patronat Français* (Paris, 1963), p. 192. For the opportunities created for the petite bourgeoisie by the expanding commodification of the economy, see D. Johnson, 'The Social Unity and Factionalisation of the Middle Class', in D. Johnson et al., *Class and Social Development: A New Theory of the Middle Class* (London, 1982), pp. 200–2, and Nord, *Paris Shopkeepers*, pp. 82–95.

dustry: no capitalist, however inhumane, dared to drive his workers as unrelentingly as petits bourgeois drove their spouses, their sons and daughters, their few employees, and themselves.[25] At the same time, trade union success in protecting working-class wages against deflation during the 'Great Depression' and then the unions' achievements in increasing salaries and reducing working-hours during the prosperous 1890s, when coupled with social reforms of the *Belle Époque* such as limitations on child labour (applied almost exclusively to large enterprises) and the institutionalisation of the ten-hour day in businesses subject to government inspection, contributed to the relative advantage enjoyed by small business, almost entirely non-unionised and unregulated. Governed by their polemical purposes, French Marxists blinded themselves to the ways in which the entrepreneurial rules had changed to favour smaller players. Coldly contemptuous of syndicalism's supposedly defensive stance against capital, ferociously hostile to social reformism and its associated class-collaborationist politics, Guesdists refused to recognise the transformations of the French labour regime which so reduced the flexibility and exploitative potential of big business, and hence failed to perceive, much less understand, the entrenched persistence, even dynamic growth, of the entrepreneurial petite bourgeoisie within the interstices of French capitalism.

The technologies of the second industrial revolution – technologies which, for Guesdists, ensured the ruin of artisanal workshops at the hands of mass production – likewise fostered small-scale enterprise in many sectors of the industrial economy. Paul Brousse, a perennial thorn-in-the-side of Marxist doctrinaires, pointed out that electricity, for instance, powered small workshops more easily than steam-engines had ever driven factories – an aspect of the second industrial revolution which would revolutionise the scale of production, just as the original coal-fired first industrial revolution had transformed productive scale, albeit in the opposite direction. The POF, unimpressed and annoyed, denounced Brousse's discovery, without evidence or serious discussion, as a 'reactionary illusion'.[26]

[25] D. Bertaux and I. Bertaux-Wiame, 'Artisanal Bakery in France: How it Lives and Why it Survives', in F. Bechhofer and B. Elliott (eds.), *The Petite Bourgeoisie: Comparative Studies of the Uneasy Stratum* (New York, 1981), pp. 161–2.

[26] Anonymous, 'Illusion Réactionnaire', *Le Socialiste*, 28 August 1886. For a somewhat more considered discussion of the issue, see E. Massard, 'L'Électricité et la Concentration Économique', *L'Égalité*, 8 January 1882. Brousse seems to have been quite correct, according to M. Lévy-Leboyer, 'Innovation and Business Strategies in Nineteenth and

Nevertheless, the proliferation of small-scale but capital-intensive enterprise during the *Belle Époque*, proliferation symbolised by ranks of sewing machines in Parisian sweatshops and sophisticated power-driven machinery in provincial engineering works, validated Brousse's perception. Even a new and soon to be highly concentrated industry such as automobile production ensured that tens of thousands of blacksmiths enjoyed a brilliant future as motor mechanics, whatever the effect upon carriage makers. The technological transformation of the French economy during the *Fin de Siècle* encouraged the expansion and transformation of the French petite bourgeoisie, not its decline.[27] Guesdists, however, mistook the metamorphosis of the middle class for terminal illness.

Why did Guesdists, obsessed by their myth of a moribund middle class, disregard the petite bourgeoisie's general survival and occasional vitality? Once again, in the habitual mode of Guesdist ideology, polemical imperatives prevailed over sociological insight. While erecting their impressive ideological edifice, French Marxists *needed* the imminent demise of the petite bourgeoisie, and, like ideologues of every persuasion, they allowed their needs to govern their perceptions. But why this need? Why did the POF so desperately crave the destruction of the petite bourgeoisie? In the metahistorical perspective which prevailed within the Parti Ouvrier, the survival of any significant number of small businesspeople, necessarily resistant to proletarian militancy and socialist ideals, impeded the rise of socialism and sustained democratic anti-collectivism: the disappearance of the petite bourgeoisie, Guesde hoped, would eliminate 'the shock absorber which cushions the collisions between employees and employers, between proletarians and capitalists, henceforth forced into direct contact and engaged in a battle as inevitable as liberating'.[28] Anticipating their revolution, Guesdists dreamed of the final confrontation between a tiny and therefore doomed bourgeoisie and an all-encompassing and therefore victorious proletariat, a dream in which 'the disappearance of the middle class' constituted 'a necessity for the collectivist transformation of

---

Twentieth-Century France', in E. Carter et al. (eds.), *Enterprise and Entrepreneurs in Nineteenth and Twentieth-Century France* (London, 1976), p. 98.

[27] G. Jacquemet, *Belleville au XIXᵉ Siècle: Du Faubourg à la Ville* (Paris, 1984), pp. 293–317 and p. 384.

[28] J. Guesde, 'La Fin de la Crise', *Le Citoyen*, 25 January 1882.

society'.[29] Dreaming, Guesdists fantasised the imminent and inevitable demise of the petite bourgeoisie.

Yet this explanation raises a further question: why did the Parti Ouvrier perceive the 'middle class' as an obstacle to socialist aspirations? Recent French experience, after all, systematically challenged this perception: the Communard armies of 1871 had included thousands of middle-class shopkeepers and master artisans as well as tens of thousands of proletarians, and the petit-bourgeois militants of the 1880s, notably in still radical Paris, sympathised with the nascent labour movement and evolved their own quasi-socialist commitments. On occasion, Guesdists recognised the revolutionary credentials of the petite bourgeoisie, which had revolted 'against the great industrial bourgeois in 1848, against wealthy speculators in 1870, against governmental corruption in 1887 ... and, finally, just recently, against monopoly power, which [petits bourgeois] naively attribute to the Jews alone'.[30] Nevertheless, French Marxists, apparently indifferent as to whether Parisian shopkeepers voted for 'radical-socialist' democrats in the 1880s or for anti-socialist nationalists in 1900, consistently distrusted and disparaged petit-bourgeois politics. How did the Parti Ouvrier rationalise this ungenerous hostility? For once sensitive to the implications of their rhetoric beyond the boundaries of their immediate proletarian constituency, Guesdists realised that the socialist onslaught upon 'private property in the means of production', although directed against capitalist exploitation, also alienated the non-capitalist petite bourgeoisie, whose very existence depended upon ownership (albeit small-scale ownership) of the means of production and exchange. 'The spectre of the "collectivist barracks" and the division of property',[31] a phantom cleverly manipulated by liberal ideologues, ensured that small businesspeople, against their own best interests, marshalled themselves as 'guardians of capitalism'.[32] Otherwise inoffensive grocers were terrified into becoming 'socialism's worst enemies, since they view[ed] it as a threat to individual property'.[33] Guesdists,

[29] J. Guesde, *Le Collectivisme* (Lille, 1891), p. 13.

[30] C. Bonnier, 'Opposition', *Le Socialiste*, 3 June 1900 – a reaction to the Nationalists' victory in the Paris municipal elections. Interestingly, Bonnier attributed this Rightward shift to the 'Ministerialist' flirtation with the haut-bourgeois Republicans. For the petit-bourgeois revolutionary tradition, see Nord, *Paris Shopkeepers*, chapter 6.

[31] J. Guesde and P. Lafargue, *Le Programme du Parti Ouvrier* (Paris, undated), p. 127.

[32] R. Chauvin, *Sans Patrie* (Lille, 1894), p. 21. The liberal discovery of petit-bourgeois defence as an effective anti-socialist strategy is described in Nord, *Paris Shopkeepers*, pp. 473–4.

[33] J. Phalippou, 'Petit Commerce, Coopératives et Socialisme', *Le Socialiste*, 12 March 1899.

indeed, concluded that the petite bourgeoisie, *because* of its economic and social vulnerability to the capitalist order, dedicated itself with particular enthusiasm to social conservation: petits bourgeois, hopelessly clutching their residual superiority over the working class, clung to the bourgeois property system more obsessively than did the haute bourgeoisie itself, 'conservative passion being ... in inverse proportion to the extent of one's property'.[34]

Apart from their overt political role, petits bourgeois, according to Guesdist ideologists, served the bourgeoisie merely by occupying a transitional position between capital and labour. The middle class, because it was a *middle* class, diffused the sharp antagonisms which otherwise turned proletarians against bourgeois: socialists would recruit few followers so long as workers confused Schneider of Creusot with their local grocer. Middle-class independence also tempted workers to better their lot by abandoning their class: working-class solidarity, the precondition for any challenge to the reign of capital, would remain an ideological fantasy so long as enterprising workers hoped to escape proletarian dependency by buying a café or opening their own workshop; the mere existence of the petite bourgeoisie ensured that able and energetic workers, the natural leaders of their class, would opt for individual solutions to their exploitation by capitalists and their domination by capital. Social mobility into the middle class obscured class structure and obviated class conflict.

These interchanges at the margin between the petite bourgeoisie and the proletariat legitimised anti-socialist politics: individual entrepreneurship trumped collectivist politics in the contest played between socialists and liberal-democrats for the allegiance of labour aristocrats. And the characteristic individualism of entrepreneurial petits bourgeois and socially mobile workers substantiated the 'end of class' rhetoric of the ruling liberals, who argued that the social promotion exemplified by ascension from the working class into the petite bourgeoisie and from the petite bourgeoisie into the bourgeoisie had forever ended the exclusive privilege which alone defined a class society. Outraged by these challenges to their revolutionary

---

[34] J. Guesde, 'Le Grand Révolutionnaire', *Le Cri du Peuple*, 12 July 1886. For the determinants of this petit-bourgeois passion for property-ownership, see Bechhofer and Elliott, 'Persistence and Change', pp. 80–1 and pp. 96–9. There is a good empirical description of this passion in F.-P. Codaccioni, *De l'Inégalité Sociale dans une Grande Ville Industrielle: Le Drame de Lille de 1850 à 1914* (Lille, 1976), p. 372 and Haupt, 'The Petite Bourgeoisie', p. 107.

project, Guesdists denounced advocacy of property-owning independence as pernicious 'imbecility and dishonesty'.[35] In searching
for the origins of the proletarian 'false consciousness' which frustrated socialist politics, however, French Marxists unhappily conceded that distressingly large numbers of workers would necessarily
succumb to anti-collectivist 'imbecility and dishonesty' so long as the
petit-bourgeois mirage shimmered on the proletarian horizon. No
wonder Guesdists consoled themselves with their own false consciousness of imminent and inevitable petit-bourgeois decease.

As always, the mentalities of the French working class conditioned
the Parti Ouvrier's social imagination: the ugly animosities which
sometimes divided proletarians from petits bourgeois reinforced the
Guesdists' ideological hostility towards small business. The myth of
the paternal and harmonious artisanal workshop, a myth cultivated
as assiduously by conservative as by radical critics of the bourgeoisie,
contrasted sadly with petit-bourgeois practice. Small employers
survived and thrived because they eluded the state-imposed regulations, trade union-imposed restraints, and self-imposed paternalism
which curtailed the exploitativeness of large-scale entrepreneurship
– their small-scale entrepreneurship constituting a distinct (and
distinctly exploitative) 'mode of production' hardly designed to
foster amity between 'master and man'. Despite the ideals and
illusions of Le Play's sociology, face-to-face relations of production
failed to ensure social solidarity: small workshops, owned by rapacious masters and staffed by embittered journeymen, occasioned
some of the most intense, if least noticed, labour conflicts of the *Belle
Époque*.

Just as the age-old conflict between 'master and man' persisted
alongside the novel struggle between capitalist and proletarian, so
the contemporaneous conflict between proletarian consumers and
petit-bourgeois shopkeepers boasted a long ancestry. The poor had
always suspected, usually correctly, that the retailers who served
them practised profiteering and petty fraud. Nineteenth-century
urban crowds, during periods of economic crisis, may no longer have

---

[35] J. Guesde, 'Imbécile et Malhonnête', *Le Cri du Peuple*, 30 April 1886. The political
implications of petit-bourgeois aspirations are analysed in F. Bechhofer et al., 'The Petits
Bourgeois in the Class Structure: The Case of the Small Shopkeepers', in F. Parkin (ed.),
The Social Analysis of Class Structure (London, 1974), pp. 103–28. For the anti-collectivist
utility of the petite bourgeoisie in France, see Nord, 'Le Mouvement des Petits Commerçants et la Politique en France', p. 52, and S. Berstein and A. Prost, 'Radicalisme et Couches
Moyennes', pp. 85–115.

automatically vented their fears and hatred upon bakers, but shopkeepers of every kind remained suspect in working-class faubourgs. This suspicion intensified in proportion to the *Fin de Siècle's* price inflation and the rapid commodification of society, inflation and commodification which inextricably enmeshed workers in the cash nexus, while the astonishing proliferation of retail outlets, which imposed unbearable competitive pressure upon marginal shopkeepers, inevitably generalised sharp practice and consequent proletarian hostility.[36] Determined to undermine the anti-collectivist myth of a unified 'urban people' indifferent to class divisions, the Parti Ouvrier gleefully exploited the everyday war between desperate petit-bourgeois retailers and impoverished working-class shoppers. Commenting on statistics which illustrated the huge differentials between wholesale and retail prices, *Le Socialiste* promised its proletarian readers that 'these exorbitant exactions levied by intermediaries on everyone's daily consumption will cease once the proletariat is in power; workers' municipal governments will assume responsibility for the feeding and welfare of every member of the commune'[37] – a promise hardly calculated to inspire shopkeeper socialism.

If working-class resentment of the labour practices of master artisans and the trading practices of retailers reinforced Guesdist hostility towards the petite bourgeoisie, then middle-class horror and hatred of socialists and labour militancy confirmed the Marxist equation of 'petit-bourgeois' with 'anti-collectivist'. Petit-bourgeois social and political evolution during the *Belle Époque* seemingly substantiated Guesdist suspicion in four ways. First, the precipitous decline of the artisanal textile, leather-goods, and metal-working industries, coupled with the prosperity and expansion of luxury crafts, shifted the balance of power within the artisanal petite bourgeoisie from trades traditionally linked with the working class towards those historically dependent upon the wealthy, a transformation with unhappy (for Marxists) political implications. The cobblers who had once shod working-class communities had identified with the labour movement and its anti-bourgeois politics; Rue

[36] Codaccioni, *De l'Inégalité Sociale*, p. 383; Pernoud, *Histoire de la Bourgeoisie en France*, pp. 584–586; E. Weber, *France: Fin de Siècle* (London, 1986), pp. 65–6; and A. Faure, 'L'Épicerie Parisienne au XIXe Siècle ou la Corporation Éclatée', *Mouvement Social*, no. 108, 1979, p. 117.

[37] Anonymous, 'Vols Bourgeois', *Le Socialiste*, 28 August 1886.

Saint-Honoré jewellers, by contrast, possessed a considerable personal interest in the wealth and well-being of their exclusive clientele.[38] French capitalism had demolished the revolutionary artisanate of the mid nineteenth century and rebuilt it to bourgeois specifications.

Second, although artisanal enterprises frequently benefited from trade union victories (almost always won at the expense of their larger competitors), small employers despised and dreaded syndicalism. Petit-bourgeois bosses realised that they survived in an economic jungle ruled by capitalist predators because they and their employees did not work to union rates or union rules: their survival might not survive syndicalist intrusion into their unorganised and unregulated workshops. At the same time, small businesspeople, personally engaged in enterprises of their own creation, resented limitation of their entrepreneurial rights with a personal passion unknown among the wealthy and powerful. The *laissez-faire* ideal of the bourgeoisie, once anathema to artisanal employers as a rationale for unfair competition, was embraced with enthusiasm once it could be turned against the labour movement. As big business, increasingly sure of its own security, began to accept the legitimacy of organised labour, small business developed a new and extreme allergy to trade unionism. The anti-labour leagues which proliferated during the *Belle Époque* reflected the fears and hatreds of small-time and small-town entrepreneurs at least as much as the paranoia of great industrialists.

Third, while the outcome of capitalist industrialisation and the rise of the 'modern' labour movement promoted artisanal conservatism, the burgeoning working-class consumer-cooperative movement and the socialist municipal services instituted during the 1890s terrified and alienated shopkeepers. The practical collectivism of the co-op and the cost-price municipal enterprise under-cut the prosperity of the petite bourgeoisie to a far greater extent than did capitalist retailing. Although every mining village and provincial textile town aspired to its cooperative store and municipal pharmacy, the great department stores of the nineteenth century hardly impinged upon retail trade outside Paris.[39] Shopkeepers who had

---

[38] P. Vigier, 'La Petite Bourgeoisie en Europe Occidentale avant 1914', *Mouvement Social*, no. 108, 1979, p. 6.

[39] For the effects of consumer coops upon petit-bourgeois attitudes towards the workers' movement, see D. Gordon, 'Liberalism and Socialism in the Nord: Eugène Motte and

once joined with their proletarian neighbours in protest against the 'economats' (company stores) imposed by paternalistic industrialists now sided with the same industrialists against the labour movement, as co-op replaced economat in the domestic economy of the working class.

Finally, the first halting steps towards the establishment of a French welfare state, taken to placate the working class, thoroughly alienated the petite bourgeoisie, which became convinced, with some justice, that it paid all the costs and enjoyed none of the benefits. The concurrent institutionalisation of cooperation between the state, capital, and organised labour – the corporatist economic programme advanced by socialist reformists and their social-liberal allies – embittered small businesspeople who had every reason to consider themselves excluded from the new social order promoted by Millerand and his allies, a social order constructed by and for big government, big business, and big labour.[40] Historians have interpreted the social-democratic transformation of capitalist society initiated at the turn of the century as pacifying the class war. But the welfare state and corporatist economics which nurtured class collaboration between labour and capital fostered class conflict between labour and the petite bourgeoisie, a contradiction born during the *Belle Époque* which would bedevil social democrats throughout the twentieth century.

Subjected to these transformations of their social milieu, hundreds of thousands of French small businesspeople, like their brethren elsewhere in continental Western Europe, abandoned the radical advocates of political democracy who had represented their cause since the eighteenth century for the rightist politics of social defence which pandered to their terror of the twentieth. Petits bourgeois' detestation of 'collectivism', their dread of trade unions, their hatred of cooperatives, their individualist rejection of nascent social democracy – all eroded a century of middle-class Leftism: petits bourgeois whose great-grandparents had been sans-culottes, whose grand-

Republican Politics in Roubaix 1898–1912', *French History*, vol. 3, 1989, pp. 316, 320, and 324; D. Reid, 'Decazeville: Company Town and Working Class Community 1826–1914', in J. Merriman (ed.), *French Cities in the Nineteenth Century* (London, 1982), pp. 204–5; Nord, 'Le Mouvement des Petits Commerçants', p. 45; M. Rebérioux, 'Les Socialistes Français et le Petit Commerce', pp. 67–9; J. Merriman, *Red City: Limoges and the French Nineteenth Century* (Oxford, 1985), p. 164; and D. Reid, *The Miners of Decazeville: A Genealogy of Deindustrialisation* (London, 1985), p. 149. For shopkeeper hatred of socialist municipal services, see Nord, *Paris Shopkeepers*, p. 363.
[40] *Ibid.*, chapter 8.

parents had supported the Montagne during the Second Republic, whose parents had fought for the Commune, turned *en masse* towards reactionary Social Catholics and proto-fascist nationalists.[41] This conversion never encompassed the entire French middle class, large elements of which maintained its long-standing commitment to radical democracy. But even 'Radical-Socialists' – authentic heirs of the Jacobins, the '48ers, and the Communards – hated revolutionary Marxism and militant trade unionism.

Despite the POF's doubts about cooperatives and trade unions and its vehement hostility towards the corporatist project of the 'Millerandists', Guesdism personified the red menace for most petits bourgeois, an unwelcome testimony to the Parti Ouvrier's prominence on the extreme Left. The archetypical expression of middle-class anti-socialism during the *Belle Époque*, the Parti Commercial et Industriel, even chose its name with self-conscious reference to the Parti Ouvrier.[42] Guesdists met hatred with hatred. Wish-fulfilment had already led them to the conviction that capitalism doomed small property, that the petite bourgeoisie, caught in the gears of industrialism, would 'be thrown into the proletariat, which consequently grows in size, misery and revolutionary potential'.[43] The bourgeoisie, once again victim of the cunning of historical reason, would expropriate the anti-collectivist middle class, thereby demolishing the last bulwark against the socialist onslaught. But, if capitalism failed to put the petits bourgeois out of their misery, socialism would eventually finish them off. 'The Parti Ouvrier', threatened Guesde, 'fully intends to expropriate all that shop-keeping petite bourgeoisie'.[44] Middle-class hostility to socialists and the labour movement provoked this ferocious rhetoric, which in turn reinforced middle-class anti-socialism, a vicious circle in which the Parti Ouvrier became hopelessly entrapped.

[41] For the Rightward shift of petit-bourgeois political opinion, see Nord, 'Le Mouvement des Petits Commerçants', pp. 48–9; Z. Sternhell, *La Droite Révolutionnaire 1885–1914: Les Origines Françaises du Fascisme* (Paris, 1978), p. 118; and Vigier, 'La Petite Bourgeoisie', pp. 9–10. But see the modification of this orthodoxy in H.-G. Haupt, 'La Petite Entreprise et la Politique en Europe au XIXᵉ Siècle', *Mouvement Social*, no. 114, 1981, p. 5.

[42] J. Bernard, 'Du Mouvement d'Organisation et de Défense du Petit Commerce Français', doctoral thesis, University of Paris, 1906, p. 86, cited in Nord, *Paris Shopkeepers*, p. 426.

[43] E. Maillard, *Le Prolétariat International et la Journée de Huit Heures* (Bordeaux, 1890), pp. 27–28.

[44] J. Guesde, 'Homéopathie Conservatrice', *Le Cri du Peuple*, 26 February 1884. It is doubtful that shopkeepers were reassured by Guesde's assurances that they would all be guaranteed jobs in socialist department stores. J. Guesde, 'Socialisez!', *Le Socialiste*, 14 January 1888.

Guesdists understood their entrapment in a cycle of hatred which could benefit only the bourgeoisie, whose champions enlisted ever more numerous petit-bourgeois foot-soldiers with every rhetorical sally by Marxist class warriors. As a consequence, the Parti Ouvrier, hoping to have its cake and eat it too, sought to placate the petits bourgeois, while still consigning individual property-ownership to the historical dustbin. This strategy *vis-à-vis* the petite bourgeoisie undoubtedly built yet another contradiction into the Guesdists' ideological edifice: an irresolvable tension between seduction and aggression. But the French Marxists had no option but to mix sugar with their vitriol as they concocted their policy towards the middle class. At the least, Guesdists recognised the electoral weight of the petite bourgeoisie in the Third Republic. 'Small scale entrepreneurs and shopkeepers' may have been 'doomed', but Guesdists knew that socialists had to 'listen to their grievances and go to their aid, since we [socialists] are going to need ... their support to seize power'.[45] Discarding the dogmatic assumption that small property-ownership necessarily implied inherent ultra-conservatism, Guesdists imagined that an anti-capitalist petite bourgeoisie might someday second the socialist working class in its struggle against the bourgeoisie.

The Marxist search for socialist petits bourgeois was neither entirely cynical nor willfully quixotic, despite the Parti Ouvrier's frequent denunciations of 'small scale entrepreneurs and shop-keepers' and the Rightward evolution of petit-bourgeois politics. Aspects of *fin-de-siècle* society sanctioned Marxist solicitation of the middle class. However menaced petits bourgeois may have believed themselves to be by 'reds' and syndicalists, they also remembered their traditional plutocratic enemies. The profound hostility of master artisans and shopkeepers towards 'capitalist monopoly' nurtured 'real' anti-capitalist socialism even among petit-bourgeois 'National Socialists', otherwise perfect exemplars of the anti-socialist middle-class politics of the *Fin de Siècle*. The Parisian petits bourgeois who voted so overwhelmingly for the nationalist Right in the Paris municipal elections of 1900 may have hated Guesdists, but they also detested banks, department stores, and industrialists.

Shopkeepers and self-employed artisans, like small employers, suffered frustration and humiliation at the hands of *fin-de-siècle*

---

[45] 'J. G.' (Guesde), 'Collectivisme et Grands Magasins', *Le Socialiste*, 5 March 1893. For the successes and failures of the Guesdist approach to the petite bourgeoisie, see C. Willard, *Le Mouvement Socialiste en France (1893–1905): Les Guesdistes* (Paris, 1965), pp. 362–6.

French capitalists. The capital accumulation necessary to accede to the haute bourgeoisie had, by the end of the nineteenth century, escalated far beyond the reach (if not the dreams) of the petite bourgeoisie, apart from an already quasi-capitalist elite of the class. No shopkeeper could seriously hope to become another Boucicaut, no blacksmith a steel baron: the Horatio Alger tales so common during the heroic age of early capitalism had degenerated into pathetic fantasies in an exclusive world of high technology and higher finance. Petits bourgeois, trapped behind their counters or workbenches, had virtually no chance of escaping into the charmed circle of wealth and power, despite the myth-making of bourgeois propagandists.

At the same time, just as the chasm between the wealth and power of the haute bourgeoisie and the penury and frustration of the petite bourgeoisie, always considerable, gaped ever wider during the late nineteenth century, so the social mentalities and life-styles of the two classes, once similar, diverged dramatically: disdain, envy, and incomprehension reinforced 'objective' conflicts of interest between large and small property-owners. Petits bourgeois, still attached to the puritan austerity of their forebears, gazed with righteous distaste and ill-concealed envy at the ostentatious opulence enjoyed by financiers and industrialists. Just as eighteenth-century bourgeois had despised the extravagance of a 'decadent' aristocracy, so the late-nineteenth-century petite bourgeoisie recoiled in horror from the conspicuous consumption of *fin-de-siècle* bourgeois 'high society'. The wealthy, in turn, disdained the narrow provincialism of middle-class mores and scorned the bad taste of petit-bourgeois culture. Puritan austerity met lavish ostentation, envy met disdain – solid grounds for class antagonism, if not class war.

Finally, the survival, even the growth of the entrepreneurial middle class disguised an appalling casualty rate among individual petits bourgeois, as the period's astounding proliferation of small businesses saturated markets, thereby fomenting cut-throat and often suicidal competition between the ever-growing hordes of marginal entrepreneurs. The arcades of Paris, shopping streets in the faubourgs, and the market squares of small towns retained, even expanded, their astonishing arrays of small shops and workshops – but their tenants changed with depressing regularity. Shopkeepers and artisans, living by and dying of the pitiless laissez-faire economics preached (but rarely practised) by the bourgeoisie, understandably perceived their individual insecurity rather than their collective vitality, and easily attributed that insecurity to the predatory practices of big business. Economic exclusion, conflicting mentalities, the anxieties of insecurity – no wonder petits bourgeois hated the 'aristocracy of wealth'.[46]

While 'material' interests and social mentalities alienated petits bourgeois from capitalists, durable ties associated the proletarian and petit-bourgeois 'popular classes'. Neighbourhood community, routine social mobility between the two classes, and similar living conditions and cultural traditions, the bonds which no longer linked bourgeois to petits bourgeois, still united petits bourgeois with workers: master artisans may have driven their journeymen and apprentices mercilessly, but those journeymen and apprentices were, frequently, their own children; shopkeepers may have exploited their working-class clients' poverty and ignorance, but thousands of proletarian families could not have survived without the weekly credit extended by their neighbourhood grocer; Marxists may have dissociated the petite bourgeoisie from the proletariat in theory, but the two classes, in everyday life, shared the stairwells of the same apartment buildings and frequented the courtyards of the same faubourgs.[47] Despite its proletarian protestations, the Parti Ouvrier itself drew most of its leadership from the petite bourgeoisie.[48] In 1895, for instance, twenty-two of the thirty-six socialist municipal councillors of Roubaix managed bistros![49] The French middle class,

---

[46] For the structural changes within capital which so reduced petit-bourgeois opportunities for upward social mobility, see A. Daumard, 'L'Évolution des Structures Sociales', pp. 344–5 and Haupt, 'The Petite Bourgeoisie', p. 106. On the relative decline of petit-bourgeois wealth as compared to that of the bourgeoisie, see A. Daumard, 'Wealth and Affluence in France since the Beginning of the Nineteenth Century', in W. Rubinstein (ed.), *Wealth and the Wealthy in the Modern World* (London, 1980), p. 103. For overcrowding of petit-bourgeois occupations and its consequences, see M. Perrot, 'Les Classes Populaires Urbaines', p. 510; Nord, *Paris Shopkeepers*, p. 198; Codaccioni, *De L'Inégalité Sociale*, pp. 188–9 and p. 200; and J. Le Yaouang, 'La Mobilité Sociale dans le Milieu Boutiquier Parisien au XIXᵉ Siècle', *Mouvement Social*, no. 108, 1979, p. 93. The seeming paradox of wide-spread individual failure and collective prosperity within the petite bourgeoisie is explained in Bechhofer and Elliott, 'Petty Property', p. 185.

[47] Haupt, 'La Petite Entreprise', p. 6; Y. Lequin, 'Le Monde des Travailleurs Manuels', in M. Agulhon (ed.), *Histoire de la France Urbaine* (Paris, 1983), vol. 4, pp. 510–11; and Haupt, 'The Petite Bourgeoisie', pp. 104–5.

[48] C. Willard, 'Contribution au Portrait du Militant Guesdiste dans les Dix Dernières Années du XIXᵉ Siècle', *Mouvement Social*, no. 33–4, 1960–1, pp. 55–66. Willard elsewhere estimates that approximately 17 per cent of the Party's militants were 'commerçants'. Willard, *Les Guesdistes*, p. 321.

[49] T. Moodie, 'The Parti Ouvrier Français 1879–1893: The Formation of a Political Sect', PhD thesis, Columbia University, 1966, p. 119.

vast in numbers and protean in its composition, never adopted a monolithically anti-proletarian posture, and French socialists and French workers, intimately associated with petits bourgeois, never embraced a uniformly hostile attitude towards the middle class.

Animated by a sense of popular solidarity, petits bourgeois repeatedly intervened against other (but larger) property-owners during the thousands of local skirmishes fought between capitalists and workers across *fin-de-siècle* France. Shopkeepers, for instance, 'carried' striking workers, granting them the credit which sustained their industrial militancy, since workers, living on the verge of subsistence, rarely saved against the prospect of unemployment, while unions, impoverished by their members' penury, rarely accumulated strike-funds.[50] The great upsurge of union organisation and strikes during the 1890s implicated thousands of shopkeepers as silent partners in their customers' militancy. At the same time, both workers and petits bourgeois hated the economats established by particularly exploitative capitalists, capitalists who thereby tied their workers to their company, reduced labour costs by providing cut-price goods, and profited from workers' consumption as well as from their production. Even when promised cheap goods and convenience by an economat, employees resented their loss of consumer freedom, while shopkeepers resented the loss of custom. As Guesdists confidently explained, this expanded exploitation of workers ensured that petits bourgeois who served working-class communities – grocers, butchers, greengrocers, and bakers – 'also became victims' of capitalist rapacity.[51] The Parti Ouvrier rejoiced whenever proletariat and petite bourgeoisie united against their common capitalist enemies, as during the great Decazeville strike of 1886, when 'a city of 10,000 people, a population of [petits] bourgeois, small manufacturers and shopkeepers, and miners ...

[50] M. Perrot, *Les Ouvriers en Grève: France 1871–1890* (Paris, 1974), vol. 1, pp. 488–9, vol 2, pp. 481–2 and pp. 535–6, and M. Perrot, 'On the Formation of the French Working Class', in I. Katznelson and A. Zolberg (eds.), *Working Class Formation: Nineteenth Century Patterns in Western Europe and the United States* (Princeton, 1986), pp. 87–8.

[51] 'Mouvement Social – Vierzon', *Le Socialiste*, 14 August 1886. For descriptions of such unity, see Perrot, *Les Ouvriers en Grève*, vol. 2, p. 489; Reid, 'Decazeville', pp. 199–201; P. Pigenet et al., *Terre des Luttes: Histoire du Mouvement Ouvrier dans le Cher* (Paris, 1977), p. 25; and M. Gillet, 'L'Affrontement des Syndicalismes Ouvriers et Patronales dans le Bassin Houiller du Nord et du Pas-de-Calais de 1884 à 1891', *Bulletin de la Société d'Histoire Moderne*, vol. 56, 1957, p. 8.

rose against the company'.[52] French Marxists hoped that, one day, all France would emulate Decazeville.

Heartened by this dream, the Parti Ouvrier solicited the support of those whom Guesdists sometimes characterised as the 'working bourgeoisie',[53] a flexible category which lent itself to almost any interpretation, since Eugène Motte himself, *bête noire* of Guesdist socialists, worked, and worked hard, at managing his textile empire. Although they refrained from extending their appeal so high into the 'working bourgeoisie', French Marxists regularly pledged to protect the 'small property, the fruit of genuinely personal labour'[54] of petits bourgeois, a pledge of protection as much directed against (their own?) socialist extremism as against capitalist rapacity. Determined to foster socialism among petits bourgeois, or at least neutralise their anti-collectivism, the POF devised an impressive repertoire of arguments for middle-class anti-capitalism. At their most extreme, Guesdists, eschewing Marx for Proudhon, even applauded proposals that the dividends of the Bank of France be abolished, thereby reducing the discount rate from three per cent to one per cent and establishing 'free and mutual credit' for small businesspeople.[55] More seriously, the Parti Ouvrier contended that petits bourgeois would profit from a strong labour movement: higher wages for workers would flow into the tills of bakers, café owners, and grocers. Addressing shopkeepers, Guesdists in the Isère pointed out that 'adequate salaries for us represent more bread, more meat, more shoes, clothing, and items of all sorts. And for you it represents greater prosperity, well-being and happiness'.[56] Avaricious bourgeois, after all, spent their ill-gotten gains in Paris or Lyons, not in Vienne. Material interests, cash in the till – what better grounds for class alliance between proletariat and petite bourgeoisie?[57]

Contemporaneous observers – from Friedrich Engels, the unofficial

[52] Anonymous, 'Decazeville', *Le Socialiste*, 6 February 1886.
[53] Electoral Manifesto for Paris, *Le Socialiste*, 19 September 1885. Such appeals were as much a part of Guesdist propaganda during the 1880s as during the 1890s, despite the analysis in Willard, *Les Guesdistes*, p. 363, which argues that they reflected the electoral opportunism of the latter period.
[54] J. Guesde, 'Le Projet Revillon-Maret', *Le Cri du Peuple*, 20 July 1884.
[55] J. Guesde, 'Banque de France et Prolétariat', *Le Socialiste*, 26 June 1892.
[56] *Droit du Peuple*, 18 February 1906, cited in R. Jonas, 'From the Radical Republic to the Social Republic: On the Origins and Nature of Socialism in Rural France 1871–1914', PhD thesis, University of California, Berkeley, 1985, p. 378.
[57] P. Lafargue, 'Le Programme Municipal', *Le Socialiste*, 9 April 1892. See Rebérioux, 'Les Socialistes Français et le Petit Commerce', p. 61 for the ways in which petit-bourgeois and proletarian interests coincided on these issues.

mentor of the POF, to *Le Temps*, the most bourgeois of newspapers –
mercilessly criticised the sporadic efforts by Guesdists to ingratiate
themselves with the petite bourgeoisie. These criticisms presupposed
that dalliance between workers and small property-owners violated
fundamental Marxist maxims, that political intercourse between
the working class and the petite bourgeoisie constituted social
miscegenation.[58] Guesdists politely ignored Engels' protests,
but furiously rejected reprimands from 'champions of capitalism
[the journalists of *Le Temps*] who [had] suddenly turned into
jealous guardians of Marxist orthodoxy'.[59] French Marxists might
rightly have been accused of self-contradiction, given their long
record of intransigent hostility towards the middle class, but they
could not be charged with betraying their principles. 'Marxist
orthodoxy' in no way precluded a socialist programme addressed to
the petite bourgeoisie. The *separation* of labour and property underpinned the Guesdists' impeccably Marxist critique of capital, while
self-employed artisans and shopkeepers *combined* the two productive
forces, albeit personally rather than collectively. Petits bourgeois
who did not employ workers could not be accused of exploiting the
proletariat, the ultimate Marxist *casus belli*. Guesdists faithfully
followed their Marxist analytic in distinguishing between 'individual
property which is exploited by its owner' and 'capitalist property
which is worked by collectivities of non-owners'.[60] French Marxists
loyally obeyed their first principles when they decided that the
former, 'which still unites labour and capital in the same hands',
should be 'sacred for even the most revolutionary of socialists'.[61]
Zévaès restated a fundamental Marxist protocol when he wrote that
'socialism did not precede economic trends, but rather followed
them and adapted itself to ... them ... so that artisans, the small-
scale entrepreneurs, will therefore retain their instruments of labour,
which they [still] work themselves'.[62] Socialists should not threaten
property-owners who were not yet capitalists. To do otherwise
would be hypocritical for a movement which 'has denounced the
iniquities of [capitalist] primitive accumulation', and, worse yet,
would 'provoke such mad terror among the middle classes, that

[58] For Engels, see 'Lettres Inédits de K. Marx and F. Engels sur le Socialisme Français', *Le Mouvement Socialiste*, vol. 35, 1913, pp. 273–95.
[59] G. Dazet, *Lois Collectivistes pour l'An 19*.. (Paris, 1907), p. 16.
[60] Anonymous, 'Le Socialisme dans les Campagnes', *Le Socialiste*, 22 July 1893.
[61] *Ibid.*
[62] A. Zévaès, 'Mensonges', *Le Socialiste*, 20 October 1894.

[they would be] definitively driven into the reactionary camp',[63] a prescient anticipation of Soviet 'primitive accumulation' and its global political impact. The social trends and ideological circumstances of the *Belle Époque* may have alienated workers from petits bourgeois and turned socialists against middle-class populists, but nothing fundamental in Marxist ideology precluded, *a priori*, socialist seduction of the petite bourgeoisie.

A minor theme in the POF's analysis of the petite bourgeoisie – a theme rarely developed with any rigour, but one replete with theoretical and polemical potential – greatly expanded the French Marxists' conception of exploitation. When using this expanded conception, Guesdists concluded that petits bourgeois, although free from the exploitation inflicted upon proletarians (petit-bourgeois labour was not yet commodified), none the less suffered capitalist rapacity through other commodity relations – a conclusion which both foreshadowed more sophisticated twentieth-century Marxist conceptions of exploitation and returned to precepts dear to mid-nineteenth-century 'mutualists'.[64] Merchant capital, according to this analysis, monopolised the wholesale supplies of artisans and shopkeepers, always to their cost, and manipulated their markets, often to their ruin. Finance capital preyed upon meagre petit-bourgeois savings, savings ruthlessly appropriated during the speculative catastrophes of the *Belle Époque*, and rationed credit in favour of capitalists, extending finance to small businesses only on extortionate terms which swept thousands of hapless petits bourgeois into the bankruptcy courts. And bourgeois landlords exacted ever-increasing commercial rents from artisans and shopkeepers, driving them off well-lit and well-heeled avenues into obscure and impoverished backstreets. Overall, in this analysis of mercantile and financial exploitation, capital reduced independent small property-owners to mere 'profit machines',[65] to the status of instruments

---

[63] H. Nivet, 'Économie et Propagande', *Le Socialiste*, 28 July – 4 August 1901.

[64] For current reconceptualisations of exploitation, see J. Roemer, 'New Directions in the Marxian Theory of Exploitation and Class', *Politics and Society*, vol. 11, 1982, pp. 256–9 and pp. 263–6 and J. Roemer, 'Exploitation, Class, and Property Relations', in T. Ball and J. Farr (eds.), *After Marx* (Cambridge, 1984), pp. 194–7. For a brilliant description of such exploitation in practice during the era of mutualism, see R. Aminzade, 'Reinterpreting Capitalist Industrialisation: A Study of Nineteenth-Century France', in J. Kaplan and C. Koepp (eds.), *Work in France: Representation, Meaning, Organisation and Practice* (London, 1986), pp. 393–417.

[65] Report of a speech by Guesde, 'Le Parti Ouvrier en France – Marseille', *Le Socialiste*, 6 October 1894.

of accumulation to be used, misused, abused, and finally discarded. At their most extreme, Guesdists asserted that 'behind their property-owning facade, [small property-owners] are as proletarian as factory workers'.[66]

This discovery of capitalist exploitation beyond the hated 'système de salaire', an uncommon achievement in Guesdist social rhetoric, 'objectively' justified the propagation of a petit-bourgeois version of socialism by a Parti Ouvrier determined to cast its net as widely as possible. Guesdists, however, never reconciled this project with their denunciations of small property-owners as agents of the bourgeoisie and natural enemies of the revolutionary working class. Why this inconsistency? The ambiguities, not to say contradictions, of the Guesdist social analytic allowed the POF, depending upon circumstances, to exploit either working-class hostility towards the petite bourgeoisie *or* the bonds which welded workers and petits bourgeois together: where proletarians resented avaricious grocers and contested domineering workshop masters, there the POF promised to expropriate the petite bourgeoisie; where petits bourgeois and workers united against their bourgeois superiors, there the Parti Ouvrier preached petit-bourgeois socialism. Rigorous Marxist theory may have required consistency, but compelling Marxist polemic thrived upon contradiction.

Guesdists, however, were confused as well as opportunistic, confused, above all, by the social and political heterogeneity of the middle class itself, a class as disrupted by its diversity as united by its characteristic combination of labour and property. Enormous differences in wealth, status, and aspirations divided the prosperous small manufacturer from the impoverished seamstress, the boulevard boutiquier from the slum costermonger, the substantial building contractor from the self-employed mason – differences which made nonsense of the amalgamation of all 'patrons' into a single category in the official statistics and political discourse of bourgeois France. The astounding diversity of the French petite bourgeoisie – dispersed over hundreds of disparate occupations, enjoying modest

---

[66] J. Guesde, 'Les Deux Armées', *Le Socialiste*, 29 July 1891. For description of capitalist exploitation of self-employed artisans, see A. Cottereau, 'Vie Quotidienne et Résistance Ouvrière à Paris en 1870', introduction to D. Poulot, *Le Sublime* (Paris, 1980), pp. 67–70; L. Berlanstein, *The Working People of Paris 1871–1914* (London, 1984), pp. 15–17; and Nord, *Paris Shopkeepers*, p. 168. For equivalent exploitation of retailers, see Haupt, 'The Petite Bourgeoisie', pp. 100–1.

wealth in some cases while suffering acute poverty in others, and awarding its allegiance across the entire political spectrum, from revolutionary socialists to the blackest reactionaries – accentuated Guesdist uncertainties.[67] Yet this heterogeneity remained untheorised, even unnoticed, in Parti Ouvrier discourse: French Marxists usually portrayed the petite bourgeoisie as a uniform mass, whether in attacking petits *bourgeois* as propertied conservatives or in recruiting *petits* bourgeois into the anti-capitalist army.

How might Guesdists have avoided this vacillation between contradictory analyses of the middle class (as either bourgeois or anti-capitalist) and equally contradictory political projects (either prospective demolition of the petite bourgeoisie or its immediate seduction)? Most obviously, French Marxists could have disaggregated the petite bourgeoisie, distinguishing between petits bourgeois irrevocably tied to capital and those potentially sympathetic to labour. The Guesdists' social analytic, if rigorously deployed, would have indicated three distinct elements within the petite bourgeoisie: a near-bourgeois group which, while working itself, exploited wage-labour; a 'middle' middle class which enjoyed a precarious independence without employing others' labour; and, finally, 'independent' outworkers with only the most illusory vestiges of property-ownership. By these criteria, the 'small' capitalist – owner perhaps of a modest engineering works, prosperous, moving easily through the expanding markets of the 1890s, and, above all, dependent upon the wage-labour of his employees – was not a 'petit bourgeois' but a small *bourgeois*, and no fit associate for Marxist class warriors. At the other extreme, the self-employed seamstress, impoverished and utterly dependent upon bourgeois contractors for her materials and her market, was not a petite *bourgeoise* but an *ouvrière*, and therefore a prime target for socialist recruitment. As for the propertied shop-keepers and artisans who employed only the labour of their immediate families, they constituted both the heart of the petite bourgeoisie and its most ambiguous element. How did the Guesdists approach these three petites bourgeoisies, so different in their social characteristics and so dissimilar according to rigorous Marxist class analysis?

The Parti Ouvrier devoted surprisingly little attention to the lowest ranks of petits bourgeois, to those who most nearly resembled

---

[67] For the enormous differences separating the various elements of the petite bourgeoisie, see Haupt, 'The Petite Bourgeoisie', p. 108.

proletarians, although their numbers greatly inflated the size of the supposedly anti-proletarian petite bourgeoisie, thereby reinforcing the arguments of anti-collectivists. The 1911 census, for instance, shifted most outworkers in the clothing trades into the category of 'patrons', thereby at one stroke increasing the number of female 'heads of enterprise' in Paris from 31,000 to 166,000![68] These seamstress 'patrons', among the worst-paid and worst-treated producers in France, laboured for derisory 'profits' (the difference between the cost of materials supplied by their contractors and the price paid for finished products), suffered unregulated working-conditions which would never have been tolerated in the worst factories, and enjoyed no social, employment, or income security whatsoever. Most of these self-employed 'petits bourgeois' were merely brutalised piece-workers, for all that they appeared to brutalise themselves. Their ownership of tools and perhaps a work-room ensured only that overhead costs had been shifted from capitalists to workers, to the disadvantage of the latter. Outworkers' 'independence', the independence of isolation and insecurity, permitted degrees of bourgeois irresponsibility and rapacity rarely experienced by 'dependent' industrial workers, increasingly organised in trade unions and protected by government regulation of working-hours and working-conditions. The pretence that *seamstresses* – labouring in overheated or frigid garrets, paid centimes for fourteen-hour working days, totally dependent upon merchant capital for their precarious livelihood – resembled the bourgeoisie and the 'real' petite bourgeoisie because they owned the means of production (often no more than a sewing machine) amounted to a cruel joke: as 'patrons, they possess[ed] only the name'.[69]

The Guesdist assertion that petits bourgeois shared the conditions, interests, and aspirations of workers, a nonsense when applied to prosperous jewellers, held good for most independent outworkers. Many of the Parisian clothing workers annexed to the *patronat* by the census of 1911 were themselves married to archetypical proletarians: the implication that a class divide ran down the marriage-bed between a self-employed seamstress and a salary-earning metal

---

[68] Berlanstein, *The Working People of Paris*, p. 6.
[69] Geva, 'Échos de l'Atelier – Le Patron', *Le Socialiste*, 5 November 1887. The classic locus of such exploitation was the clothing trades, but it existed even in 'noble' artisanal trades such as cabinetmaking, as described in L. Weissbach, 'Artisanal Responses to Artistic Decline: The Cabinetmakers of Paris in the Era of Industrialization', *Journal of Social History*, vol. 16, 1982, pp. 67–81.

worker made little or no sense. 'Independent' workers – often impoverished to the point of hunger, utterly dependent upon merchant capital, in most respects indistinguishable from proletarians – might well have swollen the socialist army with new recruits: they numbered, by conservative estimates, one and a half million in 1906.[70] Yet the Parti Ouvrier never seriously devoted itself to propaganda among the outworkers of Paris, that heartland of the putting-out system, or, even less excusably, among the numerous semi-rural independent textile workers of the Marxists' fief in the Nord.

Despite Guesdist hopes, and perhaps because of Guesdist neglect, few near-proletarian petits bourgeois joined the POF or, indeed, any other socialist or labour organisation. Most outworkers, because of the precarious independence which defined them as petit-bourgeois rather than as proletarian, remained too isolated from each other, too remote from the labour movement, and too dependent upon the merchant capitalists who supplied their materials and controlled their markets, ever to adopt a strategy of class militancy. Once, during the seventeenth and eighteenth centuries, homeworkers had constituted one of the bastions of popular protest, but they had lost the communal solidarity which had once prompted their awareness of injustice and sustained their sporadic revolts, yet without acquiring the collective organisation and collectivist consciousness of the nineteenth-century industrial working class. Their apparent resignation to dependency and exploitation, a resignation which rendered them almost invisible to eyes blinded by the fireworks of strikes and political demonstrations, accounted for the relative Guesdist disinterest in their plight. The Parti Ouvrier rarely addressed itself to the grievances of Parisian seamstresses, since those grievances were so difficult to perceive, and even more difficult to mobilise. Guesdists, once again identifying the working class with its militant minority, abandoned hundreds of thousands of potential socialists to their fate. Ironically, the Parti Ouvrier's failure to embrace the aspirations of 'independent' workers confirmed their identification as petits bourgeois, thereby encouraging anti-collectivist ideologues in their campaign against a proportionately diminished proletarian socialism.

[70] F. Caron, 'Dynamismes et Freinages de la Croissance Industrielle', in *Histoire Économique et Sociale de la France: Tome IV – L'Ère Industrielle et la Société d'Aujourd'hui (Siècle 1880–1980)*: Premier Volume – *Ambiguïtés des Débuts et Croissance Effective (Années 1880–1914)* (Paris, 1979), pp. 261–2.

If outworkers, near proletarians, enjoyed only the most tenuous links with petit-bourgeois property-ownership, the superior ranks of the 'middle class' shaded almost imperceptibly into the bourgeoisie itself. Yet, for Marxists, the dividing line between the petite bourgeoisie and the bourgeoisie should have been anything but imperceptible: employment of wage labour sharply distinguished petits bourgeois, who fructified their property with their own labour, from bourgeois, who depended upon the work of others. Small employers, small only by comparison with large employers, exploited the iniquitous 'système de salaire' which, for Guesdists, defined capitalism: small capitalists, as dependent upon wage labour as were Schneider or Motte, appeared as 'petits' bourgeois only in the thoroughly non-Marxist, even anti-Marxist, gradational sense of the term. The Parti Ouvrier, however, heedlessly discarding its characteristic analytic of property and labour, sometimes succumbed to the predominant mentality of its society, which identified all 'small' businesspeople, whether employers of wage labour or not, as 'petits' bourgeois.

Nevertheless, Parti Ouvrier ambivalence towards small-scale capitalist enterprise reflected not only conceptual muddle, but ambiguities within French entrepreneurship. Some small employers, the most grasping and irresponsible capitalists in France, treated their workers with unparalleled ruthlessness, but others, generous 'patrons' (the ambiguity of the word, meaning both boss and protector, carried its own message), breathed life into the myth of the cohesive artisanal workshop. Some small employers adored the haute bourgeoisie, to whose glories they aspired, but others led popular protests against bourgeois monopolies, from which they suffered as much as any proletarian. Some small employers defended the bourgeois values of free enterprise and the sanctity of property with the passion of parvenus, but others retained close ties with the world of labour from which so many small businesspeople had emerged.[71] Bemused by these ambiguities, Guesdists failed to delineate the border between the bourgeoisie and the petite bourgeoisie, the border where some small employers appeared more

---

[71] The social ambiguity and importance of this category is described in Vigier, 'La Petite Bourgeoisie', p. 5 and pp. 8–9 and in H.-G. Haupt, 'La Petite Bourgeoisie: Une Classe Inconnue', *Mouvement Social*, no. 108, 1979, p. 14. For solidarity between petit-bourgeois employers and their employees, see J. Charles, *Les Débuts du Mouvement Syndical à Besançon* (Paris, 1962), p. 119.

bourgeois than the bourgeoisie, while others identified not only with the petite bourgeoisie, but with the working class itself.

A certain social rationale, a rationale with some Marxist justification, further justified the Guesdists' unwillingness to consign small employers to the bourgeoisie: many small capitalists, little more than 'head workers' in *de facto* labour collectives, accumulated no capital and served largely to organise relations between their enterprises and 'real' capitalists. Entrepreneurs of this kind predominated in the construction industry, where contractors and 'their' tradesmen often exchanged roles, shared common working conditions, and resembled each other in their values and living standards.[72] These 'capitalists' easily identified with the working class into which they had often been born, to which they might return, and where they retained close working relationships, friendships, and family ties.[73] Employers so closely associated with their employees, employers who moved so easily from the working-class aristocracy to the 'patronat' and back, employers 'who worked themselves even if they had others work for them',[74] could not be casually consigned to the bourgeoisie.

Better yet (from a Marxist perspective), many small capitalists detested big capitalists, their grievances against concentrated capital inspiring a ferocious hatred of 'plutocracy', albeit a hostility couched in populist rather than socialist terms. Capitalist finance, symbolised by the Bank of France and ably seconded by the finance ministry, administered credit to the advantage of large firms, imposing the highest interest rates upon the smallest businesses, when the latter could obtain finance at all. Plutocratic speculators, supported by corrupt local governments, monopolised the land and buildings of the burgeoning commercial districts of urban France, inflating rents to levels considered intolerable by even the most prosperous small businesspeople. Merchants, the great beneficiaries of the rapidly expanding world-economy of the nineteenth century, manipulated the market in ways beyond the comprehension or control of small businesspeople, thereby systematically shifting profitability from retailing (a petit-bourgeois realm) to wholesaling (long the preserve

---

[72] Cottereau, 'Vie Quotidienne et Résistance Ouvrière', p. 69.

[73] For social solidarity between the working class and small employers, see B. Zarca, 'La Spécificité de l'Artisanat au Sein des Classes Moyennes Traditionnelles', *Revue Française de Science Politique*, vol. 32, 1982, p. 217, and Noiriel, *Les Ouvriers dans la Société Française*, p. 100.

[74] Anonymous, 'La Petite Bourgeoisie', *Le Socialiste*, 9 October 1886.

of large capital). And powerful industrialists ruthlessly dominated their subcontractors, reducing them to subservient and poorly rewarded dependency during good times and coolly observing their failure during recessions.[75] No wonder a few small employers, anti-capitalist capitalists, adhered to socialism, a phenomenon not unknown in the Parti Ouvrier itself, which included among its leaders Charles Brunellière, *armateur* of Nantes.

On the other hand, small employers, as employers, clung desperately to their quasi-bourgeois standing in society, the standing which guaranteed their fragile superiority over their workers, from whom little else distinguished them. However poor by comparison with the haute bourgeoisie, however exploited by the commercial circuit of capital, however similar to skilled workers in life-style and values, these petits bourgeois prided themselves on their status as 'patrons'. Worse yet, from the perspective of the Parti Ouvrier, they loathed the labour movement, which attacked their 'rights' as employers, detested the social reforms instituted by municipal socialists, which increased their costs, and abominated the socialist challenge to the bourgeois order, which threatened their existence as men of property. Indeed, trade union militancy, the nascent welfare state, and the violent rhetoric of the 'reds' terrified petits bourgeois more than they frightened hauts bourgeois, since small employers lacked the capital resources, political connections, and bureaucratic bulwarks employed by capitalist notables to defend their interests against the labour movement and the socialist challenge.[76] Schneiders and Mottes founded docile company unions, transferred the costs of traditional employer paternalism to the newly paternalist state, and ruthlessly coerced, corrupted, or coopted Leftist politicians. Petit-bourgeois employers could erect no such shelters against the gathering tempest.

Small employers survived in the eye of the social hurricane which engulfed bourgeois France during the late nineteenth century: apparent calm disguised furious turmoil. But, despite the nostalgic myth which glamorised paternalistic artisanal workshops and damned soulless capitalist factories (one aspect of an essentially

[75] Conflicts between large and small capital are described in H. Peiter, 'Institutions and Attitudes: The Consolidation of the Business Community in Bourgeois France 1880–1914', *Journal of Social History*, vol. 9, 1976, pp. 510–25 and Haupt, 'The Petite Bourgeoisie', p. 102.

[76] Dupeux, *La Société Française*, p. 162. For the social logic behind the extreme petit-bourgeois hostility towards socialism and the labour movement, see the analysis in N. Poulantzas, *Classes in Contemporary Capitalism* (London, 1975), pp. 140–8.

reactionary mythology enthusiastically embraced by the otherwise revolutionary Parti Ouvrier), labour conflict tormented small businesspeople at least as much as it did great capitalists: small-scale labour disputes more than made up in personal bitterness what they lacked in national political visibility. Small businesspeople, victims themselves of intense competition and narrow profit margins, imposed miserable working-conditions upon their employees and paid the lowest wages in urban France. No wonder employees of small enterprises, except for a fortunate minority, came to be known to their fellows as 'pariahs',[77] outcasts who could discover no more secure or remunerative employment. Industrial workers, however discontented with their lot, preferred their conditions to those frequently imposed upon employees of the shops and workshops of petit-bourgeois France.

How did Guesdists comprehend this discomfiting upper level of the petite bourgeoisie (or lowest level of the bourgeoisie)? No doubt they criticised the iniquities of both small and large employers in their relentless tirades against capitalist exploitation, the exploitation which presumably haunted workshops as well as coal mines and textile mills. None the less, the Parti Ouvrier invariably illustrated its polemics with the miseries of factory life and the opulence of plutocrats, never with the petty tyranny of the *atelier* and the meanness of neighbourhood building contractors. On the rare occasions when the POF mentioned small employers (and the Party often implied that few had survived capitalist concentration), they usually received sympathetic, even sycophantic, treatment. Determined to isolate the haute bourgeoisie from even its most obvious allies, Guesdists hoped, against all the evidence, that lesser capitalists might be persuaded to join the anti-capitalist crusade: 'Don't you see, you small and middling capitalists', begged Dr Albert Delon, Guesdist leader in Nîmes, 'that the losses are all yours and that the profits all go to the monopolists? Capitalist society, which you defend so stupidly, is destroying you. Try to understand that you should join the Parti Ouvrier ...'[78] Paul Lafargue, paying extravagant court to the small capitalists of Paris, foreshadowed municipally-owned grocery stores, collectivist institutions designed to reduce food

---

[77] Haupt, 'The Petite Bourgeoisie', p. 103. A. Zimbalist, 'Introduction', in A. Zimbalist (ed.), *Case Studies in the Labor Process* (New York, 1979), p. xix describes the economic logic that generated these conditions, quite apart from any wishes on the part of small employers.

[78] A. Delon, 'Et Quand il y a des Pertes! ... ', *Le Socialiste*, 29 December 1895.

prices and thereby diminish the cost of labour to employers. 'The
Parti Ouvrier', he predicted, 'by beginning the battle against
merchants and speculators, will see the still numerous small industrial bourgeoisie flock to its standard and accept its dominance.'[79]
Astonishingly, Lafargue failed to consider the repercussions of his
proposal among petit-bourgeois grocers, far more likely victims of his
gimmick than capitalist wholesalers. Guesdist municipal councils
sensibly ignored Lafargue's scheme: once in control of communal
governments, French Marxists prudently refused to meddle with the
jealously defended rights of retail traders, a more welcoming and
considerably larger constituency than the 'small industrial
bourgeoisie'.

Guesdist local governments, the locus of so many ideological
experiments during the *Fin de Siècle*, flirted outrageously with small
employers. But who were these small employers, fit subjects for
socialist seduction, and who were capitalist bourgeois, the class
enemy personified? Guesdist communes planned (although their
scheme was eventually frustrated by prefectural intervention) to
impose an employment tax upon bourgeois bosses, but flinched from
antagonising the great mass of small businesspeople who employed
one or two journeymen or shop-assistants. Parti Ouvrier mayors
decided that employers metamorphosed into capitalists once they
employed more than two workers, although they never elaborated
the rationale for this judgment – a reticence to be expected, since
Marxist theory supplied no such rationale.[80] Determined to charm
locally influential small capitalists, Guesdist municipal councillors
surreptitiously discarded the encumbering analytic of property and
labour, hoping thereby to establish an anti-capitalist alliance of
already propertyless workers and the 'expropriated of tomorrow:
small employers, small retailers, small property-owners'.[81] Ironically, Guesdists devoted far more (unavailing) effort and ingenuity
to the recruitment of these near-capitalist petits bourgeois than to
propagandising among the near-proletarian independent piece-
workers.

[79] P. Lafargue, 'Le Parti Ouvrier et l'Alimentation Publique', *La Revue Socialiste*, no. 6, 1880,
pp. 296–7.
[80] Anonymous, 'Un Taxe Démocratique', *Bulletin Mensuel de la Fédération Nationale des Élus du
Parti Ouvrier Français*, deuxième année, no. 16, 1 March 1901, p. 4.
[81] Report of a speech by Guesde in 'Mouvement Social – Alais', *L'Égalité*, 12 March 1882.

Most petits bourgeois were neither thinly disguised proletarians nor aspirant small capitalists. The 'real' petite bourgeoisie, the core of their class, enjoyed undeniable independence based upon ownership of significant productive assets (unlike the independent piece-workers below them) and exploited only their own and their families' labour (unlike the small capitalists above them). How did the Parti Ouvrier comprehend this multitude of shopkeepers and workshop artisans?

Theoretically bemused and polemically disorientated by their failure to distinguish this category from small employers or piece workers, French Marxists vacillated uncertainly between contradictory theses on the 'middle' middle class. During its most intransigent moments, the Party abused even non-capitalist petits bourgeois as conservative property owners whose mere existence reinforced bourgeois domination: only their obliteration (by capitalists in the bourgeois present or socialists in the revolutionary future) would supposedly open the road to socialism. In their more accommodating mode, French Marxists welcomed petit-bourgeois hostility towards the aristocracy of wealth, the mentality which had bound shopkeepers and independent artisans to propertyless workers since at least the eighteenth century. Well-calculated militancy, Guesdists judged, might coax this mentality away from traditional *sans-culotte* populism towards socialist anti-capitalism.[82] Needless to say, the latter approach predominated in propaganda specifically aimed at small property-owners: determined to augment the socialist army in every possible way, the Parti Ouvrier refused to abandon petits bourgeois to the bourgeoisie.

Guesdist solicitation of the middle class enjoyed minor successes: petits bourgeois sometimes adopted the politics of their proletarian neighbours in working-class communities, such as Limoges or Lille, where socialists had established local hegemony.[83] French Marxists, however, unreasonably hoped for a similar outcome on a broader scale. Indeed, the Parti Ouvrier constructed a national 'front organisation' for its petit-bourgeois fellow travellers: a 'Cercle des Commerçants Socialistes' which materialised during the election campaigns of the late 1890s, asserting that the Parti Ouvrier was the

---

[82] Solidarity between petits bourgeois and proletarians seems to have been strong as late as the 1880s. Nord, 'Le Mouvement des Petits Commerçants', p. 38.

[83] See J. Merriman, *Red City* for a predominantly working-class community which included a socialist petite bourgeoisie.

'true and only defender'[84] of the petite bourgeoisie. And the POF's cadres certainly included a substantial number of erstwhile petits bourgeois, just as the Party's proletarian militants often retreated into independent petit-bourgeois occupations, having been excluded from their trades by employer black-lists. Superficially, middle-class Marxism possessed some plausibility.

All the same, despite the Guesdists' best efforts, most shopkeepers and independent artisans, whether employers or not, detested Marxist socialism, and with reason. Victory for the Parti Ouvrier promised 'the abolition of private property in the means of production', and the subtle Guesdist distinctions between exploitative capital and non-exploitative petit-bourgeois property cut little ice. Small businesspeople, however profound their hostility towards bourgeois monopolists and however intense their dislike of plutocratic ostentation, defended bourgeois property-rights with near religious fanaticism against the communist heresy preached by Guesde.[85] Guesdist collectivism, whether embodied in the great consumer cooperatives of the Nord, in municipal pharmacies established by socialist communes, or in revolutionary rhetoric, frightened and antagonised small property-owners, who readily focused their insecurities, frustrations, and discontent upon the 'red peril'.

Only 'ministerialist' socialism (including Millerand himself, defender and representative of the Twelfth Arrondissment wine merchants) overcame this hostility in national politics, and then only because small businesspeople (and not all of them, and not for long) decided that Millerand et Cie. were not 'collectivists', that they posed no threat to property, large or small. The Parti Ouvrier, reaching the same conclusion, identified Ministerialism, the antithesis of revolutionary militancy, with 'petit-bourgeois socialism' – implicit admission that Marxist collectivism, by definition, alienated small property-owners. Challenged by this dilemma, Guesdists confronted the choice of either retreating into principled proletarian exclusivity, thereby further antagonising the petite bourgeoisie, or abandoning their distinctive 'collectivism' to gain petit-bourgeois endorsement.

---

[84] *Pas de Paroles, Des Faits* (election poster from 1898 in the Fonds Guesde, IISG, item no. 638/ 3). The organisation was not much discussed in Guesdist publications. See brief mentions in 'Le Parti Ouvrier en France – Paris', *Le Socialiste*, 20 November 1898 and Anonymous, 'Les Socialistes et le Ministère Galliffet', *Le Socialiste*, 23 July 1899. It does not seem to have been represented at the 16th Party Congress during this period.

[85] Nord, *Paris Shopkeepers*, p. 291.

They sometimes favoured the latter strategy, refusing to abandon the petite bourgeoisie to the Ministerialist class traitors. But the Parti Ouvrier, confused by the most confusing of classes, could not decide whether to solicit petits bourgeois as incipient proletarians, the 'expropriated of tomorrow', or as an authentic middle class with its own interests and ambitions. The former tactic accorded well with the Marxist conviction that capital degraded small property-owners to 'non-historic' status, with the conviction that petits bourgeois, foredoomed victims of proletarianisation, had no creative role in the present and could gain no place in either the hyper-capitalist near-future or its socialist successor. Unfortunately, this 'proletarianisation' thesis contradicted evident social trends in *fin-de-siècle* France and, worse, thoroughly alienated most petits bourgeois, who refused to reconcile themselves to their 'inevitable' demise. The alternative tactic, the construction of a distinctively petit-bourgeois socialism, might have beguiled France's millions of shopkeepers and artisans, given the considerable anti-capitalist grievances of small property-owners during the *Belle Époque*. But, once embarked upon the seduction of the petite bourgeoisie, the Parti Ouvrier risked losing its proletarian identity, thereby degenerating into a movement virtually indistinguishable from the 'petit-bourgeois' Radicals. The POF, with good reason, never unequivocally opted for one or the other of these tactical alternatives, since both options offered tempting opportunities and suffered from daunting disadvantages. The Guesdists' determination to have the best of both worlds, unfortunately, sometimes antagonised proletarians and petits bourgeois alike. Historical problems do not always come ready-supplied with solutions. The petite bourgeoisie, in its stubborn denial of proletarianisation, has presented Marxists, not least the French Marxists of the *Belle Époque*, with one of the most infuriating and insoluble of these problems.

Aristocrats, peasants, and labourers: Marxism and rural society

> The same cause producing the same effects, the concentration of
> wealth has occurred in the countryside as well as in the town,
> leading to the progressive disappearance not only of small
> properties but even of the medium ...
>
> Anonymous, 'Le Socialisme Agraire', *Le Socialiste*, 15 April
> 1891.

European Marxism dwelt in cities, with only occasional excursions
into the countryside: the doctrine's most eminent ideologues lived
their creative lives as metropolitan intellectuals, its militants devoted
their militancy to the continent's great industrial centres, and the
factory working class furnished its archetypical constituency.
Europe's peasant majority puzzled and perturbed these urban
socialists, who hoped to extend their influence into the continent's
myriad villages, but repeatedly suffered disappointment and
frustration. Anti-Marxists, indeed, have charged Marx with establishing a socialist tradition of indifference or hostility towards rural
society, which he supposedly misunderstood and despised.[1] This
charge, however, is misleading.

Marx, at least in his later years, became far more interested in
peasant society, and far more sympathetic towards its grievances
and aspirations, than anti-Marxist scholarship allows, and Marxists,
determined to plant socialism in the soil of the countryside, have
devoted endless patience and energy to debating the class status and
political potential of agrarian producers.[2] Nevertheless, intractable
conceptual problems have dogged this Marxist engagement with

---

[1] See, for example, D. Mitrany, *Marx Against the Peasants* (Durham, 1951) – a particularly
extreme and surprisingly influential example of this genre.

[2] See the analyses in H. Draper, *Karl Marx's Theory of Revolution: The Politics of Social Classes*
(New York, 1977), chapters 12–14; O. Hammen, 'Marx and the Agrarian Question',
American Historical Review, vol. 77, 1972, pp. 679–704; and H. Mayer, 'Marx, Engels and the
Politics of the Peasantry', *Cahiers de l'Institut de Science Économique Appliquée*, Série S, no. 102,
1960, pp. 91–152.

rural society. Did rural landowners constitute merely another faction of capital, or did landownership underlie a unique 'agrarian' mode of exploitation? Could the analytic of labour and property dissect rural society, or did theoretical comprehension of the countryside require its own conceptual categories? Did 'peasants' compose a class, or was 'peasant' merely a diffuse occupational identity? And how did 'rural classes' relate to their urban equivalents – landowners to bourgeois, peasants to petits bourgeois, farmworkers to proletarians?[3]

Nor was rural society merely the passive, if perplexing, object of Marxist curiosity. Europe's country-people, building upon age-old traditions, constructed a formidable alternative to the Marxist paradigm of property and labour: a concept of social conflict focusing ideological attention upon *forms* of production rather than upon *relations* of production, a concept in which 'primary' producers struggled against those who battened upon them, rather than a concept in which exploitative property owners confronted exploited workers. During the late nineteenth century, this 'agrarian' problematic not only legitimated the immemorial clash between town and country, but obscured class conflict between landowners and the landless and sustained an anti-socialist politics which successfully united village and manor against 'parasitic' urban workers and the supposedly anti-rural trade unionists and socialists who represented them. 'Country politics' clashed with class politics across the continent.

In turn, urban contempt for 'rural barbarism' – a mentality which infected many nineteenth-century working-class radicals (coexisting strangely with their common idealisation of Arcadian community) – reinforced this conservative 'agrarianism', thereby validating the agrarians' denunciation of the predatory urban (Jewish?) 'reds' who threatened rural tranquillity, prosperity, and social cohesion.[4] Marxists in principle opposed both the new agrarianism and its mirror-image in the urban disdain for country-people: the Marxist conception of the class war self-consciously transcended conflict between town and country, however conceptualised. At their most

---

3   For a sensitive and sympathetic discussion of these issues in Marxist discourse, see R. Stavenhagen, *Les Classes Sociales dans les Sociétés Agraires* (Paris, 1969).
4   The importance of the hostility between Marxism and 'agrarianism' is highlighted in D. Hodges, 'Classical Economics and Marx's Theory of Social Classes', *Indian Journal of Social Research*, vol. 2, 1961, pp. 91–5.

extreme, European Marxists totally refused to recognise the distinctive characteristics of agrarian society, thereby repudiating the urban–rural dichotomy altogether.

French agrarianism, although never achieving the political predominance of its Imperial German counterpart, flourished during the *Belle Époque*, successfully combining traditional rural resentment of urban 'parasitism' with enthusiasm for agricultural protection, paranoia about 'rural depopulation', and anti-labour and anti-socialist hysteria. Despite (or because of) the intricate interdependency of rural and urban society, French country-people increasingly succumbed to the promise of agrarian interest-group politics: they resented, as they had always resented, the urban minority who set the nation's political agenda, determined its economic policy, and moulded the 'national' culture, while their alienation from Paris deepened throughout the interminable agricultural depression of the 1880s and 1890s.[5] An incipient 'country party' – residually clerical, Republican, or nationalist, but dedicated above all else to the care and feeding of country-people – supplemented and soon supplanted the antiquated royalism and Bonapartism of French rural protest.

Inevitably, some French socialists reacted to this development by identifying the peasantry with conservative agrarianism, a movement actually initiated and led by wealthy landowners. This reaction reinforced the urban socialist movement's traditional hostility towards 'reactionary' rural society, reinforcement which in turn reinforced rural hostility towards urban 'partageux' – a vicious circle which threatened further to buttress every barricade separating revolutionary town from resentful countryside. Significantly, although socialists annually commemorated the Parisian massacres of June 1848 and May 1871, they had completely forgotten the largely rural opposition to the Bonapartist *coup d'état* of 1851, one of the most violent and wide-spread popular rebellions of the nineteenth century. Misled by its selective memories, ignoring the long

[5] The centrality of urban/rural conflict during the *Belle Époque* is described in M. Agulhon, 'Attitudes Politiques', in G. Duby and A. Wallon (eds.), *Histoire de la France Rurale:* Tome III – *Apogée et Crise de la Civilisation Paysanne 1789–1914* (Paris, 1976), p. 529. For rural solidarity *vis-à-vis* urban society, see P. Barral, 'Un Secteur Dominé: La Terre', in *Histoire Économique et Sociale de la France:* Tome IV – *L'Ère Industrielle et la Société d'Aujourd'hui (Siècle 1880–1980):* Premier Volume – *Ambiguïtés des Débuts et Croissance Effective (Années 1880–1914)* (Paris, 1979), p. 378. Barral's *Les Agrariens Français: De Méline à Pisani* (Paris, 1968) provides a superb analysis of agrarian anti-socialism and its role in consolidating the rural community behind its notables, and see H. Lebovics, *The Alliance of Iron and Wheat in the Third French Republic: Origins of the New Conservatism* (Baton Rouge, 1988).

history of rural radicalism which reached back to the great *jacqueries* of the middle ages, most of the French labour movement unwittingly seconded the agrarians' self-serving myth of innate peasant conservatism. The early works of Guesde himself exemplified this urban hostility towards 'les ruraux' who, in the embittered memories of his generation of radicals, had erected an immovable barrier against successful urban insurrection.[6] Nevertheless, Guesde's animosity towards rural society disappeared as he turned to Marxist collectivism, and his Parti Ouvrier categorically opposed both the agrarian conception of society and its anti-rural mirror-image among urban revolutionaries. Although predominantly entrenched in France's cities and industrial towns (with no more than 7 per cent of its militants classed as peasants[7]), the POF hoped to extend class conflict into the countryside, not wage indiscriminate war upon the country's thousands of villages.[8]

Given the numerical preponderance of 'les ruraux' in French society, Guesdists *had* to appeal to country-people, since an anti-socialist monopoly of village politics foreshadowed the same dismal fate for Marxists as that suffered by Parisian Jacobins, the *Démocrates-Socialistes* of the Second Republic, and the Communards.[9] Engels himself, although generally suspicious of socialist efforts to mobilise country-people, conceded that 'no lasting revolutionary transformation is possible in France *against* the will of the small peasant'.[10] The novel political order of the Third Republic reinforced the lesson taught by the bloody defeats inflicted upon Parisian radicals between 1794 and 1871: universal manhood suffrage drastically reduced the strategic advantage of metropolitan militancy and transferred at least potential political hegemony into the hands of the millions of voters scattered across rural France.[11] Lafargue himself lost the parliamentary seat he had gained in 1891 because a

---

[6] J. Guesde, *Le Livre Rouge de la Justice Rurale* (Geneva, 1872). For the deep distrust of rural society among French workers, see Y. Lequin, 'Classe Ouvrière et Idéologie dans la Région Lyonnaise à la Fin du XIXᵉ Siècle', *Mouvement Social*, no. 69, 1969, p. 16.

[7] C. Willard, *Le Mouvement Socialiste en France (1893–1905): Les Guesdistes* (Paris, 1965), p. 322.

[8] See, for a particularly telling example of this theme, G. Farjat, 'Les Ruraux', *Le Socialiste*, 10 July 1892.

[9] For commentary on this logic, see M. Jollivet, 'Sociétés Rurales et Classes Sociales', in Y. Tavernier et al. (eds.), *L'Univers Politique des Paysans dans la France Contemporaine* (Paris, 1972), pp. 79–106 and P. Gratton, 'Le Mouvement Ouvrier et la Question Agraire de 1870 à 1947', in *ibid.*, pp. 163–4.

[10] F. Engels, 'The Peasant Question in France and Germany', in K. Marx and F. Engels, *Selected Works* (Moscow, 1970), vol. 3, p. 468 (Engels' stress).

[11] G. Walter, *Histoire des Paysans de France* (Paris, 1963), p. 415, for the transformation.

subsequent gerrymander incorporated reliably anti-socialist rural votes into his constituency.

Nor did the countryside's political mobilisation benefit the agrarian Right alone. Throwing off the tutelage of rural notables, many French peasants prided themselves on their new status as the touchstone of democratic legitimacy, and discovered novel ways of converting their political potency into social and economic advantage. But, as peasants threw themselves into the brave new world of mass parties and economic interest-groups, they refused to abandon more 'primitive' modes of political representation: the revolt which swept the vineyards of the Midi in the early twentieth century constituted the most wide-spread rural uprising since the *Grande Peur* of 1789, while the woodcutters of central France conducted a veritable *jacquerie* against the landowners and merchants who exploited their labour.[12] French Marxists, whether in search of electoral support or revolutionary *élan*, could not ignore peasant politics. Nor did they.[13] Socialists, the Guesdists decided, could find building material for their political edifice in fields as well as in factories.

In exploring this insight, a few Guesdists decided that 'it's the countryside which now has the most to suffer from the present economic system, and it's from the countryside that . . . the decisive blow will come which will destroy that system',[14] a perception which foreshadowed the 'third world' Marxism of the twentieth century. At its most extreme, this enthusiasm for rural rebellion evolved into a socialist agrarianism which maintained that, 'despite the imperfections of their organisation, country-people are motivated by a vigour and determination of which the industrial proletariat – drained and depressed by the surplus labour extracted in capitalist factories – is all too often incapable'.[15] Guesdists never accorded a similar revolutionary priority over the proletariat to any other class. The POF may have forgotten the long French tradition of rural rebellion, and the great socialist peasant revolutions of the

---

[12] E. Weber, *Peasants into Frenchmen: The Modernization of Rural France 1870–1914* (Stanford, 1976), pp. 276–7. Gratton attributes the socialists' increased interest in the peasantry during the *Belle Époque* to this quasi-revolutionary militancy. P. Gratton, *Les Luttes de Classes dans les Campagnes* (Paris, 1971), pp. 24–25.

[13] See, for an example of this concern, the 'Enquête Socialiste sur la Situation des Classes Agricoles' (1892). Items 627/1 – 628/1 in the Fonds Guesde of the IISG.

[14] 'B.' (C. Bonnier), 'La Crise Agricole', *Le Socialiste*, 5 March 1893.

[15] P.-M. André, 'Les Grèves: Les Travailleurs Agricoles', *Le Socialiste*, 4–11 December 1904.

twentieth century still lay in the future, but Guesdist iconographers, inspired more by hope than history, would have thoroughly approved of adding the peasants' sickle to the workers' hammer.

How did Guesdists conceptualise the rural society from which they expected so much? Despite lapses, such as occasional references to the 'classe agricole',[16] French Marxists repudiated the identification of town and country as distinct and coherent social entities, the separation of urban and rural which justified the separatism of the conservative agrarians. On the other hand, the POF acknowledged the traditions and concerns which distinguished rural from urban society, admitting that country-people possessed 'interests, needs, and modes of expression different from those of the town'.[17] Ignoring these peculiarities, reducing villages to mere bucolic equivalents of industrial faubourgs, would alienate potential socialists. These conflicting imperatives – the need to challenge agrarian separatism, coupled with recognition of the distinctiveness of the countryside – resulted in an unstable and untheorised compromise: application of the analytic of property and labour to rural society, but an application distinct from that directed to the urban social order. This conceptual strategy divided the countryside into a 'rural bourgeoisie' of large land-owners, a rural 'middle class' of smallholders working their own land, and a propertyless rural proletariat – 'three classes or, more exactly, three class fragments'[18] analogous to, but distinct from, the Marxist urban typology of capitalists, petits bourgeois, and workers.[19]

A 'rural bourgeoisie'? This oxymoron suggests a solution to 'the mystery of the vanishing aristocracy'. Aristocratic land-owners, the *bêtes noires* of virtually every revolutionary since 1789, almost completely disappeared from the Parti Ouvrier's depictions of its society. On the few occasions when Guesdists noticed the presence of an aristocracy in *fin-de-siècle* France, they emphasised aristocratic social 'impotence', a characteristic 'of classes which ... have exhausted their function'. These classes, according to the Guesdists, 'may linger

---

16 'B.' (C. Bonnier), 'La Crise Agricole', *Le Socialiste*, 5 March 1893.
17 Anonymous, 'La Propagande Agricole', *Le Socialiste*, 18 October 1893.
18 J. Guesde, 'L'Oeuvre de Marseille', *Le Socialiste*, 10 October 1892.
19 Guesdists reiterated this typology in virtually every one of their publications directed towards the peasantry. See the archetypical instance in Adéodat Compère-Morel's *La Vérité aux Paysans par un Campagnard* (Paris, 1897).

for a time, but are necessarily obliterated by social evolution'.[20] Aristocrats, in other words, had become that archetypical 'non-historic class' – a ruling elite without a society to rule. How could the château, that hallowed symbol of oppression and exploitation, have so easily and completely vanished from Marxist portrayals of the French landscape?

According to the Parti Ouvrier, bourgeois rather than aristocrats ruled the countryside, a natural outcome of France's 'transition from feudalism to capitalism'. In one Marxist scenario, triumphant capitalists had long ago obliterated the aristocracy, as urban specu-lators exploited the free market in land imposed by the bourgeois triumph of 1789 to appropriate the estates of a moribund nobility. In the Guesdists' alternative scenario, the bourgeoisie had gradually assimilated the nobility (and been assimilated to it) as aristocrats metamorphosed into rural entrepreneurs virtually indistinguishable from bankers or merchants. In either scenario, the antiquated ruling class of the *ancien régime* had long ago forfeited its historical force and social centrality. The Guesdists' contemptuous dismissal of the aristocracy carried conviction, since the 'persistence of the Old European Order' certainly did not characterise *fin-de-siècle* France, whatever the circumstances further east.[21] 'Real' aristocrats, or at least the most prominent of their caste, had become virtually indistinguishable from the haute bourgeoisie: nobles added their cachet and connections to company boards, while bankers and industrialists aped the aristocratic life-style on their country estates; early-nineteenth-century class distinctions between aristocrats and bourgeois in patterns of property ownership, recruitment to the civil service, styles of high society, and the sharing of marriage beds diminished as the century progressed, and virtually disappeared during the *Belle Époque*; and the aristocratic and bourgeois quarters of French cities coalesced, their wealthy inhabitants assuming the common status of 'proprietor'.[22] As businesspeople purchased titles

---

[20] Anonymous, 'Jules Guesde dans le Midi', *Le Socialiste*, 10 June 1893.

[21] A. Daumard, 'Wealth and Affluence in France since the Beginning of the Nineteenth Century', in W. Rubinstein (ed.), *Wealth and the Wealthy in the Modern World* (London, 1980), pp. 105–6 and Lebovics, *The Alliance of Iron and Wheat in the Third French Republic*, pp. 78–81. For telling illustrations of this widely accepted thesis, see P. Bernard, *Économie et Sociologie de la Seine-et-Marne 1850–1950* (Paris, 1953), pp. 177–8 and P. Barral, *Le Département de l'Isère sous la IIIᵉ République: Histoire Sociale et Politique* (Paris, 1962), p. 100.

[22] For the merger of enterprise and aristocracy, see A. Daumard, 'L'Évolution des Structures Sociales en France à l'Époque de l'Industrialisation', *Revue Historique*, vol. 247, 1972, pp. 339–41 and P. Sorlin, *La Société Française 1840–1914* (Paris, 1969), p. 123. For the gradual

and nobles played the stockmarket, as aristocratic mine-owners and bourgeois industrialists fought together against increasingly assertive working-class communities, the centuries-old and always somewhat fictitious conflict between revolutionary bourgeois and reactionary aristocrats degenerated from high historic drama to gossip column trivia.

Guesdists never embarked upon a serious analysis of these economic and cultural relations between château and counting house: the Parti Ouvrier's dismissal of the aristocracy derived not so much from 'empirical' observation as from a manoeuvre in the Marxist war against 'bourgeois democracy'. Throughout the history of the early Third Republic, from the successful battle against the 'Republic of the Dukes' during the 1870s until the furious conflicts of the Dreyfus Affair, many socialists and all Radicals advocated Republican unity against the menace of 'feudal reaction'. Scheming nobles, abetted by a reactionary clergy, supposedly plotted to restore the monarchy in politics, reestablish an authoritarian hierarchy in society, and recover their hereditary privileges within their communities, thereby posing a deadly threat to Radical and socialist alike. According to this rhetoric, Republicans, whatever their class, had to stand together against the machinations of aristocratic reaction, as they had stood together against the counter-revolution in 1793, Charles X in 1830, Louis Philippe in 1848, Louis Napoleon in 1851, and MacMahon in 1877 – thereby implanting a tradition of solidarity which sustained populist neo-Jacobinism, the most vital alternative to working-class socialism, well into the twentieth century.

The Parti Ouvrier categorically rejected this myth, both as historical interpretation and as political strategy: for French Marxists, the 'bourgeois' Republic, whether in the hands of Jacobins, 48ers, or Third Republic Radicals, was itself reactionary – mere window-dressing concealing the bleak reality of exploitation, dedicated only to the preservation of bourgeois property, always more than willing to ally with remnants of the Old Order against the working class. 'Are not the remnants of the feudal regime represented by the agrarian bourgeoisie merged ... into the financial and

---

assimilation of aristocratic life-style by the bourgeoisie and *vice versa*, see T. Zeldin, *France 1848–1945: Ambition and Love* (Oxford, 1979), pp. 16–17. The role of neighbourhood in the merger of French elites is discussed in F.-P. Codaccioni, *De l'Inégalité Sociale dans une Grande Ville Industrielle: Le Drame de Lille de 1850 à 1914* (Lille, 1976), p. 186, and pp. 355–6.

industrial bourgeoisie in a genuine feudalism?'[23] demanded Guesdists, enraged by Radical and 'Radical-Socialist' efforts to ensnare the working class in the defence of one 'capitalist faction' against another.

Cynical Radicals undoubtedly manipulated aristocratic bogeymen to suit their own purposes: a revival of the *ancien régime* during the late nineteenth century smacked more of democratic scaremongering or self-indulgent rightist fantasy than of practical politics. Nevertheless, a traditional aristocracy – truncated, demoralised, and isolated, but genuine enough – did indeed survive in the more 'backward' regions of the West and the Massif Central, struggling to preserve local vestiges of the old order, if not necessarily to restore aristocratic hegemony over France as a whole. More seriously, a conflict of 'world-historical' significance divided those of the French elite, by no means all aristocrats, who aspired to a modernised *ancien régime* of industrial corporatism and populist authoritarianism from others among the wealthy and powerful, by no means all bourgeois, who supported the liberal order which guaranteed their wealth and power through formal equality moderated by property ownership and mediated by the market.[24] The POF was right: aristocrats no longer ruled France. But they had left a potent ideological legacy.

The Parti Ouvrier, however, never acknowledged the survival of aristocrats in their remote Breton lairs, nor recognised the all-important dispute between aristocratic authority and bourgeois liberty raging within the European ruling class, a dispute not finally resolved until the beautiful spring of 1945. Survival of a *genuine* feudalism distinct from the bourgeoisie, even survival of an ersatz aristocratic ideology, would have disrupted the simple pattern of class war between capital and labour, thereby dislocating the clear alternative between bourgeois liberalism and working-class socialism. Refusing to recognise such complications, the Parti Ouvrier campaigned instead against a rhetorical 'aristocracy' of wealthy capital owners, an ideological construct which conveniently ob-

---

[23] A. Zévaès, 'La Nouvelle Méthode', *Le Socialiste*, 2 and 9 December 1900.

[24] R. Gibson, 'The French Nobility in the Nineteenth Century', in J. Howorth and P. Cherny (eds.), *Elites in France: Origins, Reproduction, and Power* (New York, 1981), pp. 5–45, and A. Daumard, 'Puissance et Inquiétudes de la Société Bourgeoise', in *Histoire Économique et Sociale de la France: Tome IV – L'Ère Industrielle et la Société d'Aujourd'hui (Siècle 1880–1980): Premier Volume – Ambiguïtés des Débuts et Croissance Effective (Années 1880–1914)* (Paris, 1979), pp. 424 and 432.

scured the surviving aristocrats and reviving aristocratic ideals of the late nineteenth century.[25]

Rural landowners, however, represented an interpretive enigma, even when understood as merely one of the 'different elements of the bourgeoisie'.[26] How distinct were landlords from the (other?) lords of capital? What relationship prevailed between agrarian land-ownership and (other?) varieties of bourgeois property in *fin-de-siècle* France? Confused by both the complications of its society and the ambiguities of its doctrine, the Parti Ouvrier never decided whether irreconcilable conflict separated rent from profit, or whether land-ownership, commerce, finance, and industry melded easily into a virtually homogeneous bourgeoisie.

This quandary paralysed Guesdist analyses of agricultural protection, on occasion interpreted as dividing 'landowners from industrialists',[27] but on other occasions presented as a general bourgeois plot to exploit the working class. Nor did the Parti Ouvrier's metahistorical vision, usually more complex and sophisticated than the movement's sociology of the *fin-de-siècle* bourgeoisie, contribute a great deal to the POF's comprehension of landownership. Occasional Guesdist forays into nineteenth-century French social history did identify the 'two great fractions of the bourgeoisie which have ruled successively since the Restoration: the rural element of large landed property, and the urban element of great industrial property'.[28] Marx himself, Guesdists realised, had ascribed a specific identity to landownership, and had employed the conflict between legitimist landowners and Orleanist industrialists to explain the crises of mid-nineteenth-century France.[29] But French Marxists, unwilling to explore the implications of multiple elites, failed to elaborate this interpretive strategy, which they might have applied to the conflicts which disrupted establishment politics during the 1890s: the career of Méline, exemplary late-nineteenth-century agrarian protectionist, no less than that of Thiers, Marx's exemplar, illustrated at least

---

[25] The Guesdists tapped a powerful polemical tradition with this approach to the French plutocracy: the identification of all the wealthy as aristocrats, a tradition that dated from at least the sans-culottes. See W. Sewell, *Work and Revolution in France: The Language of Labour from the Old Regime to 1848* (Cambridge, 1980), p. 111 for the tradition, and A. Daumard, 'L'Évolution des Structures Sociales', pp. 341–2 for its survival into the *Belle Époque*.

[26] Anonymous, 'Entente Cordiale', *Le Socialiste*, 5 February 1887.

[27] J. Guesde, *Le Socialisme au Jour le Jour* (Paris, 1899), p. 46.

[28] Éd. Fortin, 'Un Anniversaire', *Le Socialiste*, 12 February 1899.

[29] The distinction between landed capital and finance and industrial capital informs the social analysis in *The Class Struggles in France* and *The Eighteenth Brumaire of Louis Bonaparte*.

factional conflict within bourgeois politics, and perhaps the illusory nature of 'bourgeois' politics as a self-sufficient explanation of the French polity.

By and large, French Marxists denied landownership a constitutive role in society, despite the obvious conflicts of interest between real estate and portfolio investment which distinguished landowners from the rest of the propertied elite: industrialists and merchants, no less than the landless poor, suffered from high rents, and manufacturers disliked agricultural protection almost as much as their workers hated the resultant inflation of food prices.[30] Why did French Marxists neglect this issue? The most obvious answer to this question would be 'empirical'. Might Guesdists have ignored landowners simply because agricultural real estate had lost its traditional centrality in French fortunes?[31] Bourgeois (and aristocrats) did, after all, increasingly abandon rural landownership to less financially discriminating small-holders during the *Belle Époque*, as the rural depression diverted the flow of investment from agricultural land to stocks and bonds.[32]

Guesdist discourse, however, provides no evidence to justify this thesis: the Parti Ouvrier blissfully ignored the trends in investment which so diminished rural capital during the 1880s and 1890s. French Marxists even asserted that the opposite tendency prevailed in the French countryside, that 'having monopolised commerce . . . [and] industry, capitalism now also monopolises productive land'.[33] The Guesdists' indictment of rural capital, the primary source of the POF's appeal to peasants and farm workers, necessarily described *increasing* bourgeois domination of agricultural landownership. French Marxists would have seriously weakened their denunciations of the 'agrarian bourgeoisie' if they had recognised a capitalist withdrawal from the countryside. Polemical efficacy, that absolute Guesdist priority, required the incorporation of rural landowners, with their strengths, weaknesses, and peculiarities, into the all-

[30] G. Dupeux, *La Société Française 1789–1970* (Paris, 1972), p. 164, and Sorlin, *La Société Française*, p. 52 stress the importance of this conflict between rent and profit.

[31] G. Palmade, *Capitalisme et Capitalistes Français au XIXᵉ Siècle'*, (Paris, 1961), p. 204, and Sorlin, *La Société Française*, p. 134.

[32] M. Agulhon, 'La Transformation du Monde Paysan', in G. Duby and A. Wallon (eds.), *Histoire de la France Rurale: Tome III – Apogée et Crise de la Civilisation Paysanne 1789–1914* (Paris, 1976), p. 474 and G. Dupeux, *Aspects de l'Histoire Sociale et Politique du Loir-et-Cher 1848–1914* (Paris, 1962), p. 574.

[33] Compère-Morel, *La Vérité aux Paysans par un Campagnard*, p. 12.

conquering but essentially abstract bourgeoisie which dominated the Marxist social vision.

Guesdists, alert for possible recruits, paid far more attention to the 'rural working class' than they did to agrarian capitalists, a preoccupation with agricultural labour which stemmed from two factors: the Marxists' conviction that capitalist exploitation would soon proletarianise the entire countryside, and their faith that the resulting rural proletariat offered socialists their natural clientele in France's thousands of villages. Technological and organisational innovations, according to the Parti Ouvrier, would soon revolutionise agriculture as they had revolutionised industry, dispossessed peasants would follow hand-loom weavers into the all-engulfing maw of capitalist concentration, and the resulting proletarianised countryside would raise the red flag of socialist revolution against its exploiters. Peasants and proletarians would become socially and politically indistinguishable, both classes propertyless victims of capital, both natural supporters of the Parti Ouvrier.

In retrospect, the Guesdist fantasy of factory farming and massed rural wage-labour advancing against capital behind socialist banners appears laughably self-deluding: far from becoming industrialised and proletarianised, small-scale technologies and an entrepreneurial (and predominantly conservative) land-owning peasantry have characterised French agriculture throughout the twentieth century, as they did throughout the nineteenth. How could Guesdists have so deluded themselves? Admittedly, certain trends during the *Belle Époque* reinforced Parti Ouvrier illusions: the marginal small-holders who had traditionally supplemented their inadequate farming income with sporadic wage-labour disappeared in favour of permanent agricultural workers, while some rural occupations, such as woodcutting, began to manifest all the classic symptoms of proletarianisation.[34] And a few regions of rural France, such as the endless wheat fields of the Brie or the phyloxera-devastated vineyards of Languedoc, evolved towards large-scale

---

[34] See Bernard, *Économie et Sociologie de la Seine-et-Marne*, pp. 73–77 for the creation of the modern farm worker at the expense of the dwarf peasant, and, for the woodcutters, Gratton, *Les Luttes de Classes*, pp. 61–63 and A. Kriegel, 'À la Conquête du Prolétariat Rural: Les Bûcherons et leurs Syndicats au Tournant du Siècle', in A. Kriegel, *Le Pain et les Roses: Jalons pour une Histoire des Socialismes* (Paris, 1968), pp. 51–60.

farming based upon hired labour.[35] A rural society as large and diverse as that of France, suitably interpreted, provided evidence for virtually any hypothesis, however incredible.

For the Guesdist imagery of agrarian proletarianisation *was* incredible. Far from increasing, the absolute number of agricultural wage-labourers had declined from approximately 3 million to $2\frac{1}{2}$ million between 1882 and 1892, and their proportional share of the rural population diminished even more dramatically – trends which would accelerate into the twentieth century.[36] This 'deproletarianisation' derived from the 'capital logic' of French farming, from the very interaction of labour and property deployed by the Marxist POF in its social analyses. Yet Guesdists completely ignored the relativities between urban and rural wages which, much to the advantage of the former during the agricultural depression, ensured a veritable flood of labour from village to city, while workers who remained on the land exploited the exodus to increase their wages and improve their conditions, thereby restricting the market for their labour and further reducing their numbers.[37] Guesdist preoccupation with the 'rural proletariat'[38] derived not from observation of the French countryside, nor from theoretical understanding of agricultural economics, but from an *a priori* conviction that socialism relied upon proletarianisation for its triumph. The Marxist prediction of an all-encompassing rural working class depended upon hope rather than theoretical or empirical insight.

None the less, quite apart from Guesdist wish-fulfilment, millions of rural labourers continued to labour in the French countryside, constituting one of the nation's largest occupational categories: by some estimations, farm labourers outnumbered urban industrial

---

35 For Languedoc, see L. Frader, 'Socialists, Syndicalists and the Peasant Question in the Aude', *Journal of Social History*, vol. 19, 1986, p. 452, and J. Smith, 'Work Routine and Social Structure in a French Village: Cruzy in the Nineteenth Century', *Journal of Interdisciplinary History*, vol. 5, 1975, p. 370.

36 F. Langlois, *Les Salariés Agricoles en France* (Paris, 1962), p. 9.

37 A. Cabanis, *Introduction à l'Histoire Économique et Sociale de la France au XIXᵉ et XXᵉ Siècle* (Toulouse, 1977), p. 140, and the analysis in Barral, *Le Département de l'Isère*, p. 129.

38 There was a significant ambiguity in Guesdist social terminology *vis-à-vis* rural labourers. While references to the 'prolétariat rural' were clear and unequivocal, the party also used the ambiguous term 'travailleurs des campagnes' to refer to its potential audience in the countryside – a category which potentially included the working but propertied peasantry. See the subtle shifts between the two usages in A. Compère-Morel, *Les Propos d'un Rural* (Beauvais, 1902).

workers.[39] The Parti Ouvrier might reasonably have hoped for massive reinforcements from the countryside, always assuming that 'worker' unproblematically equalled 'socialist'. Unfortunately for the prospects of agrarian socialism, rural labour, despite abysmal wages and conditions, proved surprisingly resistant to mobilisation against capital: trade unionism did expand in the countryside during the *Fin de Siècle*, but unions enjoyed far less popularity among village labourers than among other workers; agricultural employees did protest sporadically against poor pay and poor treatment, but usually resisted their employers by 'moving on' rather than by collective action; and, despite ties of kinship and community between urban and rural labour, agricultural workers shared the general rural distrust of city folk, including union organisers and socialist politicians.[40] Structural transformations of rural society enhanced this resistance. Against every Marxist expectation, significant numbers of agricultural labourers acquired land, and even larger numbers aspired to landownership.[41] Worse yet, from a Marxist perspective, specialised agricultural workers, increasingly migratory and thereby divorced from the community solidarity which had once sustained plebeian rural politics, proved considerably less militant and less prone to anti-capitalist protest than the marginal farmers whose part-time labour they had replaced – a striking refutation of the over-simple equation of socialism with proletarians.[42]

Guesdists rarely recognised these discouraging complications: workers were workers, they assumed, and rural workers would inevitably follow their urban counterparts into the socialist movement. At the most, the Parti Ouvrier conceded that the dispersed pattern of rural employment made mobilisation of agricultural

[39] The Guesdists themselves pointed out the predominance of rural over urban labour. See, for instance, A. Zévaès, 'Dans les Campagnes', *Le Socialiste*, 27 December 1896.

[40] On labour militancy among rural workers, see Cabanis, *Introduction à l'Histoire Économique et Sociale de la France*, p. 200; for agrarian strikes, Gratton, *Les Luttes de Classes*, pp. 84–98 and P. Pigenet et al., *Terre des Luttes: Histoire du Mouvement Ouvrier dans le Cher* (Paris, 1977), pp. 44–7; and for the ambiguous pattern of hostility and community prevailing in the relationship between urban and rural workers, J. Merriman, 'Incident at the Statue of the Virgin Mary: The Conflict of Old and New in Nineteenth-Century Limoges', in J. Merriman (ed.), *Consciousness and Class Experience in Nineteenth-Century Europe* (New York, 1979), pp. 134–6.

[41] M. Burns, *Rural Society and French Politics: Boulangism and the Dreyfus Affair 1886–1900* (Princeton, 1984), p. 23.

[42] Bernard, *Économie et Sociologie de la Seine-et-Marne*, pp. 183–4. For critique of this thesis, see J. Sagnes, *Le Mouvement Ouvrier en Languedoc: Syndicalistes et Socialistes de l'Hérault de la Fondation des Bourses du Travail à la Naissance du Parti Communiste* (Toulouse, 1980), p. 31.

labourers in their villages more difficult than recruitment of industrial workers in their faubourgs: the Party contrasted the latter, 'the working class properly defined', with the former, 'more numerous but more scattered'.[43] Guesdists underestimated even this problem, however, since rural workers, despite their number, were scattered indeed, with an average of *one* farm labourer per rural property in 1892. Even the largest agricultural enterprises, those which came closest to the Guesdist imagery of the factory farm, rarely employed more than a few workers on a permanent basis, however many they may have hired seasonally.[44] At the end of the nineteenth century, only 250 farms employed more than fifty workers, 45,000 between six and fifty, and no fewer than 1,300,000 between one and six.[45] In this sense, farm labourers resembled servants, not least in the virtually familial solidarity which sometimes united employers and employees,[46] rather than industrial workers, creatures of capitalist concentration by definition. The Parti Ouvrier never despaired of its rural prospects, despite 'the many forms in which rural property is exploited, the dispersal of the agrarian proletariat, and the diverse ways in which it sells its labour power ... as well as the fact that capital is less obvious than in the cities, albeit just as malignant'.[47] Guesdists even contended that rural capitalism was 'more malignant than its urban counterpart, inflicting living conditions and servitude virtually unknown among urban workers'.[48] Surely, French Marxists asked themselves, agricultural labour must rebel against these conditions! Surely rural labourers would find their way to the Parti Ouvrier? Socialist hope, so characteristic of the perennially optimistic POF, prevailed over sociological realism.

How did the Guesdists justify this hope? Most often, the Parti Ouvrier relied upon its *a priori* conviction that 'worker', in essence, equalled 'socialist'. But Guesdists also expected rural labourers to join the socialist crusade as they developed increasingly sturdy bonds with better organised industrial workers: the demonstration effect of urban militancy would evoke agricultural trade unionism and socialism. Such bonds between urban and rural labour already existed. The Parti Ouvrier noticed with approval and anticipation

[43] J. Guesde, 'L'Oeuvre de Marseille', *Le Socialiste*, 10 October 1892.
[44] Barral, 'Un Secteur Dominé', p. 353.   [45] Dupeux, *La Société Française*, p. 164.
[46] Burns, *Rural Society and French Politics*, pp. 29–30.
[47] Compère-Morel, *Les Propos d'un Rural*, p. 3.
[48] R. Lavigne, 'Le Congrès Corporatif de Nantes', *Le Socialiste*, 13 October 1894.

the complex seasonal migrations, such as that of the stone masons of central France to the building sites of Paris, which integrated rural proletarians into the urban labour market and associated them with their city comrades.[49] These transients sometimes alienated the settled urban workers with whom they competed for work (occasionally to the extent of riot and murder) and rarely participated in the labour militancy associated with their temporary occupations. But the Parti Ouvrier, despite these discouraging circumstances, planned to establish trade unions which recruited both urban and rural workers, wherever their place of residence at any particular moment. 'It's through these mixed unions', Henri Ghesquière predicted, 'that we'll be able to infiltrate socialist ideas [into the countryside], so that, by the circulation of workers created by the productive process, there will operate an analogous circulation of the socialist infection'.[50] The requirements of such ideological germ warfare far exceeded the meagre organisational resources of the Parti Ouvrier. It never came to fruition, although the informal contacts established by labour migration undoubtedly did nurture the little agrarian socialism which finally germinated in rural France.[51]

One final lacuna characterised Guesdist discussions of the rural working class: systematic neglect of the country artisanate, despite its traditionally central part in village politics.[52] The Parti Ouvrier regularly equated rural workers with agricultural labourers: the ploughman personified the agrarian proletariat in Guesdist imagery of the French countryside. Yet many sectors of French enterprise, from remnants of the past such as lacework in Picardy to more novel decentralised capitalism such as watch-making in the Jura, 'farmed' work to village employees. Cottage-industry not only survived but thrived during the *Belle Époque*, despite its apparently antiquated origins in seventeenth and eighteenth-century 'proto-industrialisation'.[53] And agriculture itself sustained hundreds of thousands of

[49] H. Ghesquière, 'Le Socialisme dans les Campagnes', *Le Socialiste,* 19 May 1894.

[50] *Ibid.*

[51] A. Chatelain, 'Les Migrants Temporaires et la Propagation des Idées Révolutionnaires en France au XIXe Siècle', *1848: Revue des Révolutions Contemporaines*, no. 188, 1951, pp. 6–18.

[52] There was only one serious reference to the rural artisanate in decades of Guesdist commentary on agrarian society. Anonymous, 'La Propagande Agricole', *Le Socialiste*, 18 October 1893.

[53] M. Hanagan, 'Urbanisation, Worker Settlement Patterns, and Social Protest in Nineteenth-Century France', in J. Merriman (ed.), *French Cities in the Nineteenth Century* (London, 1982), p. 222.

coopers, blacksmiths, builders, and other artisans[54] – all of them
vital to the health and prosperity of the rural economy, and many of
them fully as 'proletarian' as their urban equivalents. Why did
French Marxists ignore the myriad semi-proletarianised small-
holders engaged in cottage industry and the hundreds of thousands
of independent and not-so-independent artisans who serviced the
agrarian economy? These outworkers and artisans, after all, had
furnished more than their share of rural political protest throughout
the nineteenth century, often leading their villages against local
notables and metropolitan predators.

Guesdist neglect had its reasons. Rural artisans, despite their local
influence, never constituted an organised and coherent force within
the French polity, if only because the nature of their work dispersed
them across the French countryside, isolating them from each other
and precluding sustained mobilisation on a national scale. The Parti
Ouvrier, which regularly underestimated or even ignored the political potential of other proletarians incapable of disciplined militancy,
characteristically discounted the scattered rural artisans. At the
same time, despite the vitality of the putting-out system in areas such
as the Jura or the Stéphanois, urban manufacturing undoubtedly
reduced the overall importance of cottage industry within the
French economy and destroyed some traditional rural manufacturing activities altogether, particularly water-powered and charcoal-
burning metallurgy.[55] New technologies and new forms of labour
organisation had long since driven the spinning wheel from rural
cottages, while the last hand-looms disappeared from the countryside during the *Belle Époque* itself, to the advantage of the great textile
mills which exemplified the Guesdist conception of capitalist industry.[56] This decline in outworking undoubtedly diminished rural
social radicalism, as the marginal peasants who had once contracted
their surplus labour to metropolitan entrepreneurs migrated to the

54 For an enumeration of these trades, see Anonymous, 'La Propagande Agricole', *Le Socialiste*,
   18 October 1893.
55 M. Agulhon, 'La Transformation du Monde Paysan', p. 499 and J. Kergoat, 'France', in
   M. van der Linden and J. Rojahn (eds.), *The Formation of Labour Movements 1870–1914: An
   International Perspective* (Leiden, 1990), vol. 1, p. 166.
56 For the collapse of the rural artisanate, see Sorlin, *La Société Française*, p. 164; G. Desert, 'La
   Grande Dépression de l'Agriculture', in G. Duby and A. Wallon (eds.), *Histoire de la France
   Rurale:* Tome III – *Apogée et Crise de la Civilisation Paysanne 1789–1914* (Paris, 1976), p. 399;
   and Barral, 'Un Secteur Dominé', pp. 365–70.

cities, there to swell the ranks of the factory-fodder which Guesdists implicitly identified as the 'real' proletariat.[57]

None the less, French Marxists grossly exaggerated the forces which diminished the power and presence of the rural artisanate: the Parti Ouvrier systematically reduced 'rural society' to 'agricultural society' (a reduction which explains the Party's preoccupation with agricultural labourers), thereby ignoring hundreds of thousands of potential recruits to the Party's cause. Caught in their absolutist version of Marxist political economy, Guesdists assumed, *a priori,* that the onslaught of capital concentration had already reduced the countryside to agricultural production alone. A rural worker, in this reductionist perspective, ploughed fields or pruned vineyards, but never fabricated watches, built barns, mended barrels, or made lace. The French countryside did indeed 'industrialise' during the *Fin de Siècle* (in that the rural economy increasingly specialised in agricultural production), but a host of non-agricultural workers survived in French villages. Once again, the Parti Ouvrier, over-reacting to its valid insights, maintaining its faith in the irresistible force of capitalist industrialisation, misunderstood its society and thereby missed an opportunity.

The Guesdist seduction of rural workers failed dismally. Agricultural labourers, who rarely involved themselves in national politics at the best of times, if politicised usually supported the class-collaborationist conservatism urged upon them by their employers, while the more independent and radical of the rural artisanate eventually gravitated towards revolutionary syndicalism rather than Marxist socialism.[58] Ignoring these discouraging trends, Guesdists never abandoned their expectation that agricultural labour would flood into the POF, that proletarianised villages would bedeck themselves with red flags, that the dispossessed of the countryside would second the revolutionary struggle of the urban dispossessed. Unfortunately for French Marxists, the agrarian political economy of the *Belle Époque* rendered these expectations increasingly illusory;

---

[57] M. Hanagan, 'Agriculture and Industry in the Nineteenth-Century Stéphanois: Household Employment Patterns and the Rise of the Industrial Proletariat', in M. Hanagan and C. Stephenson (eds.), *Proletarians and Protest: The Roots of Class Formation in an Industrializing World* (New York, 1986), pp. 93 and 100. This exodus to industrial France may have reinforced the social radicalism of the urban working class. For a superb analysis of the question of the 'agrarian origins' of French socialism, see D. Gallie, *Social Inequality and Class Radicalism in France and Britain* (Cambridge, 1983), pp. 206–23.

[58] Gratton, *Les Luttes de Classes*, pp. 159 and 403.

the radicalised small-holders and cottage workers of mid-century gradually abandoned economically distressed villages for the more prosperous cities, and agricultural labourers declined in number (while improving their conditions) and spurned radical politics.[59] The Parti Ouvrier not only failed to develop a strategy appropriate to these social and political transformations of rural society, but remained virtually oblivious of them.

Most countrypeople in France neither enjoyed the wealth and power of agrarian capitalists nor suffered the dependency and insecurity of rural wage-labourers: the independent agricultural enterprise of small property-owners and tenants, an archetypical peasantry of rural small-holders, predominated throughout the French country-side during the *Belle Époque*, a predominance sustained well into the twentieth century. How did Guesdists, so uncertain when confronted by small property-owners of any kind, approach this 'agrarian middle class'[60] of landowning peasants and tenant farmers, by far the largest social category in late-nineteenth-century France?

On the whole, French Marxists treated the peasantry as a rural equivalent of the urban petite bourgeoisie: peasants, like petits bourgeois, combined property-ownership and labour, thereby distinguishing themselves from parasitic agrarian capitalists and propertyless rural proletarians, just as urban petits bourgeois distinguished themselves from bourgeois and workers. 'We divide agrarian property', Paul Louis wrote, 'into two categories: capitalist property founded upon others' labour, characterised by the separation of ownership of the instruments of labour from labour itself; and, on the other hand, small-scale property founded upon personal endeavour and characterised by the union of capital [a mistaken characterisation of non-capitalist productive property] and labour'.[61] According to the POF, the peasantry would share the unenviable fate of the petite bourgeoisie, condemned to agonising death by capitalist concentration. Confident in the 'scientific' revela-

---

[59] E. Labrousse, 'The Evolution of Peasant Society in France from the Eighteenth Century to the Present', in E. Acomb and M. Brown (eds.), *French Society and Culture Since the Old Regime* (New York, 1966), pp. 44–66, and the acutely analysed local example of the process in R. Aldrich, *Economy and Society in Burgundy Since 1850* (London, 1984), chapters 3 and 6.

[60] J. Guesde, 'Crédit-Assassin', *Le Cri du Peuple*, 23 April 1884.

[61] P. Louis, 'De Quelques Points de Doctrine', *Le Socialiste*, 7 January 1899.

tions of its metahistorical perspective, the Parti Ouvrier predicted 'the continual and inevitable dispossession of the owner-cultivator, who [thereby] becomes part of the rural proletariat and is destined to take the same road to social liberation'.[62] Even the Party's allegedly reformist agrarian programme of 1894 began with the assertion that 'an agricultural order founded upon small-scale property is doomed'.[63] The peasantry, as in similar Guesdist analyses of the petite bourgeoisie, had withered into a 'non-historic class': peasants could anticipate no independent future under either capitalism or socialism, and played a small enough role in the bourgeois present.

The technological transformation of agricultural production during the late nineteenth century supposedly justified this Guesdist conviction: French Marxists became convinced that novel agricultural machinery, chemical fertilisers, and similar innovations foreshadowed universal rural proletarianisation. The introduction of steam-powered threshing machines excited French Marxists almost as much as did insurrectionary strikes among rural wood-cutters: both phenomena supposedly manifested the relentless capital logic which heralded a radiant socialist dawn on the Arcadian horizon. According to the Parti Ouvrier, the wave of technical innovation which inundated the French countryside during the last decades of the nineteenth century, agriculture's own industrial revolution, threatened the 'rural middle class' with the same fate inflicted upon the textile artisanate by the factory: 'factory farming' would crush the peasant at his plough as surely as the cotton mill had overwhelmed the cottager at her spinning wheel, opening the way towards a rural version of the socialist mode of production.[64]

How did the POF sustain this conviction, which, in retrospect, seems so misguided? The movement employed a combination of carefully selected evidence and *a priori* argument, those mutually reinforcing gambits of all ideological discourse. Highly-developed agricultural districts such as the Brie (empirically) illustrated the conversion of small-scale farming into large-scale capital-intensive agriculture worked by wage-labour, and a prosperous capitalist

[62] Le Conseil National, '10ème Congrès National du Parti Ouvrier', (Manifesto in file 1892, AN F7 12.490).

[63] *Douzième Congrès National du Parti Ouvrier Français, tenu à Nantes du 14 au 16 Septembre 1894* (Lille, 1894), p. 19.

[64] Compère-Morel, 'Petite et Grande Propriété', *Le Socialiste*, 6–13 October 1901.

farmer could obviously (*a priori*) purchase a steam harvester more easily than could a penurious small-holder.[65] That steam harvester, according to the Parti Ouvrier, would drive the peasant along the same road which the cottage spinner had followed – the road to the proletariat.

Guesdists intended to demonstrate beyond all doubt that capitalist concentration indeed ravaged the countryside, that the Brie foretold the fate of rural France. They triumphantly flourished official statistics, the testimony of the bourgeois state itself, to prove that the 4 per cent of rural proprietors who each held more than forty hectares of land already owned almost half of rural France.[66] Unfortunately for Guesdist credibility, the same statistics also indicated the extreme fragmentation of rural enterprise: no fewer than 5·67 million separate properties contributed to the rural economy in 1882, and virtually the same number (5·5 million) survived in 1908, three-quarters of them owner-operated.[67] Landownership in the French countryside, like property ownership in general during the *Belle Époque*, remained highly inegalitarian, but not to the extent of bourgeois monopoly or aristocratic oligarchy. Rural wealth, bourgeois or aristocratic, coexisted with a genuine property-owning peasant democracy.[68]

French Marxists not only discounted this evidence but blissfully ignored the economic logic which guaranteed the survival and even the triumph of the peasantry in its struggle against agrarian capitalism. Peasant land-hunger, always a potent force, during the long years of the rural depression bid up the price of farmland far beyond its 'real' value to capital. Responding to this opportunity, landowners broke up large properties to realise the difference between the value of their land (relative to other investments) and the 'irrational' prices paid for additions to peasant farms.[69] Under these

---

[65] Bernard, *Économie et Sociologie de la Seine-et-Marne*, pp. 178–84, and Gratton, *Les Luttes de Classes*, pp. 244–5 provide regional examples of genuinely capitalist agriculture. See Walter, *Histoire des Paysans de France*, p. 420 for the distribution of technological innovation.

[66] For an analysis of these statistics, see Barral, 'Un Secteur Dominé', p. 369.

[67] A. Cabanis, *Introduction à l'Histoire Économique et Sociale de la France*, p. 138 for absolute numbers, and J. Lhomme, 'La Crise Agricole à la Fin du XIXᵉ Siècle en France: Essai d'Interprétation Économique et Sociale', *Revue Économique*, vol. 21, 1970, p. 539, for the pattern of ownership.

[68] P. McPhee, 'A Reconsideration of the "Peasantry" of Nineteenth-Century France', *Peasant Studies*, vol. 9, 1981, p. 6. I am deeply indebted to Peter McPhee for his comments on this chapter.

[69] Sorlin, *La Société Française*, p. 24.

circumstances, 'capital logic' ensured fragmentation of farm land rather than its concentration, although the Parti Ouvrier never followed this logic to its conclusion.

Guesdists also misunderstood the social impact of the genuinely revolutionary agricultural techniques introduced during the late nineteenth century: medium-sized farmers, or even small-holders (through cooperatives), *could* afford chemical fertilisers and threshing machines; the relationship between farmers and agricultural machinery differed profoundly from that between handloom weavers and textile mills.[70] Nor could the industrial labour process, the minute division of labour and close supervision of workers, function in agriculture: rural capitalists (apart from tropical-plantation owners in the colonies) failed to impose economies of scale and labour-cheapening organisational innovations upon their highly dispersed and largely autonomous workforces, although Guesdists refused to admit as much.[71]

Finally, just as self-employed shopkeepers and artisans inflicted appalling working conditions upon themselves and accepted abysmal levels of profitability, so peasant families worked dawn to dusk for tiny returns – a self-imposed labour regime inconceivable with hired agricultural workers, particularly in the constricted rural labour market of the *Belle Époque*. Overall, patterns of property-ownership and trends in commodity and labour markets ensured the triumph, not of capitalism, but of petty commodity production, the 'mode of production' characteristic of an independent peasantry.[72] Agrarian bourgeois and agricultural proletarians, the lead actors in the Guesdists' rustic drama, would play the role of 'nonhistoric' classes in twentieth-century French villages, not the peasants, who would eventually bestride the stage to the virtual exclusion of other players.

[70] C. Servolin, 'L'Absorption de l'Agriculture dans le Mode de Production Capitaliste', in Y. Tavernier et al. (eds.), *L'Univers Politique des Paysans dans la France Contemporaine* (Paris, 1972), pp. 44–5.

[71] *Ibid.*, pp. 41–77. There seems to have been an inverse correlation between the size of a rural enterprise and its productivity, according to P. McPhee, 'A Reconsideration of the Peasantry in Nineteenth-Century France', p. 16.

[72] See Eugene Weber's demolition of the class polarisation thesis in his *Peasants into Frenchmen*, pp. 244–7. See also G. Gavignaud, 'À Propos des Voies de Passage de "l'Agriculture Paysanne" à "l'Agriculture Capitaliste": Note sur le Cas des Viticulteurs Roussillonnais', *Mouvement Social*, no. 104, 1978, pp. 31–42. There is a good analysis of the capital logic of agriculture in H. Friedmann, 'World Market, State and Family Farm: Social Bases of Household Production in the Era of Wage Labour', *Comparative Studies in Society and History*, vol. 20, 1978, pp. 545–86.

Already challenged during the 1890s by the stubborn endurance
of rural small-holders, Guesdists sometimes denied the evidence of
their senses, dismissing the survival of millions of peasant proprietors
as a social 'optical illusion'. In pursuing this obscurantist strategy,
the Parti Ouvrier denounced official statistics for identifying tiny
garden-plots owned by labourers as 'farms', a tactic supposedly
intended to inflate the number of land-owning peasants.[73] This
inflation, whatever its intent, certainly characterised 'bourgeois'
interpretations of census returns, but the distortion declined in
significance throughout the *Fin de Siècle*, as the number of garden-
plots owned by agricultural labourers declined along with the
number of their owners. The traditional symbiosis between 'capitalist' agriculture, dependent upon hired labour, and 'dwarf holdings',
reliant upon supplementary wage-labour, ensured that the one
would dwindle with the other.[74] But Guesdists, self-righteously
outraged by others' manipulation of statistics, ignored this trend,
which contradicted their own interpretation of agricultural concentration and agrarian proletarianisation.

At a more fundamental level, Guesdists angrily criticised the
many contemporaneous analyses of rural political economy which
demonstrated the impossibility of capitalist concentration in agriculture – analyses favoured by anti-collectivists of every persuasion,
from Legitimist conservatives to democratic Radicals, each as determined as the other to exclude proletarianisation from the countryside. Adéodat Compère-Morel, the intelligent and prolific Guesdist
expert on rural affairs, repeatedly denounced the 'bourgeois' contention that agrarian economics inhibited concentration of rural enterprise, that the factory-scale mechanisation and extreme division of
labour characteristic of urban industry would never blossom from
the soil of the French countryside. Compère-Morel's repudiation of
these anti-collectivist arguments, however, always focused upon
mechanisation, and completely disregarded the social relations of
production, an approach which systematically avoided the most

[73] Compère-Morel, 'La Coopération dans les Milieux Agricoles', *Le Socialiste*, 22 February – 1
March 1903. Official statistics indeed greatly underestimated the concentration of agricultural property, since statisticians counted properties rather than proprietors, who often
owned more than one farm. P. Bernard, *Économie et Sociologie de la Seine-et-Marne*, p. 179.
[74] R. Jonas, 'From the Radical Republic to the Social Republic: On the Origins and Nature
of Socialism in Rural France 1871–1914', PhD thesis, University of California, Berkeley,
1985, pp. 41–2.

telling evidence against the Marxist theses on rural capitalism.[75] Yet Compère-Morel's efforts to unravel the agrarian political economy shone by comparison with those of other French Marxists, who resolved the rural conundrums implicit in their doctrine by ignoring them altogether.

Guesdists depended upon their conception of rural proletarianisation to sustain their revolutionary convictions: they had no intention of seeking evidence which refuted proletarianisation or considering theory which denied its possibility. The Parti Ouvrier's favoured conception of the transition to socialism stipulated a society divided into a tiny parasitic bourgeoisie and an all-inclusive proletariat. The permanence of the peasantry, therefore, would thwart the social polarisation which supposedly guaranteed the eventual advent of socialist revolution. At their most sectarian, French Marxists presumed that anyone who opposed or impeded this polarisation of society – particularly petits bourgeois and peasants, classes desperate to preserve their independence and property – must also oppose and impede the Parti Ouvrier. Peasants, in this Manichean view of history, served as the 'rear-guard of the bourgeoisie'[76] and erected, in Guesde's words, an 'insurmountable obstacle to our communist demands'.[77] Their proletarianisation would swell the ranks of the socialist army and demolish an otherwise impassable barrier against working-class revolution.

Yet no amount of ideological casuistry could obliterate the stubborn persistence of the peasantry, which may have been mortally wounded by capitalism, but which seemed to be taking its own good time in dying. Sociological realism, forced upon the French Marxists by their difficulties in penetrating the rural electorate, sometimes prevailed against mechanistic exaggeration of the power of capital, that characteristic flaw in the Guesdists' analyses of their society.

[75] See, for example, Compère-Morel, 'La Question Agraire', *Le Socialiste*, 27 September – 4 October 1903, where the author actually notes his opponent's stress on the impossibility of capitalist labour organisation in agriculture, and then proceeds to ignore the point in favour of a long discussion of agricultural machinery and rural credit.

[76] Ch. V. (Charles Vérecque), 'Une Victoire', *Bulletin Mensuel de la Fédération Nationale des Élus du Parti Ouvrier Français*, Première Année, no. 7, 1 June 1900, p. 1.

[77] J. Guesde, 'La Fin de la France par la Propriété', *Le Cri du Peuple*, 10 March 1884. This article illustrates an interesting sub-theme in the Guesdist analysis of the peasantry, in which the 'artificial' bourgeois preservation of the land-owning peasant as a barrier to socialism caused the low natality of the French countryside, as families sought to preserve their small-holding from parcellisation: a dynamic which Guesde believed would lead to 'a cossack or Prussian France within a century'.

Even Gabriel Deville's introduction to his abridgement of *Capital*, one of the earliest and most authoritative Guesdist texts on capitalist political economy, briefly conceded that 'large-scale enterprise has [as yet] been little developed ... in rural society'.[78] The POF's pathbreaking Congress of Nantes, which finalised the Party's agrarian programme, operated on the clearly-expressed assumption that 'in France at least, it's not the case ... that the means of production in agriculture are concentrated in the hands of capital such that they can only be returned to producers in a collectivist ... order, since the means of production are in many cases [still] owned by the producers themselves'.[79] The peasantry might disappear in the long-run, but the Parti Ouvrier had to survive in the France of its time, a France with many more peasants than proletarians. As long as the established order could rely upon peasant support against the socialist challenge, so long would the bourgeois *status quo* prevail, whether in elections, those training exercises of the class war, or in any conceivable revolutionary crisis. Guesdists could not afford to abandon the peasantry to the bourgeoisie, even as a 'rear-guard'. The POF, in its here and now as distinct from a hypothetical hyper-capitalist future, had to solicit peasant small-holders in their own right and in their own interest, rather than as prospective proletarians.

Guesdists based this solicitation upon their conviction that, although the peasantry had (momentarily) escaped expropriation by capital, it could not escape capitalist rapacity altogether. The Parti Ouvrier, in this conciliatory mode, depicted peasants as exploited, oppressed and impoverished – no less victims of capitalism than rural labourers. Once committed to this polemical tactic, French Marxists nonchalantly reversed their usual depiction of capitalist concentration in the countryside, contending that it was actually the fragmentation of rural enterprise and the dispersal of agrarian property-ownership which facilitated bourgeois exploitation of the peasantry.[80] How did the POF sustain this contention,

---

[78] G. Deville, 'Aperçu sur le Socialisme Scientifique', introduction to *Le Capital de Karl Marx* (Paris, undated, but 1883), p. 14. Landauer is incorrect in correlating the Guesdists' supposed shift to reformism in the 1890s with this perception. G. Landauer, 'The Guesdists and the Small Farmer: Early Erosion of French Marxism', *International Review of Social History*, vol. 6, 1961, p. 214.

[79] *Douzième Congrès National*, pp. 18–19.

[80] See, for example, A. Delon, *Essai de Propagande Socialiste dans les Campagnes* (Paris, undated), pp. 3–8.

a rare instance of Guesdists detecting capitalist exploitation apart from wage-labour?

As with its similar observations on the petite bourgeoisie, the Parti Ouvrier emphasised the depredations of the credit system: usury, Guesdists asserted, allowed bourgeois to 'share the product with the peasant to whom they have temporarily left ownership of the fields'.[81] According to this thesis, landowning peasants, however 'independent' as property owners, actually laboured to enrich parasitic mortgage-holders. This proposition carried conviction during the *Belle Époque*, which was anything but *belle* for the multitude of small land-owners who lived under constant menace of bankruptcy. No less than 96 per cent of peasant proprietors were indebted during this period, many to a crippling degree.[82] Indebtedness widened and deepened throughout the 1880s and 1890s, as farmers responded to the collapsing prices of the agricultural depression by borrowing to expand their output, a strategy whose considerable success further depressed prices and thereby rendered loan repayments increasingly difficult.[83] But Guesdist reasoning, despite its potential empirical force, still relied upon an *a priori* presumption: if bourgeois had not yet expropriated the peasantry, then bourgeois must benefit from its survival. Mesmerised by the awesome advance of capital, French Marxists could not imagine that the bourgeoisie might stumble in its march towards absolute mastery of French society, particularly if tripped up by the humble small-holder.

Reassured by their metahistorical certainties, Guesdists invested their hopes in an assault upon rural usury: the peasants of the *Belle Époque*, in Guesdist fantasies of the near future, would rally to the socialist revolution against bourgeois money-lenders, just as eighteenth-century peasants had rallied to the bourgeois revolution against feudal exactions. Unfortunately for the POF, peasant hatred of usurers, however intense, could not be successfully turned against the bourgeoisie as a whole: even 'bimetallism', that naive challenge to the 'cross of gold' upon which small producers suffered crucifixion

---

[81] Anonymous, 'Expropriation Économique de la Bourgeoisie', *Le Socialiste*, 12 September 1885.

[82] F. de Saint-Genis, *La Propriété Rurale en France* (Paris, 1902), pp. 261–2, cited in Willard, *Les Guesdistes*, p. 366.

[83] Barral, 'Un Secteur Dominé', p. 369, and Lhomme, 'La Crise Agricole', p. 547. Capital could benefit considerably from this 'self-exploitation' of small property. See the demonstrations of this point in C. Servolin, 'L'Absorption de l'Agriculture', and P.-P. Rey, 'Matérialisme Historique et Luttes de Classe', in P.-P. Rey, *Les Alliances de Classes* (Paris, 1966), pp. 24–41.

during the *Fin de Siècle*, enticed many more French farmers than did the nationalisation of the means of production.[84] Unaware of Guesdist blandishments or unwilling to trust urban 'partageux', most peasant proprietors staunchly defended the established property system of bourgeois France, however burdensome their mortgages.

Guesdists formulated other and more substantial arguments against the bourgeoisie and its role in rural society, arguments equally designed to foster small-holder anti-capitalism. In particular, the Parti Ouvrier emphasised peasants' vulnerability to the capitalist commodification of social relations, their subordination to the ravenous market which had already, according to French Marxists, devoured most petits bourgeois. Characteristically over-estimating capitalist might, the POF contended that rural producers, from the most marginal cottager to the most prosperous farmer, suffered from the soon-to-be fatal depredations of merchant capital, which had replaced the easy ambience of local markets with the impersonal ruthlessness of the world market. Peasants no longer met small traders on equal, albeit hostile, terms; instead, great trading firms sold fertilisers and equipment to farmers at monopoly prices, but purchased farmers' produce at prices determined by the cheapest producers anywhere, whether in Argentina or Australia. According to the French Marxists, peasants, unable to comprehend, much less manipulate, the global markets created by the nineteenth-century transport revolution, would soon fall easy prey to concentrated mercantile capital, the primary beneficiary and proximate cause of the period's agrarian depression.

As with Guesdist indictments of rural indebtedness, this thesis possessed a superficial plausibility: the rapid commodification of rural production during the nineteenth century had indeed destroyed traditional patterns of village solidarity, intensified peasant individualism, and extended the reign of impersonal market forces – all to the advantage of urban commerce.[85] Rural *gemeinschaft* had eroded, to be replaced by a predatory *gesselschaft*, a transformation with predictable consequences. The traditional sanctions which had

---

[84] For the popularity of 'funny money' solutions to peasant problems during the *Belle Époque*, see P. Barral, 'Un Secteur Dominé', p. 370.

[85] On the breakdown of communal solidarities, see A. Soboul, 'La Communauté Rurale (XVIIIᵉ – XIXᵉ Siècles): Problèmes de Base', *Revue de Synthèse*, vol. 78, 1957, pp. 283–307. For the increasing individualism of the French peasants, and its consequences in rural society, see Dupeux, *La Société Française*, pp. 163–164.

restrained *ancien régime* grain merchants in local market towns did not deter the great international trading companies of the late nineteenth century, free now to pillage the hapless small-holder at their pleasure.

As village communities disintegrated, however, peasants erected a new framework of rural self-defence and peasant self-assertion, a framework which would eventually endow them with unprecedented local autonomy and national authority. Throughout rural France, small producers banded together in cooperatives which short-circuited the power of merchant capital, while peasants in their hundreds of thousands joined agrarian interest-groups which aggressively asserted rural interests in prefectures, in Parisian ministries and during elections. This vigorous flowering of agricultural cooperatives and agrarian interest-groups ultimately constituted peasant proprietors as one of the best organised, best represented, and best defended social groups in France, a development which flatly contradicted the Marxist conviction that peasants composed yet another non-historic class, incapable of self-awareness or self-defence. By 1891, approximately 900 rural co-ops with nearly a million members extended their framework of mutuality over the countryside – a rapidly developing social movement not only larger than the contemporaneous trade unions, but considerably more successful in defending its constituency.[86] Insofar as the Parti Ouvrier showed any awareness of this phenomenon, it casually assumed that 'sooner or later these agricultural unions will fall into our hands just like their predecessors, the workers' unions'.[87] Guesdists, however, remained largely oblivious of the nascent peasant movement, whose mere existence demolished so many cherished Marxist suppositions.

No excuse existed for Guesdist neglect of this phenomenon, since one of the most prominent regional leaders of the POF, Charles Brunellière of Nantes, had helped to establish the highly successful vineyard cooperatives of the lower Loire, providing the beleaguered tenant farmers of the district with advice and support during the difficult formative years of their collective enterprise. His articles on

---

[86] Walter, *Histoire des Paysans de France*, p. 421. For agrarian interest group organisation and the power with which it endowed peasants, see M. Agulhon, 'Attitudes Politiques', pp. 519–26. There is a good description of the transition from traditional village community to cooperation in Gavignaud, 'À Propos des Voies de Passage', p. 39.

[87] C. Bonnier, 'La Question Agricole', *Le Socialiste*, 29 January 1899. And this during the ascendancy of revolutionary syndicalism!

'Le Mouvement Agraire en Bretagne' appeared in *Le Socialiste* throughout the 1890s, conveying an almost weekly account of the initial tribulations of the peasantry of the Loire-Inférieure, their dogged resistance to their exploiters, and their eventual triumph over grasping landlords.[88] But Brunellière himself failed to draw any general conclusions from this experience, apart from the banal observation that peasants resented the depredations of local land-owners and metropolitan bourgeois, while the Parti Ouvrier, as it published a running account of the rise and success of an exemplary rural cooperative movement, completely ignored this proof that peasants, even during a catastrophic rural depression, could decisively defeat the predators who stalked them.

Finally, apart from their indictment of rural usury and the depredations of agrarian merchant capital, Guesdists stressed, as the decisive proposition in their study of the capitalist exploitation of rural small-holders, the inevitability of conflict between peasants and absentee landowners – an age-old conflict now, according to the POF, embodied in a final climactic battle between farmers and bourgeois. As with the other elements of the Parti Ouvrier effort to turn the rural population against the bourgeoisie, this thesis had force: 47 per cent of France's agricultural land was rented;[89] hundreds of thousands of peasant families relied upon land leased from absentee landlords, many of them urban bourgeois; and the collapse of agricultural prices during the 1880s and 1890s accentuated the brutal war which had raged for generations between landowners and their tenants, as hard-pressed farmers desperately demanded rent reductions to match their diminishing cash flow, while equally desperate landowners struggled to defend their incomes.[90]

None the less, the Parti Ouvrier badly misjudged landlord-tenant antagonisms, which were neither as irreconcilable nor as simple as Guesdists believed. Asking himself whether 'tenant farmers working others' land with hired hands and agricultural labourers' were

---

[88] This episode in the fascinating career of Brunellière is described in C. Willard, 'Introduction', to C. Willard (ed.), *La Correspondance de Charles Brunellière: Socialiste Nantais 1880–1917* (Paris, 1968), pp. 18–19 and Y. Guin, *Le Mouvement Ouvrier Nantais* (Paris, 1976), pp. 274–7.

[89] P. McPhee, 'A Reconsideration of the "Peasantry" in Nineteenth-Century France', p. 13.

[90] See G. Desert, 'La Grande Dépression de l'Agriculture', p. 402 and M. Jollivet, 'Sociétés Rurales et Classes Sociales', pp. 88–9 for the conflict between land-owners and their tenants. For the ubiquity of peasant hatred of the large land-owners who controlled access to their primary 'means of production', see Weber, *Peasants Into Frenchmen*, pp. 247–54.

amenable to socialist mobilisation, Guesde decided that the answer was 'yes, since they share [with other rural people] a common enemy, the large landowner, the agrarian capitalist'.[91] 'Hired hands'? 'Agricultural labourers'? Surely Guesde described agrarian capitalists? Misunderstanding of rural social relations certainly characterised Guesdist attacks upon 'métayage' (sharecropping), a system indicted by the POF as a particularly exploitative subordination of productive tenant farmer to parasitic absentee landowner. But sharecroppers, many of them already wealthy employers, actually benefited from the declining prices typical of the agricultural depression, at least by comparison with tenants locked into fixed money-rentals.[92] More generally, Guesdists trod upon dangerous ground when they sought the support of tenant farmers of any kind. Wealthy farmers rented far more acreage than poor peasants rented or owned: the average tenant farmed twice as much land as that owned by the average peasant proprietor.[93] Although portrayed in Guesdist mythology as pathetic victims of capitalist exploitation, tenants often dominated their villages, employed much of the countryside's hired labour, and lorded over impecunious small-holders. Ensconced in substantial farmhouses, surrounded by accumulated capital in farm equipment and livestock, they resembled English 'farmers'. They were the authentic 'rural bourgeoisie'. For all their landlessness, tenant farmers never constituted a potential socialist constituency, however fraught their relationship with absentee landowners.[94]

The Parti Ouvrier's elaborate agrarian programme of 1894 – a programme which offered the peasantry taxation reform, cuts in mortgage rates, and cheap credit – exemplified this carelessness or opportunism by appealing to rural producers in general, whatever their status according to the Marxist analytic of labour and

[91] J. Guesde, 'L'Oeuvre de Marseille', *Le Socialiste*, 10 October 1892.
[92] S. Sokoloff, 'Land Tenure and Political Tendency in Rural France: The Case of the Sharecropper', *European Studies Review*, vol. 10, 1980, pp. 357–81, with a critique of the Guesdist approach, p. 374.
[93] Barral, 'Un Secteur Dominé', p. 353.
[94] The problem of the politics of tenancy is analysed in A. Stinchcombe, 'Agricultural Enterprise and Rural Class Relations', *American Journal of Sociology*, vol. 67, 1961, pp. 165–76 (which stresses the relative radicalism of tenants) and W. Brustein, 'A Regional Mode-of-Production Analysis of Political Behaviour: The Cases of Western and Mediterranean France', *Politics and Society*, vol. 10, 1981, pp. 380–1 (which points out the anti-socialist tendencies of tenant farmers). The Guesdists may have misunderstood tenancy because of the peculiarities of *métayage* in their stronghold of the Allier, where tenants were unrepresentatively radical, according to Willard, *Les Guesdistes*, p. 265.

property.[95] The Programme evoked criticism from purists within the Party itself, uneasy at concessions to property; protests from Engels, shocked by what he perceived as blatant opportunism; and mockery from knowledgeable conservatives, determined to exploit a supposed gap between Marxist theory and Guesdist practice.[96] No doubt themselves secretly troubled by the implications of their new programme, leading Guesdists furiously rejected these criticisms, whether well-intended or mischievous. How, they demanded of their critics, did peasant small-holders differ from self-employed artisans, workers who had long held a respected place in the socialist pantheon?

Although recruitment of self-employed small-holders, who exploited no one, could indeed be easily justified, both canonically and by tradition, soliciting the support of 'farmers of all orders'[97] potentially extended the socialist constituency well into the ranks of the agrarian bourgeoisie. However misguided their own confusion between agrarian capitalists and rural small-holders, Engels and *Le Temps* indicated, from their different perspectives, that a similar confusion existed among Guesdists, a confusion both questionable in principle and futile in practice (prosperous farmers never supported the POF). This sterile conceptual blunder incurred unfortunate consequences: it contributed to the derailment of the parallel Guesdist campaign to organise and mobilise the rural working class, whose most grasping and oppressive employers were often local farmers, hard-pressed themselves and determined to squeeze every centime of profit from their employees' labour.[98] Worse yet, from a

---

[95] P. Lafargue, *Programme Agricole du Parti Ouvrier Français* (Paris, 1895). The *Programme* was widely diffused in the countryside, even in patois (according to Gratton, *Les Luttes de Classes*, p. 99).

[96] For an internal Guesdist critique of the agrarian programme which resembles that of Engels, see Bach, 'La Concentration des Capitaux', *Le Socialiste*, 5 February 1899. For Engels, see his 'La Question Agraire et le Socialisme: Critique du Programme du "Parti Ouvrier Français"', *Le Mouvement Socialiste*, nos. 43–4, 1900, pp. 391–400. The Guesdists became particularly angry when they were criticised for abandoning Marxism by anti-Marxists such as the editorialists of *Le Temps*. See A. Zévaès, 'Mensonges', *Le Socialiste*, 20 October 1894.

[97] P. Lafargue, 'La Propriété Paysanne et l'Évolution Économique', *L'Ère Nouvelle*, November 1894, p. 298.

[98] For a defence of the Guesdist appeal to the small land-owner, see J. Pinset, 'Quelques Problèmes du Socialisme en France vers 1900', *Revue d'Histoire Économique et Sociale*, vol. 36, 1958, p. 351, and T. Judt, *Socialism in Provence 1871–1914: A Study of the Origins of the Modern French Left* (Cambridge, 1979), p. 301 (there is an interesting critique of Judt's point in E. Berenson, 'Socialism in the Countryside? A Review Article', *Comparative Studies in Society and History*, vol. 23, 1981, pp. 278–84). For evidence that Guesdist support for rural small

Marxist perspective, amalgamation of prosperous farmers and the workers they employed into the same 'populist' protest movement inevitably led towards class-collaboration, towards what the Parti Ouvrier's Ernest Ferroul, once he became leader of the Confédération Générale des Vignerons du Midi, thoughtlessly praised as the 'fraternal alliance of capital and labour'.[99]

Guesdist 'opportunism', the POF's virtually indiscrimate search for support in the countryside, has been ascribed to the Party's electoral excesses of the 1890s, to the Guesdists' determination to gain as many votes as possible from whatever quarter possible, if necessary at the expense of Marxist principles.[100] No doubt electoral opportunism partially explains the intensification of the Parti Ouvrier's rural propaganda during these years, but opportunism need not account for a transformation of the movement's overall agrarian strategy, which hardly changed between the 1880s and the 1890s. From the very inception of their movement, Guesdists had sought the support of rural entrepreneurs: at the Congress of Roanne, at the foundation in 1882 of the Parti Ouvrier as a distinct Marxist party, Guesdists had already promised to support the 'peasant proprietor'[101] in his every effort to resist bourgeois exploitation of the countryside, a promise not invented but only reiterated during the 1890s. In the same way, periodic denunciations of the peasantry as the bulwark of the bourgeoisie punctuated the supposedly opportunist years between the electoral break-through of

property compromised efforts to organise the rural proletariat, see L. Frader, 'Paysannerie et Syndicalisme Révolutionnaire: Les Ouvriers Viticoles de Coursan (1850–1914)', *Cahiers d'Histoire de L'Institut Maurice Thorez*, no. 28, 1978, pp. 21–3 and S. Derruau-Bonniol, 'Le Socialisme dans l'Allier de 1848 à 1914', *Cahiers d'Histoire*, vol. 2, 1957, pp. 155–7. For the objective conflicts between farmers and labourers which made the Guesdist choice between peasants and proletarians so critical, see Servolin, 'L'Absorption de l'Agriculture', pp. 75–77.

99 Ferroul, reported in the *Petit Méridional*, 14 August 1907, cited in L. Frader, 'Socialists, Syndicalists and the Peasant Question in the Aude', p. 461.

100 C. Landauer, 'The Guesdists and the Small Farmer', pp. 212–25 and Willard, *Les Guesdistes*, pp. 362–3 and 366–74.

101 And see Lafargue's very explicit argument that it was ridiculous to propose the nationalisation of small peasant property and that peasant landowners should be attracted to socialism by reforms such as debt reduction and agricultural credit, an argument which clearly foreshadowed the POF agrarian programme of the 1890s. P. Lafargue, untitled, *L'Égalité*, 12 February 1882. During the 1890s the Guesdists repeatedly refuted charges that they had abandoned revolutionary purity, pointing out that the programme merely formalised what had been party policy from the beginning. See, for example, Anonymous,'Mensonges Opportunistes', *Le Socialiste*, 31 March 1894, and J. Guesde, 'Ni Contradiction ni Variation', *Le Socialiste*, 4 March 1894.

1892–93 and the Millerand Affair, as they had characterised the sectarian 1880s. Like other aspects of the Parti Ouvrier's ideology, gyration between contradictory approaches to the peasant problem – fevered denunciation of peasants as property-obsessed conservatives, coupled with earnest solicitation of their support for the anti-capitalist crusade – arose as much from permanent yet conflicting polemical necessities as from particular circumstances.

The Party's gyrations largely failed their polemical purpose. As peasants mobilised during the 1890s, they opted for the democratic populism of the Radical Party or the anti-Republican populism of the demagogic Right, but only rarely for Marxist socialism: social mentalities founded upon peasant property-ownership usually eclipsed the anti-bourgeois solidarity of land and labour advocated by the POF.[102] Guesdist hopes were sporadically rewarded: land-owning peasants, particularly in traditionally 'red' regions of the Midi, did join the POF, while entire villages in the distressed woodcutting districts of central France and in the crisis-ridden vineyards of Languedoc and Provence voted for the Party during the 1890s, although their loyalty proved far more ephemeral than that of the Parti Ouvrier's urban cohorts. Historians, refighting the polemical battles of the *Belle Époque*, still debate the political choices made by the French countryside during the *Fin de Siècle*, and today's socialist-voting villages in the Midi and central France demonstrate that the Guesdists did not altogether miscalculate the peasants' collectivist potential. Nevertheless, over-optimistic Marxist expectations that the peasantry as a whole would 'find its natural ally and leader in the urban proletariat'[103] suffered disappointment, if only because the Parti Ouvrier considerably overestimated the anti-capitalist interests of the French rural community and grossly

[102] P. Barral, 'Un Secteur Dominé', pp. 375–6 for the overall anti-socialist aspects of peasant politics; Z. Sternhell, *La Droite Révolutionaire 1885–1914: Les Origines Françaises du Fascisme* (Paris, 1978), pp. 250–1 for peasant proto-fascism; and Barral, *Le Département de l'Isère*, p. 144 for the virulent anti-socialism of even Radical peasant politics.

[103] 'B.' (C. Bonnier), 'La Fabrique dans les Villages', *Le Socialiste*, 13 November 1886. Later Guesdist commentary on the peasantry was notably less enthusiastic than that of the 1880s and 1890s. See the markedly disillusioned analyses in A. Compère-Morel, *La Question Agraire et le Socialisme en France* (Paris, 1912) and P. Louis, *L'Avenir du Socialisme* (Paris, 1905), p. 284. For the historical debate, see T. Judt, 'The Development of Socialism in France: The Example of the Var', *Historical Journal*, vol. 18, 1975, pp. 74–5; R. Sandstrom, 'Socialism in the French Countryside: A Continuing Debate', *Historical Journal*, vol. 21, 1978, pp. 685–91; and T. Judt, 'Socialism in the French Countryside: A Reply', *Historical Journal*, vol. 21, 1978, pp. 693–5.

underestimated the peasantry's ability to defend itself without recourse to socialism.

Guesdist overtures to the petite bourgeoisie and the peasantry depended upon the possibilities and difficulties posed by a 'class alliance' between these non-proletarians and the proletariat, an issue which had troubled Marx himself and still today bemuses Marxist theorists.[104] Should the socialist party, a genuine Parti *Ouvrier*, have been limited to workers, or should it have sought the support of anyone with anti-capitalist interests, even those whose class status rested upon property-ownership? And, if small property-owners could have been recruited to the socialist cause, marshalled into the war against large property-owners, how should they have been enticed by socialist recruiting-sergeants: as incipient proletarians, or as distinct classes with distinct interests? Guesdists, like Marx himself, failed to formulate consistent answers to these all-important questions.

At their most sectarian, Guesdists renounced any contact with small property-owners, whether petit-bourgeois or peasant. The Parti Ouvrier, when operating in this mode, indicted non-proletarian France as a 'single reactionary mass',[105] a mass irrevocably dedicated to the defence of bourgeois property, unremittingly hostile to the working class, and utterly inimical to the socialist movement. Consorting with peasants and petits bourgeois would corrupt the proletariat; the compromises associated with class alliances would compromise socialism itself. French Marxists, at their most *pur et dur*, held that 'the working class [will] be able to win its own victory' only when 'fighting alone for its own ends'.[106] If socialists sought their constituency not only in factories but in the shops, workshops, and farms of petit-bourgeois and peasant France, their socialism would, according to this thesis, degenerate into a flaccid populism. Socialism, thus betrayed, would have lost its *raison d'être* as the doctrine of class war.

None the less, social sectarianism, although deeply satisfying to doctrinaires, could rarely be sustained. Small property-owners, the

---

[104] For the importance of this issue in Marxist theory and Marxist politics, see H. Draper, *The Politics of Social Classes*, Part II; F. Bon and M.-A. Burnier, *Classe Ouvrière et Révolution* (Paris, 1971), p. 154; and A. Hunt, 'Theory and Politics in the Identification of the Working Class', in A. Hunt (ed.), *Class and Class Structure* (London, 1977), p. 81.

[105] Anonymous, 'La Masse Réactionnaire', *Le Socialiste*, 7 July 1894.

[106] J. Guesde, 'Les Aveux', *Le Cri du Peuple*, 7 September 1886.

millions of shopkeepers and self-employed artisans who shared the cities with the industrial working class and the yet more numerous small-holders who predominated in the countryside, were too valuable a prize to be abandoned without a struggle. They may have been doomed to extinction in the long term, according to the Marxists' metahistorical *telos*, but, in the inescapable present, their intervention frequently decided the daily conflicts between proletarian socialists and bourgeois conservatives. As a consequence, Guesdists sometimes subsumed the working class, petite bourgeoisie, and peasantry in a vast and amorphous union of 'all those who work',[107] a purely rhetorical solution to the problem of class alliances.

The Parti Ouvrier, in a populist frenzy, occasionally forgot its proletarian identity altogether: 'our socialism is inclusive with regard to categories, classes and individuals', proclaimed Compère-Morel, happily dreaming of a cohesive socialist countryside, 'which is to say that it embraces ... all those who suffer'.[108] At its most ecumenical, the POF strove to encompass 'factory workers and farmers, proletarians and small property-owners, the most manual of labourers as well as the most intellectual', a fusion of classes and occupations founded upon a 'true miracle ... whereby a union of views and wills ... takes place within a society as conflict-ridden as ours and among so many irreducible differences – but differences none the less reduced by the socialist synthesis'.[109] This strategy, based upon the mobilisation of 'the dispossessed of tomorrow as well as the dispossessed of today',[110] led, at its most extreme, to the attempted Guesdist seduction of small capitalists and rich farmers. After all, Lucien Deslinières suggested in an undoctrinaire moment, 'physical and moral misery ... is not exclusively characteristic of the working class. The other classes also share it, although to a lesser degree. Almost everyone will benefit from the coming change'.[111]

[107] 'Le Parti Ouvrier en France – Isère', *Le Socialiste*, 25 February 1900. For a useful discussion of this vacillation between class sectarianism and all-inclusive populism in Marxist social thought, see A. Kriegel, 'Fonction Révolutionnaire de la Classe Ouvrière et Ouvriérisme', in *Conjoncture Économique/Structures Sociales: Hommage à Ernest Labrousse* (Paris, 1974), p. 520.

[108] Compère-Morel, *La Vérité aux Paysans par un Campagnard*, p. 31. For an insightful discussion of the problems Marxists face by diluting their class paradigm in order to appeal outside the working class, see E. Wood, 'Marxism without Class Struggle?', *The Socialist Register*, 1983, pp. 239–71.

[109] J. Guesde, 'À Nantes', *Le Socialiste*, 29 September 1894.

[110] J. Guesde, 'L'Élection d'Aujourd'hui', *Le Citoyen*, 27 February 1882.

[111] L. Deslinières, *L'Application du Système Collectiviste* (Paris, 1899), p. 17.

Periodically, despite its own often expressed warnings against opportunism, Marxism dissolved back into the democratic radicalism from
which socialism had originally been precipitated.

More often, however, the Parti Ouvrier avoided full commitment
to either proletarian exclusivity or indiscriminate populism, seeking
instead to have the best of both worlds. Playing this gambit to its
conclusion, Guesdists exploited the anti-bourgeois sentiments of
small property-owners, but refused to sacrifice the class identity of
the POF to their potential partners: 'let us accept alliances', advised
Compère-Morel, 'but never forget our doctrines. The first should be
put at the service of the second'.[112] After all, Guesdists reassured
themselves, the relentless advance of the capitalist mode of production ensured that small property-owners would have no options
apart from socialism: they could either throw themselves upon the
mercy of the ascendant working class, or succumb to the depredations of the voracious bourgeoisie. Forced into a choice between
socialism or extinction, peasants and petits bourgeois would necessarily choose the former, a necessity which guaranteed that 'this
mass [of small property-owners] is very useful to us as an auxiliary
army. But, basically, we are able to do without them, while they
cannot survive without our help. This being the case, we no longer
suffer the risk of being diverted or hindered [by class alliances]'.[113]
'This being the case', socialists could seduce small property-owners
without fear of compromising entanglements. Unfortunately, the
Parti Ouvrier's recurrent deviations towards social sectarianism or
ecumenical populism, its inability successfully to supplement its
devoted marriage to the proletariat with passionate petit-bourgeois
and peasant affairs, indicated the hopelessly unrealistic nature of this
overconfident assumption.

[112] A. Compère-Morel, *Du Socialisme* (Breteuil, 1894), p. 3.
[113] 'B.', 'La Conquête des Pouvoirs Publics', *Le Socialiste*, 3 January 1897.

CHAPTER 12

Sales clerks and savants: Marxists encounter the 'new middle class'

> The socialist party's historic mission is to transfer everything
> which is still healthy in today's society into the collectivist
> order ...
>
> C. Brunellière, 'Bourgeoisie ou Ploutocratie', *Le Socialiste*,
> 14 May 1899.

The Marxist paradigm has comfortably accommodated manual
workers and capitalists, who have respectively personified the proletarian revolutionary class and the bourgeois ruling class in the
drama of historical materialism. Even petits bourgeois and peasants,
marshalled into the supporting cast, have found their role in this
Marxist dramaturgy, albeit with considerable jostling and confusion. By contrast, the 'new middle class' – the incoherent melange of
'white-collar' employees entrusted with the administrative, managerial, clerical, and cultural tasks of 'advanced' capitalist societies –
has posed intractable practical difficulties for socialist militants and
insoluble conceptual problems for Marxist theorists. Were they
workers? Were they mere auxilliaries of the bourgeoisie? Or did they
constitute a 'new class' in their own right? Could they be recruited
into the socialist crusade? Marx himself never satisfactorily
answered, or even addressed, these questions, and the explosive
growth of the new middle class, by far the most rapidly expanding
stratum in capitalist society over the past century, has supposedly
indicated a major and perhaps fatal flaw in Marxism's theory of
social development and politics of social revolution.[1]

Since Marx's day, few ideologues, whether theorists or polemicists, have ignored the new middle class. It has evoked an astonishing range of messianic hopes and dystopian fears, including the
fashionable liberal equation of a white-collar world with 'post-

---

[1] See the debate collected in P. Walker (ed.), *Between Labour and Capital* (London, 1979).

industrial' (read 'post-socialist') society, the 'neo-Marxist' faith in technical and professional personnel as the cutting edge of late-twentieth-century socialist militancy, and the post-modernist indictment of professionals, scientists and administrators as the embodiments of oppressive and exclusionary social rationality.[2] The term, the new 'middle class', has itself become an object of angry debate. Marxists have rejected the expression, instead identifying its referent as the 'new *working* class', while anti-socialists have clung to the 'middle-class' denotation – an ostensibly lexical dispute which has, in practice, marked the on-going struggle between socialists and liberals for the political allegiance of white-collar employees.[3] What tactics have Marxists adopted in this contest? How have they conceived the class status of non-manual employees?

At their most socially sectarian and exclusive, Marxists have denounced the new middle class for exercising capitalist authority in the workplace, battening upon the surplus value extracted from workers by capital, and imposing bourgeois values upon society through educational and cultural disciplines.[4] 'Neo-Marxists' have criticised Marx himself for indiscriminately melding white-collar managerial and technical staff with 'real' (manual) workers in an overly inclusive proletariat, thereby disarming labour against the predations of the parasitic 'new class'.[5] Theorists have justified this neo-Marxist hostility towards the new middle class by establishing a sharp distinction between the 'unproductive' labour of white-collar workers and the 'productive' labour of the 'real' working class, a distinction essentially based upon the conviction that 'paper pushing' has less social value than metal bashing, or even that the former consumes rather than produces value. At their most simplistic, Marxists have contrasted 'productive' providers of material goods,

[2] M. Oppenheimer, 'The Political Missions of the Middle Strata', in D. Johnson et al., *Class and Social Development: A New Theory of the Middle Class* (London, 1982), pp. 109–32. For the 'new middle class' as the 'new working class' of the neo-Marxists, see S. Mallet, *La Nouvelle Classe Ouvrière* (Paris, 1969). There is a useful overview of these problems in B. Hindess, *Politics and Class Analysis* (Oxford, 1987), pp. 54–65.

[3] G. Ross, 'Marxism and the New Middle Classes: French Critiques', *Theory and Society*, vol. 5, 1978, p. 164.

[4] The influential work of Nicos Poulantzas sums up this tradition. See N. Poulantzas, 'On Social Classes', *New Left Review*, no. 78, 1973, pp. 37–9, and N. Poulantzas, 'The New Petty Bourgeoisie', in A. Hunt (ed.), *Class and Class Structure* (London, 1977), pp. 113–24.

[5] See, for instance, C. Mouffe, 'Working Class Hegemony and the Struggle for Socialism', *Studies in Political Economy*, no. 12, 1983, pp. 7–26.

the working class, with 'unproductive' providers of non-material services, the new middle class. But most often theorists and polemicists have simply assumed that 'worker' equals 'manual worker', thereby eliding one of the most important issues in the conceptualisation of social hierarchy.[6] Entrenched working-class 'manualism' (the *ouvriérisme* of the *Belle Époque*) has undoubtedly reinforced this otherwise highly abstract thesis, as Marxists tapped the resentment of 'blue-collar' workers toward supposedly superior 'white-collar' employees. None the less, manualism, although occasionally appealing as polemic, contradicts the classic Marxist paradigm of property and labour, which systematically precludes categorical distinction between manual and mental work, between the waged and the salaried, between white collar and blue collar.[7]

Another common socialist critique of the new middle class, one more in keeping with Marx's own theses, has distinguished white-collar employees from the proletariat by the former's consumption of surplus value extracted from the latter. In this interpretation, capitalists pay their 'non-productive' employees, as they pay their servants, out of revenue (profits, taxes, and personal income) rather than out of capital: the pay of typists depends upon their bosses' successful exploitation of 'genuine' workers; civil servants' salaries depend upon the extraction of wealth from 'real' producers; doctors' fees fluctuate with the rate of profit. As a 'surplus consuming class', the interests of white-collar employees conflict with those of the proletariat: the resources of the two classes vary inversely, the new middle class thereby possessing a vested interest in successful capitalist exploitation.[8]

---

[6] For a characteristic untheorised reduction of 'worker' to 'manual worker', see A. Przeworski and J. Sprague, *Paper Stones: A History of Electoral Socialism* (Chicago, 1986), where the authors' entire critique of the Marxist tradition turns upon this non-Marxist assumption, an assumption shared by the authors and inaccurately ascribed to their subject.

[7] P. Meiksins, 'Productive and Unproductive Labour and Marx's Theory of Classes', *Review of Radical Political Economics*, vol. 13, 1981, pp. 32–42.

[8] For the concept of a 'surplus consuming class', see M. Nicolaus, 'Proletariat and Middle Class in Marx: Hegelian Choreography and the Capitalist Dialectic', *Studies on the Left*, vol. 7, 1967, pp. 22–50. The antagonism between workers and surplus consumers is described in P. Sweezy, *A Theory of Capitalist Development* (London, 1946), pp. 283–286. There are useful discussions of the issue in D. Hodges, 'The New Class in Marxian Sociology', *Indian Journal of Social Research*, vol. 3, 1962, pp. 14–32; I. Gough, 'Marx's Theory of Productive and Unproductive Labour', *New Left Review*, no. 76, 1972, pp. 47–72; S. Resnick and R. Wolff, *Knowledge and Class: A Marxian Critique of Political Economy* (Chicago, 1987), pp. 132–41; and J. O'Connor, 'Productive and Unproductive Labor', *Politics and Society*, vol. 5, 1975, pp. 297–336.

Other Marxists have dismissed these theses as a 'conceptual gerrymander',[9] a misuse of value theory which flatly contradicts the fundamental Marxist analytic of property and labour.[10] According to their alternative criteria, the new middle class, a stratum of propertyless wage-earners subjected to the same processes of 'proletarianisation' inflicted upon manual workers, constitutes an integral part of the proletariat. A typist – regimented, mechanised, and waged – is no less a worker than a cotton-mill operative.[11] Pursuing this argument, some Marxists have contended that the distinction between manual and mental labour which informs most conceptions of the new middle class contradicts the all-important Marxist theory of the 'collective worker', the integral combination of the disparate forms of labour characteristic of large-scale enterprise in advanced capitalist society.[12] Indeed, for some Marxists, *only* the managerial, technical, and administrative skills of this 'new *working* class' endows the proletariat with the prowess to overcome capitalism and the capacity to construct a post-capitalist society: a proletariat reduced to its manual residue would never, *could* never, escape the clutches of capital.[13]

How did Guesdists handle these vital issues? Unlike Marx and his generation of socialists, French Marxists fully understood the importance of the non-manual working class, estimated by Guesde in 1891 at 'more than 900 thousand employees'.[14] *Fin-de-siècle* France experienced a precocious development of both private and public bureaucracies, a development founded upon the expansion of 'white-collar' employment of sales personnel, clerks, managers, and bureaucrats; upon the second industrial revolution's vastly increased

9 A. Cottrell, *Social Classes in Marxist Theory* (London, 1984), p. 91. Cottrell has an excellent discussion (pp. 60–6) of the reasons why most of 'the new middle class' must be included in the working class.

10 There are good critiques of the unproductive/productive labour dichotomy in J. Harrison, 'Productive and Unproductive Labour in Marx's Political Economy', *Bulletin of the Conference of Socialist Economists*, no. 6, 1973, pp. 70–82 and E. Hunt, 'The Categories of Productive and Unproductive Labour in Marxist Economic Theory', *Science and Society*, vol. 43, 1979, pp. 303–25.

11 H. Braverman, *Labor and Monopoly Capital: The Degradation of Work in the Twentieth Century* (New York, 1974), Part 4.

12 C. Anderson, *The Political Economy of Social Class* (Englewood Cliffs, 1974), pp. 125–34, and P. Meiksins, 'Beyond the Boundary Question', *New Left Review*, no. 157, 1986, pp. 101–20.

13 S. Mallet, 'Les Nouvelles Réalités Sociales', *Cahiers du Centre d'Études Socialistes*, nos. 7–8, 1961, pp. 3–21.

14 Report of a speech by Guesde, in 'La Réunion des Employés à Lille', *Le Socialiste*, 24 October 1891.

demand for technical, scientific, and engineering personnel; and upon the appearance of previously unknown occupations such as typist or telephone operator. The number of 'employees' (as distinct from manual workers) grew from 772,000 in 1876 to 1,869,000 in 1911, an increase of 142 per cent, in contrast to a growth of only 7 per cent among *ouvriers* during the same period.[15] *Ouvriers* maintained their share of the waged labour force between 1881 and 1901 (increasing from 75·9 per cent to 76·5 per cent of employment), but employees increased their share from 11·3 per cent to 15·5 per cent (at the expense of servants, who declined from 12·6 per cent to 7·8 per cent of wage labour).[16] Where there had been 10 employees to every 240 workers in 1866, there were 10 to every 145 in 1906.[17] Guesdists could hardly ignore this transformation of the 'salariat' – their favourite term for the socialist constituency, a term which explicitly designated both manual and mental workers.

None the less, French Marxists sometimes managed to overlook the new middle class altogether, implicitly equating the entire 'salariat' with manual workers. On rare occasions, Guesdists even succumbed to the 'ouvriériste' hostility towards non-manual labour which permeated their working-class constituency. Lafargue protested that 'physiologically, there's never been any distinction between manual and mental labour. Socially, however, it's a means whereby lawyers, priests, financiers, industrialists, merchants, and proprietors convince people that they fulfil a superior function requiring elite qualities, qualities which workers don't have and can't acquire.'[18] Elaborating this critique, the Parti Ouvrier denounced the mental/manual dichotomy as a bourgeois plot: 'capitalism embraces unproductive workers in order to make them parasitic upon property', *Le Socialiste* contended. 'These intellectuals [the Guesdist journal continued], overpaid for doing nothing, obviously have the same interest in the perpetuation of the existing social order as does the bourgeoisie. The bourgeoisie thus diminishes

[15] A. Daumard, 'L'Évolution des Structures Sociales en France à l'Époque de l'Industrialisation 1815–1914', *Revue Historique*, vol. 247, 1972, p. 330.
[16] J. Maréchal and J. Lecaillon, *La Répartition du Revenu National: Les Salariés* (Genin, 1958), p. 149.
[17] M. Perrot, 'Les Classes Populaires Urbaines', in *Histoire Économique et Sociale de la France: Tome IV – L'Ère Industrielle et la Société d'Aujourd'hui (Siècle 1880–1980): Premier Volume – Ambiguïtés des Débuts et Croissance Effective (Années 1880–1914)* (Paris, 1979), p. 462.
[18] P. Lafargue, untitled, *L'Égalité*, 1 January 1882.

the number of rebels and conceals the shameful exploitation of the most numerous class'.[19] Guesdists had discovered the 'surplus consuming class' and its malignant purpose.

This overt hostility towards 'brain workers', however, rarely surfaced in Parti Ouvrier rhetoric: stakes in the competition for the allegiance of the new middle class were too high for socialists to forfeit the game before it began. By and large, Guesdists – determined to recruit professionals, managers, intellectuals, clerks, and administrative and technical staff to their cause – held that white-collar employees constituted an integral part of the proletariat, at least insofar as they sold their labour and thereby acceded to the 'salariat'. 'When communists speak of the working class', Lafargue asserted, 'they always mean the salaried class, the class which sells its labour-power to be used at will by an employer – as muscle power for a navvy, or as intellectual endeavour for the porcelain painter, the chemist, the agronomist, the engineer, the foreman, etc'.[20] Lafargue's contention withstands scrutiny: if Parti Ouvrier rhetoric sometimes suggested an equation between the proletariat and manual factory workers, virtually every explicit analysis of the working class by Guesdists included white-collar employees within the proletarian ranks.

Guesdists even maintained (against overwhelming evidence) that the capitalist mode of production had already reduced most 'intellectual endeavour' to the penury and subjection supposedly characteristic of manual labour. The capitalist mechanisms which had pulverised the privileges of skilled workers, according to the POF, also ground down white-collar employees. In particular, the educational system constructed by the Third Republic ensured that 'the overproduction of intellectual producers – necessarily unemployed – will one day or another, but soon and inevitably, become the Revolution'.[21] Proletarianised mental labour might even hold the

---

[19] P. Myrens, 'Les Deux Morales', *Le Socialiste*, 7–14 July 1901.

[20] P. Lafargue, 'La Politique de la Bourgeoisie', *L'Égalité*, 18 December 1881. It was patently not the case, as argued by Przeworski and Sprague, that, in contrast to today's neo-Marxists, earlier generations of the Marxist tradition assumed that 'the new middle class' was 'not necessary for production, that they were not a lawful product of capitalist development'. Przeworski and Sprague, *Paper Stones*, p. 43.

[21] J. Guesde, 'Instruction Subversive', *Le Socialiste*, 31 July 1898. The provision of educated labour actually lagged behind demand during the *Belle Époque*, with consequent improvements in the already considerable relative advantages of 'brain workers' over manual labour. A. Daumard, 'L'Évolution des Structures Sociales en France à l'Époque de l'Industrialisation', pp. 345–6.

key to ultimate socialist victory, since 'this new labour reserve army
[of intellectual producers] will not, unlike the other [of manual
labour], allow itself to be unresistingly decimated by misery and
unemployment [a rare recognition of labourers' often passive response to their lot]'.[22] Guesdists had discovered the 'new working
class', the supposedly 'neo'-Marxist embodiment of revolutionary
energy and socialist enterprise.

Like twentieth-century theorists of the 'new working class',
Guesdists conceptualised mental labour within the ample bounds of
the 'collective worker', within that 'collectivity . . . of producers'[23]
which, with the development of large-scale industry, had replaced
the personally integrated skills of the artisan. 'Great industrial
organisms', *L'Égalité* explained, 'require the combined energies of an
army of salaried workers, all chained by the same capitalist exploitation, although they are differentiated by their various forms of
labour power'.[24] The most significant differentiation of workers'
labour power separated knowledge and command from execu-
tion: 'since manual workers are reduced to mere cogs in the
machine', Lafargue reminded his readers, 'it's necessary to create
intellectual workers – directors, administrators, foremen, engineers,
chemists, agronomists, etc'.[25] In the Guesdists' metahistorical
perspective,

artisanal industry . . . combined manual labour and intellectual labour in
the same producer. Capitalist production has dissociated the two functions:
on the one hand placing the manual labourers . . . and on the other
intellectual workers (engineers, chemists, administrators, etc.). But these
two categories of workers, however different and contrasted they may be by
their education and mentalities, are fused together, to the point where
capitalist industry could no more function without salaried intellectuals
than without manual workers.[26]

[22] J. Guesde, *Le Socialisme au Jour le Jour* (Paris, 1899), pp. 309–10. But the Parti Ouvrier
usually responded badly to others' suggestions that 'intellectuals' had become the real
revolutionary force in society: 'If the great mass awaiting liberation were to be convinced of
this, the proletariat would be paralysed for centuries'. E. Montusès, 'Science et Révolution',
Le Socialiste, 1–8 December 1901.
[23] P. Lafargue, *Le Communisme et l'Évolution Économique* (Lille, 1892), p. 5.
[24] 'P.L.' (Lafargue), untitled, *L'Égalité*, 1 January 1882.
[25] P. Lafargue, in P. Lafargue and l'Abbé Naudet, *Conférence Contradictoire du 28 Novembre 1892,
à l'Hippodrome Lillois* (Lille, 1892), p. 17.
[26] P. Lafargue, 'Le Socialisme et les Intellectuels', *Le Socialiste*, 3 June 1900.

'Intellectual workers', once incorporated as cogs in the great mechanism of the 'collective worker', became as proletarian as any manual labourer.

Expanding upon this insight, Guesdists maintained that the imminent proletarian revolution and the resultant socialist mode of production both depended upon the 'concentration of all manual and intellectual activities in ... the proletariat'.[27] The Parti Ouvrier rejected both the horny-handed antipathy to 'brain workers' characteristic of its 'ouvriériste' competitors in the POSR and the 'socialism of the intellectuals' typical of Independents who invested their hopes in an enlightened intelligentsia. According to Marxist criteria, socialist militancy would fail and socialist aspirations prove futile so long as 'one makes distinctions within the salariat, [or] if the revolutionary party limits itself to a single category of workers described as manual'.[28] The POF even underwent 'Leninist' spasms (the Lenin of *What Is To Be Done?* rather than the Lenin of *State and Revolution*) during which its militants, many themselves archetypical members of the new middle class, insisted that the revolutionary cause depended upon members of the 'intelligentsia', who, alienated from their bourgeois origins, 'enter the workers' movement, bringing with them their talents, education, and fighting spirit'.[29]

Guesdists contended that France would only, could only, attain socialism by reuniting blue-collar and white-collar, hands and brains, the waged and the salaried – the limbs of labour dismembered by capitalist industrialisation. Categorical rejection of 'ouvriériste' exclusivity conditioned virtually every Guesdist encounter with the new middle class. Guesde, himself a journalist and son of a schoolmaster, exemplified his movement when he testified that the Parti Ouvrier

does not distinguish and has never distinguished – and never will distinguish without committing suicide – among those fighting for the political and economic expropriation of the bourgeoisie, between so-called manual workers and the others. First, there is no such thing as exclusively manual

[27] J. Guesde, *Le Problème et la Solution: Les Huit Heures à la Chambre* (Paris, 1895), p. 12.
[28] Report of a speech by Guesde, *Le Socialiste*, 13 November 1886. For the POSR's approach, see C. Willard, *Le Mouvement Socialiste en France (1893–1905): Les Guesdistes* (Paris, 1965), pp. 396–8 and, for the Independents, see J. Logue, *Léon Blum: The Formative Years* (De Kalb, 1973), chapters 4–5.
[29] 'C.B.' (Bonnier), 'L'Étudiant', *Le Socialiste*, 10 July 1886.

labour, since all muscular activity is necessarily accompanied by mental activity, in the same way that the most intellectual activity, no less necessarily, is accompanied by muscular activity of the eyes, the hand, and so on. Second, if the Parti Ouvrier is a class party, and it prides itself on just that identity, the class which it seeks to organise and prepare for its great destiny is not limited to labourers [but rather to] the entire class of wage earners, that is to say all those contributing to industrial, commercial, agricultural, and scientific production, without themselves owning the means of production. It [the POF's constituency] encompasses engineers as well as navvies; station chiefs as well as linesmen; Claude Bernard and Pasteur as well as laboratory assistants. And it's because [the socialist movement] encompasses . . . both the intellectual and manual capacities of society – excluding only useless and malignant unproductive consumers – that the salaried producers, united in the Parti Ouvrier, may make their revolution, are ripe for a new civilisation . . . Amputate the more intellectual elements of [the movement], reduce it to only the manual workers, and it will be capable only of uprisings which will be sterile even if successful.[30]

Guesde and his comrades reiterated this argument under the most varied circumstances. Rejection of 'manualism', despite occasional lapses, remained one of the most significant constants in Guesdist discourse.

Nevertheless, just as the Parti Ouvrier excluded lumpenproletarians from the working class, despite their lack of property, so it excluded selected 'brain workers' from the potentially socialist 'salariat', despite their labour. Guesdists sought to have their cake and eat it too, recruiting among white-collar employees at will, yet tapping working-class hatred of 'bourgeois' elements of the new middle class, 'unproductive workers occupied in satisfying the . . . depraved tastes of capitalists and in defending their property'.[31] As Lafargue asserted,

because of its vicious organisation, capitalist society contains many parasites and superfluous individuals – those who, although exercising a profession, don't participate directly in production. In a collectivist society it will still be necessary to place goods before consumers and . . . provide auxiliary services such as social assistance, public hygiene, education, etc. Nevertheless, since the collectivist order will bring organisation in place of anarchy, as it will utilise resources according to the teaching of science, the number of these non-producers will be infinitely less than it is today.[32]

30 J. Guesde, 'Pas d'Erreur!', *Le Cri du Peuple*, 4 May 1884.
31 'Zn.', 'Le Développement Économique des États-Unis d'Amérique dans la Dizaine de 1870–1880', *Le Socialiste*, 24 April 1886.
32 P. Lafargue, 'Collectivisme et Production', *Le Socialiste*, 18 June 1899.

'Superfluous individuals ... who ... don't participate directly in production'? 'Non-producers'? Despite these hints, French Marxists avoided the intricacies and improbabilities of Marx's under-developed theory of productive labour. If nothing else, it made little political sense to classify social workers ('social assistance'), nurses ('public hygiene') and teachers ('education') as 'parasites and superfluous persons'. How, then, did Guesdists distinguish between necessary 'non-productive' workers and quasi-bourgeois 'parasites'?

Two criteria sufficed: one's role in the class war between bour-geoisie and proletariat, and one's place (or lack thereof) in the impending socialist mode of production. The Parti Ouvrier freely admitted that 'we'll need engineers, chemists, doctors, administra-tors, etc. under communism, just as much as under capitalism',[33] and confessed the absurdity of excluding such occupations from the socialist movement. Unfortunately, these criteria sometimes de-generated into equation of the saved of the socialist millennium with Parti Ouvrier supporters in the capitalist present. Confronted by a hostile journalist from a 'bourgeois' journal who questioned whether socialism would benefit a worker like himself, Guesde replied that 'in the new order you'll learn not to confuse journalists ... with salaried *producers* [Guesde's stress] and that, in order to class yourself (as you're doing) in that latter group, it's not enough to be in the pay of one or several capitalists, no more than it's enough, when you're a woman, to be maintained by a banker'.[34] Guesde may have won this round, but his rhetoric hardly represented a considered appre-ciation of the class status of reporters under capitalism, much less of their future under socialism. After all, Guesde himself had spent a lifetime in the editorial room. Fortunately, Guesdist analyses rarely sank to these depths. By and large, the POF considered 'all those who personally play a socially useful role'[35] as fit for socialism, whatever their immediate personal allegiances. But which elements of the new middle class – that astonishingly heterogeneous amalgam of professionals, intellectuals, civil servants, scientists and techni-cians, managers, and clerical and sales staff – played 'a socially

[33] J. Guesde, 'À d'Autres', *Le Cri du Peuple*, 11 September 1886.
[34] J. Guesde, 'Notre Réponse', *L'Égalité*, 10 March 1880.
[35] Anonymous, 'Franchise', *Bulletin Mensuel de la Fédération Nationale des Élus du Parti Ouvrier Français*, première année, no. 6, 1 May 1900, p. 5.

useful role' in capitalist society, and which might contribute to the socialist future?

Sales and clerical personnel, the most rapidly expanding wage-earning category in modern capitalist societies, have mustered the big battalions of the new middle class. Writing before the development of capitalist retailing and the modern office, Marx had paid scant attention to these employees, although he predicted their proliferation.[36] His followers, however, facing the prospect of a society with more white-collar employees than blue-collar workers, have devoted considerable attention to the status of this ambiguous category of the labour force, albeit without reaching any consensus. Some Marxists, altogether deserting the struggle for the allegiance of white-collar workers, have retreated into 'manualist' resentment of 'employees' (their use of this term, as distinct from 'workers', indicates withdrawal from the paradigm of labour and property), thereby abandoning typists and sales clerks to the bourgeoisie they supposedly serve. Others have welcomed sales and clerical personnel to the proletariat, contending that these workers, like any factory hand, sell their labour power, own no productive property apart from that labour, and suffer the proletarianising processes of the capitalist mode of production – deskilling, mechanisation, and managerial domination. Typing pools, these Marxists have argued, differ not at all from textile mills.[37]

The Parti Ouvrier could not ignore this interpretive dilemma, given the spectacular growth of sales and clerical employment during the *Belle Époque* – growth driven by the rapid development of the public service and private management, the invention of the typewriter and the telephone, and the expansion of large-scale capitalist retailing.[38] Bemused by these rapid changes, French

[36]　K. Marx, *Capital* (Moscow, 1959), vol. 3, pp. 292–301.

[37]　For discussion of Marxist ideology and this element of the 'new middle class', see E. Glennand and R. Feldberg, 'Degraded and Deskilled: The Proletarianisation of Clerical Work', *Social Problems*, vol. 25, 1977, pp. 52–64; D. Hodges, 'The Intermediate Classes in Marxist Theory', *Science and Society*, vol. 28, 1961, pp. 23–37; A. Harris, 'Pure Capitalism and the Disappearance of the Middle Class', *Journal of Political Economy*, vol. 47, 1939, pp. 328–56; and G. Carchedi, 'Reproduction of Social Classes at the Level of Production Relations', in *On the Economic Identification of Social Classes* (London, 1977), pp. 161–213.

[38]　C. Fohlen and F. Bédarida, *Histoire Générale du Travail* (Paris, 1962), p. 357 and F.-P. Codaccioni, *De l'Inégalité Sociale dans une Grande Ville Industrielle: Le Drame de Lille de 1850 à 1914* (Lille, 1976), p. 195.

socialists and labour militants puzzled over the place of shop assistants, typists, telephone operators, and clerks in French society. Were they proletarians, white-collar workers essentially indistinguishable from their blue-collar associates? Did they emerge from the petite bourgeoisie, and retain links with that ubiquitous class? Or were they merely the lowest rank of the hated bourgeoisie? Answers to these questions proved surprisingly elusive.

On the one hand, manual labour and routine sales and clerical work merged: the salaries of the lower ranks of 'white-collar' employment rarely exceeded the wages of skilled manual workers; employees and workers both sold their labour to capitalists; and close ties of community and family linked the upper ranks of the working class with lesser clerical and sales staff – all justifications for the inclusion of at least this element of the new middle class within the proletariat. On the other hand, many white-collar workers, even at the lowest level, enjoyed conditions of employment – promotional opportunities, fringe benefits, and security of tenure – which sharply differentiated them from manual labour and associated them with their employers.[39] No simple criteria could resolve the Guesdists' dilemma.

As a consequence, Guesdist discourse on sales and clerical employees vacillated uncertainly between hostility and enthusiasm, reflecting both equivocations in Marxist theory and ambiguities in French society. Dismayed by upwardly-mobile postal employees, deferential bank clerks, and frivolous shop assistants, the Parti Ouvrier sometimes contrasted these unproletarian white-collar employees with 'genuine workers', and complained that 'only a tiny minority [of clerical and sales employees] have come over to socialism', that 'they all too often align themselves with their employers'.[40] The POF, comparing Lille with Paris, ruefully admitted that 'the diffusion of collectivist doctrine occurs far more slowly in commercial areas than it does in industrial regions'.[41] French Marxists have doubted that Galeries Lafayette would

---

[39] Y. Lequin, *Les Ouvriers de la Région Lyonnaise: Formation de la Classe Ouvrière Régionale* (Lyons, 1977), pp. 198 and 204; L. Berlanstein, *The Working People of Paris 1871–1914* (London, 1984), pp. 112–9; M. Perrot, 'Les Classes Populaires Urbaines', p. 462; and J. Scott, *The Glassworkers of Carmaux: French Craftsmen and Political Action in a Nineteenth-Century City* (Cambridge, Mass., 1974), pp. 190–1.

[40] J. Guesde, 'Jules Guesde devant ses Électeurs – Discours de Guesde', *Le Socialiste*, 1 September 1894.

[41] 'Le Parti Ouvrier en France – Bordeaux', *Le Socialiste*, 29 January 1899.

ever raise its levy for the working-class campaign against the bourgeoisie.

Wide-spread working-class enmity towards office employees and shop assistants, perceived as looking down upon 'mere' workers, reinforced Guesdist doubts.[42] A Parisian department store sales-lady earned almost four times as much as the average female worker in the city, allowing her to ape her bourgeois clients and lord it over her proletarian sisters, while senior clerical and sales staff maintained close personal ties with their employers, and willingly represented capitalist authority and interests in the work-place. Sales-ladies and clerks often came from ambitious property-owning petit-bourgeois and farming families, hardly seed-beds of proletarian identity.[43] And office and shop employees, emulating their employers, strove for a bourgeois life-style, adopted individualist career strategies, and disdained trade union 'collectivism', while their 'professional associations' (they avoided even the rhetoric of working-class militancy) hymned the praises of class collaboration.[44] No wonder Guesdist ideologists hesitated before appealing to these 'workers'.

Despite their hesitations, Guesdists refused to abandon these 'proletarians in frock coats' to the class enemy. Indeed, a white-collar employee was, according to Guesde, 'in reality, even more of a serf than the [manual] worker'.[45] In any explicit enumeration of working-class occupations, the POF almost always included 'employés de commerce, de magazin, et de bazar',[46] notwithstanding their regressive social consciousness and resistance to socialist mobilisation. No wonder. By Guesde's own figures, 'commercial employees, salesmen, etc.' numbered 922,892 at the beginning of the

---

[42] Y. Lequin, 'Classe Ouvrière et Idéologie dans la Région Lyonnaise à la Fin du XIXe Siècle', *Mouvement Social*, no. 69, 1969, pp. 3–20; Perrot, 'Les Classes Populaires Urbaines', p. 461; and M. Perrot, 'On the Formation of the French Working Class', in I. Katznelson and A. Zolberg (eds.), *Working Class Formation: Nineteenth-Century Patterns in Western Europe and the United States* (Princeton, 1986), p. 99.

[43] For sales-clerks, see T. McBride, 'A Woman's World: Department Stores and the Evolution of Women's Employment 1870–1920', *French Historical Studies*, vol. 10, 1978, p. 675. P. Delon, *Les Employés* (Paris, 1969), p. 17, and Berlanstein, *The Working People of Paris*, p. 110, comment on employee/employer bonds, and see *ibid.*, pp. 32–3 for recruitment.

[44] P. Barral, *Le Département de l'Isère sous la IIIe République: Histoire Sociale et Politique* (Paris, 1962), p. 197, and Delon, *Les Employés*, pp. 17 and pp. 52–3.

[45] Anonymous, Report of a speech by Guesde – 'La Réunion des Employés à Lille', *Le Socialiste*, 24 October 1891.

[46] Anonymous, 'Les Employés de Commerce', *Bulletin Mensuel de la Fédération Nationale des Élus du Parti Ouvrier Français*, première année, no. 6, 1 May 1900, p. 3.

1890s, an overflowing reservoir of workers waiting to be tapped by enterprising socialists.[47] How did Guesdists justify this inclusion of white-collar employees in the proletariat, an inclusion which contradicted so many social assumptions in *fin-de-siècle* France, assumptions as common among employees as among workers? As so often in other cases, the Parti Ouvrier fell back upon its materialist determinism, dismissing the mentalities of French society in favour of its 'realities'. Marxists contended (with considerable justification) that, apart from a small elite, clerical and sales employees suffered dreadful treatment at the hands of their employers, enduring interminable working-hours, despotic supervision, and miserable salaries.[48] Guesdists, who never tired of depicting the 'making of the white-collar working class', even asserted that 'the employee has ... greater motives [than a manual worker] for wishing to escape his terrible conditions ... and join the party which is fighting against exploitation'.[49] Motive perhaps, but not motivation: white-collar sales-clerks and clerical employees never joined the Parti Ouvrier in great numbers, preferring the democratic Radicals or the clerical or nationalist Right.[50] Even property-owning shopkeepers outnumbered 'proletarian' commercial employees in the ranks of the POF.[51] For all the Guesdists' deterministic self-assurance, the essentially petit-bourgeois mentalities of the *fin-de-siècle* middle class prevailed over its proletarian 'material conditions'.

The problematical class allegiance of clerks posed a further perplexity: the enigmatic status of 'civil servants'. The state has always employed more white-collar workers than any other institution, thereby presenting a double dilemma for Marxists, perennially confused as they were by both the place of the state in the social order and the status of white-collar employees in society. Marx himself eventually concluded that state employees were genuine workers, even when they served the 'bourgeois state'. Engels, on the other hand, influenced by the rhetoric of Russian Populism,

---

[47] J. Guesde, 'Les Deux Armées', *Le Socialiste*, 29 July 1891.
[48] For these conditions, see Perrot, 'Les Classes Populaires Urbaines', p. 491; Berlanstein, *The Working People of Paris*, pp. 31 and 65–6; and C. Lesselier, 'Employées de Grands Magasins à Paris (avant 1914)', *Mouvement Social*, no. 105, 1978, pp. 109 and 112–5.
[49] Anonymous, Report of a speech by Guesde – 'La Réunion des Employés à Lille', *Le Socialiste*, 24 October 1891.
[50] Willard, *Les Guesdistes*, pp. 320–1.
[51] *Ibid.*, p. 252.

suggested on one occasion that bureaucrats constituted 'a real social estate' with its own predatory class interest. And both founding fathers of Marxism sometimes simplistically assumed that public employees belonged to whichever class ruled the state, that the (civil) servants of the ruling class were automatically breveted into that class. Subsequent Marxist social thought has perpetuated these interpretive dilemmas, indicting bureaucrats as a parasitic caste preying upon 'civil society' (including the bourgeoisie), incorporating them into the capitalist (or communist) ruling class, or courting them as proletarian employees of society's biggest boss.[52]

Themselves confronting the most centralised state on earth, Guesdists exemplified both the perennial Marxist interest in public servants and the endemic Marxist confusion over their class status. Rapid expansion of the already extensive French state sustained this interest and accentuated this confusion: public employment virtually doubled from approximately 700,000 in 1870 to over 1,300,000 in 1906, while actual civil servants ('bureaucrats', as distinct from public employees such as teachers and soldiers) increased from 210,000 to 410,000 during the same period.[53] Guesdists themselves, after their municipal electoral victories of the early 1890s, assumed responsibility for small-scale civil services scattered across France, while communal employees, impelled by either enthusiasm for municipal socialism or opportunist careerism, flooded into the POF, considerably altering the Party's social composition. Seizing upon this incipient symbiosis of socialist politics and public employment, the Marxists' liberal enemies tarred the POF with the dreaded charge of 'fonctionnarisme', although Guesdists (unlike the ruling liberals) bore no direct responsibility for the hypertrophy of the central state.

This indictment, the charge that socialism equalled bureaucracy, undoubtedly motivated the crudest Guesdist assessment of the class

---

[52] For Marx on civil servants as workers, see K. Marx, *Theories of Surplus Value* (London, 1969), vol. 1, p. 159, and for Engels, F. Engels, 'On Social Relations in Russia', in K. Marx and F. Engels, *Selected Works* (Moscow, 1969), vol. 2, p. 390. The problems Marxists have encountered with this category are discussed in G. Therborn, 'Problems of Class Analysis', in B. Matthews (ed.), *Marx: A Hundred Years On* (London, 1983), pp. 177–9; G. Carchedi, 'The Economic Identification of the State Employees', in *On the Economic Identification of Social Classes* (London, 1977), pp. 127–42; E. Wright, *Classes* (London, 1985), pp. 89–91; and R. Crompton and J. Gubbay, *Economy and Class Structure* (London, 1977), pp. 120–3.
[53] Perrot, 'Les Classes Populaires Urbaines', p. 462 for state employment. For civil servants in particular, see P. Sorlin, *La Société Française 1840–1914* (Paris, 1969), p. 91.

status of state employees: the Parti Ouvrier simply reversed the indictment by blaming 'fonctionnarisme' upon capitalism.[54] Socialism, French Marxists contended, far from accelerating the malignant spread of the state, alone offered a cure for the 'bureaucratic leprosy'[55] afflicting France. Carried away by this polemical manoeuvre, Guesdists ended by equating the civil service with the bourgeoisie, just as they identified the state with capital.

What do you think [asked Guesde] the bourgeoisie can do with its sons, cousins and nephews, particularly now that most occupations are overloaded, when 'independent careers' evaporate under conditions of increasingly centralised industry and commerce, leaving room only for white or blue-collared proletarians who are equally subordinate and miserable? Social conservation demands a share of the governmental cake, in the form of employment, for these 'inclassables', if one doesn't wish to see them turn ... against their own class.[56]

In other words, bourgeois bureaucracy amounted to little more than 'jobs for the boys'. At their most extreme, Guesdists decided that 'all bureaucrats, all state employees ... are no better than the kept women of capital',[57] a conclusion worthy of the most simple-minded anarchist.

Guesdists, however, could not sustain this extreme position, particularly as the municipal employees of Roubaix, Lille, Montluçon, and other Parti Ouvrier mini-states inundated the POF. Public employees in general, but particularly well-liked and well-respected 'fonctionnaires' such as teachers and public health personnel, could not be indicted as parasitic pensioners of the bourgeoisie without reducing Guesdist support and damaging Guesdist credibility. Abandoning their critique of bourgeois bureaucracy in the face of these circumstances, French Marxists hopefully scrutinised the public service for signs of proletarianisation, and inevitably found them. They rejoiced, for instance, to discover seventy applicants for every opening in the Prefectural Service of the Department of the Seine, an indication (at least for Marxists) that the labour market would soon reduce even bureaucrats to the alienated lot of factory workers.[58] And the first stirrings of civil service trade

54 See, for instance, J. Phalippou, 'Fonctionnarisme Bourgeois et Socialisme', *Le Socialiste*, 4 December 1898.
55 J. Phalippou, 'Dépopulation et Socialisme', *Le Socialiste*, 18 December 1898.
56 J. Guesde, 'Fonctionnarisme Obligatoire', *Le Cri du Peuple*, 22 January 1887.
57 C. Bonnier, 'Les Agents du Capital', *Le Socialiste*, 15 December 1895.
58 Anonymous, 'Prolétariat Intellectuel', *Le Socialiste*, 10 July 1892.

unionism, a novel phenomenon of the *Belle Époque*, delighted Guesdists beyond measure, above all when governments rejected public employee salary increases because granting them would set a bad example for the private sector – a demonstration, according to *Le Socialiste*, of the inextricable connection between the fate of the state's employees and that of workers in general.[59]

Convinced by their own arguments, Guesdists happily opened their Party to civil servants. Flying to the other extreme from their equation of bourgeois and bureaucrat, French Marxists even contended that state employees, dedicated in principle (if not yet in practice) to the 'general interest', must soon join the POF *en masse*. Civil servants would eventually serve only socialism, once they realised that only socialism served the public good in a world otherwise corrupted by capitalist anarchy and greed.[60] The Parti Ouvrier hoped that its own municipal governments foreshadowed this embryonic socialist public service, as Guesdists replaced 'those dangerous auxiliaries [the civil servants inherited from previous 'bourgeois' town administrations] with some of our own – voluntary déclassés who have left the bourgeoisie to serve in the ranks of the people'.[61] Despite its periodic denunciations of 'fonctionnarisme', the POF clearly presaged the twentieth-century Parti Socialiste Français (so firmly based upon constituencies of state employees), if not the late 'party-states' of Eastern Europe.

The most prestigious, if not the most powerful, element of the new middle class has been the 'intelligentsia' – the cultural and intellectual elite of modern society, heir to most of the status and much of the authority stripped from a moribund clergy. Marxist ideologues – themselves intellectuals, sometimes of considerable distinction – have cultivated a peculiar love–hate relationship with their own stratum of society. Some have pridefully contended that socialism would not exist without the intelligentsia, that intellectuals stimulated the revolutionary ideas and ideals without which proletarian force and

---

[59] Anonymous, untitled, *Le Socialiste*, 4 March 1900. For the rise of labour militancy among state employees during the Guesdists' period, see A. Daumard, 'Puissance et Inquiétudes de la Société Bourgeoise', in *Histoire Économique et Sociale de la France: Tome IV – L'Ère Industrielle et la Société d'Aujourd'hui (Siècle 1880–1980): Premier Volume – Ambiguïtés des Débuts et Croissance Effective (Années 1880–1914)* (Paris, 1979), pp. 448–9.

[60] G. Deville, *Principes Socialistes* (Paris, 1896), pp. 63–71.

[61] Anonymous, 'Les Secrétaires de Mairie', *Bulletin Mensuel de la Fédération Nationale des Élus du Parti Ouvrier Français*, Deuxième Année, no. 20, 1 July 1901, p. 4.

will would remain impotent. Others have indicted intellectuals as agents of capitalist domination, as the agents responsible for the elitist mentalities, exclusive culture, and individualistic values which have reinforced bourgeois hegemony over society. Marx himself, in his most reductionist moments, ascribed this 'superstructural stratum' to whichever class the intelligentsia served: an intellectual born to the working class but serving capital became irretrievably bourgeois; an intellectual (such as Marx himself) born to the bourgeoisie but serving the working class became impeccably proletarian. The relationship between intellectuals and workers has vexed Marxist theorists for more than a century, whatever solution they have adopted to the conundrum of the intelligentsia's class status.[62]

Intellectuals' relationship with the proletariat and with the socialist movement preoccupied Left-wing France during the *Fin de Siècle*, a period when socialists successfully recruited among prominent writers and artists and finally penetrated the Université. Their success elicited an assertive 'socialism of the intellectuals' represented by figures such as Lucien Herr (librarian of the elitist École Normale Supérieure, *éminence grise* of academic socialism, theorist of the syndicalist POSR) and Jean Jaurès himself (professor and charismatic leader of the anti-Guesdist Independent Socialists).[63] What was the Parti Ouvrier's response to this influx of eminent and not so eminent intellectuals? Very occasionally, the POF, unable to compete with the Independent Socialists or even the smaller socialist sects for the allegiance of the intelligentsia, resorted to the *ouvriériste* invective usually practised by the Marxists' syndicalist enemies. Intellectuals, in this rhetoric, were depicted as despicable bourgeois parasites: 'whether in amusing themselves or in working', Guesde

[62] For the tradition of intelligentsia leadership in Marxist social and political thought, see S. Avineri, 'Marx and the Intellectuals', *Journal of the History of Ideas*, vol. 28, 1967, pp. 269–78, and for the alternative tradition of hostility towards intellectuals, see N. Poulantzas, *Political Power and Social Classes* (London, 1973), while Marx's views on the question are described in H. Draper, *Karl Marx's Theory of Revolution: The Politics of Social Classes* (New York, 1978), pp. 481–572. There is a useful overview of the problem in E. Wright, 'Intellectuals and the Working Class', *Insurgent Sociologist*, vol. 8, 1978, pp. 5–18.

[63] D. Lindenberg and P.-A. Mayer, *Lucien Herr: Le Socialisme et son Destin* (Paris, 1977); S. Gosch, 'Socialism and the Intellectuals in France 1890–1914', PhD thesis, Rutgers University, 1972; L. Portis, *Les Classes Sociales en France: Un Débat Inachevé (1789–1989)* (Paris, 1988), chapter 4; C. Prochasson, 'Sur la Réception du Marxisme en France: Le Cas Andler (1890–1920)', *Revue de Synthèse*, no. 110, 1989, pp. 85–108; and M. Moissonnier, 'Le Mouvement Ouvrier Français et les Intellectuels avant la Première Guerre Mondiale', *Cahiers d'Histoire de l'Institut Maurice Thorez*, no. 15, 1976, pp. 12–34. Gosch points out (pp. 49–61) that the Guesdists devoted far more effort to resolving the problem of worker/intellectual relations than did any of the other French socialist groups.

fulminated, '[intellectuals] work and play at the expense of the workers'.[64]

Less simplistically, Guesdists suggested that intellectual work, abstracted from society and remote from the travails of the common people, necessarily divorced its practitioners from the proletariat. 'Intellectuals understand neither the social question nor the class war', asserted Charles Bonnier (graduate of the prestigious École des Chartes and a Lycée professor). 'This is because they are so specialised and have devoted so much of their insight, critical spirit, and analytical ability to abstractions that they have nothing left for the events of the real world'.[65] The Parti Ouvrier suspected that the esoteric education and the elitist professional experience of most intellectuals fostered individualism rather than collectivism, that even the anti-capitalist intelligentsia did not grasp the real (Marxist) meaning of socialism.[66]

A particularly violent outburst of Parti Ouvrier anti-intellectualism erupted at the turn of the century, at the apogee of the clash between the Guesdists' 'materialism' and the idealist 'socialism of the intellectuals'.[67] Jean Jaurès, archetypical socialist intellectual and exemplary political idealist, may or may not have understood the 'real' meaning of socialism, but he certainly repudiated Marxist economic reductionism and its associated revolutionary intransigence. Deeply wounded by the disdainful criticisms of professorial idealists, Guesdists riposted by denouncing 'Ministerialist' intellectuals as unconscious (or possibly conscious) agents of bourgeois corruption. And, quite apart from the polemics occasioned by the Millerand Affair, French Marxists, voicing common working-class resentments, detested the patronising assumption that socialist intellectuals 'elevated' the workers' movement with their superior attainments and their institutions of working-class enlightenment (such as the 'Universités Populaires'). Labour, according to the Guesdists, needed disciplined organisation against bourgeois domination and militant awareness of capitalist exploitation, not cultural cultivation and classical rhetoric.[68]

---

[64] J. Guesde, 'Divorce Obligatoire', *Le Cri du Peuple*, 31 December 1883.

[65] C. Bonnier, 'Prolétaires et Savants', *Le Socialiste*, 22 April 1900.

[66] P. Lafargue, *Le Socialisme et les Intellectuels* (Paris, 1900), pp. 7–14.

[67] G. Lefranc, *Jaurès et le Socialisme des Intellectuels* (Paris, 1968) is excellent on this issue.

[68] P. Lafargue, 'Les Universités Populaires', *Le Socialiste*, 11 March 1900. For a discussion of these institutions and their class-collaborationist foundations, see Portis, *Les Classes Sociales en France*, pp. 65–8.

Nevertheless, despite these factional conflicts and cultural resentments, Guesdists usually eschewed anti-intellectualism: not for them the systematic hostility towards education and culture so common among anarchists and revolutionary syndicalists. After all, prominent Guesdist leaders such as Lafargue and Bonnier themselves hovered on the margins of the French intelligentsia. Rather than search for an authentically working-class culture with which to replace the elitist pretensions and hierarchical practices of the bankrupt bourgeois intelligentsia, the Parti Ouvrier contended, against all the evidence, that most intellectuals had already broken with the bourgeoisie, with which they had little in common, that intellectuals would soon merge with the proletariat, which they increasingly resembled. 'Confusion' of the bourgeoisie with the intelligentsia had supposedly been carefully cultivated by bourgeois ideologists 'in order to give themselves an intellectual veneer and to cover their baseness', a fraud which depended upon the thoroughly illegitimate fusion of 'exploiters' with 'scholars, engineers, writers, artists, and other intellectuals'.[69]

In reality, according to the Parti Ouvrier, capital exploited intellectuals just as it exploited manual workers: in the new world of the 'second industrial revolution', capitalists relied upon 'not only a manual proletariat, but an intellectual proletariat as well – which, having done its studies in the various higher educational institutions, is condemned to the same labour and low salaries as the manual worker or the labourer'.[70] Bourgeois bought and sold ideas as they traded in other commodities, and those who produced the intellectual products sold by capitalists – writers, artists, composers, and scientists – must, therefore, eventually degenerate into propertyless proletarians selling their labour for sustenance, into educated proletarians no different in essence from illiterate labourers.[71] Thus, Lafargue contended, 'if intellectuals were aware of their own interests, they would come over *en masse* to socialism, not through philanthropy, but ... in order to fulfil their class obligations'.[72] Capitalism had supposedly reduced the intelligentsia to merely another faction of the working-class aristocracy which would, like

[69] C. Brunellière, 'Bourgeoisie ou Ploutocratie', *Le Socialiste*, 14 May 1899.
[70] Anonymous, 'Augmentation du Prolétariat Intellectuel', *Le Socialiste*, 7 August 1886.
[71] Bracke, 'À Travers la Semaine', *Le Socialiste*, 22 February– 1 March 1903.
[72] P. Lafargue, 'Le Socialisme et les Intellectuels', *Le Socialiste*, 3 June 1900.

other categories of elite workers, soon merge indistinguishably into an increasingly homogeneous and revolutionary proletariat.

These 'travailleurs supérieurs', however, differed in kind from most other working-class victims of the bourgeoisie: their critical spirit and educated perspective precluded the dull despair and dogged patience which inhibited the militancy of blue-collar workers. Once intellectuals 'came over to socialism', they would be 'less resigned [than manual workers] and thus much more perilous to the capitalist order, because [they] are more developed intellectually'.[73] Following this logic to its conclusion, Guesdists occasionally ended as 'Leninists' who expected the intelligentsia to knead indispensable revolutionary yeast into resistant proletarian dough: the 'intelligent elite of the salaried class, composed of chemists, engineers, agronomists, mechanics, administrators, foremen, etc.' would eventually 'direct the social revolution'.[74] A revolutionary Guesdist 'socialism of the intellectuals' evolved as one (albeit unrepresentative) outcome of the Parti Ouvrier's rejection of *ouvriériste* anti-intellectualism.

Finally, on rare occasions, Guesdists held that intellectuals, neither servile agents of the bourgeoisie nor incipient proletarians, constituted a separate class with its own interests, consciousness, and purposes. Commenting on the class composition of the Paris Commune, Guesde wrote that,

if the bourgeoisie was represented, it was by its 'déclassés', by its proletarians, so to speak – journalists and students who live by their labour, and whose cerebral activity, like the muscular activity of the working class, is subordinated ... to a capital which it doesn't possess. This is so much the case that it cannot be contested that a new social element, a new class, is entering the line ...[75]

Having discovered the 'new class', how did Guesdists react to its potential historic role? Twentieth-century Marxists, increasingly obsessed with 'the professional managerial class', have ascribed a bewildering array of vocations to its members, from the revolutionary transcendence of bourgeois society to the disciplining and punishing of the proletarian 'other'. For their part, Guesdists systematically occluded conflicts of interest between the intelligentsia and the working class, instead advocating alliance between

[73] J. Guesde, 'Faites vos Malles!', *Le Socialiste*, 3 September 1887.
[74] P. Lafargue, 'Les Services Publics', *Le Socialiste*, 18 March 1891.
[75] J. Guesde, 'Le 18 Mars', *Le Socialiste*, 15–22 March 1905.

intellectuals and proletarians, urging the partnership of 'intellectuals and manual workers, the force of thought and material force, science and labour'.[76] Guesdists refused to surrender the intelligentsia, whether conceived as educated proletarians or as a class with its own interests, to the armies of the bourgeois class enemy.

Of all intellectuals, educators, whether the intellectual elite of the École Normale Supérieure or humble village schoolmistresses, most preoccupied French Marxists. Both Marxist theory and French circumstances motivated this Guesdist preoccupation: education played an increasingly vital role in the reproduction of the capitalist social order, while the rapidly expanding teaching profession of the Third Republic, and particularly the primary-school teachers so vital to the new Republican regime of universal education, offered socialists a fertile field for recruitment. Apart from a tiny bourgeois elite, largely concentrated in the Parisian *grandes écoles*, teachers in the state school system, although they owed their new prominence to the educational reforms of French liberals, tended to be drawn from the 'popular classes', suffer poor pay and worse conditions, and share a vocation of public service and social idealism – all circumstances conducive to social radicalism.[77] How did Guesdists exploit this heaven-sent opportunity?

Despite their almost unconditional enthusiasm for education, French Marxists occasionally revealed reservations about certain educators. In particular, Guesdists launched ferocious attacks upon the scholarly elite of the Parisian *grandes écoles*. 'According to Marx's definition', Charles Bonnier warned readers of *Le Socialiste*, '[such scholars] come just below the courtesan among the salaried defenders of capital'.[78] The Parti Ouvrier, with some justice, regarded the professors of the Collège de France as scholarly mercenaries in the service of the bourgeois Republic, hired guns in the war of ideas. But, although this disdain and distrust sometimes extended to lycée professors, Guesdists adored the humble primary-school teachers, the *instituteurs* they hailed on one occasion as 'the only intellectuals in whom we have any interest'.[79] Guesdists

[76] Report of a speech by Krauss (Guesdist deputy for Lyons) at Lunel – 'Parti Ouvrier en France', *Le Socialiste*, 21 May 1899.
[77] There is a good description of the role of teachers as socialist militants in G. Dupeux, *Aspects de l'Histoire Sociale et Politique du Loir-et-Cher 1848–1914* (Paris, 1962), p. 608.
[78] C. Bonnier, 'Pierre de Touche', *Le Socialiste*, 25 March 1900.
[79] Anonymous, 'Nos Intellectuels', *Le Socialiste*, 7 August 1898.

contended that teachers, no less than manual workers, endured exploitation by capital (although the Parti Ouvrier never explained how these public servants produced surplus value for capitalists).[80] More credibly, Guesdists promised teachers a respected place in the future social order: they would constitute 'one of the most honoured [groups] in ... [socialist] society'.[81] This enthusiasm had little to do with analyses of 'objective' class interest. Guesdists simply hoped that thousands of poorly paid but highly respected *instituteurs* would ultimately embrace the socialist cause, bringing with them their considerable local influence and cultural prestige. For once, history has realised Guesdist hopes: the teaching profession has become a bastion of twentieth-century French socialism, an outcome foreshadowed by Marxist rhetoric during the *Fin de Siècle*.

So much for teachers. But what of their students? If the Parti Ouvrier courted *instituteurs*, it hardly mentioned their pupils: not for French Marxists the libertarian eccentricities of 'kids lib'. But the Parti Ouvrier could not completely ignore the students of the lycées and the university faculties, given their riotous presence on the Left Bank and their traditional prominence in the great Parisian revolts of the nineteenth century, revolts which had repeatedly linked radical students to revolutionary working people. Many socialist militants hoped that history would repeat itself, that student unrest would trigger the coming revolution, a not unreasonable hope in view of the violent student protests of the *Belle Époque*.[82]

Guesdists, however, repudiated these expectations: they regularly depicted university and lycée students as pampered scions of the bourgeoisie, as privileged malcontents rather than potential heroes of the barricades. Even the atypical revolutionary minority of students (and Guesdists portrayed the majority as womanising wastrels) only dallied with socialism, as their less serious fellows dallied with seamstresses: they made the least reliable of socialist recruits, the most untrustworthy of revolutionary militants.[83] According to the Parti Ouvrier, the faculties' mid-century enthusiasm for revolution, the enthusiasm symbolised by Delacroix's

[80] Anonymous, 'Les Instituteurs', *Le Socialiste*, 16 November 1890.
[81] *Ibid.*
[82] Y. Cohen, 'Avoir Vingt Ans en 1900: À la Recherche d'un Nouveau Socialisme', *Mouvement Social*, no. 120, 1982, p. 26.
[83] Anonymous, 'L'Étudiant', *Le Socialiste*, 3 July 1886.

bohemian student following *Liberty Leading the People*, had evaporated once an austere socialist *ouvrière*, rather than the enticing semi-nude symbol of bourgeois democracy, had assumed revolutionary leadership: the student 'elite of the bourgeoisie', under circumstances which threatened their parents' fortunes and power, 'formed the most reactionary part [of that class]'.[84] If students hoped to join the POF, they 'would have to abandon all their bourgeois assumptions and above all their identity as students'.[85]

Why this bitter Guesdist hatred of students and intense distrust of student protest? After all, a surprisingly large proportion of the Guesdist leadership, including Marxist luminaries such as Lafargue, Deville, and Charles Bonnier, had themselves once studied as 'bourgeois students', and Lafargue, in his day, had participated in the incendiary student protests against the Second Empire.[86] French Marxism had itself been born during the 1870s in those incubators of dissidence: the student cafés of the Left Bank. And a small student movement, firmly based upon the Parisian faculties, promoted the Parti Ouvrier in student circles during the 1890s and bequeathed the Party promising young militants, including Alexandre Zévaès, who, for a time (until his defection to the Ministerialists), reigned as Guesde's heir apparent.[87] For that matter, Guesdists might have spared a thought for the young Karl Marx – notorious brawler, drinker and dueller of the University of Bonn. From its beginning, 'bourgeois' students had contributed mightily to the development of Marxist socialism.

None the less, lycée and university students, a tiny and select proportion of their age group, were indeed overwhelmingly bourgeois in origin. The politically *engagé* students of the *Fin de Siècle*, a small ideological minority of a small social minority, increasingly championed the virulently anti-socialist nationalist movement, while most Leftist students spurned the materialist and determinist Marxism of the POF in favour of the idealism and voluntarism of the anarchists and the Independent Socialists. However impressive his command of proletarian audiences, Guesde could not hope to

---

84 'B' (Bonnier), 'Les Étudiants', *Le Socialiste*, 9 April 1892.
85 'B' (Bonnier), 'L'Association des Étudiants', *Le Socialiste*, 23 December 1893.
86 See the biographical material in Willard, *Les Guesdistes*, pp. 603–51.
87 See the discussion in 'D.', 'Le Groupe Collectiviste Révolutionnaire des Étudiants de Paris', *Le Socialiste*, 30 April 1893. There is a useful study of the weakness of the Marxist student movement in J. Maitron, 'Le Groupe des Étudiants Socialistes Révolutionnaires Internationalistes de Paris (1892–1902)', *Mouvement Social*, no. 46, 1964.

compete against Jean Jaurès in the ambiance of *l'Université*. Given
their congenital inability (or unwillingness) to adapt their rhetoric
to the values and traditions of the lycées and faculties, Guesdists
turned against even the forlorn socialist student group which
supported the POF. 'Students', French Marxists argued, 'don't
constitute a social and professional category in their own right. As a
result, they don't have any special interests to defend, nor special
demands to formulate. [Socialist student groups] would lead to
the formation of a sort of intellectual aristocracy in the socialist
party, which must not distinguish between brain workers and
manual workers'.[88] The uneasy relationship between Marxist socialists and radical students, a relationship compounded of mutual
distrust and mutual incomprehension, dates from long before May
1968.

Guesdists may have despised 'bourgeois' students, but they adored
scientists, engineers, and technicians – those heroes of the industrial
age. The Parti Ouvrier, flushed with naive enthusiasm for science
and technology, displayed none of today's 'neo-Marxist' hostility
towards scientists and technical personnel, supposedly the prime
agents and proximate beneficiaries of industrial relations of production, of the deskilling of workers.[89] Decades of Guesdist publication
produced not a single criticism of scientists and technologists, much
less of science and technology. Yet Guesdists might well have
distrusted the technical elite of the Third Republic: engineers, if not
scientists, had already assumed extensive authority over manual
workers during the *Belle Époque* (French capitalists had no need of
Frederick Taylor's advice to appreciate the value of 'scientific'
management), and an engineering education had already become a
highly desirable background for ambitious young men with entrepreneurial ambitions. The Saint-Simonian radicalism which had
once pervaded the École Polytechnique had, by the *Fin de Siècle*,

---

[88] Anonymous, 'Refus Motivé', *L'Ère Nouvelle*, March 1894, p. 422.
[89] For a discussion of Marxist attitudes towards technical personnel, see A. Gorz, 'Technology, Technicians and Class Struggle', in A. Gorz (ed.), *The Division of Labour: The
Labour Process and Class Struggle in Modern Capitalism* (Brighton, 1976), pp. 175–6 and D.
Johnson, 'The Social Unity and Factionalisation of the Middle Class', in D. Johnson
et al., *Class and Social Development: A New Theory of the Middle Class* (London, 1982), pp.
196–200.

long since given way to bourgeois conformism.[90] Engineers, like the much-reviled Watrin of Decazeville notoriety, were among the most hated enemies of the working class.[91]

Nevertheless, despite the managerial role of authoritarian engineers such as the unfortunate Watrin and the ideological role of bourgeois scientific heroes such as Louis Pasteur, Guesdists simply presumed that engineers and scientists constituted integral components of the industrial 'collective worker', the vast and vastly complicated productive entity in which 'chemists, engineers, men armed with modern science, cooperate, along with manual workers, in [capital's] enrichment'.[92] Technical and scientific personnel, propertyless producers whatever their political choices, were unconditionally accorded the status of *bona fide* proletarians, fit subjects for socialist recruiting. Why did Guesdists extend this unreserved welcome to an element of the new middle class so supportive of bourgeois hegemony over society and so vital to capitalist exploitation in the economy?

First, French Marxists refused to equate scientific industrialism and industrial capitalism: just as the Parti Ouvrier dissociated technology from capital, so the Party dissociated technologists from capitalists. Scientists and engineers, no less than navvies and textile workers, might join the anti-capitalist crusade preached by the POF. Persuaded of the capitalist labour market's self-destructive propensities, Guesdists convinced themselves that the breakneck expansion of technical education during the *Belle Époque*, one of the great achievements of the period's educational reforms, had already flooded the labour market with scientific manpower, thereby eroding the last occupational advantages enjoyed by scientists, engineers, and technicians, those 'proletarians of the intellect'.[93] The proud man of science would follow the arrogant guildmaster into capital's prison; proletarianised engineers and technicians, finally understanding their fate, would enrol themselves in the Parti Ouvrier; and

---

[90] R. Priouret, *Origines du Patronat Français* (Paris, 1963), pp. 191–2; P. Fridenson, 'Un Tournant Taylorien de la Société Française (1904–1918)', *Annales: Économies, Sociétés, Civilisations*, vol. 42, 1987, pp. 1031–60; and P. Cayez, 'Quelques Aspects du Patronat Lyonnais pendant la Deuxième Étape de l'Industrialisation', in M. Lévy-Leboyer (ed.), *Le Patronat de la Seconde Industrialisation* (Paris, 1979), pp. 195–6.

[91] M. Perrot, *Les Ouvriers en Grève: France 1871–1890* (Paris, 1974), vol. 2, pp. 671–2.

[92] Anonymous, 'Edward Aveling', *Le Socialiste*, 20 February 1886.

[93] Anonymous, 'Prolétariat Intellectuel', *Le Socialiste*, 12 December 1885.

the mixture of 'brain workers' with manual labourers would serve as an indispensable catalyst in the transition to a new and higher mode of production. Like most nineteenth-century Marxists, Guesdists were convinced that, because socialism had become 'scientific', scientists would become socialists.[94]

If twentieth-century 'Western Marxists' have abandoned this characteristic Second International infatuation with science and scientists, they have, on the rebound, fallen in love with art and artists: instead of scientists and engineers, composers, novelists, poets, and painters have fascinated our century's Marxist ideologues. The Parti Ouvrier, however, foreshadowed none of the enthusiasms associated with the Frankfurt School or 'Anglo-Marxism'. Apart from Lafargue in his most scholarly mode, Guesdists virtually ignored the 'creative' intelligentsia and, on the rare occasions when they wrote of artists and writers, displayed considerable reserve towards these 'upper servants of the wealthy classes'.[95] The French cultural elite, from the Parti Ouvrier's perspective, served the bourgeoisie, just as Medieval artists had served the Church. But, unlike the ecclesiastical and aristocratic patrons of the Middle Ages and the Renaissance, capitalists corrupted the art which they commissioned. Guesdists, who often criticised contemporaneous culture while ignoring its creators, repeatedly denounced the vulgarity and triviality of French writing and art, the 'inevitable' result of culture's subordination to the degenerate taste of a decaying bourgeoisie.[96]

On many of the sporadic occasions when it noticed artists and writers, the Parti Ouvrier portrayed them as even more contemptible than the culture they created, since the 'creative intelligentsia' allegedly despised the workers whose labour supplied the leisure and resources necessary for poetry and painting, those 'useless activities'.[97] The 'works' of artists ignored, when they did not denigrate,

---

94 M. Rebérioux, 'La Littérature Socialisante et la Représentation du Future en France au Tournant du Siècle', in *Histoire Sociale, Sensibilités Collectives et Mentalités: Mélanges Robert Mandrou* (Paris, 1985), p. 415.

95 P. Lafargue, 'Propos Socialistes', *Le Socialiste*, 4 March 1891. There is a fascinating analysis of the socialists' response to 'high culture' during this period in M. Rebérioux, 'Avant-garde Esthétique et Avant-garde Politique: Le Socialisme Français entre 1890 et 1914', in *Esthétique et Marxisme* (Paris, 1974), pp. 21–39. She stresses (pp. 32–3) the connection between artists and anarchism, another factor alienating the Guesdists from the cultural avant-guard.

96 See, for instance, G. Crépin, 'L'Art Bourgeois', *Le Socialiste*, 11 March 1891.

97 'C.B.' (Bonnier), 'Socialisme et Art', *Le Socialiste*, 4 December 1886.

the honour and dignity of real work and real workers. 'Artists', asserted the Parti Ouvrier, 'don't understand, can't understand, the needs of the daily struggle, of organisation and discipline'. Their involvement with the workers' movement 'risk[ed] introducing confusion into the minds of the real combatants of the class war, where the rare flower of art does not grow'.[98] The 'higher' culture of the intelligentsia, according to the POF, was either irrelevant or inimical to the workers' cause. Guesdists looked forward to the day when progress would finally allow socialist society to dispense with '[artistic] talent, the last refuge of inequality'.[99]

The Parti Ouvrier occasionally moderated this ferocious rejection of bourgeois art and artists. In their more tolerant moments, Guesdists decided that members of the cultural elite, despite their anarchic individualism and traditional subservience to the bourgeoisie, might eventually mobilise themselves as 'indispensable auxiliaries'[100] of the socialist movement. The creative intelligentsia, French Marxists hoped, *must* eventually realise that only socialists promised a society 'which will liberate the artist from the yoke of money and capital'.[101] Capitalism, the 'most oppressive milieu which has ever existed for art and the artist',[102] *must* eventually alienate all except the most insensitive of writers. The cultural elite would rebel against a regime in which

everything is bought and sold, in which everything becomes the subject of speculative manipulation: genius and erudition as much as shoes and cattle, one's conscience and vote as much as chemical fertilisers and apples. Art should be the most noble expression and the most superior formulation of the human spirit, but nothing prevents it from being subjected to this general rule.[103]

Guesdists exploited their period's unease about the commercialisation of culture, a theme otherwise favoured by elitist conservatives.

The POF also argued, more in keeping with its Marxist convictions (and with Marx's life-long love of 'higher' culture), that the creative intelligentsia not only produced commodities, and the most noble of commodities, but that the bourgeoisie appropriated them

[98] C. Bonnier, 'Art et Socialisme', *Le Socialiste*, 22 April 1900.
[99] E. Massard, 'L'Électricité et la Concentration Économique', *L'Égalité*, 8 January 1882.
[100] C. Bonnier, 'Art et Socialisme', *Le Socialiste*, 22 April 1900.
[101] 'B.', 'Gendelettres et Socialistes', *Le Socialiste*, 10 June 1891.
[102] J. Guesde, 'Préface', to A. Baju, *Principes du Socialisme* (Paris, 1893), pp. 3–4.
[103] P. Grados, 'L'Art Falsifié', *Le Socialiste*, 27 September–4 October 1903.

for its own profit: even painters and poets suffered proletarianisation, or at least reduction to the dismal lot of petits bourgeois, those
unfortunate 'profit machines' of capital. The copyright laws themselves supposedly demonstrated this bourgeois exploitation of cultural creativity: owners of textile mills and their heirs possessed their
factories in perpetuity, but owners of copyrights, in due time, lost
their intellectual property to rapacious publishers.[104] Guesdists
hoped that the creative intelligentsia would come to understand its
true class interest, would comprehend that 'the liberation of art
depends upon the liberation of labour'.[105] But this appealing portrait of artistic proletarianisation rarely featured in Parti Ouvrier
discourse. Most Guesdists, most of the time, believed that artists
preferred their gilded bourgeois cages to socialist liberation, that
writers sold themselves to the bourgeoisie with the same enthusiasm
with which they sold their manuscripts to bourgeois publishers.

If Guesdists largely neglected the creative intelligentsia, they
almost completely ignored the ancient 'free professions' of law and
medicine. Why this astonishing disinterest in two of the most
prestigious and influential occupations in French society? Regarding
the legal profession, French Marxists presumed, usually by implication, that 'lawyer' equalled 'bourgeois', that the law functioned as
an integral component of capital, as its superstructural manifestation, so to speak. Virtually every Guesdist reference (few as they
were) to lawyers was ferociously hostile: French Marxists assumed
that 'when you consult a lawyer, you most often consult an
enemy'.[106] The Guesdists' equation of the law with bourgeois wealth
was solidly grounded: most advocates indeed served capital, and the
legal system as a whole protected bourgeois property and power
from threat, whether the threat of petty thievery or of revolution.[107]
A society lawyer like René Waldeck-Rousseau exemplified this
symbiosis of law and capital: he not only represented capitalist
interests in court, but in politics as well, pleading the cases of some of
France's wealthiest companies while advancing through the
Chamber of Deputies to the Council of Ministers and eventually to

---

[104] P. Lafargue, 'Le Socialisme et les Intellectuels', *Le Socialiste*, 15 April and 22 April 1900.
[105] J. Guesde, 'Préface', in Baju, *Principes du Socialisme*, pp. 3–4.
[106] P. Lafargue, 'Le Programme Municipal', *Le Socialiste*, 9 April 1892.
[107] T. Johnson, 'The Professions in the Class Structure', in R. Scase (ed.), *Industrial Society: Class, Cleavage, and Control* (London, 1977), pp. 93–110, and M. Oppenheimer, 'The Proletarianisation of the Professional', in P. Holmes (ed.), *Professionalisation and Social Change* (Keele, 1973), pp. 213–27.

the Matignon itself. The term 'bourgeoisie', in its characteristic (non-Marxist) French usage, reinforced this equation by amalgamating capital-owners and their legal advisors into a single identity. Lawyers may not have been capitalists (owners of productive property worked by others), but they saw themselves and were seen by others as unconditionally *bourgeois*.[108]

All the same, many legal professionals eked out an existence as remote from that of a wealthy company-lawyer like Waldeck-Rousseau as a cobbler's lot was from that of the owner of a footwear factory, and some lawyers (including prominent figures such as Alexandre Millerand) represented socialists and workers when they appeared before the courts. Guesde and Lafargue, with most other prominent Guesdists, had themselves benefited from the professional services of radical advocates. But personal exposure to sympathetic lawyers failed to modify the simplistic Guesdist equation between the legal profession and capital, an equation which violated both socialist experience and the Marxist analytic of labour and property. The 'common sense' of the time, which assimilated lawyers to the bourgeoisie and the bourgeoisie to capital, prevented the Guesdists from comprehending or even perceiving the ambiguous actuality of the law, that double-edged sword which has so often turned in the hands of its bourgeois owners.

The medical profession also virtually disappeared from the French Marxists' portrayal of their society, apart from passing references such as *Le Socialiste*'s characterisation of capital's victims as 'labourers without work, teachers without schools, [and] doctors without patients'.[109] This neglect of doctors seems even more culpable than the Guesdists' superficial approach to lawyers, given the long and still vigorous tradition of medical radicalism in *fin-de-siècle* France (Lafargue himself had undergone medical training, as had the Possibilist Paul Brousse and the 'Blanquist' Édouard Vaillant).[110] None the less, doctors (not to mention such paramedical personnel as nurses and midwives), received virtually no mention in Guesdist discourse. Even the common, though thoroughly non-Marxist, equation of bourgeois and professional applied by Guesdists to the legal profession never featured in Guesdist discourse *vis-à-vis* doctors, perhaps because medicos, unlike lawyers, played no

---

[108] Y. Lequin, 'Les Villes et l'Industrie: L'Émergence d'une Autre France', in Y. Lequin (ed.), *Histoire des Français XIX–XXᵉ Siècles: La Société* (Paris, 1983), pp. 333–4.
[109] Geva, 'La Petite Industrie', *Le Socialiste*, 6 August 1887.
[110] C. Baudelot et al., *La Petite Bourgeoisie en France* (Paris, 1974), pp. 33–5.

obvious role in the defence of capital. During decades of polemic, the Parti Ouvrier failed to allocate *any* social role to doctors, one of the most astonishing voids in the Party's otherwise panoramic ideological perspective.

The 'independent' status of most legal and medical practitioners ('proletarianisation' had hardly touched either profession) may to some extent explain Guesdist disinterest in the 'free professions'. French Marxists easily assimilated lawyers and doctors, entrepreneurs managing their own practices, to the bourgeoisie, thereby forgetting the all-important distinction between skills and knowledge (even those protected by professional monopoly) and capitalist property. French society offered the Parti Ouvrier few incentives to develop a more nuanced analysis of the 'free professions': the Guesdists' proletarian constituency, unable to afford professional services in an era before a national health service and legal aid, 'enjoyed' little contact with lawyers and doctors, except during unwelcome moments in court or during medical examination upon conscription. All the same, neglect of the ancient professional elites of law and healing, the most powerful element of the not-so-new middle class, seriously weakened Parti Ouvrier comprehension of French society, although this oversight may have strengthened Guesdist polemics by obscuring two of the most socially enigmatic occupations in Third Republic France.

Finally, how did French Marxists approach the managerial staff of modern capitalist enterprise – *les cadres*, as they eventually came to be known in twentieth-century French parlance? Guesdists worried incessantly about the social implications of the 'bureaucratic tendency'[111] of modern production, a 'tendency' embodied in the establishment of a vast array of 'foremen, managers, supervisors, and other gaolers, who are multiplying simply because they have to replace the personal commitment of the workers with the eye and fist of the employer or his agents'.[112] These worries arose naturally enough during the *Belle Époque*. Socialists and labour militants could hardly ignore the increasingly bureaucratic organisation of the French 'second industrial revolution'. Although workers may have

[111] J. Guesde, *Services Publics et Socialisme* (Paris, 1884), p. 26.
[112] J. Guesde, 'Un Mabouliste', *Le Socialiste*, 27 January 1894. For an excellent critique of the 'managerial revolution' thesis from the perspective of the 'collective worker', see Meiksins, 'Beyond the Boundary Question', pp. 111–13.

had few contacts with the legal or medical professions, hundreds of thousands of them suffered the close supervision and rigorous discipline imposed by the novel managerial hierarchies of 'big business' – the innovative social technology which paralleled the novel material technologies of the time, a time during which 'Taylorism' seconded electricity and the internal combustion engine as the driving forces of the new productive order.[113] How did the Guesdists interpret the rise of modern management?

Unlike many twentieth-century neo-Marxists – convinced that managers not only represent capital but embody it, even to the exclusion of traditional property-owners – the Parti Ouvrier shared Marx's assumption that 'all labour in which many individuals cooperate necessarily requires a commanding will to coordinate and unify the process ... This is a productive job, which must be performed in every combined mode of production'.[114] Salaried managerial staff, in other words, constituted merely another group of labour aristocrats, alienated from the rest of the proletariat by their high salaries, exclusive privileges and hierarchical consciousness, but no less proletarian for that. 'All these administrators', Guesde and Lafargue maintained in their authoritative commentary on the Party Programme, 'are only salaried workers like the proletarians they direct and from whom they are [only] distinguished by their higher pay'.[115] Although the Guesdists were convinced that the worker-owners of the future would require far fewer (elected) managers than did capitalism,[116] they were also sure

---

[113] Daumard, 'L'Évolution des Structures Sociales en France', pp. 331–2. Modern management hierarchies, however, were little developed in the northern textile industry, usually the Guesdists' exemplar of capitalism. L. Marty, *Chanter pour Survivre: Culture Ouvrière, Travail et Techniques dans le Textile – Roubaix 1850–1914* (Lille, 1982), pp. 262–6.

[114] K. Marx, *Capital* (Moscow, 1959), vol. 3, p. 383. See also F. Engels, 'On Authority', in K. Marx and F. Engels, *Collected Works* (London, 1988), vol. 23, pp. 422–5. For equations of managerial authority and capitalism, which completely abandon property for power as the criterion of capitalism, see G. Salaman, 'Managing the Frontier of Control', in A. Giddens and G. MacKenzie (eds.), *Social Class and the Division of Labour: Essays in Honour of Ilya Neustadt* (Cambridge, 1982), p. 19, and C. Colliot-Thélène, 'Contribution à une Analyse des Classes Sociales', *Critique de l'Économie Politique*, no. 21, 1975, pp. 118–26. And, for an attempted compromise between Marx's thesis and that of the neo-Marxists, see G. Carchedi, 'On the Economic Identification of the New Middle Class', *Economy and Society*, vol. 4, 1975, pp. 1–86. There is a useful overview of these debates in Resnick and Wolff, *Knowledge and Class*, pp. 129–30.

[115] J. Guesde and P. Lafargue, *Le Programme du Parti Ouvrier: Son Histoire, Ses Considérants, Ses Articles* (Paris, undated, but 1883), pp. 36–7.

[116] Guesde argued that the socialist mode of production would need less management and supervisory labour for two reasons: 'workers working for themselves will have no need to be urged to work quickly and well, and because of the election of [the supervisors] who remain,

that managers would survive into the new mode of production, thoroughly integrated within the socialist 'collective worker'. For the Parti Ouvrier, managerial staff neither belonged to the bourgeoisie nor constituted an embryonic 'new class.' Guesdists would have detested Burnhamian predictions of a 'managerial revolution' in which managers represented a nascent ruling class destined to supplant the rentier bourgeoisie.[117] That role had already been allocated – to the proletariat.

Uncharacteristically pessimistic, however, French Marxists had little hope that managerial personnel would rally to the socialist cause. Managers served capital as 'the most privileged element of salaried labour', and therefore 'believe that they are an integral part of the capitalist class, although they only serve its interests. On every occasion they defend it against the working class, of which they are the worst enemies. This category of intellectuals can never be brought over to socialism, since their interests are too closely tied to those of the capitalists'.[118] Managerial personnel indeed identified with their employers during the *Belle Époque*, and shared the general bourgeois attitude towards 'real' workers of condescending patronage mingled wih distate and fear.[119] From the other side of the shop-floor, manual and even clerical employees often hated their supervisors far more than they hated their employers, particularly in large enterprises where capital had become increasingly remote and impersonal. Managerial disdain met proletarian resentment in a self-reinforcing spiral of contempt and contention.

None the less, Guesdists rarely allowed the prevailing mentalities of *fin-de-siècle* France to restrain their imperialistic expansion of the proletariat. Neither managerial elitism and authoritarianism nor working-class resentment and hostility necessarily precluded Marxist solicitation of salaried managers. And, indeed, the POF occasionally anticipated conversions along the road to the socialist Damascus among these Sauls of capital. After all, Guesdists argued, the bourgeoisie exploited its managerial servants (despite their high

chosen by those supervised, rather than against them'. J. Guesde, 'Un Mabouliste', *Le Socialiste*, 17 January 1894.

[117] For this prediction, see J. Goldthorpe, 'On the Service Class', in A. Giddens and G. MacKenzie (eds.), *Social Class and the Division of Labour* (Cambridge, 1982), pp. 167–71.

[118] Lafargue, *Le Socialisme et les Intellectuels*, p. 14.

[119] For useful descriptions of the vast chasm separating workers and managers during the *Belle Époque*, see F.-P. Codaccioni, *De l'Inégalité Sociale*, pp. 181–2 and 349–50; Perrot, *Les Ouvriers en Grève*, vol. 2, pp. 671–2; and Barral, *Le Département de l'Isère*, p. 179.

salaries) just as it exploited its proletarian serfs. Dissecting the 1880 annual report of the mines of Montrambert, for instance, Guesde demonstrated that 'the miners, including employees, managers, and the director, have themselves received . . . only 874,025 francs, while the stock-owners pocketed 4,124,945 francs'.[120] Surely even the managers and the director would come to resent such exploitation?

Characteristically, Guesdists concluded that capital accumulation, the *raison d'être* of the bourgeoisie, would undermine bourgeois defences, including capitalists' need to retain the loyalty of their managerial officer corps:

the necessities of any large-scale enterprise [*L'Égalité* asserted] have created within the proletarian mass an elite of scientific and administrative abilities upon which are devolved all administrative and directive responsibilities. This elite could constitute an intermediate class between the great mass of the proletarians and the capitalist bourgeoisie, and become the instrument of reaction. Capitalist rapacity, however, forces it into the proletariat and keeps it there.[121]

Guesdists anticipated that the high capacities of the managerial elite would eventually stimulate revolutionary militancy: once managers understood the contradiction between their centrality in the modern relations of production and their subordination to parasitic capital, they would enlist in the Marxists' crusade against the bourgeoisie. 'Capitalists', warned *Le Socialiste* on the occasion of the violent Decazeville strike of 1886, 'beware the day of vengeance! Your servants, the engineers, managers, and foremen, will be the most hating, the most ferocious [of your enemies]'.[122] Parti Ouvrier doubts, however, proved more accurate than Parti Ouvrier hopes: the Party never enjoyed an influx of revolutionary managing directors.

What underlying themes emerge from the Guesdists' disparate response to the almost infinitely varied new middle class? The first impression is one of theoretical chaos, a chaos in which intense hostility towards the white-collar occupations engaged in the administration and reproduction of the bourgeois order mingled indiscriminately with uncritical enthusiasm for property-less wage-

---

[120] J. Guesde, 'Morale et Action', *Le Citoyen*, undated clipping in the Fonds Guesde, IISG, no. 600/1.
[121] Anonymous, 'Constitution du Prolétariat', *L'Égalité*, 18 March 1880.
[122] Anonymous, 'Decazeville', *Le Socialiste*, 6 February 1886.

earners, however educated, elitist, or remote from manual labour
(even army officers might become socialists![123]). Political considerations and the prevailing social mentalities of the *Belle Époque*
frequently overrode the imperatives of the Marxists' productivist
paradigm: the Parti Ouvrier embraced teachers with open arms,
however remote their role from capitalist production, while generally distrusting managers, a category as vital to the industrial order
as any manual employee. Nevertheless, a hazy pattern emerges from
this conceptual muddle: elements of the new middle class which
contributed to the 'collective worker' – particularly clerical, scientific, and technical staff – received Guesdist attention and favour;
those more remote from production – artists, lawyers, doctors, and
even students (despite their long tradition of radicalism) – suffered
ridicule and contempt, when they were noticed at all. The Parti
Ouvrier assimilated the former social strata to the proletariat, and
relegated the latter to the bourgeoisie. In the last analysis, Guesdists,
although fascinated by particular categories of white-collar
employees, refused to recognise a 'new middle class' as such. Its
'discovery' as an autonomous force in society awaited twentieth-
century neo-Marxism.

[123] See the article by 'Un Saint-Cyrien Socialiste', 'Armée Révolutionnaire', *Le Socialiste*, 13–20
July 1902.

CHAPTER 13

The proletarian revolution: from pauperisation to utopia

Both for the production on a mass scale of this communist consciousness, and for the success of the cause itself, the alteration of men on a mass scale is necessary, an alteration which can only take place in a practical movement, a *revolution;* the revolution is necessary, therefore, not only because the *ruling* class cannot be overthrown in any other way, but also because the class *overthrowing* it can only in a revolution succeed in ridding itself of all the muck of ages and become fitted to found society anew.

> K. Marx and F. Engels, *The German Ideology*, in K. Marx and
> F. Engels, *Collected Works* (London, 1976), vol. 5, pp. 52–3.

Marxism's theory of transition between modes of production, the doctrine's fundamental concept of revolution, presupposes a moribund ruling class to be overthrown and an aspiring revolutionary class to assume its place. According to this historical *telos*, militant proletarians constitute the revolutionary class within the capitalist mode of production, and their proliferation presages the inevitable transition to socialism. Just as feudal rulers had once been displaced by bourgeois revolutionaries representing forces and relations of production with greater power and potential than those which aristocrats embodied, so bourgeois rulers face defeat at the hands of working-class revolutionaries who represent further progress towards human mastery of the natural and social worlds.[1] This conviction – the faith that the proletariat had become 'the revolutionary class, which, once formed, will shatter the old social milieu in which it has grown ... and sally forth into the historic unknown'[2] – governed the Guesdists' metahistorical vision absolutely,

---

[1] For a penetrating discussion of the problems associated with this concept of a 'revolutionary class', see D. Friedman, 'Marx's Perspective on the Objective Class Structure', *Polity*, vol. 6, 1974, pp. 318–44.

[2] Anonymous, 'Évolution-Révolution', *L'Égalité*, 2 March 1880.

giving meaning to the past, purpose to the present, and a goal to the future.

Marxist faith in the proletarian mission has sometimes wavered, provoking doubts with cataclysmic consequences for the doctrine. Without a revolutionary proletariat to sustain its expectations, Marxism has lost its meaning and Marxists their *raison d'être*. In his less messianic moments, Marx himself doubted the revolutionary capacity of the working class, thereby lapsing into what has been described as 'nightmare Marxism'.[3] At his most pessimistic, he concluded that 'the advance of capitalist production develops a working-class, which by education, tradition, habit, looks upon the conditions of that mode of production as self-evident laws of Nature. The organisation of the capitalist process of production, once fully developed, breaks down all resistance'.[4] Even the Marxists' pervasive analogy between the revolutionary bourgeoisie of the past and the aspiring working class of the present fails to convince. The premise that ownership of the means of production confers social hegemony and political authority, one of the defining axioms of Marxist ideology and one of the doctrine's most incontestable postulates, suggests that workers' dispossession by capital eliminates or at least seriously diminishes the proletariat's capacity for historical self-assertion.[5] The Guesdists themselves, usually oblivious of their doctrine's dilemmas, realised that equation of the bourgeois revolution (firmly based upon possession of the means of production) with the proletarian revolution (aimed at their seizure) did not compare like with like.[6]

Nightmares certainly troubled Guesdists. 'One can imagine', admitted Albert Delon, 'the monstrous possibility [in France] of a sort of slave-system, like that reigning at Montceau-les-Mines, in Creusot, and elsewhere'.[7] The Schneiders might rule forever, not

3 A. Gouldner, *The Two Marxisms: Contradictions and Anomalies in the Development of Theory* (London, 1980), chapter 13.
4 K. Marx, *Capital* (Moscow, 1954), vol. 1, p. 689.
5 A. Touraine, 'L'Évolution de la Classe Ouvrière et l'Idée du Socialisme', *Esprit*, vol. 24, 1956, pp. 692–705.
6 É. Fortin, 'Différence Révolutionnaire', *Le Socialiste*, 2 October 1898. For devastating critiques of the analogy between the revolutionary bourgeoisie and the contemporary proletariat, see J. Monnerot, 'Est-ce l'Avènement du Prolétariat?', in R. Aron (ed.), *De Marx à Marxisme* (Paris, 1948), pp. 165–201; H. Lubasz, 'Marx's Conception of the Revolutionary Proletariat', *Praxis*, vol. 5, 1969, pp. 288–90; and K. Kumar, 'Can Workers by Revolutionary?', *European Journal of Political Research*, vol. 6, 1978, pp. 357–79.
7 A. Delon, 'Une Trahison', *Le Socialiste*, 19 January 1896.

over Le Creusot alone, but over all France – a nightmarish vision indeed. The Parti Ouvrier built its socialism upon resolute refusal of this vision: the Party firmly rejected the heretical suggestion that the mechanisms of capitalist exploitation guaranteed their own persistence, that the self-perpetuation and self-expansion of capital doomed workers to an endless prospect of bourgeois dominance and capitalist exploitation. Nevertheless, this daunting prospect must have returned to haunt the Parti Ouvrier with every electoral frustration, every failed May Day demonstration, every defeated strike. Nightmares undoubtedly prompted many of the French Marxists' innumerable assertions that the proletariat *must* become revolutionary, assertions reiterated as the Guesdists' hopes beat down their experience, as their need defeated their fears.

The 'monstrous possibility' of proletarian failure assumed three equally terrifying guises in Guesdist visions of the future. First, the POF, like Marx, dreaded the habituation of workers to the capitalist order. Imagining the social world viewed from a proletarian perspective, Lafargue wrote of

the worker who, still a child, enters the factory to spend his adolescence and his mature years in gaining his daily bread, who sees all about him workers of both sexes leading the same hard existence, who knows that his father and his father's father lived and worked the same way – this worker cannot imagine that things might change. Despairing, he accepts his lot with patience, and ends by being satisfied when he has work and enough to eat.[8]

Routine might accustom workers to even the most exploitative and despotic productive order. Secondly, Guesdists feared the grinding brutality of industrial capitalism, the ruthless subordination of labour to the inhuman pace of the machine and the inhumane despotism of the supervisor, inhumanities which would gradually undermine workers' capacity for revolutionary self-assertion and which might eventually completely erode their ability to establish or even imagine an alternative mode of production. 'The workers and *compagnons* of the last century', Lafargue confessed, 'had a proud understanding of their class interest which our proletarians, broken by labour and misery, have yet to recover'.[9] Finally, foreshadowing Marcuse's theory of 'repressive desublimation', Guesdists

---

[8] P. Lafargue, 'L'Évolution de la Propriété', *Le Socialiste*, 23 November 1890.
[9] P. Lafargue, 'L'Autonomie', *L'Égalité*, 1 January 1882.

denounced the fleeting self-indulgence nurtured by bourgeois show-men, the escapism which threatened to oust revolution as the workers' escape-route from an intolerable society. As *Le Socialiste,* itself sober to the point of austerity, lamented: 'a popular clientele has been created in our large cities for a certain genre of novels replete with crimes, police adventures, and picturesque events. The bourgeoisie has encouraged the development of this silly and demoralising literature. It occupies the popular consciousness, paci-fies it and turns it from the study of its true class interest'.[10] Routine, brutalisation, escapism – these fearsome apparitions evoked the nightmares which troubled French Marxists as the Parti Ouvrier awaited the socialist revolution, nightmares which all too often became waking reality in the working-class world of the *'Belle' Époque,* a world in which many, perhaps most, workers refused to contemplate their future – sure that it promised only misery, unable to imagine an alternative, living for the moment as the only realistic way to live.[11] None the less, Guesdists rarely succumbed to meta-historical despair. When they asked themselves the question, 'how could the working class *not* go directly to the source of its travails, capitalism, and extirpate it once and for all?',[12] they refused to contemplate a possible abortion of the proletariat's historic mission: they answered their own rhetorical query with the conviction that workers *had* to extirpate the iniquitous system which appropriated their labour, that workers *had* to aspire to an alternative social order.

How have Marxists convinced themselves that the working class *must* revolt against capital, despite the stratagems and strengths of the bourgeoisie? Several alternative theses on proletarian revolution have developed within the Marxist tradition, all of which found some echo in Guesdist discourse. One thesis originated with the 'young Marx' and has predominated within the 'Western Marxism' which claims his legacy: workers would inaugurate the socialist utopia because they embodied ecumenical humanity in its age-old struggle against avaricious particularism, because they possessed an antidote to the irrational egotism which otherwise poisoned bour-geois society. As Marx elaborated this argument, in one of his most

---

[10] Anonymous, 'Sapho', *Le Socialiste,* 2 January 1886.
[11] L. Marty, *Chanter pour Survivre: Culture Ouvrière, Travail et Techniques dans le Textile – Roubaix 1850–1914* (Lille, 1982), pp. 194–6.
[12] J. Guesde, 'Un Meeting Pratique', *Le Cri du Peuple,* 14 January 1884.

famous and mystifying passages, the positive possibility of revolutionary emancipation depended upon

> the formation of a class with *radical chains*, a class of civil society which is not a class of civil society, an estate which is the dissolution of all estates, a sphere which has a universal character by its universal suffering and claims no *particular right* because no *particular wrong* but *wrong generally* is perpetrated against it; which can no longer invoke a *historical* but only a *human* title; which does not stand in any one-sided antithesis to the consequences but in an all-round antithesis to the premises of the German state; a sphere, finally, which cannot emancipate itself without emancipating itself from all other spheres of society and thereby emancipating all other spheres of society; which, in a word, is the *complete loss* of man and hence can win itself only through the *complete rewinning of man*. This dissolution of society as a particular estate is the *proletariat*.[13]

This conception of the revolutionary proletariat complements the Marxist critique of bourgeois alienation, and manifests similar moral strengths and sociological weaknesses. The working class shines forth transfigured as a secular redeemer, but also as a *deus ex machina* without social referents. Indeed, precisely this lack of specific interests identifies the 'philosophical' proletariat as the representative of universal humanity, fit protagonist of a transcendental historical destiny.

Unlike twentieth-century 'Western Marxists', Guesdists rarely favoured this conception of the revolutionary working class. They enjoyed only the most limited access to the works of the young Marx, expressed little interest in the Hegelian philosophy which had sustained his imagery of transcendence, and maintained too close a relationship with the labour movement to conceive of workers as a social *tabula rasa*. French Marxists very occasionally did hail workers as 'the champions of the entire species' who represented 'the general interest of humanity'.[14] Even the astringent Guesde could write that workers' 'particular interests as a class engaged in its own liberation coincide with the general interest, thus transforming the proletariat ... into the champion of all humanity'.[15] But this rhetoric meshed poorly or not at all with the Guesdist concepts of class interest and class conflict, leading instead to the conclusion that the working class

---

[13] K. Marx, *Contribution to Critique of Hegel's Philosophy of Right: Introduction*, in K. Marx and F. Engels, *Collected Works* (London, 1975), vol. 3, p. 186 (Marx's stress).

[14] J. Guesde, *Le Collectivisme: Conférence de Jules Guesde à la Société d'Études Sociales et Politiques de Bruxelles sous la Présidence de M. Montefiore Levy, Sénateur, le 7 Mars 1891* (Lille, 1891), pp. 3–13.

[15] *Ibid.*, p. 18.

embodied not 'a class revolution, but ... a humanist revolution' which would triumph 'in the interests of all human beings without distinction'.[16] This ideal of a 'humanist revolution' which would appeal as much to bourgeois as to proletarians imbued the rhetoric of non-Marxist socialists such as Benoît Malon and Lucien Herr, and sharply distinguished them from the militants of the Parti Ouvrier. Guesdists detested their opponents' sentimental ideals, and would have been horrified by the 'young Marx', if they had ever encountered him.

The 'mature' Marx had sought the origins of socialist revolution and the foundations of a socialist mode of production within the mechanisms of capital itself, not in the logic of human nature.[17] This 'materialistic' perspective has dominated most Marxist conceptions of the transition to socialism: workers would initiate the new social order because they embodied particular revolutionary interests, not because they objectified the universal human essence.[18] Nevertheless, neither Marx nor his successors developed a fully coherent 'economistic' theory of the revolutionary proletariat. Instead, they have proposed several alternative revolutionary 'interests' which would supposedly propel the working class towards the transcendence of capitalism.

A rhetoric of 'pauperisation' has long pervaded Marxist revolutionary discourse, representing the most dramatic but least credible of the interests supposedly driving proletarians towards socialism. According to Marx, 'the modern labourer ... instead of rising with the progress of industry, sinks deeper and deeper below the conditions of existence of his own class. He becomes a pauper, and pauperism develops more rapidly than population and wealth'.[19] According to this thesis, workers share an obvious interest in overthrowing a capitalist mode of production which systematically

[16] C. Vérecque, 'Notre Révolution', *Le Socialiste*, 27 February – 3 March 1901. Even in this article, Vérecque made it quite clear that only workers could initiate this universalistic revolution.
[17] O. Berland, 'Radical Chains: The Marxian Concept of the Proletarian Mission', *Studies on the Left*, vol. 6, 1966, p. 41. This conception of a 'mature' and 'young' Marx does not deny continuities between the two, but takes it for granted that Marx's thought changed considerably over some forty years of sustained elaboration.
[18] For the contrast, see E. Wright, *Class, Crisis and the State* (London, 1978), p. 110.
[19] K. Marx, *The Communist Manifesto*, in K. Marx and F. Engels, *Collected Works* (London, 1976), vol. 6, p. 78. See the discussion of this thesis in R. Meek, 'Marx's "Doctrine of Increasing Misery"', in R. Meek, *Economics and Ideology and Other Essays* (London, 1967), pp. 113–28.

reduces them to penury. The concept of pauperisation complemented Marx's theory of capitalist crises, and has understandably
attracted Marxist ideologists and their audiences during periods of
depression and declining living standards, including the 'Great
Depression' of the 1880s which conditioned the early years of the
Parti Ouvrier. None the less, the theory has always raised serious
problems, not the least of which has been the secular trend toward
rising real wages which has understandably undermined the conviction that 'pauperism develops more rapidly than population and
wealth'.[20] Worse yet, Marxists have had to admit that paupers,
however pitiful, make unlikely revolutionaries and even less likely
agents of historical progress.[21] Conceding the theory's empirical
implausibility and political impracticality, they have often had
to retreat from the seductive simplicities of revolutionary
impoverishment.

Marx himself led this retreat, supplying the more sophisticated
theory of 'relative' pauperisation as an alternative conceptualisation
of the revolutionary proletariat. The absolute level of working-class
welfare is irrelevant in this conception, since 'in proportion as capital
accumulates, the lot of the labourer, *be his payment high or low*, must
grow worse'.[22] According to the protocols of relative pauperisation,
relativities between the bourgeoisie and the working class, not
working-class living standards in themselves, define proletarian
poverty: capitalism has impoverished workers because bourgeois
wealth has increased more rapidly than that of the proletariat. The
textile worker in a *fin-de-siècle* spinning mill may have enjoyed a
marginally higher standard of living than her artisanal great-grand-
mother, but her capitalist employer accumulated infinitely greater
wealth than her ancestor's master had ever dreamed of.[23] She underwent (relative) impoverishment, even as she became 'better off'.

Nevertheless, this thesis, although powerful as social and historical theory, has suffered from two crippling weaknesses. First, it
presupposes, improbably, that workers whose absolute standard of

[20] This critique is discussed in J. Cousins, 'Some Problems in the Concept of the "Proletariat"', *Mens en Maatschappij*, vol. 46, 1971, pp. 211–12.
[21] For this point, see the superb discussion in Barrington Moore's *Injustice: The Social Bases of
Obedience and Revolt* (London, 1978), pp. 143–4.
[22] Marx, *Capital*, vol. 1, pp. 386–7 (my italics).
[23] For discussion of this thesis, see T. Sowell, 'Marx's "Increasing Misery" Doctrine', *American
Economic Review*, vol. 50, 1960, pp. 111–20; D. Hodges, 'Marx's General Law of Capitalist
Development', *Études de Marxologie*, no. 176, 1966, pp. 121–35; and M. Nicolaus, 'The
Unknown Marx', in C. Oglesley (ed.), *The New Left Reader* (New York, 1969), pp. 98–9.

living has improved would perceive the overall distribution of income clearly enough to resent their 'relative impoverishment'. Assessment of national income distribution by class daunts the econometric late twentieth century, and hardly existed in *fin-de-siècle* France, even among academic economists, much less among working-class autodidacts. Second, the theory of relative pauperisation assumes that workers' resentment of the deteriorating income differential between themselves and their exploiters, if this mentality could be inculcated at all, furnishes sufficient motive for revolutionary militancy – a most unlikely assumption. Absolute pauperisation, despite its empirical implausibility, at least implied a credible revolutionary desperation. By contrast, relative pauperisation implied, at most, resentment and envy: 'restore our differentials!' – a most unlikely revolutionary slogan. Both fundamental suppositions underpinning this theory of proletarian militancy, that relative pauperisation manifests itself to its victims and that it fosters revolutionary aspirations, have failed in practice, despite the theory's deserved popularity with sociologists.[24]

The theory of pauperisation, often in its most simplistic form, dominated the Guesdist conception of the revolutionary class interest which supposedly motivated proletarian militancy and which would eventually determine the transition from capitalism to socialism. On occasion, the POF even accepted Lassalle's 'iron law of wages', an extreme interpretation of pauperisation in which the capitalist labour market necessarily reduces wages to minimum subsistence levels, thereby dooming workers to absolute poverty. This 'Lassalleanism' predominated in the nascent Guesdist movement during the 1870s before Guesde, at least, had fully assimilated a vulgarised Marxist political economy, and continued to appear in Guesdist rhetoric throughout the depression-wracked 1880s.[25] This enthusiasm for the 'iron law' may have reflected the early theoretical 'immaturity' of the movement or its unthinking response to the dismal economic circumstances of the 'Great Depression'. But Lassalleanism never completely disappeared from Guesdist rhetoric,

[24] See the discussions in M. Mann, *Consciousness and Action Among the Western Working Class* (London, 1973), p. 70, and A. Przeworski, 'Material Interests, Class Compromise, and the State', in A. Przeworski, *Capitalism and Social Democracy* (Cambridge, 1985), pp. 171–203.
[25] Guesde's most Lassallean work was *La Loi des Salaires et ses Conséquences* (Paris, 1879), a book written before Guesde's full assimilation of Marxist precepts, but nevertheless republished three times between 1878 and 1906.

even during periods of prosperity. Alexandre Zévaès, by no means a simpleton, wrote as late as 1893 that 'the law which limits a worker's remuneration to the minimum for survival and reproduction is increasingly becoming an "iron" reality. If there was a time when it did not work with all the rigour described by Lassalle, it was when it was formulated by the fathers of political economy at the beginning of the century'.[26] Some Guesdists actually outdid Lassalle, finding his theory too *optimistic*. Rather than 'an unbreakable law of iron' which maintained workers at bare subsistence levels, Lafargue, for instance, discovered 'a compressive law . . . which grasps the worker in a physical and moral vice and compels him to reduce his needs'.[27] Capitalism not only reduced wages to a subsistence minimum, but inexorably reduced that minimum, thereby impoverishing the meaning of subsistence itself.

The iniquitous results of pauperisation, 'larger and larger fortunes confront[ing] increasingly lamentable working-class misery',[28] supposedly supplied the proletariat with every motive for revolution. Wretches with nothing to lose and everything to gain – famished, dressed in rags, housed in crumbling slums – *must* revolt against the system which so impoverished them. Having described (in an article graphically entitled 'Misère!') the appalling conditions characteristic of French industrial *faubourgs*, *Le Socialiste* concluded that 'there's an enormous number of malcontents in capitalist societies who are . . . ready to throw themselves into revolutionary adventures. The lot of the workers is so bad that it couldn't get any worse. As in Marx and Engels' *Communist Manifesto*, the workers have nothing to lose but their chains'.[29] Virtually every issue of the Guesdist press, every Guesdist pamphlet, every Guesdist parliamentary intervention painted harrowing pictures of proletarian wretchedness and poverty, portrayals of a dire social catastrophe which not only condemned bourgeois society as intolerable but doomed capitalism to death at the hands of its destitute victims.

At their most extreme, Guesdists appeared to believe that the very existence of revolutionary socialism depended upon impoverishment and destitution, a crude economic determinism which implied that a

[26] A. Zévaès, 'M. Drumont et le Socialisme', *Le Socialiste*, 11 October 1893.
[27] P. Lafargue, 'La Loi d'Airain', *Le Socialiste*, 29 January 1899.
[28] Anonymous, 'Franchise', *Bulletin Mensuel de la Fédération Nationale des Élus du Parti Ouvrier Français*, première année, no. 6, 1 May 1900, p. 5.
[29] Anonymous, 'Misère!', *Le Socialiste*, 14 August 1886.

prosperous proletariat must be a quiescent proletariat. When the
Belgian socialist Vandervelde criticised Lassalleanism in 1898, maintaining that its 'iron law' grossly misrepresented the real tendencies
of capitalist society, *Le Socialiste* responded that 'to deprive ourselves
of an axiom holding the key to this vitally important economic
phenomenon would be a major and unpardonable error. It would
frivolously lend support to the schemes of socialism's enemies, since it
would undermine the entire traditional system of collectivism'.[30]
Like a growing number of liberal optimists, who expected working-
class prosperity to reconcile workers to their place in the polity,
many Guesdists decided that a well-fed, well-dressed, and well-
housed proletariat would pose little threat to capital. No wonder
French Marxists clung, against all evidence, to the comforting
conviction that capitalism would not, even could not, allow the
slightest degree of proletarian well-being.

Despite the *a priori* certainties of Lassalleanism, the more theoretically sensitive Guesdists abandoned the 'iron law', at least in its most
simplistic form.[31] After all, the real income of the average worker
had virtually doubled during the nineteenth century, and this
improvement, if anything, accelerated during the *Fin de Siècle*. For
the first time, meat appeared regularly on workers' tables, the
Sunday suit became a normal part of working-class wardrobes, and
even housing, the most recalcitrant aspect of proletarian poverty,
lost some of its bleakness as Leftist municipal governments embarked
upon programmes of 'urban improvement'.[32] The Guesdist imagery
of absolute 'pauperisation' may have reflected workers' fears, but it
bore little relationship to their experience. Clinging to the rhetoric of
misery and destitution, while the working class took its first tentative
steps into the consumer society, hardly enhanced Marxist
credibility.

Nevertheless, like Marx himself, the POF refused to abandon

[30] P. Louis, 'De Quelques Points de Doctrine', *Le Socialiste*, 25 December 1898.
[31] It is emphatically not the case that the Guesdists were unswervingly Lassallean, as claimed
in D. Lindenberg, *Le Marxisme Introuvable* (Paris, 1975), pp. 56 and 59–60.
[32] The secular evolution of real wages is described in G. Weill, 'Le Rôle des Facteurs
Structurels dans l'Évolution des Rémunérations Salariales au XIXᵉ Siècle', *Revue Économique*, vol. 10, 1959, p. 238. For the indications of rising real wages during the *Fin de Siècle*, see
Y. Lequin, *Les Ouvriers de la Région Lyonnaise (1848–1914): Les Intérêts de Classe et la République*
(Lyons, 1977), pp. 22–9, 31–9, and 60–7. There is a useful critique of Guesdist blindness to
these trends in C. Willard, *Le Mouvement Socialiste en France (1893–1905): Les Guesdistes* (Paris,
1965), pp. 171–2.

'pauperisation' altogether. Challenged by incontrovertible evidence of improving working-class living standards as France emerged from the 'Great Depression', Guesdists developed a complex and surprisingly sophisticated theory of relative pauperisation. At the most basic level, this theory stressed the ever-widening gap between workers' incomes, even when these had increased in absolute terms, and bourgeois wealth. 'I'm quite willing to admit', confessed Gabriel Deville,

that there has been an improvement over the past while. All the same, what does such a comparison prove? You don't bother with such things if you remember that well-being is basically relative. In order to give an accurate account of the improvement or degradation of working-class conditions, you don't compare what they now consume with what they once consumed, but the gap existing then and now between the condition of the proletariat and that of the capitalists.[33]

According to this formulation, French proletarians sank ever deeper into poverty not because of how little they possessed, but because of the deteriorating ratio between their slowly increasing comfort and the burgeoning luxury of the bourgeoisie: workers rented larger flats, while their employers bought country houses; proletarians finally began to eat meat, while their bosses ate caviar; seamstresses could afford Sunday dresses, while their bourgeois customers wore mink.

At first sight, this thesis suffered from none of the empirical implausibility of 'absolute pauperisation'. Income relativities between labour and capital indeed shifted to the advantage of the latter during the *Belle Époque*, as profits and dividends increased from 34 per cent of national income in 1860 to 40 per cent in 1913.[34] Some of this increase in the capitalist share of national wealth took place at the expense of non-proletarian groups, particularly in rural society. But the bourgeois opulence of the *Fin de Siècle* undoubtedly did diminish the relative value of the working-class share of the French GNP. The resulting 'relative pauperisation' of the proletariat manifested itself even in the height of military recruits: working-class conscripts were taller in comparison to those of earlier years, a sure sign of an improved standard of living, but they were also markedly shorter relative to bourgeois youths.[35]

All the same, the polemical (as opposed to sociological) force of

[33] G. Deville, *Principes Socialistes* (Paris, 1896), pp. 123–4.
[34] P. Sorlin, *La Société Française 1840–1914* (Paris, 1969), p. 134.
[35] Y. Lequin, *Les Intérêts de Classe et la République*, pp. 42–44.

this thesis depended upon workers' awareness of the actual wealth of
the bourgeoisie, and of its evolution over several decades in relation
to their own. These requirements became increasingly improbable
as the gulf of incomprehension separating the working class from the
bourgeoisie gaped ever wider. Increasing residential segregation of
labour and wealth, coupled with the separation of management and
ownership which so reduced contact between employees and
employers during the 'second industrial revolution', ensured that
workers knew little about their betters' life-style and less about their
incomes. Only once did the Guesdists themselves support their
theory of relative pauperisation with serious evidence, whether
statistical or anecdotal: *Le Socialiste* maintained in 1895 that France's
national wealth had tripled during the preceding fifty years, while
workers' income had stagnated – supposed evidence of an enormous
shift of relative wealth towards the bourgeoisie.[36] But deteriorating
relativities between the classes, unlike the wounds of absolute
poverty, remained statistical abstractions, and presented few
rhetorical opportunities for Parti Ouvrier propaganda: starving
children made better copy than did shifts in national income
distribution. No wonder Guesdists clung to their theory of absolute
pauperisation, despite its implausibility.

Nevertheless, the Parti Ouvrier struggled to reinforce its conception of relative pauperisation with more obvious miseries than
deteriorating but abstract relativities. First, Guesdists discovered
that standards of living depended upon gradually changing definitions of subsistence itself, as the affluence of one period became the
poverty of another. Heartened by this discovery, Guesdists emphasised that, although workers' incomes might have increased during
the nineteenth century, their needs had inflated even more rapidly –
a combination resulting in relative impoverishment. 'It's ridiculous',
Deville contended, 'to argue from workers' life-styles in two different
epochs, one in which the non-satisfaction of needs derived from the
fact that those needs were unknown, and another where needs have
been acquired but not satisfied'.[37] The 'progress' of capitalism had
progressively transformed the Lassallean subsistence minimum itself.
According to Paul Louis, 'it's evident that the living standard of a
worker in 1898 requires more complex . . . satisfactions than those of

---

[36] An assessment based upon figures in Gide's *Traité d'Économie Politique*, cited in A. Delon, 'Et
Quand Il y a des Pertes!', *Le Socialiste*, 29 December 1895.
[37] G. Deville, 'L'État et le Socialisme', *Le Socialiste*, 2 June 1895.

a worker in 1825 or 1850. A good many things which would have seemed superfluous to our fathers fifty years ago are absolute necessities for us'.[38] This version of 'relative impoverishment' possessed considerable theoretical force. Although workers of the *Belle Époque* undoubtedly dressed better and ate more than their grandparents, the pressure to sustain these improved conditions proved at least as demanding as the mid-century struggle for subsistence: higher incomes only 'created further needs, needs previously unknown'.[39] Guesdists had discovered the rat-race.

Second, Guesdists decided that increasing working-class needs within a capitalist economy did not necessarily imply a more affluent proletarian life-style. The consumption of commodities, however expanded, sometimes failed to compensate for the decline in the self-sufficiency which had characterised traditional working-class survival strategies. The miner who had once killed a hog every year now depended upon the butcher: his expenditures upon meat increased; his consumption of pork declined.[40] In other words, the irresistible advance of the capitalist commodity market, under some circumstances, combined apparent enhancement of the working-class standard of living with genuine impoverishment. Unfortunately, the Guesdists' neglect of consumption in favour of production inhibited development of this complex argument, an argument which led back towards absolute pauperisation, towards the discovery of an absolute, rather than relative, compression of living standards.

Finally, 'relative impoverishment', in the hands of the Parti Ouvrier, measured the relativities between work and income: increasing wages, Guesdists asserted, came at the price of disproportionately intensified labour. Ernest Montusès, a Guesdist militant from Montluçon, admitted that 'it seems one eats better bread and more meat. That's quite possible, for some. But work has intensified, and nourishment can improve without succouring the body. What's certain is that work has become harder, more exhausting, and that the worker gives a few more hours of his sad life to the capitalist Minotaur'.[41] A constant search for higher productivity certainly

---

[38] P. Louis, 'De Quelques Points de Doctrine', *Le Socialiste*, 25 December 1898. There is an explicit description (based upon an official inquiry) of how expanding working-class income was devoured by expanding needs in 'Dr. Z.', 'L'Enquête', *Le Socialiste*, 11 May 1891.

[39] 'C. B.' (Bonnier), 'La Fabrique dans les Villages', *Le Socialiste*, 13 November 1886.

[40] R. Trempé, *Les Mineurs de Carmaux 1848–1914* (Paris, 1971), vol. 1, pp. 413 and 415.

[41] E. Montusès, 'Science et Révolution', *Le Socialiste*, 1–3 December 1901.

pervaded French workplaces during the *Belle Époque*, and the higher wages enjoyed by some workers often reflected a greatly intensified labour process. Many workers received surprisingly meagre reward for the vastly expanded output generated by their mastery of novel technologies and their subjection to new labour disciplines.[42] The glass-blower who had doubled his output understandably resented a 10 per cent wage increase: he well understood the meaning of relative impoverishment. Guesdists successfully tapped working-class resentment of the ever-accelerating 'speed-up' which drove the 'second industrial revolution'. They denigrated the workers' share of the resultant prosperity and highlighted the capitalists' appropriation of the lion's share of the gains.

Changing relativities between the wealth of the bourgeoisie and that of the proletariat, changing relativities between past and present working-class needs, changing relativities between productivity and pay – Guesdists exploited all three of these incitements to revolution. The resulting conception of 'relative pauperisation' undoubtedly satisfies twentieth-century scholarly prejudices rather better than does 'absolute pauperisation': it conforms to the apparent 'realities' of the French economy during the *Belle Époque*, and demonstrates a more sophisticated comprehension of the 'standard of living' problem. But 'relative pauperisation', because of its theoretical complexity and remoteness from workers' everyday 'lived experience', offered Guesdist polemicists only the most pallid opportunities for anti-capitalist propaganda. As journalists and pamphleteers, devoted to the telling phrase rather than to intellectual rigour, they understandably preferred a rhetoric of social criticism in which 'the lot of workers is so bad that it couldn't get any worse'.

Finally, once having conceded that capitalism had not reduced its workers to paupers, Guesdists retreated to the solidly defensible assertion that workers prospered not *because* of capitalism, but *in spite* of it. Absolute impoverishment, they argued, endured in the logic of capital, even if proletarian resistance mitigated the tendency of the system 'to reduce salaries to the minimum possible'.[43] Driven by the imperatives of the market, capitalists necessarily sought to reduce labour costs to subsistence levels, or even below them. They might not always succeed, but they would always try: the 'iron law of

---

[42] Sorlin, *La Société Française*, p. 185, and G. Dupeux, *La Société Française 1789–1970* (Paris, 1972), p. 175.

[43] Deville, *Principes Socialistes*, pp. 129–30.

salaries' persisted as the 'tendential law of capitalism'.[44] That some workers improved their standard of living, despite capitalism, no more disproved the 'iron law' than the flight of birds disproved the law of gravity. Socialist revolution alone might abolish the constant *tendency* towards pauperisation inherent in the capitalist mode of production.[45]

No doubt dismayed by the accumulating epicycles in their Ptolemaic theory of pauperisation, Guesdists sometimes abandoned the concept altogether, whether in its absolute, relative, or tendential variants, dismissing it as 'that simplistic approach'[46] to revolution. As so often with Guesdist discourse, this abandonment of an otherwise cherished thesis largely depended upon polemical circumstances. Lassalle (and Guesde) had used the 'iron law' to denounce an economic system which supposedly frustrated any improvements in wages. French capitalists, however, deployed the same 'law' to fend off their employees' wage-demands, arguing that, since workers could not significantly improve their wages, given the nature of the labour market, they should resign themselves to their lot. French Marxists had themselves exploited a similar argument against syndicalists, but angrily repudiated it when encountered in the hands of the bourgeoisie.[47]

The Parti Ouvrier attacked the 'iron law' even more scathingly when it appeared in anarchist hands. Working-class libertarians advocated sabotage, terrorism, and spontaneous revolt as the only tactics left to the impoverished victims of capital – an implicit and sometimes explicit critique of the Marxists' programme of patient political education and systematic class mobilisation. In response, Guesdists, unperturbed by self-contradiction, abandoned Lassalleianism altogether, maintaining that poverty created 'only beggars and anarchists'[48] and that 'the proletarian revolution could not be a [mere] slave revolt'[49] against suffering. Dismayed by anarchist deployment of the 'iron law', French Marxists even completely reversed themselves, arguing convincingly that pauperisation

[44] P. Lafargue, 'Le Parti Ouvrier et l'Alimentation Publique', *La Revue Socialiste*, no. 4, 1890, p. 218. Guesde, often characterised as particularly Lassallean in his political economy, also described the iron law as tendential rather than absolute. See J. Guesde, 'Théorie et Pratique', *Le Citoyen*, 18 May 1882.

[45] Anonymous, 'Le Minimum de Salaire', *Le Socialiste*, 28 July 1894.

[46] A. Baju, *Principes du Socialisme* (Paris, 1893), p. 6.

[47] J. Guesde, 'Bêtise Triple', *Le Cri du Peuple*, 25 December 1884.

[48] J. Guesde, *Double Réponse à MM. de Mun et Deschanel* (Paris, 1900), p. 8.

[49] P.-M. André, 'Pour les 3–8', *Le Socialiste*, 25 December – 8 January 1905.

actually *impeded* revolution. In the words of Alexandre Zévaès, 'continuous suffering and extended and intensifying misery are far from being, as the anarchists would believe, a stimulus to revolt ... Instead, they depress morale, breed stupidity, and create resignation and prostration rather than courage and readiness for action'.[50] Upon consideration, Guesdists decided that pauperisation also laid highly insecure foundations for the impending socialist order. Adéodat Compère-Morel, perhaps sensitised to the improbability of an indigents' revolution by his long association with the land-owning peasantry, concluded that 'it's not with paupers suffering from empty stomachs that one builds a new society. Hatred of the present isn't enough to construct a better world; it's necessary, above all, to possess the power and the knowledge required for that task'.[51] Once having forgotten its long infatuation with the revolutionary consequences of pauperisation, the POF maintained that only working-class *well-being* led towards socialism. Charles Brunellière, for instance, asserted that,

far from expecting any movement towards liberation on the part of the proletariat caused by its growing misery, the Parti Ouvrier has never ceased [!] to affirm and reaffirm that the less a class is starved and oppressed the more capable it will be of self-emancipation. That is why we are eagerly seeking the immediate reforms which may give the workers the strength to organise against the bourgeoisie today and the ability to seize political power tomorrow.[52]

Guesdists affirmed that, 'unlike anarchists, the Parti Ouvrier ... doesn't rely upon the intensification or generalisation of poverty'.[53] Consistency rarely troubled Guesdist propagandists.

At first glance, emphasis upon working-class vigour rather than working-class impoverishment furnished the POF with powerful arguments. Evidence suggests that proletarian prosperity indeed empowered working-class militancy: textile workers in the Nord challenged their employers not during the depths of their mid-nineteenth-century misery, but as their conditions improved during the latter part of the century; prosperous artisanal workers enlisted in the socialist army far more readily than did poverty-stricken

[50] A. Zévaès, 'Collectivisme et Réformes', *Le Socialiste*, 7 July 1895.
[51] A. Compère-Morel, 'Paysan et Socialiste', *Le Socialiste*, 10–17 April 1904.
[52] C. Brunellière, 'La Semaine', *Le Socialiste*, 22 July 1900.
[53] *Douzième Congrès National du Parti Ouvrier Français, tenu à Nantes du 14 au 16 Septembre 1894* (Lille, 1894), p. 20.

labourers.[54] Guesdists, however, systematically avoided the equally convincing argument that, while misery gave workers motive but not opportunity for militancy, prosperity gave them opportunity but not motive. Determined optimists, French Marxists never noted a working-class oscillation between impotent poverty and affluent quiescence. The Parti Ouvrier, secure in its Marxist convictions, maintained that capitalist exploitation, in itself, *always* justified the socialist revolution. Abandoning decades of propaganda on the theme of pauperisation, Édouard Fortin concluded that

even if we were to admit that the bourgeoisie could guarantee every worker his employment, even if we were to admit that these latter could benefit from technological progress in the same proportion as the capitalists, even if we were to admit that the rate of exploitation could diminish, as the 'standard of living' of all the workers grew more rapidly than labour productivity, the problem of wage labour's abolition would remain.[55]

In the end, Guesdists reduced their theory of pauperisation to irrelevancy: workers would challenge capitalist exploitation whether they were poor or prosperous.

Once having reached this conclusion, Guesdists turned to an alternative theory of the revolutionary proletariat and the transition to socialism, a theory in which workers would inherit the world not because of what capitalists had done to them, but because of what capitalists no longer did for themselves.[56] Management of the productive process, once the prerogative of capital and the source of its legitimacy, had devolved onto salaried workers: capitalists had withdrawn into opulent parasitism while the vital capacities of society accumulated in the hands of the proletariat. Thus, just as an entrepreneurial bourgeoisie had overthrown a superannuated aristocracy, so the working class would overthrow rentier capitalism. Marx, summing up his optimistic teleology of progressive productive forces, had depicted the hegemonic class of the future: 'we

[54] J.-P. Courtheoux, 'Naissance d'une Conscience de Classe dans le Prolétariat Textile du Nord 1830–1870', *Revue Économique*, vol. 8, 1957, p. 119; M. Hanagan, 'Organisation du Travail et Action Revendicative: Verriers et Métallurgistes de Rive-de-Giers à la Fin du XIXᵉ Siècle', *Cahiers d'Histoire*, vol. 26, 1981, pp. 9–10; and J.-P. Brunet, *Saint-Denis: La Ville Rouge – Socialisme et Communisme en Banlieu Ouvrier 1890–1939* (Paris, 1980), pp. 101–2.

[55] É. Fortin, 'La Grande Industrie', *Le Devenir Social*, nos. 8–9, 1896, p. 706.

[56] It was not the case for the Guesdists that 'the theory of increasing misery is a necessary element of the dialectic mechanism of history and therefore an indispensable part of Marxist philosophy', as alleged in C. Landauer, 'The Guesdists and the Small Farmer: Early Erosion of French Marxism', *International Review of Social History*, vol. 6, 1961, p. 215.

know that to work well the newfangled forces of society, they only want to be mastered by newfangled men – and such are the working men. They are as much the invention of modern times as machinery itself'.[57] A 'collective worker' embodying all the managerial, technical and manual needs of the productive apparatus would rule the new world created by machinery – a theory of proletarian revolution which complemented the Marxist conception of 'monopoly capitalism'.

Marxists have too often assumed that, once workers come to desire the destruction of capitalism, they will necessarily have the capacity to achieve that aspiration – a *non sequitur* of massive proportions.[58] Unlike the various theories of pauperisation, the concept of the revolutionary 'collective worker' avoids this flaw: what better revolutionary class could be imagined than a proletariat exercising the managerial, technical, and administrative functions once performed by the bourgeoisie, but excluded from the wealth, prestige, and privilege traditionally associated with these functions?[59] Anti-Marxists have, none the less, vigorously attacked this conception of revolutionary dynamics, with liberals contending that conflict over authority divides the 'collective worker' far more than the class war opposes the 'salariat' to capital, while the libertarian Left, accentuating this conflict over authority and widening the divisions within the 'salariat', has denounced the very idea of a 'collective worker' as a mystification of the subordination of 'real workers' to a 'new bourgeoisie' of planners, technicians, and managers.[60] All the same, the concept of a revolutionary collective worker has withstood criticism far better than has the theory of pauperisation, so that the *capacity* of the working class has complemented, or even replaced, the *condition* of the working class in most contemporary Marxist conceptions of proletarian revolution.

The POF developed several theories of the transition to socialism based upon the capacity of the working class, not all of which

[57] K. Marx, *Speech at the Anniversary of the People's Paper*, in K. Marx and F. Engels, *Collected Works* (London, 1980), vol. 14, p. 656.

[58] A. Levine and E. Wright, 'Rationality and Class Struggle', *New Left Review*, no. 123, 1980, pp. 47–68 is a good analysis of this fallacy.

[59] For Marx's most explicit discussion of the 'collective worker', see the so-called 'lost chapter' of *Capital*: 'Results of the Immediate Process of Production', *Capital* (Penguin edition, London, 1976), vol. 1, p. 1040.

[60] For an example of the liberal critique, see R. Dahrendorf, *Class and Class Conflict in Industrial Society* (Stanford, 1959), p. 136, and, for that of the libertarians, C. Castoriadis, 'On the History of the Workers' Movement', *Telos*, no. 30, 1976–7, pp. 3–42.

depended upon the concept of the 'collective worker'. In their rare 'ouvriériste' moments, Guesdists held that 'any cook can rule the state', that even the most impoverished and brutalised workers of the Roubaisian textile industry surpassed their parasitic employers in administrative capacity. The monthly bulletin published for Parti Ouvrier deputies and municipal councillors, few of them manual workers, asserted that

the worker is a born administrator. Keeping your head above water is administration like any other, and more difficult than most. Making ends meet and holding them together with enormous effort, saving here in order to spend there, clothing oneself, shoeing oneself, feeding an entire family and facing illnesses with such a salary – that's showing administrative capacity far superior to some bourgeois who has his affairs managed by employees, aside from signing papers.[61]

After all, French Marxists pointed out, workers managed cooperatives, trade unions, and socialist municipalities. When the working class had acquired 'sufficient self-confidence and self-consciousness', Guesdists predicted, 'it will no longer limit its efforts to the management of a bakery, a trade union or a town. It will be able to seize . . . the controls of that great machine which is society'.[62] Today Roubaix, tomorrow the world!

Fortunately for their credibility, Guesdists rarely relied upon the simplistic assumption that workers – although impoverished, brutalised, and debased – none the less displayed all the attributes of an aspirant ruling class. In more sophisticated Parti Ouvrier analyses, proletarian potential derived from the working class's incorporation of the 'intellectual elite responsible for the supervision and control of production'.[63] As Lafargue noted in his aptly titled *Le Communisme et l'Évolution Économique*, 'the working class is charged with producing everything and, at the same time, with directing all production. Today it is the only useful class and it remains only for it to . . . administer the political interests of the nation'.[64] The Guesdist interpretation of the 'new middle class' as essentially a 'new working class' thoroughly integrated into the 'collective worker' underpinned this concept of the transition to socialism: scientists and technicians,

[61] Anonymous, 'Les Ouvriers au Conseil Municipal', *Bulletin Mensuel de la Fédération Nationale des Élus du Parti Ouvrier Français*, Première Année, no. 7, 1 June 1900, p. 4.
[62] Maussa, 'Sur le Terrain', *Le Socialiste*, 27 March – 3 April 1904.
[63] G. Deville, *Philosophie du Socialisme* (Paris, 1886), p. 30.
[64] P. Lafargue, *Le Communisme et l'Évolution Économique* (Lille, 1892), p. 23.

managers and civil servants, teachers, intellectuals and artists – all had been proletarianised, their talents and capacities concentrated in the working class. In Guesde's words,

That which allows the immediate transformation of the capitalist order into a collectivist or communist order is that every kind of labour – manual, administrative, managerial, and scientific – is carried out by salaried workers. There lies the chance to eliminate the capitalist class, now useless, but a chance which will be missed if one amputates any element of this salaried class, if the revolutionary party limits itself to only those workers labelled as manual.[65]

The 'new working class' constituted the proletarian officer corps without which the class war could hardly be fought, and never won.

On the face of it, this conception of the revolutionary proletariat depended upon hope rather than evidence: only a tiny elite of workers displayed much capacity or even interest in management and administration, most French capitalists had by no means abandoned productive entrepreneurship for luxurious parasitism, and solidarity between the 'mental' and manual elements of the 'collective worker' existed largely in the socialist imagination.[66] All the same, the faith that workers would revolt because of their unrewarded capacities suffused Guesdist discourse, no doubt because of its *a priori* plausibility, given Marxist assumptions about the capitalist mode of production. But the theory of proletarian capacities also conferred an invaluable polemical advantage: it projected the image of studious, conscientious, honest workers, both 'blue-collar' and 'white-collar', fit not only to mind their own affairs but those of society as a whole, an image ideally calculated to refute the common bourgeois assumption that 'the proletariat lacks the intelligence to assume what is referred to as the responsibilities of power'.[67] This imagery of the omnicompetent proletariat not only

---

[65] Report of a speech by Guesde, *Le Socialiste*, 13 November 1886.
[66] See the critique in A. Touraine, *La Conscience Ouvrière* (Paris, 1966), pp. 322–4 and the evidence in A. Daumard, 'L'Évolution des Structures Sociales en France à l'Époque de l'Industrialisation 1815–1914', *Revue Historique*, vol. 247, 1972, p. 326; A. Daumard, 'Les Structures Bourgeoises en France à l'Époque Contemporaine: Évolution ou Permanence?', in *Conjoncture Économique/Structures Sociales: Hommage à Ernest Labrousse* (Paris, 1974), p. 456; and R. Girault, 'Existe-t-elle une Bourgeoisie d'Affaires Dynamique en France avant 1914?', *Bulletin de la Société d'Histoire Moderne*, vol. 68, 1969, p. 4.
[67] G. Maillet, 'Le Parti Ouvrier et le Pouvoir Municipal', *Bulletin Mensuel de la Fédération Nationale des Élus du Parti Ouvrier Français*, deuxième année, no. 20, 1 July 1901, p. 2. For the prevalence of this contempt towards workers among employers, who tended to see their employees as irresponsible minors, see J. Lambert, *Le Patron: De l'Avènement à la Contestation* (Paris, 1969), pp. 89–91.

buttressed a theory of socialist revolution, but furnished French workers with a powerful and much-needed weapon against the condescension of their social 'superiors'.

While the theories of pauperisation and of the collective worker jostled each other for precedence in the Guesdists' conception of the revolutionary working class, a third thesis transcended both. This most fundamental Marxist concept of the proletariat and its role in the transition to the socialist mode of production has depended neither upon the condition of the working class nor upon its capacities, but upon a vision of the future, upon a utopia.[68] Proletarians, after all, could not opt for or against the capitalist *status quo* without some idea of the socialist morrow, and socialists could only recruit for the revolution by identifying those with an 'interest in the [prospective] triumph of socialism'.[69] The saved and the damned of capitalist society identified themselves by their pre-destined place within the future socialist mode of production, that secular vision of the heavenly city. In this thesis, the proletarian revolution and the socialist utopia merged into a teleological whole.

Nevertheless, Marxists have resisted utopianism. Marx himself had asserted that the socialist 'utopia', defined as a classless society, already existed in embryo within the proletariat, since 'the condition for the emancipation of the working class is the abolition of all classes'.[70] Once socialists perceived this working-class acorn, a hard reality evident to the naked eye, they would not have to puzzle themselves over the misty branching of the ultimate socialist oak tree.[71] Contemptuous of the fantasies of Fourier and the Saint-Simonians, Marxists have consistently refused to predict the positive actuality of classlessness. The construction of the future, they have contended, should be left to the future. As a consequence, Marxists

[68] For discussion of Marxist utopianism, see B. Ollman, 'Marx's Vision of Communism', in *Social and Sexual Revolution: Essays on Marx and Reich* (Boston, 1979), p. 51; C. Siriani, 'Production and Power in a Classless Society: A Critical Analysis of the Utopian Dimensions of Marxist Theory', *Socialist Review*, no. 59, 1981, pp. 33–82; and I. Wallerstein, 'Marxism as Utopias: Evolving Ideologies', *American Journal of Sociology*, vol. 91, 1986, pp. 1,295–308.

[69] Deville, *Principes Socialistes*, p. 68. For the importance of a vision of the future in any critique of the present, see M. Rebérioux, 'Demain: Les Ouvrières et l'Avenir au Tournant du Siècle', *Revue du Nord*, vol. 63, 1981, p. 667, note 60.

[70] K. Marx, *The Poverty of Philosophy*, in K. Marx and F. Engels, *Collected Works* (London, 1976), vol. 6, p. 212.

[71] There is a good discussion of this teleology in G. Cohen, 'The Workers and the Word: Why Marx Had the Right to Think He was Right', *Praxis*, vol. 4, 1968, pp. 376–90.

have unthinkingly elaborated an entirely negative utopia founded upon the *abolition* of capitalist property, the *absence* of commodity exchange, and the *end* of the state.[72] This refusal to delineate the contours of the socialist promised land has had its advantages: unlike the great utopian socialists of the early nineteenth century, Marxists have not bogged down in 'planning the sewerage of utopia'. But critics have convincingly indicted this unwillingness to depict the future as an enormous confidence trick, a promise literally without substance.[73]

Guesdists, in the best Marxist tradition, professed a clear conception of the future socialist society immanent in the capitalist present: they even meticulously calculated the percentage of the French population fit for the socialist paradise.[74] Despite this feigned precision, however, the POF refused to elaborate 'the logical phantom'[75] of a full-scale utopia, contending that the gateway to the socialist tomorrow opened from the capitalist today, that workers needed no other map than the Marxist critique of capital to guide them in their march towards liberation. According to Lafargue, 'we refuse to furnish descriptions of the Jerusalem into which civilised humanity will soon enter. We limit ourselves to theoretically demolishing the capitalist hell, while waiting to demolish it in practice. To each generation its task: those who come after us will build the communist society upon the terrain which we have cleared'.[76] Convinced that the construction of ideal futures contradicted its novel 'scientific' socialism, the Parti Ouvrier denounced Guesdists such as Lucien Deslinières and Georges Dazet who had innocently indulged in utopian speculation.[77] French Marxists foreshadowed a 'paradise on earth',[78] but self-imposed strictures confined Guesdists to descriptions of the capitalist inferno.

[72] A. Cottrell, *Social Classes in Marxist Theory* (London, 1984), p. 24.
[73] S. Lukes, 'Marxism and Utopianism', in P. Alexander and R. Gill (eds.), *Utopia* (London, 1984), pp. 153–67 and Siriani, 'Production and Power', p. 49, pp. 53–5 and 65–6.
[74] E. Fortin, 'Le Prix d'une Première Classe', *Le Socialiste*, 15 December 1895. For a useful discussion of the POF's attitude towards utopianism, see M. Rebérioux, 'La Littérature Socialisante et la Représentation du Future en France au Tournant du Siècle', in *Histoire Sociale, Sensibilités Collectives et Mentalités: Mélanges Robert Mandrou* (Paris, 1983), p. 408.
[75] Anonymous, 'Anarchie et Socialisme', *Le Socialiste*, 27 October 1895.
[76] P. Lafargue, 'Le Problème Social', *Le Socialiste*, 2 September 1900.
[77] L. Deslinières, *Entretiens Socialistes* (Paris, 1901), and G. Dazet, *Lois Collectivistes pour l'An 19...* (Paris, 1907). See Deslinières' response to his critics in 'Un Réponse', *Le Socialiste*, 27 October 1901 – 3 November 1901, where he naively argues that he cannot see anything wrong with developing his personal utopia, since the Party had yet to adopt an official one!
[78] P. Lafargue, untitled, *L'Égalité*, 29 January 1882.

All the same, Guesdist discourse, as it accumulated over the decades, revealed the vague outlines of an alternative society: two generations of Marxist propaganda inadvertently disclosed a series of untheorised presuppositions about the socialist future. First, Guesdists abjured the Arcadian nostalgia of most preceding utopias: not for them the retreat from urban industrialism into rural self-sufficiency which had seduced so many working-class dreamers. The Parti Ouvrier's ideal tomorrow, as far as it could be discerned, depended upon and would further enhance the enormous productivity of modern industry. In the future dimension of the Guesdists' metahistory, industrial capitalism, condemned by its stifling relations of production, would surrender to industrial socialism, heir to its all-powerful forces of production. Proletarians would unseat the bourgeois ruling class precisely because workers embodied all the productive capacities of capitalism, capacities potentially freed from their encumbering bourgeois integument. Guesdists fiercely denounced the capitalists, who,

in order to indulge their vices and their beastly tastes, and in order to defend their property, withdraw from production and condemn to unproductiveness an enormous number of citizens. The rich are parasites upon whom live an innumerable army of further parasites: prostitutes, venal writers ... male and female servants, etc. The army, the police, prison guards and legal personnel are engaged in work without social utility which has the sole purpose of defending capitalist property. All the workers in the luxury trades, who are among the worst paid, can be, once [the bourgeoisie] has been suppressed, returned to production which is useful to the great mass of citizens.[79]

Just as the bourgeoisie had liberated the productivity of capitalist society by expropriating the accumulated wealth of monasteries and the wasted patrimonies of aristocrats, so socialists would discard the decadent bourgeoisie and its parasitic lackeys, thereby unleashing previously unimaginable forces of production.

Second, society's vessel would not only sail more freely once its hull had been scraped clean of bourgeois encrustations, but social-

---

[79] Anonymous, untitled, *Le Socialiste*, 13 February 1886. Some of these exercises in labour redistribution implied interesting problems: 'There are 1,609,432 servants in France. This figure will certainly descend to around a million under collectivism, resulting in the suppression of some 600,000 useless workers'. 'L.', 'Collectivisme et Production', *Le Socialiste*, 18 June 1899. The collectivist employers of the remaining million servants are not specified.

History and class conflict

ism, navigating by reason rather than by the blind caprice of competition, would steer clear of the squalls and maelstroms of the market. Individuals and firms would no longer strive blindly against each other, frustrating their own projects and disrupting society. Instead, economies of scale and rational organisation and planning, pioneered by individual capitalist firms but absent from capitalism as a system, would be extended to the entire socialist mode of production: 'socialist industry will be to large-scale capitalist industry what large-scale capitalist industry was to small-scale production. Nothing will be able to stand against *France Incorporated*.'[80] Guesdists envisaged an economy in which 'statistical commissions would formulate, on the basis of previous years' figures, the needs of consumption. These formulations, centralised and completed by the addition of general charges, would be the guidelines for production, which unified management would easily balance against effective demand'.[81] In this Guesdist vision of the future, society would transcend the crises, uncertainties, and irrationalities inherent in the market economy by generalising the orderly discipline of individual capitalist firms to society as a whole. At its most impoverished, this Saint-Simonian Guesdism foreshadowed little more than an orderly technocracy: *'this social control of production* – which will put an end to bourgeois anarchy – *is the sum of socialism.'*[82]

Finally, socialism would prove infinitely more productive than capitalism. Its 'employees', now joint proprietors of France Inc., would work enthusiastically for an enterprise which belonged to them rather than to their exploiters. The 'incentives' so beloved of bourgeois ideologists, but largely confined to property-owners within the capitalist mode of production, would finally be extended to every producer, now 'co-proprietors of all social wealth'.[83] Socialism would eliminate the barriers to productivity engendered by the 'complete indifference of the worker towards his work'[84] under capitalism. Responding to liberal assertions that socialism would destroy incentive and create nothing but universal poverty, Guesdists contended that socialism would actually unleash an unprecedented burst of productivity, as everyone gained an imme-

[80] J. Guesde, 'À Calais', *Le Socialiste*, 20 March 1892 (Guesde's stress).
[81] G. Deville, *Cours d'Économie Sociale: L'Évolution du Capital* (Paris, undated), p. 15.
[82] Anonymous, 'Anarchie et Socialisme', *Le Socialiste*, 27 February 1886 (stress in original).
[83] P. Lafargue, 'Le Problème Social', *Le Socialiste*, 2 September 1900.
[84] P. Lafargue, 'La Participation', *L'Égalité*, 30 April 1882.

diate interest in the productive order. Once everyone was their own capitalist, everyone, including the former capitalists, would be able to live as capitalists had once lived.[85] The socialist mode of production, unencumbered by parasitism, rationally organised, and stimulated by universal 'profit-sharing', would construct a world of plenty, a world where 'men and women ... will drink good wine to their hearts' content, and leave water to livestock'.[86] The land of Cockayne lay just beyond the socialist horizon.

Guesdist imagery of the future, however, suffered from an internal contradiction which has plagued Marxist ideology throughout its history: the contradiction between rational organisation and producers' democracy.[87] On the one hand, the Parti Ouvrier predicated its rudimentary utopia upon centralised planning and unified social ownership of the means of production ('France Inc.'); but, on the other hand, French Marxists embellished their socialist vision with the prospect that workers would own and manage their own workshops, free from others' authority. This Guesdist ambiguity, characteristically, reinforced and was reinforced by ambiguous working-class mentalities. Vacillation between authoritarian rationalism and libertarian self-management reflected two very different working-class responses to capitalism: workers both abominated anarchic capitalist macro-economics, above all the repetitive crises occasioned by market irrationalities, and detested dictatorial capitalist micro-economics, above all the destruction of workers' autonomy within individual firms. The proletariat dreamed of a social order which would guarantee both their security and their autonomy. The Guesdist utopia, through its contradictions, vowed to fulfil these otherwise tragically incompatible aspirations.[88]

Guesdists championed 'workers' control', albeit less often in the nebulous socialist future than in the capitalist present. They proposed self-governing institutions such as works-councils, prefigurations of twentieth-century 'council-communism', which, 'in

[85] P. Lafargue, 'Le Problème Social', *Le Socialiste*, 2 September 1900.
[86] Anonymous, 'La Récolte de Vin et de Cidre et le Communisme', *Le Socialiste*, 16 January 1886.
[87] For critique of this alternation between planning and workers' control, see J. Cohen, *Class and Civil Society: The Limits of Marxian Critical Theory* (Oxford, 1982), pp. 49 and 105–6.
[88] French labour sometimes feared the Marxist ideal of unified central economic planning (see B. Moss, *The Origins of the French Labor Movement 1830–1914: The Socialism of Skilled Workers* (Berkeley, 1976), pp. 21–2) but was also attracted to the idea of stable and waste-free socialist rationalism (see Rebérioux, 'La Littérature Socialisante et la Représentation du Future', pp. 416–18).

habituating the workers to collective action would prepare the way
to the new order where, restored to society, the means of production
will be entrusted to the exclusive management of the workers'.[89]
The Parti Ouvrier fully understood that the Third Republic would
never countenance such a violation of employers' command over
their enterprises: property rights and managerial authority
remained sacrosanct in the 'bourgeois Republic'. But Guesdist
proposals that workers obtain a degree of self-government within
their workplaces, for this very reason, served an invaluable rhetorical purpose: such proposals demonstrated, by their impossibility,
that the Republican regime of liberty, equality and fraternity
stopped at the factory gate. Guesdists, carried away by the force of
this polemic, occasionally lapsed into full-blown anarchosyndicalism, otherwise anathema to French Marxists. The POF actually
proposed that 'in the near future, unions ... take in hand the
management of the nation's entire production'[90] – an instance of the
powerful (non-Marxist) myth which would sustain the syndicalist
generation between 1900 and 1920. But, whether in syndicalist mode
or not, the Guesdist utopia seduced with its promise of a 'republic in
the factory' where, 'elected by workers, the "heads of industry" will
cease to be masters and despots and become simple collaborators'.[91]

Guesdists, none the less, suffered qualms about this utopia of self-
governing producers. At the least, they decided that 'the revolutionary government [a rare reference to the post-revolutionary
state] will have to guarantee that the workers to whom it has confided
a nationalised instrument [of production] possess all the qualities
required for its effective functioning'.[92] Why these qualms? Once
again, Guesdist rhetoric obeyed polemical necessity: transfer of
ownership from capitalists to workers, of coal mines from mine-
owners to miners, echoed the programmes of the Possibilists and
anarchosyndicalists – those fraternal enemies of Marxist socialism.[93]
In their hands, workers' control served as a weapon against
the Guesdist programme of centralised and disciplined proletarian

[89] Anonymous, untitled, *L'Égalité*, 16 April 1882.
[90] P. Lafargue, 'Le Congrès des Ouvrières et Ouvriers des Manufactures de Tabacs', *Le Socialiste*, 18 December 1892.
[91] J. Guesde, 'À Calais', *Le Socialiste*, 14 February 1892.
[92] P. Lafargue, 'Le Communisme et les Services Publics', *L'Égalité*, 2 July 1882.
[93] D. Stafford, *From Anarchism to Reformism: A Study of the Political Activities of Paul Brousse Within the First International and the French Socialist Movement 1870–1890* (Toronto, 1971), pp. 169–98, and J. Maitron, *Histoire du Mouvement Anarchiste en France (1880–1914)* (Paris, 1955), pp. 494–514.

politics: workers' self-management challenged both capitalist economics *and* Marxist socialism.

French Marxists, however, could not rubbish this popular ideal
without forfeiting working-class sympathy and support. They developed a simple solution to this dilemma: Guesdists accepted, even
demanded, workers' *control* of production, but condemned workers'
ownership of their workplaces. The POF insisted upon the nationalisation of industry – 'the social appropriation of the means of
production, excluding all varieties of private property, not only
individual, but corporative [in the social rather than commercial
sense] or professional'[94] – rather than the transfer of individual
enterprises from capitalists to groups of workers. How could
Guesdists justify this stance, which flatly contradicted the equation
of ownership and power which they applied in their critique of
bourgeois society?

First, French Marxists argued that the worker self-management
championed by the revolutionary syndicalists or the producers' co-
ops favoured by mutualists would generate 'the same disorder
associated with individual property' and thereby preclude the
'regulation, the *ordering* of production'.[95] As a consequence, the
ordered social rationality embodied in 'France Inc.' would collapse
as worker-proprietors lapsed into their own 'anarchy of production'.
Worse yet, the ownership of the means of production by trade
unions, as proposed by revolutionary syndicalists, or their possession
by corporative bodies representing workers in particular enterprises,
as advocated by the mutualists, would disrupt the unity of the
working class, the prerequisite of revolution and guarantee of
socialism.[96] Guesdists imagined a nightmare political economy in
which coal miners quarrelled with railway workers over freight
rates, metallurgical and engineering workers came to blows over the
supply of steel, while farm-workers and the urban proletariat fought
over the price of bread: anarchy would reign, and socialism would
succumb to the fatal disorders which had disrupted capitalism.

At its worst, proletarian ownership of individual firms or entire
industries would enable workers to exploit other workers. Denouncing the slogan 'the mine for the miners', a slogan which enjoyed

[94] J. Guesde, 'La Déchéance', *Le Cri du Peuple*, 10 March 1886.
[95] Anonymous, 'Mines et Mineurs', *Le Socialiste*, 13 March 1886 (stress in the original).
[96] G. Deville, 'Aperçu sur le Socialisme Scientifique', introduction to *Le Capital de Karl Marx*
(Paris, 1883), p. 21.

considerable popularity among both coal miners and anti-Marxist reformists, Guesde asserted 'the impossibility ... of leaving a commodity as essential ... as coal to individual interest or speculation. Like the capitalist companies, workers' societies would perceive only profits, rather than coal, to be mined in their new monopoly'.[97] Marxists saw no point in replacing workers' exploitation by capitalists with workers' exploitation by other workers.[98] According to *Le Socialiste*, Guesdists could not accept

the *mine for the miners*, just as we cannot accept the *tool for the worker, the land for the peasant*. This fragmentation of the means of production between different categories of workers, far from realising our ideal, is as antisocialist as impracticable – corporative property ... would lead to the same evils, the same disorder, as individual property: the struggle for existence between men, with its wounded and dead, overproduction, etc. What socialism seeks ... is the mine – like everything else – for society ... This social or integral appropriation of the mean of production will alone permit the control, the *organisation* of production.[99]

Thus Guesdists, seeking the best of both worlds, simultaneously endorsed workers' control of individual enterprises and common ownership and planning of the means of production, an economic order in which 'the nation ... will produce what is necessary for the needs of its citizens and divide the product equitably among them'.[100] The Parti Ouvrier never explained how it intended to combine central planning of needs and equitable distribution of goods with workers' self-management.

What did the Parti Ouvrier understand by dividing 'the product equitably'? If workers' control and common ownership would structure socialist production, what of socialist distribution? At their most simplistic, Guesdists demagogically promised that every worker would automatically and immediately receive the 'full product of his labour', that age-old demand of the labour movement (and target of Marx's attack in *The Critique of the Gotha Programme*). Socialism would 'leave the entire product of his labour to the labourer, now his own

[97] J. Guesde, 'Dans le Vide', *Le Cri du Peuple*, 18 April 1886. For the ways in which the programme of 'the mine for the miners' could be used against the socialist Left, see D. Reid, *The Miners of Decazeville: A Genealogy of Deindustrialisation* (London, 1985), pp. 102–4 and 284.

[98] J. Guesde, *En Garde! Contre les Contrafaçons, les Mirages et la Fausse Monnaie des Réformes Bourgeoises* (Paris, 1911), pp. 69–70.

[99] Anonymous, 'Mines et Mineurs', *Le Socialiste*, 13 March 1886 (stress in original).

[100] A. Delon, 'Et Quand Il y a des Pertes!', *Le Socialiste*, 29 December 1895.

boss'.[101] Guesdists sweetened this pledge with their over-simplified notion of enterprise finance: they never factored reinvestment or overhead costs into their frequent analyses of capitalist balance sheets. These exercises divided enterprises' net income into two categories, wages and profits, and equated the latter with the proprietors' personal consumption. This equation grossly exaggerated prospective proletarian gains from a socialist expropriation of capital: suppression of dividends would at least triple wages, according to Guesdist calculations.[102]

On other occasions, however, Guesdists admitted that workers would have to contribute towards 'social charges or the general costs of society'[103] – investment, care of the aged, children and the infirm, and general infrastructural costs. In some Guesdist projections, a socialist economic authority would appropriate *all* the fruits of production, concentrating them under its command before redistributing them for consumption and investment.[104] At the least, 'the law of capitalist surplus value will be mastered ... by the nationalisation of the means of production. Surplus value will then be social'.[105] Workers, in other words, would continue to produce a surplus over and above the cost of their immediate sustenance, and this surplus would continue to be appropriated, albeit by nationalised industries rather than by capitalists. Socialist redistribution might guarantee that workers would ultimately 'receive the full product of their labour', but this 'equitable division of the product' hardly assumed the shape envisaged by generations of exploited proletarians. Guesdists, secure in their socialist faith, never imagined that workers might resist appropriation of the surplus by 'France Inc.' as they had once resisted its appropriation by capitalists.

However Guesdists conceived of equitable distribution, it never involved price mechanisms and commodity markets. 'Commerce', Lafargue commented, 'did not exist in the communist and collectivist societies of savages or barbarians, and it will cease to exist when humanity once again achieves communism'.[106] In the Marxist utopia, 'exchange values, designed for barter or buying and selling, will have disappeared, leaving only use values. Society, like the

[101] 'Le Parti Ouvrier en France – Tourcoing', *Le Socialiste*, 12 March 1893.
[102] 'P. L.' (Lafargue), 'La Compagnie du Gaz Parisien', *Le Socialiste*, 30 April 1893.
[103] J. Guesde, 'Quatrième Leçon à un Professeur', *L'Égalité*, 22 January 1882.
[104] J. Bertrand, 'De Quoi Je Me Mêle!', *Le Socialiste*, 1 October 1899.
[105] P. Lafargue, 'La Plus-Value Capitaliste', *L'Égalité*, 26 March 1882.
[106] P. Lafargue, 'Propos Socialiste', *Le Socialiste*, 4 March 1891.

family or the former tribe, will produce for itself alone, in order to satisfy the needs of its members'.[107] The Parti Ouvrier had too often denounced the market as rationing for the rich to contemplate 'market socialism'. Commodity exchange remained anathema to Guesdists, despite the prospective abolition of the bourgeois property regime which determined the distribution of goods by prior distribution of affluence and poverty. Marxist neglect of exchange relations in favour of production relations, the neglect which so often crippled Guesdist social understanding, in this case failed to insulate the Parti Ouvrier against an unfortunate equation of markets with capitalism.

Having eschewed the calculus of supply and demand, how would 'society...satisfy the needs of members'? The Parti Ouvrier self-consciously abjured the dream of 'to each according to his needs and from each according to his abilities'. Guesdists well understood that only an eventual communism of absolute plenty, a distant prospect far beyond the transition to socialism, would render distributional dilemmas irrelevant in that ultimate utopia where 'consumption by some will not restrain or limit consumption by others'.[108] French Marxists admitted that rewards would necessarily differ under socialism, although they would differ without the iniquitous distortions present in bourgeois society. Nevertheless, the Parti Ouvrier never seriously addressed the distributional ramifications of socialist inequality. At the most, Guesdists suggested that the allocation of goods within the socialist mode of production would depend upon equal division of the product for equal time of labour,[109] a suggestion which skirted the all-important questions of measurement and quality.

Finally, the centralist assumptions of the Guesdist conception of a socialist mode of production led directly to the problem of the state. Who would represent the collective ownership of the means of production? Who would be responsible for planning? Who would appropriate and distribute the wealth produced within the new system? Certainly not individuals, in the 'collectivist' new economic order. Certainly not the victorious socialist party, since, as 'a class party, it will disappear with the disappearance of classes. A party of

---

[107] Anonymous, 'Pitre ou Fou', *Le Socialiste*, 20 November 1886.
[108] J. Guesde, reported in 'Sur Une Formule Prétendue Communiste', *Le Socialiste*, 22 October 1887.
[109] J. Guesde, 'Quelques Effets de la Loi sur l'Enseignement Primaire Obligatoire', *L'Égalité*, 1 April 1882.

struggle, it will disappear once the goal of that struggle – the political and economic expropriation of the bourgeoisie – has been attained'.[110] Only the socialist state, *de jure* owner and *de facto* manager of socialised wealth, could provide an answer to these questions. Guesdists, however, avoided this obvious response. Why their circumspection? First, because Marxists associated the state with class oppression, and have always uncompromisingly promised the destruction of the former with the suppression of the latter.[111] Second, because the Guesdists had fiercely denounced state enterprise ever since their formative struggle against Brousse's programme of *services publics*, and had consistently criticised existing state-owned industries such as the navy's arsenals or the factories of the state tobacco monopoly. 'The state', Guesdists had argued, 'because it is the largest possible boss, is also the worst of bosses'.[112] The Parti Ouvrier simultaneously foreshadowed the end of centralised political authority, and presaged a centrally planned economy. By implication, the Marxist critique of the state and the Marxist ideal of social rationality contradicted each other, one of the most damning ambiguities in the Parti Ouvrier's ideological construct.

Fully aware of the self-contradictions in the Marxist utopia, liberal and anarchist enemies of the Parti Ouvrier regularly accused French Marxists of covertly planning a statist authoritarianism. Once forced onto the defensive, Guesdists responded that the socialist revolution would necessarily abolish the state, along with the class antagonisms which had engendered political authority across the millennia. 'How many times do we have to repeat', complained *Le Socialiste*, 'that the state, which is only the domination of a class over another class, will disappear, must disappear, when

---

[110] *Septième Congrès National du Parti Ouvrier, tenu à Roubaix du Samedi 29 Mars au Lundi 7 Avril 1884* (Paris, undated), p. 20.

[111] D. Tarschys, *Beyond the State: The Future Polity in Classical and Soviet Marxism* (Stockholm, 1971), chapter 2, and H. Draper, 'The Death of the State in Marx and Engels', *The Socialist Register*, 1970, pp. 281–307.

[112] P. Lafargue, 'Le Congrès des Ouvrières et Ouvriers des Manufactures de Tabacs', *Le Socialiste*, 18 December 1892. Guesdists remained bitterly hostile to nationalisations and state ownership under capitalism, seen as merely 'collective capitalist exploitation, unified and centralised'. J. Guesde, 'Le Socialisme du *Temps*', *Le Cri du Peuple*, 20 May 1884. This was because 'nationalised industries' within the capitalist mode of production 'unite', against the workers, in the same bourgeois hands, the power of economic exploitation and the power of political oppression'. J. Guesde, untitled, *Le Socialiste*, 28 February 1892. What is more, nationalised industry would exploit the public through its monopoly power, since it would not be subjected to the constraints of competition. P.-M. André, 'Congrès Ouvriers: Les Allumettiers', *Le Socialiste*, 7–14 June 1903.

classes disappear?'[113] Better yet, the socialist revolution, according to French Marxists, would end not only the class war, but all the other conflicts which had bloodied human history: socialism would mark the 'end [of] all strife' and finally establish complete 'social peace'.[114] Sectarianism, racism, sexism, nationalism – all these provocations to murder arose from bourgeois malevolence and capitalist irrationality, and all would vanish with the establishment of the socialist mode of production. The socialist revolution was 'the sole but general cure for all the past and present ills of society';[115] it would finally 'put an end to all the miseries – whether material or mental – by eliminating the last regime of exploitation which spawns them';[116] once workers were 'co-proprietors' of the means of production, 'every antagonism would end, instituting [general] social peace'.[117] As the Guesdist auto-didact Jean-Baptiste Lebas summed up the hopes of his fellow workers, 'once [we] ... have seized power and have ... socialised the means of production, the causes of disorder and social conflict will disappear. There will no longer be any antagonisms within society, for conflicting class interests will have given place to common interests; while individual interests will be identical to the general interest'.[118] Forecasts that the socialist mode of production would require an all-powerful authoritarian state outraged Guesdists. Only wilful ignorance or ill-will, they riposted, could possibly elicit this prediction, since socialism would actually install universal harmony[119] and could therefore dispense with the Hobbesian Leviathan. Despite their disavowal of utopian speculation, Guesdists were utopians indeed.

The Guesdist conception of the revolutionary proletariat promised that workers would usher in a new world of 'liberty, dignity ... and joy for [all] the members of the human family, finally reconciled [by socialism]'.[120] Despite its millenarian allure, however, this rationale for the transition to socialism remained as problem-ridden as those based upon working-class conditions or capacities.

113 Anonymous, 'Anarchie et Socialisme', *Le Socialiste*, 27 February 1886.
114 Transcript of a speech by Guesde, 'Mouvement Social: France – Lyon', *L'Égalité*, 12 March 1882.
115 'J. G.' (Guesde), 'Un à Compte', *L'Égalité*, 18 June 1882.
116 Éd. Fortin, 'Un Anniversaire', *Le Socialiste*, 12 February 1899.
117 C. Vérecque, 'Les Syndicats Mixtes', *Le Socialiste*, 15 September 1894.
118 J. Vingtras (J.-B. Lebas), *Socialisme et Patriotisme* (Lille, 1900), p. 31.
119 See the argument by 'E.F.' (buttressed by *Anti-Dühring* and *The Poverty of Philosophy*) in 'Le Socialisme Vaincu', *Le Socialiste*, 28 November 1885.
120 Éd. Fortin, 'Droits et Devoir', *Le Socialiste*, 11 February 1900.

The Parti Ouvrier supplied a most unsatisfactory prospectus of its promised land. Was socialism to develop as a disciplined order founded upon a centralised socialist rationality, or would it evolve as a libertarian free-for-all of self-governing producers? How could goods be allocated without the market? And what of public authority and the 'revolutionary state'? Guesdists self-consciously refused to seriously address these questions – not for them the system-building of a Fourier or a Saint-Simon. Unfortunately, Marxist rejection of systematic speculation opened the way for incoherent dreaming. Incoherence, however, undoubtedly bolstered Guesdist polemics: the ambiguity of the Marxist utopia enhanced its appeal, since the Parti Ouvrier could satisfy its constituency's most contradictory aspirations – an advantage which would last only so long as socialism remained prospect rather than reality.

The Parti Ouvrier exploited all three of its interconnected theories of the revolutionary proletariat: one based upon the condition of the working class, driven to revolt by impoverishment and exploitation; a second sustained by the capacities of the proletariat, repository of the productive and administrative capabilities abandoned by a decadent bourgeoisie; and a third, transcending the other two, which evoked the utopian advantages of the prospective socialist mode of production. In some respects, these theses supported each other: the working class would achieve its utopia both because its conditions under capitalism impelled it towards socialist revolution, and because its capacities enabled the construction of a socialist mode of production. All the same, contradictions frequently arose between these alternative theories of proletarian revolution: a pauperised working class, brutalised and exploited by capital, evinced little obvious capacity for revolution, and even less for the construction of socialism. Guesdists, to their distress, never experienced the travails inherent in the establishment of a new mode of production. None the less, their theory of the revolutionary proletariat, as rhetoric, foreshadowed the traumas of the great twentieth-century revolutions and the disappointments of 'actually existing socialism'.

Conclusion

In reality, the actual property owners stand on one side and the propertyless communist proletarians on the other. This opposition becomes keener day by day and is rapidly driving to a crisis. If, then, the theoretical representatives of the proletariat wish their literary activity to have any practical effect, they must first and foremost insist that all phrases are dropped which tend to dim the sharpness of the opposition.

> Karl Marx and Frederick Engels, *The German Ideology*, in
> K. Marx and F. Engels, *Collected Works* (London, 1976),
> vol. 5, p. 469.

Come on, comrades, bravely into the breach. Make your propaganda, continually recruit more propagandists, that's where we have to concentrate all our energies ... Tomorrow ... once the human soul has been rescued from the economic forces which repress it, we can don the armour of Don Quixote, we can be generous, we can be sentimental; but today, to put an end to things, we have no other care but to bitterly pursue the bitter class struggle.

> P. Larlat-Bénaben, 'Que Peut-on Attendre des Réformes?',
> *Bulletin Mensuel des Élus Socialistes*, deuxième année, October
> 1901.

The Guesdists' rise to predominance within the working-class Left marked a turning-point in French political history: the birth of a powerful alternative to liberalism within the 'party of the Enlightenment', the constitution of an ideological force equivalent in impact and import to the liberal reconstruction of bourgeois social consciousness during the eighteenth century. As the French embodiment of the Second International's 'Orthodox Marxism', the Parti Ouvrier elaborated a novel discourse of social criticism and socialist affirmation which obscured landmarks that had once towered over the social vista, illuminated hitherto obscure recesses of society, and revalued values which had previously compelled unquestioning assent – thereby empowering Marxism's adepts to challenge the established social order and aspire to a transcendent future. French Marxists applied their lexicon of 'class' – the vocabulary of 'class consciousness' in the realm of reflection, the idiom of 'class conflict' in the arena of deeds – within a grammar of social analysis which disrupted the tradition-hallowed dialogue between liberal Republicans and their conservative enemies, while supplementing, if not entirely supplanting, the populist discourse of radical democrats. The Parti Ouvrier's often-criticised 'schematism, idealisation and rhetoric'[1] blasted apart the French political culture, clearing space for the working class to erect its own ideological edifice – indeed allowing the working class to construct itself, to constitute itself as a historical force, as a subject in its own right rather than a subjected object of capitalist manipulation and exploitation, of bourgeois pity and contempt.

What 'tools of discourse'[2] did Guesdists employ to demolish the ideological *ancien régime*? How did they build their socialist political culture upon the rubble of the nineteenth-century discursive order? Crudely, according to the sophisticated standards of today's 'Western Marxism'. Guesdists worked with the Second International's much-maligned 'determinism' and 'materialism', supposedly obsolescent ideological implements which have been roundly criticised by social theorists in general and by twentieth-century Marxists in particular. Yet the POF's theoretical crudity complemented, even enhanced, the Party's considerable polemical force. Guesdists may have been philosophically simplistic and historiographically naive, but their fundamental (fundamentalist?) world-view empowered a forceful intervention in their society. Their 'materialist' focus upon 'objective interests' and their 'determinist' metahistorical faith armoured them against disappointment and demoralisation as they struggled to convert the French proletariat to their version of socialism: Guesdists knew that workers' essential 'material' interests

[1] 'Transformative capacity is preserved only on condition that the ideas which it conveys become opinions, that thought loses rigour in order to enhance its social efficacy... Schematism, idealisation and rhetoric are the prices to be paid for the social efficacy of ideas.' P. Ricoeur, 'Science and Ideology', in P. Ricoeur, *Hermeneutics and the Human Sciences* (Cambridge, 1981), p. 227.

[2] 'A discourse is a set of tools. People use these tools to forge the identities that provide the basis for their collective social practices. As such, the tools of discourse are a mechanism for the formation of group action. The content of a discourse is simply the constellation of uses to which it is regularly put.' S. Bowles and H. Gintis, *Democracy and Capitalism: Property, Community and the Contradictions of Modern Social Thought* (New York, 1986), p. 153.

would 'inevitably' prevail over transient 'false consciousness', that history was on the side of socialism – convictions which sustained the French Marxists during defeats which would have shattered a less messianic movement.

If the Guesdists' primitive philosophy laid the crude but solid foundations of their discursive fortress, then the 'property question' furnished the rhetorical dynamite which razed the old order. The Parti Ouvrier's characteristic reduction of social hierarchy to the explosive combination of property-ownership and labour-power shattered every customary understanding of rank and authority, tearing asunder the individualist and corporative identities which had animated French politics since the eighteenth century. Simultaneously, the Guesdists' analytic of labour and property reconstituted social usage into a rhetoric of 'modes of production'. The permutations of the 'capitalist mode of production' articulated the French Marxists' ideological construct – governing the Parti Ouvrier's angry imagery of its times, structuring the movement's teleological comprehension of the pre-capitalist past, evoking the Party's prophetic vision of the socialist utopia. Guesdism engendered a socially potent critique of capitalism, just as the social potency of capitalism engendered Guesdism.[3]

Social radicals have censured the wealthy since Old Testament times. For their part, pre-Marxist French social revolutionaries, from Babeuf to Blanqui, had damned capitalism as inequitable and iniquitous. Where, then, the novelty of Guesdism? Its novelty was Marxism's: the contention that workers might challenge the capitalist mode of production only through the structural logic of the system's internal contradictions, that the social revolution would arise as much out of capital's achievements as against its crimes. Guesdists denounced as self-serving bourgeois illusion the liberal conviction that capitalism had inaugurated universal freedom. They

---

[3] One must avoid falling into the absurd idealism which argues that 'it was the acceptance of this myth [Marxism], not capitalism, which was responsible for the support given by a segment of the European working class to a revolutionary socialist programme at the turn of the century'. T. Tholfsen, *Ideology and Revolution in Modern Europe: An Essay on the Role of Ideas in History* (New York, 1984), p. 74. At its worst, reduction of class to merely an interpersonal rhetoric may result in absurdities such as 'if there is an escape from "class", it must come, not by ignoring it, but by thinking it through, as a prelude to *unthinking* it; and in this project it could be said that, up to now, these [modernist] novels have been our most helpful guide'. P. Furbank, *Unholy Pleasures or the Idea of Social Class* (Oxford, 1985), p. 143. If only Roubaisian textile workers had read Proust rather than Guesde, they could have easily escaped the travails of their class . . .

ridiculed as reactionary mystification or superannuated folly the conservative and anarchist advocacy of retreat to a precapitalist corporative or communitarian order. And Guesdists dismissed as petit-bourgeois fantasy, if not bourgeois fraud, the democratic expectation that a triumphant Republican state would beget 'capitalism with a human face'. According to the Parti Ouvrier, every commodity transaction, every recruit to the wage-labour force, every extension of the credit system intensified capital's voracity. Nothing and no one could withstand capitalism's ravening progress towards social dominion. This awe-struck estimation of capitalism as the evil demiurge of modernity, the heartless heart of society, constituted the most distinctive attribute of Guesdist ideology, its very essence.

The Guesdists' portrayal of capitalism's dominion, although productive of terrifying imagery and powerful polemic, none the less obscured fundamental aspects of French society. Above all, the Parti Ouvrier grossly underestimated plebeian defiance of capital's aggressions. The barriers to industrialism's minute division of labour which precluded capitalist transformation of many sectors of the economy, the intense self-exploitation which shielded the petite bourgeoisie and peasantry against capitalist expropriation, the time-honoured conventions which frustrated capital's encroachment into traditional trades – these formidable barricades against the capitalist onslaught rarely if ever appeared in Guesdist analyses of the French economy and polity. Capital may have ruled *fin-de-siècle* France, as the Parti Ouvrier asserted, but it did not rule unchallenged and unchecked. Guesdists themselves successfully organised workers' resistance to capitalism – founding trade unions and cooperatives, mobilising workers against bourgeois command of the state, establishing miniature social democracies in their municipal strongholds – all the while arguing that resistance short of socialist revolution was virtually inconceivable.

The Parti Ouvrier's delineation of capitalist political economy itself wavered between apparently contradictory theses. On the one hand, Guesdists contended that capitalism inexorably effaced every social identity apart from class, that traditional occupational or ethnic identities, for instance, vaporised in the furnace breath of the onrushing capitalist monster. Once subjected to capital, skilled tradesmen would learn to think of themselves as workers rather than as tradesmen, French workers would eventually see themselves as workers rather than as Frenchmen or Frenchwomen. On the other hand, frustrated by the stubborn persistence of obstacles to militant class consciousness, the Parti Ouvrier attributed these anomalous survivals to capitalist cunning. According to French Marxists, labour aristocrats escaped deskilling because capitalists needed working-class minions; the 'bourgeois state' propagated proletarian chauvinism to divide the workers of the world. Cleverly managed, these apparently contradictory rhetorical strategies served the Guesdists well: the myth of a homogenising proletariat permitted indiscriminate socialist mobilisation of the most diverse and even antagonistic fractions of the French working class, while the spectre of bourgeois manipulation damned workers who resisted recruitment into the class war.

In addressing 'bourgeois France', Guesdists above all else preached Marxism's revelation of the exploitative relationship between industrial capitalists and industrial workers, the apparently contractual relationship which concealed property-owners' coercion of the propertyless, the coercion which engendered bourgeois power and proletarian dependency. Yet the force of this revelation blinded Guesdists to other aspects of their society, even to other aspects of bourgeois rule. In fixing attention upon the domination and exploitation inherent in capitalist production, Guesdists lost sight of the domination and exploitation inherent in capitalist exchange. As a result, the Parti Ouvrier's analyses of French society grossly underestimated the domain of commerce and finance, including their dominion over French industrialists. By placing proletarians and proletarianisation at the centre of their social science, Guesdists unwittingly limited their appeal among small property-owners, thereby restricting socialist penetration into the laborious world of rural small-holders and urban artisans and shopkeepers, plebeians with their own grievances against French capitalism, but grievances remote from the Parti Ouvrier's 'productivist' proletarian socialism.

The POF neglected the peasantry and petite bourgeoisie largely because Guesdists believed that peasants and petits bourgeois had no place in the future and little importance in the present. Capitalism, according to the French Marxists' version of 'primitive accumulation', throve by dispossessing peasants and expropriating petits bourgeois, by reducing hapless farmers and doomed shopkeepers to propertyless proletarians. All France awaited the unhappy fate of Roubaix, a polarised society where thousands of impoverished workers laboured to enrich a few dozen already opulent employers. But all France also awaited Roubaix's good fortune as the Bethlehem of a secular salvation, as modern socialism's birthplace where workers had coalesced into a class-conscious community, entrusted their interests and aspirations to an independent proletarian political party, and seized (municipal) power from their bourgeois rulers. A revolutionary socialist mode of production would emerge once workers across France emulated their pioneering Roubaisian comrades; the proletariat would inaugurate a social order founded upon the enormous productive power of industrial capitalism, but a social order freed from capitalism's parasitic bourgeoisie.

Yet the Parti Ouvrier's conception of the revolutionary proletariat generated as many ambiguities and contradictions as did the POF's perception of capitalism. Guesdists tended to equate the working class with its militant and class-conscious minority, and implicitly subsumed all workers in an anonymous mass of factory hands – political and social reductions which impoverished Guesdist theory even while enhancing Guesdist polemic. Despite the homogenising tendencies of capitalist industrialisation, the French working class remained astonishingly diverse: highly skilled and highly paid craftsmen contrasted with unskilled and impoverished navvies; well-read and highly politicised Lyonnais compositors apparently had little in common with illiterate and disoriented Vosgian mill-hands; community-tied coal miners in Pas-de-Calais mining villages differed profoundly from itinerant Limousin masons on Parisian building sites. Indeed, millions of workers disappeared completely into the yawning chasm separating the Guesdist imagery of an undifferentiated industrial proletariat from the rich diversity of French working-class society: servants, one of the largest occupational categories of the French 'salariat', were relegated to the despised lumpenproletariat; building workers, who escaped the industrial labour processes which Guesdists implicitly generalised throughout the working class, hardly appeared in Guesdist discourse; farm labourers, virtually impervious to trade unionism and socialist militancy, received meagre treatment quite out of proportion to their number; and outworkers, although numerous and impoverished, were dismissed by Parti Ouvrier recruiting officers as if seamstresses actually were 'patrons', as the French census misleadingly identified them. Nor did the Guesdists develop a serious sociology of the industrial working class itself, cheerfully ignoring the complex internal differentiation of the factory proletariat, the intricate patterns of gender, skill, and tradition which so often frustrated the Marxist admonition 'Workers Unite!' French Marxists portrayed a working class more akin to their wishes than to their experience: a working class unified in its social being and thereby united in its political aspirations.

Thus, the Guesdists imagined their social world, a realm ruled by an all-powerful capitalism which none the less nurtured its own nemesis in an increasingly homogeneous, all-inclusive, and militant proletariat. This metahistorical scenario was thoroughly Manichean, yet all the more compelling for its division of the present and future into an evil empire of capitalist damnation and a promised land of socialist salvation. Every affliction of French society, from the ravages of tuberculosis in proletarian slums to the cultured decadence of Parisian high society, could be attributed to capitalism, and every aspiration entertained by the exploited and dominated, from simple job-security to the ultimate attainment of social harmony, was to be fulfilled by socialism. Hence the peculiar extremism of the Guesdists' social imagery, which reflected not so much immediate French 'reality' as the hopes and fears of French workers – millenarian hopes for a 'Social Republic' which would finally accord liberty, equality and fraternity to the plebeians who had been so long excluded by capitalist greed and bourgeois arrogance from those revolutionary conquests; dire fears of imminent pauperisation and brutalisation at the hands of a triumphant capitalist plutocracy.[4] Insofar as hopes and fears accord meaning to experience and draw individuals and masses into the future, the Guesdists' Marxism constituted one of history's most potent ideological visions.

Visionary rather than soberly 'scientific' (despite its Victorian pretensions to scientific truth), Guesdism manifested all the attributes of polemical as opposed to theoretical ideology: not for the Parti Ouvrier sober dialogue with its antagonists, reflexive self-criticism, or the search for evidence which might challenge the movement's defining axioms. According to Guesdists, their enemies were absolutely wrong, they themselves were absolutely right, and evidence which might 'disconfirm' their ideas and ideals did not exist. Guesdists subscribed to a fighting creed, a crusading faith which promised to annihilate the false consciousness which held French proletarians in thrall. Identities which impeded this cause

---

[4] This contradictory mentality has received little analysis, but see L. Portis, *Les Classes Sociales en France: Un Débat Inachevé (1789–1989)* (Paris, 1988), p. 77.

were to be destroyed if possible, annexed if necessary: workers who identified with their trade had to discard this corporative identity in favour of militant class consciousness, or accept that only proletarian socialism could defend their trade against capitalist deskilling; proudly patriotic workers had to recognise that the proletariat had no country apart from its class, or understand that only a triumphant socialism could realise the true French genius; female workers should accept that their gender was irrelevant in the all-important class war, or concede that only socialist revolution could embody their womanly interests. Guesdism defined itself in combat. Every competitor for the proletariat's allegiance was to be discredited. Born in battle against anti-collectivist Republicans, anti-socialist mutualists and anti-Marxist socialists, the Parti Ouvrier matured during its long struggle against Radicals and anarchists, and finally triumphed after its near-fatal duel with Jaurésien reformism.

The Guesdists' tactics during this long campaign were extraordinarily fluid, even opportunistic. Despite its reputation for dogmatism, the Parti Ouvrier shifted effortlessly between narrow social sectarianism and eclectic populism, between revolutionary intransigence and reformist pragmatism. This amazing flexibility occasionally reflected changing circumstances: 'electoralism' understandably appealed rather more to the victorious POF of 1893 than to the defeated Parti Ouvrier of 1885. But most often alternative tactics were pursued simultaneously, and with no obvious awareness of self-contradiction. Marxist theory, even Marxist dogma, allowed far more variation than scholars have acknowledged. The Party's doctrine, for instance, encouraged Guesdists to attack the democratic Third Republic as a rampart of bourgeois hegemony even as they defended it as a precondition of the transition from democracy to social democracy. These difficult manoeuvres offered great rewards, but also great dangers. When successful, Guesdist 'flexibility' achieved the best of both worlds, tapping workers' alienation from the 'bourgeois' Republic, for instance, while seconding their traditional commitment to Republican democracy. But the same tactics, when unsuccessful, could antagonise virtually everyone, including disoriented Guesdists.

Thus the surface text of Guesdist discourse: self-confident socialist militancy embodying the vulgar 'economistic' Marxism of the Second International, the providential determinism of Marxism's 'Golden Age'. But the Parti Ouvrier's discursive strategies, when closely examined, reveal an alternative text, a profoundly pessimistic vision in which the interests of capital easily prevailed over the interests of labour, in which the least contact between workers and bourgeois subordinated the former to the latter. Hence the apparent contradictions which structured Parti Ouvrier polemic: the Guesdists' determined advocacy of working-class industrial organisation as the foundation of proletarian class formation, but also their ferocious hostility to 'collective bargaining', which would 'inevitably' advantage employers; their committed promotion of workers' political mobilisation as the decisive manoeuvre in the class war, but also their profound dread of 'bourgeois democracy', which would 'inevitably' coopt working-class militants. The Parti Ouvrier's pathological aversion to the 'secondary campaigns' (campaigns 'secondary' to the class war) which associated workers with bourgeois revealed the French Marxists' conviction that such associations, if sustained, 'inevitably' consolidated bourgeois hegemony.

Guesdists adored triumphal language: they never wearied of predicting tomorrow's bourgeois debacle, never tired of proclaiming the imminent proletarian victory. Yet the troubling ambiguities which crept into their every prediction and proclamation testified to the French Marxists' apprehension of a working-class rout, to their insecure dependence upon a proletarian constituency which had been plundered, brutalised, and manipulated for generations. Guesdism constituted, if nothing else, 'an ideology of compensation'[5] for French workers, who received little enough compensation from their thoroughly bourgeois society. Despoiled by capitalist economics, excluded from establishment politics, demeaned by bourgeois culture, proletarians, 'the defeated in the great historical drama',[6] had every reason to seek sanctuary in the Parti Ouvrier's rhetorical bunker. For their part, Guesdists, having seized their bridgehead within French society, entrenched themselves in working-class fortresses: self-sufficient citadels armoured against capital's assaults, impervious to bourgeois ruses, secured against capitalist infiltration – a social Maginot Line designed for an interminable war of attrition rather than a conquering final offensive.

---

[5] D. Lindenberg, *Le Marxisme Introuvable* (Paris, 1975), p. 66.

[6] Éd. Fortin, 'Un Anniversaire', *Le Socialiste*, 12 February 1899. After the repeated failure of challenges to bourgeois rule in nineteenth-century France, it was understandable that (in Terdiman's ironic reversal of Marx's irony) 'the criticism of weapons had of necessity to be replaced by the weapon of criticism'. R. Terdiman, *Discourse/Counter-Discourse: The Theory and Practice of Symbolic Resistance in Nineteenth-Century France* (Ithaca, 1985), p. 67.

The Guesdists succeeded, but not as they would have wished: a century after their first victories, France remains a 'bourgeois democracy', capital still rules the economy, socialist revolution continues to recede beyond the historical horizon. Yet half of France today votes for parties which trace their origins to the POF, the social-democratic reforms pioneered by Guesdist municipalities have been generalised throughout the nation, the terms of political debate are those imposed by the Parti Ouvrier at the turn of the century. The class war still rages, although no longer to socialist advantage, as today's capitalism presses its most sustained and successful counter-attack since the first Marxist offensives of the late nineteenth century. In the face of this onslaught, the Guesdists' fortresses still stand as they have stood for a century, scattered across the bleak terrain of industrial France, besieged, battered and breached, but none the less sheltering their proletarian garrisons against the worst depredations of capital, forcing the French bourgeoisie to manoeuvre outside their fields of fire, providing bases for occasional socialist sorties against capitalism's entrenchments.

This defensive achievement has won few plaudits. The massive bastions thrown up by the Marxists of the Second International have been harshly criticised by Leninist tacticians, advocates of a 'last push' which would finally break the bourgeois front. For their part, social democrats have denigrated the Parti Ouvrier's anti-capitalist intransigence, assuming that the class war is over, that it need not have been fought, that the Guesdists' elaborate fortifications stand forlornly as relics of a phoney war. Perhaps. But the aggressive Leninists who advanced so resolutely during the crisis years between 1914 and 1945 today disband as capitalism luxuriates in another *Belle Époque,* while the pacific social democracy of the post-crisis generation falters as capital arrogantly abrogates clause after clause of the inconclusive peace treaty signed at Godesberg. Our moment evokes memories of the 1880s, not of 1917 or 1959. Historians, social theorists, and militants who recognise that, 'in the absence of wealth, without the support of tradition, and militarily weak, a democratic social movement depends upon political discourse as its synthesizing force'[7] should respect the Guesdists' heavily armoured socialism, the socialism which first marshalled workers into a coherent class, first constituted working-class interests

---

[7] Bowles and Gintis, *Democracy and Capitalism,* p. 155.

to challenge the iron laws of capital, first promised that the transient triumph of the propertied augured the inevitable victory of the propertyless – the socialism of martial spirit, material interest, and millenarian hope which today's Left signally lacks, the socialism of Marxism at work.

Bibliographical note

The footnotes detail the evidential foundation of this study, with the first mention of a source in any chapter providing its complete bibliographical details. The following Note furnishes a selective discussion of the more important source materials.

Prolific journalists and pamphleteers, Guesdists published thousands of pages during the decades between 1882 and 1905, thereby unwittingly bestowing an invaluable legacy upon historians of Marxist ideology. The overwhelming dimensions of this corpus – a daunting abundance of books, pamphlets, newspapers, and journals – inevitably imposes selectivity upon its student.[1] What principles have governed this process of discrimination and exclusion? *Marxism at Work* – as a 'symptomatic reading' of the Guesdist texts, an analysis of the 'problematic' which governed the Guesdists' perception of social order[2] – neglects the organisational development of the Parti Ouvrier (a subject superbly elucidated by Claude Willard's *Le Mouvement Socialiste en France (1893–1905): Les Guesdistes*, Paris, 1965) and ignores the movement's view of the world beyond France, except where organisational considerations or foreign events

[1] And thereby potentially engenders the intellectual crime of 'converting some scattered or quite incidental remarks . . . into 'doctrine' on one or more mandatory themes'. Q. Skinner, 'Meaning and Understanding in the History of Ideas', *History and Theory*, vol. 8, 1969, p. 7. Unfortunately, despite the pretensions of various schools of 'content analysis', there is no methodology which allows us to indisputably demonstrate 'the rigorous, objective character of our argument', the goal assigned in R. Robin, 'Langage et Idéologies', in J. Guilhaumou et al., *Langage et Idéologies: Le Discours comme Objet de l'Histoire* (Paris, 1974), p. 3. Only close reading and rereading of the texts, their illumination by as many theoretical perspectives as possible, and comparison with other sources, both primary and secondary, insure against the discovery of what is not really present in the texts and against exaggeration or undervaluation of what *is* present.

[2] This methodology derives to some extent from that proposed by Louis Althusser and Étienne Balibar in *Reading Capital* (London, 1970), pp. 13–30. The goal of this study, however, is not only the discovery and elucidation of the Guesdist 'problematic', but its historical comprehension – a most un-Althusserian, even anti-Althusserian, project.

significantly influenced Guesdist comprehension of French society. This study, therefore, concentrates upon primary material which illuminates the Parti Ouvrier's ideological presuppositions and their consequences in Guesdist theory and polemic.

Despite their well-deserved reputation as vulgarisers, Guesdists did contribute substantial theoretical works to the Marxist corpus, such as Lafargue's influential study of the role of the stock exchange in equalising the rate of profit. The Parti Ouvrier, however, characteristically embodied its ideological militancy in newspapers and pamphlets, media accessible to the Party's inadequately educated, impoverished, and overburdened audience, an audience unlikely to read scholarly monographs. The Parti Ouvrier's journalistic ephemerae and insubstantial pamphlets, although slight by comparison with *La Fonction Économique de la Bourse*, none the less deserve serious consideration. A single issue of a socialist newspaper often profoundly influenced its proletarian owner, who read, reread, and recalled it for months, shared the tattered treasure with friends and family, and retailed its contents in bistro and workplace.[3] Hence the overwhelming importance of the Guesdist weeklies, *L'Égalité* and *Le Socialiste*. Week after week, month after month, year after year, the Parti Ouvrier distributed their small grey pages throughout working-class France, never in large numbers, but with dogged tenacity and a constant message: the all-importance of the class war, the necessity of socialism, and the inevitability of proletarian revolution. Claude Willard is undoubtedly correct that 'it is above all through [these newspapers] that the historian may come to know the ideology and propaganda of [the POF]'.[4] Guesdist contributions to other newspapers such as *Le Citoyen*, *Le Petit Sou*, *La Petite République*, and (particularly) *Le Cri du Peuple* have also proven useful, as have

[3] For an instance of the spread of Guesdist socialism in this way, see R. Simler, 'Gustave Delory et les Débuts du Mouvement Socialiste à Lille et dans la Région du Nord sous la Troisième République', *Les Pays-Bas Français*, 1982, p. 115.

[4] C. Willard, '*L'Égalité* et *Le Socialiste* jusqu'en 1905', in *Collection Complète de l'Égalité et Le Socialiste* (Paris, 1974), vol. 1, page unnumbered, but p. 1. The importance of these weeklies in the articulation and the diffusion of Guesdism is further stressed in C. Willard, *Le Mouvement Socialiste en France (1893–1905): Les Guesdistes* (Paris, 1965), pp. 144–6; J. Girault, 'Les Guesdistes, le Deuxième *Égalité* et le Commune', *International Review of Social History*, vol. 17, 1972, pp. 421–50; and M. Perrot, 'Le Premier Journal Marxiste Français: *L'Égalité* de Jules Guesde', *L'Actualité de l'Histoire*, no. 28, 1959, pp. 1–26. It is worth stressing that there were relatively few legal constraints upon political journalism after the passing of the 1881 press laws, so that Guesdist polemic was rarely constrained to 'pull its punches', according to J. Kergoat, 'France', in M. van der Linden and J. Rojahn (eds.), *The Formation of Labour Movements 1870–1914: An International Perspective* (Leiden, 1990), vol. 1, pp. 163–90.

Figure 4 'À l'Assaut de la Bastille Capitaliste' (From *Le Socialiste*, 28 April 1895)

the little-consulted *Bulletins* of the Fédération Nationale des Syndicats and the Fédération Nationale des Élus du Parti Ouvrier
Français. Apart from the important *Réveil du Nord* and *Le Travailleur*,
which represented the POF in the Nord, the movement's provincial
press tended to reproduce material from *L'Égalité* and *Le Socialiste*,
and offers little extra insight into the intricacies of Marxist ideology,
however useful as sources for the Parti Ouvrier's political implantation. Guesdist contributions to monthlies and bimonthlies such as
Le Devenir Social, *L'Ère Nouvelle*, *Études Socialistes*, *l'Idée Nouvelle*, *Le
Mouvement Socialiste*, and *La Revue Socialiste* are often revealing.
Pamphlets, themselves usually based upon previous journalism, and
comptes rendus of party congresses also furnish invaluable insight into
the ideas and ideals characteristic of popular Marxism during the
Belle Époque, while police reports deposited in the Archives Nationales and the Archives of the Paris Préfecture de Police describe
debates and speeches, the public occasions so vital to the political
culture of the late nineteenth century.[5]

These texts must be studied in context, their 'meaning' evinced by
their place within Parti Ouvrier discourse and their relationship to
the society which shaped that discourse and in turn was shaped by it.
Fortunately, numerous historians have studied the Parti Ouvrier,
although their works, from the official (and laudatory) SFIO history
of the POF by Alexandre Zévaès (*Histoire des Partis Socialistes en
France: Les Guesdistes*, Paris, 1911) to recent 'New Left' demolitions of
Second International Marxism in France (D. Lindenberg, *Le Marxisme Introuvable*, Paris, 1975 and T. Paquot, *Les Faiseurs de Nuages:
Essai sur la Genèse des Marxismes Français 1880–1914*, Paris, 1980), have
repeatedly fallen prey to ungoverned political *partis pris*. Ideological
commitment, however, has not always inhibited serious scholarship.
Claude Willard's superb *Les Guesdistes* exemplifies political history at
its best, despite (or because of) its unabashed Leninism. Willard's
book, and less substantial but still useful studies of the POF (S.
Bernstein, *The Beginnings of Marxian Socialism in France*, New York,

---

[5] Guesde addressed some 1,200 political meetings between 1882 and 1900, according to A.
Compère-Morel, *Jules Guesde* (Paris, 1937), p. 258. For the enormous impact of this effort,
necessarily undervalued given the nature of our sources, see Willard, *Les Guesdistes*, p. 32; M.
Perrot, 'La Classe Ouvrière au Temps de Jaurès', in *Jaurès et la Classe Ouvrière* (Paris, 1981),
p. 78; and J. Quellien, 'Contribution à l'Histoire du Mouvement Ouvrier en Basse-
Normandie: La Naissance du Mouvement Ouvrier Bas-Normand à la Fin du XIXe Siècle',
Annales du Normandie, vol. 23, 1983, pp. 50–4, which demonstrates how a single speech could
implant socialism throughout a previously barren region.

1933 and M. Dommanget, *L'Introduction du Marxisme en France*, Lausanne, 1969) – although they concentrate upon party building, factional conflict, and the Guesdists' place in the political history of the Third Republic – have constructed a solid foundation for a study of Guesdist ideology, a foundation reinforced by the contextual works of historians such as Tony Judt (*Marxism and the French Left: Studies in Labour and Politics in France 1830–1981*, Oxford, 1986) or Madeleine Rebérioux. These works constitute a necessary but not sufficient condition for decipherment of the intricacies of Marxist discourse in France during the *Belle Époque*, that thoroughly neglected subject.[6]

Such an analysis presupposes detailed knowledge of *fin-de-siècle* society. This knowledge, at the least, highlights aspects of the French social order which Guesdists ignored or neglected – lacunae in Guesdist discourse which reveal as much about the Parti Ouvrier's Marxism as do characteristic Guesdist obsessions, but which may not (unlike the obsessions) be deduced from the primary sources. What is more, the ambiguities and contradictions of Guesdist ideology mirrored the myriad ambiguities and contradictions of the Guesdists' milieu in a complex play of reflection, distortion and occlusion.[7] Here the analyst must depend unapologetically upon the work of others: *fin-de-siècle* France, the outcome of tens of millions of lives striving to achieve their individual and collective ends over several decades, might exhaust the energy and ingenuity of hundreds, if not thousands, of historians before surrendering its secrets. Fortunately, historians have scrutinised few other times and places with equivalent intensity and dedication or with equal rigour and sophistication: Yves Lequin (*Les Ouvriers de la Région Lyonnaise 1848–1914*, Lyons, 1977), Michelle Perrot (*Les Ouvriers en Grève: France 1871–1890*, Paris, 1974), or Joan Scott (*The Glassworkers of Carmaux: French Craftsmen and Political Action in a Nineteenth-Century City*, Cambridge, Mass., 1974) – to name only a few from a distinguished company – have written exemplary works of social

---

6 Michelle Perrot bemoans Willard's inattention in *Les Guesdistes* to the Guesdists' ideas and language. M. Perrot, 'Les Guesdistes: Controverses sur l'Introduction du Marxisme en France', *Annales: Économies, Sociétés, Civilisations*, vol. 22, 1967, p. 705.

7 For the need to 'situate' socialist ideological development within the relevant social history, see E. Hobsbawm, 'The Formation of the Industrial Working Classes: Some Problems', *Troisième Conférence Internationale d'Histoire Économique – Munich 1965* (Paris, 1968), vol. 1, p. 175. But see the useful warning against the reductionism often associated with 'contextualism' in B. Moss, 'Workers' Ideology and French Social History', *International Labor and Working Class History*, no. 11, 1977, pp. 26–30.

history which have greatly enhanced scholars' comprehension of the world the Guesdists knew. In particular, the proliferation of local and regional studies of French communities during the *Belle Époque* – a genre the titles of which now number in the many dozens, if not hundreds – has constituted a resource without which this study would have been impossible.

Finally, theoretical works have served as sharp (if sometimes treacherous) instruments with which to dissect French Marxism. These sources – proudly hermetic in their esoteric terminologies, unapologetically sectarian in their theoretical allegiances, unforgivingly technical in their disciplinary methodologies – sometimes infuriate. Yet their conceptual intransigence and finely-honed arguments stimulate insight, criticism, and self-criticism – qualities necessary for any historian of ideas, and doubly necessary for a historian of Marxist ideas. This study has been particularly well-served by recent reconceptualisations of ideology, benefiting from the work of, amongst others, Fredric Jameson, J. G. A. Pocock, Paul Ricoeur, and Quentin Skinner. Books and articles on Marxism, of course, proliferate more rapidly than the most industrious scholar could ever read them, even if he or she ignored the Marxist self-criticisms and non-Marxist critiques of Marxism which already burden library shelves. *Marxism at Work*, therefore, has selectively exploited analyses of class and class conflict, that central Guesdist theme, and focused upon works devoted to the Marxist engagement with issues which preoccupied the Parti Ouvrier, such as the capitalist labour process or the fate of the petite bourgeoisie. The original conception of this project was heavily influenced by the still valuable works of Frank Parkin (*Class Inequality and Political Order*, London, 1971) and Anthony Giddens (*The Class Structure of Advanced Societies*, London, 1973), and its further development has been conditioned by continuing critical engagement with the apparently endless and endlessly stimulating debates between contemporary Marxists and critics of Marxism such as Ellen Meiksins Wood, Erik Olin Wright, Jon Elster, and Adam Przeworksi.

Index

Adler, Victor 22
agricultural labourers, 44, 399–406
Aigues-Mortes, 160–1
Allemane, Jean, 39, 218
Allemanists *see* Parti Ouvrier Socialiste
    Révolutionnaire
Allier (department of), 44
Althusser, Louis, xv, 12, 29, 73
America, 198, 207, 289, 291
anarchism, 32–5, 43, 47, 87–8, 90, 109, 123,
    146, 218, 220, 236, 240, 243, 250, 259,
    263–4, 267–8, 273, 279, 280–6, 292,
    297, 330, 439, 443, 447, 473–4, 489,
    499
anarchosyndicalism *see* revolutionary
    syndicalism
André, Paul, 196, 241, 307
Anti-Dühring, 24
anti-semites, 87, 123 *see also* Nationalists
Anzin, 36
aristocracy, 89, 318, 322, 324, 393–7, 475,
    481
army officers, 302, 458
artists, 450–2
Aubervilliers, 46
Austro-Marxism, 22

Babeuf, Gracchus, 25, 67, 126, 494
Bad Godesberg, Congress of SPD (1959),
    501
Bakunin, Michael, 50, 88, 278, 285
Bank of France, 319, 373, 381
Barberet, Joseph, 184
Barrès, Maurice, 51, 152–3, 161, 318–9
Basly, Émile, 186, 245
Bastille Day, 81, 228
Bauer, Otto, 22
Belgium, 159, 219
Belleville, 46, 149
Belleville Programme, 207, 256

Bernstein, Eduard, 338
Blanc, Louis, 228
Blanqui, Auguste, 38, 494
Blanquists, 38–9, 46, 189, 249, 251
Blum, Léon, 253
Bonapartism, 148, 204, 208, 210, 247, 390
Bon Marché (department store), 315, 359
Bonnier, Charles, xix, 30, 34, 57–8, 92, 151,
    166, 186, 194, 255, 271, 275, 288, 291,
    442–3, 445, 447
Bordeaux, 49, 308, 312
Boucicaut, Aristide, 315, 370
Boulanger crisis, 38–9, 51, 188–9, 225, 227,
    230–2
Bourgeois, Léon, 93, 207, 256, 258, 271,
    277
Bourses du Travail, 188, 218
Bracke *see* Desrousseaux, Alexandre-Marie
Briand, Aristide, 217, 221
Brie, 399, 407
Brousse, Paul, 35, 52, 161, 241, 249, 258,
    274, 283, 298, 360, 453, 489
Broussists *see* Possibilists
Brunellière, Charles, 97, 382, 415–6, 474
*Bulletin Mensuel de la Fédération Nationale des
    Élus du Parti Ouvrier Français*, 275–6
Burke, Edmund, 20

Cail, Jean-François, 132
Calais, 338
campagnonnages, 183
Capital, 21, 25, 30, 44, 67, 79, 311, 313, 324,
    412
capital accumulation, 62, 100–4, 370
capital concentration, 62, 103, 118–24,
    133–4, 199, 354 *see also* monopoly
    capitalism
Carrette, Henri, 190
Carmaux, 192
Casimir-Perier, Jean-Paul-Pierre, 225

Cercle des Commerçants Socialistes, 385–6
Chalon-sur-Saône, 54
Chambers of Commerce, 306
Chambord, Henri, comte de, 189
Champ de Mars Massacre, 228
Christian Democrats, 47, 50, 87, 91, 93, 123, 171, 203, 205–7, 368
Le Citoyen, 504
civil servants, 236–8, 302, 437–40
class alliances, 421–3
class collaboration, 173–8, 289
class consciousness, 14, 42–4, 77–84
Clemenceau, Georges, 34, 89, 207, 237, 286–8
collective worker, 107, 125, 136, 138, 427, 430, 449, 456, 458, 475–9
Collège de France, 445
Combes, Émile, 293
Commentery, 40, 274
commodity exchange *see* exchange relations
commodity fetishism, 324
Commune, 31, 41, 127, 228, 275, 278, 362, 368, 390–1
Le Communisme et l'Évolution Économique, 477
Communist Manifesto, 44, 323, 467
Compère-Morel, Adéodat, 71, 216, 410, 422–3, 474
Confédération Générale des Vignerons du Midi, 419
Confédération Générale du Travail, 218, 293
Conseil Supérieur du Travail, 121
cooperatives, 209–17, 235, 278, 366–7, 386, 409, 415–16, 485
corporatism, 90–93, 104–5, 205–6, 396
Courbevoie, 275
Creusot *see* Le Creusot
Le Cri du Peuple, 504
criminality, 147, 152–3, 284, 327
crisis theory, 199, 330–9, 465
Critique of the Gotha Programme, 486

Darwinism, 300–1
Dazet, Georges, 480
Decazeville, 36, 138, 192, 204, 372–3, 449, 457
Dejean, Lucien, 177
Delcluze, Marc, 338
Delon, Albert, 383
democracy, xvii, 226–34, 353–4, 395, 499
Dépêche de Toulouse, xvii
deskilling, 62, 104–6, 128, 181, 200, 409–10
Deslinières, Lucien, 422, 480
Desrousseaux, Alexandre-Marie, 259, 328
Le Devenir Social, 506

Deville, Gabriel, 25, 89, 213, 228, 272, 281, 287, 311, 412, 447, 469–70
doctors, 453
domestic industry, 127, 377–9, 403–5
Dormoy, Jean, 24, 112
Dreyfus Affair, 51, 188, 225, 231–2, 307, 395
Le Droit à la Paresse, 65
Drumont, Édouard, 51, 61, 225, 318–19
Dupuy, Charles, 271
Duval restaurants, 122

Ebert, Friedrich, 253
École des Chartes, 442
École Normale Supérieure, 441, 445
École Polytechnique, 448
ecology, 328–9
Economist, 303
Économiste Français, 41, 60, 303
egalitarianism, 84–8, 131, 331, 352–4
l'Égalité, xviii, 32, 35, 68, 182, 430, 504
elections, 36, 188–9, 263–8, 285, 288, 352, 369, 391–2, 412, 415, 419, 499
Engels, Frederick, 24, 27, 32, 39, 73, 97, 140, 246, 287, 319, 373–4, 391, 418, 437–8
engineers, 448–50
L'Ère Nouvelle, 506
Études Socialistes, 506
exchange relations, 61, 84–5, 154–6, 214, 328, 359, 365, 375–6, 414–16, 486–8, 496

false consciousness, 80–2, 133, 265–7, 324, 364, 462, 494
Farjat, Gabriel, 219
Fédération du Textile, 47, 170, 187, 197
Fédération Nationale des Élus du Parti Ouvrier Français, 506
Fédération Nationale des Syndicats, 40, 113, 182, 184, 186, 188–90, 196, 218, 240, 280, 283, 506
Ferroul, Ernest, 74, 277, 419
Ferry, Jules, 189, 291
finance capital, 61, 302, 310–12, 316–19, 333, 357–8, 375, 381, 413–14
Flaissières, Siméon, 176
La Fonction Économique de la Bourse, 341, 504
Fortin, Édouard, 100, 212, 354, 475
Foucault, Michel, 15, 280
Fougères, 86
Fourier, Charles, 479, 491
Fourmies, 36, 40, 54, 76, 228, 231, 306
Frankfurt School, 22, 450
free trade, 37, 248–9, 307–8, 312, 334, 390, 397

Galliffet, Gaston, 52
Gambetta, Léon, 34, 89, 189, 237
Gard (department of), 44
gender *see* women
general strike, 218, 264
generational conflict, 164–7
George, Henry, 320
Ghesquière, Henri, 82, 131, 403
Gide, Charles, 356
Grados, Paul, 131, 341
Gramsci, Antonio, 13, 21
Grave, Jean, 284
Great Depression (of the 1880s), 37–8, 145, 197, 336, 360, 465–6, 469
Greffier, Léon, 219
Grenoble, 47, 117, 345–6
Guesde, Jules, xii, xvi, xix, 24, 26, 28–33, 36, 42, 46, 49, 51, 69, 81, 89, 100, 114–16, 130, 161, 175, 177, 186, 189, 214, 233, 236, 242, 245, 255, 264, 267–8, 270, 275, 287, 293, 303, 306, 308, 316, 321, 324, 341, 354, 368, 386, 391, 411, 417, 427, 431, 433, 436, 441, 444, 447–8, 453, 455, 457, 463, 466, 473, 486
Guizot, François, 225–6

Halévy, Daniel, xv
Hegel, G. W. F., 16, 28, 463
Herr, Lucien, 35, 441, 464
Hilferding, Rudolf, 100, 317, 340
historical theory, 69–70, 261–2, 297, 302, 397, 459–602, 479
Hobsbawm, Eric, 22
Holland, 313

L'Idée Nouvelle, 506
Independent Socialists, 52, 189, 233, 241, 247, 249, 258, 270, 277, 431, 441, 447
industrial capital, 302, 311–13, 318, 382
intellectuals, 53, 440–5
Internationale, 24
L'Intransigeant, 89
iron law of wages, 143, 466–75
Isère (department of), 219, 373
Italians, 159–60
Ivry-sur-Seine, 275

Jacobins, 228, 286, 391, 395
Jaurès, Jean, 26, 52–3, 59, 89, 189, 218–9, 227, 233, 250, 283, 441–2, 448, 499
July Monarchy, 237
Jura (department of), 357, 403

Keufer, Auguste, 190
Kropotkin, Peter, 284

labour, theory of, 63–6
labour aristocracy, 139–44, 147, 249, 443, 455
Lafargue, Laura, 24
Lafargue, Paul, xix, 24, 29, 31–2, 36, 39, 41, 49, 60, 65–6, 68, 70, 89, 100, 103, 105, 111, 114, 135, 140, 149, 166, 186, 210, 215, 233, 245, 262, 264, 287, 298, 304, 308, 314, 324–6, 328, 330, 332, 341, 344, 383–4, 391, 428–30, 432, 443, 447, 450, 453, 455, 461, 467, 477, 480, 487, 504
Lagardelle, Hubert, 221
Languedoc, 48, 157, 399, 420
Lassalleanism, 305, 307 *see also* iron law of wages
lawyers, 302–3, 452–3
Lebas, Jean-Baptiste, 490
Le Chapelier Law, 207, 228
Le Creusot, 7, 43, 204, 305, 314, 460–1
Le Havre, 314
Le Havre, Congress of (1880), 33
Lenin, Vladimir, 22, 100, 242, 252, 300, 431, 444, 501
Leo XIII, 50, 58
Le Play, Frédéric, 364
Leroy-Beaulieu, Paul, 41, 60
La Libre Parole, 81
Lille, 41, 47–8, 87, 121, 143, 149, 165, 170, 248, 275, 277–8, 308, 385, 435, 439
Lille, Congress of (1890), 40
Limoges, 385
Locke, John, 20
Loire-Inférieure (department of), 415–16
Longwy, 346
Lorraine, 47–8, 118, 157, 346, 359
Loubet, Émile, 63
Louis, Paul, 406, 470
Louis Napoleon, 148, 225–6
Luddism, 114, 118
Lukács, Georg, 14, 16
lumpenproletariat, 147–54, 161, 284, 301
Luxemburg, Rosa, 22, 252
Lyons, 44, 47, 117, 190, 211, 248, 308, 312, 314–15
Lyons, Congress of (1891), 82

Maillard, Étienne, 79
Malon, Benoît, 35, 59, 464
managerial authority, 62, 90, 103, 107–10, 128, 135–9, 181, 200, 342–4, 347–8, 409, 454–7
Manchester, 329
Mannheim, Karl, 16
marchandage, 142

Marcuse, Herbert, 80, 297, 461
Marseilles, 176, 275, 312, 314
Marseilles, congress of (1879), 32, 182, 208, 293
Marseilles, congress of (1892), 187
Martinique, 54
Marx, Karl, xii–xiii, 20–2, 24–8, 30–3, 55, 64, 73–5, 77, 86, 88, 97, 99–101, 104, 111, 114, 127, 134, 136, 140, 147–8, 155, 164, 173, 180, 182, 190–1, 210, 223–4, 226, 241, 243, 245, 254, 260, 285, 287, 289, 297, 301–3, 310, 319, 322–4, 341, 354–5, 373, 388, 397, 421, 424–5, 434, 437, 441, 447, 451, 455, 460, 464–5, 468, 475, 479, 486
Massif Central, 396
materialism, 30, 56–61, 82–4, 99, 255, 299, 326, 437, 447, 464, 493–4
mechanisation *see* technology
Méline, Jules, 37, 248, 307–9, 397
mercantile capital, 61, 302, 310–12, 313–16, 318, 375, 381, 414–15
Merrheim, Alphonse, 221
Meslier, Jean, 280
Midi, 40, 48, 392, 420
Millerand, Alexandre, 35, 49, 52, 54, 207, 241, 247, 249–50, 256–8, 272–3, 277, 367, 386, 442, 453
Ministerialists, 35, 52, 93, 140, 192, 250, 254, 277, 304, 386, 442, 447
monarchists, 34, 49, 51, 188, 204, 208, 225, 227, 230–1, 237, 247, 330, 390, 410
monopoly capitalism, 37, 340–2, 357, 476
  see also capital concentration
Montceau-les-Mines, 54, 192, 460
Montluçon, 24, 41, 45, 274, 278, 439, 471
Montluçon, congress of FNS (1887), 219
Montusès, Ernest, 471
Motte, Eugène, 43, 67, 236, 264, 305, 309, 313–14, 347–8, 373
Le Mouvement Socialiste, 506
Mun, Albert de, 93
municipal socialism, 40–1, 274–9, 288–9, 366–7, 384, 386, 438
mutualism, 61–2, 108, 182, 203, 209–17, 235, 250, 333, 485, 499

Nantes, 97, 382, 415
Nantes, congress of POF (1894), 412
Nantes, congress of FNS (1894), 190, 218
Narbonne, 74, 277
nationalism, 144, 156–63
Nationalists, 34, 47, 51, 91, 93, 203, 205–7, 230–1, 233, 304, 307, 318, 356, 362, 368–9, 437, 447

Nîmes, 383
Nord (department of), 44, 49, 112, 157, 170, 190, 197, 206, 308–9, 379, 386, 474
Normandy, 44

Opportunists, 34, 39, 52, 189, 207–8, 228, 247, 290, 308
ouvriérisme, 245, 426, 428, 431, 441, 477

Panama Scandal, 41, 337–8, 358
Pareto, Vilfredo, 88, 130
Paris, 26, 44, 46, 121–2, 156, 161, 170, 190, 212, 272, 274, 278, 319–20, 343, 357, 362, 369–70, 378–9, 383–4, 386, 403, 435
parliamentarianism, 268–74, 285
Parti Commercial et Industriel, 368
Parti Ouvrier Socialiste Révolutionnaire, 39, 189, 249, 431, 441
Parti Radical et Radical-Socialiste *see* Radicals
Parti Socialiste Révolutionnaire *see* Blanquists
party theory, 224, 241–51, 488–9
Pas-de-Calais (department of), 44
Pasteur, Louis, 449
paternalism, 122, 174–5, 203–5, 364
pauperisation, 142, 464–73
Pelletan, Camille, 34, 287
Pelloutier, Fernand, 190, 217, 220, 283
Le Petit Sou, 506
La Petite République, 504
Picardy, 403
populism, 50, 88–90, 286–93, 353–4, 381, 419, 421–2, 499
Possibilists, 35, 39, 46, 52, 135, 140, 156, 169, 210, 239, 241, 249–50, 258, 274–5, 278, 320, 484
Pouget, Émile, 186
Printemps (department store), 316, 357, 359
production relations, 61–3, 91, 104–6
Progressistes *see* Opportunists
prostitution, 151–3, 327, 329, 331
protection *see* free trade
Proudhon, Pierre-Joseph, 50, 62, 67, 109, 123, 210–11, 235, 285, 373
Provence, 48, 157

Radicals, xvii, 32–5, 39, 49–50, 79, 85, 87–90, 120, 123–4, 129, 207, 221, 225, 228, 230, 232–3, 235, 237, 243, 247–8, 250, 256, 258, 270, 277, 280, 286–93, 308, 353, 356, 368, 387, 395–6, 410, 420, 437, 499

Ralliement, 58, 308
Ravachol (François-Auguste Koenigstein), 35, 273, 283, 286
real-estate capital, 310–11, 319–21, 375, 381, 397–9
Reclus, Élisée, 35, 284
Renard, Victor, 47, 187
Renouvier, Charles, xv, 58
Réveil du Nord, 506
Revisionism, 52, 338
revolutionary syndicalism, 40, 108–9, 182, 185, 188, 190, 203, 217–21, 233, 235, 240, 259, 264, 273, 405, 443, 484–5
La Revue Socialiste, 506
Rigola, Rinaldo, 160
Roanne, 47, 62, 125
Roanne, congress of (1882), 33, 184, 419
Rochefort, Henri, 89
Romilly, congress of (1895), 24
Rothschilds, 121
Roubaix, xvi, 41–2, 44–6, 48, 52, 62, 117, 121, 125, 157, 165, 170, 190, 212, 215, 236, 267, 270, 274, 276–7, 305, 308–9, 312, 314, 319, 346, 348, 355, 371, 459, 477, 496–7
Rouvier, Maurice, 236

Saint-Denis, 46
Saint-Étienne, 311–12, 404
Sainte-Pélagie Prison, 229, 280
Saint-Simon, Henri, 63, 126, 448, 479, 482, 491
Say's Law, 336
Schneiders of Creusot, 43, 121, 305, 363, 460
scientists, 443–50
Secrétariats du Travail, 183
Seine (department of), 439
Separation Crisis, 53
servants, 150–1
sharecropping, 417
social Catholicism *see* Christian Democrats
social mobility, 129–34, 139–40, 352, 363, 435
social reform *see* welfare reform
Socialism: Utopian and Scientific, 24
Le Socialiste, xvii–xviii, 7, 53, 68, 81, 88, 112, 145, 159–60, 169, 175–6, 182, 184, 195, 228–9, 233, 237, 242, 247, 262, 303, 307, 316, 328–9, 335, 341, 357, 365, 416, 428, 440, 445, 453, 457, 462–3, 467–8, 470, 486, 489, 504
Solidarism, 50, 91, 203, 207, 258, 277, 289
Sorel, Georges, 26, 29, 41
state, theory of, 200–2, 224, 234–41, 437, 484, 489–91

strikes, 36–7, 54, 80, 128, 144, 157–8, 169–71, 182, 191–202, 217–21, 240, 278, 289, 372
students, 446–8

taxation, 87, 320, 334
Taylorism, 37, 107–8, 137, 143, 221, 448, 455
teachers, 433, 439, 445–6
technology, 37, 62, 103, 110–18, 128, 181, 199–200, 358–61, 399, 407–10, 448–50, 472
Le Temps, 374, 418
Theories of Surplus Value, xiii, 150
Thiers, Adolphe, 246, 397
Thivrier, Christophe, 272
Tolain, Henri, 246
Toulouse, 177
Tourcoing, 197, 308
Tour du Pin, René de la, 288
Le Travailleur, 506
Treich, Édouard, 219
Les Trusts Américains, xix, 341

unemployment, 144–7, 214
Union des Chambres Syndicales Ouvrières de France, 208
United Kingdom, 140, 185, 202, 313
Universités Populaires, 442
utopia, 66, 117, 124, 336, 355, 479–91

Vaillant, Édouard, 26, 39, 251, 453
Valenciennes, 86
Valette, Aline, 83
value theory, 28, 31, 67, 100, 150, 330, 426–7
Vandervelde, Émile, 468
Var (department of), 46
Venice, 313
Vérecque, Charles, 123
Vienne, 373

Waldeck-Rousseau, René, 35, 52, 192, 207, 225, 231, 237, 247, 257, 271, 288
Watrin, Jules, 138–9, 449
welfare reform, 41, 52, 149, 154, 165–6, 253–9, 276, 292, 333–4, 367, 382
white collar employees, 45, 314–15, 350–1, 434–7
women, 69, 83, 155–9, 164, 167–74, 257–8
workers' control, 109, 483–6

Zévaès, Alexandre, 52, 177, 374, 447, 467, 474